MW01352520

Saxon Phonics 1

An Incremental Development

Home Study Teacher's Manual

Lorna Simmons

with

Linda Calvert

Saxon Publishers, Inc.

Phonics 1: An Incremental Development

Home Study Teacher's Manual

Printed in the United States of America

ISBN: 978-1-5657-7175-8

Editor: Julie Webster

Pre-Press Manager: Travis Rose

Production Coordinator: Joan Coleman

Illustrators: Dan Lawler, Sean Pruitt, and T.J. Brannon

Graphic Artist: Johnna Pulis

Typesetter: Johnna Pulis

Proofreaders: Mary Burleson, Edward Burr, and Anna Maria Rodriguez

11 21 13 14 15 4331 20 19 18 17 16

4500639079

Reaching us via the Internet

WWW: http://www.saxonpub.com

E-mail: info@saxonpub.com

Saxon Publishers, Inc.

Contents

Introductory Material

Lessons

PROGRAM OVERVIEW

Phonics 1 is a success-oriented program that enables most students to develop a solid foundation in phonics and thus become successful readers. In keeping with the Saxon philosophy, the phonics series builds on prior learning. New learning is presented in increments and each increment is reviewed every day for the entire year. This provides every student with the exposure he or she needs to achieve success.

Phonics 1 is designed as a supplemental program and may be used with any other reading program. Hence, the proper objective of *Phonics 1* is to provide students with the information they need to be able to read independently. There has been no attempt to include the type of quality literature most first grade teachers use to further their students' desire to read. The goal of *Phonics 1* is for all first graders to be able to read not only what the teacher assigns, but also anything else they might choose to read on their own.

When to Begin the Program

You may begin as soon as possible. However, in order for the student to benefit from the instructional content in *Phonics 1*, he or she must have attained a level of conceptual development called *phonemic awareness.* (Phonemic awareness is the awareness that words are composed of separate sounds and the ability to hear and manipulate those sounds. It is important to note that **phonemic awareness precedes effective phonics instruction.**) Phonemic awareness is taught in isolation during the first seventy lessons and is embedded in the lessons thereafter.

Pacing

Proper pacing is very important if the student is to succeed. Under normal circumstances, **five lessons (four lessons and an assessment) should be completed each week.** The fifth day of the week (assessment day) can also be used to reteach a difficult lesson, play games, or review areas where the student needs more practice. Teaching a lesson (which includes the presentation of new learning and review of decks, as well as alphabet, phonemic awareness, and spelling sounds activities), should take about forty-five minutes. If you sense that a lesson has exceeded the student's attention span, stop the lesson and continue it later in the day.

All other components (worksheet, practice, assessment, and reading activities), as well as individual remediation, take place *in addition* to the forty-five-minute time slot allocated for the lesson. Although these components are written to flow directly from one to the next, each can be done in isolation. Be sure, however, that you do not neglect any of them.

Slowing or Accelerating the Program

It is usually best to teach one lesson a day, using the suggested reinforcement activities when the student's weak areas are detected. The student can work in your choice of a basal reader. Allow the student who can read easily to do so. The average student can be guided through the reading. A student with learning difficulties can have the basal read to him or her and participate in all activities to ensure that he or she is presented with the new vocabulary and concepts. When the student's reading skills improve, the other areas will not have been neglected.

Whatever modifications are made to the program, you must not neglect the built-in continuous review that is crucial to the program's success. While it is not necessary for the student to achieve mastery of previously taught material before moving on to new material, adherence to the review process ensures that the student who has not mastered a skill will be given many subsequent opportunities to do so.

Handwriting Instruction

Handwriting instruction is provided in *Phonics 1*. Although there is some controversy regarding the appropriate style of handwriting to teach in first grade, *Phonics 1* accommodates most ideologies.

The choice of a handwriting style is left up to you. Two different styles are provided on the alphabet strip: a D'Nealian-style alphabet is featured on one side, a block-style alphabet on the other.

The letters shown on the worksheets, letter tiles, charts, and reader booklets are modeled after Times-Roman (the standard print in newspapers), which is what the student will see when reading. To become a successful reader, the student must understand the correlation between "reading" styles and "handwriting" styles (e.g., **a** is the same as **ɑ**, **g** is the same as **g**, etc.).

Any student who is physically unable to write can point to letters on the alphabet strip or use letter tiles to indicate what letter he or she would write.

Teaching Tools

The **teaching tools** for *Phonics 1* include the Review Decks, the Kid Cards, the Rule Book, and the audiotape. Specific instructions for their use are as follows:

Review Decks

The letter, picture, spelling, sight word, and affix cards form the Review Decks. The **letter cards** review each letter/letter cluster taught, helping the student learn the letter names and recognize letters/letter clusters in print. The **picture cards** feature illustrations that represent "keywords," which are used to remind the student of specific letter sounds he or she may have forgotten. Each **spelling card** instructs you to give a specific sound. The correct student response is indicated. Some spelling cards will never have more than one correct response. Others may have multiple responses as new material is taught. The additional responses are indicated on the cards by listing the lesson numbers after which the new responses should be given. The **sight word cards** are used to review some common words that do not follow the rules that have been taught; the student must learn to recognize these words by sight. The **affix cards** are used to review the prefixes and suffixes introduced throughout the year.

The Review Decks are used by you during instruction and directed activities, but are not intended for use by the student independently. The cards are introduced one by one and contain only that material to which the student has been exposed.

In order to prevent the student from memorizing card sequences, the cards should be reviewed in random order each time. The letter, spelling, sight word, and affix cards should be shuffled before being reviewed. The picture deck requires a different procedure. Within the picture deck, cards that represent different sounds made by the same letter (or letters) should always remain together (after they have been introduced, of course). Some of these cards must also be shown in a particular sequence. The card sequence required is indicated in the lessons and below:

2, 3, 98	(short, long, and schwa sounds of *o*)
6, 7	(short and long sounds of *i*)
9, 10, 65, 95	(short, long, schwa, and /ŏ/ sounds of *a*)
12, 13	(unvoiced and voiced sounds of *s*)
17, 80	(hard and soft sounds of *g*)
20, 63	(hard and soft sounds of *c*)
23, 24	(short and long sounds of *e*)
26, 27	(voiced and unvoiced digraph *th*)
30, 31	(short and long sounds of *u*)

41, 42	(two sounds of digraph *oo*)
51, 52	(two sounds of vowel *y*)
59, 96	(two sounds of combination *or*)
58, 91, 92	(three sounds of digraph *ch*)
57, 97	(two sounds of combination *ar*)
64, 74	(two sounds of digraph *ow*)
66, 67, 68	(three sounds of digraph *ea*)
73, 102	(two sounds of digraph *ou*)
86, 87	(two sounds of digraph *ie*)
88, 89	(two sounds of final, stable syllable *-sion*)
99, 100	(two sounds of digraph *ei*)

The picture deck can be rearranged every day as you review it. Make two discard piles and alternate between them until you reach a group of cards that must remain together. Place these cards in one of the discard piles (it doesn't matter which one). Try to distribute "groups" evenly between both piles. When you complete the deck, simply stack one discard pile on top of the other; the deck is now ready for tomorrow's review.

The letter, picture, spelling, sight word, and affix decks should not be mixed. Paper clips will keep them separate for a time; rubber bands will become necessary as the decks grow. (You may want to obtain a small box or shoe carton in which to store the card decks.)

As the school year progresses and the student masters the easier sounds and spellings, individual cards may be retired. Beginning in Lesson 70 (and periodically thereafter), suggestions are made about which cards to retire. You may retire any or all of the cards indicated *if the student has mastered them.* Do not remove cards other than those suggested. The retired cards are reviewed once a week (in lieu of the active cards).

Alphabet/Accent Decks (Sections 1, 2, and 3) are used to help the student practice accenting given syllables without the added task of sounding out new words. The cards use small alphabet sequences and thus serve the additional purpose of reinforcing the alphabet order.

Kid Cards

The Kid Cards are made up of orange letter cards, purple word cards, red picture cards, green action cards, white blend cards, and blue word cards. They are used in both teacher-guided and independent activities and games. They are often used for reinforcement of previously taught material and are especially beneficial when used to engage an unmotivated student. (See "Kid Card Games" in the appendix for more information.) As with the Review Decks, the student will use only those cards containing material to which he or she has already been exposed.

The Kid Cards should be stored in a similar manner to the Review Decks (the orange, purple, green, red, white, and blue cards rubber-banded separately).

Rule Book

The Rule Book contains a variety of charts that explain many of the rules used in phonics. It includes **rule charts** (explaining the rules for coding vowels and spelling), **syllable division charts** (demonstrating the procedure for dividing words into syllables to make them easier to decode), and **letter cluster charts** (containing the letter clusters and their keywords). The charts are perforated and may be removed and hung on the wall *after they are introduced* so that the student may refer to them more easily. **Regardless of whether you remove the charts or keep them in the booklet, the contents of the Rule Book should be available to the student during every lesson and assessment.**

Audiotape

To aid in the pronunciation of the letter sounds, an audiotape containing a spoken example of each sound is provided in the kit. The tape allows you to hear the sound(s) of each letter or letter cluster as it should be pronounced; however, please be aware that differences in pronunciation occur throughout the country, and any modifications necessary to reflect the dialect spoken in your area should be made. Please note that not all of the sounds included on this tape are taught in *Phonics 1*. The tape is intended for teacher use only.

Student Materials

The **student materials** for *Phonics 1* include an alphabet strip, letter tiles, readers, a workbook, and an Irregular Spelling Booklet. Specific instructions for the various components are as follows:

Alphabet Strip

The alphabet strip features D'Nealian-style letters on one side, block-style letters on the other. Above each letter is a small, colorful picture representing that letter's keyword. The strip is laminated for durability.

Letter Tiles

The student will receive a complete set of 32 letter tiles (26 letters plus 6 blank tiles). The tiles will be used in numerous ways during both teacher-directed and independent activities. The punch-out tiles are stamped on sturdy plastic-coated cardboard sheets and feature capital letters on one side, lowercase on the other.

It will be necessary to provide a container for the set of tiles. A plastic butter tub, heavy-duty zip-lock plastic bag, or small box will be suitable. You will add the appropriate tile or tiles as indicated by the lesson directions. (As always, the student works only with the letters he or she has learned.)

If a tile is lost, use a permanent marker to write the missing letter on one of the blank tiles.

Worksheets

Each day, the student will be given a worksheet to complete. The worksheets provide practice that reinforces new learning and also review previously learned material. The worksheets are usually teacher-directed but are occasionally completed independently. Worksheets are backed by a page of homework. **Although they are not graded, you should always check the worksheets and have the student correct any errors before completing the homework.** Each worksheet contains a short note that outlines the information presented that day.

Spelling Sound Sheets

The student will use the spelling sound sheets to record sounds given by you during spelling sound activities. Each sheet contains numbered lines to assist the student as he or she writes the letters. The number of sounds increases from one (in Lesson 1) to forty-eight (in Lesson 139). **Like the worksheets, the spelling sound sheets are not graded, but they should be checked for accuracy.**

Spelling Word Lists and Spelling Tests

Once a week (beginning in Lesson 16), the student is given a list of words to practice. Each list contains words that are made of only those sounds that have been taught. At the end of the week, the student is tested on those words.

Readers

The student constructs these small booklets before reading (and coloring) them. (See "Reader Assembly Instructions" on page xxii.) Fifty-two readers will be distributed during the program. The readers tell simple stories using only those words made from letters/letter clusters and vowel rules to which the student has been exposed. A small box in which to store the readers is also provided. You are encouraged to use the readers to practice with the student.

Irregular Spelling Booklet

The Irregular Spelling Booklet contains words in which sounds are spelled "irregularly" (i.e., in a manner used less than fifteen percent of the time). The booklet also contains special spelling lists: "wild colt" words, "ghost letters," irregular floss words, sight words, etc. Once the booklet is introduced (in Lesson 16), the student should keep the booklet nearby so that it may be referred to easily (even during spelling tests or assessments).

Classroom Preparation

Very little classroom preparation is required. The alphabet strip should be taped at the top of the table or desk where the student will be doing handwriting activities. (Or if you prefer, distribute and collect the strip each day.) Once the Rule Book and Irregular Spelling Booklet are introduced, they will be needed daily. Finally, a pencil should be available for every lesson.

You might consider placing window adhesive tabs on the various sections of the teacher's manual (e.g., the list of materials, the lessons, the reading word list, the Kid Card games, etc.). This will make it easier to refer to those sections quickly.

Assessments

Oral and **written assessments** are built into the program; they occur at five-lesson intervals (from Lesson 10 to Lesson 140). The written assessments are given first: you will read the instructions aloud and the student will write his or her answers. The oral assessments are short, individual interviews that may take place at any time during the day.

Each assessment tests concepts and skills that have been practiced for approximately ten days. A student is considered "successful" if he or she answers at least eighty percent of the questions correctly. If the student does not achieve eighty percent accuracy on any given assessment, identify the concepts he or she finds difficult and spend some time reinforcing those concepts with recommended activities before moving on.

Grading and Recording Strategies

Assessments and spelling tests have been provided to help you evaluate the student's progress and make adjustments in the teaching plan accordingly. If you choose to assign grades, please give the student as many points as possible for work attempted. For example, the word "cage" is coded as follows:

cāġe̸

When grading this word, do not mark the word completely wrong if the student forgets to include one or two coding marks, such as the k-back on the *c* or the dot over the *g*; instead, you might consider merely subtracting one point or even half a point for each coding "mistake." The most important point is to correct and then review any mistakes with the student. Remember, the ultimate goal is reading, not coding; coding merely facilitates the reading process but becomes less necessary as the student gains skill in reading.

Items that might be graded:

Assessments: Written and oral sections combine to form one grade per assessment. Review any mistakes with the student.

Spelling Tests: Grade each spelling test; then return to the student.

Items that should not be graded:

Worksheets: Always correct any mistakes before assigning homework.

Homework: Check for accuracy; then return to the student.

Spelling Sound Sheets: Check for accuracy while the student works.

Spelling Lists: As each new spelling list is presented, the student will check his or her own work.

Reinforcement of Learning Throughout the Day

Take advantage of opportunities to reinforce new learning throughout the day. Use time that would otherwise be wasted (when standing in line at the grocery store or while stopped at a traffic light, for example) to ask quick questions: "What letter did we learn today?" "What sound does that letter make?" "Give me a word that begins with the letter ___." "Look around. Do you see anything that begins with the letter ___?" "Give me a two- (or three-) syllable word."

Other curriculum areas hold numerous opportunities to reinforce coding/reading skills. For example, rather than simply presenting new vocabulary, code new words on the chalkboard and help the student sound them out. Of course this is possible only to the extent of the student's current knowledge, but even the simplest coding (and your assistance) will encourage the student to attempt pronunciation.

Letters and words are especially suited to graphs. Graph the occurrence of individual letters within a given paragraph, the number of one-syllable, two-syllable, and three-syllable words in any context (family members' names, for example), or student-generated lists of particular things (animals, foods, cities, etc., that begin with *a*, *b*, *c*, …).

Pronunciation

The chart below shows both the phonetic coding (for pronunciation) and the keyword for each sound. When pronouncing the letter sounds, be sure to use pure and crisp diction. Most importantly, do not add extra vowel sounds. For example, the pure sound of the letter *t* is /t/, not /tŭh/.

Pronunciation Chart

LETTERS	SOUNDS	EXAMPLES	LETTERS	SOUNDS	EXAMPLES
a	/ă/	apple	o	/ŏ/	ostrich
	/ā/	acorn		/ō/	open
b	/b/, not bŭh	belt	p	/p/, not pŭh	pencil
c	/k/, not kŭh	carrot	qu	/kw/	quilt
	/s/, not sŭh	circle	r	/r/, not rŭh or /er/	rabbit
d	/d/, not dŭh	doughnut	s	/s/, not sŭh	sock
e	/ĕ/	egg		/z/, not zŭh	rose
	/ē/	equal	t	/t/, not tŭh	tent
f	/f/, not fŭh	feet	u	/ŭ/	umbrella
g	/g/, not gŭh	goggles		/ū/	unicorn
	/j/, not jŭh	giraffe		/o͞o/	rule
h	/h/, not hŭh	hair	v	/v/, not vŭh	vest
i	/ĭ/	igloo	w	/w/, not wŭh	wagon
	/ī/	ivy	x	/ks/	fox
j	/j/, not jŭh	jet	y	/y/, not yŭh	yarn
k	/k/, not kŭh	kite		/ī/	cry
l	/l/, not lŭh	lion		/ē/	candy
m	/m/, not mŭh	mask		/ĭ/	symbol
n	/n/, not nŭh	nest	z	/z/, not zŭh	zipper

Coding Charts

The charts shown on the following pages briefly summarize the rules for coding and spelling that will be introduced throughout the year.

Basic Coding

To Code	Use	Example	Introduced in Lesson
Accented syllables	Accent marks	no´	3
C's that make a /k/ sound, as in "cat"	K-backs	cat	21
C's that make a /s/ sound, as in "cell"	Cedillas	çell	78
Combinations; diphthongs	Arcs	ar	63; 89
Digraphs; trigraphs; quadrigraphs	Underlines	sh	28; 64; 126
Final, stable syllables	Brackets	[fle	56
Long vowel sounds	Macrons	nō	3
Schwa vowel sounds (rhymes with vowel sound in "sun," as in "some," "about," and "won")	Schwas	o̊ (or ə)	18
Scribal *o*'s	Schwas	o̊	133
Short vowel sounds	Breves	lŏg	2
Sight words	Circles	are	16
Silent letters	Slash marks	makø	41
Suffixes	Boxes	work|ing	12
Syllables	Syllable division lines	cac|tus	24
Voiced sounds	Voice lines	his	11

Vowel Rules

Rule	Coding Examples	Introduced in Lesson
A vowel followed by a consonant is short; code it with a breve.	lŏg căt sĭt	2
An open, accented vowel is long; code it with a macron.	nō´ mē´ ī´ gō´	3
A vowel followed by a consonant and a silent *e* is long; code the vowel with a macron and cross out the silent *e*.	nāmø hōpø līkø	41
An open, unaccented vowel can make a schwa sound. The letters *e*, *o*, and *u* can also make long sounds. The letter *i* can also make a short sound.	bå|năn´|å ē|rāsø´ hō|tĕl´ Jū|lȳ´ dĭ|vīdø´	*a*—84 *e, o, u*—114 *i*—134

Spelling Rules

Rule	Example	Introduced in Lesson
To spell the /ch/ sound in the final position: ▪ Use the letters *tch* after a short vowel. ▪ Use the letters *ch* after anything else.	match pooch bench	116
To spell the /j/ sound in the initial position: ▪ Use the letter *j* before the letters *a*, *o*, or *u*. ▪ Use the letter *g* before the letters *e*, *i*, or *y*.	jam joke giant	109
To spell the /j/ sound in the final position: ▪ Use the letters *dge* after a short vowel. ▪ Use the letters *ge* after anything else.	edge lunge cage	117
To spell the /k/ sound in the initial position: ▪ Use the letter *k* before the letters *e*, *i*, or *y*. ▪ Use the letter *c* before *a*, *o*, *u*, or any consonant.	keg kid silky cat cot cut crop	22
To spell the /k/ sound in the final position: ▪ Use the letters *ck* after a short vowel. ▪ Use the letter *k* after a consonant or two vowels. ▪ Use the letters *ke* after a long vowel. ▪ Use the letter *c* at the end of a word with two or more syllables.	lock milk look make Atlantic	29
The /ŏ/ sound before the letter *l* is usually spelled with the letter *a*.	tall salt false	128
The /ŏ/ sound after the letters *w* or *qu* is usually spelled with the letter *a*.	watch qualm	127
To spell the /s/ sound in the final position: ▪ Use the letters *ss* after a short vowel. ▪ Use the letters *ce* after a long vowel. ▪ Use the letters *se* after a consonant or two vowels.	boss ice false loose	78
To spell the /v/ sound in the final position: ▪ Use the letters *ve*.	wave live solve	53
Changing Rule: ▪ If a word ends with a vowel *y*, change the *y* to an *i* before adding a suffix (except for those suffixes that begin with *i*). ▪ Do not change *y* if it comes after a vowel.	silly + ness = silliness muddy + ing = muddying play + ed = played	134
Dropping Rule: When a word ends with a "silent *e*," drop the *e* before adding a vowel suffix.	make + ing = making	88
Doubling Rule: When the final syllable of a word is accented and ends with one vowel and one consonant, double the final consonant before adding a vowel suffix.	hit + ing = hitting	111
When a consonant suffix is added to a word, just put the word and the suffix together.	red + ness = redness	88
Floss Rule: When a one-syllable root word has a short vowel sound followed by the sound /f/, /l/, or /s/, it is usually spelled *ff*, *ll*, or *ss*.	puff doll pass	52

Syllable Division Patterns

Pattern	Variation	Example	Introduced in Lesson
vccv	vc´|cv	napkin	24
	vc|cv´	inject	39
vcv	v´|cv	baby	81
	vc´|v	river	107
	v|cv´	erase	84
vccvccv	vc|cvc´|cv	important	92
vcccv	vc|ccv´	explain	99
	vc´|ccv	emblem	
	vcc´|cv	pumpkin	

Digraphs

Digraph	Coding	Example	Introduced in Lesson
ai	āi̸	rain	68
au	au	sauce	101
aw	aw	straw	102
ay	āy̸	hay	69
ch	ch	cheese	72
	ch̸	chord	123
	çh	chef	
ck	c̸k	lock	28
ea	ēa̸	leaf	86
	ĕa̸	thread	87
	e̸ā	break	
ee	ēe̸	sheep	34
ei	ēi̸	receipt	137
	ei	veil	
ew	ew	cashew	138
ey	ēy̸	key	106
gn	g̸n	gnat	112
ie	īe̸	pie	119
	i̸ē	shield	
kn	k̸n	knot	112

Digraphs (Continued)

Digraph	Coding	Example	Introduced in Lesson
ng	ng	lung	32
oa	ōa̸	soap	104
oe	ōe̸	toe	104
oo	oo	hook	49
		tooth	
ou	o̸ū	soup	138
ow	ōw̸	bow	79
ph	ph	phone	108
sh	sh	shark	48
th	th	feather	31
	th	thimble	
ue	ūe̸	glue	94
wr	w̸r	wreath	112

Trigraphs

Trigraph	Coding	Example	Introduced in Lesson
dge	d̸ge̸	bridge	117
igh	īg̸h̸	light	64
tch	t̸ch	patch	116

Quadrigraph

Quadrigraph	Coding	Example	Introduced in Lesson
eigh	eigh	sleigh	126

Diphthongs

Diphthong	Coding	Example	Introduced in Lesson
oi	oi	oil	89
ou	ou	mouse	97
ow	ow	cow	97
oy	oy	toy	89

Combinations

Combination	Coding	Example	Introduced in Lesson
ar	ar	arm	71
		dollar	132
er	er	butter	63
ir	ir	shirt	76
or	or	fork	73
		doctor	132
		worm	
qu	qu	quail	74
ur	ur	purse	77
wh	wh	whale	124

Final, Stable Syllables

Final, Stable Syllable	Coding	Example	Introduced in Lesson
-ble	´[blę	bubble	56
-cle	´[clę	uncle	59
-dle	´[dlę	candle	57
-fle	´[flę	ruffle	57
-gle	´[glę	bugle	58
-kle	´[klę	buckle	59
-ple	´[plę	staple	57
-sion	´[sion	television	121
		mission	
-sle	´[slę	hassle	59
-tion	´[tion	lotion	93
-tle	´[tlę	bottle	58
-ture	´[ture	picture	122
-zle	´[zlę	puzzle	59

Prefixes

Letters	Definition	Example	Introduced in Lesson
dis-	not, opposite	dislike	139
pre-	before	presoak	139
un-	not	uneven	129
	reversing	unpack	

Suffixes

Letters	Definition	Example	Introduced in Lesson
-ed	past tense	jumped	33
-er	more than	shorter	131
	one who	baker	
-es	plural	bushes	96
-est	most, superlative	biggest	131
-ful	full of	peaceful	136
	quantity	cupful	
-ing	action	jumping	32
-less	without	hatless	67
-ly	like	kingly	67
	how	quickly	
	occurring	weekly	
-ness	condition of	redness	67
-s	plural	trees	12
-y	like	healthy	62
	state of	angry	
	place that	saddlery	
	small	puppy	

Reader Assembly Instructions

1. Bend the reader back and forth along the top perforation line several times.

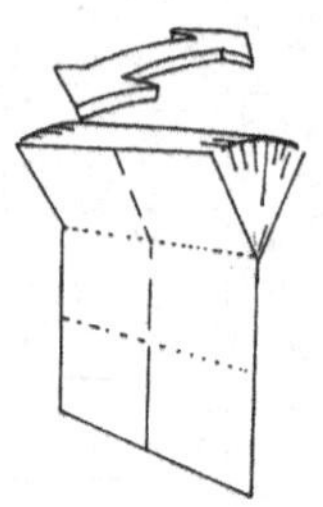

2. Repeat at the lower perforation line.

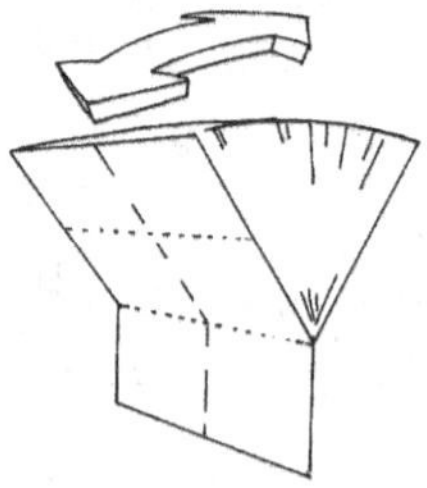

3. Hold the page so that the tree illustration faces you.

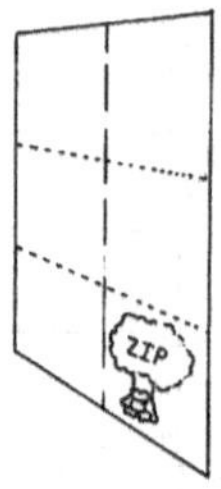

4. Fold the top of the page down (toward you) along the top perforation line.

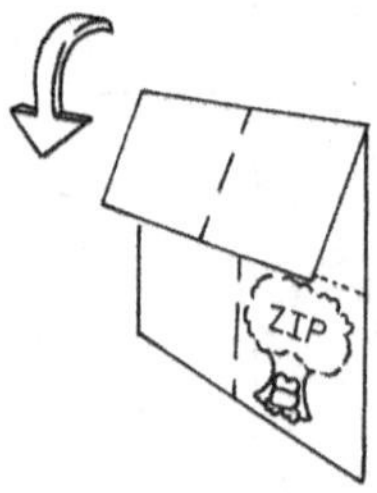

5. At the lower perforation line, fold the top perforation of the reader back (away from you) so that the tree remains facing you.

6. Now fold the left half back to form a booklet, with the tree as the cover illustration. Place a small rubber band around the spine, or staple it. Then separate the pages along the top and bottom perforation lines.

Glossary

accent the syllable receiving the primary stress in a word

affix a word element, such as a prefix or a suffix, that is appended to a root word

blend two consonants that slide together so smoothly that you can hardly hear each sound

breve a coding mark used to indicate a vowel's short sound (e.g., ăpple)

cedilla a coding mark on the letter *c* to indicate its soft sound (e.g., çent)

changing rule a spelling rule stating that when a root word ends with the vowel *y*, change *y* to *i* before adding a suffix, except for suffixes beginning with *i* (e.g., silliness)

code to mark a word with symbols (such as a breve, macron, etc.) to give information about how to pronounce the word

combination two letters that come together to make an unexpected sound (e.g., quick)

consonant suffix a suffix that begins with a consonant (e.g., -less)

derivative a root word with something added to it (e.g., a suffix or prefix)

digraph two letters that come together to make one sound (e.g., lock)

diphthong two vowel sounds that come together so quickly that they are considered one syllable (e.g., foil)

doubling rule a spelling rule stating that when the final syllable of a root word is accented, and it ends with one vowel and one consonant, double the final consonant before adding a vowel suffix (e.g., hitting)

dropping rule a spelling rule stating that when a root word ends with a "silent *e*," drop the *e* before adding a vowel suffix (e.g., making)

final the last sound or letter(s) in a word

final silent *e* an *e* in the final position of an English root word, usually silent

final, stable syllable a nonphonetic syllable that occurs in the final position frequently enough to be considered stable (e.g., crum ble)

floss rule a spelling rule stating that the letters *f*, *l*, and *s* are doubled after a short vowel in a one-syllable root word (e.g., puff, hill, boss)

ghost letters letters whose sounds are no longer pronounced in certain letter combinations (e.g., gnat, knife, wrote)

initial the first sound or letter(s) in a word

k-back a vertical line on the back of a *c* that represents the /k/ sound (e.g., cat)

macron a coding mark used to indicate a vowel's long sound (e.g., ācorn)

medial the middle sound(s) or letter(s) in a word

open vowel a vowel that is not followed by a consonant within its syllable (e.g., no)

possessive *s* an apostrophe *s* added to a word to show ownership

prefix a letter or group of letters added to the beginning of a root word that changes the meaning or usage of the word

quadrigraph four letters that come together to make one sound (e.g., sleigh)

regular for reading the sound that a letter or group of letters makes at least 85% of the time

regular for spelling the spelling that occurs for a particular sound at least 85% of the time

root word a word with no prefix or suffix added

schwa a code mark placed over a vowel to indicate the /ŭ/ sound (e.g., thė)

sight word a word in which all or part does not follow phonetic rules

sneaky *e* the *e* in vowel rule v̄–ɇ; it makes the vowel say its long sound (e.g., makɇ)

suffix a letter or group of letters added to the end of a root word that changes the meaning or usage of the word

syllable a word or part of a word that contains only one vowel sound and is made by one impulse of the voice

syllable division the breaking of a word into separate syllables to make decoding (pronunciation) easier

trigraph three letters that come together to make one sound (e.g., light)

twin consonants two adjacent consonants that are just alike

voiced sound a sound that requires use of the vocal cords; a vibration is felt

voice line a horizontal line through the middle of a letter, representing a voiced sound (e.g., rose)

vowel rules rules that determine a vowel's sound in a given situation in a syllable:
1. a vowel followed by a consonant is short;
2. a vowel that is open and accented is long;
3. vowel-consonant-*e*, where the silent *e* makes the vowel long

vowel suffix a suffix that beings with a vowel (e.g., -ing)

wild colt words words containing the letters *i* or *o* followed by two consonants in which the vowels are pronounced with their long sounds (e.g., wild)

List of Materials

Week 1

Lesson 1
alphabet strip
rubber band
tin can or plastic foam cup
Spelling Sound Sheet 1
letter tile in a container
Letter Card 1
Picture Card 1
Spelling Card 1
Worksheet 1

Lesson 2
Review Decks
Spelling Sound Sheet 2
Letter Card 2
Picture Card 2
Spelling Card 2
Worksheet 2
Rule Book

Lesson 3
Review Decks
Spelling Sound Sheet 3
container of letter tiles
Picture Card 3
Spelling Card 3
Worksheet 3

Lesson 4
ball
Review Decks
Spelling Sound Sheet 4
container of letter tiles
Letter Card 3
Picture Card 4
Spelling Card 4
Worksheet 4

Lesson 5
Review Decks
Spelling Sound Sheet 5
container of letter tiles
Letter Card 4
pencil in a sack
Picture Card 5
Spelling Card 5
Worksheet 5

Week 2

Lesson 6
Review Decks
Spelling Sound Sheet 6
container of letter tiles
Letter Card 5
Picture Cards 6–7
Spelling Cards 6–7
Worksheet 6

Lesson 7
Review Decks
Spelling Sound Sheet 7
container of letter tiles
Letter Card 6
Picture Card 8
Spelling Card 8
Worksheet 7

Lesson 8
Review Decks
Spelling Sound Sheet 8
container of letter tiles
Letter Card 7
apple in a sack
Picture Cards 9–10
Spelling Cards 9–10
Worksheet 8

Lesson 9
Review Decks
Spelling Sound Sheet 9
container of letter tiles
Letter Card 8
zipper in a sack
Picture Card 11
Spelling Card 11
Worksheet 9

Lesson 10
Review Decks
Assessment 1
Assessment 1 Recording Form
Kid Cards
tokens

WEEK 3

*Lesson **11***
- Review Decks
- Spelling Sound Sheet 10
- container of letter tiles
- Letter Card 9
- sock in a sack
- Picture Cards 12–13
- Spelling Card 12
- Worksheet 11

*Lesson **12***
- Review Decks
- Spelling Sound Sheet 11
- gingersnaps
- Affix Card 1
- Worksheet 12
- Reader 1 (*Zip*)
- colored pencils
- Reader Collection Box

*Lesson **13***
- ball
- Review Decks
- Spelling Sound Sheet 12
- tokens or colored pencil
- Letter Card 10
- doughnut in a sack
- Picture Card 14
- Spelling Card 13
- Worksheet 13

*Lesson **14***
- Review Decks
- Spelling Sound Sheet 13
- container of letter tiles
- Letter Card 11
- Picture Card 15
- Spelling Card 14
- Worksheet 14
- Reader 2 (*Nat and Don*)
- colored pencils

*Lesson **15***
- Review Decks
- Assessment 2
- Assessment 2 Recording Form
- Kid Cards
- tokens

WEEK 4

*Lesson **16***
- Review Decks
- Letter Card 12
- wig in a sack
- Picture Card 16
- container of letter tiles
- Spelling Card 15
- Sight Word Card 1
- Irregular Spelling Booklet
- Worksheet 16
- Spelling List 1

*Lesson **17***
- Review Decks
- Spelling Sound Sheet 14
- container of letter tiles
- Letter Card 13
- goggles in a sack
- Picture Card 17
- Spelling Card 16
- Worksheet 17
- Reader 3 (*Ann and Sal in the Sand*)
- colored pencils

*Lesson **18***
- ball
- Review Decks
- Spelling Sound Sheet 15
- container of letter tiles
- Letter Card 14
- Picture Card 18
- Spelling Card 17
- Worksheet 18

*Lesson **19***
- container of letter tiles
- Review Decks
- Spelling Sound Sheet 16
- Letter Card 15
- Picture Card 19
- Spelling Card 18
- Worksheet 19
- Reader 4 (*Zip and the Ant*)
- colored pencils

*Lesson **20***
- Review Decks
- Assessment 3
- Spelling Test 1
- Assessment 3 Recording Form
- Kid Cards
- tokens

WEEK 5

*Lesson **21***
- Review Decks
- Spelling Sound Sheet 17
- container of letter tiles
- Letter Card 16
- carrot in a sack
- Picture Card 20
- Worksheet 21
- Sight Word Cards 2–3
- Spelling List 2

Lesson **22**
Review Decks
Spelling Sound Sheet 18
Worksheet 22
Sight Word Card 4
Reader 5 (*Lost at the Pond*)
colored pencils

Lesson **23**
ball
Review Decks
Spelling Sound Sheet 19
tokens or colored pencil
Letter Card 17
Picture Card 21
container of letter tiles
Spelling Card 19
Sight Word Card 5
Worksheet 23

Lesson **24**
container of letter tiles
Review Decks
Spelling Sound Sheet 20
Worksheet 24
Rule Book
Reader 6 (*Sass*)
colored pencils

Lesson **25**
Review Decks
Assessment 4
Spelling Test 2
Assessment 4 Recording Form
Kid Cards
tokens

Week 6

Lesson **26**
Review Decks
Spelling Sound Sheet 21
container of letter tiles
Letter Card 18
Picture Card 22
Spelling Card 20
Worksheet 26
Spelling List 3

Lesson **27**
Review Decks
Spelling Sound Sheet 22
container of letter tiles
Letter Card 19
Picture Cards 23–24
Spelling Cards 21–22
Worksheet 27
Reader 7 (*Mom*)
colored pencils

Lesson **28**
ball
Review Decks
container of letter tiles
Letter Card 20
lock in a sack
Picture Card 25
Worksheet 28

Lesson **29**
container of letter tiles
Review Decks
Spelling Sound Sheet 23
Worksheet 29
Sight Word Card 6
Reader 8 (*Nick's Kid*)
colored pencils

Lesson **30**
Review Decks
Assessment 5
Spelling Test 3
Assessment 5 Recording Form
Kid Cards
tokens

Week 7

Lesson **31**
Review Decks
Spelling Sound Sheet 24
Letter Card 21
feathers and a thimble in a sack
Picture Cards 26–27
Spelling Cards 23–24
Worksheet 31
Sight Word Card 7
Spelling List 4

Lesson **32**
Review Decks
Spelling Sound Sheet 25
Letter Card 22
Picture Card 28
Spelling Card 25
Affix Card 2
Worksheet 32
Sight Word Card 8
Reader 9 (*A CK Spelling Test*)
colored pencils

Lesson **33**
ball
Review Decks
Spelling Sound Sheet 26
tokens or colored pencil
Affix Card 3
Worksheet 33

Lesson ***34*** Review Decks
Spelling Sound Sheet 27
Letter Card 23
Picture Card 29
Worksheet 34
Sight Word Cards 9–11
Reader 10 (*Who Sleeps Where?*)
colored pencils

Lesson ***35*** ball
Review Decks
Assessment 6
Spelling Test 4
Assessment 6 Recording Form
Kid Cards
tokens

WEEK 8

Lesson ***36*** Review Decks
Spelling Sound Sheet 28
Sight Word Card 12
Worksheet 36
Spelling List 5

Lesson ***37*** Review Decks
Spelling Sound Sheet 29
container of letter tiles
Letter Card 24
Picture Cards 30–31
Spelling Cards 26–27
Worksheet 37
Sight Word Card 13
Reader 11 (*Zip's Mess*)
colored pencils

Lesson ***38*** ball
Activity Sheet 1
Review Decks
Spelling Sound Sheet 30
container of letter tiles
Letter Card 25
Picture Card 32
Spelling Card 28
Sight Word Card 14
Worksheet 38

Lesson ***39*** container of letter tiles
Review Decks
Worksheet 39
Reader 12 (*Spilled Milk*)
colored pencils

Lesson ***40*** Review Decks
Assessment 7
Spelling Test 5
Assessment 7 Recording Form
Kid Cards
tokens

WEEK 9

Lesson ***41*** Review Decks
Spelling Sound Sheet 31
3 index cards
Letter Card 26
Picture Card 33
Sight Word Card 15
Worksheet 41
Spelling List 6

Lesson ***42*** Review Decks
Spelling Sound Sheet 32
2 index cards
Letter Cards 27–28
Picture Cards 34–35
cube in a sack
Worksheet 42
Reader 13 (*Zip Gets a Beef Bone*)
colored pencils

Lesson ***43*** ball
Review Decks
Spelling Sound Sheet 33
tokens or colored pencil
2 index cards
Letter Cards 29–30
dime in a sack
Picture Cards 36–37
Sight Word Card 16
Worksheet 43

Lesson ***44*** container of letter tiles
Review Decks
Spelling Sound Sheet 34
Worksheet 44
Reader 14 (*Huck's Raft*)
colored pencils

Lesson ***45*** Review Decks
Assessment 8
Spelling Test 6
Assessment 8 Recording Form
Kid Cards
tokens

Week 10

Lesson **46**
Review Decks
Spelling Sound Sheet 35
container of letter tiles
Letter Card 31
Picture Card 38
Spelling Card 29
Worksheet 46
Spelling List 7

Lesson **47**
Review Decks
Spelling Sound Sheet 36
container of letter tiles
Letter Card 32
yarn in a sack
Picture Card 39
Spelling Card 30
Worksheet 47
Reader 15 (*A Flat on Bill's Bus*)
colored pencils

Lesson **48**
Review Decks
Letter Card 33
Picture Card 40
Spelling Card 31
Worksheet 48

Lesson **49**
container of letter tiles
Review Decks
Spelling Sound Sheet 37
Letter Card 34
Picture Cards 41–42
Spelling Cards 32–33
Worksheet 49
Sight Word Card 17
Reader 16 (*A Picnic in the Woods*)
colored pencils

Lesson **50**
Review Decks
Assessment 9
Spelling Test 7
Assessment 9 Recording Form
Kid Cards
tokens

Week 11

Lesson **51**
Review Decks
Spelling Sound Sheet 38
container of letter tiles
Letter Card 35
Picture Card 43
Spelling Card 34
Sight Word Card 18
Worksheet 51
Spelling List 8

Lesson **52**
Review Decks
Spelling Sound Sheet 39
Worksheet 52
Reader 17 (*Fig Jam*)
colored pencils
fig cookies

Lesson **53**
Alphabet/Accent Deck (Section 1)
Review Decks
Spelling Sound Sheet 40
tokens or colored pencil
Letter Card 36
Picture Card 44
Spelling Card 35
Sight Word Card 19
Worksheet 53

Lesson **54**
container of letter tiles
Review Decks
Spelling Sound Sheet 41
Worksheet 54
Reader 18 (*Deb's Dogs*)
colored pencils

Lesson **55**
ball
Review Decks
Assessment 10
Spelling Test 8
Assessment 10 Recording Form
Kid Cards
tokens

Week 12

Lesson **56**
container of letter tiles
Review Decks
Spelling Sound Sheet 42
Letter Card 37
Picture Card 45
liquid bubbles and bubble maker
Spelling Card 36
Worksheet 56
Spelling List 9

Lesson **57**
Alphabet/Accent Deck (Section 1)
Review Decks
Spelling Sound Sheet 43
Letter Cards 38–40
Picture Cards 46–48
candles in a sack
Worksheet 57

Sight Word Card 20
Reader 19 (*Jogging Josh*)
colored pencils

Lesson **58** 4 index cards
Review Decks
Letter Cards 41–42
bottle in a sack
Picture Cards 49–50
Sight Word Card 21
Worksheet 58

Lesson **59** Alphabet/Accent Deck (Section 1)
Review Decks
Spelling Sound Sheet 44
Worksheet 59
Reader 20 (*Mom's Cake*)
colored pencils

Lesson **60** Alphabet/Accent Deck (Section 1)
Review Decks
Assessment 11
Spelling Test 9
Assessment 11 Recording Form
Kid Cards
tokens

WEEK 13

Lesson **61** container of letter tiles
Review Decks
Spelling Sound Sheet 45
Letter Card 43
Picture Card 51
Sight Word Card 22
Worksheet 61
Spelling List 10

Lesson **62** Alphabet/Accent Deck (Section 1)
Review Decks
Spelling Sound Sheet 46
Affix Card 4
wrapped candy in a sack
Picture Card 52
Worksheet 62
Reader 21 (*The Tale of Rex Rabbit*)
colored pencils

Lesson **63** 6 index cards
Review Decks
Spelling Sound Sheet 47
tokens or colored pencil
Letter Card 44
Picture Card 53
Spelling Card 37
Sight Word Cards 23–24
Worksheet 63

Lesson **64** Alphabet/Accent Deck (Section 1)
Review Decks
Spelling Sound Sheet 48
Letter Card 45
Picture Card 54
Worksheet 64
Sight Word Card 25
Reader 22 (*What Will Uncle Dave Make?*)
colored pencils

Lesson **65** assorted items
Review Decks
Assessment 12
Spelling Test 10
Assessment 12 Recording Form
Kid Cards
tokens

WEEK 14

Lesson **66** container of letter tiles
Review Decks
Spelling Sound Sheet 49
Worksheet 66
Spelling List 11

Lesson **67** Alphabet/Accent Deck (Section 1)
Review Decks
Spelling Sound Sheet 50
Affix Cards 5–7
Sight Word Cards 26–27
Worksheet 67
Reader 23 (*Ann and the Dentist*)
colored pencils

Lesson **68** Review Decks
Letter Card 46
Picture Card 55
Sight Word Cards 28–29
Worksheet 68

Lesson **69** Alphabet/Accent Deck (Section 1)
Review Decks
Spelling Sound Sheet 51
Letter Card 47
Picture Card 56
Worksheet 69
Reader 24 (*A Wet Picnic*)
colored pencils

Lesson ***70*** ball
Review Decks
Assessment 13
Spelling Test 11
Assessment 13 Recording Form
Kid Cards
tokens

Lesson ***75*** Alphabet/Accent Deck (Section 1)
Review Decks
Assessment 14
Spelling Test 12
Assessment 14 Recording Form
Kid Cards
tokens

WEEK 15

Lesson ***71*** container of letter tiles
Review Decks
Spelling Sound Sheet 52
Letter Card 48
Picture Card 57
Spelling Card 38
Sight Word Card 30
Worksheet 71
Spelling List 12

Lesson ***72*** Alphabet/Accent Deck (Section 1)
Retired Decks
Affix Deck
Spelling Sound Sheet 53
Letter Card 49
Picture Card 58
Spelling Card 39
Sight Word Card 31
Worksheet 72
Reader 25 (*Chester*)
colored pencils

Lesson ***73*** Activity Sheet 2
Review Decks
Spelling Sound Sheet 54
tokens or colored pencil
Letter Card 50
Picture Card 59
Spelling Card 40
Worksheet 73

Lesson ***74*** Alphabet/Accent Deck (Section 1)
Review Decks
Spelling Sound Sheet 55
container of letter tiles
Letter Card 51
Picture Card 60
Spelling Card 41
Sight Word Cards 32–33
Worksheet 74
Reader 26 (*Copper*)
colored pencils

WEEK 16

Lesson ***76*** container of letter tiles
Review Decks
Spelling Sound Sheet 56
Letter Card 52
Picture Card 61
Sight Word Cards 34–37
Worksheet 76
Spelling List 13

Lesson ***77*** Alphabet/Accent Deck (Section 1)
Retired Decks
Affix Deck
Spelling Sound Sheet 57
Letter Card 53
purse in a sack
Picture Card 62
Worksheet 77
Reader 27 (*Beth Cuts a Tooth*)
colored pencils

Lesson ***78*** Activity Sheet 3
Review Decks
Picture Card 63
Sight Word Card 38
Worksheet 78

Lesson ***79*** Alphabet/Accent Deck (Section 1)
Review Decks
Spelling Sound Sheet 58
Letter Card 54
Picture Card 64
Worksheet 79
Reader 28 (*Chester's Bath*)
colored pencils

Lesson ***80*** ball
Review Decks
Assessment 15
Spelling Test 13
Assessment 15 Recording Form
Kid Cards
tokens

Week 17

Lesson ***81***
- container of letter tiles
- Review Decks
- Spelling Sound Sheet 59
- Sight Word Card 39
- Worksheet 81
- Spelling List 14

Lesson ***82***
- Alphabet/Accent Deck (Section 1)
- Retired Decks
- Affix Deck
- Spelling Sound Sheet 60
- Sight Word Cards 40–41
- Worksheet 82
- Reader 29 (*Jon Helps Dad*)
- colored pencils

Lesson ***83***
- container of letter tiles
- Review Decks
- Spelling Sound Sheet 61
- tokens or colored pencil
- Worksheet 83

Lesson ***84***
- Alphabet/Accent Deck (Section 1)
- Review Decks
- Spelling Sound Sheet 62
- banana in a sack
- Picture Card 65
- Worksheet 84
- Reader 30 (*Kerry's Bike*)
- colored pencils

Lesson ***85***
- container of letter tiles
- Review Decks
- Assessment 16
- Spelling Test 14
- Assessment 16 Recording Form
- Kid Cards
- tokens

Week 18

Lesson ***86***
- container of letter tiles
- Review Decks
- Spelling Sound Sheet 63
- Letter Card 55
- leaves in a sack
- Picture Card 66
- Worksheet 86
- Spelling List 15

Lesson ***87***
- Alphabet/Accent Deck (Section 1)
- Retired Decks
- Affix Deck
- Spelling Sound Sheet 64
- spool of thread in a sack
- Picture Cards 67–68
- small, brittle stick
- Sight Word Cards 42–43
- Worksheet 87
- Reader 31 (*Nubbin*)
- colored pencils

Lesson ***88***
- 12 index cards
- Review Decks
- Worksheet 88

Lesson ***89***
- Alphabet/Accent Deck (Section 1)
- Review Decks
- Spelling Sound Sheet 65
- Letter Cards 56–57
- Picture Cards 69–70
- toy in a sack
- Spelling Card 42
- Sight Word Cards 44–46
- Worksheet 89
- Reader 32 (*Bobby*)
- colored pencils

Lesson ***90***
- assorted items
- Review Decks
- Assessment 17
- Spelling Test 15
- Assessment 17 Recording Form
- Kid Cards
- tokens

Week 19

Lesson ***91***
- container of letter tiles
- Review Decks
- Spelling Sound Sheet 66
- Worksheet 91
- Spelling List 16

Lesson ***92***
- Alphabet/Accent Deck (Section 1)
- Retired Decks
- Affix Deck
- Spelling Sound Sheet 67
- Sight Word Cards 47–48
- Worksheet 92
- Reader 33 (*Ming and Grandmother*)
- colored pencils

Lesson ***93***
- Activity Sheet 4
- Review Decks
- Spelling Sound Sheet 68
- tokens or colored pencil

Letter Card 58
bottle of hand lotion in a sack
Picture Card 71
Spelling Card 43
Sight Word Cards 49–51
Worksheet 93

Lesson ***94*** Alphabet/Accent Deck (Section 1)
Review Decks
Spelling Sound Sheet 69
Letter Card 59
bottle of glue in a sack
Picture Card 72
Worksheet 94
Reader 34 (*Jordan and Morgan*)
colored pencils

Lesson ***95*** ball
Review Decks
Assessment 18
Spelling Test 16
Assessment 18 Recording Form
Kid Cards
tokens

Week 20

Lesson ***96*** container of letter tiles
Review Decks
Spelling Sound Sheet 70
Affix Card 8
Worksheet 96
Spelling List 17

Lesson ***97*** Alphabet/Accent Deck (Section 2)
Retired Decks
Affix Deck
Spelling Sound Sheet 71
Letter Card 60
toy mouse in a sack
Picture Cards 73–74
Spelling Card 44
Sight Word Card 52
Worksheet 97
Reader 35 (*Mike on a Jet*)
colored pencils

Lesson ***98*** Activity Sheet 5
Review Decks
Worksheet 98

Lesson ***99*** Alphabet/Accent Deck (Section 1)
Review Decks
Spelling Sound Sheet 72
Sight Word Card 53
Worksheet 99
Reader 36 (*Chester and Hudson*)
colored pencils

Lesson ***100*** assorted items
Review Decks
Assessment 19
Spelling Test 17
Assessment 19 Recording Form
Kid Cards
tokens

Week 21

Lesson ***101*** container of letter tiles
Review Decks
Spelling Sound Sheet 73
Letter Card 61
Picture Card 75
Spelling Card 45
Sight Word Card 54
Worksheet 101
Spelling List 18

Lesson ***102*** Alphabet/Accent Deck (Section 2)
Retired Decks
Affix Deck
Spelling Sound Sheet 74
Letter Card 62
straws in a sack
Picture Card 76
Sight Word Cards 55–56
Worksheet 102
Reader 37 (*Frank Goes Camping*)
colored pencils

Lesson ***103*** container of letter tiles
Review Decks
Spelling Sound Sheet 75
tokens or colored pencil
Worksheet 103

Lesson ***104*** Alphabet/Accent Deck (Section 1)
Review Decks
Spelling Sound Sheet 76
Letter Card 63
bar of soap in a sack
Picture Card 77
Sight Word Cards 57–58
Worksheet 104
Reader 38 (*The Apartment Building*)
colored pencils

Lesson **105** container of letter tiles
Review Decks
Assessment 20
Spelling Test 18
Assessment 20 Recording Form
Kid Cards
tokens

Week 22

Lesson **106** container of letter tiles
Review Decks
Spelling Sound Sheet 77
Letter Card 64
keys in a sack
Picture Card 78
Worksheet 106
Spelling List 19

Lesson **107** Alphabet/Accent Deck (Section 1)
Retired Decks
Affix Deck
Spelling Sound Sheet 78
Sight Word Card 59
Worksheet 107
Reader 39 (*Punkin Gets a Surprise*)
colored pencils

Lesson **108** Activity Sheet 6
Review Decks
Letter Card 65
phone receiver, child's telephone, or a tape of a phone ringing
Picture Card 79
Worksheet 108

Lesson **109** Alphabet/Accent Deck (Section 2)
Review Decks
Spelling Sound Sheet 79
Picture Card 80
Worksheet 109
Reader 40 (*Roger the Rat*)
colored pencils

Lesson **110** Alphabet/Accent Deck (Section 2)
Review Decks
Assessment 21
Spelling Test 19
Assessment 21 Recording Form
Kid Cards
tokens

Week 23

Lesson **111** container of letter tiles
Review Decks
Worksheet 111
Spelling List 20

Lesson **112** Alphabet/Accent Deck (Section 1)
Retired Decks
Affix Deck
Spelling Sound Sheet 80
Letter Cards 66–68
knotted rope in a sack
Picture Cards 81–83
Sight Word Cards 60–61
Worksheet 112
Reader 41 (*Carlo is Sick*)
colored pencils

Lesson **113** assorted items
Review Decks
Spelling Sound Sheet 81
tokens or colored pencil
Worksheet 113

Lesson **114** Alphabet/Accent Deck (Section 2)
Review Decks
Spelling Sound Sheet 82
Sight Word Cards 62–64
Worksheet 114
Reader 42 (*Amber at the Beach*)
colored pencils

Lesson **115** Alphabet/Accent Deck (Section 2)
Review Decks
Assessment 22
Spelling Test 20
Assessment 22 Recording Form
Kid Cards
tokens

Week 24

Lesson **116** container of letter tiles
Review Decks
Letter Card 69
a patch in a sack
Picture Card 84
Sight Word Card 65
Worksheet 116
Spelling List 21

Lesson **117** Alphabet/Accent Deck (Section 2)
Retired Decks
Affix Deck

Spelling Sound Sheet 83
Letter Card 70
Picture Card 85
Sight Word Card 66
Worksheet 117
Reader 43 (*Butterscotch*)
colored pencils

Lesson **118** Activity Sheet 7
Review Decks
Worksheet 118

Lesson **119** Alphabet/Accent Deck (Section 1)
Review Decks
Spelling Sound Sheet 84
Letter Card 71
Picture Cards 86–87
Sight Word Card 67
Worksheet 119
Reader 44 (*Summer and Minnie*)
colored pencils

Lesson **120** Alphabet/Accent Deck (Section 2)
Review Decks
Assessment 23
Spelling Test 21
Assessment 23 Recording Form
Kid Cards
tokens

Week 25

Lesson **121** container of letter tiles
Review Decks
Letter Card 72
Picture Cards 88–89
Spelling Card 46
Worksheet 121
Spelling List 22

Lesson **122** Alphabet/Accent Deck (Section 3)
Retired Decks
Affix Deck
Spelling Sound Sheet 85
Letter Card 73
Picture Card 90
Spelling Card 47
Sight Word Cards 68–69
Worksheet 122
Reader 45 (*Stan and Steve*)
colored pencils

Lesson **123** purple Kid Cards
Review Decks
Spelling Sound Sheet 86
tokens or colored pencil
Sight Word Card 70
Picture Cards 91–92
Worksheet 123

Lesson **124** Alphabet/Accent Deck (any section)
Review Decks
Spelling Sound Sheet 87
Letter Card 74
Picture Card 93
Spelling Card 48
Sight Word Cards 71–72
Worksheet 124
Reader 46 (*Carly's Collection*)
colored pencils

Lesson **125** Alphabet/Accent Deck (Section 3)
Review Decks
Assessment 24
Spelling Test 22
Assessment 24 Recording Form
Kid Cards
tokens

Week 26

Lesson **126** container of letter tiles
Review Decks
Letter Card 75
Picture Card 94
Worksheet 126
Spelling List 23

Lesson **127** Alphabet/Accent Deck (any section)
Retired Decks
Affix Deck
Spelling Sound Sheet 88
Picture Card 95
Sight Word Cards 73–75
Worksheet 127
Reader 47 (*Bo and the Bagel*)
colored pencils

Lesson **128** purple Kid Cards
Review Decks
Spelling Sound Sheet 89
tokens or colored pencil
Sight Word Card 76
Worksheet 128

Lesson ***129*** Alphabet/Accent Deck (any section)
Review Decks
Spelling Sound Sheet 90
Affix Card 9
Worksheet 129
Reader 48 (*A Long Car Trip*)
colored pencils

Lesson ***130*** Alphabet/Accent Deck (any section)
Review Decks
Assessment 25
Spelling Test 23
Assessment 25 Recording Form
Kid Cards
tokens

WEEK 27

Lesson ***131*** container of letter tiles
Review Decks
Affix Cards 10–11
Worksheet 131
Spelling List 24

Lesson ***132*** Alphabet/Accent Deck (any section)
Retired Decks
Affix Deck
Spelling Sound Sheet 91
Picture Cards 96–97
dollar in a sack
Sight Word Cards 77–78
Worksheet 132
Reader 49 (*The Big Fight*)
colored pencils

Lesson ***133*** purple Kid Cards
Review Decks
Spelling Sound Sheet 92
tokens or colored pencil
sponge in a sack
Picture Card 98
Worksheet 133

Lesson ***134*** Alphabet/Accent Deck (any section)
Review Decks
Spelling Sound Sheet 93
Sight Word Cards 79–80
Worksheet 134
Reader 50 (*Hudson Goes to Work*)
colored pencils

Lesson ***135*** Alphabet/Accent Deck (any section)
Review Decks
Assessment 26
Spelling Test 24
Assessment 26 Recording Form
Kid Cards
tokens

WEEK 28

Lesson ***136*** container of letter tiles
Review Decks
Affix Card 12
Worksheet 136
Spelling List 25

Lesson ***137*** Alphabet/Accent Deck (any section)
Retired Decks
Affix Deck
Spelling Sound Sheet 94
Letter Card 76
receipt in a sack
Picture Cards 99–100
Sight Word Cards 81–82
Worksheet 137
Reader 51 (*Grandpa John*)
colored pencils

Lesson ***138*** purple Kid Cards
Review Decks
Letter Card 77
Picture Cards 101–102
cashew nuts
Worksheet 138

Lesson ***139*** Alphabet/Accent Deck (any section)
Review Decks
Spelling Sound Sheet 95
Affix Cards 13–14
Sight Word Cards 83–84
Worksheet 139
Reader 52 (*A New Home*)
colored pencils

Lesson ***140*** container of letter tiles
Review Decks
Assessment 27
Spelling Test 25
Assessment 27 Recording Form
Kid Cards
tokens

LESSON 1 — The Letter *N*

lesson preparation

materials

alphabet strip

rubber band

tin can or plastic foam cup

Spelling Sound Sheet 1

letter tile in a container (see *the night before*)

Letter Card 1

Picture Card 1

Spelling Card 1

Worksheet 1

new concepts

vowel

consonant

capital

initial

echo

vibration

voiced

unvoiced

the night before

- If you have not read the information that precedes this lesson, do so now.
- Stretch a rubber band lengthwise around the can or cup. For this lesson, tin cans work better than plastic foam cups, but may be harder to find.
- Punch out the *n* letter tile. Put it in a container such as a plastic butter tub, bag with a zip top, or small box. You will be adding new letter tiles periodically.

ALPHABET ACTIVITY

- The student should be seated with the alphabet strip.
- **Note:** The alphabet strip should be available in every lesson and during every assessment. You may want to tape it to the desk or table top where the student will be working, or you may choose to distribute and collect it again each day.

  "This is called an 'alphabet strip.' Let's look at it."

  "There are two kinds of letters that make up our alphabet. They are vowels and consonants."

  "The vowels are a, e, i, o, and u. Did you notice that the vowels are the letters in red?"

- Point to each vowel to show that it is printed in red.
- **Note:** The letter *y* is treated as a consonant until Lesson 61.

  "All of the other letters are called consonants."

"Let's point to each letter and say the whole alphabet. Put your index finger on 'a' and say the names with me."

- Demonstrate which finger is the index finger. Then begin reciting the alphabet.
- Try to set a steady pace so the student cannot sing the alphabet. Although students who attended kindergarten should know the letters, some will not. Do not be concerned if the student cannot stay on the correct letter. If you find the student on the wrong letter, just show him or her where you are, and continue.

PHONEMIC AWARENESS

- **Objective:** To identify initial sounds in spoken words.

  "I am going to say some words. See if you can tell me the beginning sound in these words."

- When giving words, it helps to exaggerate the sound you want identified.
- Point to your mouth as you say the following words: table, too, timber.
- Some students will have difficulty isolating the sounds. Slowly repeat the words until the student can answer. Then ask:

  "What sound do you hear at the beginning of these words?" */t/*

- **Note:** A letter appearing between parallel lines (e.g., /t/) stands for the *sound* of the letter rather than the letter name. If the student responds with the name of the letter, ask again: "What sound do you hear?" Make sure the student is giving the pure sound of *t* and not pronouncing it with a short *u* sound, as in /tŭh/. (For help pronouncing the precise letter sounds, refer to the audiotape.)
- Point to your mouth and say the following words: lost, lemon, lollipop.

  "What sound do you hear at the beginning of these words?" */l/*

- Point to your mouth and say the following words: no, nine, nifty.

  "What sound do you hear at the beginning of these words?" */n/*

- Point to your mouth and say the following words: paper, petunia, people.

  "What sound do you hear at the beginning of these words?" */p/*

NEW LEARNING

- The student should be seated where he/she can see the chalkboard.

  "I am going to use your name to teach something today. Your first name is (Kim) and your last name is (Jones)."

- Write the student's name on the chalkboard.

  "Let's look at your name. What is the first letter in your first name?" *(K)*

  "Names are special, so we use a special type of letter. We call it a 'capital' letter."

- Write a capital (K) under the student's first name.

"This is a capital (K). What is the first letter in your last name?" *(J)*

"The first letter in your last name is a (j). What kind of special letter do we use?" *capital letter*

- Write a capital (J) under the student's last name.

"These are the initials in your name. They are called initials because they come at the beginning of your name. The word 'initial' means 'beginning.' "

- Repeat this activity with your own name. Encourage the student to come to the chalkboard and write his/her initials. Later in the day, have the student return to the chalkboard to circle his/her initials.
- The student should be seated for the remainder of this activity.

"Have you ever been to the mountains or hills where you can yell 'Hello!' and the mountains yell 'Hello!' back?"

- If the student has not been to the mountains, give another example of an echo, such as an echo in a large, empty room.

"This is called an 'echo.' There will be many times this year when you are going to act like the mountains and 'echo' words back to me."

"Let's practice echoing. I'll say 'Hello!' to you and I want you to echo 'Hello!' back to me. Hellooooooo!" *Hello!*

"Now I'm going to say some words to you and I want you to echo them back to me. Listen for the sound that is the same in the beginning, or initial, position of each word."

- Point to your mouth as you say each word.

"Echo after me. Note." *note* ***"Numb."*** *numb* ***"Nip."*** *nip*

"What sound do you hear in the beginning, or initial, position?" */n/*

- If necessary, slowly repeat the words until the student can answer. Make sure the student is giving the pure sound of *n* and not pronouncing it with a short *u* sound, as in /nŭh/. (If desired, refer to the audiotape for the precise sound.)

"/N/ is the sound you hear in the initial position of these words."

- Get out the can or cup with a rubber band stretched over the end. Begin plucking the rubber band as if it were a guitar string.

"Watch what this (can) does when I pluck it like a guitar. What do you notice about the rubber band?" *it moves*

"That is what your vocal cords do when you make certain sounds."

"Now I want you to try plucking this rubber band and see if it moves."

- Give the student the (can) and have him/her pluck the rubber band.

"Feel the (can) and tell me what you notice." *it wiggles, tickles, or vibrates*

"The wiggling or tickling you feel is called 'vibration.' "

"There is a part of our body that is like a can."

- Put your hands around your neck to show its cylindrical shape.

  "We have vocal cords inside our necks that are similar to rubber bands because they vibrate. Put your four fingertips on the front of your neck and say /n/. See if you feel your throat vibrating like the (can) did."

- Demonstrate; then allow a moment for the student to try.

  "When a letter sound makes your vocal cords vibrate, it is called a 'voiced sound.' Since /n/ vibrates, it is a voiced sound."

  "Let's try a sound that is unvoiced. An unvoiced sound won't make your vocal cords vibrate. Say /s/." */s/*

  "/S/ is unvoiced because the vocal cords do not vibrate."

  "I am going to write some words on the chalkboard."

- Write the following words on the chalkboard: not, nap, net.

  "What letter do you see that might be making the /n/ sound?" *n*

- If the student does not know the name of the letter, say it for him/her.

  "N is the first letter in all of these words, so we can see that n must be the letter used to spell the /n/ sound."

  "Look at your alphabet strip. Can you tell me if n is a vowel or a consonant?" *consonant*

  "That's right. We know that a, e, i, o, and u are vowels, so n must be a consonant."

HANDWRITING/LETTER TILES

- The student should be seated where he/she can write comfortably.
- Write a capital *N* on the chalkboard.

  "This is a capital letter N. Let's practice skywriting capital N's before you write them on your paper."

- Demonstrate how to skywrite letters. The student should keep his/her arms as straight as possible. Do not let the student bend his/her wrists or elbows when forming the letter shapes. Each letter should be about two feet tall. Provide assistance as needed.
- Give the student **Spelling Sound Sheet 1.**

  "Leave your pencil on your desk until I tell you to pick it up."

  "This is called a spelling sound sheet. We will practice writing our new letter on this paper."

- Draw handwriting lines on the chalkboard:

  "These are handwriting lines like you have on your paper."

- Write a capital *N* on the handwriting lines in the handwriting you want the student to learn.

  "Now pick up your pencil. Find the first line on your paper and practice writing capital N's like I wrote this one on the chalkboard."

  "Say the name of the letter each time you write it."

- Allow a few minutes for the student to practice writing capital *N*'s. Provide assistance as necessary.

  "Put your pencil back on your desk."

- Write a lowercase *n* on the handwriting lines in the handwriting you want the student to learn.

  "This is a lowercase letter n."

- Have the student practice skywriting lowercase *n*'s.

  "Now pick up your pencil and practice writing lowercase n's on the second line of your paper. Say the name of the letter each time you write it."

- Again, provide assistance as necessary.
- Have the student set the spelling sound sheet aside for use later in the lesson.
- Leave the handwriting lines and letters on the chalkboard for the remainder of the lesson.
- Give the student the container with the *n* letter tile inside.

  "This is a letter tile. Today I have given you an n."

  "Take out your n letter tile and look at each side. One side has a capital N and the other side has a lowercase n."

- Allow time for the student to examine the letter tile.

  "Hold your letter tile up in the air. Turn it so I can see the capital N."

  "Now turn it so I can see the lowercase n."

- Have the student replace the tile in the container and put it away.
- Reinforce the name, sound, and shape of the letter *n* throughout the day. (See the introductory material for suggestions.)

New Deck Cards

- Show the student **Letter Card 1.**

  "What letter is this?" *n*

- Hold up **Picture Card 1** but keep the picture covered with your hand (or the letter card).

  "I have a card with a picture on it that begins with the /n/ sound."

  "I am going to describe it to you. See if you can guess what the picture is."

"These are made with twigs, grass, hair, or string. Birds make their homes and lay their eggs here. What do you think the picture is?" *nest*

"That's right. From now on, we will use the word 'nest' to help us remember the /n/ sound. 'Nest' is our 'keyword' for the /n/ sound."

"A keyword is a word that contains our new sound and helps us remember the new sound."

- Show the student **Picture Card 1,** and then point to the picture of a nest on the alphabet strip.

"The word 'nest' helps us remember the /n/ sound because it begins with /n/."

"Find your spelling sound sheet."

"Find the #1 on your paper and put your finger on it."

- Hold up **Spelling Card 1** so that only you can see what is written.
- Hand signals that accompany this sequence are as follows: 1. Point to your mouth as you say the sound; 2. Point to the student to indicate that he/she is to echo the sound; 3. Extend your hand palm up as you ask for the name of the letter that makes the sound; 4. Point straight down to indicate that the student is to write the letter. The student will eventually follow the hand signals without verbal cues.

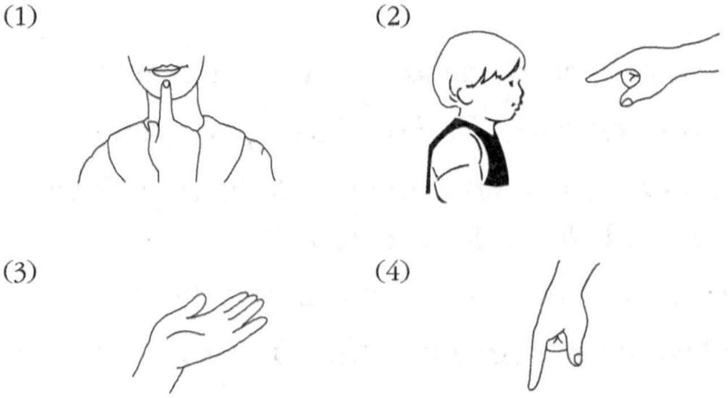

- Follow the instructions on the card, or use the following verbal cues until the student is familiar with the procedure:

"Echo this sound: /n/." */n/*

"What letter makes this sound?" *n*

"Write the lowercase letter n on the line by #1."

- **Note:** If the student has extreme difficulty writing, have him/her manipulate letter tiles instead of writing letters. The goal of the spelling card activities is to spell sounds correctly, not to write letters perfectly.
- Check the spelling sound sheet for accuracy.
- **Note:** The letter, picture, and spelling cards used in this lesson form what will now be referred to as the "Review Decks." See the introductory material for tips on deck maintenance.

WORKSHEET

- Seat the student where he/she can write comfortably.

  "I am going to give you your first worksheet. On most days, we will have a worksheet after our lesson."

- Write "Worksheet 1" on the chalkboard. Then hold up the worksheet and point to "Worksheet 1" at the top of the page.

  "When I give you the worksheet, find the side that has 'worksheet' written on it."

- Give the student **Worksheet 1.** Make sure he/she turns to the correct side.

  "This is the side we will do together."

  "Find the #1 on your paper. Tell me what the picture is." *nest*

  "Can you tell me the sound in the initial, or beginning, position of 'nest'?" */n/*

  "Write the lowercase letter that says /n/ on the line under #1."

- Repeat this procedure with #2 (nose), #3 (nap), #4 (necklace), #5 (net), and #6 (neck).
- As the student works, provide help as needed. Help the student correct any incorrect answers. Then initial the worksheet in the space provided.
- **Note:** Always make sure the worksheet is corrected before the student begins the homework. The worksheet serves as a guide to help complete the homework.

HOMEWORK

"Turn your paper over. This is the side that you will do by yourself."

"Put your finger on the top row of handwriting lines. Write your best capital N on the line so I will know what a capital N should look like."

- Have the student write a lowercase letter *n* on the second handwriting line.
- Make sure that the student has written the letters correctly (to the best of his or her ability). He/She will use them as guides when completing the homework.

  "Do you know what to do on the rest of the homework paper?"

- Discuss the homework pictures to make sure the student understands the word each one represents: #1 (nurse), #2 (needle), #3 (napkin), #4 (newspaper), #5 (number), and #6 (nag).

  "If you need help, look at the worksheet side. There will usually be an activity on the worksheet side that is similar to your homework."

  "When you finish your paper, I will check it for you and initial it in the space provided."

- The student may complete the homework now or later in the day. If possible, allow the student to complete the homework independently. When the student is through, help him/her correct any incorrect answers. Then initial the homework in the space provided.

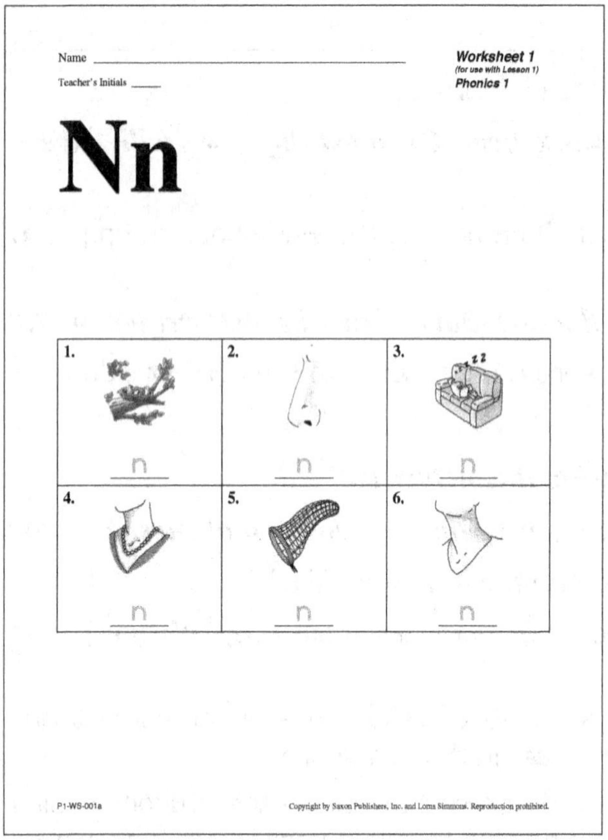

Name ______________________

Teacher's Initials _____

Worksheet 1
(for use with Lesson 1)
Phonics 1

Nn

1. n	2. n	3. n
4. n	5. n	6. n

P1-WS-001a

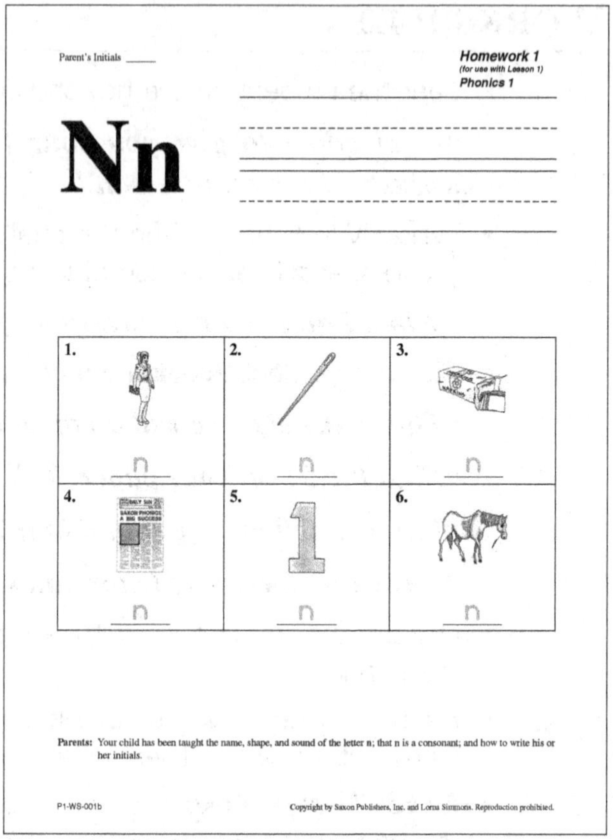

Parent's Initials _____

Homework 1
(for use with Lesson 1)
Phonics 1

Nn

1. n	2. n	3. n
4. n	5. n	6. n

Parents: Your child has been taught the name, shape, and sound of the letter n; that n is a consonant; and how to write his or her initials.

P1-WS-001b

LESSON 2 — The Letter *O*, Part 1

lesson preparation

materials

Review Decks
Spelling Sound Sheet 2
Letter Card 2
Picture Card 2
Spelling Card 2
Worksheet 2
Rule Book

new concepts

final
short vowel sound
breve
coding
blending
vowel rule

ALPHABET ACTIVITY

- The student should be seated with the alphabet strip.
- **Reminder:** The alphabet strip should be available in every lesson.

"Let's look at the alphabet strip."

"What two kinds of letters make up our alphabet?" *vowels and consonants*

"What do we call the letters in red?" *vowels*

"All of the other letters are called _________?" *consonants*

"If the alphabet had an initial, what letter would it be?" *a*

"Where do you think the final letter would be?" *at the end*

"The word 'final' means 'at the end.' "

"So the final letter of the alphabet is _________?" *z*

"Let's point to each letter and say the whole alphabet."

"Put your index finger on 'a' and say the names with me."

- Try to set a steady pace so the student cannot sing the alphabet. Although students who attended kindergarten should know the letters, some will not. Do not be concerned if the student cannot stay on the correct letter. If you find the student on the wrong letter, just show him or her where you are, and continue.

PHONEMIC AWARENESS

- **Objective:** To identify initial sounds in spoken words.

  "I am going to say some words. See if you can tell me the initial, or beginning, sound in these words."
- When giving words to the student, it helps to exaggerate the sound you want identified.
- Point to your mouth as you say the following words: me, most, mud.
- Some students will have difficulty isolating the sounds. Slowly repeat the words until the student can answer. Then ask:

  "What sound do you hear at the beginning of these words?" */m/*
- Be sure to have the student tell you the sound, not the letter name.
- Point to your mouth and say the following words: ostrich, often, otter.

  "What sound do you hear at the beginning of these words?" */ŏ/*
- Point to your mouth and say the following words: be, boast, batch.

  "What sound do you hear at the beginning of these words?" */b/*
- Point to your mouth and say the following words: right, read, rat.

  "What sound do you hear at the beginning of these words?" */r/*

REVIEW OF DECKS

- The student should be seated where he/she can write comfortably.
- Show the student **Letter Card 1.**

  "What letter is this?" *n*
- Show the student **Picture Card 1** and point to the nest.

  "What is the initial sound we hear in 'nest'?" */n/*

  "The word 'nest' is our keyword for n because we hear the /n/ sound at the beginning of the word."
- Point to the letter *n* on the picture card.

  "What is the sound the letter n makes?" */n/*
- Give the student **Spelling Sound Sheet 2.**

  "Find the #1 on your paper and put your finger there."
- Hold up **Spelling Card 1** so that only you can see what is written.
- Hand signals that accompany this sequence are as follows: 1. Point to your mouth as you say the sound; 2. Point to the student to indicate that he/she is to echo the sound; 3. Extend your hand palm up as you ask for the name of the letter that makes the sound; 4. Point straight down to indicate that the student is to write the letter. The student will eventually follow the hand signals without verbal cues.

- Follow the instructions on the card, or use the following verbal cues until the student is familiar with the procedure:

  "Echo this sound: /n/." */n/*

  "What letter makes this sound?" *n*

  "Write the lowercase letter n on the line by #1."

- Write a lowercase *n* on the chalkboard in case the student has forgotten how to make an *n*.
- Have the student set the spelling sound sheet aside for use later in the lesson.

New Learning

"I am going to say some words to you and I want you to echo them back to me. Listen for the sound that is the same at the beginning of each word."

- Point to your mouth as you say each word.

  "Echo after me. Off." *off* ***"On."*** *on* ***"Odd."*** *odd*

  "What sound do you hear in the initial position?" */ŏ/*

- If necessary, slowly repeat the words until the student can answer.
- **Note:** A letter appearing between parallel lines (e.g., /ŏ/) stands for the *sound* of the letter rather than the letter name. If the student responds with the name of the letter, ask again: "What sound do you hear?"

  "/Ŏ/ is the sound that you hear in the initial, or beginning, position of these words."

  "Put your fingertips on the front of your neck and say /ŏ/. See if you feel any vibration. When a letter sound makes your vocal cords vibrate, it is a voiced sound."

  "Is this sound voiced or unvoiced?" *voiced*

  "Since /ŏ/ vibrates, it is a voiced sound."

  "I am going to write these words on the chalkboard."

- Write the following words on the chalkboard: off, on, odd.

  "What letter do you see that might be making the /ŏ/ sound?" *o*

- If the student does not know the name of the letter, say it for him/her.

  "O is the first letter in all of these words, so we can see that o must be the letter used to spell the /ŏ/ sound."

  "Look at your alphabet strip. Can you tell me if o is a vowel or a consonant?" *vowel*

  "That's right. We know that a, e, i, o and u are vowels, so o is a vowel."

HANDWRITING

- The student should be seated where he/she can write comfortably.
- Write a capital *O* on the chalkboard.

  "This is a capital O. Let's practice skywriting capital O's before we write them on our paper."
- Have the student practice skywriting capital *O*'s. The student should keep his/her elbows and wrists locked and make each letter about two feet tall.

  "Find your spelling sound sheet. Leave your pencil on your desk until I tell you to pick it up."
- Draw handwriting lines on the chalkboard.

  "These are handwriting lines like you have on your paper."
- Write a capital *O* on the handwriting lines in the handwriting you want the student to learn.

  "Now pick up your pencil. Find the first line on your paper and practice writing capital O's like I wrote this one on the chalkboard."

  "Say the name of the letter each time you write it."
- Allow a few minutes for the student to practice writing capital *O*'s. Provide assistance as necessary.

  "Put your pencil back on your desk."
- Write a lowercase *o* on the handwriting lines in the handwriting you want the student to learn.

  "This is a lowercase letter o."
- Have the student practice skywriting lowercase *o*'s.

  "Now pick up your pencil and practice writing lowercase o's on the second line of your paper. Say the name of the letter each time you write it."
- Have the student set the spelling sound sheet aside for use later in the lesson.
- Leave the handwriting lines and letters on the chalkboard for the remainder of the lesson.

NEW DECK CARDS

- Show the student **Letter Card 2.**

  "What letter is this?" *o*
- Hold up **Picture Card 2** but keep the picture covered with your hand (or the letter card).

  "I have a card with a picture on it that begins with the /ŏ/ sound."

  "I am going to describe it to you. See if you can guess what the picture is."

  "This is a bird. It has two toes and a long neck. This bird is known for putting its head in the ground. What do you think the picture is?" *ostrich*

"That's right. The keyword is 'ostrich' and the sound we have learned is /ŏ/."

- Show the student **Picture Card 2,** and then point to the picture of an ostrich on the alphabet strip.

  "The word 'ostrich' helps us remember the /ŏ/ sound because it begins with the /ŏ/ sound."

  "Can you tell me if the letter o is a vowel or a consonant?" *vowel*

  "That's right! Find your spelling sound sheet again."

  "Find the #2 on your paper and put your finger on it."

- Hold up **Spelling Card 2** so only you can see what is written. Using the hand signals described earlier, follow the instructions on the card. (Or use the following verbal cues until the student is familiar with the procedure.)

  "Echo this sound: /ŏ/." */ŏ/*

  "What letter makes this sound?" *o*

  "Write the lowercase letter o on the line by #2."

- **Note:** If the student has extreme difficulty writing, have him/her manipulate letter tiles instead of writing letters. The goal of the spelling card activities is to spell sounds correctly, not to write letters perfectly.
- Check the spelling sound sheet for accuracy.
- **Note:** Add the new letter, picture, and spelling cards to the Review Decks.

WORKSHEET

- The student should be seated where he/she can write comfortably.
- Write "Worksheet 2" on the chalkboard. Then hold up the worksheet and point to "Worksheet 2" at the top of the page.

  "When I give you the worksheet, find the side that has 'worksheet' written on it."

- Give the student **Worksheet 2.** Make sure he/she turns to the correct side.

  "This is the side we will do together."

  "Find the #1 on your paper. Tell me what the picture is." *octopus*

  "Can you tell me the sound in the initial, or beginning, position of 'octopus'?" */ŏ/*

  "Write the lowercase letter that says /ŏ/ on the line under #1."

- Repeat this procedure with #2 (ostrich) and #3 (numbers).
- Write the word "on" on the chalkboard.

  "Do you see a vowel in this word?" *yes, an o*

  "Do you see anything after the o?" *yes, an n*

- Point to the *n*.

  "Is n a vowel or a consonant?" *a consonant*

  "When a vowel is followed by a consonant, the vowel is short."

- Point to the *o*.

  "This vowel has a consonant after it, so it is short. We will code it with a breve. A breve looks like a smile."
- Put a breve over the *o*: ŏn.

  "We code letters to help us remember the sounds they make. When a vowel has a breve over it, it makes its short sound, like the /ŏ/ in 'ostrich.' "
- Point to the *n*.

  "What is the sound of this letter?" */n/*

  "Let's blend these two sounds together and see what word they make."
- Blending is the process of combining sounds to form words. Say the first sound, /ŏ/, and do not let go of that sound until you "blend" into the /n/ sound. The student will discover that the word is "on."

  "When we read, we blend the sounds of letters together to form words, like the word 'on.' "

  "Can you use the word 'on' in a sentence?" *expect various answers*

  "Look at the word by #4 on your paper."

  "Is there a vowel in this word?" *yes*

  "When a vowel is followed by a consonant, the vowel is short."

  "Code the vowel on your paper with a breve."
- Point to the breve on the chalkboard to remind the student how to make one.

  "Let's try to blend the sounds in this word together."
- Say the first sound, /ŏ/, and do not let go of that sound until you "blend" into the /n/ sound.

  "What is the word?" *on*

  "Do you see a picture of something that is on?" *yes*

  "Draw a line from the word 'on' to the picture of something that is on."
- Allow time for the student to do this. Then hold up the **Rule Book.**

  "I'm going to give you a new book today. This book will help you remember many of the new things you're going to be learning this year."
- Allow a few minutes for the student to examine the Rule Book.

  "Now turn to page 1."
- Show the student **Rule Chart 1.** Point to the letters as you explain:

  "V stands for any vowel, and c stands for any consonant."

  "You can use this rule chart anytime you need help coding vowels."
- **Note:** The Rule Book should be kept in an area where the student has immediate access to it (even during the worksheet and assessment activities). You might prefer to remove each rule chart after it is introduced and hang it on the wall; otherwise, store the book with the materials needed daily (i.e., the alphabet strip

and a pencil). However you choose to store the Rule Book, its contents should always be readily available to the student.

- Refer to **Rule Chart 1** every time the student codes so he/she will learn to refer to the chart when help is needed.
- As the student works, provide help as needed. Help the student correct any incorrect answers. Then initial the worksheet in the space provided.
- **Note:** Always make sure the worksheet is corrected before the student begins the homework. The worksheet serves as a guide to help complete the homework.

HOMEWORK

"Turn your paper over to the homework side."

"Put your finger on the top row of handwriting lines. Write your best capital O on the line so I will know what a capital O should look like."

- Have the student write a lowercase letter *o* on the second handwriting line.
- Make sure that the student has written the letters correctly (to the best of his or her ability). He/She will use them as guides when completing the homework.

"Do you know what to do on the rest of the homework paper?"

- Discuss the homework pictures to make sure the student understands the word each one represents: #1 (ostrich), #2 (ox), #3 (newspaper), #4 (nose), #5 (something "off"), and #6 (octopus).

"If you need help, look at the worksheet side. There will usually be an activity on the worksheet side that is similar to your homework."

"When you finish your paper, I will check it for you and initial it in the space provided."

- The student may complete the homework now or later in the day. If possible, allow the student to complete the homework independently. When the student is through, help him/her correct any incorrect answers. Then initial the homework in the space provided.

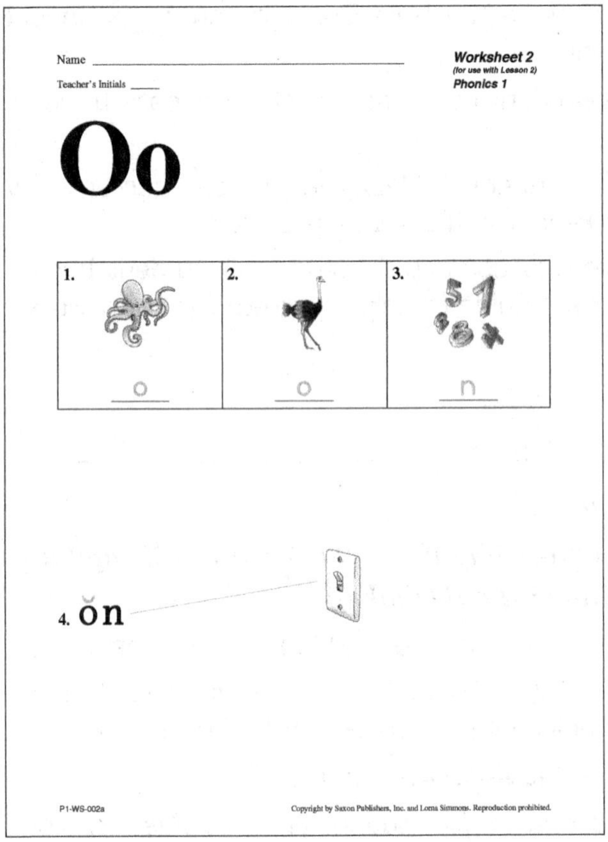

Name ______________________ **Worksheet 2** *(for use with Lesson 2)* **Phonics 1**

Teacher's Initials ____

Oo

1.	2.	3.
o	o	n

4. ŏn

P1-WS-002a

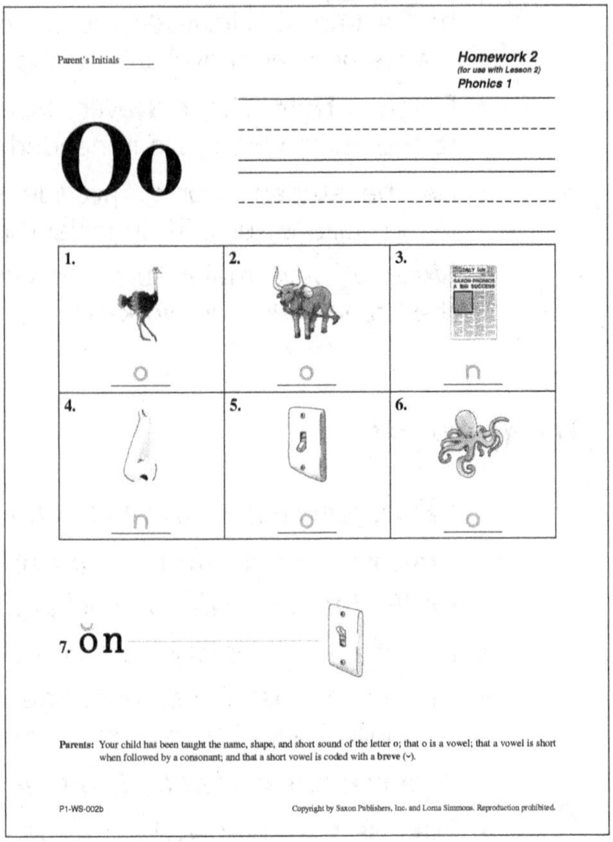

Parent's Initials ____ **Homework 2** *(for use with Lesson 2)* **Phonics 1**

Oo

1.	2.	3.
o	o	n
4.	**5.**	**6.**
n	o	o

7. ŏn

Parents: Your child has been taught the name, shape, and short sound of the letter o; that o is a vowel; that a vowel is short when followed by a consonant; and that a short vowel is coded with a **breve** (˘).

P1-WS-002b

LESSON 3 — The Letter *O*, Part 2

lesson preparation

materials

Review Decks

Spelling Sound Sheet 3

container of letter tiles

Picture Card 3

Spelling Card 3

Worksheet 3

new concepts

long vowel sound

macron

accent mark

the night before

- Add the *o* letter tile to the student's container.

ALPHABET ACTIVITY

- The student should be seated with the alphabet strip.

  "Let's look at the alphabet strip."

  "Do you know how many letters are in the alphabet?" *expect various answers*

  "Put your index finger on 'a' and count the letters with me."

- Point to each letter on the alphabet strip as you count the letters in the alphabet.

  "What two kinds of letters make up our alphabet?" *vowels and consonants*

  "Name the vowels." *a, e, i, o, and u*

  "All of the other letters are called _________?" *consonants*

  "Let's point to each letter and say the whole alphabet."

  "Put your index finger on 'a' and say the names with me."

- Try to set a steady pace so the student cannot sing the alphabet.

  "The initial, or beginning, letter of the alphabet is _____?" *a*

  "The final, or last, letter of the alphabet is _____?" *z*

Phonemic Awareness

- **Objective:** To identify initial sounds in spoken words.

  "I am going to say some words. See if you can tell me the initial, or beginning, sound in these words."
- When giving words to the student, it helps to exaggerate the sound you want identified.
- Point to your mouth as you say the following words: chip, chair, cheese.
- Some students will have difficulty isolating the sounds. Slowly repeat the words until the student can answer. Then ask:

  "What sound do you hear at the beginning of these words?" */ch/*
- Be sure to have the student tell you the sound, not the letter name(s).
- Point to your mouth and say the following words: ship, share, she.

  "What sound do you hear at the beginning of these words?" */sh/*
- Point to your mouth and say the following words: thin, thank, thumb.

  "What sound do you hear at the beginning of these words?" */th/*
- Continue with additional words as time permits.

Review of Decks

- The student should be seated where he/she can write comfortably.
- Show the student **Letter Cards 1** and **2** in random order.

  "Name the letters."
- The student should name the letter on each letter card.
- Show the student **Picture Cards 1** and **2** in random order.

  "Name the keyword and sound for each card."
- The student should name the keyword and sound for each picture card.
- Give the student **Spelling Sound Sheet 3.**
- Call out the sounds on **Spelling Cards 1** and **2** in random order. Hand signals that accompany this sequence are as follows: 1. Point to your mouth as you say the sound; 2. Point to the student to indicate that he/she is to echo the sound; 3. Extend your hand palm up as you ask for the name of the letter that makes the sound; 4. Point straight down to indicate that the student is to write the letter. The student will eventually follow the hand signals without verbal cues.
- The student should echo each sound and name the letter that makes the sound as he/she writes the letter on the spelling sound sheet.
- Check the student's response after each card.
- Have the student set the spelling sound sheet aside for use later in the lesson.

NEW LEARNING

"Can you tell me a word that starts with the short sound of the letter o?" *expect various answers*

"The short sound of the vowel o is /ŏ/."

"Vowels have at least two sounds, a long sound and a short sound."

"Today we are going to work with words that start with the long sound of o."

"I am going to say some words to you and I want you to echo them back to me. Listen for the sound that is the same at the beginning, or initial, position of each word."

- Point to your mouth as you say each word.

"Echo after me. Oval." *oval* ***"Over."*** *over* ***"Open."*** *open*

"What sound do you hear in the initial position?" */ō/*

- If necessary, slowly repeat the words until the student can answer.

"That's right. The sound you hear in the initial position is /ō/."

"Put your fingertips on the front of your neck and say /ō/. See if you feel any vibration."

"Is this sound voiced or unvoiced?" *voiced*

"Since /ō/ vibrates, it is a voiced sound."

- Write the following words on the chalkboard: no, so, go.

"What letter do you see that might be making the /ō/ sound?" *o*

- If the student does not know the name of the letter, say it for him/her.

"O is the second letter in all of these words, so we can see that o must be the letter used to spell the /ō/ sound."

"Look at your alphabet strip. Can you tell me if o is a vowel or a consonant?" *vowel*

LETTER TILES

- Give the student the container of letter tiles.

"Today I've given you a new letter tile."

"Find your o letter tile and look at it. One side has a capital O and the other side has a lowercase o."

- Allow time for the student to examine the new letter tile.

"Hold your letter tile up in the air. Turn it so I can see the capital O."

"Now turn it so I can see the lowercase o."

"See if you can use your letter tiles to spell the word 'on.' "

- Make sure the student has arranged the tiles correctly.
- Have the student replace the tiles in the container and put it away.
- Reinforce the name, sound, and shape of the letter *o* throughout the day. (See the introductory material for suggestions.)

NEW DECK CARDS

- **Reminder:** The Rule Book should be available in every lesson.
- Show the student **Letter Card 2.**

  "What letter is this?" *o*

- Hold up **Picture Card 3** but keep the picture covered with your hand (or the letter card).

  "I have a card with a picture on it that begins with the /ō/ sound, which is also this vowel's name."

  "I am going to describe this picture to you. See if you can guess what it is."

  "This is what you do to a door if you want to go outside. You would do this to a window if you wanted some fresh air. We do it to the wrappers on things we want to eat, and on your birthday, you get to do it to your presents. What do you think the picture is?" *open*

  "That's right. The keyword is 'open' and the sound we have learned is /ō/."

- Show the student **Picture Card 3.**

  "The word 'open' helps us remember the long sound of o because it begins with the /ō/ sound."

  "Find your spelling sound sheet."

  "Find the #3 on your paper and put your finger on it."

- Hold up **Spelling Card 3** so only you can see what is written. Using the hand signals described earlier, follow the instructions on the card. (Or use the following verbal cues until the student is familiar with the procedure.)

  "Echo this sound: /ō/." /ō/

  "What letter makes this sound?" *o*

  "Write the lowercase letter o on the line by #3."

- **Note:** If the student has extreme difficulty writing, have him/her manipulate letter tiles instead of writing letters. The goal of the spelling card activities is to spell sounds correctly, not to write letters perfectly.
- Check the spelling sound sheet for accuracy.
- **Note:** Add the new picture and spelling cards to the Review Decks. Always keep **Picture Card 3** behind **Picture Card 2** to help the student remember that the letter *o* has two sounds. (The picture deck is the only deck wherein certain cards must remain together. See the introductory material for specific information.)

WORKSHEET

- The student should be seated where he/she can write comfortably.
- Write "Worksheet 3" on the chalkboard. Then hold up the worksheet and point to "Worksheet 3" at the top of the page.

  "When I give you the worksheet, find the side that has 'worksheet' written on it."
- Give the student **Worksheet 3.** Make sure he/she turns to the correct side.

  "Find the #1 on your paper. Can you tell me what the picture is?" *open*

  "Can you tell me the sound in the initial, or beginning, position of 'open'?" */ō/*

  "Write the lowercase letter that says /ō/ on the line under #1."
- Repeat this procedure with #2 (nickel) and #3 (otter).
- Write the word "no" on the chalkboard.

  "Do you see a vowel in this word?" *yes*

  "Is this vowel followed by a consonant?" *no*

  "When a vowel is not followed by a consonant, it is long. We code it with a macron. A macron looks just like a straight line."
- Put a macron over the *o*: nō.

  "This vowel is also accented because 'no' is a one-syllable word. All one-syllable words will carry an accent. We will discuss accent more later, but for now we know that when the vowel is not followed by a consonant, we will code it with an accent mark."
- Put an accent mark over the *o*: nō´. Point to the *o*.

  "When a vowel is long and is coded with a macron, it says its name."

  "What is the name of this letter?" *o*

  "Then /ō/ is the sound it will make."

  "Let's try blending this word. Remember, the vowel says /ō/ instead of /ŏ/."
- Say the first sound, /n/, and do not let go of that sound until you "blend" into the /ō/ sound. The student will discover that the word is "no."
- **Note:** The following activity is written to take place in a room where the door is on the student's right. If your room is situated differently, locate another opening (window, closet door, etc.) that is to the student's right. If this is not possible, relocate the student to the left of the door.
- If the door to the room is shut, open it now.

  "Let's pretend that I am the letter o."

  "Without a consonant to stop me, I can say my name as long as I want."
- Make an extended /ō/ sound as you walk toward the door. As you reach the door, say:

  "The letter o can even decide to leave if there's no consonant to stop it."

- Resume the extended /ō/ sound as you walk out the door. After a moment, return and shut the door behind you.

"But what happens if o runs into a consonant?" *it says its short sound*

"That's right. Watch the letter o try to leave this time."

- Make another extended /ō/ sound as you walk toward the door. When you reach the closed door, bump into it and change the /ō/ sound to /ŏ/ (expressed as a disappointed "aaahhh").
- If desired, allow the student to play the "o" role.

"Get out your Rule Book and turn to page 1."

- **Note:** If the rule charts are removed, it may occasionally be necessary to modify the dialogue in the lessons accordingly.
- Point to **Rule Chart 1** as you say the following:

"When a vowel is followed by a consonant, it is closed, like the door, and the vowel is short."

"Now turn to page 2."

- Point to **Rule Chart 2** as you say the following:

"When an accented vowel is not followed by a consonant, it is open, and the vowel is long."

- Now point to the symbols on **Rule Chart 2** as you explain:

"V stands for any vowel, and the arrow means there is no consonant after it."

"You may refer to this rule chart anytime you need help coding vowels."

- Again, you may prefer to remove each rule chart after it is introduced and hang it on the wall for easy reference.
- Refer to **Rule Charts 1** and **2** whenever the student codes to help him/her learn where to look when help with coding is needed.

"Since you know how to spell three sounds, we are going to have our first spelling test. You'll be surprised how easy it is to spell when you know the letters that spell sounds."

"Put your finger by #4 on your paper. The word we are going to spell is 'no.' What is the first sound in 'no'?" */n/*

"That's right! What letter makes the /n/ sound?" *n*

"Write an n on the first line by #4."

"What is the last sound in the word 'no'?" */ō/*

"What letter makes the /ō/ sound?" *o*

"Write an o on the second line by #4."

"Look, we spelled 'no'!"

- Repeat the procedure with #5 (on).

"Read the words and see if the picture matches any of the words."

"When you are finished, draw a line from one of the words to the picture it matches."

- As the student works, provide help as needed. Help the student correct any incorrect answers. Then initial the worksheet in the space provided.
- Some time during the day, ask the student to read some or all of the words on the worksheet. Although coding is important, the ultimate goal is reading, so the student, especially if he/she is having difficulty, should read to someone every day.
- **Note:** Always make sure the worksheet is corrected before the student begins the homework. The worksheet serves as a guide to help complete the homework.

HOMEWORK

"Turn your paper over to the homework side."

"Put your finger on the top row of handwriting lines. Write your best lowercase o on the line so I will know what a lowercase o should look like."

- Have the student write a lowercase letter *n* on the second handwriting line.
- Make sure that the student has written the letters correctly (to the best of his or her ability). He/She will use them as guides when completing the homework.

"Do you know what to do on the rest of the homework paper?"

- Discuss the homework pictures to make sure the student understands the word each one represents: #1 (oatmeal), #2 (nut), #3 (something "off"), #4 (needle), #5 (ostrich), and #6 (open).

"If you need help, look at the worksheet side. There will usually be an activity on the worksheet side that is similar to your homework."

"When you finish your paper, I will check it for you and initial it in the space provided."

- The student may complete the homework now or later in the day. If possible, allow the student to do this independently. Help him/her correct any incorrect answers. Then initial the homework in the space provided.

Name ____________________ **Worksheet 3** *(for use with Lesson 3)* *Phonics 1*

Teacher's Initials _____

Oo

1.	2.	3.
o	n	o

4. n o

5. o n

P1-WS-003a

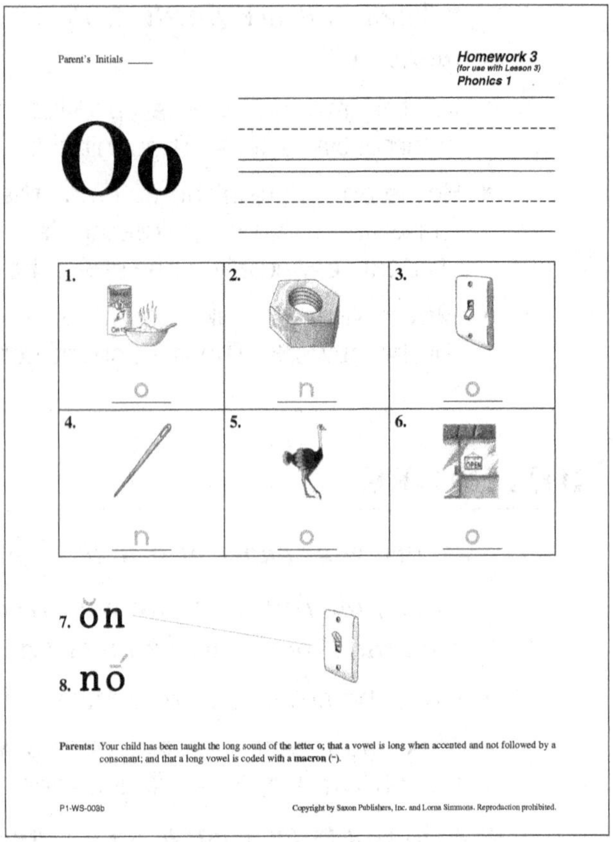

Parent's Initials _____ **Homework 3** *(for use with Lesson 3)* *Phonics 1*

Oo

1.	2.	3.
o	n	o
4.	**5.**	**6.**
n	o	o

7. ŏn

8. nṓ

Parents: Your child has been taught the long sound of the letter o; that a vowel is long when accented and not followed by a consonant; and that a long vowel is coded with a **macron** (¯).

P1-WS-003b

Lesson 4 — The Letter *T*

lesson preparation

materials

ball

Review Decks

Spelling Sound Sheet 4

container of letter tiles

Letter Card 3

Picture Card 4

Spelling Card 4

Worksheet 4

the night before

- Locate a ball the student can roll easily. An inexpensive plastic ball will work well.
- Add the *t* letter tile to the student's container.

Alphabet Activity

- The student should be seated with the alphabet strip.

"Let's look at the alphabet strip."

"How many letters are in the alphabet?" *26*

"What two kinds of letters make up our alphabet?" *vowels and consonants*

"Name the vowels." *a, e, i, o, and u*

"All of the other letters are called _________?" *consonants*

"The initial, or beginning, letter of the alphabet is _____?" *a*

"The final, or last, letter of the alphabet is _____?" *z*

"Let's sit down and play with this ball."

"We'll say the alphabet while we roll the ball."

"I'll begin with 'A' and roll the ball to you. After you catch the ball, say 'B' and roll the ball back to me. We'll continue until we complete the alphabet."

- Recite the alphabet as you roll the ball back and forth to the student.
- Have the student return to his/her seat.

Phonemic Awareness

- **Objective:** To identify initial sounds in spoken words.

  "I am going to say some words. See if you can tell me the initial, or beginning, sound in these words."
- When giving words to the student, it helps to exaggerate the sound you want identified.
- Point to your mouth as you say the following words: side, suds, sand.
- Some students will have difficulty isolating the sounds. Slowly repeat the words until the student can answer. Then ask:

  "What sound do you hear at the beginning of these words?" */s/*
- Be sure to have the student tell you the sound, not the letter name.
- Point to your mouth and say the following words: tap, turn, toss.

  "What sound do you hear at the beginning of these words?" */t/*
- Point to your mouth and say the following words: pat, port, picnic.

  "What sound do you hear at the beginning of these words?" */p/*
- Point to your mouth and say the following words: nose, neat, nephew.

  "What sound do you hear at the beginning of these words?" */n/*
- Continue with additional words as time permits.

Review of Decks

- The student should be seated where he/she can write comfortably.
- Show the student **Letter Cards 1** and **2** in random order.

  "Name the letters."
- The student should name the letter on each letter card.
- Show the student **Picture Cards 1–3** in random order.

  "Name the keyword and sound for each card."
- The student should name the keyword and sound for each picture card.
- Give the student **Spelling Sound Sheet 4.**
- Call out the sounds on **Spelling Cards 1–3** in random order. Hand signals that accompany this sequence are as follows: 1. Point to your mouth as you say the sound; 2. Point to the student to indicate that he/she is to echo the sound; 3. Extend your hand palm up as you ask for the name of the letter that makes the sound; 4. Point straight down to indicate that the student is to write the letter. The student will eventually follow the hand signals without verbal cues.
- The student should echo each sound and name the letter that makes the sound as he/she writes the letter on the spelling sound sheet.
- Have the student set the spelling sound sheet aside for use later in the lesson.

New Learning

"I am going to say some words to you and I want you to echo them back to me. Listen for the sound that is the same at the beginning, or initial, position of each word."

- Point to your mouth as you say each word.

"Echo after me. Top." *top* ***"Tin."*** *tin* ***"Tub."*** *tub*

- Slowly repeat the words until the student can answer the following question:

"What sound do you hear in the initial position?" /t/

- **Note:** A letter appearing between parallel lines (e.g., /t/) stands for the *sound* of the letter rather than the letter name. If the student responds with the name of the letter, ask again: "What sound do you hear?" Make sure the student is giving the pure sound of *t* and not pronouncing it with a short *u* sound, as in /tŭh/. (If desired, refer to the audiotape for the precise sound.)

"That's right. The sound you hear in the initial position is /t/."

"Put your fingertips on the front of your neck and say /t/. See if you feel any vibration."

"Is this sound voiced or unvoiced?" *unvoiced*

"Since /t/ doesn't vibrate, it is an unvoiced sound."

- Write the following words on the chalkboard: top, tin, tub.

"What letter do you see that might be making the /t/ sound?" *t*

- If the student does not know the name of the letter, say it for him/her.

"T is the first letter in all of these words, so we can see that t must be the letter used to spell the /t/ sound."

"Look at your alphabet strip. Can you tell me if t is a vowel or a consonant?" *consonant*

Handwriting/Letter Tiles

- The student should be seated where he/she can write comfortably.
- Write a capital *T* on the chalkboard.

"This is a capital letter T. Let's practice skywriting capital T's before we write them on our paper."

- Have the student practice skywriting capital *T*'s. The student should keep his/her elbows and wrists locked and make each letter about two feet tall.

"Find your spelling sound sheet. Leave your pencil on your desk until I tell you to pick it up."

- Draw handwriting lines on the chalkboard.

"These are handwriting lines like you have on your paper."

- Write a capital *T* on the handwriting lines in the handwriting you want the student to learn.

  "Now pick up your pencil. Find the first line on your paper and practice writing capital T's like I wrote this one on the chalkboard."

  "Say the name of the letter each time you write it."

- Allow a few minutes for the student to practice writing capital *T*'s. Provide assistance as necessary.

  "Put your pencil back on your desk."

- Write a lowercase *t* on the handwriting lines in the handwriting you want the student to learn.

  "This is a lowercase letter t."

- Have the student practice skywriting lowercase *t*'s.

  "Now pick up your pencil and practice writing lowercase t's on the second line of your paper. Say the name of the letter each time you write it."

- Have the student set the spelling sound sheet aside for use later in the lesson.
- Leave the handwriting lines and letters on the chalkboard for the remainder of the lesson.
- Give the student the container of letter tiles.

  "Today I've given you a new letter tile."

  "Find and look at your t letter tile. One side has a capital T and the other side has a lowercase t."

- Allow time for the student to examine the new letter tile.

  "Hold your letter tile up in the air. Turn it so I can see the capital T."

  "Now turn it so I can see the lowercase t."

  "See if you can spell the word 'not.' "

  "Now take one letter away to make the word 'no.' "

- Check to see that the student is moving the tiles correctly.
- Have the student replace the tiles in the container and put it away.
- Reinforce the name, sound, and shape of the letter *t* throughout the day. (See the introductory material for suggestions.)

NEW DECK CARDS

- Show the student **Letter Card 3.**

  "What letter is this?" *t*

- Hold up **Picture Card 4** but keep the picture covered with your hand (or the letter card).

  "I have a card with a picture on it that begins with the /t/ sound."

"I am going to describe it for you. See if you can guess what the picture is."

"This is something that you sleep in when you go camping. It has a flap for a door. It is held up with stakes. What do you think the picture is?" *tent*

"That's right. The keyword is 'tent' and the sound we have learned is /t/."

- Show the student **Picture Card 4,** and then point to the picture of a tent on the alphabet strip.

"The word 'tent' helps us remember the /t/ sound because it begins with /t/."

"Find your spelling sound sheet."

"Find the #4 on your paper and put your finger on it."

- Hold up **Spelling Card 4** so that only you can see what is written. Using the hand signals described earlier, follow the instructions on the card. (Or use the following verbal cues until the student is familiar with the procedure.)

"Echo this sound: /t/." */t/*

"What letter makes this sound?" *t*

"Write the lowercase letter t on the line by #4."

- Check the spelling sound sheet for accuracy.
- **Note:** Add the new letter, picture, and spelling cards to the Review Decks.

WORKSHEET

- The student should be seated where he/she can write comfortably.
- Write "Worksheet 4" on the chalkboard. Then hold up the worksheet and point to "Worksheet 4" at the top of the page.

"When I give you the worksheet, find the side that has 'worksheet' written on it."

- Give the student **Worksheet 4.** Make sure he/she turns to the correct side.

"Find the #1 on your paper. Can you tell me what the picture is?" *tiger*

"What is the sound in the initial position of 'tiger'?" */t/*

"Write the lowercase letter that says /t/ on the line under #1."

- Repeat this procedure with #2 (ox) and #3 (turkey).
- Write the word "not" on the chalkboard.

"Do you see a vowel in this word?" *yes, an o*

"Do you see anything after the o?" *yes, a t*

"Is t a vowel or a consonant?" *a consonant*

"That's right. T is a consonant. When a vowel has a consonant after it, the vowel is short. Does this vowel have a consonant after it?" *yes*

"Yes, this vowel is short, so we will code it with a breve. A breve looks like a smile."

- Put a breve over the *o*: nŏt.

- Point to the *n*.

  "What is the sound of this letter?" */n/*

- Point to the *o*.

  "What is the short sound of o?" */ŏ/*

- Point to the *t*.

  "What is the sound of this letter?" */t/*

  "Let's blend these three sounds together and see what word they make."

- Say the first sound, /n/, and do not let go of that sound until you "blend" into the /ŏ/ sound; then immediately add the /t/ sound. The student will discover that the word is "not."

  "When we read, we blend the sounds of the letters to form words, like the word 'not.' "

  "Can you use the word 'not' in a sentence?" *expect various answers; explain "knot," if necessary*

  "Look at the word by #4 on your paper."

  "Put your finger under the vowel."

  "When we code a vowel, we mark it to show what sound it makes."

  "How are we going to code this vowel?" *short; with a breve*

  "Why?" *it has a consonant after it*

  "Code the vowel with a breve and blend the three sounds."

  "What is the word?" *not*

  "Code the vowel in the word by #5."

- Allow time for the student to do this. Provide assistance, if necessary.
- Write the word "no" on the chalkboard.

  "Look at the word by #6 on your paper."

  "Do you see a vowel in this word?" *yes*

  "Is this vowel followed by a consonant?" *no*

  "This vowel has a consonant before it, but that consonant won't change the vowel sound."

  "When an accented vowel is open, it is long. We code it with a macron."

- If necessary, use the phrase "is not followed by a consonant" in addition to the word "open." However, the student should quickly learn to refer to these vowels simply as "open."

  "Code the vowel on your paper with a macron and an accent mark."

- Demonstrate by putting a macron and an accent mark over the *o* on the chalkboard: nō´.
- Point to the *o*.

"The name of this letter is _____?" *o*

"Then the sound it will make is _____?" */ō/*

"Let's try blending this word. Remember, the vowel says /ō/ instead of /ŏ/."

- Help the student blend the word "no" by starting with the /n/ sound and holding onto it until he/she "blends" into the /ō/ sound. The student will discover that the word is "no."

"Can you use the word 'no' in a sentence?" *expect various answers*

"Read the words and see if the picture matches any of the words."

"When you are finished, draw a line from one of the words to the picture it matches."

- Check to see if the student has drawn the line correctly.

"Now, since you know how to spell four sounds we are going to have another spelling test."

"Put your finger by #7 on your paper. The word we are going to spell is 'on.' What is the first sound in 'on'?" */ŏ/*

"That's right! What letter makes the /ŏ/ sound?" *o*

"Write a lowercase letter o on the first line by #7."

"What is the last sound in the word 'on'?" */n/*

"What letter makes the /n/ sound?" *n*

"Write a lowercase letter n on the second line by #7."

"Look, we spelled 'on'!"

- Repeat the procedure with #8 (not) and #9 (no).
- As the student works, provide help as needed. Help the student correct any incorrect answers. Then initial the worksheet in the space provided.
- Some time during the day, ask the student to read some or all of the words on the worksheet. Although coding is important, the ultimate goal is reading, so the student, especially if he/she is having difficulty, should read to someone every day.
- **Note:** Always make sure the worksheet is corrected before the student begins the homework. The worksheet serves as a guide to help complete the homework.

HOMEWORK

"Turn your paper over to the homework side."

"Put your finger on the top row of handwriting lines. Write your best capital T on the line so I will know what a capital T should look like."

- Have the student write a lowercase letter *t* on the second handwriting line.
- Make sure that the student has written the letters correctly (to the best of his or her ability). He/She will use them as guides when completing the homework.

"Do you know what to do on the rest of the homework paper?"

- Discuss the homework pictures to make sure the student understands the word each one represents: #1 (tooth), #2 (tub), and #3 (net).

  "If you need help, look at the worksheet side. There will usually be an activity on the worksheet side that is similar to your homework."

  "When you finish your paper, I will check it for you and initial it in the space provided."

- Either now or later in the day, the student should complete the homework independently (if possible). Help the student correct any incorrect answers. Then initial the homework in the space provided.

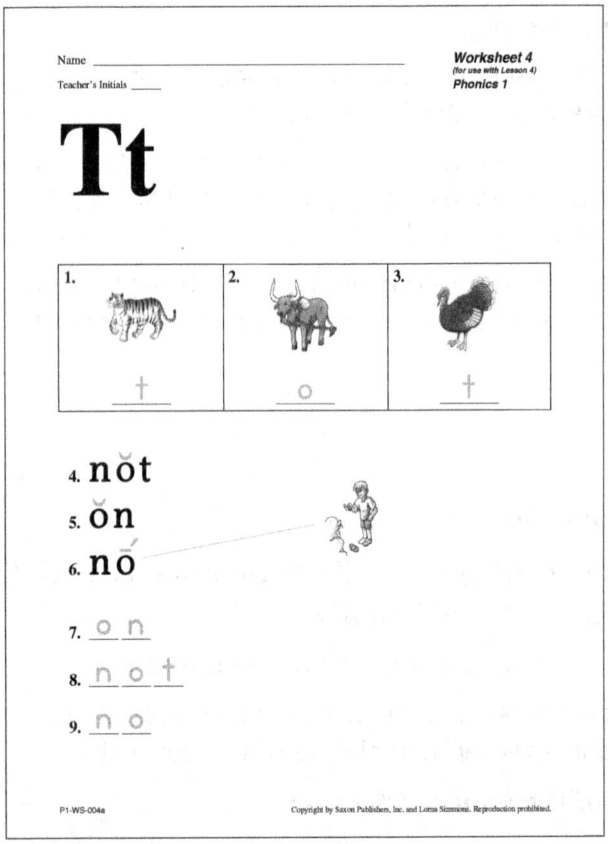

Name ______

Teacher's Initials ____

Worksheet 4
(for use with Lesson 4)
Phonics 1

Tt

1. t
2. o
3. t

4. nŏt
5. ŏn
6. nó

7. o n
8. n o t
9. n o

P1-WS-004a

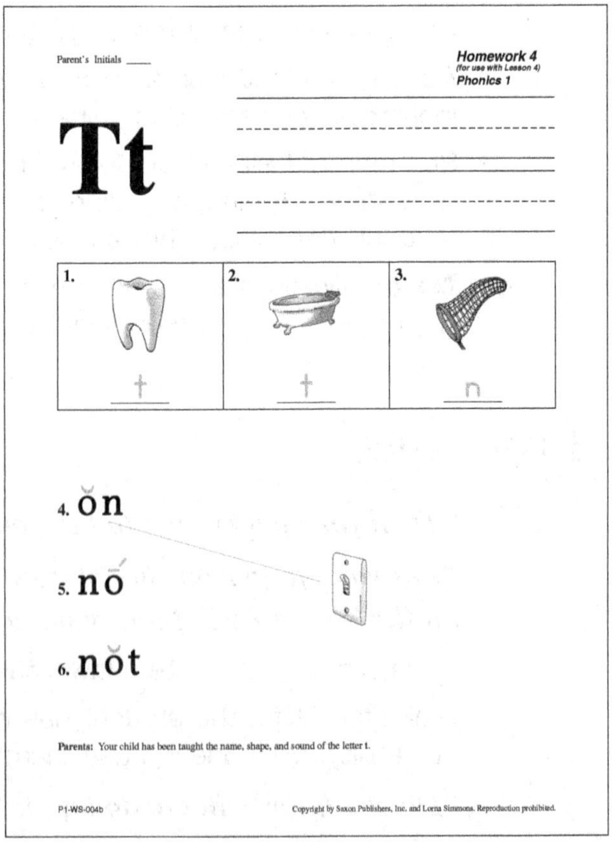

Parent's Initials ____

Homework 4
(for use with Lesson 4)
Phonics 1

Tt

1. t
2. t
3. n

4. ŏn
5. nó
6. nŏt

Parents: Your child has been taught the name, shape, and sound of the letter t.

P1-WS-004b

Lesson 5

The Letter *P*

lesson preparation

materials

Review Decks

Spelling Sound Sheet 5

container of letter tiles

Letter Card 4

pencil in a sack (see *the night before*)

Picture Card 5

Spelling Card 5

Worksheet 5

the night before

- Put a pencil in a sack for the student to use to "discover" the new keyword. Make sure the pencil does not have a sharp point. If possible, do not allow the student to see what you place inside the sack.
- Add the *p* letter tile to the student's container.

Alphabet Activity

- The student should be seated with the alphabet strip.

  "Let's look at the alphabet strip."

  "How many letters are in the alphabet?" *26*

  "How many letters are vowels?" *5*

- Let the student count the vowels, if necessary.

  "All of the other letters are called _________?" *consonants*

  "The initial, or beginning, letter of the alphabet is _____?" *a*

  "The final, or last, letter of the alphabet is _____?" *z*

  "Let's stand up."

  "Let's say the alphabet and jump up in the air when we say the vowels."

- Try to set a steady pace so the student cannot sing the alphabet.

PHONEMIC AWARENESS

- **Objective:** To identify initial sounds in spoken words.

  "I am going to say some words. See if you can tell me the initial, or beginning, sound in these words."

- Point to your mouth as you say the following words: top, tear, tug, tar.
- Some students will have difficulty isolating the sounds. Slowly repeat the words until the student can answer. Then ask:

  "What sound do you hear at the beginning of these words?" */t/*

- Be sure to have the student tell you the sound, not the letter name.
- Point to your mouth and say the following words: nip, name, nose, nest.

  "What sound do you hear at the beginning of these words?" */n/*

- Point to your mouth and say the following words: ostrich, octopus, otter, off.

  "What sound do you hear at the beginning of these words?" */ŏ/*

- Point to your mouth and say the following words: pop, pan, pest, part.

  "What sound do you hear at the beginning of these words?" */p/*

- Continue with additional words as time permits.

REVIEW OF DECKS

"As we review the letter deck today, I want you to stand up when the letter card is a vowel and sit down when it is a consonant."

- Show the student **Letter Cards 1–3** in random order.

  "Name the letters."

- The student should name the letter on each letter card, standing up or sitting down as required.
- Show the student **Picture Cards 1–4** in random order.

  "Name the keyword and sound for each card."

- The student should name the keyword and sound for each picture card.
- Seat the student where he/she can write comfortably. Give the student **Spelling Sound Sheet 5.**
- Call out the sounds on **Spelling Cards 1–4** in random order. Hand signals that accompany this sequence are as follows: 1. Point to your mouth as you say the sound; 2. Point to the student to indicate that he/she is to echo the sound; 3. Extend your hand palm up as you ask for the name of the letter that makes the sound; 4. Point straight down to indicate that the student is to write the letter. The student will eventually follow the hand signals without verbal cues.
- The student should echo each sound and name the letter that makes the sound as he/she writes the letter on the spelling sound sheet.
- Have the student set the spelling sound sheet aside for use later in the lesson.

NEW LEARNING

"I am going to say some words to you and I want you to echo them back to me. Listen for the sound that is the same at the beginning, or initial, position of each word."

- Point to your mouth as you say each word.

"Echo after me. Past." *past* ***"Popcorn."*** *popcorn* ***"Pancake."*** *pancake*

- Slowly repeat the words until the student can answer the following question:

"What sound do you hear in the initial position?" */p/*

- **Note:** A letter appearing between parallel lines (e.g., /p/) stands for the *sound* of the letter rather than the letter name. If the student responds with the name of the letter, ask again: "What sound do you hear?" Make sure the student is giving the pure sound of *p* and not pronouncing it with a short *u* sound, as in /pŭh/. (If desired, refer to the audiotape for the precise sound.)

"That's right. The sound you hear in the initial position is /p/."

"Put your fingertips on the front of your neck and say /p/. See if you feel any vibration."

"Is this sound voiced or unvoiced?" *unvoiced*

"Since /p/ doesn't vibrate, it is an unvoiced sound."

- Write the following words on the chalkboard: pan, pig, pond.

"What letter do you see that might be making the /p/ sound?" *p*

- If the student does not know the name of the letter, say it for him/her.

"P is the first letter in all of these words, so we can see that p must be the letter used to spell the /p/ sound."

"Look at your alphabet strip. Can you tell me if p is a vowel or a consonant?" *consonant*

HANDWRITING/LETTER TILES

- The student should be seated where he/she can write comfortably.
- Write a capital *P* on the chalkboard.

"This is a capital letter P. Let's practice skywriting capital P's before we write them on our paper."

- Have the student practice skywriting capital *P*'s. The student should keep his/her elbows and wrists locked and make each letter about two feet tall.

"Find your spelling sound sheet. Leave your pencil on your desk until I tell you to pick it up."

- Draw handwriting lines on the chalkboard.

"These are handwriting lines like you have on your paper."

- Write a capital *P* on the handwriting lines in the handwriting you want the student to learn.

  "Now pick up your pencil. Find the first line on your paper and practice writing capital P's like I wrote this one on the chalkboard."

  "Say the name of the letter each time you write it."

- Allow a few minutes for the student to practice writing capital *P*'s. Provide assistance as necessary.

  "Put your pencil back on your desk."

- Write a lowercase *p* on the handwriting lines in the handwriting you want the student to learn.

  "This is a lowercase letter p."

- Have the student practice skywriting lowercase *p*'s.

  "Now pick up your pencil and practice writing lowercase p's on the second line of your paper. Say the name of the letter each time you write it."

- Have the student set the spelling sound sheet aside for use later in the lesson.
- Leave the handwriting lines and letters on the chalkboard for the remainder of the lesson.
- Give the student the container of letter tiles.

  "Today I've given you a new letter tile."

  "Find and look at your p letter tile. One side has a capital P and the other side has a lowercase p."

- Allow time for the student to examine the new letter tile.

  "Hold your letter tile up in the air. Turn it so I can see the capital P."

  "Now turn it so I can see the lowercase p."

  "See if you can spell the word 'top.' "

  "Now try to spell the word 'no.' "

  "This time, spell the word 'pot.' "

- Check to see that the student is moving the tiles correctly.
- Have the student replace the tiles in the container and put it away.
- Reinforce the name, sound, and shape of the letter *p* throughout the day. (See the introductory material for suggestions.)

NEW DECK CARDS

- Show the student **Letter Card 4.**

  "What letter is this?" p

- Show the student the sack with a pencil inside.

  "We're going to do something really fun today. I have a sack that contains a clue to our new keyword. Don't look in the sack, but put your hand inside and see if you can feel what is inside the sack."

- Allow the student a chance to feel inside the sack.

  "I'm going to count to three. On three, whisper what you think is in the sack."

  "One, two, three." *pencil*

  "That's right. The keyword is 'pencil' and the sound we have learned is /p/."

- Show the student **Picture Card 5,** and then point to the picture of a pencil on the alphabet strip.

  "The word 'pencil' helps us remember the /p/ sound because it begins with /p/."

  "Find your spelling sound sheet."

  "Find the #5 on your paper and put your finger on it."

- Hold up **Spelling Card 5** so only you can see what is written. Using the hand signals described earlier, follow the instructions on the card. (Or use the following verbal cues until the student is familiar with the procedure.)

  "Echo this sound: /p/." */p/*

  "What letter makes this sound?" *p*

  "Write the lowercase letter p on the line by #5."

- Check the spelling sound sheet for accuracy.
- If desired, sharpen the new pencil for use on the worksheet.
- **Note:** Add the new letter, picture, and spelling cards to the Review Decks.

WORKSHEET

- The student should be seated where he/she can write comfortably.
- Write "Worksheet 5" on the chalkboard. Then hold up the worksheet and point to "Worksheet 5" at the top of the page.

  "When I give you the worksheet, find the side that has 'worksheet' written on it."

- Give the student **Worksheet 5.** Make sure he/she turns to the correct side.

  "Find the #1 on your paper. Can you tell me what the picture is?" *pig*

  "Can you tell me the sound in the initial position of 'pig'?" */p/*

  "Write the lowercase letter that says /p/ on the line under #1."

- Repeat this procedure with #2 (peacock) and #3 (pan).
- Write the word "pot" on the chalkboard.

  "Do you see a vowel in this word?" *yes, an o*

  "Do you see anything after the o?" *yes, a t*

- Point to the *t*.

  "Is t a vowel or a consonant?" *consonant*

  "That's right. When a vowel is followed by a consonant, the vowel is short. We code it with a breve."

  "Repeat that with me." *when a vowel is followed by a consonant, the vowel is short; we code it with a breve*

- Point to the *o* in "pot."

  "Does this vowel have a consonant after it?" *yes*

  "Yes. This vowel is short, so we will code it with a breve."
- Put a breve over the *o*: pŏt.
- Point to the *p*.

  "What is the sound of this letter?" */p/*
- Point to the *o*.

  "What is the short sound of o?" */ŏ/*
- Point to the *t*.

  "What is the sound of this letter?" */t/*

  "Let's blend these three sounds together and see what word they make."
- Say the first sound, /p/, and do not let go of that sound until you "blend" into the /ŏ/ sound; then immediately add the /t/ sound. The student will discover that the word is "pot." If necessary, define the word.

  "Can you give me a sentence with the word 'pot' in it?" *expect various answers*

  "Look at the word by #4 on your paper."

  "Put your finger under the vowel."

  "How are we going to code this vowel?" *short; with a breve*

  "Why?" *it has a consonant after it*

  "Code the vowel with a breve and blend the three sounds."

  "What is the word?" *pot*
- Provide assistance, if necessary.

  "Code the vowels in the words by #5 and #6."

  "Read the words and see if the picture matches any of the words."

  "When you are finished, draw a line from one of the words to the picture it matches."
- Check to see if the student has drawn the line correctly.

  "We are going to have another spelling test."

  "Put your finger by #7 on your paper. The word we are going to spell is 'pop.' What is the first sound in 'pop'?" */p/*

  "That's right. What letter makes the /p/ sound?" *p*

  "Write a lowercase p on the first line by #7."

  "What is the middle sound in the word 'pop'?" */ŏ/*

  "Write a lowercase o on the second line by #7."

  "What is the last sound in the word 'pop'?" */p/*

  "What letter makes the /p/ sound?" *p*

  "Write a p on the last line by #7."

"Look, we spelled 'pop'!"

- Repeat the procedure with #8 (no) and #9 (not).

"Look at the picture by #10. Who can tell me what this is?" pop

"Think about the sounds in the word 'pop.' Try to spell the word on the lines next to the picture."

- Allow time for the student to do this.

"On the homework side you will find two more problems like #10. You must guess the picture and then spell it on the lines under the picture. You will only be spelling with the letters we have learned. They are n, o, t, and p."

- As the student works, provide help as needed. Help the student correct any incorrect answers. Then initial the worksheet in the space provided.
- Some time during the day, ask the student to read some or all of the words on the worksheet. Although coding is important, the ultimate goal is reading, so the student, especially if he/she is having difficulty, should read to someone every day.
- **Note:** Always make sure the worksheet is corrected before the student begins the homework. The worksheet serves as a guide to help complete the homework.

HOMEWORK

"Turn your paper over to the homework side."

"Put your finger on the top row of handwriting lines. Write your best capital P on the line so I will know what a capital P should look like."

- Have the student write a lowercase letter *p* on the second handwriting line.
- Make sure that the student has written the letters correctly (to the best of his or her ability). He/She will use them as guides when completing the homework.

"Do you know what to do on the rest of the homework paper?"

- Discuss the homework pictures to make sure the student understands the word each one represents: #1 (pencil), #2 (piano), and #3 (puppy).

"If you need help, look at the worksheet side. There will usually be an activity on the worksheet side that is similar to your homework."

"When you finish your paper, I will check it for you and initial it in the space provided."

- Either now or later in the day, the student should complete the homework independently (if possible). Help the student correct any incorrect answers. Then initial the homework in the space provided.

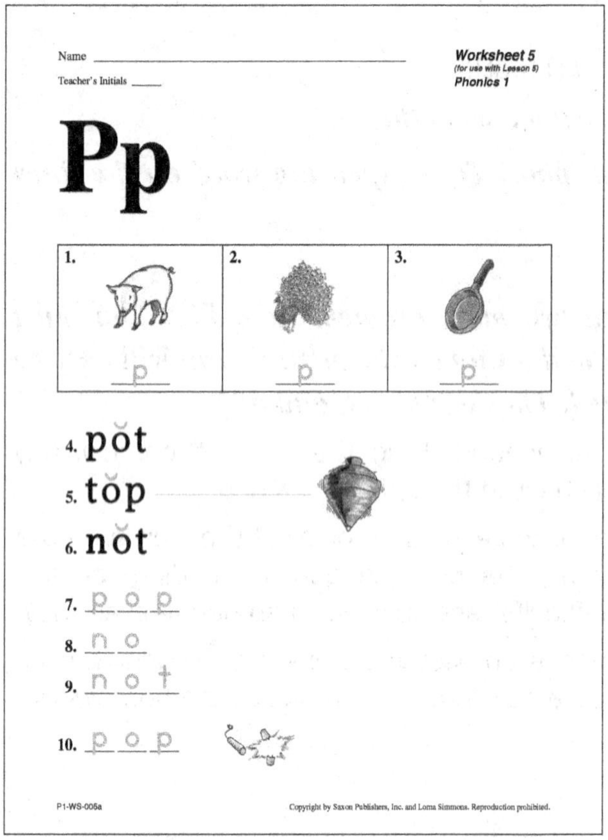

Name ______________________________ **Worksheet 5** (for use with Lesson 5) **Phonics 1**

Teacher's Initials _____

Pp

1.	2.	3.
p	p	p

4. pŏt
5. tŏp
6. nŏt

7. p o p
8. n o
9. n o t
10. p o p

P1-WS-005a

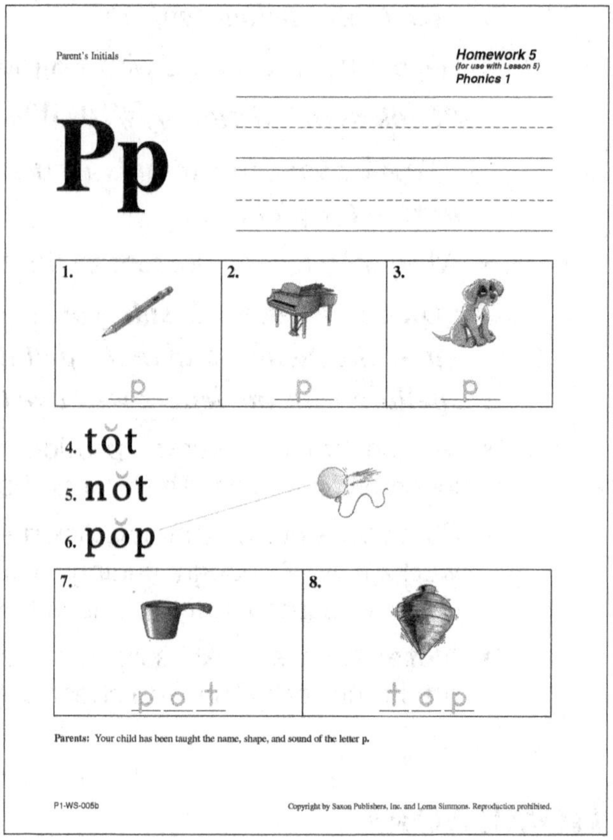

Parent's Initials _____ **Homework 5** (for use with Lesson 5) **Phonics 1**

Pp

1.	2.	3.
p	p	p

4. tŏt
5. nŏt
6. pŏp

7.	8.
p o t	t o p

Parents: Your child has been taught the name, shape, and sound of the letter p.

P1-WS-005b

LESSON 6 — The Letter *I*

lesson preparation

materials

Review Decks

Spelling Sound Sheet 6

container of letter tiles

Letter Card 5

Picture Cards 6–7

Spelling Cards 6–7

Worksheet 6

new concepts

twin consonants

the night before

- Add the *i* letter tile to the student's container.

ALPHABET ACTIVITY

- The student should be seated with the alphabet strip.

  "Let's look at the alphabet strip."

  "How many letters are in the alphabet?" *26*

  "The letters in red are called _________?" *vowels*

  "All of the other letters are called _________?" *consonants*

  "Let's point to each letter and say the whole alphabet."

  "Put your index finger on 'a' and say the names with me."

- Try to set a steady pace so the student cannot sing the alphabet.

  "The initial letter of the alphabet is _____?" *a*

  "The final, or last, letter of the alphabet is _____?" *z*

PHONEMIC AWARENESS

- **Objective:** To identify final sounds in spoken words.

  "I am going to say some words. See if you can tell me the final, or ending, sound in these words."

- When giving words to the student, it helps to exaggerate the sound you want identified.
- Point to your mouth as you say the following words: big, hug, pig, hog.
- Some students will have difficulty isolating the sounds. Slowly repeat the words until the student can answer. Then ask:

  "What sound do you hear in the final position of these words?" */g/*
- Be sure to have the student tell you the sound, not the letter name.
- Point to your mouth and say the following words: fill, smell, pull.

  "What sound do you hear in the final position of these words?" */l/*
- Point to your mouth and say the following words: sit, flat, hot.

  "What sound do you hear in the final position of these words?" */t/*
- Point to your mouth and say the following words: snow, toe, grow.

  "What sound do you hear in the final position of these words?" */ō/*
- Continue with additional words as time permits.

REVIEW OF DECKS

- The student should be seated where he/she can write comfortably.
- Show the student **Letter Cards 1–4** in random order.

  "Name the letters."
- The student should name the letter on each letter card.
- Show the student **Picture Cards 1–5** in random order.

  "Name the keyword and sound for each card."
- The student should name the keyword and sound for each picture card.
- Give the student **Spelling Sound Sheet 6.**
- Call out the sounds on **Spelling Cards 1–5** in random order. Hand signals that accompany this sequence are as follows: 1. Point to your mouth as you say the sound; 2. Point to the student to indicate that he/she is to echo the sound; 3. Extend your hand palm up as you ask for the name of the letter that makes the sound; 4. Point straight down to indicate that the student is to write the letter. The student will eventually follow the hand signals without verbal cues.
- The student should echo each sound and name the letter that makes the sound as he/she writes the letter on the spelling sound sheet.
- Have the student set the spelling sound sheet aside for use later in the lesson.

NEW LEARNING

"I am going to say some words to you and I want you to echo them back to me. Listen for the sound that is the same at the beginning, or initial, position of each word."

- Point to your mouth as you say each word.

"Echo after me. It." *it* ***"Ill."*** *ill* ***"If."*** *if*

- Slowly repeat the words until the student can answer the following question:

"What sound do you hear in the initial position?" */ĭ/*

- **Note:** A letter appearing between parallel lines (e.g., /ĭ/) stands for the *sound* of the letter rather than the letter name. If the student responds with the name of the letter, ask again: "What sound do you hear?"

"That's right. The sound you hear in the initial position is /ĭ/."

"Put your fingertips on the front of your neck and say /ĭ/. See if you feel any vibration."

"Is this sound voiced or unvoiced?" *voiced*

"Since /ĭ/ vibrates, it is a voiced sound."

- Write the following words on the chalkboard: it, in, ill.

"What letter do you see that might be making the /ĭ/ sound?" *i*

- If the student does not know the name of the letter, say it for him/her.

"I is the first letter in all of these words, so we can see that i must be the letter used to spell the /ĭ/ sound."

"Can you tell me the long sound of i?" */ī/*

"That's right! The long i says its name."

"Look at your alphabet strip. Can you tell me if i is a vowel or a consonant?" *vowel*

HANDWRITING/LETTER TILES

- The student should be seated where he/she can write comfortably.
- Write a capital *I* on the chalkboard.

"This is a capital I. Let's practice skywriting capital I's before we write them on our paper."

- Have the student practice skywriting capital *I*'s. The student should keep his/her elbows and wrists locked and make each letter about two feet tall.

"Find your spelling sound sheet. Leave your pencil on your desk until I tell you to pick it up."

- Draw handwriting lines on the chalkboard.

"These are handwriting lines like you have on your paper."

- Write a capital *I* on the handwriting lines in the handwriting you want the student to learn.

"Now pick up your pencil. Find the first line on your paper and practice writing capital I's like I wrote this one on the chalkboard."

"Say the name of the letter each time you write it."

- Allow a few minutes for the student to practice writing capital *I*'s. Provide assistance as necessary.

  "Put your pencil back on your desk."

- Write a lowercase *i* on the handwriting lines in the handwriting you want the student to learn.

  "This is a lowercase i."

- Have the student practice skywriting lowercase *i*'s.

  "Now pick up your pencil and practice writing lowercase i's on the second line of your paper. Say the name of the letter each time you write it."

- Have the student set the spelling sound sheet aside for use later in the lesson.
- Leave the handwriting lines and letters on the chalkboard for the remainder of the lesson.
- Give the student the container of letter tiles.

  "Today I've given you a new letter tile."

  "Find and look at your i letter tile. One side has a capital I and the other side has a lowercase i."

- Allow time for the student to examine the new letter tile.

  "Hold your letter tile up in the air. Turn it so I can see the capital I."

  "Now turn it so I can see the lowercase i."

  "See if you can spell the word 'tip.' "

  "Now spell the word 'not.' "

  "This time, spell the word 'pit.' "

- Check to see that the student is moving the tiles correctly.
- Have the student replace the tiles in the container and put it away.
- Reinforce the name, sound, and shape of the letter *i* throughout the day. (See the introductory material for suggestions.)

New Deck Cards

- Show the student **Letter Card 5.**

  "What letter is this?" *i*

- Hold up **Picture Card 6** but keep the picture covered with your hand (or the letter card).

  "I have a card with a picture on it that begins with the /ĭ/ sound."

  "I am going to describe it for you. See if you can guess what the picture is."

  "This is a house that is made of ice. This house is only found where it is very cold. Eskimos live in these kinds of houses when they travel. What do you think the picture is?" *igloo*

"That's right. The keyword is 'igloo' and the sound we have learned is /ĭ/."

- Show the student **Picture Card 6,** and then point to the picture of an igloo on the alphabet strip.

"The word 'igloo' helps us remember the /ĭ/ sound because it begins with /ĭ/."

"Since the letter i also has a long sound, we need another card."

"I have a card with a picture on it that begins with the long /ī/ sound. See if you can guess what the picture is."

"This is green. It is a plant. It grows indoors and outdoors. Sometimes you see this growing on the sides of old stone houses. What do you think the picture is?" *ivy*

"That's right. The keyword is 'ivy' and the sound we have learned is /ī/."

- Show the student **Picture Card 7.**

"The word 'ivy' helps us remember the /ī/ sound because it begins with /ī/."

"We will keep these cards together in our review deck to help us remember that the letter i can make two sounds."

"Find your spelling sound sheet."

"Find the #6 on your paper and put your finger on it."

- Hold up **Spelling Card 6** so only you can see what is written. Using the hand signals described in previous lessons, follow the instructions on the card.
- Repeat the procedure with **Spelling Card 7.**
- Check the student's response after each card.
- **Note:** Add the new letter, picture, and spelling cards to the Review Decks. Always keep **Picture Card 7** behind **Picture Card 6** to help the student remember that the letter *i* has two sounds. (The picture deck is the only deck wherein certain cards must remain together. See the introductory material for specific information.)

BOARDWORK

"Let's practice coding some words like the ones you'll have on your worksheet."

- Write the word "tint" on the chalkboard.

"Do you see a vowel in this word?" *yes, an i*

"Do you see anything after the i?" *yes, an n*

"Is n a vowel or a consonant?" *consonant*

"That's right. N is a consonant because a, e, i, o, and u are the vowels and the rest of the letters are consonants."

- Say the vowel rule (below) as you write it on the chalkboard: v̆c.

  "A vowel followed by a consonant is short; code it with a breve. Repeat that with me."

- Point to the chalkboard as the student repeats the vowel rule with you.
- Say the second vowel rule (below) as you write it on the chalkboard: v̄′→.

  "The second vowel rule says, 'An open, accented vowel is long; code it with a macron.' Repeat that with me."

- Point to the chalkboard as the student repeats the vowel rule with you.

  "Does this vowel have a consonant after it?" *yes*

  "A vowel followed by a consonant is short, so we will code it with a _____?" *breve*

- Put a breve over the *i*: tĭnt.
- Point to the initial *t*.

  "What is the sound of this letter?" */t/*

- Point to the *i*.

  "What is the sound of this letter?" */ĭ/*

- Point to the *n*.

  "What is the sound of this letter?" */n/*

- Point to the final *t*.

  "What is the sound of this letter?" */t/*

  "Let's blend these four sounds together and see what word they make."

- Say the first sound, /t/, and do not let go of that sound until you "blend" into the /ĭ/ sound. Continue saying that sound until you "blend" into the /n/ sound; then immediately add the /t/ sound. Help the student by moving your finger from left to right under the letters as you add the sounds.

  "What is the word?" *tint*

- Define the word, if necessary.

  "Can you use the word 'tint' in a sentence?" *expect various answers*

- Write the word "inn" on the chalkboard.

  "Which letter is a vowel?" *i*

  "How do we code it?" *short; with a breve*

  "This word has twin consonants."

  "Do you know what a twin is?" *expect various answers*

  "A twin consonant is two consonants that are just alike and next to each other."

  "When we have twin consonants, we cross out one of the letters because the two letters only make one sound."

- Cross out the second *n*: ĭn~~n~~.

"Can you read this word?" *expect various attempts*

- If the student answers incorrectly, encourage him/her with responses such as "Nice try!" or "Good idea!" or a similar phrase. If possible, find part of the response that was correct and dignify the answer. It is important that the student be willing to participate and will risk offering a possibly incorrect answer.

"Now you are ready to practice on your own."

WORKSHEET

- The student should be seated where he/she can write comfortably.
- Write "Worksheet 6" on the chalkboard. Then hold up the worksheet and point to "Worksheet 6" at the top of the page.

"When I give you the worksheet, find the side that has 'worksheet' written on it."

- Give the student **Worksheet 6.** Make sure he/she turns to the correct side.

"Using the rules we just practiced, code the words by #1, #2, and #3."

"After you have coded these words, blend the sounds in each word and figure out what the words are."

"When you are finished, draw a line from one of the words to the picture it matches."

- Provide assistance as needed.

"Let's try spelling a few words. Put your finger by #4. The first word we are going to spell is 'no.' What is the first sound in the word 'no'?" */n/*

"Write the lowercase letter that says /n/ on the first line by #4."

"What is the next sound in the word 'no'?" */ō/*

"Write the lowercase letter that says /ō/ on the second line by #4."

"What is the word you wrote?" *no*

- Repeat the procedure with #5 (not) and #6 (tin).

"Look at the picture by #7 and tell me what it is." *pot*

"Can you tell me what the picture by #8 is?" *top*

"Think about the sounds in the words 'pot' and 'top.' Try to spell each word on the lines under the pictures."

- As the student works, provide help as needed. Help the student correct any incorrect answers. Then initial the worksheet in the space provided.
- Some time during the day, ask the student to read from the worksheet or homework.
- **Note:** Always make sure the worksheet is corrected before the student begins the homework. The worksheet serves as a guide to help complete the homework.

HOMEWORK

"Turn your paper over to the homework side."

"Put your finger on the top row of handwriting lines. Write your best capital I on the line so I will know what a capital I should look like."

- Have the student write a lowercase letter *i* on the second handwriting line.
- Make sure that the student has written the letters correctly (to the best of his or her ability). He/She will use them as guides when completing the homework.

"On your homework, you'll find two places just like #7 and #8 on the worksheet side. Decide what the picture is and then spell it on the lines under the picture. You will only be spelling with the letters we've learned."

- Discuss the homework pictures to make sure the student understands the word each one represents: #4 (pop) and #5 (pin).
- Either now or later in the day, the student should complete the homework independently (if possible). Help the student correct any incorrect answers. Then initial the homework in the space provided.

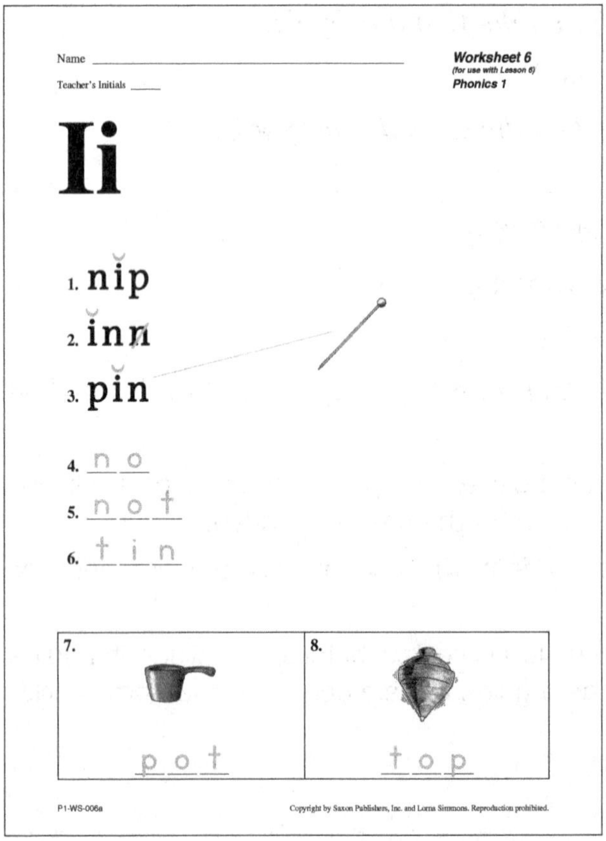

Name ______________________

Teacher's Initials ____

Worksheet 6
(for use with Lesson 6)
Phonics 1

Ii

1. nĭp
2. ĭnn
3. pĭn
4. n o
5. n o t
6. t i n
7. p o t
8. t o p

P1-WS-006a

Copyright by Saxon Publishers, Inc. and Lorna Simmons. Reproduction prohibited.

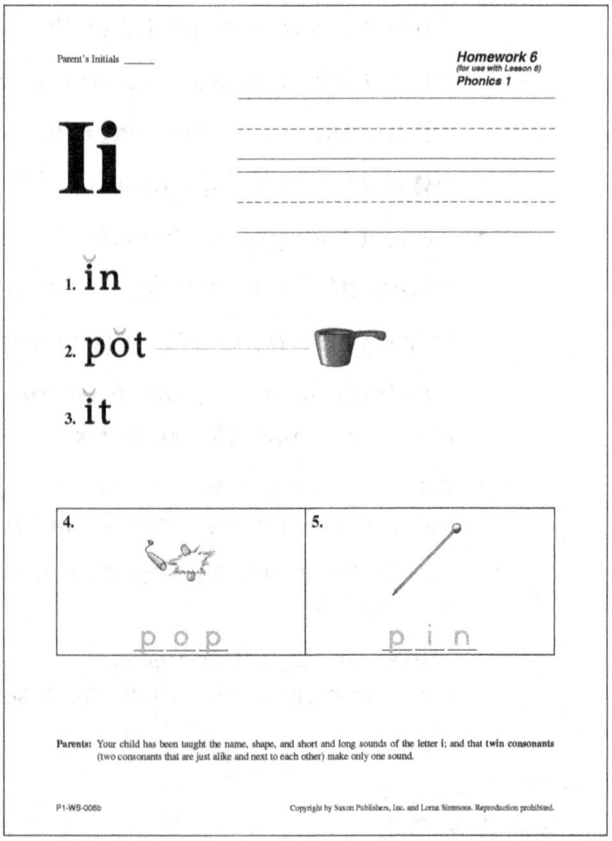

Parent's Initials ____

Homework 6
(for use with Lesson 6)
Phonics 1

Ii

1. ĭn
2. pŏt
3. ĭt
4. p o p
5. p i n

Parents: Your child has been taught the name, shape, and short and long sounds of the letter i; and that **twin consonants** (two consonants that are just alike and next to each other) make only one sound.

P1-WS-006b

Copyright by Saxon Publishers, Inc. and Lorna Simmons. Reproduction prohibited.

Lesson 7 — The Letter *L*

lesson preparation

materials

Review Decks

Spelling Sound Sheet 7

container of letter tiles

Letter Card 6

Picture Card 8

Spelling Card 8

Worksheet 7

new concepts

blends

the night before

- Add the *l* letter tile to the student's container.

Alphabet Activity

- The student should be standing.

  "When we recite the alphabet today, we're going to (sit down, squat, jump up, etc.) as we say every other letter."

- Begin reciting the alphabet with the student. As you say every other letter, perform whatever physical activity you chose.

Phonemic Awareness

- **Objective:** To identify final sounds in spoken words.

  "I am going to say some words. See if you can tell me the final, or ending, sound in these words."

- When giving words to the student, it helps to exaggerate the sound you want identified.
- Point to your mouth as you say the following words: mad, fed, rod, mud.
- Some students will have difficulty isolating the sounds. Slowly repeat the words until the student can answer. Then ask:

  "What sound do you hear in the final position of these words?" */d/*

- Be sure to have the student tell you the sound, not the letter name.

- Point to your mouth and say the following words: high, cry, my, lie.

  "What sound do you hear in the final position of these words?" */ī/*
- Point to your mouth and say the following words: fin, ban, done, bone.

  "What sound do you hear in the final position of these words?" */n/*
- Point to your mouth and say the following words: fudge, cage, wedge, badge.

  "What sound do you hear in the final position of these words?" */j/*
- Continue with additional words as time permits.

Review of Decks

- The student should be seated where he/she can write comfortably.
- Show the student **Letter Cards 1–5** in random order.

  "Name the letters."
- The student should name the letter on each letter card.
- Show the student **Picture Cards 1–7** in random order.

  "Name the keyword and sound for each card."
- The student should name the keyword and sound for each picture card.
- Give the student **Spelling Sound Sheet 7.**
- Call out the sounds on **Spelling Cards 1–7** in random order. Using the hand signals described in previous lessons, follow the instructions on the cards.
- The student should echo each sound and name the letter that makes the sound as he/she writes the letter on the spelling sound sheet.
- Have the student set the spelling sound sheet aside for use later in the lesson.

New Learning

"I am going to say some words to you and I want you to echo them back to me. Listen for the sound that is the same at the beginning, or initial, position of each word."

- Point to your mouth as you say each word.

  "Echo after me. Lip." *lip* ***"Lot."*** *lot* ***"Lit."*** *lit*
- Slowly repeat the words until the student can answer the following question:

  "What sound do you hear in the initial position?" */l/*
- **Note:** A letter appearing between parallel lines (e.g., /l/) stands for the *sound* of the letter rather than the letter name. If the student responds with the name of the letter, ask again: "What sound do you hear?" Make sure the student is giving the pure sound of *l* and not pronouncing it with a short *u* sound, as in /lŭh/.

  "That's right. The sound you hear in the initial position is /l/."

"Put your fingertips on the front of your neck and say /l/. See if you feel any vibration."

"Is this sound voiced or unvoiced?" *voiced*

"Since /l/ vibrates, it is a voiced sound."

- Write the following words on the chalkboard: lip, lot, lit.

"What letter do you see that might be making the /l/ sound?" *l*

- If the student does not know the name of the letter, say it for him/her.

"L is the first letter in all of these words, so we can see that l must be the letter used to spell the /l/ sound."

"Look at your alphabet strip. Can you tell me if l is a vowel or a consonant?" *consonant*

HANDWRITING/LETTER TILES

- The student should be seated where he/she can write comfortably.
- Write a capital *L* on the chalkboard.

"This is a capital L. Let's practice skywriting capital L's before we write them on our paper."

- Have the student practice skywriting capital *L*'s.

"Find your spelling sound sheet. Leave your pencil on your desk until I tell you to pick it up."

- Draw handwriting lines on the chalkboard.

"These are handwriting lines like you have on your paper."

- Write a capital *L* on the handwriting lines in the handwriting you want the student to learn.

"Now pick up your pencil. Find the first line on your paper and practice writing capital L's like I wrote this one on the chalkboard."

"Say the name of the letter each time you write it."

- Allow a few minutes for the student to practice writing capital *L*'s.

"Put your pencil back on your desk."

- Now write a lowercase *l* on the handwriting lines in the handwriting you want the student to learn.

"This is a lowercase l."

- Have the student practice skywriting lowercase *l*'s.

"Now pick up your pencil and practice writing lowercase l's on the second line of your paper. Say the name of the letter each time you write it."

- Have the student set the spelling sound sheet aside for use later in the lesson.

- Leave the handwriting lines and letters on the chalkboard for the remainder of the lesson.
- Give the student the container of letter tiles.

  "Today I've given you a new letter tile."

  "Find and look at your l letter tile. One side has a capital L and the other side has a lowercase l."
- Allow time for the student to examine the new letter tile.

  "Hold your letter tile up in the air. Turn it so I can see the capital L."

  "Now turn it so I can see the lowercase l."

  "Use your letter tiles to spell the word 'lot.' "
- Repeat with the following words: lip, tin.
- Check to see that the student is moving the tiles correctly.
- Additional words may be found in the Spelling Word List in the appendix. Remember that the student cannot spell words in which letters are repeated. (He/she has only one of each tile.)
- Have the student replace the tiles in the container and put it away.
- Reinforce the name, sound, and shape of the letter *l* throughout the day. (See the introductory material for suggestions.)

NEW DECK CARDS

- Show the student **Letter Card 6.**

  "What letter is this?" *l*
- Hold up **Picture Card 8** but keep the picture covered with your hand (or the letter card).

  "I have a card with a picture on it that begins with the /l/ sound."

  "I am going to describe it for you. See if you can guess what the picture is."

  "This is a large animal. It has a mane. It is very dangerous. People call this animal the king of the jungle. What do you think the picture is?" *lion*

  "That's right. The keyword is 'lion' and the sound we have learned is /l/."
- Show the student **Picture Card 8,** and then point to the picture of a lion on the alphabet strip.

  "The word 'lion' helps us remember the /l/ sound because it begins with /l/."

  "Find your spelling sound sheet."

  "Find the #8 on your paper and put your finger on it."
- Hold up **Spelling Card 8** so only you can see what is written. Using the hand signals described in previous lessons, follow the instructions on the card.
- Check the spelling sound sheet for accuracy.
- **Note:** Add the new letter, picture, and spelling cards to the Review Decks.

Boardwork

"Let's practice coding some words like the ones you'll have on your worksheet."

- Write the word "lit" on the chalkboard.

"Do you see a vowel in this word?" *yes, an i*

"Do you see anything after the i?" *yes, a t*

"Is t a vowel or a consonant?" *consonant*

"That's right. T is a consonant because we know that a, e, i, o, and u are vowels and the rest of the letters are consonants."

- Say the vowel rule (below) as you write it on the chalkboard: v̆c.

"A vowel followed by a consonant is short; code it with a breve. Repeat that with me."

- Point to the chalkboard as the student repeats the vowel rule with you.
- Say the second vowel rule (below) as you write it on the chalkboard: v̄′→.

"The second vowel rule says, 'An open, accented vowel is long; code it with a macron.' Repeat that with me."

- Point to the chalkboard as the student repeats the vowel rule with you.
- Point to the *i* in "lit."

"Does this vowel have a consonant after it?" *yes*

"How should we code this vowel?" *with a breve, short*

"This vowel is short, so we will code it with a breve."

- Put a breve over the *i*: lĭt.
- Point to the *l*.

"What is the sound of this letter?" */l/*

- Point to the *i*.

"What is the short sound of i?" */ĭ/*

- Point to the *t*.

"What is the sound of this letter?" */t/*

"Let's blend these three sounds together and see what word they make."

- Say the first sound, /l/, and do not let go of that sound until you "blend" into the /ĭ/ sound; then immediately add the /t/ sound.

"What is the word?" *lit*

"Can you use the word 'lit' in a sentence?" *expect various answers*

- Write the word "no" on the chalkboard.

"Do you see a vowel in this word?" *yes, an o*

"Do you see anything after the o?" *no*

"Which vowel rule will work on this word?" *a vowel that is not followed by a consonant and is accented is long; we code long vowels with macrons*

"That's right. This vowel will be long because it's not followed by a consonant."

- Code the vowel and mark the accent: nō′.

"What sound does long o make?" */ō/*

"Now blend the two sounds. What is the word?" *no*

"Since we have learned the letter l, we can talk about something new."

- Write the word "plop" on the chalkboard.

"Which letter is a vowel?" *o*

"How do we code the o?" *with a breve*

- Code the vowel with a breve: plŏp.

"Can you read this word?" *expect various attempts*

"The first two letters in this word, p and l, are called a blend. A blend is two consonants that slide together so smoothly that you can hardly hear each sound."

"We will be learning a lot of blends, but we don't code them because you don't need to know any special sounds to read them."

WORKSHEET

- The student should be seated where he/she can write comfortably.
- Write "Worksheet 7" on the chalkboard. Then hold up the worksheet and point to "Worksheet 7" at the top of the page.

"When I give you the worksheet, find the side that has 'worksheet' written on it."

- Give the student **Worksheet 7.** Make sure the student turns to the correct side.

"Using the rules we just practiced, code the words by #1, #2, and #3."

"After you have coded these words, blend the sounds in each word and figure out what the words are."

"When you are finished, draw a line from one of the words to the picture it matches."

- Allow time for the student to do this.

"Let's try spelling a few words. Put your finger by #4. The first word we are going to spell is 'pop.' What is the first sound in the word 'pop'?" */p/*

"Write the lowercase letter that says /p/ on the first line by #4."

"What is the next sound in the word 'pop'?" */ŏ/*

"Write the lowercase letter that says /ŏ/ on the second line by #4."

"What is the last sound in the word 'pop'?" */p/*

"Write the lowercase letter that says /p/ on the last line by #4."

"What is the word you wrote?" *pop*

- Repeat the procedure with #5 (tip) and #6 (plot). Give special attention to the *pl* blend.

  "Look at the picture by #7 and tell me what it is." *something "on"*

  "Can you tell me what the picture by #8 is?" *pot*

  "Can you tell me what the picture by #9 is?" *nip*

  "Think about the sounds in the words 'on,' 'pot,' and 'nip.' Try to spell each word on the lines under the pictures."

  "On the homework side, you'll find three places just like #7, #8, and #9. Decide what the picture is and then spell it on the lines under the picture. You will only be spelling with the letters we've learned."

- As the student works, provide help as needed. Help the student correct any incorrect answers. Then initial the worksheet in the space provided.
- Some time during the day, ask the student to read from the worksheet or homework.
- **Note:** Always make sure the worksheet is corrected before the student begins the homework. The worksheet serves as a guide to help complete the homework.

HOMEWORK

"Turn your paper over to the homework side."

"Put your finger on the top row of handwriting lines. Write your best capital L on these lines so I will know what a capital L should look like."

- Have the student write a lowercase letter *l* on the second handwriting line.
- Make sure that the student has written the letters correctly (to the best of his or her ability). He/She will use them as guides when completing the homework.

  "Do you know what to do on the rest of the homework paper?"

- Discuss the homework pictures to make sure the student understands the word each one represents: #5 (pin), #6 (no), and #7 (top).

  "When you finish your paper, I will check it for you and initial it in the space provided."

- Either now or later in the day, the student should complete the homework independently (if possible). Help the student correct any incorrect answers. Then initial the homework in the space provided.

Name ____________________

Teacher's Initials ____

Worksheet 7
(for use with Lesson 7)
Phonics 1

Ll

1. tĭlt
2. lĭp
3. lĭnt

4. pop
5. tip
6. plot

7.	8.	9.
 on	 pot	 nip

P1-WS-007a

Parent's Initials ____

Homework 7
(for use with Lesson 7)
Phonics 1

Ll

1. ĭll
2. ŏn
3. lŏt
4. pĭn

5.	6.	7.
 pin	 no	 top

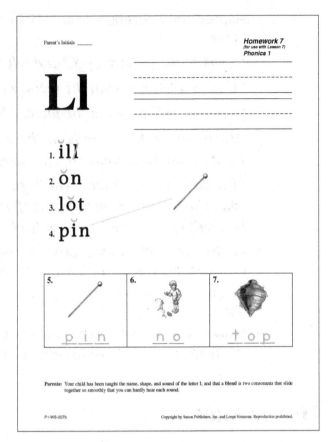

Parents: Your child has been taught the name, shape, and sound of the letter l; and that a **blend** is two consonants that slide together so smoothly that you can hardly hear each sound.

P1-WS-007b

LESSON 8 — The Letter *A*

lesson preparation

materials

Review Decks

Spelling Sound Sheet 8

container of letter tiles

Letter Card 7

apple in a sack (see *the night before*)

Picture Cards 9–10

Spelling Cards 9–10

Worksheet 8

the night before

- Put an apple in a sack for the student to use to "discover" the new keyword. If possible, do not allow the student to see you do this.
- Punch out the *a* letter tile, but do not add it to the container yet.

ALPHABET ACTIVITY

- The student should be standing.

  "Let's do something fun with the alphabet today."

  "First, let's make room to do jumping jacks."
- Demonstrate jumping jacks, if necessary.

  "We'll say the alphabet together. Every time we jump up and put our hands over our heads, we'll say a letter. Ready? A, B, C, …."
- Have the student return to his/her seat.

PHONEMIC AWARENESS

- **Objective:** To identify final sounds in spoken words.

  "I am going to say some words. See if you can tell me the final, or ending, sound in these words."
- When giving words, it helps to exaggerate the sound you want identified.
- Point to your mouth as you say the following words: rub, tab, bib.

- Some students will have difficulty isolating the sounds. Slowly repeat the words until the student can answer. Then ask:

  "What sound do you hear in the final position of these words?" */b/*
- Be sure to have the student tell you the sound, not the letter name.
- Point to your mouth and say the following words: snap, flip, hop.

  "What sound do you hear in the final position of these words?" */p/*
- Point to your mouth and say the following words: rim, arm, ham.

  "What sound do you hear in the final position of these words?" */m/*
- Point to your mouth and say the following words: staff, puff, off.

  "What sound do you hear in the final position of these words?" */f/*
- Continue with additional words as time permits.

Review of Decks

- The student should be seated at a table or desk.
- Show the student **Letter Cards 1–6** in random order.

  "Name the letters."
- The student should name the letter on each letter card.
- Show the student **Picture Cards 1–8** in random order.

  "Name the keyword and sound for each card."
- The student should name the keyword and sound for each picture card.
- Give the student **Spelling Sound Sheet 8** and the container of letter tiles. (Do not give the student the *a* letter tile yet.)

  "Take out your letter tiles and put them in a row in front of you."

  "I'm going to call out some sounds. After you echo the sound and name the letter, find the tile with that letter on it. On your spelling sound sheet, there will be a place for that sound. Put the letter tile on that space."

  "If I give you a sound that's made by a letter you've already used, move that letter tile to the new space."
- Call out the sound on any one of **Spelling Cards 1–8.**
- Check to see that the student chooses and places the tile correctly.
- As you call out the rest of the sounds on **Spelling Cards 1–8** (in random order), make sure the student is placing the tiles correctly.

  "Put your letter tiles back in the container."
- Have the student set the spelling sound sheet and letter tile container aside for use later in the lesson.

New Learning

"I am going to say some words to you and I want you to echo them back to me. Listen for the sound that is the same in the beginning, or initial, position of each word."

- Point to your mouth as you say each word.

"Echo after me. As." *as* ***"Add."*** *add* ***"After."*** *after*

- Slowly repeat the words until the student can answer the following question:

"What sound do you hear in the initial position?" */ă/*

- **Note:** A letter appearing between parallel lines (e.g., /ă/) stands for the *sound* of the letter rather than the letter name. If the student responds with the name of the letter, ask again: "What sound do you hear?"

"That's right. The sound you hear in the initial position is /ă/. Put your fingertips on the front of your neck and say /ă/. See if you feel any vibration."

"Is this sound voiced or unvoiced?" *voiced*

"Since /ă/ vibrates, it is a voiced sound."

- Write the following words on the chalkboard: as, and, ask.

"What letter do you see that might be making the /ă/ sound?" *a*

- If the student does not know the name of the letter, say it for him/her.

"A is the first letter in all of these words, so we can see that a must be the letter used to spell the /ă/ sound. Can you tell me the long sound of a?" */ā/*

"That's right! The long a says its name."

"Look at your alphabet strip. Can you tell me if a is a vowel or a consonant?" *vowel*

Handwriting/Letter Tiles

- The student should be seated where he/she can write comfortably.
- Write a capital *A* on the chalkboard.

"This is a capital A. Let's practice skywriting capital A's before we write them on our paper."

- Have the student practice skywriting capital *A*'s. The student should keep his/her elbows and wrists locked and make each letter about two feet tall.

"Find your spelling sound sheet. Leave your pencil on your desk until I tell you to pick it up."

- Draw handwriting lines on the chalkboard.

"These are handwriting lines like you have on your paper."

- Write a capital *A* on the handwriting lines in the handwriting you want the student to learn.

  "Now pick up your pencil. Find the first line on your paper and practice writing capital A's like I wrote this one on the chalkboard. Say the name of the letter each time you write it."

- Allow a few minutes for the student to practice writing capital *A*'s.

  "Put your pencil back on your desk."

- Now write a lowercase *a* on the handwriting lines in the handwriting you want the student to learn.

  "This is a lowercase a."

- Have the student practice skywriting lowercase *a*'s.

  "Now pick up your pencil and practice writing lowercase a's on the second line of your paper. Say the name of the letter each time you write it."

- Provide assistance as necessary. Then have the student set the spelling sound sheet aside for use later in the lesson.
- Leave the handwriting lines and letters on the chalkboard for the remainder of the lesson.
- Have the student find the container of letter tiles.

  "Today I'm giving you a new letter tile."

- Give the student the *a* letter tile.

  "Look at your a letter tile. One side has a capital A and the other side has a lowercase a."

- Allow time for the student to examine the new letter tile.

  "Hold your letter tile up in the air. Turn it so I can see the capital A."

  "Now turn it so I can see the lowercase a."

- Have the student spell the following words with the letter tiles: at, nap, plant. Choose additional words from the Spelling Word List, if desired.
- Check to see that the student is moving the tiles correctly.
- Have the student replace the tiles in the container and put it away.
- Reinforce the name, sound, and shape of the letter *a* throughout the day. (See the introductory material for suggestions.)

New Deck Cards

- Show the student **Letter Card 7.**

  "What letter is this?" *a*

  "I have another sack today. It contains a clue to our new keyword. Don't look in the sack, but put your hand inside and see if you can guess what is inside."

- Allow the student a chance to feel inside the sack.

- When the student has felt inside the sack, show **Picture Card 9** and ask:

  "Were you right?"

  "The keyword is 'apple' and the sound we have learned is /ă/."

- Point to the picture of an apple on the alphabet strip.

  "The word 'apple' helps us remember the /ă/ sound because it begins with the /ă/ sound."

- If desired, allow the student to eat the apple after the lesson.

  "The short sound of the vowel a is /ă/. But vowels have at least two sounds, so we need another card."

  "I have a card with a picture on it that begins with the long /ā/ sound. See if you can guess what the picture is."

  "This is something that grows on oak trees. They are small and round. Squirrels like them a lot. They have little 'caps' on them. What do you think the picture is?" *acorn*

  "That's right. The keyword is 'acorn' and the sound we have learned is /ā/."

- Show the student **Picture Card 10.**

  "The word 'acorn' helps us remember the /ā/ sound because it begins with /ā/."

  "We will keep these cards together in our review deck to help us remember that the letter a has two sounds."

  "Find your spelling sound sheet. Find the #1 on your paper and put your finger on it."

- Hold up **Spelling Card 9** so only you can see what is written. Using the hand signals, follow the instructions on the card.
- Repeat the procedure with **Spelling Card 10.**
- Check the student's response after each card.
- **Note:** Add the new letter, picture, and spelling cards to the Review Decks. Always keep **Picture Card 10** behind **Picture Card 9** to help the student remember that the letter *a* has two sounds.

BOARDWORK

"Let's practice coding some words like the ones you'll have on your worksheet."

- Write the word "nap" on the chalkboard.

  "Do you see a vowel in this word?" *yes, an a*

  "Do you see anything after the a?" *yes, a p*

  "Is p a vowel or a consonant?" *consonant*

  "That's right. P is a consonant because a, e, i, o and u are the vowels and the rest of the letters are consonants."

"Get out your Rule Book and turn to page 1."

"A vowel followed by a consonant is short; code it with a breve. Repeat that with me."

- Point to **Rule Chart 1** as the student repeats the vowel rule with you.

"Now turn to page 2."

"The second vowel rule says, 'An open, accented vowel is long; code it with a macron.' Repeat that with me."

- Point to **Rule Chart 2** as the student repeats the second vowel rule with you.
- Point to the *a* in "nap."

"Does this vowel have a consonant after it?" *yes*

"How should we code this vowel?" *with a breve*

- Put a breve over the *a*: năp. Point to the *n*.

"What is the sound of this letter?" */n/*

- Point to the *a*.

"What is the short sound of a?" */ă/*

- Point to the *p*.

"What is the sound of this letter?" */p/*

"Let's blend these three sounds together and see what word they make."

- Say the first sound, /n/, and do not let go of that sound until you "blend" into the /ă/ sound; then immediately add the /p/ sound. Help the student by moving your finger from left to right under the letters as you add the sounds.

"What is the word?" *nap*

"Can you use the word 'nap' in a sentence?" *expect various answers*

- Write the word "ill" on the chalkboard.

"How do we code this word?" *code the i with a breve because it is followed by a consonant; mark out one of the l's because it is a twin consonant*

- Code the word: ĭll̸.

Worksheet

- The student should be seated where he/she can write comfortably.
- Write "Worksheet 8" on the chalkboard. Then hold up the worksheet and point to "Worksheet 8" at the top of the page.

"When I give you the worksheet, find the side that has 'worksheet' written on it."

- Give the student **Worksheet 8.** Make sure the student turns to the correct side.

"Using the rules we just practiced, code the words by #1, #2, and #3."

"After you have coded these words, blend the sounds in each word and figure out what the words are. When you are finished, draw a line from one of the words to the picture it matches."

- Provide assistance as necessary.

"Let's try spelling a few words. Put your finger by #4. The first word we are going to spell is 'at.' What is the first sound in the word 'at'?" /ă/

"Write the lowercase letter that says /ă/ on the first line by #4."

"What is the next sound in the word 'at'?" /t/

"Write the lowercase letter that says /t/ on the second line by #4."

"What is the word you wrote?" *at*

- Repeat the procedure with #5 (not) and #6 (pit).

"Look at the picture by #7 and tell me what it is." *lip*

"Can you tell me what the picture by #8 is?" *pin*

"Think about the sounds in the words 'lip' and 'pin.' Try to spell the words on the lines under the pictures."

- Allow time for the student to do this.

"On the homework side, you'll find two more problems like #7 and #8. You must guess what the picture is and then spell the word on the lines under the picture. You will only be spelling with the letters we have learned."

- As the student works, provide help as needed. If necessary, help the student by giving him/her the letter sounds individually. Help the student correct any incorrect answers. Then initial the worksheet in the space provided.
- Some time during the day, ask the student to read from the worksheet or homework. Although coding is important, the ultimate goal is reading, so the student, especially if he/she is having difficulty, should read to someone every day.
- **Note:** Always make sure the worksheet is corrected before the student begins the homework. The worksheet serves as a guide to help complete the homework.

HOMEWORK

"Turn your paper over to the homework side."

"Put your finger on the top row of handwriting lines. Write your best capital A on the line so I will know what a capital A should look like."

- Have the student write a lowercase letter *a* on the second handwriting line.
- Make sure that the student has written the letters correctly (to the best of his or her ability). He/She will use them as guides when completing the homework.

"Do you know what to do on the rest of the homework paper?"

- Discuss the homework pictures to make sure the student understands the word each one represents: #5 (top) and #6 (on).

"When you finish your paper, I will check it for you and initial it in the space provided."

- Either now or later in the day, the student should complete the homework independently (if possible). Help the student correct any incorrect answers. Then initial the homework in the space provided.

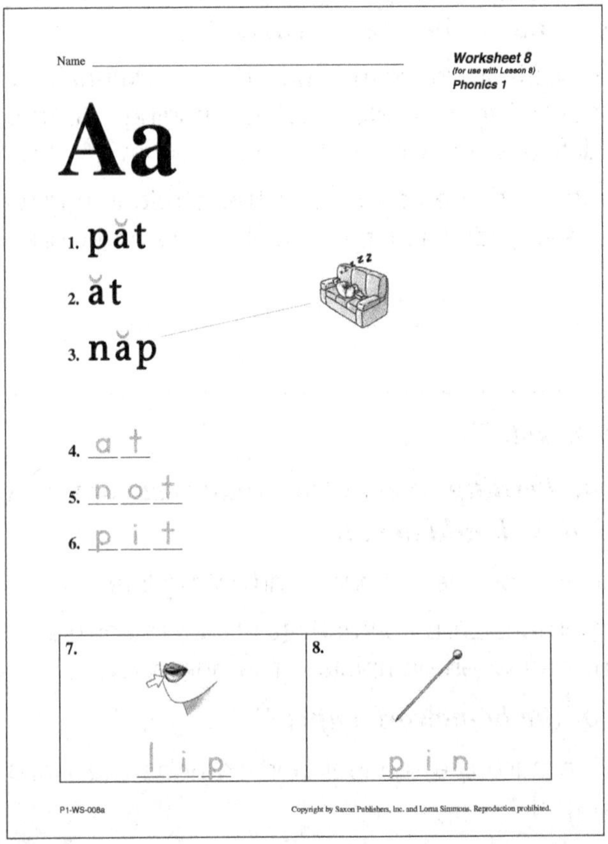

Name ______________________

Worksheet 8
(for use with Lesson 8)
Phonics 1

Aa

1. păt
2. ăt
3. năp

4. at
5. not
6. pit

7. lip
8. pin

P1-WS-008a

Copyright by Saxon Publishers, Inc. and Lorna Simmons. Reproduction prohibited.

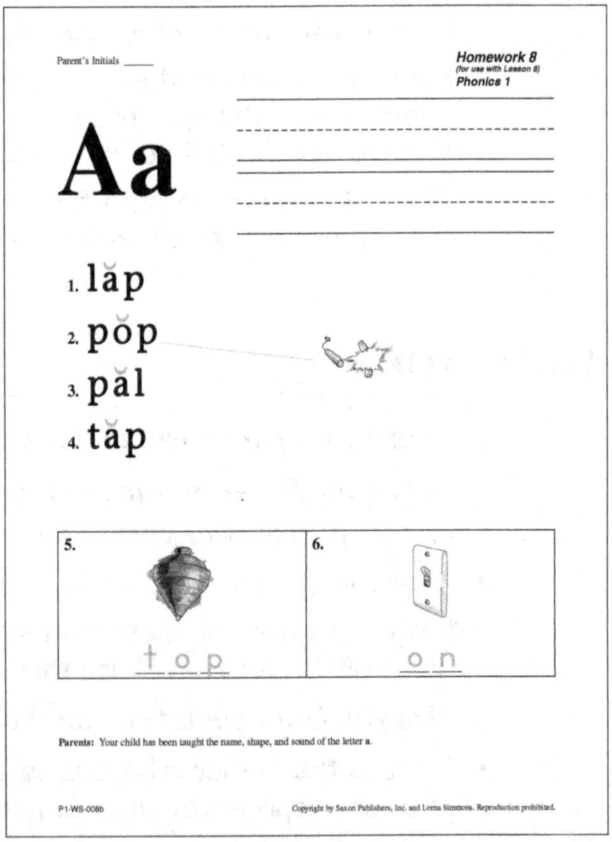

Parent's Initials _____

Homework 8
(for use with Lesson 8)
Phonics 1

Aa

1. lăp
2. pŏp
3. păl
4. tăp

5. top
6. on

Parents: Your child has been taught the name, shape, and sound of the letter a.

P1-WS-008b

Copyright by Saxon Publishers, Inc. and Lorna Simmons. Reproduction prohibited.

LESSON 9 — The Letter *Z*

> **lesson preparation**
>
> **materials**
>
> Review Decks
>
> Spelling Sound Sheet 9
>
> container of letter tiles
>
> Letter Card 8
>
> zipper in a sack (see *the night before*)
>
> Picture Card 11
>
> Spelling Card 11
>
> Worksheet 9
>
> **the night before**
>
> - Put a zipper in a sack for the student to use to "discover" the new keyword. If possible, do not allow the student to see you do this.
> - Add the *z* letter tile to the student's container.

ALPHABET ACTIVITY

- The student should be seated with the alphabet strip.

  "How many letters are in the alphabet?" *26*

  "What two kinds of letters make up our alphabet?" *vowels and consonants*

  "Name the vowels." *a, e, i, o, and u*

  "All of the other letters are called _________?" *consonants*

  "We're going to do something special when we say the alphabet. Every time we say a consonant, we'll sit and whisper it. Every time we say a vowel, we'll stand and say it loudly."

PHONEMIC AWARENESS

- **Objective:** To identify final sounds in spoken words.

  "I am going to say some words. See if you can tell me the final, or ending, sound in these words."

- When giving words to the student, it helps to exaggerate the sound you want identified.
- Point to your mouth as you say the following words: stuff, laugh, stiff.
- Some students will have difficulty isolating the sounds. Slowly repeat the words until the student can answer. Then ask:

  "What sound do you hear in the final position of these words?" */f/*
- Be sure to have the student tell you the sound, not the letter name.
- Point to your mouth and say the following words: pass, hiss, boss.

  "What sound do you hear in the final position of these words?" */s/*
- Point to your mouth and say the following words: pack, sick, luck.

  "What sound do you hear in the final position of these words?" */k/*
- Point to your mouth and say the following words: fox, six, sax.

  "What sound do you hear in the final position of these words?" */ks/*
- Continue with additional words as time permits.

REVIEW OF DECKS

- The student should be seated where he/she can write comfortably.
- Show the student **Letter Cards 1–7** in random order.

  "Name the letters."
- The student should name the letter on each letter card.
- Show the student **Picture Cards 1–10** in random order.

  "Name the keyword and sound for each card."
- The student should name the keyword and sound for each picture card.
- Give the student **Spelling Sound Sheet 9.**
- Call out the sounds on **Spelling Cards 1–10** in random order. Using the hand signals described in previous lessons, follow the instructions on the cards.
- The student should echo each sound and name the letter that makes the sound as he/she writes the letter on the spelling sound sheet.
- Have the student set the spelling sound sheet aside for use later in the lesson.

NEW LEARNING

"I am going to say some words to you and I want you to echo them back to me. Listen for the sound that is the same in the beginning, or initial, position of each word."

- Point to your mouth as you say each word.

"Echo after me. Zoo." *zoo* ***"Zebra."*** *zebra* ***"Zigzag."*** *zigzag*

- Slowly repeat the words until the student can answer the following question:

  "What sound do you hear in the initial position?" */z/*

- **Note:** A letter appearing between parallel lines (e.g., /z/) stands for the *sound* of the letter rather than the letter name. Make sure the student is giving the pure sound of *z* and not pronouncing it with a short *u* sound, as in /zŭh/.

  "That's right. The sound you hear in the initial position is /z/."

  "Put your fingertips on the front of your neck and say /z/. See if you feel any vibration."

  "Is this sound voiced or unvoiced?" *voiced*

  "Since /z/ vibrates, it is a voiced sound."

- Write the following words on the chalkboard: zoo, zebra, zigzag.

  "What letter do you see that might be making the /z/ sound?" *z*

- If the student does not know the name of the letter, say it for him/her.

  "Z is the first letter in all of these words, so we can see that z must be the letter used to spell the /z/ sound."

  "Look at your alphabet strip. Can you tell me if z is a vowel or a consonant?" *consonant*

HANDWRITING/LETTER TILES

- The student should be seated where he/she can write comfortably.
- Write a capital *Z* on the chalkboard.

  "This is a capital Z. Let's practice skywriting capital Z's before we write them on our paper."

- Have the student practice skywriting capital *Z*'s.

  "Find your spelling sound sheet. Leave your pencil on your desk until I tell you to pick it up."

- Draw handwriting lines on the chalkboard.

  "These are handwriting lines like you have on your paper."

- Write a capital *Z* on the handwriting lines in the handwriting you want the student to learn.

  "Now pick up your pencil. Find the first line on your paper and practice writing capital Z's like I wrote this one on the chalkboard."

  "Say the name of the letter each time you write it."

- Allow a few minutes for the student to practice writing capital *Z*'s.

  "Put your pencil back on your desk."

- Now write a lowercase *z* on the handwriting lines in the handwriting you want the student to learn.

"This is a lowercase z."

- Have the student practice skywriting lowercase *z*'s.

  "Now pick up your pencil and practice writing lowercase z's on the second line of your paper. Say the name of the letter each time you write it."

- Have the student set the spelling sound sheet aside for use later in the lesson.
- Leave the handwriting lines and letters on the chalkboard for the remainder of the lesson.
- Give the student the container of letter tiles.

  "Today I've given you a new letter tile."

  "Find your z letter tile and look at it. One side has a capital Z and the other side has a lowercase z."

- Allow time for the student to examine the new letter tile.

  "Hold your letter tile up in the air. Turn it so I can see the capital Z."

  "Now turn it so I can see the lowercase z."

  "Spell the word 'zip' with your letter tiles."

  "Change one letter to make the word 'zap.' "

  "Now change another letter to make the word 'tap.' "

- Check to see that the student is moving the tiles correctly. Choose additional words from the Spelling Word List, if desired.
- Have the student replace the tiles in the container and put it away.
- Reinforce the name, sound, and shape of the letter *z* throughout the day. (See the introductory material for suggestions.)

New Deck Cards

- Show the student **Letter Card 8.**

  "What letter is this?" *z*

  "I have another sack today. It contains a clue to our new keyword. Don't look in the sack, but put your hand inside and see if you can guess what is inside."

- Allow the student a chance to feel inside the sack.

  "I'm going to count to three. On three, whisper what you think is in the sack."

  "One, two, three." *zipper*

  "That's right. The keyword is 'zipper' and the sound we have learned is /z/."

- Show the student **Picture Card 11,** and then point to the picture of the zipper on the alphabet strip.

  "The word 'zipper' helps us remember the /z/ sound because it begins with /z/."

  "Find your spelling sound sheet."

"Find the #11 on your paper and put your finger on it."

- Hold up **Spelling Card 11** so only you can see what is written. Using the hand signals, follow the instructions on the card.
- Check the student's response.
- **Note:** Add the new letter, picture, and spelling cards to the Review Decks.

BOARDWORK

"Let's practice coding some words like the ones you'll have on your worksheet."

- Write the word "zip" on the chalkboard.

"Do you see a vowel in this word?" *yes, an i*

"Do you see anything after the i?" *yes, a p*

"Is p a vowel or a consonant?" *consonant*

"That's right. P is a consonant because a, e, i, o, and u are vowels and the rest of the letters are consonants."

"A vowel followed by a consonant is short; code it with a breve. Repeat that with me."

- Point to **Rule Chart 1** as the student repeats the vowel rule with you.

"The second vowel rule says, 'An open, accented vowel is long; code it with a macron.' Repeat that with me."

- Point to **Rule Chart 2** as the student repeats the second vowel rule with you.
- Point to the *i* in "zip."

"Does this vowel have a consonant after it?" *yes*

"How should we code this vowel?" *with a breve*

- Put a breve over the *i*: zĭp. Point to the *z*.

"What is the sound of this letter?" */z/*

- Point to the *i*.

"What is the short sound of this letter?" */ĭ/*

- Point to the *p*.

"What is the sound of this letter?" */p/*

"Let's blend these three sounds together and see what word they make."

- Blend the sounds with the student. If the student has difficulty blending, it is sometimes helpful to cover up the letters before the vowel. Read the remaining portion of the word, and then add the preceding consonants, one at a time.

"What is the word?" *zip*

"Can you use the word 'zip' in a sentence?" *expect various answers*

- Write the word "no" on the chalkboard.

"Do you see a vowel in this word?" *yes, an o*

"Do you see anything after the o?" *no*

"Which vowel rule will work on this word?" *an open, accented vowel is long (v̄′→)*

"Good answer! This vowel will be long because it's not followed by a consonant. Code the vowel and mark the accent."

- Allow time for the student to come to the chalkboard and do this: nō′.

"What sound does a long o make?" */ō/*

"Now blend the two sounds together. What word do they make?" *no*

- Write the word "till" on the chalkboard.

"I see two things that need to be coded in this word. Can you help me?" *short i and twin consonants*

"That's right. We need a breve on the i, and we need to mark out one of the consonants to remind us to read only one of them."

- Code the word: tĭl~~l~~.

WORKSHEET

- The student should be seated where he/she can write comfortably.
- Write "Worksheet 9" on the chalkboard. Then hold up the worksheet and point to "Worksheet 9" at the top of the page.

"When I give you the worksheet, find the side that has 'worksheet' written on it."

- Give the student **Worksheet 9.** Make sure the student turns to the correct side.

"Using the rules we just practiced, code the words by #1, #2, and #3."

"After you have coded these words, blend the sounds in each word and figure out what the words are."

"When you are finished, draw a line from one of the words to the picture it matches."

- Provide assistance as necessary.

"Let's try spelling a few words. Put your finger by #4. The first word we are going to spell is 'lit.' What is the first sound in the word 'lit'?" */l/*

"Write the lowercase letter that says /l/ on the first line by #4."

"What is the next sound in the word 'lit'?" */ĭ/*

"Write the lowercase letter that says /ĭ/ on the second line by #4."

"What is the last sound in the word 'lit'?" */t/*

"Write the lowercase letter that says /t/ on the third line by #4."

"What is the word you wrote?" *lit*

- Repeat the procedure with #5 (top) and #6 (no).

"Look at the picture by #7 and tell me what it is." *something on*

"Can you tell me what the picture by #8 is?" *zip*

"Think about the sounds in the words 'on' and 'zip.' Try to spell the words on the lines under the pictures."

- Allow time for the student to do this.

"On the homework side, you'll find three more problems like #7 and #8. You must guess what the picture is and then spell the word on the lines under the picture. You will only be spelling with the letters we have learned."

- As the student works, provide help as needed. If necessary, give the letter sounds individually. Help the student correct any incorrect answers. Then initial the worksheet in the space provided.
- Some time during the day, ask the student to read from the worksheet or homework.
- **Note:** Always make sure the worksheet is corrected before the student begins the homework. The worksheet serves as a guide to help complete the homework.

HOMEWORK

"Turn your paper over to the homework side."

"Put your finger on the top row of handwriting lines. Write your best capital Z on the line so I will know what a capital Z should look like."

- Have the student write a lowercase letter *z* on the second handwriting line.
- Make sure that the student has written the letters correctly (to the best of his or her ability). He/She will use them as guides when completing the homework.

"Do you know what to do on the rest of the homework paper?"

- Discuss the homework pictures to make sure the student understands the word each one represents: #5 (pop), #6 (nap), and #7 (pan).

"When you finish your paper, I will check it for you and initial it in the space provided."

- Either now or later in the day, the student should complete the homework independently (if possible). Help the student correct any incorrect answers. Then initial the homework in the space provided.

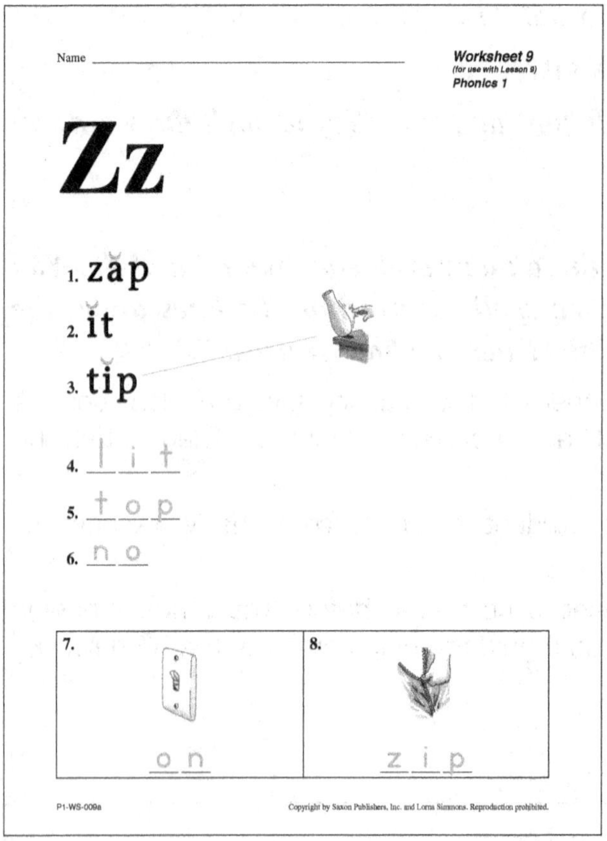

Name ____________________

Worksheet 9
(for use with Lesson 9)
Phonics 1

Zz

1. zăp
2. ĭt
3. tĭp

4. l i t
5. t o p
6. n o

7. o n
8. z i p

P1-WS-009a

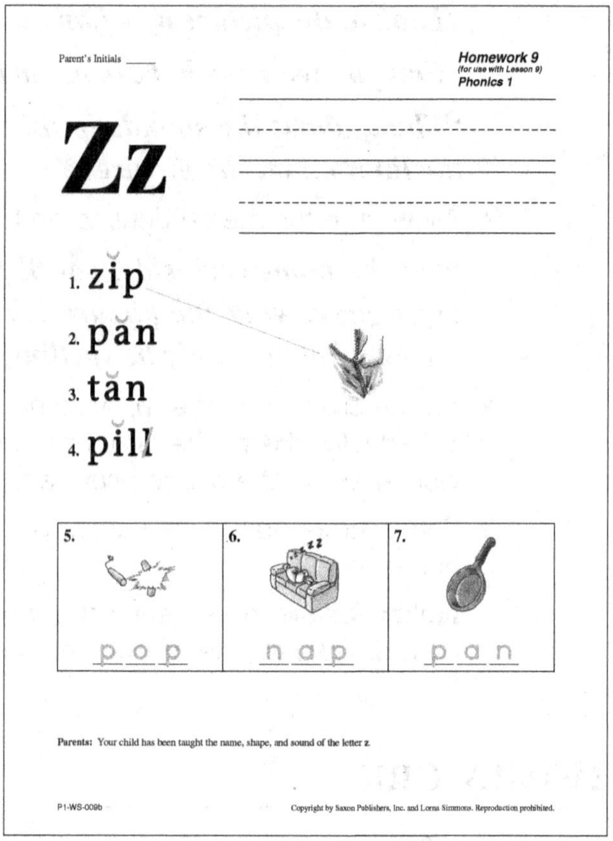

Parent's Initials _____

Homework 9
(for use with Lesson 9)
Phonics 1

Zz

1. zĭp
2. păn
3. tăn
4. pĭll

5. p o p
6. n a p
7. p a n

Parents: Your child has been taught the name, shape, and sound of the letter z.

P1-WS-009b

LESSON 10 — Assessment

lesson preparation

materials

Review Decks

Assessment 1

Assessment 1 Recording Form

Kid Cards

tokens

the night before

- Separate the Kid Cards marked "Lesson 10."
- Select some small objects to use as game tokens (approximately 12). If you choose tokens that will be collected and reused, occasionally substitute "fun" tokens (small wrapped candies, goldfish-shaped crackers, cereal pieces, etc.).

ALPHABET ACTIVITY

- The student should be seated.

  "We're going to do something special with the alphabet today."

  "I will be the consonant team and you will be the vowel team. When we recite the alphabet, you'll say the vowels and I'll say the consonants."

- As you say the alphabet, point to the student when it is his/her time to recite.
- If time permits, swap letters.

PHONEMIC AWARENESS

- **Objective:** To identify final sounds in spoken words.

  "I am going to say some words. See if you can tell me the final, or ending, sound in these words."

- When giving words, it helps to exaggerate the sound you want identified.
- Point to your mouth as you say the following words: mail, pill, haul, kneel.
- Some students will have difficulty isolating the sounds. Slowly repeat the words until the student can answer. Then ask:

  "What sound do you hear in the final position of these words?" */l/*

- Be sure to have the student tell you the sound, not the letter name.
- Point to your mouth and say the following words: fuzz, quiz, was, says.

  "What sound do you hear in the final position of these words?" */z/*
- Point to your mouth and say the following words: hat, sit, what, fought.

  "What sound do you hear in the final position of these words?" */t/*
- Point to your mouth and say the following words: play, stay, weigh, day.

  "What sound do you hear in the final position of these words?" */ā/*
- Continue with additional words as time permits.

REVIEW OF DECKS

- Show the student **Letter Cards 1–8** in random order. The student should name the letter on each card.
- Show the student **Picture Cards 1–11** in random order. The student should name the keyword and sound for each card.

WRITTEN ASSESSMENT

- Beginning with this lesson, there will be written and oral assessments every fifth lesson. Each assessment covers material that was taught at least one week earlier. It is expected that the student will master at least 80% of the concepts on the assessments. See the introductory material for general information regarding assessments, grading, and record keeping.

  "Today we are going to see if you remember the letters and sounds we have been practicing."
- Give the student **Assessment 1.**
- **Section I:**

  "Today, we will write our spelling deck responses on this paper."

  "I'm going to give you a sound. Write the letter that makes that sound on the line by #1."
- Give the following sounds in the order shown: /t/, /ŏ/, /n/, /p/.
- The student should write the letter that makes each sound on lines 1–4.
- **Section II:**

  "Put your finger on #5."

  "Look at the letter by #5."

  "Find the picture of the keyword for this sound."

  "Draw a line from the letter to the keyword."
- Repeat with #6, #7, and #8. Allow a few minutes for the student to work.
- The pictures (from top to bottom) are as follows: nest, ostrich, pencil, tent.

- **Section III:**

  "Put your finger on #9."

  "Code the words by #9, #10, #11, and #12."

  "When you have finished coding, show your paper to me."
- This paper will be used during the oral portion of the assessment.

ORAL ASSESSMENT

- Oral assessments are short interviews that occur during independent work time. It is important to complete them promptly (today, if possible) in order to identify any areas of weakness and begin remediation.
- Use the assessment and the following dialogue to complete the oral portion.
- **Section IV:**

  "I'm going to say some words. Tell me the sound you hear in the initial position."
- Point to your mouth and say the following words: nice, new, nut, need.
- Write the student's response on the line by #13.
- Repeat with #14 (tip, two, take, tub); #15 (odd, on, off, ox); and #16 (pest, pad, post, pipe).
- **Section V:**
- Show the student the letter by #17.

  "What is this letter?"
- Write the student's response on the adjacent line.
- Repeat with #18, #19, and #20.
- **Section VI:**

  "Look at the word by #21. Read this word for me."
- Record the student's response on the adjacent line.
- Repeat with #22, #23, #24, and #25.

ASSESSMENT EVALUATION

- Grade the assessment and record the results on **Assessment 1 Recording Form.** Check off the boxes to indicate mastery (i.e., the section was completed with 100% accuracy).
- **Note:** If you choose to grade the assessments, try to give as many points as possible for work attempted. Do not grade the coding marks too severely, especially secondary marks like accents, voice lines, and k-backs. The most important coding marks to look for are breves, macrons, and syllable division lines.
- See the introductory material for detailed information regarding grading and recording procedures.

- Use the assessment results to identify those skills in which the student is weak. Practice those skills by playing Kid Card games. Listed below are games appropriate for remediation in selected areas. See the "Games and Activities" section in the appendix for the directions for each game.
- **Section I:** Play "Spelling Deck Perfection" or "Sound Scamper."
- **Section II:** Play "Keyword and Sound" or "Letter/Sound Identification."
- **Section III:** Play "Chalkboard Challenge."
- **Section IV:** Play "Sound Solutions." (*Note*: This game is usually played with the red Kid Cards. However, since these cards have not been introduced, play with any available pictures, such as pictures in a basal reader, a magazine, a poster on the wall, etc.)
- **Section V:** Play "Letter Deck Data" or "Letter/Sound Identification."
- **Section VI:** Play "Word Blend" (with blue Kid Cards).
- When the student seems more secure in areas that had previously proven difficult, retest him/her (in those areas only) and indicate on the recording form any sections the student has subsequently mastered.
- Try to help the student achieve mastery of all the sections before the next assessment.

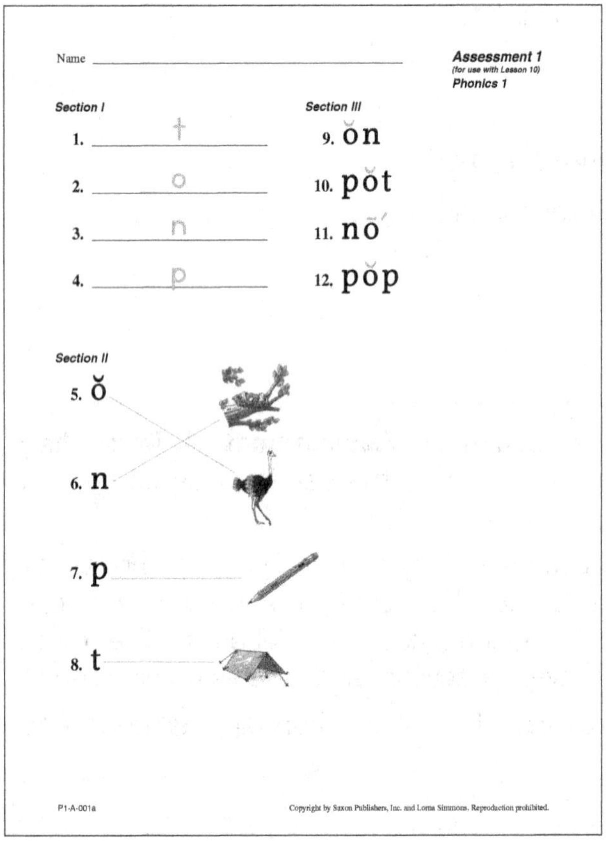

Name ______________________

Assessment 1
(for use with Lesson 10)
Phonics 1

Section I

1. t
2. o
3. n
4. p

Section II

5. ŏ
6. n
7. p
8. t

Section III

9. ŏn
10. pŏt
11. nō´
12. pŏp

P1-A-001a

Copyright by Saxon Publishers, Inc. and Lorna Simmons. Reproduction prohibited.

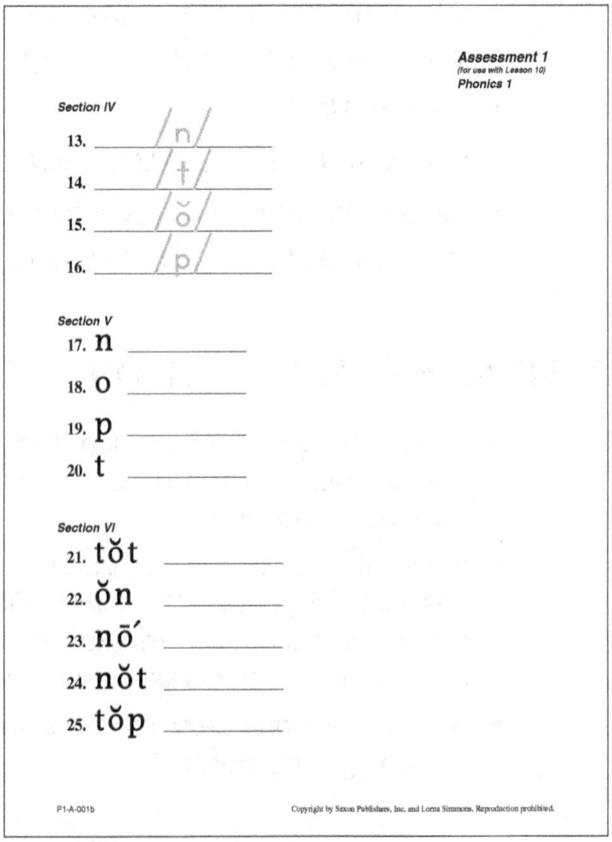

Assessment 1
(for use with Lesson 10)
Phonics 1

Section IV

13. /n/
14. /t/
15. /ŏ/
16. /p/

Section V

17. n ______
18. o ______
19. p ______
20. t ______

Section VI

21. tŏt ______
22. ŏn ______
23. nō´ ______
24. nŏt ______
25. tŏp ______

P1-A-001b

Copyright by Saxon Publishers, Inc. and Lorna Simmons. Reproduction prohibited.

LESSON 11 — The Letter *S*

lesson preparation

materials

Review Decks

Spelling Sound Sheet 10

container of letter tiles

Letter Card 9

sock in a sack (see *the night before*)

Picture Cards 12–13

Spelling Card 12

Worksheet 11

new concepts

medial

voice line

comma

the night before

- Put a sock in a sack for the student to use to "discover" the new keyword. If possible, do not allow the student to see you do this.
- Add the *s* letter tile to the student's container.

ALPHABET ACTIVITY

- The student should be seated with the alphabet strip.

  "Let's point to each letter and say the whole alphabet. Put your index finger on 'a' and say the names with me."

- Try to set a steady pace so the student cannot sing the alphabet.

  "The initial letter of the alphabet is _____?" *a*

  "The final letter of the alphabet is _____?" *z*

  "The medial letters are all of the letters between a and z, or the letters in the middle. Can you name a medial letter?" *any letter from b to y*

PHONEMIC AWARENESS

- **Objective:** To identify medial sounds in spoken words.

  "I am going to say some words. See if you can tell me the medial, or middle, sound in these words."

- It helps to exaggerate the sound you want the student to identify. Point to your mouth as you say the following words: pat, can, bad. Slowly repeat the words until the student can answer. Then ask:

  "What sound do you hear in the medial position of these words?" /ă/
- Repeat with hot, sod, pop (/ŏ/); sip, bid, pin (/ĭ/); mud, bug, fun (/ŭ/).
- Continue with additional words as time permits.

Review of Decks

- The student should be seated where he/she can write comfortably.
- Show the student **Letter Cards 1–8** in random order. The student should name the letter on each letter card.
- Show the student **Picture Cards 1–11** in random order. The student should name the keyword and sound for each picture card.
- Give the student **Spelling Sound Sheet 10.**
- Call out the sounds on **Spelling Cards 1–11** in random order. The student should echo each sound and name the letter that makes the sound as he/she writes the letter on the spelling sound sheet.
- Check the student's response after each card.
- Have the student set the spelling sound sheet aside for use later in the lesson.

New Learning

"I am going to say some words to you and I want you to echo them back to me. Listen for the sound that is the same in the beginning, or initial, position of each word."

- Point to your mouth as you say each word.

  "Echo after me. Soup." *soup* ***"Sea."*** *sea* ***"Same."*** *same*
- Slowly repeat the words until the student can answer the following question:

  "What sound do you hear in the initial position?" /s/
- **Note:** Make sure the student is giving the pure sound of *s* and not pronouncing it with a short *u* sound, as in /sŭh/.

  "That's right. The sound you hear in the initial position is /s/."

  "Put your fingertips on the front of your neck and say /s/. See if you feel any vibration."

  "Is this sound voiced or unvoiced?" *unvoiced*

  "Since /s/ doesn't vibrate, it is an unvoiced sound."
- Write the following words on the chalkboard: sip, sit, Sal.

  "What letter do you see that might be making the /s/ sound?" *s*

- If the student does not know the name of the letter, say it for him/her.

  "S is the first letter in all of these words, so we can see that s must be the letter used to spell the /s/ sound."

  "Look at your alphabet strip. Is s a vowel or a consonant?" *consonant*

  "I want you to echo some more words. This time, listen for the sound in the final position."

  "Echo after me. Is." *is* ***"As."*** *as* ***"Has."*** *has*

  "What sound do you hear in the final position?" */z/*

- Write the words on the chalkboard: is, as, has.

  "What letter is making the final sound?" *s*

  "How many sounds does s make?" *two*

  "What are the sounds?" */s/ and /z/*

  "That's right. When we read words, we need to remember that s has two sounds."

  "The /s/ sound is unvoiced, but the /z/ sound is voiced."

  "Put your fingertips on the front of your neck and say /z/."

  "This sound is voiced, isn't it?"

  "There's a special code mark we put on the voiced s to help us remember that it is voiced. It is called a voice line. It looks like this."

- Write an *s* on the chalkboard and draw a voice line through it: ~~s~~.

  "When we code words, we can try both sounds of s and mark a voice line when we hear a voiced s."

- Demonstrate with the word "has": ha~~s~~.
- **Optional:** Explain to the student that in some cases both the voiced and the unvoiced *s* will make legitimate (but different) words (e.g., his/hiss), but a doubled *s* will always make the /s/ sound.

HANDWRITING/LETTER TILES

- The student should be seated where he/she can write comfortably.
- Write a capital *S* on the chalkboard.

  "This is a capital S. Let's practice skywriting capital S's before we write them on our paper."

- Have the student practice skywriting capital *S*'s.

  "Find your spelling sound sheet."

- Draw handwriting lines on the chalkboard. Write a capital *S* on the handwriting lines in the handwriting you want the student to learn.

"Find the first handwriting line on your paper and practice writing capital S's like I wrote this one on the chalkboard."

"Say the name of the letter each time you write it."

- Allow a few minutes for the student to practice writing capital *S*'s.
- Write a lowercase *s* on the handwriting lines in the handwriting you want the student to learn.

"This is a lowercase s."

- Have the student practice skywriting lowercase *s*'s.

"Now practice writing lowercase s's on the second handwriting line. Say the name of the letter each time you write it."

- Have the student set the spelling sound sheet aside for use later in the lesson.
- Leave the handwriting lines and letters on the chalkboard for the remainder of the lesson.
- Give the student the container of letter tiles.

"Today I've given you a new letter tile."

"Find your s letter tile and look at it. One side has a capital S and the other side has a lowercase s."

- Allow time for the student to examine the new letter tile.

"Hold your letter tile up in the air. Turn it so I can see the capital S."

"Now turn it so I can see the lowercase s."

"Spell the word 'sip' with your letter tiles."

- Continue with the following words: so, snap. Choose additional words from the Spelling Word List, if desired.
- Have the student replace the tiles in the container and put it away.
- Reinforce the name, sound, and shape of the letter *s* throughout the day.

NEW DECK CARDS

- Pull **Spelling Card 11** from the Review Deck.
- Show the student **Letter Card 9.**

"What letter is this?" s

"I have another sack today. It contains a clue to our new keyword. Don't look in the sack, but put your hand inside and see if you can guess what is inside."

- Allow the student a chance to feel inside the sack.

"I'm going to count to three. On three, whisper what you think is in the sack."

"One, two, three." *sock*

"That's right. The keyword is 'sock' and the sound we have learned is /s/."

- Show the student **Picture Card 12,** and then point to the picture of a sock on the alphabet strip.

  "The word 'sock' helps us remember the /s/ sound because it begins with /s/."

  "Since the letter s also has another sound, we need another card."

  "I have a card with a picture on it that ends with the /z/ sound of the letter s. See if you can guess what the picture is."

  "This is a flower you would find in a garden. It is beautiful, but if you're not careful, it could hurt you. Sometimes a boy sends a dozen of these to a girl to show her he likes her. They come in many colors and smell very nice. What do you think the picture is?" *rose*

  "The keyword is 'rose' and the sound we have learned is /z/."

- Show the student **Picture Card 13.**

  "The word 'rose' helps us remember the /z/ sound because it contains the /z/ sound."

  "We will keep these cards together in our review deck to help us remember that the letter s has two sounds."

  "Find your spelling sound sheet."

  "Find the #12 on your paper and put your finger on it."

- Hold up **Spelling Card 11** so that only you can see what is written.

  "Echo this sound: /z/." */z/*

  "What letter makes this sound?" *the student will probably answer "z"*

  "Write the lowercase letter z on the line by #12."

  "What other letter makes the /z/ sound?" *s*

  "Write the lowercase letter s on the line after the z."

- Write the following on the chalkboard: *z s.*

  "Z and s both make the /z/ sound. But it's not 'z-s.' We need something to separate them to show that they are two different spellings. Let's put a comma between them and say 'z comma s' when we write it. A comma means a slight pause."

- Put a comma between the letters: *z, s.*

  "From now on, this will be your new response to the /z/ sound."

- Hold up **Spelling Card 12** so only you can see what is written. Using the hand signals, follow the instructions on the card.
- Check the spelling sound sheet for accuracy.
- **Note:** Add the new letter, picture, and spelling cards to the Review Decks (and re-insert **Spelling Card 11**). Always keep **Picture Card 13** behind **Picture Card 12** to help the student remember that the letter *s* has two sounds.

BOARDWORK

"Let's practice coding some words like the ones you'll have on your worksheet."

- Write the word "spill" on the chalkboard.

"Do you see a vowel in this word?" *yes, an i*

"Do you see anything after the i?" *yes, ll*

"Is there something special I need to do to one of these l's?" *mark one out because we only read one of them*

"How will we code the i?" *short; breve*

- Point to **Rule Chart 1.**

"How do we know it is short?" *it is followed by a consonant*

- Code the word as the student instructs: spĭll.

"What is this word?" *spill*

"Can you give me a sentence with the word 'spill' in it?" *expect various answers*

"We have a new blend in this word. Can you tell me what it is?" *sp*

"Good job. We can now make other blends with the letter s."

- Write the following on the chalkboard: *sp, sn, sl, spl, st.*

"These are the new blends we will see as we read."

- Write the word "so" on the chalkboard.

"Does this word have a vowel?" *yes, an o*

- Point to **Rule Chart 2.**

"Is this vowel going to be short or long?" *long*

"How do you know?" *it is not followed by a consonant*

"That's right. What else do I need to mark on this word?" *the accent*

- Code the word as the student instructs: sō´.

"What is this word?" *so*

"Can you give me a sentence with the word 'so' in it?" *expect various answers*

WORKSHEET

- The student should be seated where he/she can write comfortably.
- Write "Worksheet 11" on the chalkboard. Then hold up the worksheet and point to "Worksheet 11" at the top of the page.

"When I give you the worksheet, find the side that has 'worksheet' written on it."

- Give the student **Worksheet 11.** Make sure the student turns to the correct side.

"Using the rules we just practiced, code the words by #1, #2, and #3."

"After you have coded these words, blend the sounds in each word and figure out what the words are."

"When you are finished, draw a line from one of the words to the picture it matches."

- Assist the student as necessary.

"Let's try spelling a few words. Put your finger by #4. The first word we are going to spell is 'pat.' What is the first sound in the word 'pat'?" /p/

"Write the letter that says /p/ on the first line by #4."

"What is the next sound in the word 'pat'?" /ă/

"Write the letter that says /ă/ on the second line by #4."

"What is the final sound in the word 'pat'?" /t/

"Write the letter that says /t/ on the third line by #4."

"What is the word you wrote?" pat

- Repeat the procedure with #5 (tip) and #6 (so).

"Look at the picture by #7 and tell me what it is." list

"Can you tell me what the picture by #8 is?" spot

"Think about the sounds in the words 'list' and 'spot.' Try to spell the words on the lines under the pictures."

- Allow time for the student to do this.

"On the homework side, you'll find three more problems like #7 and #8. You must guess what the picture is and then spell that word on the lines under the picture. You will only be spelling with the letters we have learned."

- As the student works, provide help as needed. Help the student correct any incorrect answers. Then initial the worksheet in the space provided.
- Some time during the day, ask the student to read from the worksheet or homework.
- **Note:** Always make sure the worksheet is corrected before the student begins the homework. The worksheet serves as a guide to help complete the homework.

HOMEWORK

"Turn your paper over to the homework side."

"Put your finger on the top row of handwriting lines. Write your best capital S on these lines so I will know what a capital S should look like."

- Have the student write a lowercase letter *s* on the second handwriting line.
- Make sure that the student has written the letters correctly (to the best of his or her ability). He/She will use them as guides when completing the homework.

"Do you know what to do on the rest of the homework paper?"

Lesson 11

- Discuss the homework pictures to make sure the student understands the word each one represents: #5 (sap), #6 (zip), and #7 (top).

  "When you finish your paper, I will check it for you and initial it in the space provided."

- Either now or later in the day, the student should complete the homework independently (if possible). Help the student correct any incorrect answers. Then initial the homework in the space provided.
- If possible, take time to play the Kid Card games listed in Lesson 10.

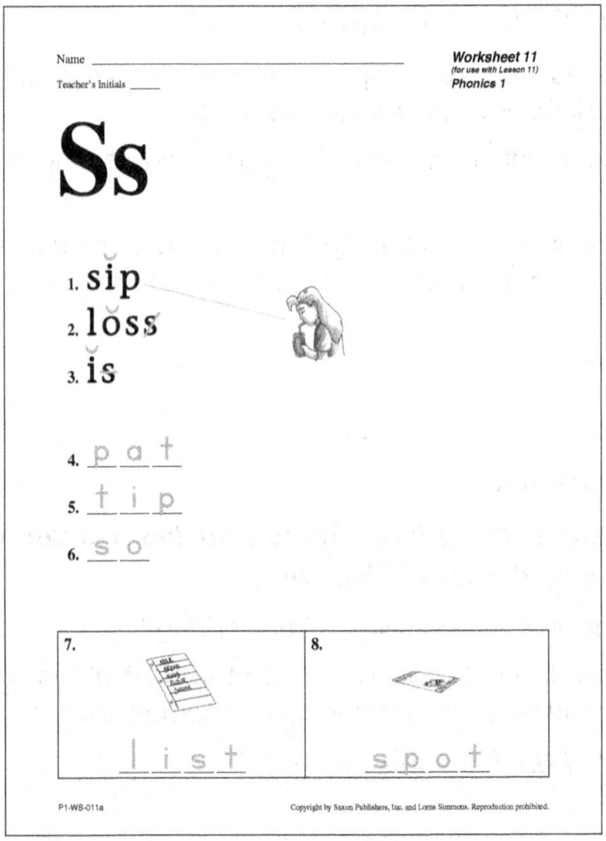
Name ______

Teacher's Initials ____

Worksheet 11
(for use with Lesson 11)
Phonics 1

Ss

1. sip
2. loss
3. is

4. pat
5. tip
6. so

7. list
8. spot

P1-WS-011a

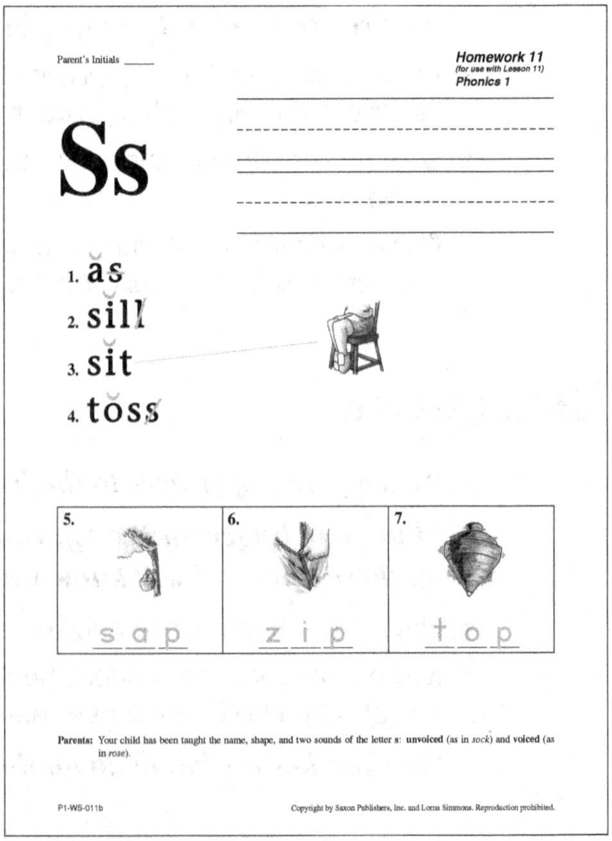
Parent's Initials ____

Homework 11
(for use with Lesson 11)
Phonics 1

Ss

1. as
2. sill
3. sit
4. toss

5. sap
6. zip
7. top

Parents: Your child has been taught the name, shape, and two sounds of the letter s: **unvoiced** (as in *sock*) and **voiced** (as in *rose*).

P1-WS-011b

LESSON 12

Suffix *-s*

lesson preparation

materials

Review Decks
Spelling Sound Sheet 11
gingersnaps (see *the night before*)
Affix Card 1
Worksheet 12
Reader 1 (*Zip*)
colored pencils
Reader Collection Box

new concepts

plural
root word
suffix
temporary sight words
derivative
sentence
exclamation point

the night before

- Buy enough gingersnaps for the student to have a handful. If the student has dietary restrictions, provide a substitute snack.

ALPHABET ACTIVITY

- The student should be standing.

  "Let's say the alphabet as we touch our toes."

  "We'll say a letter each time we bend over."

- Say the alphabet; then have the student return to his/her seat.

PHONEMIC AWARENESS

- **Objective:** To identify medial sounds in spoken words.

  "I am going to say some words. See if you can tell me the medial, or middle, sound in these words."

- It helps to exaggerate the sound you want the student to identify. Point to your mouth as you say the following words: mad, cat, fan. Slowly repeat the words until the student can answer. Then ask:

  "What sound do you hear in the medial position of these words?" */ă/*

- Point to your mouth and say the following words: mop, hot, top.

"What sound do you hear in the medial position of these words?" */ŏ/*

- Point to your mouth and say the following words: rip, lid, fin.

"What sound do you hear in the medial position of these words?" */ĭ/*

- Point to your mouth and say the following words: made, cake, late.

"What sound do you hear in the medial position of these words?" */ā/*

- Continue with additional words as time permits.

Review of Decks

- The student should be seated where he/she can write comfortably.
- Show the student **Letter Cards 1–9** in random order. The student should name the letter on each letter card.
- Show the student **Picture Cards 1–13** in random order. The student should name the keyword and sound for each picture card.
- Give the student **Spelling Sound Sheet 11.**
- Call out the sounds on **Spelling Cards 1–12** in random order. The student should echo each sound and name the letter or letters that make the sound as he/she writes the letter(s) on the spelling sound sheet.
- Check the student's response after each card.

New Learning

- Have gingersnaps handy. They will be referred to as "snaps" for today's lesson.

"You look really hungry today. I think I should give you something to eat before we begin. I have some gingersnaps."

"Would you like a snap, or snaps?"

- If the student says "snap," give him/her one. If the student says "snaps," give him/her a handful.

"Did you get as many as you wanted?"

- The student should have discovered that saying "snap" resulted in one cookie or that saying "snaps" resulted in a handful of cookies.
- Write the words "snap" and "snaps" on the chalkboard.

"What is the difference between 'snap' and 'snaps'?" */s/ at the end*

"What do you think the /s/ means?" *more than one*

"That's right. When s is added to the end of a word, it makes the word plural. This means 'more than one.' "

- Cover the suffix *-s* with your hand or a piece of paper.

"If we take away the suffix -s, we still have a whole word. It's called the root word."

"What is the root word of 'snaps'?" *snap*

"When we code, we code everything around the root word first. What will we code first in the word 'snaps'?" *suffix -s*

"That's right. When we find an s on the end of a word, and it means more than one, we'll box it because it is a suffix."

- Box the *s* in "snaps": snap[s].

"Our new word, 'snaps,' is called a derivative. It's a root word with a suffix."

"A suffix is something that is added to the end of a word that changes the meaning of the word."

- Write the following words on the chalkboard and code them as indicated:

pǐn[s] pŏt[s]

- Point to the first word.

"What is this word?" *pins*

"Is the s voiced or unvoiced?" *voiced*

"How do we code a voiced s?" *put a line through it*

- Point to the second word.

"What is this word?" *pots*

"Is the s voiced or unvoiced?" *unvoiced*

"Do we code unvoiced s's?" *no*

"Can you figure out when the s is voiced and when it is unvoiced?"

"When s follows a voiced letter, it is voiced, as in 'pins.' When it follows an unvoiced letter, it is unvoiced, as in 'pots.' "

- Offer more "snaps" to the student if he/she said "snap" the first time.

New Deck Cards

- Show the student **Affix Card 1.**

"We have a brand new card today. It is a suffix -s card."

"I am going to put it in our Review Decks so you will remember suffix -s."

"When you see this card, I want you to say 'suffix -s.' "

- **Note:** Add the new affix card to the Review Decks.

Boardwork

"Let's practice coding some words like the ones you'll have on your worksheet."

- Write the word "pots" on the chalkboard.

"Do you see a suffix in this word?" *yes, an s*

"How will we code the suffix?" *box it*

"Do you see a vowel in this word?" *yes, an o*

"Do you see anything after the o?" *yes, a t*

"How will we code the o?" *short; breve*

- Point to **Rule Chart 1.**

"How do we know it is short?" *it is followed by a consonant*

- Code the word as the student instructs: pŏt[s].

"What is this word?" *pots*

"Can you give me a sentence with the word 'pots' in it?" *expect various answers*

WORKSHEET

- The student should be seated where he/she can write comfortably.
- Write "Worksheet 12" on the chalkboard. Then hold up the worksheet and point to "Worksheet 12" at the top of the page.

"When I give you the worksheet, find the side that has 'worksheet' written on it."

- Give the student **Worksheet 12.** Make sure the student turns to the correct side.

"Using the rules we just practiced, code the words by #1, #2, and #3."

"After you have coded these words, blend the sounds in each word and figure out what the words are."

"When you are finished, draw a line from one of the words to the picture it matches."

- Assist the student as necessary.

"Let's try spelling a few words. Put your finger by #4. The first word we are going to spell is 'taps.' What is the first sound in the word 'taps'?" */t/*

"Write the letter that says /t/ on the first line by #4."

"What is the next sound in the word 'taps'?" */ă/*

"Write the letter that says /ă/ on the second line by #4."

"What is the next sound in the word 'taps'?" */p/*

"Write the letter that says /p/ on the third line by #4."

"What is the last sound in the word 'taps'?" */s/*

"Write the letter that says /s/ on the fourth line by #4."

"What is the word that you wrote?" *taps*

- Repeat the procedure with #5 (sat) and #6 (nips).

"Find the #7 on your page and put your finger there."

"Draw me a picture of this word: circles."

- See if the student draws more than one circle (showing comprehension of suffix -*s*).
- Help the student correct any incorrect answers. Then initial the worksheet in the space provided.
- Some time during the day, ask the student to read from the worksheet or homework.
- **Note:** Always make sure the worksheet is corrected before the student begins the homework. The worksheet serves as a guide to help complete the homework.

HOMEWORK

"Turn your paper over to the homework side."

"Do you know what to do on the homework paper?"

- Discuss the homework pictures to make sure the student understands the word each one represents: #4 (pots) and #5 (pits).

"When you finish your paper, I will check it for you and initial it in the space provided."

- Either now or later in the day, the student should complete the homework independently (if possible). Help the student correct any incorrect answers. Then initial the homework in the space provided.

READER

- Write the words "The End" on the chalkboard.

"Have you ever seen these words at the end of a book or at the end of a television show or movie?" *expect various answers*

- If the student cannot tell you the words "The End," say the words for him/her.
- Hold up **Reader 1.**

"Today, you will be making your own book."

"You will see these two words at the end of the book. They will tell you that the story is over."

"Sometimes we will use words before we have talked about all of their sounds. These words will be called 'temporary sight words.' "

"We will have to remember them by sight because we cannot sound them out yet. They are temporary, meaning 'just for a little while.' "

- Give the student **Reader 1 (*Zip*)** and some colored pencils.
- Assist the student as necessary as he/she completes the following steps:

"Hold up your page so that the tree is facing you."

"Now put your finger on the top dotted line."

"Carefully fold the paper along this dotted line toward you so that it lines up with the bottom dotted line."

"Now fold the top half of the sheet back along the dotted line."

"Hold your book so the tree is facing you again. Then put your finger on the dotted line down the center of the page."

"Fold the book backward along this dotted line so that the tree will still be facing you when you're finished."

- When the student completes this last step, either put a rubber band around the book's spine or staple the spine.

"Next, carefully separate the pages along the perforated lines at the top and bottom."

- Demonstrate how to separate the pages.

"Let's check the page numbers to see if they are in the correct order."

- Demonstrate how to check that the book's page numbers are in order.

"Look, we made a book!"

- Point to the book's title.

"Can you tell me what this book is called?" *Zip*

"Open to page 1 and put your fingers on the words. This is a sentence. A sentence is a group of words that makes a complete thought. A sentence always begins with a capital letter and ends with a period, question mark, or exclamation point."

- Put an exclamation point on the chalkboard.

"This is an exclamation point. It means that you should read the sentence with great emphasis."

- Illustrate with phrases such as "Oh no!", "Look out!", and "Hooray!" If desired, allow the student to offer his/her own exclamatory sentences.

"You'll see some exclamation points in the reader today."

"Read your book to yourself. When you are finished reading, color the pictures. Write your name on the book so I will know who colored it."

"When you are finished, I will ask you to read your book to me."

- Give the student the **Reader Collection Box** and help him or her assemble it following the instructions on the box.

"This box will hold your readers. We're going to have a lot more of them, and by the end of the year, your box will be full."

- Some time during the day, have the student read the reader to you.
- If possible, take time to play the Kid Card games listed in Lesson 10.

Lesson 12

Name ____________________

Teacher's Initials _____

Worksheet 12
(for use with Lesson 12)
Phonics 1

-S

1. tips
2. sills
3. pans

4. t a p s
5. s a t
6. n i p s

7.

P1-WS-012a

Parent's Initials _____

Homework 12
(for use with Lesson 12)
Phonics 1

-S

1. pops
2. pins
3. tops

4.  p o t s

5.  p i t s

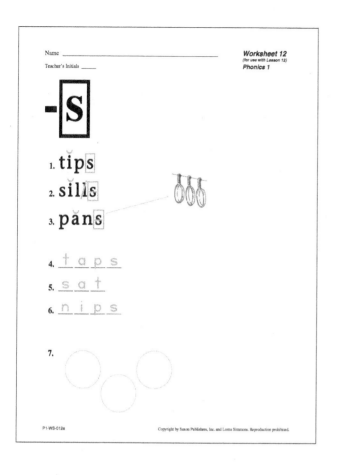

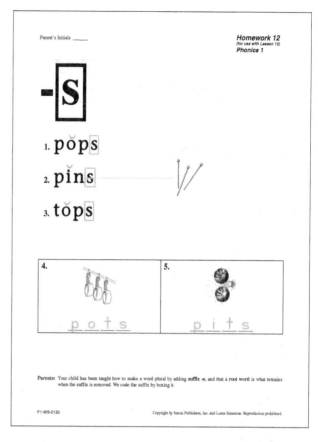

Parents: Your child has been taught how to make a word plural by adding **suffix -s**; and that a **root word** is what remains when the suffix is removed. We code the suffix by boxing it.

P1-WS-012b

LESSON 13 — The Letter *D*

lesson preparation

materials

ball

Review Decks

Spelling Sound Sheet 12

tokens or colored pencil

Letter Card 10

doughnut in a sack (see *the night before*)

Picture Card 14

Spelling Card 13

Worksheet 13

the night before

- Put a doughnut in a thin plastic bag, then in a sack, for the student to use to "discover" the new keyword. If the student has dietary restrictions, use the riddle format to describe the new keyword.
- Add the *d* letter tile to the student's container.

ALPHABET ACTIVITY

- You and the student should be seated on the floor with the ball.

  "Let's say the alphabet while we roll this ball."

  "I'll begin with 'A' and roll the ball to you. After you catch the ball, say 'B' and roll the ball back to me. We'll continue until we complete the alphabet."
- Recite the alphabet as you and the student roll the ball.
- Have the student return to his/her seat.

PHONEMIC AWARENESS

- **Objective:** To identify medial sounds in spoken words.

  "I am going to say some words. See if you can tell me the medial, or middle, sound in these words."

- It helps to exaggerate the sound you want the student to identify. Point to your mouth as you say the following words: weave, lean, beet, meal. Slowly repeat the words until the student can answer. Then ask:

  "What sound do you hear in the medial position of these words?" /ē/

- Point to your mouth and say the following words: bet, leg, neck, wed.

  "What sound do you hear in the medial position of these words?" /ĕ/

- Point to your mouth and say the following words: rope, boat, moan, poke.

  "What sound do you hear in the medial position of these words?" /ō/

- Point to your mouth and say the following words: pipe, line, fight, ride.

  "What sound do you hear in the medial position of these words?" /ī/

- Continue with additional words as time permits.

REVIEW OF DECKS

- The student should be seated where he/she can write comfortably.
- Show the student **Letter Cards 1–9** in random order. The student should name the letter on each letter card.
- Show the student **Affix Card 1.**

  "What is this called?" *suffix -s*

- Show the student **Picture Cards 1–13** in random order. The student should name the keyword and sound for each picture card.
- Give the student **Spelling Sound Sheet 12** and at least twelve tokens (or a colored pencil).

  "Today we are going to play Bingo!"

  "I am going to call out a spelling sound. Cover (or draw a big X on) the letter that spells that sound on your spelling sound sheet."

  "When you cover (or X out) all of the letters on one line, either up and down, across, or from corner to corner, call out Bingo!"

- Demonstrate, if necessary.

  "Let's begin: /t/."

- Continue, calling out the following sounds: /n/, /ĭ/, /ŏ/, /p/, /l/, /ă/, /s/, /ī/, /z/, /ō/, /ā/, /f/.
- The student should Bingo by the time all the sounds have been called out.
- Collect the tokens (or colored pencil) and the spelling sound sheet. If you used tokens and the spelling sound sheet is unmarked, keep it available for practice.

NEW LEARNING

"I am going to say some words to you and I want you to echo them back to me. Listen for the sound that is the same in the initial position of each word."

- Point to your mouth as you say each word.

"Echo after me. Do." *do* ***"Door."*** *door* ***"Deep."*** *deep*

- Slowly repeat the words until the student can answer the following question:

"What sound do you hear in the initial position?" */d/*

- **Note:** Make sure the student is giving the pure sound of *d* and not pronouncing it with a short *u* sound, as in /dŭh/.

"That's right. The sound you hear in the initial position is /d/."

"Put your fingertips on the front of your neck and say /d/. See if you feel any vibration."

"Is this sound voiced or unvoiced?" *voiced*

"Since /d/ vibrates, it is a voiced sound."

- Write the following words on the chalkboard: dip, dad, dot.

"What letter do you see that might be making the /d/ sound?" *d*

- If the student does not know the name of the letter, say it for him/her.

"D is the first letter in all of these words, so we can see that d must be the letter used to spell the /d/ sound."

"Look at your alphabet strip. Can you tell me if d is a vowel or a consonant?" *consonant*

NEW DECK CARDS

- Show the student **Letter Card 10.**

"What letter is this?" *d*

"I have another sack today. It contains a clue to our new keyword. Don't look in the sack, but put your hand inside and see if you can guess the new keyword."

- Allow the student a chance to feel inside the sack.

"I'm going to count to three. On three, whisper what you think is in the sack."

"One, two, three." *doughnut*

"That's right. The keyword is 'doughnut' and the sound we have learned is /d/."

- Show the student **Picture Card 14,** and then point to the picture of a doughnut on the alphabet strip.

"The word 'doughnut' helps us remember the /d/ sound because it begins with the /d/ sound."

- **Note:** If you have provided a doughnut for the student to eat, tell the student to put the sack away until later.
- Give the student the container of letter tiles.

  "Today I've given you another letter tile."

  "Find your d letter tile and look at it. One side has a capital D and the other side has a lowercase d."

- Allow time for the student to examine the new letter tile.

  "Hold your letter tile up in the air. Turn it so I can see the capital D."

  "Now turn it so I can see the lowercase d."

  "Spell the word 'tad' with your letter tiles."

- Continue with the following words: nod, slid. Choose additional words from the Spelling Word List, if desired.
- Have the student replace the tiles in the container and put it away.
- Reinforce the name, sound, and shape of the letter *d* throughout the day.
- Hold up **Spelling Card 13** so that only you can see what is written. Follow the instructions on the card and have the student write the letter with his/her finger on the desktop, or skywrite the letter in the air.
- **Note:** Add the new letter, picture, and spelling cards to the Review Decks.

BOARDWORK

"Let's practice coding some words like the ones you'll have on your worksheet."

- Write the word "pill" on the chalkboard.

  "Do you see a vowel in this word?" *yes, an i*

  "Do you see anything after the i?" *yes, ll*

  "Is there something special I need to do to one of these l's?" *mark one out because we only read one of them*

  "How will we code the i?" *short; breve*

- Point to **Rule Chart 1.**

  "How do we know it is short?" *it is followed by a consonant*

- Code the word as the student instructs: pĭl~~l~~.

  "What is this word?" *pill*

  "Can you give me a sentence with the word 'pill' in it?" *expect various answers*

WORKSHEET

- The student should be seated where he/she can write comfortably.
- Write "Worksheet 13" on the chalkboard. Then hold up the worksheet and point to "Worksheet 13" at the top of the page.

  "When I give you the worksheet, find the side that has 'worksheet' written on it."

- Give the student **Worksheet 13.** Make sure the student turns to the correct side.

  "Using the rules we just practiced, code the words by #1, #2, #3, and #4."

  "After you have coded these words, blend the sounds in each word and figure out what the words are."

  "When you are finished, draw a line from one of the words to the picture it matches."

- Assist the student as necessary.

  "Let's try spelling a few words. Put your finger by #5. The first word we are going to spell is 'dip.' What is the first sound in the word 'dip'?" */d/*

  "Write the letter that says /d/ on the first line by #5."

  "What is the next sound in the word 'dip'?" */ĭ/*

  "Write the letter that says /ĭ/ on the second line by #5."

  "What is the final sound in the word 'dip'?" */p/*

  "Write the letter that says /p/ on the third line by #5."

  "What is the word you wrote?" *dip*

- Repeat the procedure with #6 (lap) and #7 (tip).

  "Look at the picture by #8 and tell me what it is." *lid*

  "What is the picture by #9?" *pod*

  "Think about the sounds in the words 'lid' and 'pod.' Try to spell the words on the lines under the pictures."

- Allow time for the student to do this.
- As the student works, provide help as needed. If necessary, help the student by giving him/her the letter sounds individually. Help the student correct any incorrect answers. Then initial the worksheet in the space provided.
- Some time during the day, ask the student to read from the worksheet or homework.
- **Note:** Always make sure the worksheet is corrected before the student begins the homework. The worksheet serves as a guide to help complete the homework.

HOMEWORK

"Turn your paper over to the homework side."

"Put your finger on the top row of handwriting lines. Write your best capital D on these lines so I will know what a capital D should look like."

- Have the student write a lowercase letter *d* on the second handwriting line.
- Make sure that the student has written the letters correctly (to the best of his or her ability). He/She will use them as guides when completing the homework.

"Do you know what to do on the rest of the homework paper?"

- Discuss the homework pictures to make sure the student understands the word each one represents: #7 (pin), #8 (pan), and #9 (sap).

"When you finish your paper, I will check it for you and initial it in the space provided."

- Either now or later in the day, the student should complete the homework independently (if possible). Help the student correct any incorrect answers. Then initial the homework in the space provided.
- **Optional:** If you provided a doughnut for the student, allow the student to eat it now (or when time permits).
- If possible, take time to play the Kid Card games listed in Lesson 10.

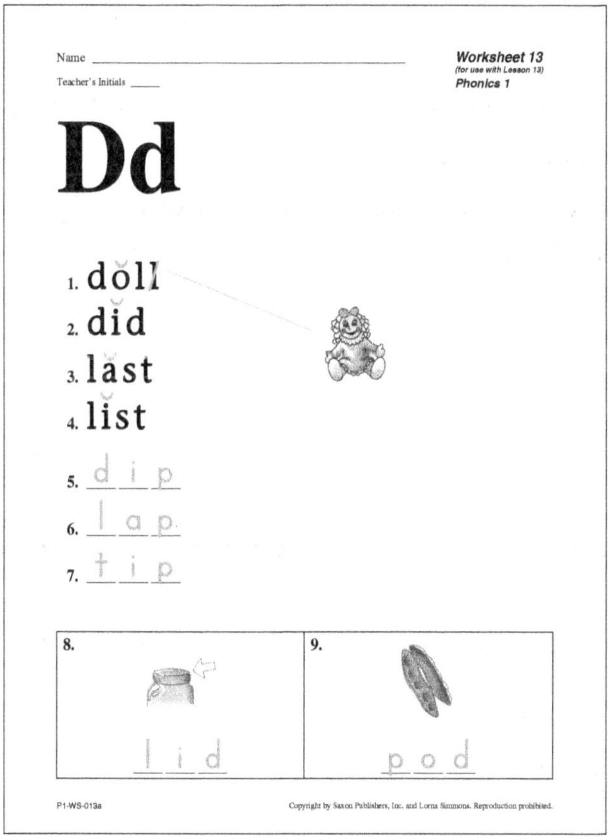

Name ______

Teacher's Initials ____

Worksheet 13
(for use with Lesson 13)
Phonics 1

Dd

1. dŏll
2. dĭd
3. lăst
4. lĭst
5. d i p
6. l a p
7. t i p

8. l i d

9. p o d

P1-WS-013a

Copyright by Saxon Publishers, Inc. and Lorna Simmons. Reproduction prohibited.

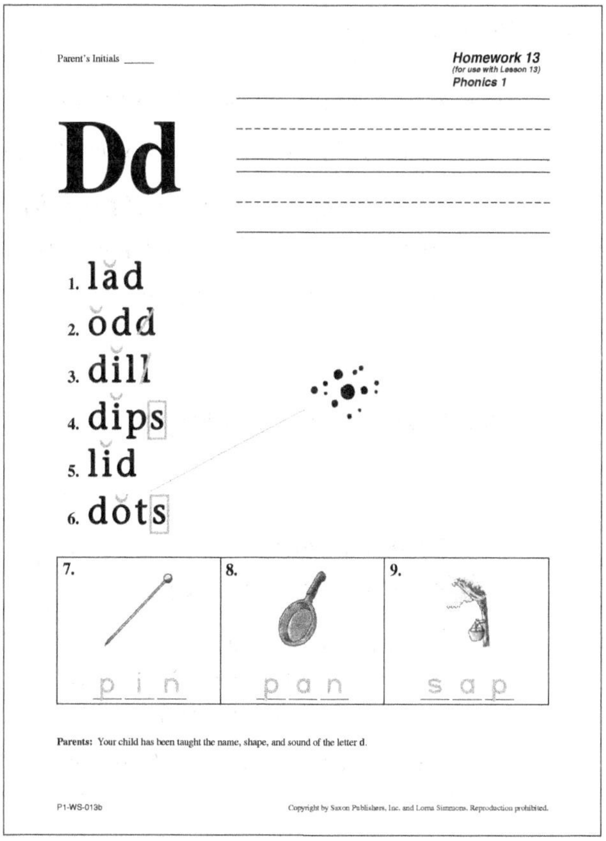

Parent's Initials ____

Homework 13
(for use with Lesson 13)
Phonics 1

Dd

1. lăd
2. ŏdd
3. dĭll
4. dĭps
5. lĭd
6. dŏts

7. p i n

8. p a n

9. s a p

Parents: Your child has been taught the name, shape, and sound of the letter d.

P1-WS-013b

Copyright by Saxon Publishers, Inc. and Lorna Simmons. Reproduction prohibited.

LESSON 14 — The Letter *F*

lesson preparation

materials

Review Decks
Spelling Sound Sheet 13
container of letter tiles
Letter Card 11
Picture Card 15
Spelling Card 14
Worksheet 14
Reader 2 (*Nat and Don*)
colored pencils

the night before

- Add the *f* letter tile to the container.

ALPHABET ACTIVITY

- The student should be standing in an area where he/she can move around freely.

  "Let's do jumping jacks with the alphabet today."

  "We'll say the alphabet together. Every time we jump up and put our hands over our head, we'll say a letter. Ready? A, B, C, …."

- Have the student return to his/her seat.

PHONEMIC AWARENESS

- **Objective:** To identify blended sounds in spoken words.

  "I am going to say some words. See if you can tell me the blend in the initial position in these words."

- It helps to exaggerate the sound you want the student to identify. Point to your mouth as you say the following words: play, plop, plant, plug. Slowly repeat the words until the student can answer. Then ask:

  "What blend do you hear in the initial position of these words?" */pl/*

- Be sure to have the student tell you the sound of the blend, not the letter names.
- Point to your mouth and say the following words: snail, snip, sneak, snoop.

  "What blend do you hear in the initial position of these words?" */sn/*
- Repeat with the following blends: /sp/ (spot, speak, spun, spoke); /sl/ (sleep, slung, slow, slide); and /st/ (stop, steep, step, stone).

  "The next one is a three-letter blend. It's really hard. See if you can tell me the blend."
- Point to your mouth and say the following words: splash, split, splurge, spleen.

  "What blend do you hear in the initial position of these words?" */spl/*
- Continue with additional words as time permits.

Review of Decks

- The student should be seated where he/she can write comfortably.
- Show the student **Letter Cards 1–10** in random order. The student should name the letter on each letter card.
- Show the student **Affix Card 1.**

  "What is this called?" *suffix -s*
- Show the student **Picture Cards 1–14** in random order. The student should name the keyword and sound for each picture card.
- Give the student **Spelling Sound Sheet 13.**
- Call out the sounds on **Spelling Cards 1–13** in random order. The student should echo each sound and name the letter or letters that make the sound as he/she writes the letter(s) on the spelling sound sheet.
- Have the student set the spelling sound sheet aside for use later in the lesson.

New Learning

"I am going to say some words to you and I want you to echo them back to me. Listen for the sound that is the same in the initial position of each word."

- Point to your mouth as you say each word.

  "Echo after me. Fig." *fig* ***"Fast."*** *fast* ***"Fall."*** *fall*

  "What sound do you hear in the initial position?" */f/*
- **Note:** Make sure the student is giving the pure sound of *f* and not pronouncing it with a short *u* sound, as in /fŭh/.

  "That's right. The sound you hear in the initial position of these words is /f/."

  "Put your fingertips on the front of your neck and say /f/. See if you feel any vibration."

  "Is this sound voiced or unvoiced?" *unvoiced*

"Since /f/ does not vibrate, it is an unvoiced sound."

- Write the following words on the chalkboard: fan, fog, fill.

"What letter do you see that might be making the /f/ sound?" *f*

- If the student does not know the name of the letter, say it for him/her.

"F is the first letter in all of these words, so we can see that f must be the letter used to spell the /f/ sound."

"Look at your alphabet strip. Can you tell me if f is a vowel or a consonant?" *consonant*

HANDWRITING/LETTER TILES

- The student should be seated where he/she can write comfortably.
- Write a capital *F* on the chalkboard.

"This is a capital F. Let's practice skywriting capital F's before we write them on our paper."

- Have the student practice skywriting capital *F*'s. The student should keep his/her elbows and wrists locked and make each letter about two feet tall.

"Find your spelling sound sheet. Leave your pencil on your desk until I tell you to pick it up."

- Draw handwriting lines on the chalkboard. Write a capital *F* on the handwriting lines in the handwriting you want the student to learn.

"Now pick up your pencil. Find the first handwriting line and practice writing capital F's like I wrote this one on the chalkboard. Say the name of the letter each time you write it."

- Allow a few minutes for the student to practice writing capital *F*'s.

"Put your pencil back on your desk."

- Now write a lowercase *f* on the handwriting lines in the handwriting you want the student to learn.

"This is a lowercase f."

- Have the student practice skywriting lowercase *f*'s.

"Now pick up your pencil and practice writing lowercase f's on the second handwriting line. Say the name of the letter each time you write it."

- Have the student set the spelling sound sheet aside for use later in the lesson.
- Leave the handwriting lines and letters on the chalkboard for the remainder of the lesson.
- Give the student the container of letter tiles.

"Today I've given you another letter tile."

"Find your f letter tile and look at it. One side has a capital F and the other side has a lowercase f."

- Allow time for the student to examine the new letter tile.

"Hold your letter tile up in the air. Turn it so I can see the capital F."

"Now turn it so I can see the lowercase f."

"Spell the word 'fan' with your letter tiles."

- Continue with the following words: if, soft. Choose additional words from the Spelling Word List, if desired.
- Have the student replace the tiles in the container and put it away.
- Reinforce the name, sound, and shape of the letter *f* throughout the day.

NEW DECK CARDS

- Show the student **Letter Card 11.**

"What letter is this?" *f*

- Hold up **Picture Card 15** but keep the picture covered with your hand (or the letter card).

"I have a card with a picture on it that begins with the /f/ sound."

"I am going to describe it for you. See if you can guess what the picture is."

"Most people have two of these. They are important if we want to go somewhere. People put socks on them to keep them warm. What do you think the picture is?" *feet*

"That's right. The keyword is 'feet' and the sound we have learned is /f/."

- Show the student **Picture Card 15,** and then point to the picture of feet on the alphabet strip.

"The word 'feet' helps us remember the /f/ sound because it begins with /f/."

"Find your spelling sound sheet. Find #14 and put your finger on it."

- Hold up **Spelling Card 14** so only you can see what is written. Using the hand signals, follow the instructions on the card.
- Check the spelling sound sheet for accuracy.
- **Note:** Add the new letter, picture, and spelling cards to the Review Decks.

BOARDWORK

"Let's practice coding some words like the ones you'll have on your worksheet."

"Before we begin, let's review the two vowel rules."

"The first vowel rule says, 'A vowel followed by a consonant is short. Code it with a breve.' Repeat that with me."

- Point to **Rule Chart 1** as the student repeats the vowel rule with you.

  "The second vowel rule says, 'An open, accented vowel is long. Code it with a macron.' Repeat that with me."

- Point to **Rule Chart 2** as the student repeats the vowel rule with you.
- Write the word "pans" on the chalkboard.

  "What part of this word will we code first?" *suffix -s; put a box around it*

  "Do you see a vowel in this word?" *yes, an a*

  "Do you see anything after the a?" *yes, an n*

  "How should we code the a?" *with a breve*

  "Why?" *it is followed by a consonant*

- Code the word as the student instructs: păn[s].

  "What is this word?" *pans*

  "What does the suffix -s mean?" *plural; more than one*

- Cover the *s* with your hand or a piece of paper.

  "Take away the suffix -s. What is the root word?" *pan*

  "How many pans is that?" *one pan*

- Show the *s* again.

  "And with the suffix -s?" *more than one pan*

  "Can you give me a sentence with the word 'pans' in it?" *expect various answers*

- Write the word "fill" on the chalkboard.

  "How should I code this word?"

- Code the word as the student instructs: fĭl/.

  "What is the word?" *fill*

- Write "fl" on the chalkboard.

  "We have a new blend today: fl. Can you think of a word that begins with fl?"

- Lead the student to some of the following blends: flag, fly, flower, floss, flew, flake, flirt, float, flame, flea, flight, flutter, flume, flip-flop, flute.

WORKSHEET

- The student should be seated where he/she can write comfortably.
- Write "Worksheet 14" on the chalkboard. Then hold up the worksheet and point to "Worksheet 14" at the top of the page.

  "When I give you the worksheet, find the side that has 'worksheet' written on it."

- Give the student **Worksheet 14.** Make sure the student turns to the correct side.

  "Using the rules we just practiced, code the words by #1, #2, #3, and #4."

"After you have coded these words, blend the sounds in each word and figure out what the words are. When you are finished, draw a line from one of the words to the picture it matches."

- Assist the student as necessary.

"It's spelling time! Put your finger by #5. The first word we are going to spell is 'snap.' Let's unblend that word together by saying the sounds we hear. The sounds we hear are /s/, /n/, /ă/, /p/."

- Hold up a finger for each sound to help the student remember how many sounds are in the word.

"What letters spell those sounds?"

- Point to one of your fingers each time the student spells a sound.

"S … n … a … p."

- Have the student repeat the spelling as he/she writes the letters in the four spaces by #5.

"What is the word you wrote?" *snap*

- Repeat the procedure with #6 (snip) and #7 (last).

"Look at the picture by #8 and tell me what it is." *list*

"Spell that word on the lines beside the picture."

- Allow time for the student to do this.

"Now put your finger on #9. This is a sentence. Remember, a sentence is a group of words that makes a complete thought. A sentence always begins with a capital letter and ends with a period, question mark, or exclamation point."

"Read the sentence to yourself. If you come to a word you don't know, code the word to help you figure it out."

"Do you see one of our temporary sight words in this sentence?" *yes, "the"*

"Let's circle it to help us remember that since we can't code it yet, we have to remember it by sight."

"You will get a chance to read for me when I check your paper."

- As the student works, provide help as needed. Listen to the student read and help correct any incorrect answers. Then initial the worksheet in the space provided.
- It is very important that the student has many chances to read to you and that you give your complete attention as he/she does so. Daily reading allows the student to become more secure in applying what he/she has learned.
- **Note:** Always make sure the worksheet is corrected before the student begins the homework. The worksheet serves as a guide to help complete the homework.

HOMEWORK

"Turn your paper over to the homework side."

"Put your finger on the top row of handwriting lines. Write your best capital F on these lines so I will know what a capital F should look like."

- Have the student write a lowercase letter *f* on the second handwriting line.
- Make sure that the student has written the letters correctly (to the best of his or her ability). He/She will use them as guides when completing the homework.

"Do you know what to do on the rest of the homework paper?"

- Discuss the homework pictures to make sure the student understands the word each one represents: #7 (fan), #8 (fin), and #9 (snap).

"When you finish your paper, I will check it for you and initial it in the space provided."

- Either now or later in the day, the student should complete the homework independently (if possible). Help the student correct any incorrect answers. Then initial the homework in the space provided.

READER

- Give the student **Reader 2 (*Nat and Don*)** and some colored pencils.

"We're going to make another book today."

- Assist the student as necessary as he/she completes the following steps:

"Hold up your page so that the tree is facing you."

"Now put your finger on the top dotted line."

"Carefully fold the paper along this dotted line toward you so that it lines up with the bottom dotted line."

"Now fold the top half of the sheet back along the dotted line."

"Hold your book so the tree is facing you again. Then put your finger on the dotted line down the center of the page."

"Fold the book backward along this dotted line so that the tree will still be facing you when you're finished."

- When the student completes this last step, either put a rubber band around the book's spine or staple the spine.

"Next, carefully separate the pages along the perforated lines at the top and bottom."

- Demonstrate how to separate the pages.

"Let's check the page numbers to see if they are in the correct order."

- Demonstrate how to check that the book's page numbers are in order.

"Look, we made another book! What's the title?" *Nat and Don*

"I want you to read your book to yourself. When you are finished reading, color the pictures. Write your name on the book so I will know who colored it."

"Keep your book handy because I will be asking you to read it for me."

- Some time during the day, have the student read the reader to you.
- If possible, take time to play the Kid Card games listed in Lesson 10. Try to see that the student is prepared for tomorrow's assessment.

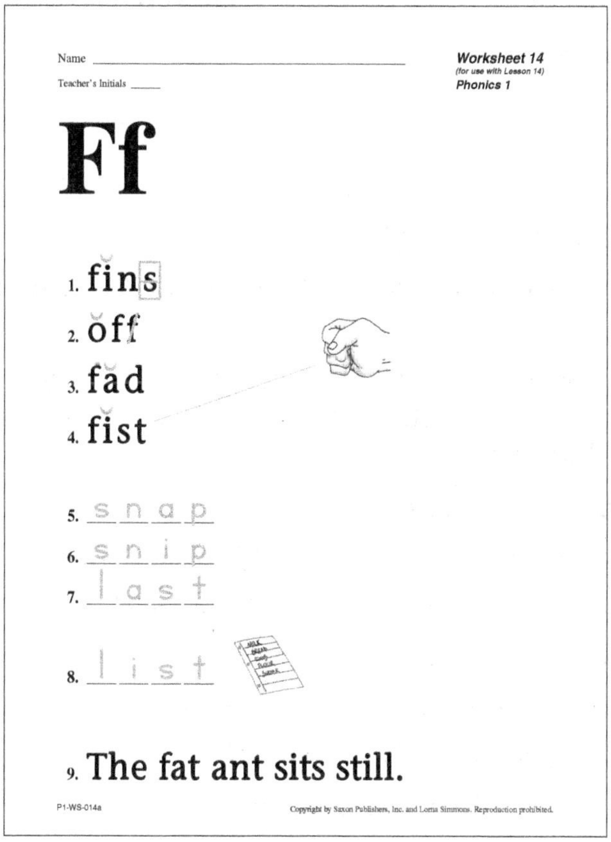

Name ____________

Teacher's Initials ____

Worksheet 14
(for use with Lesson 14)
Phonics 1

Ff

1. fins
2. off
3. fad
4. fist
5. snap
6. snip
7. last
8. list
9. The fat ant sits still.

P1-WS-014a

Parent's Initials ____

Homework 14
(for use with Lesson 14)
Phonics 1

Ff

1. fit
2. fizz
3. fans
4. fond
5. fast
6. The ant sits on sand.

7.	8.	9.
fan	fin	snap

Parents: Your child has been taught the name, shape, and sound of the letter f; and that a sentence is a group of words that makes a complete thought.

P1-WS-014b

LESSON 15 **Assessment**

lesson preparation

materials

Review Decks

Assessment 2

Assessment 2 Recording Form

Kid Cards

tokens

the night before

- Separate the Kid Cards marked "Lesson 15."

ALPHABET ACTIVITY

- The student should be seated with the alphabet strip.

  "Let's do something special when we say the alphabet today. Every time we say a consonant, we'll sit and whisper it. But we'll stand up and yell the vowels."

  "Look at your alphabet strip if you need to."

PHONEMIC AWARENESS

- **Objective:** To identify blended sounds in spoken words.

  "I'm going to say some words. See if you can tell me the blend in the initial position in these words."

- It helps to exaggerate the sound you want the student to identify. Point to your mouth as you say the following words: slow, slosh, slur, slip. Slowly repeat the words until the student can answer. Then ask:

  "What blend do you hear in the initial position of these words?" */sl/*

- Be sure to have the student tell you the sound of the blend, not the letter names.

- Point to your mouth and say the following words: snip, snow, snake, snug.

  "What blend do you hear in the initial position of these words?" */sn/*

- Point to your mouth and say the following words: pledge, plow, plump, plot.

  "What blend do you hear in the initial position of these words?" */pl/*

- Point to your mouth and say the following words: spell, spike, spark, spade.

"What blend do you hear in the initial position of these words?" /sp/

- Point to your mouth and say the following words: stir, stock, state, stem.

  "What blend do you hear in the initial position of these words?" /st/

- Continue with additional words as time permits.

Review of Decks

"As we review the letter deck today, I want you to say the name of the letter, and then tell me the keyword and sound of the letter."

- Show the student **Letter Cards 1–11** in random order.
- Make sure the student says the name of the letter, and then the keyword and sound. For example:

The correct response to Letter Card 9 (*s*) should be:

"*S*, sock, /s/; rose, /z/."

The correct response to Letter Card 7 (*a*) should be:

"*A*, apple, /ă/; acorn, /ā/."

Written Assessment

"Today we are going to see if you remember the letters and sounds we have been practicing."

- Give the student **Assessment 2.**
- **Section I:**

  "I'm going to say a sound. Write the letter that makes that sound on the line by #1."

- Give the following sounds in the order shown: /ă/, /ĭ/, /l/, /z/.
- The student should write the letter(s) that makes each sound on lines 1–4.
- **Section II:**

  "Look at the letter by #5."

  "Find the picture of the keyword for this sound."

  "Draw a line from the letter to the keyword."

- Repeat with #6, #7, and #8. Allow a few minutes for the student to work.
- The pictures (from top to bottom) are as follows: zipper, apple, lion, igloo.
- **Section III:**

  "Put your finger on #9."

  "Code the words by #9, #10, #11, and #12."

  "When you have finished coding, show your paper to me."

- This paper will be used during the oral portion of the assessment.

ORAL ASSESSMENT

- Oral assessments are short interviews that occur during independent work time. It is important to complete them promptly (today, if possible) in order to identify any areas of weakness and begin remediation.
- Use the assessment and the following dialogue to complete the oral portion.
- **Section IV:**

  "I'm going to say some words. Tell me the sound you hear in the initial position."
- Point to your mouth and say the following words: lid, lamp, lost, late.
- Write the student's response on the line by #13. (If the student responds with the letter name, ask again for the *sound.*)
- Repeat with #14 (at, add, attic, after); #15 (in, it, ill, if); and #16 (zap, zip, zoom, zig).
- **Section V:**
- Show the student the letter by #17.

  "What is this letter?"
- Write the student's response on the adjacent line.
- Repeat with #18, #19, and #20.
- **Section VI:**

  "Look at the word by #21. Read this word for me."
- Record the student's response on the adjacent line.
- Repeat with #22, #23, #24, and #25.

ASSESSMENT EVALUATION

- Grade the assessment and record the results on **Assessment 2 Recording Form.** Check off the boxes to indicate mastery (i.e., the section was completed with 100% accuracy).
- **Note:** If you choose to grade the assessments, try to give as many points as possible for work attempted. Do not grade the coding marks too severely, especially secondary marks like accents, voice lines, and k-backs. The most important coding marks to look for are breves, macrons, and syllable division lines.
- See the introductory material for detailed information regarding grading and recording procedures.
- Use the assessment results to identify those skills in which the student is weak. Practice those skills by playing Kid Card games.
- Add the Kid Cards marked "Lesson 15" to the existing decks. Listed below are games appropriate for remediation in selected areas. See "Games and Activities" for the directions for each game.
- **Section I:** Play "Spelling Deck Perfection" or "Sound Scamper," or have the student use the letter tiles to spell words you give from the Spelling Word List.

- **Section II:** Play "Keyword and Sound" or "Letter/Sound Identification."
- **Section III:** Play "Chalkboard Challenge."
- **Section IV:** Play "Sound Solutions" with any available pictures. (See Lesson 10.)
- **Section V:** Play "Letter Deck Data" or "Letter/Sound Identification."
- **Section VI:** Play "Word Blend" (with blue Kid Cards).
- When the student seems more secure in areas that had previously proven difficult, retest him/her (in those areas only) and indicate on the recording form any sections the student has subsequently mastered.
- Try to help the student achieve mastery of all the sections before the next assessment.
- If the student is having difficulty with a particular skill, keep his or her practice activities at the most basic level so the chance of success is greater.

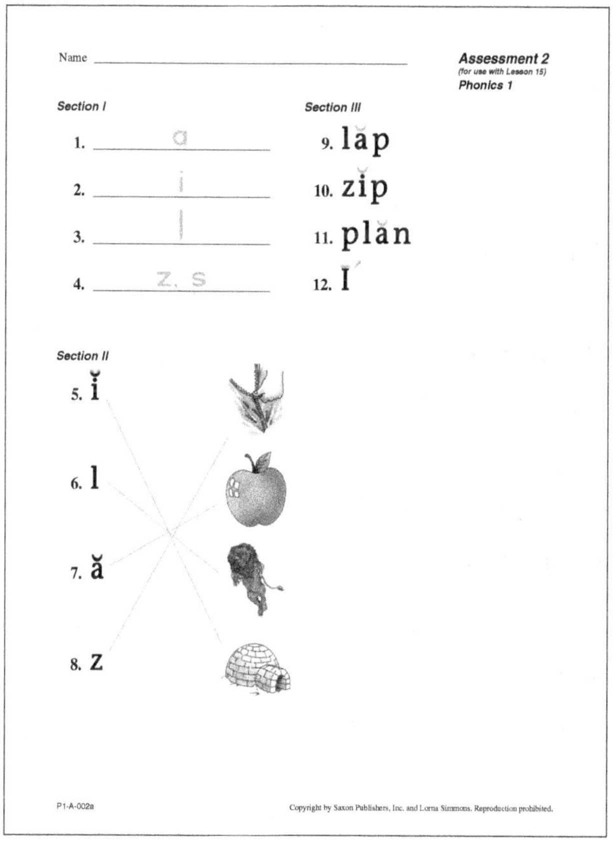
Name ______________________

Assessment 2
(for use with Lesson 15)
Phonics 1

Section I
1. a
2. i
3. l
4. z, s

Section III
9. lăp
10. zĭp
11. plăn
12. Ī́

Section II
5. ĭ
6. l
7. ă
8. z

P1-A-002a

Copyright by Saxon Publishers, Inc. and Lorna Simmons. Reproduction prohibited.

Assessment 2
(for use with Lesson 15)
Phonics 1

Section IV
13. /l/
14. /ă/
15. /ĭ/
16. /z/

Section V
17. z ________
18. i ________
19. a ________
20. l ________

Section VI
21. zăp ________
22. lĭp ________
23. Ī́ ________
24. pŏp ________
25. năp ________

P1-A-002b

Copyright by Saxon Publishers, Inc. and Lorna Simmons. Reproduction prohibited.

LESSON 16 — The Letter *H*

lesson preparation

materials

Review Decks

Letter Card 12

wig in a sack (see *the night before*)

Picture Card 16

container of letter tiles

Spelling Card 15

Sight Word Card 1

Irregular Spelling Booklet

Worksheet 16

Spelling List 1

new concepts

sight word

the night before

- Put a wig (or some doll's hair) in a sack for the student to use to "discover" the new keyword. If possible, do not allow the student to see you do this.
- Add the *h* letter tile to the student's container.

ALPHABET ACTIVITY

- The student should be seated with the alphabet strip.

  "How many letters are in the alphabet?" *26*

  "What two kinds of letters make up our alphabet?" *vowels and consonants*

  "A, e, i, o, and u are called ________?" *vowels*

  "All of the other letters are called ________?" *consonants*

  "Let's point to each letter and say the whole alphabet."

- Try to set a steady pace so the student cannot sing the alphabet.

  "The initial letter of the alphabet is _____?" *a*

  "The final letter of the alphabet is _____?" *z*

  "What are the medial letters of the alphabet?" *all letters b–y*

PHONEMIC AWARENESS

- **Objective:** To identify the number of sounds in spoken words.

  "We are going to start listening to sounds in words to decide how many sounds we hear. Let's try the word 'it.' We'll unblend it first. Hold up a finger for each sound."

- Hold up a finger as you say each sound.

  "/ĭ/, /t/. How many sounds do you hear?" *two*

- Remember to have the student listen for the *sounds* in the words, not the letters.

  "Let's try the word 'pan.' First we'll unblend it."

  "/P/, /ă/, /n/. How many sounds do you hear?" *three*

- Continue with the following words: sand, list, in, tip, rag.

REVIEW OF DECKS

- Show the student **Letter Cards 1–11** in random order. The student should name the letter on each letter card.
- Show the student **Affix Card 1.**

  "What do we call this?" *suffix -s*

- Show the student **Picture Cards 1–15** in random order. The student should name the keyword and sound for each picture card.
- **Note:** The usual spelling sounds activity will not take place today. An alternate activity occurs later in the lesson.

NEW LEARNING

"I am going to say some words to you and I want you to echo them back to me. Listen for the sound that is the same in the initial position of each word."

- Point to your mouth as you say each word.

  "Echo after me. Heavy." *heavy* ***"Hiccup."*** *hiccup* ***"Handsome."*** *handsome*

- Slowly repeat the words until the student can answer the following question:

  "What sound do you hear in the initial position?" */h/*

- **Note:** Make sure the student is giving the pure sound of *h* and not pronouncing it with a short *u* sound, as in /hŭh/.

  "That's right. The sound you hear in the initial position is /h/."

  "Put your fingertips on the front of your neck and say /h/. See if you feel any vibration."

  "Is this sound voiced or unvoiced?" *unvoiced*

"Since /h/ doesn't vibrate, it is an unvoiced sound."

- Write the following words on the chalkboard: hat, hop, hen.

  "What letter do you see that might be making the /h/ sound?" *h*

- If the student does not know the name of the letter, say it for him/her.

  "H is the first letter in all of these words, so we can see that h must be the letter used to spell the /h/ sound."

  "Look at your alphabet strip. Can you tell me if h is a vowel or a consonant?" *consonant*

New Deck Cards

- Show the student **Letter Card 12.**

  "What letter is this?" *h*

  "I have another sack today. It contains a clue to our new keyword. Don't look in the sack, but put your hand inside and see if you can guess what is inside. Keep in mind that the object in the sack starts with the /h/ sound."

- Allow the student a chance to feel inside the sack.

  "I'm going to count to three. On three, point to what you think is in the sack."

  "One, two, three." *the student should point to his/her hair*

  "That's right. The keyword is 'hair' and the sound we have learned is /h/."

- Show the student **Picture Card 16,** and then point to the picture of hair on the alphabet strip.

  "The word 'hair' helps us remember the /h/ sound because it begins with /h/."

- Give the student the container of letter tiles.

  "Today I've given you another letter tile."

  "Find your h letter tile and look at it. One side has a capital H and the other side has a lowercase h."

- Allow time for the student to examine the new letter tile.

  "Hold your letter tile up in the air. Turn it so I can see the capital H."

  "Now turn it so I can see the lowercase h."

  "Spell the word 'had' with your letter tiles."

  "Now spell the word 'hi.' "

  "Add two tiles to make the word 'hint.' "

- Choose additional words from the Spelling Word List, if desired.

  "Put your h letter tile into the container and shake it up."

  "Now, pull out a letter tile."

"I want you to give the sound of your letter. Then I will echo that sound and tell you the letter that makes that sound."

- The student should pull out each letter tile, one at a time, and say its sound. You should echo the sound and name the letter. This activity will help you determine how well the student knows the sounds of the letters.
- Have the student replace the tiles in the container and put it away.
- Hold up **Spelling Card 15** so that only you can see what is written. Follow the instructions on the card. Have the student write the letter with his/her finger on the desktop, or skywrite the letter.
- Reinforce the name, sound, and shape of the letter *h* throughout the day.
- **Note:** Add the new letter, picture, and spelling cards to the Review Decks.

BOARDWORK

"Today we have a new sight word. This sight word isn't temporary."

- Write the word "oh" on the chalkboard.

"Do you know this sight word?" *expect various answers*

"The word is 'oh.' Can you use 'oh' in a sentence?" *expect various answers*

"This is a sight word because the o is followed by a consonant but it is not short, and the h is silent."

"This word will never follow the rules, so we are going to have a list of words that will always be sight words."

- Show the student **Sight Word Card 1.**

"We will add this card to our Review Deck so we can review it daily."

"I have a booklet for you that contains many sight words."

"You can look in this booklet to find out how to spell these words."

"We will be going through this booklet many times this year."

- Give the student the **Irregular Spelling Booklet.**

"Write your name on your booklet."

- Allow time for the student to do this.

"Turn to the first page. This page is called the 'Table of Contents.' Have you ever used a table of contents before?"

"A table of contents tells us the names of chapters or sections of a book. It also tells us on what page those chapters or sections begin."

"See if you can tell me where to find sight words."

- Allow time for the student to examine the table of contents.

"The sight words begin on page 35. Let's turn to page 35 and look at them."

- Allow time for the student to examine the list of sight words (pages 35–39).

- **Note:** The sight word charts in this booklet contain every sight word that will be introduced in first grade. They also contain other common words the student may encounter while reading, but may not be able to decode.

  "See if you can find the sight word 'oh.' "

- Provide assistance as necessary.

  "You may refer to your booklet whenever you need help spelling words. If we find other words that don't follow the rules, we will write them in this book so we will remember that they are exceptions to the rule."

  "Do you know what it means to be an exception to the rule?" *expect various answers*

  "An exception to the rule is something that does not follow the rule."

- Collect the Irregular Spelling Booklet.
- **Note:** The student should be allowed to refer to this booklet at any time, so it should be stored at the student's desk or another area where it is readily accessible.

  "Let's practice coding some words like the ones you'll have on your worksheet."

  "First, can you say the vowel rules with me?"

- Point to **Rule Chart 1** as the student repeats the vowel rule with you.

  "A vowel followed by a consonant is short; code it with a breve."

- Point to **Rule Chart 2** as the student repeats the second vowel rule with you.

  "An open, accented vowel is long; code it with a macron."

- Write the word "still" on the chalkboard.

  "Can you help me code this word?"

- Code the word as the student instructs: stĭll.

  "What is this word?" *still*

- Write the word "ponds" on the chalkboard.

  "Can you help me code this word?"

- Code the word as the student instructs: pŏnds.

  "What is this word?" *ponds*

  "Can you give me a sentence with one of these words in it?" *expect various answers*

- Write the word "pass" on the chalkboard.

  "Can you help me code this word?"

- Code the word as the student instructs: păss.
- **Note:** The student may want to box the second *s* in "pass." If so, point out that when a word ends in two *s*'s, the last *s* is not a suffix. Code the *s*'s as twin consonants. (Do not feel you need to explain that when a root word ends with *s*, the suffix is *-es*. This concept will be taught in a later lesson.)
- **Note:** Add **Sight Word Card 1** to the Review Decks.

WORKSHEET

- The student should be seated where he/she can write comfortably.
- Write "Worksheet 16" on the chalkboard. Then hold up the worksheet and point to "Worksheet 16" at the top of the page.

  "When I give you the worksheet, find the side that has 'worksheet' written on it."
- Give the student **Worksheet 16.** Make sure the student turns to the correct side.

  "Using the rules we just practiced, code the words by #1 through #6."

  "After you have coded these words, blend the sounds in each word and figure out what the words are."
- Assist the student as necessary.

  "Beside #7 and #8 are two sentences. Read the sentences to yourself. If you come to a word you don't know, code the word to help you figure it out. Be sure to circle the sight words to help you remember that we can't code them. Then draw a line from one of the sentences to the picture it matches."
- Allow time for the student to work.

  "It's time to spell some words. Put your finger by #9. The first word we are going to spell is 'sand.' "

  "Let's unblend that word together. The sounds we hear are /s/, /ă/, /n/, /d/."
- Hold up a finger for each sound.

  "Let's spell those sounds."
- Point to one of your fingers each time the student spells a sound.

  "S … a … n … d."

  "Now spell the word again and write the letters as you say them."
- Allow time for the student to work.

  "What word did you write?" *sand*
- Repeat the procedure with #10 (hip), #11 (past), and #12 (lift).

  "Look at the picture above #13 and tell me what it is." *list*

  "Think about the sounds in the word and spell them on the lines under the picture."
- As the student works, provide help as needed. Listen to the student read both the words and the sentences; then help correct any incorrect answers. Initial the worksheet in the space provided.
- It is very important that the student be given many chances to read to you and that you give your complete attention as he/she does so. Daily reading allows the student to become more secure in applying what has been learned.
- **Note:** Always make sure the worksheet is corrected before the student begins the homework. The worksheet serves as a guide to help complete the homework.

HOMEWORK

"Turn your paper over to the homework side."

"Put your finger on the top row of handwriting lines. Write your best capital H on the line so I will know what a capital H should look like."

- Have the student write a lowercase letter *h* on the second handwriting line.
- Make sure that the student has written the letters correctly (to the best of his or her ability). He/She will use them as guides when completing the homework.

"Do you know what to do on the rest of the homework paper?"

"Look at the sentence by #7. Do you see a sight word? Let's circle it now so you'll remember it later."

"After the sight word, there's a comma. Do you remember what a comma means?" *a slight pause*

- Discuss the homework pictures to make sure the student understands the word each one represents: #9 (hat), #10 (hit), and #11 (pins).
- Either now or later in the day, the student should complete the homework independently (if possible). Help the student correct any incorrect answers. Then initial the homework in the space provided.

SPELLING LIST

- Fold **Spelling List 1** in half lengthwise (with the printed side facing out).

"Leave your paper just like I give it to you."

- Give the student **Spelling List 1,** folded with the blank lines facing up.

"Today I'm going to let you try your spelling words without ever seeing them."

- Call out the following words (in the order shown). Sound them out, if necessary.

  #1 (on), #2 (no), #3 (not), #4 (pop), #5 (top), #6 (I), #7 (it), #8 (in),
  #9 (pin), #10 (tip)

"Now unfold your paper and check your words."

- Check the student's work to see if he/she needs extra help with spelling.

"I want you to practice these words. We'll have a spelling test in a few days."

- If possible, take time to play the Kid Card games listed in Lesson 15.

Name ____________________

Teacher's Initials _____

Worksheet 16
(for use with Lesson 16)
Phonics 1

Hh

1. his
2. hop
3. hits
4. hill
5. hip
6. hid

7. Dot sits on the hill. 
8. A pond is on the land.

9. sand
10. hip
11. past
12. lift
13. list

P1-WS-016a

Parent's Initials _____

Homework 16
(for use with Lesson 16)
Phonics 1

Hh

1. hiss
2. had
3. hint
4. hot
5. hit
6. has

7. Oh, the pot lid is hot!
8. Toss the hat on the doll.

9.	10.	11.
 hat	 hit	 pins

Parents: Your child has been taught the name, shape, and sound of the letter **h**; that a **sight word** is a word that doesn't follow spelling rules and so must be memorized; and that sight words are circled rather than coded.

P1-WS-016b

Lesson 16

LESSON 17 — The Letter *G*

lesson preparation

materials

Review Decks
Spelling Sound Sheet 14
container of letter tiles
Letter Card 13
goggles in a sack (see *the night before*)
Picture Card 17
Spelling Card 16
Worksheet 17
Reader 3 (*Ann and Sal in the Sand*)
colored pencils

new concepts

phrase
apostrophe *s*

the night before

- **Optional:** Select a piece of music appropriate for a marching activity.
- Put some swimming or industrial goggles in a sack for the student to use to "discover" the new keyword. If possible, do not allow the student to see you do this.
- Add the *g* letter tile to the student's container.

ALPHABET ACTIVITY

"Today we're going to have an alphabet march. Let's stand up. We will say our alphabet together as we march around the room. Each time we take a step, we will say a letter."

- Lead the student in a march. Marching music can be played, if desired.
- **Optional:** Have the student march as he/she sings the alphabet song.

PHONEMIC AWARENESS

- **Objective:** To identify the number of sounds in spoken words.

  "We are going to listen for the number of sounds in words. We'll unblend the word and hold up a finger for each sound. The first word is 'late.' "
- Hold up a finger as you say each sound.

"/L/, /ā/, /t/. How many sounds do you hear?" three

- Remember to have the student listen for the *sounds* in the words, not the letters.
- Repeat with the following words: same (3), host (4), side (3), cool (3), and peak (3).

REVIEW OF DECKS

- The student should be seated where he/she can write comfortably.
- Show the student **Letter Cards 1–12** in random order. The student should name the letter on each letter card.
- Review **Affix Card 1.**
- Show the student **Picture Cards 1–16** in random order. The student should name the keyword and sound for each picture card.
- Review **Sight Word Card 1.**
- Give the student **Spelling Sound Sheet 14.**
- Call out the sounds on **Spelling Cards 1–15** in random order. The student should echo each sound and name the letter or letters that make the sound as he/she writes the letter(s) on the spelling sound sheet.
- Check the student's response after each card.
- Have the student set the spelling sound sheet aside for use later in the lesson.

NEW LEARNING

"I am going to say some words to you and I want you to echo them back to me. Listen for the sound that is the same in the initial position of each word."

- Point to your mouth as you say each word.

"Echo after me. Guest." guest *"Game."* game *"Gasoline."* gasoline

- Slowly repeat the words until the student can answer the following question:

"What sound do you hear in the initial position?" /g/

- **Note:** Make sure the student is giving the pure sound of *g* and not pronouncing it with a short *u* sound, as in /gŭh/.

"That's right. The sound you hear in the initial position is /g/."

"Put your fingertips on the front of your neck and say /g/. See if you feel any vibration."

"Is this sound voiced or unvoiced?" voiced

"Since /g/ vibrates, it is a voiced sound."

- Write the following words on the chalkboard: got, gal, gulp.

"What letter do you see that might be making the /g/ sound?" g

- If the student does not know the name of the letter, say it for him/her.

"G is the first letter in all of these words, so we can see that g must be the letter used to spell the /g/ sound."

"Look at your alphabet strip. Can you tell me if g is a vowel or a consonant?" *consonant*

HANDWRITING/LETTER TILES

- The student should be seated where he/she can write comfortably.
- Write a capital *G* on the chalkboard.

"This is a capital G. Let's practice skywriting capital G's before we write them on our paper."

- Have the student practice skywriting capital *G*'s.

"Find your spelling sound sheet. Leave your pencil on your desk until I tell you to pick it up."

- Draw handwriting lines on the chalkboard. Write a capital *G* on the handwriting lines in the handwriting you want the student to learn.

"Now pick up your pencil. Find the first line on your paper and practice writing capital G's like I wrote this one on the chalkboard. Say the name of the letter each time you write it."

- Allow a few minutes for the student to practice writing capital *G*'s.

"Put your pencil back on your desk."

- Now write a lowercase *g* on the handwriting lines in the handwriting you want the student to learn.

"This is a lowercase g."

- Have the student practice skywriting lowercase *g*'s.

"Now pick up your pencil and practice writing lowercase g's on the second line of your paper. Say the name of the letter each time you write it."

- Have the student set the spelling sound sheet aside for use later in the lesson.
- Leave the handwriting lines and letters on the chalkboard for the remainder of the lesson.
- Give the student the container of letter tiles.

"Today I've given you another letter tile."

"Find your g letter tile and look at it. One side has a capital G and the other side has a lowercase g."

- Allow time for the student to examine the new letter tile.

"Hold your letter tile up in the air. Turn it so I can see the capital G."

"Now turn it so I can see the lowercase g."

"Using your letter tiles, spell the word 'fog.' "

- Continue with the following words: go, glad. Choose additional words from the Spelling Word List, if desired.
- Have the student replace the tiles in the container and put it away.
- Reinforce the name, sound, and shape of the letter *g* throughout the day.

NEW DECK CARDS

- Show the student **Letter Card 13.**

  "What letter is this?" *g*

  "I have another sack today. It contains a clue to our new keyword. Don't look in the sack, but put your hand inside and see if you can feel what is inside the sack. Keep in mind that the object in the sack starts with the /g/ sound."
- Allow the student a chance to feel inside the sack.

  "I'm going to count to three. On three, show me with your hands but without talking what you think is in the sack."

  "One, two, three." *the student will probably circle his/her eyes with his/her fingers*

  "Do you mean 'goggles'? That's right! The keyword is 'goggles' and the sound we have learned is /g/."
- Show the student **Picture Card 17,** and then point to the picture of goggles on the alphabet strip.

  "The word 'goggles' helps us remember the /g/ sound because it begins with /g/."

  "Find your spelling sound sheet. Find #16 and put your finger on it."
- Hold up **Spelling Card 16** so only you can see what is written. Using the hand signals, follow the instructions on the card.
- Check the spelling sound sheet for accuracy.
- **Note:** Add the new letter, picture, and spelling cards to the Review Decks.

BOARDWORK

"Let's practice coding some words like the ones you'll have on your worksheet. First, can you say the vowel rules with me?"

- Point to **Rule Chart 1** as the student repeats the vowel rule with you.

  "A vowel followed by a consonant is short; code it with a breve."
- Point to **Rule Chart 2** as the student repeats the second vowel rule with you.

  "An open, accented vowel is long; code it with a macron."
- Write the word "fog" on the chalkboard.

  "Can you code this word?"

- Code the word as the student instructs: fŏg.

  "What is this word?" *fog*

  "Can you describe fog for me?"
- Write the word "hills" on the chalkboard.

  "Can you code this word?"
- Code the word as the student instructs: hĭl/s.

  "What is this word?" *hills*

  "What is the root word?" *hill*
- Write the phrase "Pat's pig" on the chalkboard.

  "This is a phrase. It is a group of words, but it doesn't express a complete thought. How will we code this phrase?"
- Code the phrase as the student instructs: Păt's pĭg.
- Explain that "apostrophe s" is not a suffix, but instead shows ownership. In this phrase, it shows that the pig belongs to Pat.

  "What does this phrase say?" *Pat's pig*

  "So the pig belongs to __________?" *Pat*
- Point to the words and the phrase on the chalkboard.

  "Can you give me a sentence using any of these words or the whole phrase?" *expect various answers*
- Write the blend "gl" on the chalkboard.

  "We have a new blend today. Can you tell me a word that begins with this blend?"
- Lead the student to some of the following words: glass, gloves, glad, glitter, glider, glob, globe, gloom, glory, gloss, glow, glue.

WORKSHEET

- The student should be seated where he/she can write comfortably.
- Write "Worksheet 17" on the chalkboard. Then hold up the worksheet and point to "Worksheet 17" at the top of the page.

  "When I give you the worksheet, find the side that has 'worksheet' written on it."
- Give the student **Worksheet 17.** Make sure the student turns to the correct side.

  "Using the rules we just practiced, code the words by #1 through #6."

  "After you have coded these words, blend the sounds in each word and figure out what the words are."
- Assist the student as necessary.

  "Beside #7 and #8 are two sentences. Read the sentences to yourself. If you come to a word you don't know, code the word to help you figure it out. Be sure to

circle the sight words to help you remember that we can't code them. Then draw a line from one of the sentences to the picture it matches."

- Allow time for the student to work.

"Now let's spell some words. Put your finger by #9. The first word we are going to spell is 'hog.' "

"Let's unblend that word together. The sounds we hear are /h/, /ŏ/, /g/."

- Hold up a finger for each sound.

"Let's spell those sounds."

- Point to one of your fingers each time the student spells a sound.

"H ... o ... g. Now spell the word again and write the letters as you say them."

- Allow time for the student to work.

"What word did you write?" *hog*

- Repeat the procedure with #10 (tags), #11 (hot), and #12 (go).

"Look at the picture above #13 and tell me what it is." *gift*

"Think about the sounds in the word and spell them on the lines under the picture."

- As the student works, provide help as needed. Listen to the student read both the words and the sentences; then help correct any incorrect answers. Initial the worksheet in the space provided.
- **Note:** Always make sure the worksheet is corrected before the student begins the homework. The worksheet serves as a guide to help complete the homework.

HOMEWORK

"Turn your paper over to the homework side."

"Put your finger on the top row of handwriting lines. Write your best capital G on the line so I will know what a capital G should look like."

- Have the student write a lowercase letter *g* on the second handwriting line.
- Make sure that the student has written the letters correctly (to the best of his or her ability). He/She will use them as guides when completing the homework.

"Do you know what to do on the rest of the homework paper?"

- Discuss the homework pictures to make sure the student understands the word each one represents: #9 (pig), #10 (gas), and #11 (flag).

"When you finish your paper, I will check it for you and initial it in the space provided."

- Either now or later in the day, the student should complete the homework independently (if possible). Help the student correct any incorrect answers. Then initial the homework in the space provided.

READER

- Give the student **Reader 3 (*Ann and Sal in the Sand*)** and some colored pencils.

  "We're going to make another book today."

- Point to the book's title.

  "Can you tell me the name of this book?" *Ann and Sal in the Sand*

  "You'll notice that on page one of this book, there's a word with an 'apostrophe s' in it."

- Write the words "Sal's pal" on the chalkboard. Point to the apostrophe.

  "This apostrophe s shows ownership."

  "What does Sal have?" *a pal*

  "Yes, he has a pal. Look for this in your story today."

- Assist the student as necessary as he/she completes the following steps:

  "Hold up your page so that the tree is facing you."

  "Now put your finger on the top dotted line."

  "Carefully fold the paper along this dotted line toward you so that it lines up with the bottom dotted line."

  "Now fold the top half of the sheet back along the dotted line."

  "Hold your book so the tree is facing you again. Then put your finger on the dotted line down the center of the page."

  "Fold the book backward along this dotted line so that the tree will still be facing you when you're finished."

- When the student completes this last step, either put a rubber band around the book's spine or staple the spine.

  "Next, carefully separate the pages along the perforated lines at the top and bottom."

- Demonstrate how to separate the pages.

  "Let's check the page numbers to see if they are in the correct order."

- Demonstrate how to check that the book's page numbers are in order.

  "Tell me again the name of this book." *Ann and Sal in the Sand*

  "I want you to read the book to yourself. When you are finished reading, color the pictures. Write your name on the book so I will know who colored it."

  "Keep your book handy because I will be asking you to read it for me."

- Some time during the day, have the student read the reader to you.
- If possible, take time to play the Kid Card games listed in Lesson 10.

Worksheet 17

Name _____
Teacher's Initials _____
Worksheet 17
(for use with Lesson 17)
Phonics 1

Gg

1. tăg
2. hăg
3. gŏt
4. zĭg
5. gĭft
6. flăg

7. Dad's pig is in his lap.
8. Dot hid the gift.

9. h o g
10. t a g s
11. h o t
12. g o

13. g i f t

Homework 17

Parent's Initials _____
Homework 17
(for use with Lesson 17)
Phonics 1

Gg

1. go
2. săg
3. fĭg
4. pĭg
5. gĭll
6. snăg

7. The pig zigs and zags.
8. The figs fill the pan.

9.	10.	11.
p i g	g a s	f l a g

Parents: Your child has been taught the name, shape, and sound of the letter g; that apostrophe s shows ownership; and that a phrase is a group of words that does not express a complete thought.

LESSON 18 The Letter *R*

lesson preparation

materials

ball

Review Decks

Spelling Sound Sheet 15

container of letter tiles

Letter Card 14

Picture Card 18

Spelling Card 17

Worksheet 18

new concepts

schwa (ə)

the night before

- Punch out the *r* letter tile, but do not add it to the student's container yet.

ALPHABET ACTIVITY

- You and the student should be seated on the floor with the ball.

  "How many letters are in the alphabet?" *26*

  "What two kinds of letters make up our alphabet?" *vowels and consonants*

  "A, e, i, o, and u are called __________?" *vowels*

  "All of the other letters are called __________?" *consonants*

  "What is the initial letter of the alphabet?" *a*

  "What is the final letter of the alphabet?" *z*

  "Let's say the alphabet while we roll this ball back and forth."

  "I'll begin with 'A' and roll the ball to you. When you catch the ball, say 'B' and roll the ball back to me. We'll continue until we complete the alphabet."

- Recite the alphabet as you and the student roll the ball back and forth.
- Have the student return to his/her seat.

PHONEMIC AWARENESS

- **Objective:** To identify the number of sounds in spoken words.

  "We are going to listen for the number of sounds in some words. We'll unblend the word and hold up a finger for each sound. The first word is 'thin.' "

- Hold up a finger as you say each sound.

  "/Th/, /ĭ/, /n/. How many sounds do you hear?" *three*

- Remember to have the student listen for the *sounds* in the words, not the letters.
- Repeat with the following words: light (3), land (4), window (5), dazzle (4), and rocket (5).

REVIEW OF DECKS

- The student should be seated at a table or a desk.
- Show the student **Letter Cards 1–13** in random order. The student should name the letter on each letter card.
- Review **Affix Card 1.**
- Show the student **Picture Cards 1–17** in random order. The student should name the keyword and sound for each picture card.
- Review **Sight Word Card 1.**
- Give the student **Spelling Sound Sheet 15** and the container of letter tiles. (Do not give the student the *r* letter tile yet.)

  "Take out your letter tiles and put them in a row in front of you."

  "I'm going to call out some sounds. After you echo the sound and name the letter, find the tile with that letter on it. On your spelling sound sheet, there will be a place for that sound. Put the letter tile on that space."

  "If I give you a sound that's made by a letter you've already used, move that letter tile to the new space."

- Call out the sound on any one of **Spelling Cards 1–16.**
- Check to see that the student chooses and places the tile correctly.
- As you call out the rest of the sounds on **Spelling Cards 1–16** (in random order), make sure the student is placing the tiles correctly.

  "Put your letter tiles back in the container."

- Have the student set the container aside for use later in the lesson.

NEW LEARNING

"I am going to say some words to you and I want you to echo them back to me. Listen for the sound that is the same in the initial position of each word."

- Point to your mouth as you say each word.

"Echo after me. Rust." *rust* ***"Recipe."*** *recipe* ***"Rag."*** *rag*

"What sound do you hear in the initial position?" */r/*

- **Note:** Make sure the student is giving the pure sound of *r* and not pronouncing it with a short *u* sound, as in /rŭh/, or like the combination /er/.

"That's right. The sound you hear in the initial position is /r/."

"Put your fingertips on the front of your neck and say /r/. See if you feel any vibration."

"Is the sound voiced or unvoiced?" *voiced*

"Since /r/ vibrates, it is a voiced sound."

- Write the following words on the chalkboard: rub, rat, rock.

"What letter do you see that might be making the /r/ sound?" *r*

- If the student does not know the name of the letter, say it for him/her.

"R is the first letter in all of these words, so we can see that r must be the letter used to spell the /r/ sound."

"Look at your alphabet strip. Can you tell me if r is a vowel or a consonant?" *consonant*

HANDWRITING/LETTER TILES

- The student should be seated where he/she can write comfortably.
- Draw handwriting lines on the chalkboard. Write a capital *R* on the handwriting lines in the handwriting you want the student to learn.

"This is a capital R. Let's practice skywriting capital R's."

- Have the student practice skywriting capital *R*'s.

"Say the name of the letter each time you write it."

- Allow a few minutes for the student to practice writing capital *R*'s.
- Now write a lowercase *r* on the handwriting lines in the handwriting you want the student to learn.

"This is a lowercase r."

- Have the student practice skywriting lowercase *r*'s.
- Leave the handwriting lines and letters on the chalkboard for the remainder of the lesson.

"Find your container of letter tiles."

"I'm going to give you another letter tile."

- Give the student the *r* letter tile.

"Look at your r letter tile. One side has a capital R and the other side has a lowercase r."

"Hold your letter tile up in the air. Turn it so I can see the capital R."

"Now turn it so I can see the lowercase r."

"Spell the word 'rat' with your letter tiles."

"Now spell the word 'rip.' "

"Now add one letter to make the word 'grip.' "

- Choose additional words from the Spelling Word List, if desired.
- Have the student replace the tiles in the container and put it away.
- Reinforce the name, sound, and shape of the letter *r* throughout the day.

NEW DECK CARDS

- Show the student **Letter Card 14.**

"What letter is this?" *r*

- Hold up **Picture Card 18** but keep the picture covered with your hand (or the letter card).

"I have a card with a picture on it that begins with the /r/ sound."

"I am going to describe it for you. See if you can guess what the picture is."

"This is a small animal. It is soft and furry. Some people have them for pets. It has long ears and likes to eat carrots. What do you think the picture is?" *rabbit*

"That's right. The keyword is 'rabbit' and the sound we have learned is /r/."

- Show the student **Picture Card 18,** and then point to the picture of a rabbit on the alphabet strip.

"The word 'rabbit' helps us remember the /r/ sound because it begins with /r/."

- Hold up **Spelling Card 17** so only you can see what is written. Follow the instructions on the card. Have the student write the letter with his/her finger on the desktop, or skywrite the letter.
- **Note:** Add the new letter, picture, and spelling cards to the Review Decks.

BOARDWORK

"Let's practice coding some words like the ones you'll have on your worksheet."

"First, can you say the vowel rules with me?"

- Point to **Rule Chart 1** as the student repeats the vowel rule with you.

"A vowel followed by a consonant is short; code it with a breve."

- Point to **Rule Chart 2** as the student repeats the second vowel rule with you.

  "An open, accented vowel is long; code it with a macron."

- Write the word "staff" on the chalkboard.

  "Can you code this word?"

- Code the word as the student instructs: stăff.

  "What is the word?" *staff*

- Write the word "frogs" on the chalkboard.

  "Can you code this word?"

- Code the word as the student instructs: frŏgs.

  "What is the word?" *frogs*

- Write the phrase "a hot pan" on the chalkboard.

  "This is another phrase. A phrase is a group of words that does not express a complete thought. How will we code this phrase?"

- Code the phrase as the student instructs: ā´ hŏt păn.

  "What is this first word?" *a*

  "If you listen to people talk, you'll notice that sometimes we say /ā/ but more often we say /ŭ/. When we read, we like to sound the same as when we talk. So we will try to read 'a' as /ŭ/. It is not incorrect to say /ā/, but we sound like more experienced readers when we say /ŭ/."

  "When a vowel says /ŭ/, we code it with a mark that looks like an upside-down e."

  "This mark is called a 'schwa.' "

- Draw a schwa (ə) on the chalkboard. Erase the macron and the accent mark. Put a schwa over the *a*: ə̊ hŏt păn.

  "If you want to show that the word 'a' is pronounced /ŭ/, code it with a schwa. This mark is hard to make, so you can just draw a circle with a line through it."

- **Note:** Since the actual schwa (ə) will be shown in all coding examples, the student must learn to recognize it. When writing, however, you and the student are free to use the substitute coding mark (⊖).

- Point to the phrase again.

  "What does this phrase say?" */ŭ/ hot pan*

  "Can you give me a sentence using any of these words or the whole phrase?" *expect various answers*

  "We have several new blends today. See if you can tell me a word that begins with each blend."

- Write the following blends on the chalkboard and lead the student to words such as those listed: /br/ (bring, broken, breath, brain); /tr/ (train, tree, trim, trunk, try); /dr/ (drive, dream, drip, dry); /gr/ (grab, green, grow, grin); and /pr/ (pretty, price, print, princess).

WORKSHEET

- The student should be seated where he/she can write comfortably.
- Write "Worksheet 18" on the chalkboard. Then hold up the worksheet and point to "Worksheet 18" at the top of the page.

"When I give you the worksheet, find the side that has 'worksheet' written on it."

- Give the student **Worksheet 18.** Make sure the student turns to the correct side.

"Using the rules we just practiced, code the words by #1 through #6."

"We'll talk about the stars a little later."

"After you have coded these words, blend the sounds in each word and figure out what the words are."

- Assist the student as necessary.

"Beside #7 and #8 are two sentences. Read the sentences to yourself. If you come to a word you don't know, code the word to help you figure it out. Be sure to circle the sight words to help you remember that we can't code them. Then draw a line from one of the sentences to the picture it matches."

- Allow time for the student to work.

"Let's spell some words. Put your finger by #9. The first word we are going to spell is 'got.' "

"Let's unblend that word together. The sounds we hear are /g/, /ŏ/, /t/."

- Hold up a finger for each sound.

"Let's spell those sounds."

- Point to one of your fingers each time the student spells a sound.

"G ... o ... t."

"Now spell the word again and write the letters as you say them."

- Allow time for the student to work.

"What word did you write?" *got*

- Repeat the procedure with #10 (snag), #11 (gift), and #12 (rip).
- As the student works, provide help as needed. Listen to the student read both the words and the sentences; then help correct any incorrect answers. Initial the worksheet in the space provided.
- Although coding is important, the ultimate goal is reading, so the student, especially if he/she is having difficulty, should read to someone every day.
- **Note:** Always make sure the worksheet is corrected before the student begins the homework. The worksheet serves as a guide to help complete the homework.

HOMEWORK

"Turn your paper over to the homework side."

"Put your finger on the top row of handwriting lines. Write your best capital R on the line so I will know what a capital R should look like."

- Have the student write a lowercase letter *r* on the second handwriting line.

- Make sure that the student has written the letters correctly (to the best of his or her ability). He/She will use them as guides when completing the homework.

"Today on your worksheet and homework, there are some words with stars by them. Ask (parent, sibling, etc.) to read four of these words to you. You should spell the words on the lines by #9 through #12."

- Some time during the day, have someone other than yourself (if possible) read any four of the starred words from the worksheet or the homework side. The student should try to spell the words on the lines by #9–#12.

"Do you know what to do on the rest of the homework paper?"

"When you finish your paper, I will check it for you and initial it in the space provided."

- Either now or later in the day, the student should complete the homework independently (if possible), except for #9–#12. Help the student correct any incorrect answers. Then initial the homework in the space provided.

- If possible, take time to play the Kid Card games listed in Lesson 15.

Name _____ Worksheet 18
(for use with Lesson 18)
Teacher's Initials _____ **Phonics 1**

Rr

★ 1. răt ★ 4. grĭt

★ 2. rĭd 5. răzz

★ 3. trŏt 6. drĭll

7. Ron has a tan rag.
8. Sid's pig is in the pond.

9. ___got___ 11. ___gift___

10. ___snag___ 12. ___rip___

P1-WS-018a Copyright by Saxon Publishers, Inc. and Lorna Simmons. Reproduction prohibited.

Parent's Initials _____ Homework 18
(for use with Lesson 18)
Phonics 1

Rr

★ 1. răg ★ 4. trĭp

★ 2. rĭd ★ 5. răft

★ 3. rŏt ★ 6. răp

7. A flag is on the hill.
8. The frog is in hot sand.

Parents: Select four of the starred words on either side of this sheet. Ask your child to write the words on the lines below.

9. _____ 11. _____

10. _____ 12. _____

Parents: Your child has been taught the name, shape, and sound of the letter r; and that the word "a" is usually pronounced "ŭ," which is the schwa (ə) sound.

P1-WS-018b Copyright by Saxon Publishers, Inc. and Lorna Simmons. Reproduction prohibited.

LESSON 19 — The Letter *K*

lesson preparation

materials

container of letter tiles

Review Decks

Spelling Sound Sheet 16

Letter Card 15

Picture Card 19

Spelling Card 18

Worksheet 19

Reader 4 (*Zip and the Ant*)

colored pencils

the night before

- Punch out the *k* letter tile, but do not add it to the student's container yet.

ALPHABET ACTIVITY

- The student should be seated with the alphabet strip.

  "Today we are going to work with the words 'before' and 'after.' "

  "Can you tell me a letter that is before p in the alphabet?" *any letter a–o*

- Allow the student to use the alphabet strip, if necessary.

  "Can you tell me a letter that is after i in the alphabet?" *any letter j–z*

- Give the student the container of letter tiles. (Do not give the student the *k* letter tile yet.)

  "I am going to write a letter on the chalkboard and I want you to pull one letter tile out of your container. When I ask you, tell me if your letter comes before or after my letter. Ready?"

- Write the letter *r* on the chalkboard. Ask the student to pull out a letter tile and tell you if the letter comes before or after the letter *r*. Repeat this procedure a few more times.

  "Let's see if we can do this a different way."

- Write the letter *o* on the chalkboard.

"Pick a letter from your container. If your letter comes after o, stand up."

- The student should stand or remain seated, depending on the letter tile drawn.
- Repeat this procedure, but have the student stand if the letter he/she draws comes *before* the letter *o*.
- Continue this activity, using either variation. Remember to use only those letters that have been taught: *n, o, t, p, i, l, a, z, s, d, f, h, g,* and *r*.
- Have the student set the letter tile container aside for use later in the lesson.

PHONEMIC AWARENESS

- **Objective:** To identify blended sounds in spoken words.

  "I am going to say some words. See if you can tell me the blend in the initial position in these words."
- Point to your mouth as you say the following words: grass, grape, gripe, ground.
- Some students will have difficulty isolating the blended sounds. Slowly repeat the words until the student can answer. Then ask:

  "What blend do you hear in the initial position of these words?" */gr/*
- Be sure to have the student tell you the sound of the blend, not the letter names.
- Point to your mouth and say the following words: bring, bright, brook, brother.

  "What blend do you hear in the initial position of these words?" */br/*
- Repeat with the following blends: /tr/ (trip, trail, trot, train); /dr/ (drive, dream, drink, dress); and /pr/ (pray, present, print, promise).

  "The next one is a three-letter blend. It's hard. See if you can tell me the blend."
- Point to your mouth and say the following words: spray, sprint, spread, spring.

  "What blend do you hear in the initial position of these words?" */spr/*
- Continue with additional words as time permits.

REVIEW OF DECKS

- The student should be seated where he/she can write comfortably.
- Show the student **Letter Cards 1–14** in random order. The student should name the letter on each letter card.
- Review **Affix Card 1.**
- Show the student **Picture Cards 1–18** in random order. The student should name the keyword and sound for each picture card.
- Review **Sight Word Card 1.**
- Give the student **Spelling Sound Sheet 16.**

- Call out the sounds on **Spelling Cards 1–17** in random order. The student should echo each sound and name the letter or letters that make the sound as he/she writes the letter(s) on the spelling sound sheet.
- Have the student set the spelling sound sheet aside for use later in the lesson.

NEW LEARNING

"I am going to say some words to you and I want you to echo them back to me. Listen for the sound that is the same in the initial position of each word."

- Point to your mouth as you say each word.

"Echo after me. Keep." *keep* ***"Kindergarten."*** *kindergarten* ***"Kitten."*** *kitten*

"What sound do you hear in the initial position?" */k/*

- **Note:** Make sure the student is giving the pure sound of *k* and not pronouncing it with a short *u* sound, as in /kŭh/.

"That's right. The sound you hear in the initial position is /k/."

"Put your fingertips on the front of your neck and say /k/. See if you feel any vibration."

"Is this sound voiced or unvoiced?" *unvoiced*

"Since /k/ doesn't vibrate, it is an unvoiced sound."

- Write the following words on the chalkboard: kid, kept, king.

"What letter do you see that might be making the /k/ sound?" *k*

- If the student does not know the name of the letter, say it for him/her.

"K is the first letter in all of these words, so we can see that k must be the letter used to spell the /k/ sound."

"Look at your alphabet strip. Can you tell me if k is a vowel or a consonant?" *consonant*

HANDWRITING/LETTER TILES

- The student should be seated where he/she can write comfortably.
- Write a capital *K* on the chalkboard.

"This is a capital K. Let's practice skywriting capital K's before we write them on our paper."

- Have the student practice skywriting capital *K*'s.

"Find your spelling sound sheet."

- Draw handwriting lines on the chalkboard. Write a capital *K* on the handwriting lines in the handwriting you want the student to learn.

"Find the first handwriting line and practice writing capital K's like I wrote this one on the chalkboard. Say the name of the letter each time you write it."

- Allow a few minutes for the student to practice writing capital *K*'s.
- Write a lowercase *k* on the handwriting lines in the handwriting you want the student to learn.

"This is a lowercase k."

- Have the student practice skywriting lowercase *k*'s.

"Now practice writing lowercase k's on the second handwriting line. Say the name of the letter each time you write it."

- Have the student set the spelling sound sheet aside for use later in the lesson.
- Leave the handwriting lines and letters on the chalkboard for the remainder of the lesson.

"Find your container of letter tiles. I am going to give you your next letter tile."

- Give the student the *k* letter tile.

"Look at your k letter tile. One side has a capital K and the other side has a lowercase k."

"Hold your letter tile up in the air. Turn it so I can see the capital K."

"Now turn it so I can see the lowercase k."

"Spell the word 'kid' with your letter tiles."

"Now change one letter to make the word 'kit.' "

"Now spell the word 'ask.' "

- Choose additional words from the Spelling Word List, if desired.
- Have the student replace the tiles in the container and put it away.
- Reinforce the name, sound, and shape of the letter *k* throughout the day.

NEW DECK CARDS

- Show the student **Letter Card 15.**

"What letter is this?" *k*

- Hold up **Picture Card 19** but keep the picture covered with your hand (or the letter card).

"I have a card with a picture on it that begins with the /k/ sound."

"I'm going to describe it for you. See if you can guess what the picture is."

"This is something that can fly. It can be many bright colors. You might see one on a windy day in the spring. It usually has a long string attached to it. What do you think the picture is?" *kite*

"That's right. The keyword is 'kite' and the sound we have learned is /k/."

- Show the student **Picture Card 19,** and then point to the picture of a kite on the alphabet strip.

  "The word 'kite' helps us remember the /k/ sound because it begins with /k/."

  "Find your spelling sound sheet. Find #18 and put your finger on it."

- Hold up **Spelling Card 18** so only you can see what is written. Using the hand signals, follow the instructions on the card.
- Check the spelling sound sheet for accuracy.
- **Note:** Add the new letter, picture, and spelling cards to the Review Decks.

BOARDWORK

"Let's practice coding some words like the ones you'll have on your worksheet."

"First, can you say the vowel rules with me?"

- Point to **Rule Chart 1** as the student repeats the vowel rule with you.

  "A vowel followed by a consonant is short; code it with a breve."

- Point to **Rule Chart 2** as the student repeats the second vowel rule with you.

  "An open, accented vowel is long; code it with a macron."

- Write the word "skits" on the chalkboard.

  "Can you code this word?"

- Code the word as the student instructs: skĭt[s].

  "What is this word?" *skits*

  "What does the suffix -s on the end mean?" *more than one*

  "What is the root word?" *skit*

- Write the word "drift" on the chalkboard.

  "Can you code this word?"

- Code the word as the student instructs: drĭft.

  "What is this word?" *drift*

- Write the phrase "the top kids" on the chalkboard.

  "This is another phrase, a group of words that does not express a complete thought. How will we code this phrase?"

- Code the phrase as the student instructs: (the) tŏp kĭd[s].

  "What does the phrase say?" *the top kids*

  "Can you give me a sentence using any of these words or the phrase?" *expect various answers*

WORKSHEET

- The student should be seated where he/she can write comfortably.
- Write "Worksheet 19" on the chalkboard. Then hold up the worksheet and point to "Worksheet 19" at the top of the page.

  "When I give you the worksheet, find the side that has 'worksheet' written on it."
- Give the student **Worksheet 19.** Make sure the student turns to the correct side.

  "Using the rules we just practiced, code the words by #1 through #6. After you have coded these words, blend the sounds in each word and figure out what the words are."
- Assist the student as necessary.

  "Beside #7 and #8 are two sentences. Read the sentences to yourself. If you come to a word you don't know, code the word to help you figure it out. Be sure to circle the sight words to help you remember that we can't code them. Then try to fill in the missing word in #8."
- Allow time for the student to work.

  "It's time to spell some words. Put your finger by #9. The first word we are going to spell is 'hats.' Let's unblend that word together. The sounds we hear are /h/, /ă/, /t/, /s/."
- Hold up a finger for each sound.

  "Let's spell those sounds."
- Point to one of your fingers each time the student spells a sound.

  "H ... a ... t ... s."

  "Now, spell the word again and write the letters as you say them."
- Allow time for the student to work.

  "What word did you write?" *hats*
- Repeat the procedure with #10 (spin), #11 (land), and #12 (fist).
- As the student works, provide help as needed. Listen to the student read both the words and the sentences; then help correct any incorrect answers. Initial the worksheet in the space provided.
- **Note:** Always make sure the worksheet is corrected before the student begins the homework. The worksheet serves as a guide to help complete the homework.

HOMEWORK

"Turn your paper over to the homework side."

"Put your finger on the top row of handwriting lines. Write your best capital K on the line so I will know what a capital K should look like."

- Have the student write a lowercase letter *k* on the second handwriting line.

- Make sure that the student has written the letters correctly (to the best of his or her ability). He/She will use them as guides when completing the homework.

  "Do you know what to do on the rest of the homework paper?"
- Discuss the homework pictures to make sure the student understands the word each one represents: #9 (kid), #10 (skip), and #11 (kit).

  "When you finish your paper, I will check it for you and initial it in the space provided."
- Either now or later in the day, the student should complete the homework independently (if possible). Help the student correct any incorrect answers. Then initial the homework in the space provided.

READER

- Give the student **Reader 4 (*Zip and the Ant*)** and some colored pencils.

  "We're going to make another book today."

  "Can you tell me the name of this book?" *Zip and the Ant*
- Assist the student as necessary as he/she completes the following steps:

  "Hold up your page so that the tree is facing you."

  "Now put your finger on the top dotted line."

  "Carefully fold the paper along this dotted line toward you so that it lines up with the bottom dotted line."

  "Now fold the top half of the sheet back along the dotted line."

  "Hold your book so the tree is facing you again. Then put your finger on the dotted line down the center of the page."

  "Fold the book backward along this dotted line so that the tree will still be facing you when you're finished."
- When the student completes this last step, either put a rubber band around the book's spine or staple the spine.

  "Next, carefully separate the pages along the perforated lines at the top and bottom."
- Demonstrate how to separate the pages.

  "Let's check the page numbers to see if they are in the correct order."
- Demonstrate how to check that the book's page numbers are in order.

  "Tell me again the name of this book." *Zip and the Ant*

  "I want you to read your book to yourself. When you are finished reading, color the pictures. Write your name on the book so I will know who colored it."

  "Keep your book handy because I will be asking you to read it for me."
- Some time during the day, have the student read the reader to you.
- If possible, take time to play the Kid Card games listed in Lesson 15. Try to see that the student is prepared for tomorrow's assessment.

Lesson 19

Name ______________________

Teacher's Initials ____

Worksheet 19
(for use with Lesson 19)
Phonics 1

Kk

1. kit
2. skip
3. silk
4. skin
5. kilt
6. kin

7. The skiff is on the pond.
8. The __pond__ has a skiff on it.

9. h a t s
10. s p i n
11. l a n d
12. f i s t

P1-WS-019a

Parent's Initials ____

Homework 19
(for use with Lesson 19)
Phonics 1

Kk

1. kid
2. kiss
3. kit
4. skit
5. skiff
6. skid

7. Grass is on the hill.
8. The hill has __grass__ on it.

9.

k i d

10.

s k i p

11.

k i t

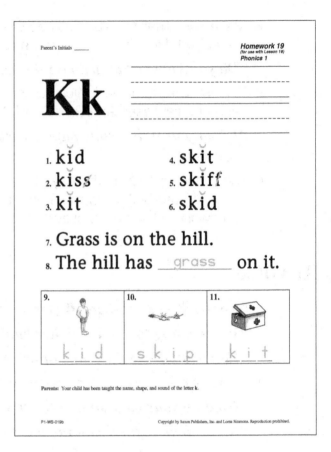

Parents: Your child has been taught the name, shape, and sound of the letter k.

P1-WS-019b

LESSON 20 — Assessment

lesson preparation

materials

Review Decks

Assessment 3

Spelling Test 1

Assessment 3 Recording Form

Kid Cards

tokens

the night before

- Separate the Kid Cards marked "Lesson 20."

ALPHABET ACTIVITY

- The student should be seated.

  "When we recite the alphabet today, you will say the consonants and I will say the vowels."

  "Ready? Let's begin."

- As you say the alphabet, point to the student when it is his/her time to recite.
- If time permits, swap letters.

PHONEMIC AWARENESS

- **Objective:** To blend sounds in spoken words.

  "Echo this blend: /st/." */st/*

  "Now can you add the long a sound to /st/?" *stay*

  "Good job! Can you add the long o sound to /st/?" *stow*

  "Let's try the blend /sn/. Can you add a long o sound to /sn/?" *snow*

- Repeat with the following:

/pr/ + long *a* = pray	/tr/ + long *e* = tree
/tr/ + long *a* = tray	/tr/ + long *i* = try
/gr/ + long *o* = grow	/gr/ + long *a* = gray
/pl/ + long *a* = play	/dr/ + long *i* = dry

Review of Decks

- Show the student **Letter Cards 1–15** in random order. The student should name the letter on each card.
- Review **Affix Card 1.**
- Show the student **Picture Cards 1–19** in random order. The student should name the keyword and sound for each picture card.
- Review **Sight Word Card 1.**

Written Assessment

"Today we are going to see if you remember the letters and sounds we have been practicing."

- Give the student **Assessment 3.**
- **Section I:**

  "Today we're going to write some words for our assessment."

  "I'm going to say a word. Write the letter that makes each sound in that word on the lines by #1."

  "The first word is 'nod.' "
- Sound the word out slowly if the student is not successful.
- Repeat with the following words in the order shown: #2 (zap), #3 (sit), #4 (list), and #5 (lips).
- **Note:** While the student spells words on assessments, be ready to point to appropriate rule charts as necessary to help the student spell the words.
- **Section II:**

  "Look at the letter by #6."

  "Find the picture of the keyword for this sound."

  "Draw a line from the letter to the keyword."
- Repeat with #7 and #8. Allow a few minutes for the student to work.
- The pictures (from top to bottom) are as follows: feet, rose, doughnut.
- **Section III:**

  "Put your finger on #9."

  "Code the words by #9 through #12."
- Allow a few minutes for the student to work.
- **Section IV:**

  "Look at the blend by #13. What sound does this blend make?" *pl*
- Repeat with #14, #15, #16, #17, and #18.
- Point to the first picture (spider) and help the student identify it. Ask the student to name the blend the picture begins with and then to draw a line from the picture to the blend.
- Repeat with each picture. The pictures (from top to bottom) are as follows: spider, slide, snake, plant, stick, flag.

"When you are finished, show your paper to me."

- This paper will be used during the oral portion of the assessment.

SPELLING TEST

- Give the student **Spelling Test 1.**
- Call out the following words (in the order shown). Sound them out, if necessary.
  #1 (in), #2 (it), #3 (top), #4 (pin), #5 (not), #6 (I), #7 (no), #8 (on), #9 (tip), #10 (pop)
- Grade and record the paper in any manner that suits your needs.

ORAL ASSESSMENT

- Oral assessments are short interviews that occur during independent work time. It is important to complete them promptly (today, if possible) in order to identify any areas of weakness and begin remediation.
- Use the assessment and the following dialogue to complete the oral portion.
- **Section V:**
- Show the student the word by #19.

  "Read this word for me."
- Write the student's response on the adjacent line.
- Repeat with #20, #21, and #22.
- **Section VI:**

  "I'm going to say some words. Tell me the sound you hear in the initial position."
- Point to your mouth and say the following words: dog, door, dime.
- Write the student's response on the line by #23. (If the student responds with the letter name, ask again for the *sound.*)
- Repeat with #24 (set, sift, seek); #25 (fun, foam, fable); and #26 (stop, spell, scoot).
- **Section VII:**
- Show the student the letter by #27.

  "Tell me the name of this letter and the sound it makes."
- Record the student's response on the adjacent line.
- Repeat with #28, #29, and #30.

ASSESSMENT EVALUATION

- Grade the assessment and record the results on **Assessment 3 Recording Form.** Check off the boxes to indicate mastery (i.e., the section was completed with 100% accuracy).
- **Note:** If you choose to grade the assessments, try to give as many points as possible for work attempted. Do not grade the coding marks too severely, especially secondary marks like accents, voice lines, and k-backs. The most important coding marks to look for are breves, macrons, and syllable division lines.

- See the introductory material for detailed information regarding grading and recording procedures.
- Use the assessment results to identify those skills in which the student is weak. Practice those skills by playing Kid Card games.
- Add the Kid Cards marked "Lesson 20" to the existing decks. Listed below are games appropriate for remediation in selected areas. See "Games and Activities" for the directions for each game.
- **Section I:** Play "Spelling Deck Perfection" or "Sound Scamper," or have the student use the letter tiles to spell words you give from the Spelling Word List.
- **Section II:** Play "Keyword and Sound" or "Letter/Sound Identification."
- **Section III:** Play "Chalkboard Challenge."
- **Section IV:** Play "Blend It."
- **Section V:** Play "Word Blend" (with blue Kid Cards).
- **Section VI:** Play "Sound Solutions."
- **Section VII:** Play "Letter Deck Data" or "Letter/Sound Identification."
- When the student seems more secure in areas that had previously proven difficult, retest him/her (in those areas only) and indicate on the recording form any sections the student has subsequently mastered.
- Try to help the student achieve mastery of all the sections before the next assessment.
- If the student is having difficulty with a particular skill, keep his or her practice activities at the most basic level so the chance of success is greater.

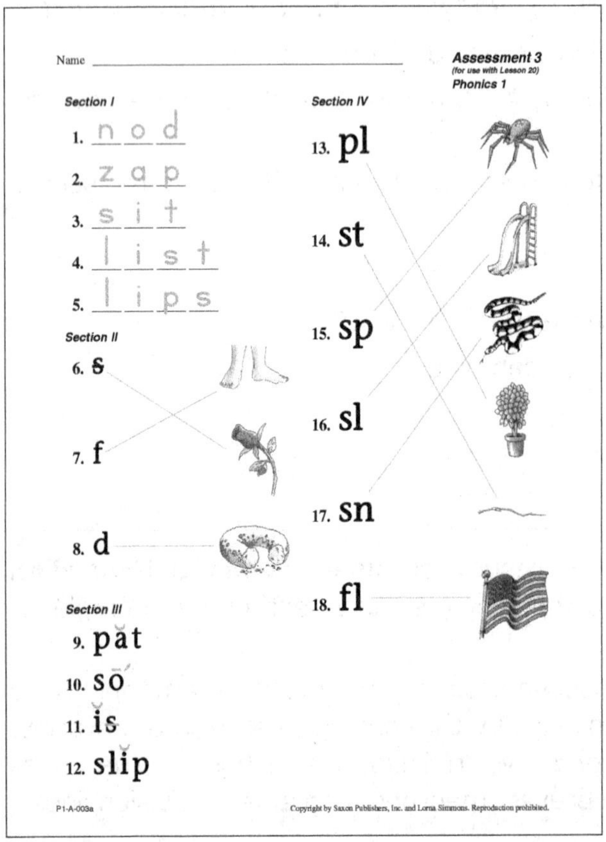

Name ______

Assessment 3 (for use with Lesson 20) Phonics 1

Section I

1. nod
2. zap
3. sit
4. list
5. lips

Section II

6. s̶
7. f
8. d

Section III

9. păt
10. sṓ
11. ĭs̶
12. slĭp

Section IV

13. pl
14. st
15. sp
16. sl
17. sn
18. fl

P1-A-003a

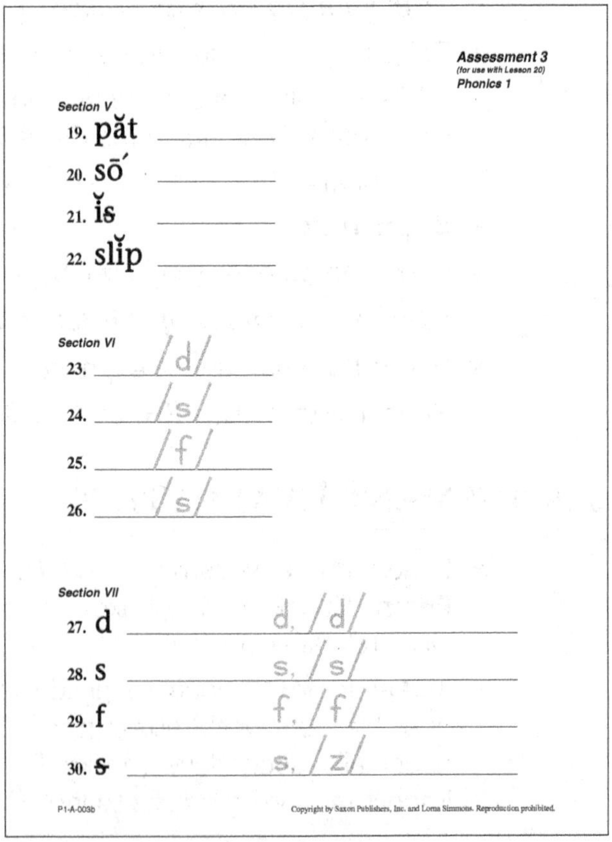

Assessment 3 (for use with Lesson 20) Phonics 1

Section V

19. păt ______
20. sṓ ______
21. ĭs̶ ______
22. slĭp ______

Section VI

23. /d/
24. /s/
25. /f/
26. /s/

Section VII

27. d — d, /d/
28. s — s, /s/
29. f — f, /f/
30. s̶ — s, /z/

P1-A-003b

LESSON 21 — The Letter *C*

lesson preparation

materials

Review Decks
Spelling Sound Sheet 17
container of letter tiles
Letter Card 16
carrot in a sack (see *the night before*)
Picture Card 20
Worksheet 21
Sight Word Cards 2–3
Spelling List 2

new concepts

syllables
k-back
question mark

the night before

- Put a carrot in a sack for the student to use to "discover" the new keyword. (Baby carrots are especially fun.)
- Add the *c* letter tile to the student's container.

ALPHABET ACTIVITY

- The student should be seated with the alphabet strip.

"How many letters are in our alphabet?" *26*

"What two kinds of letters make up our alphabet?" *vowels and consonants*

"Name the vowels." *a, e, i, o, and u*

"All of the other letters are called _________?" *consonants*

"The initial letter of the alphabet is _____?" *a*

"The final letter of the alphabet is _____?" *z*

"Can you name a medial letter?" *any letter between a and z*

PHONEMIC AWARENESS

- **Objective:** To identify syllables in spoken words.

"All words are made of parts. These parts are called 'syllables.'"

"Every word has at least one syllable and some have many more. Listen as I say a word and clap it. Tell me how many syllables you hear. Nap … kin." *two*

"Every syllable has a vowel and a vowel sound. In the word I just clapped, the first syllable was 'nap.' The second syllable was 'kin.' "

"What vowel sound do you hear in 'nap'?" */ă/*

"What vowel sound do you hear in 'kin'?" */ĭ/*

"Let's try another word. Listen to this word and decide how many times you could clap. Teach … er."

- Emphasize both syllables equally.

"Let's say the word and clap it together. Ready?" *teach … er (clap two times, once with each syllable)*

"How many parts does this word have?" *two*

"That's right! Each of these parts is a syllable. Can you say that?" *syllable*

"If the word has two parts, it has two syllables. How many syllables are in the word 'teacher'?" *two*

"Let's try another word. Echo this word and clap the parts. Sand … wich." *sand … wich (clap two times)*

"How many parts does this word have?" *two*

"How many syllables are in this word?" *two*

"Here's another word. Echo and clap the parts. E … ra … ser." *e … ra … ser (clap three times)*

"How many parts does this word have?" *three*

"How many syllables are in this word?" *three*

"Let's try one more. Echo and clap the parts. In … sect." *in … sect (clap two times)*

"How many parts does this word have?" *two*

"So how many syllables are in this word?" *two*

Review of Decks

- The student should be seated where he/she can write comfortably.
- Show the student **Letter Cards 1–15** in random order. The student should name the letter on each letter card.
- Review **Affix Card 1.**
- Show the student **Picture Cards 1–19** in random order. The student should name the keyword and sound for each picture card.
- Review **Sight Word Card 1.**
- Give the student **Spelling Sound Sheet 17.**

- Call out the sounds on **Spelling Cards 1–18** in random order. The student should echo each sound and name the letter or letters that make the sound as he/she writes the letter(s) on the spelling sound sheet.
- Check the student's response after each card.
- Have the student set the spelling sound sheet aside for use later in the lesson.

New Learning

"I am going to say some words to you and I want you to echo them back to me. Listen for the sound that is the same in the initial position of each word."

- Point to your mouth as you say each word.

"Echo after me. Catnip." *catnip* ***"Capital."*** *capital* ***"Cotton."*** *cotton*

"What sound do you hear in the initial position?" */k/*

- **Note:** This sound for the letter *c* will always be represented as /k/ because *c* borrows its sounds from the letters *k* and *s*. Make sure the student is giving the pure sound of *k* and not pronouncing it with a short *u* sound, as in /kŭh/.

"That's right. The sound you hear in the initial position is /k/. Put your fingertips on the front of your neck and say /k/. See if you feel any vibration. Is this sound voiced or unvoiced?" *unvoiced*

"Since /k/ does not vibrate, it is an unvoiced sound. We have already had this sound. Let's see if another letter is making it."

- Write the following words on the chalkboard: catnip, capital, cotton.

"What letter do you see that might be making the /k/ sound?" *c*

- If the student does not know the name of the letter, say it for him/her.

"C is the first letter in all of these words, so we can see that c must also be a letter used to spell the /k/ sound. C has to borrow its sound from the k because it does not have a sound of its own. Look at your alphabet strip. Is c a vowel or a consonant?" *consonant*

Handwriting/Letter Tiles

- The student should be seated where he/she can write comfortably.
- Write a capital *C* on the chalkboard.

"This is a capital C. Let's practice skywriting capital C's before we write them on our paper."

- Have the student practice skywriting capital *C*'s.

"Find your spelling sound sheet."

- Draw handwriting lines on the chalkboard. Write a capital *C* on the handwriting lines in the handwriting you want the student to learn.

"Find the first handwriting line on your paper and practice writing capital C's like I wrote this one on the chalkboard. Say the name of the letter each time you write it."

- Allow a few minutes for the student to practice writing capital *C*'s.
- Write a lowercase *c* on the handwriting lines in the handwriting you want the student to learn.

"This is a lowercase c."

- Have the student practice skywriting lowercase *c*'s.

"Now practice writing lowercase c's on the second handwriting line. Say the name of the letter each time you write it."

- Have the student set the spelling sound sheet aside for use later in the lesson.
- Leave the handwriting lines and letters on the chalkboard for the remainder of the lesson.
- Give the student the container of letter tiles.

"Today I've given you another letter tile."

"Find your c letter tile and look at it. One side has a capital C and the other side has a lowercase c."

- Allow time for the student to examine the new letter tile.

"Hold your letter tile up in the air. Turn it so I can see the capital C."

"Now turn it so I can see the lowercase c."

"Let's spell some words with your letter tiles. All of the words will begin with the letter c. Spell the word 'cat.' "

- Continue with the following words: cod, clap. Choose additional words from the Spelling Word List, if desired.
- Have the student replace the tiles in the container and put it away.
- Reinforce the name, sound, and shape of the letter *c* throughout the day.

New Deck Cards

- Pull **Spelling Card 18** from the Review Deck.
- Show the student **Letter Card 16.**

"What letter is this?" *c*

"I have another sack today. It contains a clue to our new keyword. Don't look in the sack, but put your hand inside and see if you can feel what is inside the sack. Keep in mind that the object in the sack starts with the /k/ sound."

- **Optional:** If a carrot was not available, use the following riddle:

"This is something that is good for your eyes. You can grow it in a garden or you can buy it in a grocery store. It is an orange vegetable and is liked a lot by our keyword for r. What do you think the keyword is?" *carrot*

"The keyword is 'carrot' and the sound we have learned is /k/."

- Show the student **Picture Card 20,** and then point to the picture of a carrot on the alphabet strip.

"The word 'carrot' helps us remember the /k/ sound because it begins with /k/."

"Notice that the c on this card has a line on the side of it. Since c does not have its own sound, we are going to put this line on it. It's called a k-back and it makes a c look like a k. It will help us remember that c makes the /k/ sound."

- Demonstrate another k-back on the chalkboard: c.

"This is how we will code the letter c that makes the /k/ sound."

"Find your spelling sound sheet. Find #19 and put your finger by it."

- Hold up **Spelling Card 18** so only you can see what is written.

"Echo this sound: /k/." */k/*

"How do we spell /k/?" *expect various answers*

- Write "k, c" on the chalkboard.

"K and c both make the /k/ sound, so when I give you the /k/ sound, you should respond 'k comma c' and write what I wrote on the chalkboard."

- The student should write the response on line #19.
- **Note:** This will be the proper response to **Spelling Card 18** until Lesson 28.
- Check the spelling sound sheet for accuracy.
- **Note:** Add the new letter and picture cards to the Review Decks (and re-insert **Spelling Card 18**).

BOARDWORK

"Let's practice coding some words like the ones you'll have on your worksheet. First, can you say the vowel rules with me?"

- Point to **Rule Chart 1** as the student repeats the vowel rule with you.

"A vowel followed by a consonant is short; code it with a breve."

- Point to **Rule Chart 2** as the student repeats the second vowel rule with you.

"An open, accented vowel is long; code it with a macron."

- Write the word "clasp" on the chalkboard.

"Can you code this word?"

- Code the word as the student instructs: clăsp.

"What is the word?" *clasp*

- Write the word "skills" on the chalkboard.

"Can you code this word?"

- Code the word as the student instructs: skĭlls.

"What is the word?" *skills*

"Can you give me a sentence using either of these words?" *expect various answers*

WORKSHEET

- The student should be seated where he/she can write comfortably.
- Give the student **Worksheet 21.** Make sure the student turns to the correct side.

"Using the rules we just practiced, code the words by #1 through #6. After you have coded these words, blend the sounds in each word and figure out what the words are."

- Assist the student as necessary.
- Write the following words on the chalkboard: what, who.

"Do you know these words?"

- If the student does not know the words, write the phonetic spellings (hwŭt, h<u>oo</u>) on the chalkboard and help the student sound them out.

"These words are 'what' and 'who.' They will always be sight words."

- Show the student **Sight Word Cards 2** and **3.**

"We will add these cards to our sight word deck. If you need help remembering them, look at the sight word charts in your Irregular Spelling Booklet."

- If desired, allow the student to get the Irregular Spelling Booklet and look up "what" and "who" in the list of sight words.

"Beside #7 and #8 are two sentences. Look at the sentence by #8. The first word is one of our new sight words. Let's draw a circle around it now to help us remember that it is a sight word and we can't code it."

"Turn your paper over to the homework side. The sentence by #8 has our other new sight word in it. Circle it now so you will remember it when you do your homework later."

"Turn your paper back to the worksheet side. Read the sentences by #7 and #8 to yourself. If you find any words you can't read, code them. The second sentence ends with a question mark. It asks a question. Write your answer on the line next to it."

- Allow time for the student to work.

"Let's try spelling some words with the /k/ sound. Sometimes we use c and sometimes we use k. Since we don't know yet when to use a k or a c, all of the words today will contain a c."

"Put your finger by #9. The first word is 'can.' "

"Let's unblend that word together. The sounds we hear are /k/, /ă/, /n/."

- Hold up a finger for each sound.

"Let's spell those sounds."

- Point to one of your fingers each time the student spells a sound.

"C ... a ... n."

"Now spell the word again and write the letters as you say them."

- Allow time for the student to work.

"What word did you write?" *can*

- Repeat the procedure with #10 (cat) and #11 (cost).

"Look at #12 and tell me what the picture is." *a flag*

"Think about the sounds in the word 'flag.' Try to spell the word on the line under the picture."

- As the student works, provide help as needed. Listen to the student read both the words and the sentences; then help correct any incorrect answers. Initial the worksheet in the space provided.
- **Note:** Always make sure the worksheet is corrected before the student begins the homework. The worksheet serves as a guide to help complete the homework.
- Add **Sight Word Cards 2** and **3** to the Sight Word Deck.

HOMEWORK

"Turn your paper over to the homework side."

"Put your finger on the top row of handwriting lines. Write your best capital C on the line so I will know what a capital C should look like."

- Have the student write a lowercase letter *c* on the second handwriting line.
- Make sure that the student has written the letters correctly (to the best of his or her ability). He/She will use them as guides when completing the homework.

"Do you know what to do on the rest of the homework paper?"

- Discuss the homework pictures to make sure the student understands the word each one represents: #9 (rat), #10 (gift), and #11 (fist).

"When you finish your paper, I will check it for you and initial it in the space provided."

- Either now or later in the day, the student should complete the homework independently (if possible). Help the student correct any incorrect answers. Then initial the homework in the space provided.

SPELLING LIST

- Fold **Spelling List 2** in half lengthwise (with the printed side facing out).

"Leave your paper just like I give it to you."

- Give the student **Spelling List 2,** folded with the blank lines facing up.

"Let's spell some more words. You can spell these words without seeing them first because you know the rules for spelling them."

- Call out the following words (in the order shown). Sound them out, if necessary.

  #1 (at), #2 (lot), #3 (lap), #4 (nap), #5 (pat), #6 (tan), #7 (lip), #8 (tap), #9 (zip), #10 (pit)

  "Now unfold your paper and check your words."

- Check the student's work to see if he/she needs extra help with spelling.

  "I want you to practice these words. We'll have a spelling test in a few days."

- If possible, take time to play the Kid Card games listed in Lesson 20.
- If you provided a carrot (or baby carrots) for the student, allow the student to eat it now (or when time permits).

Name ______________________

Teacher's Initials ____

Worksheet 21
(for use with Lesson 21)
Phonics 1

Cc

1. cŏt
2. cŏn
3. cŏd
4. scălp
5. clŏt
6. crisp

7. A cat can hiss.
8. What can hiss? ___cat___

9. ___can___
10. ___cat___
11. ___cost___

12.

___flag___

P1-WS-021a

Parent's Initials ____

Homework 21
(for use with Lesson 21)
Phonics 1

Cc

1. căp
2. căn
3. cŏp
4. căt
5. căst
6. clăp

7. Dot is on the sand hill.
8. Who is on the sand hill? ___Dot___

9.

r a t

10.

g i f t

11.

f i s t

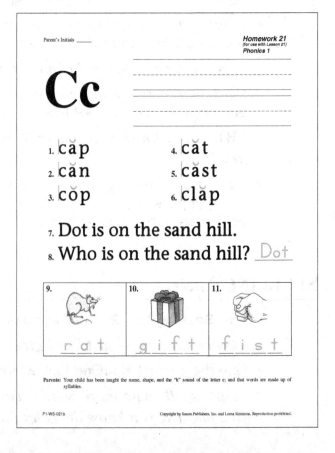

Parents: Your child has been taught the name, shape, and the "k" sound of the letter c; and that words are made up of syllables.

P1-WS-021b

LESSON 22 — Spelling with *k* and *c*

lesson preparation

materials

Review Decks

Spelling Sound Sheet 18

Worksheet 22

Sight Word Card 4

Reader 5 (*Lost at the Pond*)

colored pencils

new concepts

k and *c* spelling rule

ALPHABET ACTIVITY

- You and the student should be standing.

  "When we say the alphabet today, let's sit down on every other letter and then stand back up."

- Sit down and then stand up for every other letter.

PHONEMIC AWARENESS

- **Objective:** To identify syllables in spoken words.

  "Today I want you to give me a word. We will try to figure out how many syllables are in that word."

  "Can you think of a word?"

- Allow time for the student to respond.

  "Listen as I say the word, and then clap it. Tell me how many syllables you hear."

- Clap and say the word. Emphasize each syllable equally.

  "Every syllable has a vowel and a vowel sound. In the word I just said, what vowel sound(s) did you hear?"

- Repeat with more words suggested by the student.

REVIEW OF DECKS

- The student should be seated where he/she can write comfortably.
- Show the student **Letter Cards 1–16** in random order. The student should name the letter on each letter card.

- Review **Affix Card 1.**
- Show the student **Picture Cards 1–20** in random order. The student should name the keyword and sound for each picture card.
- Review **Sight Word Cards 1–3.**
- Give the student **Spelling Sound Sheet 18.**
- Call out the sounds on **Spelling Cards 1–18** in random order. The student should echo each sound and name the letter or letters that make the sound as he/she writes the letter(s) on the spelling sound sheet.
- Check the student's response after each card.

New Learning

- Write the following on the chalkboard: __at, __it, and __lip.

  "All of these words begin with the /k/ sound."

  "What letters have the sound of /k/?" *k and c*

  "I am going to show you a rule to use when you spell with this sound."

  "Get out your Rule Book and turn to page 3."
- Point to **Rule Chart 3** as you say the following:

  "This is called the 'K and C Spelling Rule.' "
- Point to "__at."

  "Look at this first word. This word begins with the sound of /k/."

  "Look at the letter right after the line. What is it?" *a*

  "Let's find the a on this chart."
- Point to *a*, and then move your finger back to the *c* as you say:

  "What letter do we use to spell the /k/ sound when it is followed by an a?" *c*

  "That's right! Let's try another one."
- Repeat the procedure with "__it" and "__lip."
- Discuss the letters *e* and *u*, if necessary.
- If the student seems to understand, go on to the worksheet activity. If not, have him/her practice more words on the chalkboard.
- **Note:** You might also point out page 23 in the Irregular Spelling Booklet. This page contains a few words whose /k/ spelling is irregular.

Worksheet

- The student should be seated where he/she can write comfortably.
- Give the student **Worksheet 22.** Make sure the student turns to the correct side.

  "We are going to spell some words using your new rule chart."

"The first word is 'can.' "

"Unblend 'can' with me. /K/, /ă/, /n/."

- Hold up a finger for each sound.

"What sound do you hear after the /k/ sound?" /ă/

"What letter do we use to spell the /k/ sound if it is followed by an a?" c

- Point to **Rule Chart 3.**

"This word must begin with the letter c."

- Hold up one finger.

"Write the letter c on the line by #1."

"Let's spell the rest of the word. A … n."

- Hold up two more fingers.

"Write the letters as you say them again."

- Allow time for the student to write *a* and *n*.

"What word did you write?" can

- Repeat the procedure with #2 (kin), #3 (clap), #4 (skin), and #5 (skid).

"Read the sentence by #6 to yourself. If you find a word you can't read, code it."

- Allow time for the student to read the sentence.

"Now read #7 and see if you can answer the question."

- Refer to the sight word charts in the Irregular Spelling Booklet, if necessary.
- As the student works, provide help as needed. Help the student correct any incorrect answers. Then initial the worksheet in the space provided.
- Some time during the day, ask the student to read from the worksheet or homework. Although coding is important, the ultimate goal is reading, so the student, especially if he/she is having difficulty, should read to someone every day.
- **Note:** Always make sure the worksheet is corrected before the student begins the homework. The worksheet serves as a guide to help complete the homework.

Lesson 22

HOMEWORK

"Turn your paper over to the homework side."

"Do you know what to do on the homework paper?"

- Show the student **Sight Word Card 4.**

"This is a new sight word."

"Do you know what this word is?" expect various answers

"This word is 'was.' Can you use 'was' in a sentence?"

" 'Was' will always be a sight word. Look for it in the sentence by #8 and circle it now. If you can't remember the word when you do your homework, ask me."

"We'll add this card to our sight word deck. It is also on the sight word charts in your Irregular Spelling Booklet."

- If desired, help the student find the word in the booklet.

"When you finish your paper, I will check it for you and initial it in the space provided."

- Either now or later in the day, the student should complete the homework independently (if possible). Help the student correct any incorrect answers. Then initial the homework in the space provided.
- Add **Sight Word Card 4** to the Sight Word Deck.

READER

- Give the student **Reader 5 (*Lost at the Pond*)** and some colored pencils.

"We're going to make another book today."

"Can you tell me the name of this book?" *Lost at the Pond*

- Assist the student as necessary as he/she completes the following steps:

"Hold up your page so that the tree is facing you."

"Now put your finger on the top dotted line."

"Carefully fold the paper along this dotted line toward you so that it lines up with the bottom dotted line."

"Now fold the top half of the sheet back along the dotted line."

"Hold your book so the tree is facing you again. Then put your finger on the dotted line down the center of the page."

"Fold the book backward along this dotted line so that the tree will still be facing you when you're finished."

- When the student completes this last step, either put a rubber band around the book's spine or staple the spine.

"Next, carefully separate the pages along the perforated lines at the top and bottom."

- Demonstrate how to separate the pages.

"Let's check the page numbers to see if they are in the correct order."

- Demonstrate how to check that the book's page numbers are in order.

"Tell me again the name of this book." *Lost at the Pond*

"I want you to read your book to yourself. When you are finished reading, color the pictures. Write your name on the book so I will know who colored it."

"Keep your book handy because I will be asking you to read it for me."

- Some time during the day, have the student read the reader to you.
- If possible, take time to play the Kid Card games listed in Lesson 20.

Name ______________________

Teacher's Initials ____

Worksheet 22
(for use with Lesson 22)
Phonics 1

Spelling with k and c

1. can
2. kin
3. clap
4. skin
5. skid

6. The class can plan a skit.
7. Who can plan a skit? the class

P1-WS-022a

Parent's Initials ____

Homework 22
(for use with Lesson 22)
Phonics 1

Spelling with k and c

K is found before e, i, or y.

C is found before a, o, u, or any consonant.

1. c at
2. k it
3. k iss
4. c ost
5. c lip
6. c lass

7. Dot lost the cat.
8. The cat was lost.

Parents: Your child has been taught that when spelling, "k" is found before e, i, or y, and "c" is found before a, o, u or any consonant.

P1-WS-022b

Lesson 22

LESSON 23 — The Letter *B*

lesson preparation

materials

ball

Review Decks

Spelling Sound Sheet 19

tokens or colored pencil

Letter Card 17

Picture Card 21

container of letter tiles

Spelling Card 19

Sight Word Card 5

Worksheet 23

new concepts

paired consonants

the night before

- Add the *b* letter tile to the student's container.

ALPHABET ACTIVITY

- You and the student should be seated on the floor with the ball.

  "Let's say the alphabet while we roll this ball."

  "I'll begin with 'A' and roll the ball to you. After you catch the ball, say 'B' and roll the ball back to me. We'll continue until we complete the alphabet."

- Recite the alphabet as you and the student roll the ball back and forth.
- Have the student return to his/her seat.

PHONEMIC AWARENESS

- **Objective:** To identify syllables in spoken words.

  "We are going to listen for the number of syllables in words. Hold up your fingers to show how many syllables you hear."

  "The first word is 'tab … let.' "

- Emphasize both syllables equally.

"Let's say it and clap it together."

"Ready? Tab … let." tab … let (clap two times, once with each syllable)

"Hold up your fingers to show how many parts this word has." two fingers

"That's right!"

"Let's try a different word. Echo after me and clap the parts."

"Piz … za." piz … za (clap two times)

"How many parts does this word have?" two

"How many syllables are in this word?" two

"Here's another word. Echo and clap the parts."

"Prin … ci … pal." prin … ci … pal (clap three times)

"How many parts does the word have?" three

"How many syllables are in this word?" three

- Repeat with the following words: dog (1), spaghetti (3), popcorn (2), and dollar (2).

Review of Decks

- The student should be seated where he/she can write comfortably.
- Show the student **Letter Cards 1–16** in random order. The student should name the letter on each letter card.
- Review **Affix Card 1.**
- Show the student **Picture Cards 1–20** in random order. The student should name the keyword and sound for each picture card.
- Review **Sight Word Cards 1–4.**
- Give the student **Spelling Sound Sheet 19** and at least twelve tokens (or a colored pencil).

"Today we are going to play Bingo! I am going to call out a spelling sound. Cover (or X out) the letter that spells that sound on your spelling sound sheet."

"When you cover (or X out) all of the letters on one line, either up and down, across, or from corner to corner, call out Bingo!"

- Demonstrate, if necessary.

"Let's begin: /r/."

- Continue, calling out the following sounds: /g/, /ĭ/, /f/, /d/, /z/, /ă/, /s/, /l/, /p/, /t/.
- The student should Bingo by the time all the sounds have been called out.
- Collect the tokens (or colored pencil) and the spelling sound sheet. If you used tokens and the spelling sound sheet is unmarked, keep it available for practice.

New Learning

"I'm going to say some words to you and I want you to echo them back to me. Listen for the sound that is the same in the initial position of each word."

- Point to your mouth as you say each word.

"Echo after me. Beagle." *beagle* ***"Border."*** *border* ***"Bonnet."*** *bonnet*

"What sound do you hear in the initial position?" */b/*

- **Note:** Make sure the student is giving the pure sound of *b* and not pronouncing it with a short *u* sound, as in /bŭh/.

"That's right. The sound you hear in the initial position is /b/."

"Put your fingertips on the front of your neck and say /b/. See if you feel any vibration."

"Is this sound voiced or unvoiced?" *voiced*

"Since /b/ vibrates, it is a voiced sound."

"Say the /p/ sound. Do you notice that the /p/ sound is made just like the /b/ sound, except /b/ is voiced? Let's see if /p/ is voiced."

"Put your fingertips on the front of your neck and say /p/. See if you feel any vibration."

"Is this sound voiced or unvoiced?" *unvoiced*

"P is unvoiced and b is voiced, but our mouths make these two sounds the same exact way. For that reason, p and b are called 'paired consonants.'"

"We have had two other letters that are paired consonants. I'll tell you one of them. See if you can tell me the letter that goes with it."

"Ready? The letter is d, and the sound is /d/, which is voiced."

"What other letter is made the same as d, but is unvoiced?" *t*

- Allow the student to experiment with the sounds.
- Write the following words on the chalkboard: bat, bug, bin, boss.

"What letter do you see that might be making the /b/ sound?" *b*

- If the student does not know the name of the letter, say it for him/her.

"B is the first letter in all of these words, so we can see that b must be the letter used to spell the /b/ sound."

"Is b a vowel or a consonant?" *consonant*

New Deck Cards

- Show the student **Letter Card 17.**

"What letter is this?" *b*

- Hold up **Picture Card 21** but keep the picture covered with your hand (or the letter card).

  "I have a card with a picture on it that begins with the /b/ sound."

  "I am going to describe it for you. See if you can guess what the picture is."

  "This is something that is usually made of leather, plastic, or fabric. Cowboys often have their names tooled in the back of leather ones. They have a metal connector on one end and holes punched in the other end. They are helpful if your pants are too loose. What do you think the picture is?" *belt*

  "That's right. The keyword is 'belt' and the sound we have learned is /b/."

- Show the student **Picture Card 21,** and then point to the picture of a belt on the alphabet strip.

  "The word 'belt' helps us remember the /b/ sound because it begins with /b/."

- Give the student the container of letter tiles.

  "What new letter tile do you think I have given you today?" *b*

  "Find your b letter tile and look at it. One side has a capital B and the other side has a lowercase b."

- Allow time for the student to examine the new letter tile.

  "Hold your letter tile up in the air. Turn it so I can see the capital B."

  "Now turn it so I can see the lowercase b."

  "Use your letter tiles to spell the word 'bat.' "

  "Now change one letter to make the word 'bag.' "

  "Spell the word 'rib' with your letter tiles."

  "Now add one letter to make the word 'crib.' "

- If necessary, refer the student to **Rule Chart 3.**
- Choose additional words from the Spelling Word List, if desired.
- Have the student replace the tiles in the container and put it away.
- Reinforce the name, sound, and shape of the letter *b* throughout the day.
- Hold up **Spelling Card 19** so that only you can see what is written. Follow the instructions on the card. Have the student write the letter with his/her finger on the desktop, or skywrite the letter.
- **Note:** Add the new letter, picture, and spelling cards to the Review Decks.

BOARDWORK

- Write the word "put" on the chalkboard.

  "Do you know this word?"

  "This word is 'put.' It will always be a sight word. Circle this word whenever you see it."

- Show the student **Sight Word Card 5.**

  "Can you use the word 'put' in a sentence?" *expect various answers*

  "We will add this card to our sight word deck."

- If desired, help the student locate the word in the Irregular Spelling Booklet.

  "Let's practice coding some words like the ones you'll have on your worksheet."

  "First, can you say the vowel rules with me?"

- Point to **Rule Chart 1** as the student repeats the vowel rule with you.

  "A vowel followed by a consonant is short; code it with a breve."

- Point to **Rule Chart 2** as the student repeats the second vowel rule with you.

  "An open, accented vowel is long; code it with a macron."

- Write the word "bands" on the chalkboard.

  "Can you code this word?"

- Code the word as the student instructs: bănd[s].

  "What is the word?" *bands*

  "What is the root word?" *band*

- Write the phrase "a brass pot" on the chalkboard.

  "Can you code this phrase?"

  "Do you remember how we code the word 'a' if we want to say /ŭ/?" *with an upside-down e or a circle with a line through it*

- Code the phrase as the student instructs: å brăs𝑠̸ pŏt.

- **Note:** The student may want to box the second *s* in "brass." If so, point out that when a word ends in two *s*'s, the last *s* is not a suffix. Code the *s*'s as twin consonants. (When a root word ends with *s*, the suffix is *-es*. This concept will be taught in a later lesson.)

  "What is the phrase?" *a brass pot*

  "Can you give me a sentence using either the word or the phrase?" *expect various answers*

- Add **Sight Word Card 5** to the Sight Word Deck.

WORKSHEET

- The student should be seated where he/she can write comfortably.

- Give the student **Worksheet 23.** Make sure the student turns to the correct side.

  "Using the rules we just practiced, code the words by #1 through #6."

  "After you have coded these words, blend the sounds in each word and figure out what the words are."

"Beside #7 and #8 are two sentences. Please read the sentences to yourself. If you find any words you can't read, code them. Then fill in the missing word."

- Assist the student as necessary.

"Now let's spell some words."

"Put your finger by #9. The first word is 'bag.' "

"Unblend 'bag' with me: /b/, /ă/, /g/."

- Hold up a finger for each sound.

"Let's spell these sounds. B … a … g."

- Point to one of your fingers each time the student spells a sound.

"Now spell the word again and write the letters as you say them."

- Allow time for the student to do this.

"What word did you write?" *bag*

- Repeat the procedure with #10 (rib), #11 (bat), and #12 (bran).
- As the student works, provide help as needed. Help the student correct any incorrect answers. Then initial the worksheet in the space provided.
- Some time during the day, ask the student to read from the worksheet or homework. Although coding is important, the ultimate goal is reading, so the student, especially if he/she is having difficulty, should read to someone every day.
- **Note:** Always make sure the worksheet is corrected before the student begins the homework. The worksheet serves as a guide to help complete the homework.

HOMEWORK

"Turn your paper over to the homework side."

"Put your finger on the top row of handwriting lines. Write your best capital B on the line so I will know what a capital B should look like."

- Have the student write a lowercase letter *b* on the second handwriting line.
- Make sure that the student has written the letters correctly (to the best of his or her ability). He/She will use them as guides when completing the homework.

"Do you know what to do on the rest of the homework paper?"

- Discuss the homework pictures to make sure the student understands the word each one represents: #9 (bag), #10 (bat), and #11 (lab).

"When you finish your paper, I will check it for you and initial it in the space provided."

- Either now or later in the day, the student should complete the homework independently (if possible). Help the student correct any incorrect answers. Then initial the homework in the space provided.
- If possible, take time to play the Kid Card games listed in Lesson 20.

Name _____

Teacher's Initials _____

Worksheet 23
(for use with Lesson 23)
Phonics 1

Bb

1. bĭt 4. băss
2. fĭb 5. bŏnd
3. crăb 6. blĭss

7. Dad had a big dog.
8. Dad's dog was ___big___ .

9. ___bag___
10. ___rib___
11. ___bat___
12. ___bran___

Parent's Initials _____

Homework 23
(for use with Lesson 23)
Phonics 1

Bb

1. băt 4. bĭg
2. cŏp 5. bŏss
3. bĭll 6. bănd

7. The brass band is big.
8. The ___big___ band is brass.

9.	10.	11.
b a g	b a t	b i b

Parents: Your child has been taught the name, shape, and sound of the letter b.

LESSON 24

The Rule vc′|cv

lesson preparation

materials

container of letter tiles

Review Decks

Spelling Sound Sheet 20

Worksheet 24

Rule Book (see *the night before*)

Reader 6 (*Sass*)

colored pencils

new concepts

syllable division

vc′|cv pattern

the night before

- If desired, remove Syllable Division Chart 1 from the Rule Book, cut the chart in half as shown, and tape the bottom half to the top half. (See the picture on page 169.)

ALPHABET ACTIVITY

- The student should be seated with the container of letter tiles.

  "Today we are going to work with 'before' and 'after' again."

  "I am going to write a letter on the chalkboard and I want you to pull one letter tile out of your container."

- Write the letter *n* on the chalkboard while the student selects a letter tile.

  "If your letter comes after n, stand up."

- The student should stand or remain seated, depending on the letter tile chosen.
- Write the letter *t* on the chalkboard while the student selects a new tile (and if necessary, sits back down).

  "If your letter comes before t, stand up."

- The student should stand or remain seated, depending on the letter tile chosen.
- Continue practicing the concept of "before" and "after," using only those letters that have been taught: *n, o, t, p, i, l, a, z, s, d, f, h, g, r, k, c,* and *b*.
- Have the student replace the tiles in the container and put it away.

PHONEMIC AWARENESS

- **Objective:** To identify syllables in spoken words.

  "We are going to listen for the number of syllables in words."

  "Hold up your fingers to show how many syllables you hear."

  "The first word is 'mag … ic.' "

- Emphasize both syllables equally.

  "Let's say it and clap it together."

  "Ready? Mag … ic." *mag … ic (clap two times, once with each syllable)*

  "Hold up your fingers to show how many parts this word has." *(two fingers)*

  "That's right!"

  "Let's try a different word. Echo after me and clap the parts."

  "Weath … er." *weath … er (clap two times)*

  "How many parts does this word have?" *two*

  "How many syllables are in this word?" *two*

  "Here's another word. Echo and clap the parts."

  "Lim … ou … sine." *lim … ou … sine (clap three times)*

  "How many parts does this word have?" *three*

  "How many syllables are in this word?" *three*

- Repeat with the following words: feet (1), lasagna (3), doodlebug (3), and girl (1).

REVIEW OF DECKS

- The student should be seated where he/she can write comfortably.
- Show the student **Letter Cards 1–17** in random order. The student should name the letter on each letter card.
- Review **Affix Card 1.**
- Show the student **Picture Cards 1–21** in random order. The student should name the keyword and sound for each picture card.
- Review **Sight Word Cards 1–5.**
- Give the student **Spelling Sound Sheet 20.**
- Call out the sounds on **Spelling Cards 1–19** in random order. The student should echo each sound and name the letter or letters that make the sound as he/she writes the letter(s) on the spelling sound sheet.
- Check the student's response after each card.

New Learning

- Write the words "can" and "napkins" on the chalkboard.

"What do these two words have that is alike?" *both have /k/ sound; both have an a and a final n*

"What do these two words have that is different?" *one is longer; one has a k and the other has a c; one has two vowels and the other has one*

- Accept any answer that is factual. Lead the student to the fact that one word contains one vowel and the other word contains two.

"When a word has more than one vowel sound, it has more than one syllable."

"You hear a syllable every time you hear a vowel sound."

"Let's listen for the syllables in some words."

"Echo these words and clap each time you hear a vowel sound."

- Clap once for each syllable (each time you hear a vowel).

"Bandit." *bandit (clap two times)*

"Sunshine." *sunshine (clap two times)*

"Mat." *mat (clap one time)*

"Let's see how many syllables are in the word 'napkins.'" *napkins (clap two times)*

"When a word has more than one vowel sound, we have to divide the vowel sounds. This is called 'syllable division.'"

- Point to the word "napkins."

"Is there a suffix on this word?" *yes, suffix -s*

- Box the *s* and put a voice line through it:

napkin[s]

"Is this s voiced or unvoiced?" *voiced*

"How do we know it's voiced?" *because it follows a voiced consonant*

"Other than the vowels, do we need any special code marks, such as k-backs, voice lines, or twin consonants?" *no*

"Things like k-backs, voice lines, and twin consonants are called 'givens.' They are called givens because we always code them the same way. Once we have coded the givens, we can concentrate on the vowels."

"Which letters in this word are vowels?" *a and i*

"Let's write a 'v' under each vowel."

- Write a small *v* under each vowel:

napkin[s]
 v   v

"When you have two vowels, you need to look between the vowels and see how many consonants are there."

- Use the following hand signals to illustrate the concept. Raise both of your hands and make "*v*'s" with your index and middle fingers. Then bend your wrists so the "*v*'s" point to one another. Move your hands together, drawing back your middle fingers, until your index fingers almost meet.

  "How many consonants come between the two vowels?" *two*

  "Let's write a 'c' under each consonant between the vowels."

- Write a *c* under each consonant between the vowels:

  n a p k i n [s]
  v c c v

- Point to the "vccv" pattern under the word.

  "This word has a 'vccv' pattern. That's short for 'vowel, consonant, consonant, vowel.' "

  "When we have a 'vccv' pattern, we divide the word between the two consonants."

- Draw a line between the two consonants:

  n a p | k i n [s]
  v c | c v

  "The usual place to put the accent is on the first syllable."

- Put an accent on the first syllable:

  n a p′ | k i n [s]
  v c | c v

- Point to the *a*.

  "How do we code this vowel?" *short, with a breve*

  "Why?" *because it is followed by a consonant*

- Code the *a* with a breve:

  n ă p′ | k i n [s]
  v c | c v

- Point to the *i*.

  "How do we code this vowel?" *short, with a breve*

  "Why?" *because it is followed by a consonant*

- Code the *i* with a breve:

  n ă p′ | k ĭ n [s]
  v c | c v

- Cover "kins" with your hand or a piece of paper.

  "Let's read the first syllable." *nap*

- Cover "nap."

  "Let's read the second syllable." *kins*

  "Now, let's put the two syllables together." *napkins*

  "Now say it with the accent on the first syllable." *nap′ kins*

  "Can you tell me what a napkin is?" *expect various answers*

- Leave the coded word on the chalkboard.

"I have a chart to help you through the job of dividing words."

- If you removed **Syllable Division Chart 1** and taped the two parts together, get out the chart. (It should look like the picture to the right.) If you did not detach the chart, have the student get out the Rule Book and turn to page 16.
- Briefly explain the steps on the chart. (They follow the steps used in the lesson.)
- **Note:** Hanging the chart on the wall may make it easier for the student to refer to it. Regardless of whether or not you choose to do this, the student should always be allowed to refer to this or any other coding chart.

"Dividing big words makes them a lot easier to read."

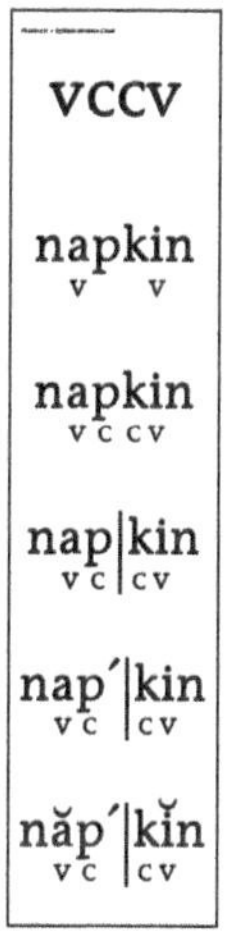

WORKSHEET

- The student should be seated where he/she can write comfortably.
- Give the student **Worksheet 24.** Make sure the student turns to the correct side.

"Let's see if you can code the first word on your worksheet."

- Observe the student as he/she attempts to code the word.
- If the student seems to understand the syllable division process, ask him/her to code #2 and #3 independently.
- If the student is having difficulty, code #2 (plastic) with him/her on the chalkboard.

"Now I want you to read the words you coded and draw a line from one of the words to the picture it matches."

- Assist the student as necessary.

"Let's try spelling a few words."

"Put your finger by #4. Write the word 'kit.' "

- Have the student refer to **Rule Chart 3,** if necessary.
- If necessary, sound the words out slowly.
- Repeat with #5 (can) and #6 (raft).

"Now read the words you wrote and draw a line from one of the words to the picture it matches."

- As the student works, provide help as needed. Help the student correct any incorrect answers. Then initial the worksheet in the space provided.
- Some time during the day, ask the student to read from the worksheet or homework. Although coding is important, the ultimate goal is reading, so the student, especially if he/she is having difficulty blending, should read to someone every day.
- **Note:** Always make sure the worksheet is corrected before the student begins the homework. The worksheet serves as a guide to help complete the homework.

HOMEWORK

"Turn your paper over to the homework side."

"(Tonight) you can teach (someone at home) how to divide a 'vccv' word. You will be the teacher."

"Do you know what to do on the homework paper?"

- If necessary, discuss the homework picture (rabbit).

"When you finish your paper, I will check it for you and initial it in the space provided."

- Either now or later in the day, the student should complete the homework independently (if possible). Help the student correct any incorrect answers. Then initial the homework in the space provided.

READER

- Give the student **Reader 6 (*Sass*)** and some colored pencils.

"We're going to make another book today."

"What is this book's title?" *Sass*

- Assist the student as necessary as he/she completes the following steps:

"Hold up your page so that the tree is facing you."

"Now put your finger on the top dotted line."

"Carefully fold the paper along this dotted line toward you so that it lines up with the bottom dotted line."

"Now fold the top half of the sheet back along the dotted line."

"Hold your book so the tree is facing you again. Then put your finger on the dotted line down the center of the page."

"Fold the book backward along this dotted line so that the tree will still be facing you when you're finished."

- When the student completes this last step, either put a rubber band around the book's spine or staple the spine.

"Next, carefully separate the pages along the perforated lines at the top and bottom."

- Demonstrate how to separate the pages.

"Let's check the page numbers to see if they are in the correct order."

- Demonstrate how to check that the book's page numbers are in order.

"The title of the book is __________?" *Sass*

"In this story, watch for words that end with apostrophe s. Remember that apostrophe s shows ownership."

"I want you to read your book to yourself. When you are finished reading, color the pictures. Write your name on the book so I will know who colored it."

"Keep your book handy because I will be asking you to read it for me."

- Some time during the day, have the student read the reader to you.
- If possible, take time to play the Kid Card games listed in Lesson 20. Try to see that the student is prepared for tomorrow's assessment.

Name ____________________

Teacher's Initials ____

Worksheet 24
(for use with Lesson 24)
Phonics 1

vć|cv

1. năp|kĭn
   v c c v
2. plăs|tĭc
   v c c v
3. pĭc|nĭc
   v c c v

4. ____ kit ____
5. ____ can ____
6. ____ raft ____

P1-WS-024a

Parent's Initials ____

Homework 24
(for use with Lesson 24)
Phonics 1

vć|cv

1. răb|bĭt
   v c c v
2. cŏn|tăct
   v c c v
3. gŏs|sĭp
   v c c v

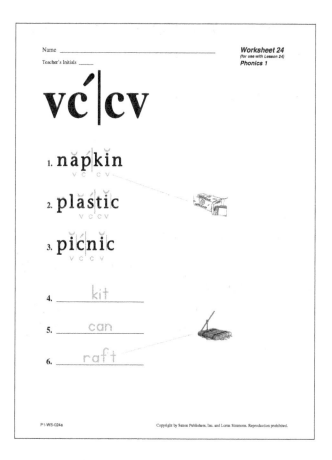

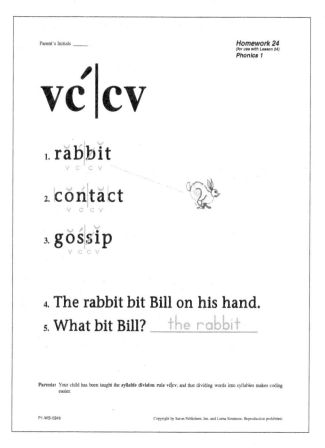

4. The rabbit bit Bill on his hand.
5. What bit Bill? ____ the rabbit ____

Parents: Your child has been taught the **syllable division rule** vć|cv; and that dividing words into syllables makes coding easier.

P1-WS-024b

Lesson 25 — Assessment

lesson preparation

materials

Review Decks

Assessment 4

Spelling Test 2

Assessment 4 Recording Form

Kid Cards

tokens

the night before

- Separate the Kid Cards marked "Lesson 25."

Alphabet Activity

- The student should be seated.

  "Today I want to see if you can say the alphabet from beginning to end."

- Allow the student to recite as much of the alphabet as possible; if necessary, help the student complete it.
- If the student needs extra motivation, give him/her a token (cereal, poker chip, small candy, etc.) for each letter.

Phonemic Awareness

- **Objective:** To identify syllables in spoken words.

  "Let's make a game of listening to the number of syllables in words."

  "I'll say some words. I want you to hold up your fingers to show how many syllables you hear. If you're right, I'll give you a point."

- Use the following words (in this order): powder (2), fantastic (3), relative (3), respect (2), investigate (4), temper (2), silver (2), January (4), September (3), remember (3), scoot (1), restful (2), shortly (2), bring (1).
- Help the student count the number of points "won."

Review of Decks

"As we review the letter deck today, I want you to say the name of the letter, and then tell me the keyword and sound of the letter."

- Show the student **Letter Cards 1–17** in random order.
- Make sure the student says the name of the letter, then the keyword and sound. For example:

The correct response to Letter Card 9 (*s*) would be:

"*S*, sock, /s/; rose, /z/."

The correct response to Letter Card 7 (*a*) would be:

"*A*, apple, /ă/; acorn, /ā/."

Written Assessment

"Today we are going to have an assessment to see if I'm doing a good job of teaching you to read."

- Give the student **Assessment 4.**
- **Section I:**

"Today we're going to write some words for our assessment."

"I'm going to say a word. Write the letter that makes each sound in that word on the lines by #1."

"Here's the first word: hot."

- If the student cannot hear the individual sounds in the word, give each sound, one at a time: /h/, /ŏ/, /t/.
- Repeat with the following words in the order shown: #2 (gas), #3 (rip), #4 (plop), and #5 (snap).
- **Note:** While the student spells words on assessments, be ready to point to appropriate rule charts as necessary to help the student spell the words.
- **Section II:**

"Look at the letter by #6."

"Find the picture of the keyword for this sound."

"Draw a line from the letter to the keyword."

- Repeat with #7, #8, and #9. Allow a few minutes for the student to work.
- The pictures (from top to bottom) are as follows: rabbit, kite, hair, goggles.
- **Section III:**

"Put your finger on #10."

"Code the words by #10 through #13."

- Allow a few minutes for the student to work.

- **Section IV:**

  "Look at the blend by #14. What sound does this blend make?" *tr*
- Repeat with #15, #16, and #17.
- Point to the first picture (drum) and help the student identify it. Ask the student to name the blend the picture begins with and then to draw a line from the picture to the blend.
- Repeat with each picture. The pictures (from top to bottom) are as follows: drum, tree, pretzel, frog.

  "When you are finished, show your paper to me."
- This paper will be used during the oral portion of the assessment.

Spelling Test

- Give the student **Spelling Test 2.**
- Call out the following words (in the order shown). Sound them out, if necessary.

  #1 (at), #2 (tap), #3 (pat), #4 (lot), #5 (lip), #6 (zip), #7 (nap), #8 (pit), #9 (tan), #10 (lap)
- Grade and record the paper in any manner that suits your needs.

Oral Assessment

- Oral assessments are short interviews that occur during independent work time. It is important to complete them promptly (today, if possible) in order to identify any areas of weakness and begin remediation.
- Use the assessment and the following dialogue to complete the oral portion.
- **Section V:**
- Show the student the word by #18.

  "Read this word for me."
- Write the student's response on the adjacent line.
- Repeat with #19, #20, and #21.
- **Section VI:**

  "I'm going to say some words. Tell me the sound you hear in the initial position."
- Point to your mouth and say the following words: rug, reef, roam.
- Write the student's response on the line by #22. (If the student responds with the letter name, ask again for the *sound.*)
- Repeat with #23 (goat, gate, gum); #24 (kite, keg, kiss); and #25 (hair, hip, host).

- **Section VII:**
- Show the student the letter by #26.

  "Tell me the name of this letter and the sound it makes."
- Write the student's response on the adjacent line.
- Repeat with #27, #28, and #29.

ASSESSMENT EVALUATION

- Grade the assessment and record the results on **Assessment 4 Recording Form.** Check off the boxes to indicate mastery (i.e., the section was completed with 100% accuracy).
- **Note:** If you choose to grade the assessments, try to give as many points as possible for work attempted. Do not grade the coding marks too severely, especially secondary marks like accents, voice lines, and k-backs. The most important coding marks to look for are breves, macrons, and syllable division lines.
- See the introductory material for detailed information regarding grading and recording procedures.
- Use the assessment results to identify those skills in which the student is weak. Practice those skills by playing Kid Card games.
- Add the Kid Cards marked "Lesson 25" to the existing decks. Listed below are games appropriate for remediation in selected areas. See "Games and Activities" for the directions for each game.
- **Section I:** Play "Spelling Deck Perfection" or "Sound Scamper," or have the student use the letter tiles to spell words you give from the Spelling Word List.
- **Section II:** Play "Keyword and Sound" or "Letter/Sound Identification."
- **Section III:** Play "Chalkboard Challenge."
- **Section IV:** Play "Blend It."
- **Section V:** Play "Word Blend" (with blue Kid Cards).
- **Section VI:** Play "Sound Solutions."
- **Section VII:** Play "Letter Deck Data" or "Letter/Sound Identification."
- When the student seems more secure in areas that had previously proven difficult, retest him/her (in those areas only) and indicate on the recording form any sections the student has subsequently mastered.
- Try to help the student achieve mastery of all the sections before the next assessment.
- If the student is having difficulty with a particular skill, keep his or her practice activities at the most basic level so the chance of success is greater.

Lesson 25

Name ______________________

Assessment 4
(for use with Lesson 25)
Phonics 1

Section I

1. h o t
2. g a s
3. r i p
4. p l o p
5. s n a p

Section II

6. k
7. r
8. g
9. h

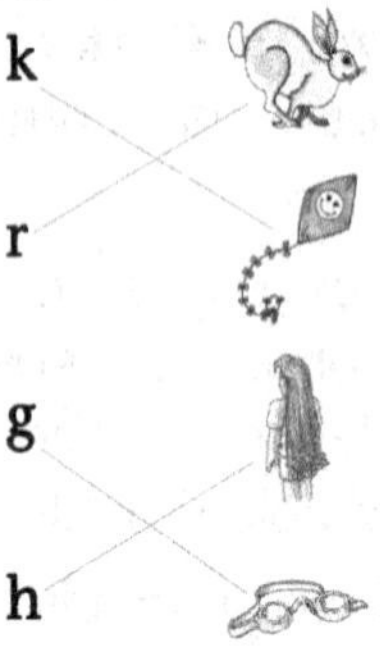

Section III

10. kĭt
11. răg
12. gṓ
13. stŏp

Section IV

14. tr
15. pr
16. dr
17. fr

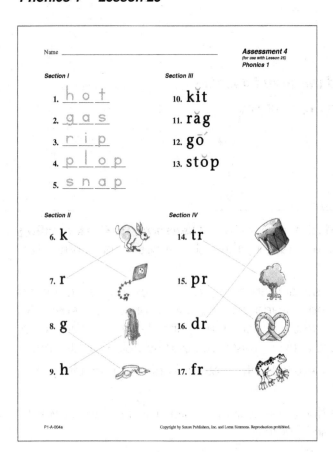

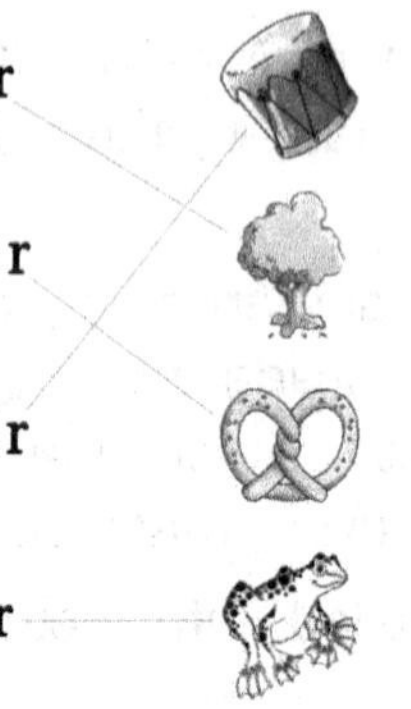

P1-A-004a

Assessment 4
(for use with Lesson 25)
Phonics 1

Section V

18. kĭt ________
19. răg ________
20. gṓ ________
21. stŏp ________

Section VI

22. /r/
23. /g/
24. /k/
25. /h/

Section VII

26. r ________ r, /r/
27. k ________ k, /k/
28. g ________ g, /g/
29. h ________ h, /h/

P1-A-004b

LESSON 26 — The Letter *M*

lesson preparation

materials	***new concepts***
Review Decks	rhyming words
Spelling Sound Sheet 21	
container of letter tiles	
Letter Card 18	
Picture Card 22	
Spelling Card 20	
Worksheet 26	
Spelling List 3	

the night before

- Add the *m* letter tile to the student's container.

ALPHABET ACTIVITY

- The student should be seated with the alphabet strip.

  "How many letters are in the alphabet?" *26*

  "What two kinds of letters make up our alphabet?" *vowels and consonants*

  "Name the vowels." *a, e, i, o, and u*

  "All of the other letters are called _________?" *consonants*

  "Let's point to each letter and say the whole alphabet."

  "The initial letter of the alphabet is _____?" *a*

  "The final letter of the alphabet is _____?" *z*

  "Can you tell me a medial letter of the alphabet?" *any letter b–y*

PHONEMIC AWARENESS

- **Objective:** To identify rhyming sounds in spoken words.

  "When words end with the same vowel and the same consonants after the vowel, they rhyme, like the words 'hat,' 'mat,' and 'pat.' "

- Write "hat," "mat," and "pat" on the chalkboard.

"Notice how all of these words end with 'at.' That's what makes them rhyming words."

"Can you think of some more words that rhyme with these words?"

- Accept any rhyming word. Let the student determine (with your help) if the words are real. If the student cannot think of any, use the following words to give him/her a start: cat, sat, bat, gnat, flat, scat, slat.

"Let's try another word. How about 'top'?"

- Examples of rhyming words: hop, mop, slop, crop, drop, shop, plop.

"Let's try one more. Sock."

- Examples of rhyming words: lock, rock, hock, stock, shock, smock, dock, mock, crock.

"Good job! We'll try some more rhymes tomorrow."

REVIEW OF DECKS

- The student should be seated where he/she can write comfortably.
- Show the student **Letter Cards 1–17** in random order. The student should name the letter on each letter card.
- Review **Affix Card 1.**
- Show the student **Picture Cards 1–21** in random order. The student should name the keyword and sound for each picture card.
- Review **Sight Word Cards 1–5.**
- Give the student **Spelling Sound Sheet 21.**
- Call out the sounds on **Spelling Cards 1–19** in random order. The student should echo each sound and name the letter or letters that make the sound as he/she writes the letter(s) on the spelling sound sheet.
- Check the student's response after each card.
- Have the student set the spelling sound sheet aside for use later in the lesson.

NEW LEARNING

"I'm going to say some words to you and I want you to echo them back to me. Listen for the sound that is the same in the initial position of each word."

- Point to your mouth as you say each word.

"Echo after me. Monkey." *monkey* ***"Mystery."*** *mystery* ***"Mouse."*** *mouse*

"What sound do you hear in the initial position?" */m/*

- **Note:** Make sure the student is giving the pure sound of *m* and not pronouncing it with a short *u* sound, as in /mŭh/.

"That's right. The sound you hear in the initial position is /m/."

"Put your fingertips on the front of your neck and say /m/. See if you feel any vibration."

"Is this sound voiced or unvoiced?" *voiced*

"Since /m/ vibrates, it is a voiced sound."

- Write the following words on the chalkboard: mat, miss, mend.

"What letter do you see that might be making the /m/ sound?" *m*

- If the student does not know the name of the letter, say it for him/her.

"M is the first letter in all of these words, so we can see that m must be the letter used to spell the /m/ sound."

"Is m a vowel or a consonant?" *consonant*

HANDWRITING/LETTER TILES

- The student should be seated where he/she can write comfortably.
- Write a capital *M* on the chalkboard.

"This is a capital M. Let's practice skywriting capital M's before we write them on our paper."

- Have the student practice skywriting capital *M*'s.

"Find your spelling sound sheet."

- Draw handwriting lines on the chalkboard.
- Write a capital *M* on the handwriting lines in the handwriting you want the student to learn.

"Find the first line on your paper and practice writing capital M's like I wrote this one on the chalkboard."

"Say the name of the letter each time you write it."

- Allow a few minutes for the student to practice writing capital *M*'s.
- Write a lowercase *m* on the handwriting lines in the handwriting you want the student to learn.

"This is a lowercase m."

- Have the student practice skywriting lowercase *m*'s.

"Now practice writing lowercase m's on the second handwriting line. Say the name of the letter each time you write it."

- Have the student set the spelling sound sheet aside for use later in the lesson.
- Leave the handwriting lines and letters on the chalkboard for the remainder of the lesson.
- Give the student the container of letter tiles.

"Today I've given you another new letter tile."

"Find your m letter tile and look at it. One side has a capital M and the other side has a lowercase m."

- Allow time for the student to examine the new letter tile.

"Hold your letter tile up in the air. Turn it so I can see the capital M."

"Now turn it so I can see the lowercase m."

"Spell the word 'mop' with your letter tiles."

"This time, spell the word 'man.' "

"Now change one letter to make the word 'can.' "

- Watch to see if the student refers to **Rule Chart 3.** Do not refer to the chart directly unless necessary.
- Choose additional words from the Spelling Word List, if desired.
- Have the student replace the tiles in the container and put it away.
- Reinforce the name, sound, and shape of the letter *m* throughout the day.

NEW DECK CARDS

- Show the student **Letter Card 18.**

"What letter is this?" *m*

- Hold up **Picture Card 22** but keep the picture covered with your hand (or the letter card).

"I have a card with a picture on it that begins with the /m/ sound."

"I am going to describe it for you. See if you can guess what the picture is."

"This is something that a person wears on his or her face. A child wears it to pretend he or she is someone else. There are lots of them in the stores the week before October 31st. What do you think the picture is?" *mask*

"That's right. The keyword is 'mask' and the sound we have learned is /m/."

- Show the student **Picture Card 22,** and then point to the picture of a mask on the alphabet strip.

"The word 'mask' helps us remember the /m/ sound because it begins with /m/."

"Find your spelling sound sheet. Find #20 and put your finger on it."

- Hold up **Spelling Card 20** so only you can see what is written. Using the hand signals, follow the instructions on the card.
- Check the spelling sound sheet for accuracy.
- **Note:** Add the new letter, picture, and spelling cards to the Review Decks.

Boardwork

"Let's practice coding some words like the ones you'll have on your worksheet."

- Write the word "class" on the chalkboard.

"Can you help me code this word?"

- Refer to the rule charts, if necessary.
- Code the word as the student instructs: clăss.
- **Note:** The student may want to box the second *s* in "class." If so, point out that when words end in two *s*'s, the last *s* is not a suffix. Code the *s*'s as twin consonants. (When a root word ends with *s*, the suffix is *-es*. This concept will be taught in a later lesson.)

"What is the word?" class

"Can you give me a sentence using the word 'class'?" expect various answers

- Write the following sentence on the chalkboard: Put on the tan mask.

"Can you help me code this sentence?"

- Code the sentence as the student instructs: (Put) ŏn (the) tăn măsk.

"What is the sentence?" Put on the tan mask.

Worksheet

- The student should be seated where he/she can write comfortably.
- Give the student **Worksheet 26.** Make sure the student turns to the correct side.

"Let's start with our spelling today."

"Put your finger by #1. The first word is 'slim.' "

"Unblend 'slim' with me." /s/ /l/ /ĭ/ /m/

- Hold up one finger for each sound.

"Let's spell those sounds." s ... l ... i ... m

- Point to one of your fingers each time the student spells a sound.

"Now spell the word again and write the letters as you say them."

- Allow time for the student to do this.

"What word did you write?" slim

- Repeat the procedure with #2 (tram), #3 (fad), and #4 (smog).

"You are ready to code and read the words on your paper."

"Find #5 on your paper. Using the rules we just practiced on the chalkboard, code the words by #5 through #8. After you have coded these words, blend the sounds in each word and figure out what each word is."

- Assist the student as necessary.

"At the bottom of the page are four sentences. Two of the sentences have missing words. If you find any words you can't read, code them. Don't forget to circle the sight words. Then see if you can fill in the missing words."

- As the student works, provide help as needed. Help the student correct any incorrect answers. Then initial the worksheet in the space provided.
- Some time during the day, ask the student to read from the worksheet or homework. Although coding is important, the ultimate goal is reading, so the student, especially if he/she is having difficulty blending, should read to someone every day.
- **Note:** Always make sure the worksheet is corrected before the student begins the homework. The worksheet serves as a guide to help complete the homework.

HOMEWORK

"Turn your paper over to the homework side."

"Put your finger on the top row of handwriting lines. Write your best capital M on the line so I will know what a capital M should look like."

- Have the student write a lowercase letter *m* on the second handwriting line.
- Make sure that the student has written the letters correctly (to the best of his or her ability). He/She will use them as guides when completing the homework.

"Do you know what to do on the rest of the homework paper?"

"When you finish your paper, I will check it for you and initial it in the space provided."

- Either now or later in the day, the student should complete the homework independently (if possible). Help the student correct any incorrect answers. Then initial the homework in the space provided.

SPELLING LIST

- Fold **Spelling List 3** in half lengthwise (with the printed side facing out).

"Leave your paper just like I give it to you."

- Give the student **Spelling List 3,** folded with the blank lines facing up.

"Let's spell some more words. You can spell these words without seeing them first because you know the rules for spelling them."

- Call out the following words (in the order shown). Sound them out, if necessary.

  #1 (so), #2 (is), #3 (as), #4 (sit), #5 (did), #6 (sad), #7 (fan), #8 (fit), #9 (if), #10 (sat)

"Now unfold your paper and check your words."

- Check the student's work to see if he/she needs extra help with spelling.

"I want you to practice these words. We'll have a spelling test in a few days."

- If possible, take time to play the Kid Card games listed in Lesson 25.

Name ____________________

Teacher's Initials ____

Worksheet 26
(for use with Lesson 26)
Phonics 1

Mm

1. slim
2. tram
3. fad
4. smog
5. mŏb
6. mŏss
7. stŏmp
8. ĭmpăct

9. Tom put the pin in the hat.
10. The hat has a pin in it.

11. Pam's bib is on the doll.
12. The doll has Pam's bib.

P1-WS-026a

Parent's Initials ____

Homework 26
(for use with Lesson 26)
Phonics 1

Mm

1. măd
2. mŏp
3. mĭtt
4. ăm
5. mĭst
6. năpkĭn

9. Tom has a fat cat.
10. Tom's cat is fat.

11. I put Tim's napkin on his lap.
12. Tim's napkin is on his lap.

Parents: Your child has been taught the name, shape, and sound of the letter **m**; and that rhyming words end with the same vowel and consonants.

P1-WS-026b

Lesson 26

LESSON 27 — The Letter *E*

lesson preparation

materials

Review Decks

Spelling Sound Sheet 22

container of letter tiles

Letter Card 19

Picture Cards 23–24

Spelling Cards 21–22

Worksheet 27

Reader 7 (*Mom*)

colored pencils

the night before

- Add the *e* letter tile to the student's container.

ALPHABET ACTIVITY

"Let's skip in place today as we say the alphabet. Stand up."

- Skipping in place is not easy! If the student has difficulty, march or hop in place instead.
- Have the student return to his/her seat.

PHONEMIC AWARENESS

- **Objective:** To identify rhyming sounds in spoken words.

"Let's work again with rhyming words."

- Write "lip" on the chalkboard.

"Can you think of some words that rhyme with 'lip'?"

- Accept any rhyming word. Let the student determine (with your help) if the words are real. If the student cannot think of any, use the following words to give him/her a start: sip, nip, hip, slip, snip, skip, grip, trip, flip, ship, dip, tip, drip.

"Let's try another word."

- Write "sand" on the chalkboard.

  "Can you think of some words that rhyme with 'sand'?"

- Examples of rhyming words: hand, band, land, grand, stand, bland.

REVIEW OF DECKS

- The student should be seated where he/she can write comfortably.
- Show the student **Letter Cards 1–18** in random order. The student should name the letter on each letter card.
- Review **Affix Card 1.**
- Show the student **Picture Cards 1–22** in random order. The student should name the keyword and sound for each picture card.
- Review **Sight Word Cards 1–5.**
- Give the student **Spelling Sound Sheet 22.**
- Call out the sounds on **Spelling Cards 1–20** in random order. The student should echo each sound and name the letter or letters that make the sound as he/she writes the letter(s) on the spelling sound sheet.
- Check the student's response after each card.
- Have the student set the spelling sound sheet aside for use later in the lesson.

NEW LEARNING

"I'm going to say some words to you and I want you to echo them back to me. Listen for the sound that is the same in the initial position of each word."

- Point to your mouth as you say each word.

  "Echo after me. Elf." *elf* ***"Estimate."*** *estimate* ***"Effort."*** *effort*

  "What sound do you hear in the initial position?" */ĕ/*

  "That's right. The sound you hear in the initial position is /ĕ/."

  "Put your fingertips on the front of your neck and say /ĕ/. See if you feel any vibration. Is this sound voiced or unvoiced?" *voiced*

  "Since /ĕ/ vibrates, it is a voiced sound."

- Write the following words on the chalkboard: elf, estimate, effort.

  "What do you see that might be making the /ĕ/ sound?" *e*

- If the student does not know the name of the letter, say it for him/her.

  "E is the first letter in all of these words, so we can see that e must be the letter used to spell the /ĕ/ sound. Is e a vowel or a consonant?" *a vowel*

HANDWRITING/LETTER TILES

- The student should be seated where he/she can write comfortably.
- Write a capital *E* on the chalkboard.

  "This is a capital E. Let's practice skywriting capital E's before we write them on our paper."
- Have the student practice skywriting capital *E*'s.

  "Find your spelling sound sheet."
- Draw handwriting lines on the chalkboard. Write a capital *E* on the handwriting lines in the handwriting you want the student to learn.

  "Find the first handwriting line on your paper and practice writing capital E's like I wrote this one on the chalkboard. Say the name of the letter each time you write it."
- Allow a few minutes for the student to practice writing capital *E*'s.
- Write a lowercase *e* on the handwriting lines in the handwriting you want the student to learn.

  "This is a lowercase e."
- Have the student practice skywriting lowercase *e*'s.

  "Now practice writing lowercase e's on the second handwriting line. Say the name of the letter each time you write it."
- Have the student set the spelling sound sheet aside for use later in the lesson.
- Leave the handwriting lines and letters on the chalkboard for the remainder of the lesson.
- Give the student the container of letter tiles.

  "What new letter tile do you think is in your container today?" *e*

  "Find your e letter tile and look at it. One side has a capital E and the other side has a lowercase e."
- Allow time for the student to examine the new letter tile.

  "Hold your letter tile up in the air. Turn it so I can see the capital E."

  "Now turn it so I can see the lowercase e."

  "Use your letter tiles to spell the word 'elm.' "

  "Now spell the word 'end.' "

  "Add one letter to spell the word 'bend.' "

  "Now change one letter tile to make the word 'tend.' "
- Choose additional words from the Spelling Word List, if desired.
- Have the student replace the tiles in the container and put it away.
- Reinforce the name, sound, and shape of the letter *e* throughout the day.

Lesson 27

New Deck Cards

- Show the student **Letter Card 19.**

  "What is the name of this letter?" e

- Hold up **Picture Card 23** but keep the picture covered with your hand (or the letter card).

  "I have a card with a picture on it that begins with the /ĕ/ sound."

  "I am going to describe it for you. See if you can guess what the picture is."

  "You would find these in a refrigerator. They are usually white, but around Easter you will see them in all colors. They are good to eat, especially with bacon and toast. What do you think the picture is?" egg

  "That's right. The keyword is 'egg' and the sound we have learned is /ĕ/."

- Show the student **Picture Card 23,** and then point to the picture of an egg on the alphabet strip.

  "The word 'egg' helps us remember the /ĕ/ sound because it begins with /ĕ/."

  "Today is a special day because we get to have another riddle. Why would we have another riddle?" e is a vowel and vowels have at least two sounds

- Hold up **Picture Card 24** but keep the picture covered with your hand (or the letter card).

  "I have a card with a picture on it that begins with the long /ē/ sound. See if you can guess what the picture is."

  "This is something you might see on a math paper. It is two straight lines that come right before the answer. What do you think the picture is?" equal

  "That's right. The keyword is 'equal' and the sound we have learned is /ē/."

- Show the student **Picture Card 24.**

  "The word 'equal' helps us remember the /ē/ sound because it begins with /ē/."

  "We will keep these cards together in our review deck to help us remember that the letter e can make two sounds."

  "Find your spelling sound sheet. Find #21 and put your finger on it."

- Hold up **Spelling Cards 21** and **22** so only you can see what is written. Using the hand signals, follow the instructions on the cards.
- Check the spelling sound sheet for accuracy.
- **Note:** Add the new letter, picture, and spelling cards to the Review Decks. Always keep **Picture Card 24** behind **Picture Card 23** to help the student remember that the letter *e* has two sounds.

Boardwork

"Let's practice coding some words like the ones you'll have on your worksheet."

- Review the rule charts, if necessary.
- Write the word "bell" on the chalkboard.

"Can you help me code this word?"

- Code the word as the student instructs: bĕl/.

"What is the word?" *bell*

"Can you give me a sentence with the word 'bell' in it?" *expect various answers*

- Write the following sentence on the chalkboard: The milk smells bad!

"Can you help me code this sentence?"

- Code the sentence as the student instructs: (The) mĭlk smĕl/s̶ băd!
- **Note:** If the student wants to box the *s* in "smells," remind him/her that the suffix -*s* means "more than one." Try to help the student understand that in this sentence, "smells" does not indicate more than one. (If you think that the student will understand subject-verb agreement, feel free to teach it. For our purposes, however, only the plural *s* will be coded.)

"Did you notice that this sentence ends with an exclamation point?"

"What is this sentence?" *The milk smells bad!*

Worksheet

- The student should be seated where he/she can write comfortably.
- Give the student **Worksheet 27.** Make sure the student turns to the correct side.

"Let's spell today with the /ĕ/ sound."

"Put your finger by #1. The first word is 'rest.' "

"Unblend 'rest' with me." */r/ /ĕ/ /s/ /t/*

- Hold up one finger for each sound.

"Let's spell those sounds." *r … e … s … t*

- Point to one of your fingers each time the student spells a sound.

"Now spell the word again and write the letters as you say them."

- Allow time for the student to do this.

"What word did you write?" *rest*

- Repeat the procedure with #2 (left), #3 (melt), #4 (crept), and #5 (best).

"Now you're ready to code and read the words on your paper."

"Find the #6 on your paper. Using the rules we just practiced on the chalkboard, code the words by #6 through #10. After you have coded these words, blend the sounds in each word and figure out what each word is."

- Assist the student as necessary.

  "At the bottom of the page are four sentences. Two of the sentences have missing words. If you find any words you can't read, code them. Don't forget to circle the sight words. Then see if you can fill in the missing words."

- As the student works, provide help as needed. Help the student correct any incorrect answers. Then initial the worksheet in the space provided.
- Some time during the day, ask the student to read from the worksheet or homework. Although coding is important, the ultimate goal is reading, so the student, especially if he/she is having difficulty blending, should read to someone every day.
- **Note:** Always make sure the worksheet is corrected before the student begins the homework. The worksheet serves as a guide to help complete the homework.

HOMEWORK

"Turn your paper over to the homework side."

"Put your finger on the top row of handwriting lines. Write your best capital E on the line so I will know what a capital E should look like."

- Have the student write a lowercase letter *e* on the second handwriting line. Make sure that the student has written the letters correctly (to the best of his or her ability). He/She will use them as guides when completing the homework.

  "Do you know what to do on the rest of the homework paper?"

  "When you finish your paper, I will check it for you and initial it in the space provided."

- Either now or later in the day, the student should complete the homework independently (if possible). Help the student correct any incorrect answers. Then initial the homework in the space provided.

READER

- Give the student **Reader 7 (*Mom*)** and some colored pencils.

  "We're going to make another book today."

  "What is this book's title?" Mom

- Assist the student as necessary as he/she completes the following steps:

  "Hold up your page so that the tree is facing you."

  "Now put your finger on the top dotted line."

  "Carefully fold the paper along this dotted line toward you so that it lines up with the bottom dotted line."

  "Now fold the top half of the sheet back along the dotted line."

  "Hold your book so the tree is facing you again. Then put your finger on the dotted line down the center of the page."

Lesson 27

"Fold the book backward along this dotted line so that the tree will still be facing you when you're finished."

- When the student completes this last step, either put a rubber band around the book's spine or staple the spine.

  "Next, carefully separate the pages along the perforated lines at the top and bottom."

- Demonstrate how to separate the pages.

  "Let's check the page numbers to see if they are in the correct order."

- Demonstrate how to check that the book's page numbers are in order.

  "The title of the book is _________?" *Mom*

  "In this story, watch for words that end with apostrophe s. Apostrophe s shows ownership."

  "Turn to the last page of your book where it says 'The End.' What do you think about the word 'end'? Is it a sight word now?" *no, now we know the short e sound*

  "I want you to read your book to yourself. When you are finished reading, color the pictures. Write your name on the book so I will know who colored it."

  "Keep your book handy because I will be asking you to read it for me."

- Some time during the day, have the student read the reader to you.
- If possible, take time to play the Kid Card games listed in Lesson 25.

Name ______________________

Teacher's Initials ____

Worksheet 27
(for use with Lesson 27)
Phonics 1

Ee

1. rest
2. left
3. melt
4. crept
5. best
6. bĕlt
7. fĕd
8. rĕnt
9. smĕll
10. ĕlms

11. Ted has a red spot on his belt.
12. The spot is red.
13. Fred, go get the mess off the desk.
14. The desk is a mess.

P1-WS-027a

Parent's Initials ____

Homework 27
(for use with Lesson 27)
Phonics 1

Ee

1. rĕd
2. tĕll
3. dĕsk
4. mĕss
5. sĕnt
6. drĕss
7. rĕst
8. pĕsts

11. The red sled has a dent in it.
12. The sled has a dent.
13. Ted sat on the bed and the pins fell off.
14. The pins fell off the bed.

Parents: Your child has been taught the name, shape, and short and long sounds of the letter e.

P1-WS-027b

LESSON 28 — Digraph *ck*

lesson preparation

materials

ball

Review Decks

container of letter tiles

Letter Card 20

lock in a sack (see *the night before*)

Picture Card 25

Worksheet 28

new concepts

digraph

the night before

- Put a lock in a sack for the student to use to "discover" the new keyword. If a lock is unavailable, use the riddle provided in the lesson script.

ALPHABET ACTIVITY

- You and the student should be seated on the floor with the ball.

  "How many letters are in the alphabet?" *26*

  "What two kinds of letters make up our alphabet?" *vowels and consonants*

  "Name the vowels." *a, e, i, o, and u*

  "All of the other letters are called _________?" *consonants*

  "The initial letter of the alphabet is _____?" *a*

  "The final letter of the alphabet is _____?" *z*

  "Let's say the alphabet while we roll this ball back and forth."

  "I'll begin with 'A' and roll the ball to you. After you catch the ball, say 'B' and roll the ball back to me. We'll continue until we complete the alphabet."

- Say the alphabet as you and the student roll the ball back and forth.
- Have the student return to his/her seat.

Phonemic Awareness

- **Objective:** To identify rhyming sounds in spoken words.

  "Let's work with rhyming words again."
- Write "pan" on the chalkboard.

  "Can you think of any words that rhyme with 'pan'?"
- Accept any rhyming word. Let the student determine (with your help) if the words are real. If the student cannot think of any, use the following words to give him/her a start: tan, fan, man, ran, ban, can, van.

  "Let's try another word."
- Write "fill" on the chalkboard.

  "Can you think of any words that rhyme with 'fill'?"
- Examples of rhyming words: bill, dill, gill, hill, mill, sill, will.

  "Let's try another word."
- Write "boss" on the chalkboard.

  "Can you think of any words that rhyme with 'boss'?"
- Examples of rhyming words: loss, moss, toss, gloss, floss, cross.

Review of Decks

- The student should be seated where he/she can write comfortably.
- Show the student **Letter Cards 1–19** in random order. The student should name the letter on each letter card.
- Review **Affix Card 1.**
- Show the student **Picture Cards 1–24** in random order. The student should name the keyword and sound for each picture card.
- Review **Sight Word Cards 1–5.**
- Give the student the container of letter tiles.

  "Take out your letter tiles and put them in a row in front of you."

  "Use your letter tiles to spell the word 'fond.' "
- Have the student return the letter tiles to the top row after each word.

  "Now spell the word 'crib.' "
- As the student works, make sure he/she is spelling the words correctly.
- Continue with the following words: pet, plod, got, zap, hint.
- Have the student replace the tiles in the container and put it away.

NEW LEARNING

"I'm going to say some words to you and I want you to echo them back to me. Listen for the sound that is the same in the final position of each word."

- Point to your mouth as you say each word.

"Echo after me. Track." *track* ***"Block."*** *block* ***"Click."*** *click*

"What sound do you hear in the final position?" */k/*

"That's right. The sound you hear in the final position is /k/."

"Put your fingertips on the front of your neck and say /k/. See if you feel any vibration."

"Is this sound voiced or unvoiced?" *unvoiced*

"Since /k/ does not vibrate, it is an unvoiced sound."

- Write the following words on the chalkboard: pack, rock, stick.

"What do you see that might be making the /k/ sound?" *ck*

"There is a ck at the end of all of these words, so ck must be the letters used to spell the /k/ sound."

"Listen carefully. How many sounds do you hear in 'pack'?" */p/ /ă/ /k/, three*

"How many letters are in the word 'pack'?" *four*

"How many sounds do you hear in the word 'rock'?" */r/ /ŏ/ /k/, three*

"How many letters are in the word 'rock'?" *four*

"How many sounds do you hear in the word 'stick'?" */s/ /t/ /ĭ/ /k/, four*

"How many letters are in the word 'stick'?" *five*

"What do you think is happening in these words?"

- Expect various answers, but lead the student to respond that *c* and *k* go together to make one sound.

"This is called a digraph. 'Di' means 'two,' and 'graph' means 'letter.' "

"A digraph is two letters …"

- Hold up your index fingers.

"… that come together …"

- Bring your fingers together until they almost touch.

"… and make one sound."

- Drop one hand.

"Repeat that with me. Let's make the hand signals, too."

- Repeat the definition and the hand signals with the student.

"When we read, we need a way to remind ourselves about digraphs."

"We'll draw a line under both letters to show that they go together."

- Draw a line under the *ck* in "pack": pa<u>ck</u>.

  "Then we'll mark out the c to remind us that ck makes just one sound."

- Mark out the *c*: pa~~c~~k.

  "Is this a vowel digraph or a consonant digraph?" *consonant, because it makes a consonant sound*

  "Is there anything else we need to code?" *put a breve over the a*

- Code the *a* with a breve: pă~~c~~k.

NEW DECK CARDS

- Pull **Spelling Card 18** from the Review Deck.
- Show the student **Letter Card 20.**

  "What letters are these?" *c and k*

  "When you see this card, say 'digraph ck.' "

  "I have another sack today. It contains a clue to our new keyword. Don't look in the sack, but put your hand inside and see if you can guess what is inside. Keep in mind that the object in the sack ends with the /k/ sound."

- Allow the student a chance to feel inside the sack.
- If a lock is unavailable, use the following riddle:

  "This is something we wouldn't need if people were honest and didn't take things that don't belong to them. This is usually made of metal. We need a key or a combination to open this. What do you think the picture is?" *lock*

- Show the student **Picture Card 25.**

  "Were you right?"

  "The keyword is 'lock' and the sound is /k/."

  "The word 'lock' helps us remember the /k/ sound because it ends with /k/."

- **Note:** The digraph and its picture are also shown in the Rule Book on page 21. The student may find it useful to refer to this chart to help remember the keywords and sounds.
- Hold up **Spelling Card 18** so only you can see what is written.

  "Echo this sound: /k/."

  "How do we spell /k/?" *k comma c*

- Write "k, c" on the chalkboard.

  "We have to add something new to this response."

  "When we talk about a certain letter or letters at the end of a word, we say that they are in the final position."

- Draw two straight lines after "k, c": k, c ||.

"These two straight lines mean 'final.' "

- Write "ck" after the lines: k, c || ck.

"This means 'final digraph ck' and now it will be part of your response when I give you the /k/ sound."

"What will you say when I give you the /k/ sound?" *k comma c final digraph ck*

- Ask the student to write the new response on the chalkboard.

"Write the letters that spell /k/."

- Leave your written response (k, c || ck) on the chalkboard so the student may refer to it.
- **Note:** This will be the proper response to **Spelling Card 18** until Lesson 36.
- **Note:** Add the new letter and picture cards to the Review Decks (and re-insert **Spelling Card 18**).

BOARDWORK

"Let's practice coding some words like the ones you'll have on your worksheet."

- Write the word "snacks" on the chalkboard.

"Can you help me code this word?"

- Code the word as the student instructs: snăcks.

"What is the word?" *snacks*

- Write the following phrase on the chalkboard: ten big problems.

"Can you help me code this phrase?"

- Code the phrase as the student instructs:

tĕn bĭg prŏb'|lĕms
v c | cv

"What is the phrase?" *ten big problems*

"Can you give me a sentence with this phrase in it?" *expect various answers*

WORKSHEET

- The student should be seated where he/she can write comfortably.
- Give the student **Worksheet 28.** Make sure the student turns to the correct side.

"Let's start with our spelling today."

"Find the #1 on your paper. The first word is 'drab.' "

"Unblend 'drab' with me." */d/ /r/ /ă/ /b/*

- Hold up one finger for each sound.

"Let's spell those sounds." *d ... r ... a ... b*

- Point to each finger as you say a letter.

  "Now spell the word again and write the letters as you say them."
- Allow time for the student to do this.

  "What word did you write?" *drab*
- Repeat the procedure with #2 (frost), #3 (trip), #4 (grasp), and #5 (brand).

  "Now you're ready to code and read the words on your paper."

  "Using the rules we just practiced on the chalkboard, code the words by #6 through #10. After you've coded all the words, try to read them."
- Assist the student as necessary.

  "At the bottom of the page are four sentences. Two of the sentences have missing words. If you find any words you can't read, code them. Don't forget to circle the sight words. Then see if you can fill in the missing words."
- As the student works, provide help as needed. Help the student correct any incorrect answers. Then initial the worksheet in the space provided.
- Some time during the day, ask the student to read from the worksheet or homework. Although coding is important, the ultimate goal is reading, so the student, especially if he/she is having difficulty blending, should read to someone every day.
- **Note:** Always make sure the worksheet is corrected before the student begins the homework. The worksheet serves as a guide to help complete the homework.

HOMEWORK

"Turn your paper over to the homework side."

"Do you know what to do on the homework paper?"

"When you finish your paper, I will check it for you and initial it in the space provided."

- Either now or later in the day, the student should complete the homework independently (if possible). Help the student correct any incorrect answers. Then initial the homework in the space provided.
- If possible, take time to play the Kid Card games listed in Lesson 25.

Name ______________________

Teacher's Initials _____

Worksheet 28
(for use with Lesson 28)
Phonics 1

ck

1. drab
2. frost
3. trip
4. grasp
5. brand
6. nick
7. trick
8. slick
9. brick
10. block

11. Ann has a red smock.
12. The red smock is Ann's.

13. The cat slept in the sack.
14. The sack had a cat in it.

P1-WS-028a

Parent's Initials _____

Homework 28
(for use with Lesson 28)
Phonics 1

ck

1. back
2. tick
3. pick
4. neck
5. track
6. clock
7. stack
8. kick

9. The black pig is sick.
10. The sick pig is black.

11. He left tracks in the sand.
12. The sand had tracks in it.

Parents: Your child has been taught **digraph ck;** that a digraph is two letters that come together to make one sound; and that digraphs are coded by underlining.

P1-WS-028b

Lesson 28

Lesson 29 — Spelling with *ck*

lesson preparation

materials

container of letter tiles
Review Decks
Spelling Sound Sheet 23
Worksheet 29
Sight Word Card 6
Reader 8 (*Nick's Kid*)
colored pencils

new concepts

alphabetizing

Alphabet Activity

- The student should be seated with the container of letter tiles.

"Let's try something new today. Take out the letters a, b, c, d, e, f, and g."

- Allow time for the student to do this.

"We are going to alphabetize these letter tiles. That means we will put them in ABC, or alphabetical, order."

"To put the letter tiles in alphabetical order, we recite the alphabet and put the letter tiles in order as we say them."

"Let's say the alphabet together as you put your letter tiles in order."

"A. Find your 'a' letter tile and push it to the top of your desk."

"B. Find the 'b' letter tile and put it after the 'a.' "

"C. Find the 'c' letter tile and put it after the 'b.' "

- Continue with *d*, *e*, *f*, and *g*.

"These letter tiles are now in alphabetical order because they are in the order of the alphabet."

"Let's check to see if we are right. Point to each letter tile as I name it."

- Write each letter on the chalkboard as you say it. The student should see that your hand moves progressively to the right.
- Have the student replace the tiles in the container and put it away.

PHONEMIC AWARENESS

- **Objective:** To identify rhyming sounds in spoken words.

  "Let's see how many rhyming words you can make for a particular word."

  "I'm going to say a word. Then tell me as many words as you can that rhyme with my word."

  "The first word is 'hat.' Can you think of a word that rhymes with 'hat'?"
- **Optional:** Record one point for each word that rhymes.
- When the student can no longer think of any rhyming words, give a new word.
- Use the following words, if desired: stop, lad, pin, fog.

REVIEW OF DECKS

- The student should be seated where he/she can write comfortably.
- Show the student **Letter Cards 1–20** in random order. The student should name the letter on each letter card.
- Review **Affix Card 1.**
- Show the student **Picture Cards 1–25** in random order. The student should name the keyword and sound for each picture card.
- Review **Sight Word Cards 1–5.**
- Give the student **Spelling Sound Sheet 23.**
- Call out the sounds on **Spelling Cards 1–22** in random order. The student should echo each sound and name the letter or letters that make the sound as he/she writes the letter(s) on the spelling sound sheet.
- Check the student's response after each card.

NEW LEARNING

- Write the following on the chalkboard: stǐ___, blă___, sŏ___.

  "All of these words end with the /k/ sound."

  "What letters could we use to spell the /k/ sound?" *k, c, or ck*

  "I am going to show you a rule to use when you spell the /k/ sound in the final position."

  "Get out your Rule Book and turn to page 4."
- Point to "stǐ___" on **Rule Chart 4** as you say the following:

  "Look at this word."

  "This word ends with the sound of /k/."

  "Look at the letter right before the line. What is it?" *i*

"Is this vowel short or long?" *short*

- Point to the *ck* and move your finger across the words "after a short vowel."

"What letters do we use to spell the /k/ sound after a short vowel?" *ck*

"That's right! Let's try another one."

- Repeat the procedure with "blă____" and "sŏ____."
- If the student seems to understand the rule, go on to the worksheet activity. If not, have the student practice more words on the chalkboard.

WORKSHEET

- The student should be seated where he/she can write comfortably.
- Give the student **Worksheet 29.** Make sure the student turns to the correct side.

"We are going to spell some words using our new rule chart."

"Put your finger by #1. The first word is 'back.'"

"Unblend 'back' with me." */b/ /ă/ /k/*

- Hold up one finger for each sound.

"Let's spell the word." *b … a … ck*

- Hold up three fingers.

"Write the first two letters. Say each letter out loud."

- Allow time for the student to write *b* and *a*.

"What sound do you hear before the /k/ sound?" */ă/*

"What letters do we use to spell the /k/ sound if it comes after a short vowel?" *ck*

"Write the letters that spell the /k/ sound after a short vowel."

"What word did you write?" *back*

- Repeat the procedure with #2 (pick), #3 (rack), #4 (dock), #5 (sack), #6 (rock), #7 (lack), and #8 (pack).
- Assist the student as necessary.

"Now you're ready to code and read the words on your paper."

"Code the words by #9 through #12. After you've coded all the words, try to read them. Watch for words with a 'vccv' pattern. They have to be divided."

- Again, assist the student as necessary.
- Show the student **Sight Word Card 6.**

"This is a new sight word."

"Do you know what this word is?" *expect various answers*

"This word is 'are.' Can you use 'are' in a sentence?" *expect various answers*

"'Are' will always be a sight word. We'll add this card to our sight word deck. The word is also on our sight word charts."

- Help the student locate the word "are" in the Irregular Spelling Booklet.

  "At the bottom of the page are two sentences. One of the sentences has two missing words. If you find any words you can't read, code them. Don't forget to circle the sight words. Then see if you can fill in the missing words."

- As the student works, provide help as needed. Help the student correct any incorrect answers. Then initial the worksheet in the space provided.
- Some time during the day, ask the student to read from the worksheet or homework. Although coding is important, the ultimate goal is reading, so the student, especially if he/she is having difficulty blending, should read to someone every day.
- **Note:** Always make sure the worksheet is corrected before the student begins the homework. The worksheet serves as a guide to help complete the homework.
- Add **Sight Word Card 6** to the Sight Word Deck.

HOMEWORK

"Turn your paper over to the homework side."

"Do you think you know what to do on the homework paper?"

- Explain that numbers 1 through 5 are all words that end with the /k/ sound, and that the student should finish spelling the words.

  "When you finish your paper, I will check it for you and initial it in the space provided."

- Either now or later in the day, the student should complete the homework independently (if possible). Help the student correct any incorrect answers. Then initial the homework in the space provided.

READER

- Give the student **Reader 8 (*Nick's Kid*)** and some colored pencils.

  "We're going to make another book today."

  "What is this book's title?" *Nick's Kid*

  "Do you remember what the 'apostrophe s' shows?" *ownership*

  "Whose kid is it?" *Nick's*

- Assist the student as necessary as he/she completes the following steps:

  "Hold up your page so that the tree is facing you."

  "Now put your finger on the top dotted line."

  "Carefully fold the paper along this dotted line toward you so that it lines up with the bottom dotted line."

  "Now fold the top half of the sheet back along the dotted line."

"Hold your book so the tree is facing you again. Then put your finger on the dotted line down the center of the page."

"Fold the book backward along this dotted line so that the tree will still be facing you when you're finished."

- When the student completes this last step, either put a rubber band around the book's spine or staple the spine.

"Next, carefully separate the pages along the perforated lines at the top and bottom."

- Demonstrate how to separate the pages.

"Let's check the page numbers to see if they are in the correct order."

- Demonstrate how to check that the book's page numbers are in order.

"The title of the book is __________?" *Nick's Kid*

"I want you to read your book to yourself. When you are finished reading, color the pictures. Write your name on the book so I will know who colored it."

"Keep your book handy because I will be asking you to read it for me."

- Some time during the day, have the student read the reader to you.
- If possible, take time to play the Kid Card games listed in Lesson 25. Try to see that the student is prepared for tomorrow's assessment.

Name ________________
Teacher's Initials ____

Worksheet 29
(for use with Lesson 29)
Phonics 1

Spelling with ck

1. back
2. pick
3. rack
4. dock
5. sack
6. rock
7. lack
8. pack

9. păt
10. slĭck
11. răbbĭt
12. rŏcks

13. Mom is back and so is Kim.
14. Mom and Kim are back.

P1-WS-029a

Parent's Initials ____

Homework 29
(for use with Lesson 29)
Phonics 1

Spelling with ck

1. blăck
2. stĭck
3. lŏck
4. sŏck
5. stăck

6. bricks
7. hŏgs
8. zĭp

9. The black dog is Kim's and the black cat is Nick's.
10. Kim has a black dog.

Parents: Your child has been taught that when spelling the "k" sound at the end of a word, **ck** follows a short vowel. **Alphabetizing** has also been introduced.

P1-WS-029b

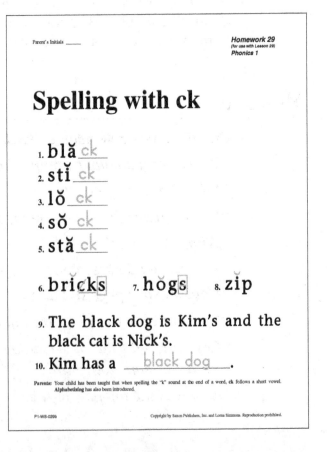

LESSON 30

Assessment

lesson preparation

materials

Review Decks

Assessment 5

Spelling Test 3

Assessment 5 Recording Form

Kid Cards

tokens

the night before

- Separate the Kid Cards marked "Lesson 30."

ALPHABET ACTIVITY

- The student should be seated.

  "Today, I want to see how well you understand the words 'before' and 'after.' "

  "I'll name a letter. Then I'll ask you to tell me a letter that comes before or after that letter."

- Select letters at random and ask the student to identify letters that come before or after yours, varying your requests between the two.

PHONEMIC AWARENESS

- **Objective:** To identify rhyming sounds in spoken words.
- The student should be seated.

  "Let's work with rhyming words one more time."

  "I'm going to say some words. I want you to stand up if the words rhyme. If they don't rhyme, remain seated."

- Give the following words, one pair at a time:

  pan/fan *(Stand.)*
  sit/fit *(Stand.)*
  hat/win *(Sit.)*
  pot/caught *(Stand.)*
  hall/fit *(Sit.)*
  most/post *(Stand.)*

- Continue with more words as time permits.

Review of Decks

- The student should be seated where he/she can write comfortably.
- Show the student **Letter Cards 1–20** in random order. The student should name the letter on each letter card.
- Review **Affix Card 1.**
- Show the student **Picture Cards 1–25** in random order. The student should name the keyword and sound for each picture card.
- Review **Sight Word Cards 1–6.**
- Play "Spelling Deck Perfection" in place of the usual spelling deck review. (See "Games and Activities" for directions.)

Written Assessment

- Seat the student where he/she can write comfortably.
- Give the student **Assessment 5.**
- **Section I:**

  "Today we are going to write some words for our assessment."

  "I'm going to say a word. Write the letter that makes each sound in that word on the lines by #1."

  "Here's the first word: kit."
- Repeat with the following words in the order shown: #2 (cap), #3 (stop), #4 (fog), and #5 (slip).
- **Note:** While the student spells words on assessments, be ready to point to appropriate rule charts as necessary to help the student spell the words.
- **Section II:**

  "Look at the letter by #6."

  "Find the picture of the keyword for this sound."

  "Draw a line from the letter to the keyword."
- Repeat with #7. Allow a few minutes for the student to work.
- The pictures (from top to bottom) are as follows: belt, carrot.
- **Section III:**

  "Put your finger on #8."

  "Code the words by #8 through #11."
- Allow a few minutes for the student to work.
- **Section IV:**

  "Look at the blend by #12. What sound does this blend make?" *gl*
- Repeat with #13, #14, #15, #16, and #17.

- Point to the first picture (skate) and help the student identify it. Ask the student to name the blend the picture begins with and then to draw a line from the picture to the blend.
- Repeat with each picture. The pictures (from top to bottom) are as follows: skate, clock, crab, glue, grapes, smoke.
- **Section V:**

  "Look at the sentences by #18."

  "Read the sentences. Then see if you can fill in the missing word."
- **Note:** If the student absolutely cannot read the sentences, read them to the student to see if he or she can answer the question.

  "When you are finished, show your paper to me."
- This paper will be used during the oral portion of the assessment.

Spelling Test

- Give the student **Spelling Test 3.**
- Call out the following words (in the order shown). Sound them out, if necessary.

  #1 (if), #2 (as), #3 (is), #4 (sat), #5 (fit), #6 (fan), #7 (did), #8 (sit), #9 (so), #10 (sad).
- Grade and record the test in any manner that suits your needs.

Oral Assessment

- Oral assessments are short interviews that occur during independent work time. It is important to complete them promptly (today, if possible) in order to identify any areas of weakness and begin remediation.
- Use the assessment and the following dialogue to complete the oral portion.
- **Section VI:**
- Point to the sight word by #19.

  "Read this sight word for me."
- Record the student's response by placing a check mark by each word he/she reads correctly.
- Repeat with #20, #21, and #22.
- **Section VII:**
- Point to the letter by #23.

  "Tell me the name of this letter and the sound it makes."
- Write the student's response on the adjacent line.
- Repeat with #24.

- **Section VIII:**

  "I'm going to say some words. Tell me the sound you hear in the initial position."
- Point to your mouth and say the following words: bite, bug, boat.
- Write the student's response on the line by #25. (If the student responds with the letter name, ask again for the *sound.*)

ASSESSMENT EVALUATION

- Grade the assessment and record the results on **Assessment 5 Recording Form.** Check off the boxes to indicate mastery (i.e., the section was completed with 100% accuracy).
- **Reminder:** If you choose to grade the assessments, try to give as many points as possible for work attempted. Do not grade the coding marks too severely, especially secondary marks like accents, twin consonants, and k-backs. The most important coding marks to look for are breves, macrons, and syllable division lines.
- See the introductory material for detailed information regarding grading and recording procedures.
- Use the assessment results to identify those skills in which the student is weak. Practice those skills by playing Kid Card games.
- Add the Kid Cards marked "Lesson 30" to the existing decks. Listed below are games appropriate for remediation in selected areas. See "Games and Activities" for the directions for each game.
- **Section I:** Play "Spelling Deck Perfection," "Sound Scamper," or have the student use the letter tiles to spell words you give from the Spelling Word List.
- **Section II:** Play "Keyword and Sound" or "Letter/Sound Identification."
- **Section III:** Play "Chalkboard Challenge."
- **Section IV:** Play "Blend It."
- **Section V:** Play "Acting Out."
- **Section VI:** Play "At First Sight."
- **Section VII:** Play "Letter/Sound Identification."
- **Section VIII:** Play "Sound Solutions."
- When the student seems more secure in areas that had previously proven difficult, retest him/her (in those areas only) and indicate on the recording form any sections the student has subsequently mastered.
- Try to help the student achieve mastery of all the sections before the next assessment.
- If the student is having difficulty with a particular skill, keep his or her practice activities at the most basic level so the chance of success is greater.

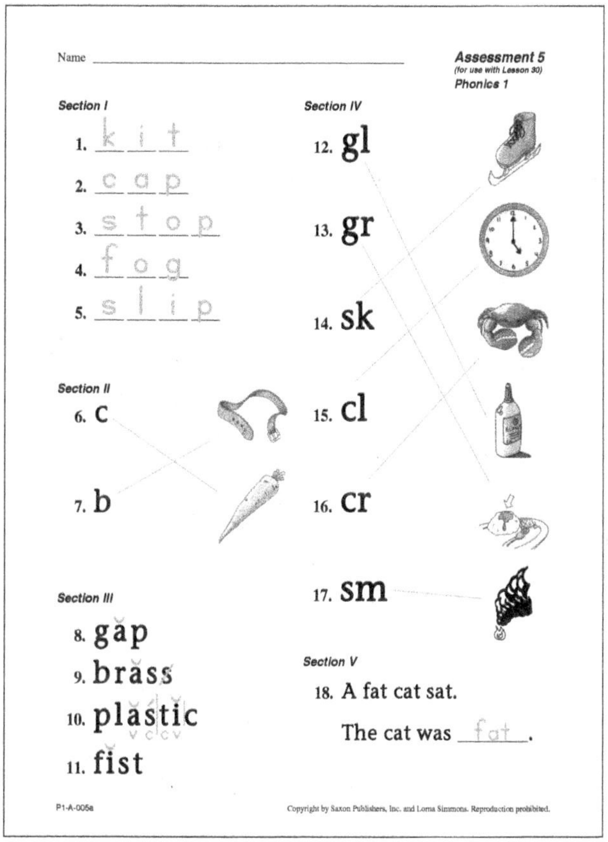

Name ____________________

Assessment 5
(for use with Lesson 30)
Phonics 1

Section I

1. k i t
2. c a p
3. s t o p
4. f o g
5. s l i p

Section II

6. c
7. b

Section III

8. găp
9. brăss
10. plăstĭc (v c c v)
11. fĭst

Section IV

12. gl
13. gr
14. sk
15. cl
16. cr
17. sm

Section V

18. A fat cat sat.
The cat was fat.

P1-A-005a

Assessment 5
(for use with Lesson 30)
Phonics 1

Section VI

19. oh ____________
20. who ____________
21. what ____________
22. was ____________

Section VII

23. c ______ c. /k/ ______
24. b ______ b. /b/ ______

Section VIII

25. ____/b/____

P1-A-005b

LESSON 31 — Digraph *th*

lesson preparation

materials

Review Decks
Spelling Sound Sheet 24
Letter Card 21
feathers and a thimble in a sack (see *the night before*)
Picture Cards 26–27
Spelling Cards 23–24
Worksheet 31
Sight Word Card 7
Spelling List 4

new concepts

compound words

the night before

- Put feathers and a thimble in a sack for the student to use to "discover" the new keywords. If possible, do not allow the student to see you do this.

ALPHABET ACTIVITY

- The student should be seated with the alphabet strip.

  "How many letters are in the alphabet?" *26*

  "What two kinds of letters make up our alphabet?" *vowels and consonants*

  "Name the vowels." *a, e, i, o, and u*

  "All of the other letters are called _________?" *consonants*

  "The initial letter of the alphabet is _____?" *a*

  "The final letter of the alphabet is _____?" *z*

  "Let's point to each letter and say the whole alphabet."

  "Put your index finger on 'a' and say the names with me."

PHONEMIC AWARENESS

- **Objective:** To identify compound words.

  "Today we are going to work with compound words."

  "A compound word is two words that come together to form one new word."

  "Say that with me."

- Repeat the definition slowly as the student says it with you.

  "I will say a compound word. Listen for the two words that make the compound word."

  "The first word is 'seaweed.' "

  "What are the two words?" *"sea" and "weed"*

  "The next word is 'notebook.' "

  "What are the two words?" *"note" and "book"*

  "The next word is 'cowbell.' "

  "What are the two words?" *"cow" and "bell"*

  "Say 'wallpaper.' " *wallpaper*

  "What are the two words?" *"wall" and "paper"*

- Continue with additional compound words as time permits.

REVIEW OF DECKS

- The student should be seated where he/she can write comfortably.
- Show the student **Letter Cards 1–20** in random order. The student should name the letter on each letter card.
- Review **Affix Card 1.**
- Show the student **Picture Cards 1–25** in random order. The student should name the keyword and sound for each picture card.
- Review **Sight Word Cards 1–6.**
- Give the student **Spelling Sound Sheet 24.**
- Call out the sounds on **Spelling Cards 1–22** in random order. The student should echo each sound and name the letter or letters that make the sound as he/she writes the letter(s) on the spelling sound sheet.
- Check the student's response after each card.
- Have the student set the spelling sound sheet aside for use later in the lesson.

NEW LEARNING

"I'm going to say some words. Echo them back to me and listen for the sound in the final position."

- Point to your mouth as you say each word.

"Echo after me. Bath." *bath* ***"Math."*** *math* ***"Moth."*** *moth*

"What sound do you hear in the final position?" */th/*

"That's right. The sound you hear in the final position is /th/."

- Write the following words on the chalkboard: bath, math, moth.

"Look at these words. What letters might be making the /th/ sound?" *th*

"Does anyone know what 'th' is called?" *a digraph*

"Is this a vowel digraph or a consonant digraph?" *consonant*

"How do we code a digraph?" *underline it*

- Underline each *th*: bath math moth.

"How do we code the vowels in these words?" *breve; short*

"Why?" *because they are followed by consonants*

- Put a breve on each vowel: băth măth mŏth.
- Point to "bath."

"What is this word?" *bath*

"Can you use the word 'bath' in a sentence?" *expect various answers*

- Have the student read the words "math" and "moth" and use them in sentences.

"I'm going to say some more words. Echo them back to me and listen for the sound in the initial position."

- Point to your mouth as you say each word.

"Echo after me. Then." *then* ***"There."*** *there* ***"Those."*** *those*

"What sound do you hear in the initial position?" */~~th~~/*

"That's right. The sound you hear is /~~th~~/. It's a different sound, isn't it?"

- Write the following words on the chalkboard: this, than, then.

"Look at these words. What letters might be making the /~~th~~/ sound?" *th*

"That's right. The digraph th can make two sounds."

"Put your fingers on your vocal cords and feel this sound: /~~th~~/."

- Make an extended /~~th~~/ sound (voiced, as in "feather") with the student.

"The vocal cords vibrate, so this sound is voiced."

"Let's try another sound of 'th': /th/."

- Make an extended /th/ sound (unvoiced, as in "thimble") with the student.

"The vocal cords don't vibrate, so this sound is unvoiced."

"We can't count on 'th' to make a certain sound in a certain position, but usually it is voiced in the medial position and unvoiced in the final position."

"In the initial position, it can make either sound. When you see a word that begins with 'th,' try the voiced sound first. If that doesn't sound right, try the unvoiced sound."

"You'll hear the voiced sound a lot more than the unvoiced sound."

"How do we code 'digraph th'?" *underline it*

- Underline each *th*: this than then.

"Is the 'th' in each of these words voiced or unvoiced?" *voiced*

"What other letter has both a voiced and an unvoiced sound?" *s*

"What mark did we make to show the voiced sound of s?" *a voice line*

"We'll do the same thing to show the voiced digraph th."

- Put a voice line through each *th*: ~~th~~is ~~th~~an ~~th~~en.

"How do we code the vowels in these words?" *breve; short*

"Why?" *because they are followed by consonants*

- Put a breve on each vowel: ~~th~~ĭs ~~th~~ăn ~~th~~ĕn.
- Point to "this."

"Can you read this word?" *this*

"Can you use the word 'this' in a sentence?" *expect various answers*

- Have the student read the words "than" and "then" and use them in sentences.
- Leave the words on the chalkboard for the remainder of the lesson.

NEW DECK CARDS

- Show the student **Letter Card 21.**

"What is this called?" *digraph th*

"I have a sack that contains a clue to our new keywords. Don't look in the sack, but put your hand inside and see if you can feel what is inside the sack."

- After allowing the student to feel inside the sack, see if he/she has guessed that the sack contains both feathers and a thimble.

"That's right. Our new keywords are 'feather' and 'thimble.'"

"Which keyword is for the unvoiced sound of 'th'?" *thimble*

- Show the student **Picture Card 27.**

"Which keyword is for the voiced sound of 'th'?" *feather*

- Show the student **Picture Card 26.**

"On the 'feather' picture card, the 'th' has a voice line through it. That helps us remember the /~~th~~/ sound."

- **Note:** The digraphs and their pictures are also shown in the Rule Book on page 21.

"Find your spelling sound sheet. Put your finger by #23."

- Hold up **Spelling Card 23** so only you can see what is written.

  "Echo this sound: /th/."

  "How do we spell the /th/ sound?" *digraph th*

  "Write the letters that make that sound on line #23."
- Hold up **Spelling Card 24** so only you can see what is written.

  "Echo this sound: /th/."

  "How do we spell the /th/ sound?" *digraph th*

  "Write the letters that make that sound on line #24."
- Check the spelling sound sheet for accuracy.
- **Note:** Add the new letter, picture, and spelling cards to the Review Decks.

BOARDWORK

"Let's practice coding some words like the ones you'll have on your worksheet."

- Review the rule charts, if necessary.
- Write the word "thick" on the chalkboard.

  "Can you help me code this word?"
- Code the word as the student instructs: thick.

  "What is the word?" *thick*

  "Does digraph th need a voice line?" *no*

  "Can you use the word 'thick' in a sentence?" *expect various answers*
- Write the following sentence on the chalkboard: The man has a moth.

  "How will we code this sentence?"
- Point to the word "the."

  "Have you noticed that we say 'the' in the same way we say 'a'? Sometimes we say /thē/, but usually we say /thŭ/."

  "We can put a schwa over the 'e' to show that we mean /ŭ/."
- Code the *e* with a schwa: The.

  "Many vowels turn into schwas and make the /ŭ/ sound when we talk."

  "How do we code digraph th?" *draw a line under it*

  "Does this digraph th need a voice line?" *yes*
- Finish coding the sentence as the student instructs: The măn hăs a mŏth.

  "What is this sentence?" *The man has a moth.*

  "What do you think about the word 'the'? Is it still a sight word?" *no, now we know how to code it*

WORKSHEET

- The student should be seated where he/she can write comfortably.
- Give the student **Worksheet 31.** Make sure the student turns to the correct side.

  "Let's spell with digraph ck. Remember, when we hear the /k/ sound after a short vowel, we use digraph ck."
- Refer the student to **Rule Chart 4.**

  "Put your finger by #1. The first word is 'rock.' "

  "Unblend 'rock' with me." */r/ /ŏ/ /k/*
- Hold up one finger for each sound.

  "Is /ŏ/ a short or long vowel sound?" *short*

  "How do we spell the /k/ sound after a short vowel sound?" *digraph ck*

  "Let's spell these sounds." *r … o … digraph ck*
- Point to each finger as you spell a sound.

  "Now spell the word again and write the letters as you say them."
- Allow time for the student to do this.

  "What word did you write?" *rock*

  "Put your finger by #2. The word is 'pack.' "

  "Unblend 'pack' with me." */p/ /ă/ /k/*
- Hold up one finger for each sound.

  "Is /ă/ a short or long vowel sound?" *short*

  "How do we spell the /k/ sound after a short vowel sound?" *digraph ck*

  "Let's spell those sounds." *p … a … digraph ck*
- Point to each finger as you spell a sound.

  "Now spell the word again and write the letters as you say them."
- Allow time for the student to do this.

  "What word did you write?" *pack*
- Repeat the procedure with #3 (moth), #4 (flock), and #5 (that).
- Assist the student as necessary.

  "Now you're ready to code and read the words on your paper."

  "Code the words by #6 through #10. After you have coded all the words, try to read them."
- Allow time for the student to do this.
- Show the student **Sight Word Card 7.**

  "This is a new sight word."

  "Do you know what this word is?" *expect various answers*

"This word is 'where.' Can you use the word 'where' in a sentence?" *expect various answers*

" 'Where' will always be a sight word. We'll add this card to our sight word deck. The word is also on our sight word charts."

- Allow time for the student to find the word in the Irregular Spelling Booklet.

"At the bottom of the page are some sentences. Two of the sentences ask questions. If you find any words you can't read, code them. Don't forget to circle the sight words. Then see if you can answer the questions."

- As the student works, provide help as needed. Help the student correct any incorrect answers. Then initial the worksheet in the space provided.
- Some time during the day, ask the student to read from the worksheet or homework. Although coding is important, the ultimate goal is reading, so the student, especially if he/she is having difficulty blending, should read to someone every day.
- **Note:** Always make sure the worksheet is corrected before the student begins the homework. The worksheet serves as a guide to help complete the homework.
- Add **Sight Word Card 7** to the Sight Word Deck.

HOMEWORK

"Turn your paper over to the homework side."

"Do you know what to do on the rest of the homework paper?"

"When you finish your paper, I will check it for you and initial it in the space provided."

- Either now or later in the day, the student should complete the homework independently (if possible). Help the student correct any incorrect answers. Then initial the homework in the space provided.

SPELLING LIST

- Fold **Spelling List 4** in half lengthwise (with the printed side facing out).

"Leave your paper just like I give it to you."

- Give the student **Spelling List 4,** folded with the blank lines facing up.

"Let's spell some more words. You can spell these words without seeing them first because you know the rules for spelling them."

- Call out the following words (in the order shown). Sound them out, if necessary.

  #1 (had), #2 (has), #3 (dog), #4 (go), #5 (got), #6 (pig), #7 (ran), #8 (hat), #9 (dig), #10 (fast)

"Now unfold your paper and check your words."

- Check the student's work to see if he/she needs extra help with spelling.

"I want you to practice these words. We'll have a spelling test in a few days."

- If possible, take time to play the Kid Card games listed in Lesson 30.

Name ____________________

Teacher's Initials ____

Worksheet 31
(for use with Lesson 31)
Phonics 1

th, th

1. rock
2. pack
3. moth
4. flock
5. that
6. this
7. cloth
8. thick
9. sick
10. test
11. The math problem is on the back.
12. Where is the math problem? on the back
13. Beth has a black cat and a red dog.
14. Who is black? Beth's cat

P1-WS-031a

Parent's Initials ____

Homework 31
(for use with Lesson 31)
Phonics 1

th, th

1. that
2. math
3. snack
4. film
5. mint
6. camp
7. thin
8. stomp
9. deck
10. black
11. Let Tom help sell the flags.
12. Who can help? Tom
13. Tim kept his pet frog in a pan.
14. Tim's pet is a frog.

Parents: Your child has been taught the two sounds of **digraph th** (voiced, as in *feather*, and unvoiced, as in *thimble*); and that a **compound word** is two words that come together to form one new word.

P1-WS-031b

LESSON 32 Digraph *ng* and Suffix *-ing*

lesson preparation

materials

Review Decks
Spelling Sound Sheet 25
Letter Card 22
Picture Card 28
Spelling Card 25
Affix Card 2
Worksheet 32
Sight Word Card 8
Reader 9 (*A CK Spelling Test*)
colored pencils

new concepts

contraction

ALPHABET ACTIVITY

- The student should be standing.

  "Let's jog in a circle today as we say the alphabet."
- Set a steady rhythm and recite the alphabet while jogging.
- Have the student return to his/her seat.

PHONEMIC AWARENESS

- **Objective:** To identify compound words.

  "Today we are going to work with compound words again."

  "A compound word is two words that come together to form one new word."

  "Say that with me."
- Repeat the definition slowly as the student says it with you.

  "I'll say a compound word. Listen for the two words that make the compound word."

  "The first word is 'lighthouse.' "

  "What are the two words?" *"light" and "house"*

  "The next word is 'earphone.' "

"What are the two words?" *"ear" and "phone"*

"The next word is 'suitcase.' "

"What are the two words?" *"suit" and "case"*

"Say 'lifeguard.' " *lifeguard*

"What are the two words?" *"life" and "guard"*

- Continue with additional compound words as time permits.

REVIEW OF DECKS

- The student should be seated where he/she can write comfortably.
- Show the student **Letter Cards 1–21** in random order. The student should name the letter on each letter card.
- Review **Affix Card 1.**
- Show the student **Picture Cards 1–27** in random order. The student should name the keyword and sound for each picture card.
- Review **Sight Word Cards 1–7.**
- Give the student **Spelling Sound Sheet 25.**
- Call out the sounds on **Spelling Cards 1–24** in random order. The student should echo each sound and name the letter or letters that make the sound as he/she writes the letter(s) on the spelling sound sheet.
- Check the student's response after each card.
- Have the student set the spelling sound sheet aside for use later in the lesson.

NEW LEARNING

"I'm going to say some words. Echo them back to me and listen for the sound in the final position."

- Point to your mouth as you say each word.

"Echo after me. Song." *song* ***"Stung."*** *stung* ***"Ring."*** *ring*

"What sound do you hear in the final position?" */ng/*

- This sound is more difficult than most to hear. Repeat the words, exaggerating the /ng/ sound, if necessary.

"That's right. The sound you hear in the final position is /ng/."

"Put your fingertips on the front of your neck and say /ng/. See if you can feel any vibration."

"Is this sound voiced or unvoiced?" *voiced*

- Write the following words on the chalkboard: song, stung, ring.

"Look at these words. What letters might be making the /ng/ sound?" *ng*

"There is an ng in all of these words, so we can see that the letters ng must be making the /ng/ sound."

"How many sounds do you hear?" *one*

"How many letters are making that one sound?" *two*

- Use the hand signals described in Lesson 28 as you say the following:

"What do we call two letters that come together to make one sound?" *a digraph*

"Is digraph ng a vowel or a consonant digraph?" *a consonant digraph, because it contains only consonants*

NEW DECK CARDS

- Show the student **Letter Card 22.**

"What do we call this?" *digraph ng*

- Hold up **Picture Card 28** but keep the picture covered with your hand (or the letter card).

"I have a card with a picture on it that ends with the /ng/ sound."

"I'm going to describe it for you. See if you can guess what the picture is."

"This is one of the organs in our body. We have two of them located near our ribs. Smoking can do damage to them. If they become damaged, we cannot breathe properly. What do you think the picture is?" *lung*

"That's right. The keyword is 'lung' and the sound we have learned is /ng/."

- Show the student **Picture Card 28.**

"The word 'lung' helps us remember the /ng/ sound because it ends with /ng/."

- **Note:** The digraph and its picture are also shown in the Rule Book on page 21.

"Find your spelling sound sheet. Put your finger by #25."

- Hold up **Spelling Card 25** so only you can see what is written.

"Echo this sound: /ng/."

"How do we spell the /ng/ sound?" *digraph ng*

"Write the letters that make that sound on line #25."

"Let's talk about this a little more. Echo these words and tell me what you hear at the end."

- Point to your mouth as you say each word.

"Echo after me. Resting." *resting* ***"Standing."*** *standing* ***"Milking."*** *milking*

"What do you hear at the end of these words?" *ing*

- Write "resting," "standing," and "milking" on the chalkboard.

"What is the same at the end of all of these words?" *ing*

- Point to "resting."

  "Look at this word. Can I cover up the 'ing' and still have a root word?" *yes*

- Repeat the procedure with "standing" and "milking."

  "What do we call something that is added to the end of a root word?" *a suffix*

  "How do we code suffixes?" *by boxing them*

- Have the student help you code the words: rĕst´[ing] stănd´[ing] mĭlk´[ing]

  "What does a suffix do to a root word?" *it changes its meaning*

  "Let's see what 'ing' means at the end of a word."

  "If I am jumping (demonstrate), when am I doing it?" *right now*

  "If I am clapping (demonstrate), when am I doing it?" *right now*

  "If I am walking (demonstrate), when am I doing it?" *right now*

  "So, what does 'ing' mean at the end of the root word?" *it is happening now*

- Show the student **Affix Card 2.**

  "What do we call this?" *suffix -ing*

- Check the spelling sound sheet for accuracy.
- **Note:** Add the new letter, picture, spelling, and affix cards to the Review Decks.

BOARDWORK

"Let's practice coding some words like the ones you'll have on your worksheet."

- Review the rule charts, if necessary.
- Write the word "helping" on the chalkboard.

  "Can you help me code this word?"

- Code the word as the student instructs: hĕlp´[ing].
- **Note:** It is not necessary to code digraph *ng* (or any other digraph) within a suffix box. Extensive coding of a word can make the word difficult to read and thus defeats its own purpose. If the student relies heavily on coding in order to read, you may choose to code each word completely. In either case, you should feel free to adapt the coding process to the student's needs.

  "What is the word?" *helping*

  "Can you use the word 'helping' in a sentence?"

- Write the word "gossiping" on the chalkboard.

  "Can you help me code this word?"

- Code the word as the student instructs:

  g ŏ s´ | s̸ ĭ p [ing]

  v c | c v

  "What is the word?" *gossiping*

- Write the following sentence on the chalkboard: The long basket is in that sink.

  "Can you help me code this sentence?"

- Code the sentence as the student instructs:

  T̶h̶e̊ lŏng băs′|kĕt i̶s̶ ĭn t̶h̶ăt sĭnk.
  vc|cv

  "What is this sentence?" *The long basket is in that sink.*

  "Say the word 'sink.'" *sink*

  "Do you notice anything strange about the sound of n in this word?" *it says /ng/*

  "This is something you will hear often. When n comes before k or the /k/ sound, it usually makes the /ng/ sound."

- **Optional:** If the student relies heavily on coding to read, code these *n*'s with "monkey tails" (ŋ). Most children will not require this coding; the correct pronunciation comes easily because the throat automatically closes to make the /ng/ sound when moving from /n/ to /k/.

  "Did you notice anything different about the sound of the letter i in 'sink'?" *it sounds like /ē/*

  "When we talk, the i before ng can sound like /ē/. Our voices do that naturally when we go from the /ĭ/ sound to the /ng/ sound. Try it with this word: thing."

- Allow the student to experiment with the sound of "ng."

  "Even though we end up saying /ē/, we will still code it as having the short sound of i because that's the sound we start with."

- **Note:** If you feel it is necessary, allow the student to experiment with *a* before an /ng/ sound. The *a* is also distorted.

- Write the word "hopping" on the chalkboard.

  "Can you help me code this word?"

- Code the word as the student instructs:

  hŏpp̸′[ing]

  "What is the word?" *hopping*

- **Note:** The final *p* in the root word "hop" has been doubled before adding the suffix. This spelling rule will be taught in Lesson 111. However, before that lesson the student will be asked to read words in which the consonant has been doubled; the student may or may not choose to cross out the second consonant in these words.

WORKSHEET

- The student should be seated where he/she can write comfortably.
- Give the student **Worksheet 32.** Make sure the student turns to the correct side.

  "Let's spell with the /k/ sound today."

"Look at Rule Chart 3. If you hear the /k/ sound at the beginning or middle of a word, we use these rules."

"When do we use k?" *before e, i, and y*

"When do we use c?" *before a, o, u, and any consonant*

"Be sure to check the rule chart if you are not sure which to use."

"Put your finger by #1. The first word is 'kid.' "

"Unblend 'kid' with me." */k/ /ĭ/ /d/*

- Hold up one finger for each sound.

"Let's spell those sounds." *k … i … d*

- Point to each finger as you spell a sound.

"Now spell the word again and write the letters as you say them."

- Allow time for the student to do this.

"What word did you write?" *kid*

- Repeat the procedure with #2 (kept), #3 (crisp), #4 (clap), and #5 (kick).

"Now you're ready to code and read the words on your paper."

"Code the words by #6 through #10. After you have coded all the words, try to read them."

- Assist the student as necessary.
- Show the student **Sight Word Card 8.**

"This is a new sight word."

"Do you know what this word is?" *expect various answers*

"The word is 'said.' Can you use the word 'said' in a sentence?" *expect various answers*

" 'Said' will always be a sight word. We'll add this card to our sight word deck. Can you find this word on our sight word charts?"

- Help the student locate the word in the Irregular Spelling Booklet.

"At the bottom of the page are some sentences. One of the sentences has a word missing, and one asks a question. If you find any words you can't read, code them. Don't forget to circle the sight words. Then see if you can fill in the missing word and answer the question."

- As the student works, provide help as needed. Help the student correct any incorrect answers. Then initial the worksheet in the space provided.
- Some time during the day, ask the student to read from the worksheet or homework. Although coding is important, the ultimate goal is reading, so the student, especially if he/she is having difficulty blending, should read to someone every day.
- **Note:** Always make sure the worksheet is corrected before the student begins the homework. The worksheet serves as a guide to help complete the homework.
- Add **Sight Word Card 8** to the Sight Word Deck.

Lesson 32

HOMEWORK

"Turn your paper over to the homework side."

"Do you think you know what to do on the homework paper?"

"Watch for suffix -ing. Always box suffixes before coding the rest of the word. Also, watch for words with a 'vccv' pattern that need to be divided."

"You'll see something new on your homework today."

- Write the contraction "can't" on the chalkboard.

"How will we code this word?"

- Code the word as the student instructs: căn't.

"Do you know what the apostrophe in this word means?"

"The apostrophe is there to show that some letters are missing. When we talk, we sometimes take short cuts. What do we mean when we say 'can't'?" *can not*

"That's right. 'Can't' is short for 'can not.' We can spell words this way, too. When we take out letters and use an apostrophe in their place, the word is called a 'contraction.' "

"When you finish your paper, I will check it for you and initial it in the space provided."

- Either now or later in the day, the student should complete the homework independently (if possible). Help the student correct any incorrect answers. Then initial the homework in the space provided.

READER

- Give the student **Reader 9 (*A CK Spelling Test*)** and some colored pencils.

"We're going to make another book today."

"What is this book's title?" *A CK Spelling Test*

- Assist the student as necessary as he/she completes the following steps:

"Hold up your page so that the tree is facing you."

"Now put your finger on the top dotted line."

"Carefully fold the paper along this dotted line toward you so that it lines up with the bottom dotted line."

"Now fold the top half of the sheet back along the dotted line."

"Hold your book so the tree is facing you again. Then put your finger on the dotted line down the center of the page."

"Fold the book backward along this dotted line so that the tree will still be facing you when you're finished."

- When the student completes this last step, either put a rubber band around the book's spine or staple the spine.

  "Next, carefully separate the pages along the perforated lines at the top and bottom."

- Demonstrate how to separate the pages.

  "Let's check the page numbers to see if they are in the correct order."

- Demonstrate how to check that the book's page numbers are in order.

  "The title of the book is ________?" *A CK Spelling Test*

  "I want you to read this book to yourself. When you come to a blank, try to fill it in with the correct spelling for the /k/ sound. When you are finished, color the pictures. Write your name on the book so I will know who colored it."

  "Keep your book handy because I will be asking you to read it for me."

- Some time during the day, have the student read the reader to you.
- If possible, take time to play the Kid Card games listed in Lesson 30.

Name ________________ **Worksheet 32** *(for use with Lesson 32)* **Phonics 1**

Teacher's Initials ____

ng, -ing

1. kid
2. kept
3. crisp
4. clap
5. kick
6. passing
7. stepping
8. honk
9. grasping
10. contacting
11. Beth kept asking and Dad still said no.
12. Who said no? Dad
13. The soft drink was fizzing in a glass.
14. The glass held a soft drink.

P1-WS-032a

Parent's Initials ____ **Homework 32** *(for use with Lesson 32)* **Phonics 1**

ng, -ing

1. bank
2. dripping
3. tricking
4. limping
5. think
6. sticks
7. snipping
8. skipping
9. happening
10. broth
11. This fog can't last long.
12. The fog can't last.
13. Mom was misting the thick plant.
14. The plant was thick.

Parents: Your child has been taught **digraph ng**; suffix **-ing** and its meaning; and that a **contraction** is formed when two words are combined/shortened and an apostrophe takes the place of missing letters.

P1-WS-032b

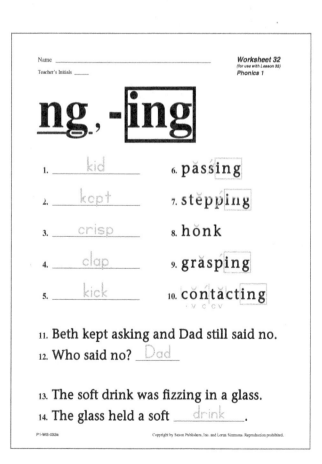

LESSON 33

Suffix -*ed*

lesson preparation

materials

ball

Review Decks

Spelling Sound Sheet 26

tokens or colored pencil

Affix Card 3

Worksheet 33

ALPHABET ACTIVITY

- You and the student should be seated on the floor with the ball.

  "Let's say the alphabet while we roll this ball."

  "I'll begin with 'A' and roll the ball to you. After you catch the ball, say 'B' and roll the ball back to me. We'll continue until we complete the alphabet."

- Recite the alphabet as you and the student roll the ball back and forth.
- Have the student return to his/her seat.

PHONEMIC AWARENESS

- **Objective:** To identify compound words.

  "We have learned that a compound word is two words that come together to form one new word. Say that with me."

- Repeat the definition slowly as the student says it with you.

  "I'll say a compound word. Listen for the two words that make the compound word."

  "The first word is 'goldfish.'"

  "What are the two words?" *"gold" and "fish"*

  "Say it without 'fish.'" *gold*

  "The next word is 'doghouse.'"

  "What are the two words?" *"dog" and "house"*

  "Say it without 'house.'" *dog*

"The next word is 'downstairs.' "

"What are the two words?" *"down" and "stairs"*

"Say it without 'stairs.' " *down*

"Say 'blueberry.' " *blueberry*

"What are the two words?" *"blue" and "berry"*

"Say it without 'berry.' " *blue*

- Continue with additional compound words as time permits.

REVIEW OF DECKS

- Seat the student at a table or a desk.
- Show the student **Letter Cards 1–22** in random order. The student should name the letter on each letter card.
- Review **Affix Cards 1–2.**
- Show the student **Picture Cards 1–28** in random order. The student should name the keyword and sound for each picture card.
- Review **Sight Word Cards 1–8.**
- Give the student **Spelling Sound Sheet 26** and at least twelve tokens (or a colored pencil).

"Let's play Bingo again!"

"When I call out the spelling sounds today, I want you to cover (or X out) the space that spells that sound."

"When you cover (or X out) all of the letters on one line, either up and down, across, or from corner to corner, call out Bingo!"

- Demonstrate, if necessary.

"Don't forget to refer to your rule charts if you need to."

"Are you ready?"

"Cover (or X out) the letters that spell the final sound in 'math.' " *th*

"Cover (or X out) the letter that spells the initial sound in 'cat.' " *c*

"Cover (or X out) the letter that spells the final sound in 'has.' " *~~s~~*

"Cover (or X out) the letter that spells the initial sound in 'mine.' " *m*

"Cover (or X out) the letter that spells the initial sound in 'risk.' " *r*

"Cover (or X out) the letters that spell the final sound in 'gruff.' " *ff*

"Cover (or X out) the letter that spells the initial sound in 'kiss.' " *k*

"Cover (or X out) the letter that spells the initial sound in 'grasshopper.' " *g*

"Cover (or X out) the letter that spells the initial sound in 'helicopter.' " *h*

- The student should Bingo by the time all the sounds have been called out.
- Collect the tokens (or colored pencil) and the spelling sound sheet. If you used tokens and the spelling sound sheet is unmarked, keep it available for practice.

NEW LEARNING

"I'm going to say some words. Echo them back to me and tell me what you hear at the end of each word."

- Point to your mouth as you say each word.

"Jumped." *jumped* ***"Puffed."*** *puffed* ***"Missed."*** *missed*

"What sound do you hear at the end of these words?" */t/*

- Write "jumped," "puffed," and "missed" on the chalkboard.

"What is the same at the end of these words?" *ed*

"Echo these words and tell me what you hear at the end."

"Rubbed." *rubbed* ***"Filled."*** *filled* ***"Tanned."*** *tanned*

"What sound do you hear at the end of these words?" */d/*

- Write "rubbed," "filled," and "tanned" on the chalkboard.

"What is the same at the end of all of these words?" *ed*

"Echo these words and tell me what you hear at the end."

"Sanded." *sanded* ***"Rusted."*** *rusted* ***"Misted."*** *misted*

"What do you hear at the end of these words?" */ĕd/*

- Write "sanded," "rusted," and "misted" on the chalkboard.

"What is the same at the end of all of these words?" *ed*

"Look at these words. Can I cover up the 'ed' on any of them and still have a root word?" *yes*

"What do we call something that is added to the end of a root word?" *a suffix*

"When we learned suffix -ing, it only had one sound. When we learned suffix -s, it could have two sounds. What do you notice about suffix -ed?" *it can make three sounds*

- The sound of suffix *-ed* is determined by the following rules:

  Suffix *-ed* says /t/ after an unvoiced letter (except *t*).

  Suffix *-ed* says /d/ after a voiced letter (except *d*).

  Suffix *-ed* says /ĕd/ when it follows the letter *t* or the letter *d*.

- **Note:** Because children seem to want every suffix *-ed* to say /ĕd/, it is helpful to give the rules that state exactly when it does so. However, your main objective is to teach the student the meaning of suffix *-ed* and that it has more than one sound.

"Some suffixes have their own vowel sound, like suffix -ing. When we add suffix -ing to a one-syllable word, we get a two-syllable word. Add suffix -ing to the word 'jump.' " *jumping*

"How many syllables does 'jumping' have?" *two*

"If a suffix doesn't have its own vowel sound, it doesn't add a syllable to the word. Add suffix -s to the word 'jump.' " *jumps*

"How many syllables does 'jumps' have?" *one*

"That's right. Suffix -s doesn't have its own vowel sound, so it doesn't add a syllable. Now add suffix -ed to 'jump.' " *jumped*

"How many syllables does 'jumped' have?" *one*

"Now try adding suffix -ed to the word 'lift.' " *lifted*

"How many syllables does 'lifted' have?" *two*

"That's right. When we add suffix -ed to a word that ends with t or d, the suffix says /ĕd/. Since /ĕd/ has its own vowel sound, it adds a syllable to the word. But the accent will almost always stay on the root word."

"What does a suffix do to a root word?" *it changes its meaning*

"When suffix -ed is added to the end of a root word, it tells us that the action described by the word has already happened."

"If I sanded the cabinet, has it already been done?" *yes*

"If I jumped on the trampoline, has it already happened?" *yes*

"If I filled the bathtub, have I already done it?" *yes*

"So, what does suffix -ed mean?" *the action has already happened*

- Show the student **Affix Card 3.**

  "What do we call this?" *suffix -ed*

- **Note:** Add the new affix card to the Affix Deck.

BOARDWORK

"Let's practice coding some words like the ones you'll have on your worksheet."

- Review the rule charts, if necessary.
- Write the word "melted" on the chalkboard.

  "Can you help me code this word?"

  "Remember, always box the suffix first."

- As with suffix *-ing* (and for the same reasons), it is usually unnecessary to code within the suffix *-ed*.
- Code the word on the chalkboard as the student instructs: mĕlt′[ed].

  "What is the word?" *melted*

"Can you use the word 'melted' in a sentence?" *expect various answers*

- Repeat the procedure with the following words and sentence:

sniff̸[ed] (suffix -*ed* says /t/)

slămm̸[ed] (suffix -*ed* says /d/)

cŏn′|tăct[ed] (suffix -*ed* says /ĕd/)
vc|cv

Bĕth fill̸[ed] the̸ sink ănd ădd̸′[ed] pŏt[s] ănd păn[s].

- **Note:** If the student is missing the suffix -*ed* spelling, consider adding suffix -*ed* as a response to **Spelling Cards 4** and **13.**

Worksheet

Lesson 33

- The student should be seated where he/she can write comfortably.
- Give the student **Worksheet 33.** Make sure the student turns to the correct side.

"Let's spell with the /ng/ sound we learned yesterday."

"Put your finger by #1. The first word is 'song.'"

"Unblend 'song' with me." */s/ /ŏ/ /ng/*

- Hold up one finger for each sound.

"Let's spell those sounds." *s … o … digraph ng*

- Point to each finger as you spell a sound.

"Now spell the word again and write the letters as you say them."

- Allow time for the student to do this.

"What word did you write?" *song*

- Repeat the procedure with #2 (bang), #3 (thing), #4 (hang), and #5 (ring).

"Now you're ready to code and read the words on your paper."

"Code the words by #6 through #10. After you have coded all the words, try to read them."

- Assist the student as necessary.

"At the bottom of the page are some sentences. One of the sentences is missing a word, and the other one asks a question. If you find any words you can't read, code them. Then see if you can fill in the missing word and answer the question."

- As the student works, provide help as needed. Help the student correct any incorrect answers. Then initial the worksheet in the space provided.
- Some time during the day, ask the student to read from the worksheet or homework. Although coding is important, the ultimate goal is reading, so the student, especially if he/she is having difficulty blending, should read to someone every day.
- **Note:** Always make sure the worksheet is corrected before the student begins the homework. The worksheet serves as a guide to help complete the homework.

HOMEWORK

"Turn your paper over to the homework side."

"Do you think you know what to do on the homework paper?"

"Watch for suffix -ed. Always box suffixes before coding the rest of the word. Also, watch for words with a 'vccv' pattern that need to be divided."

"When you finish your paper, I will check it for you and initial it in the space provided."

- Either now or later in the day, the student should complete the homework independently (if possible). Help the student correct any incorrect answers. Then initial the homework in the space provided.
- If possible, take time to play the Kid Card games listed in Lesson 30.

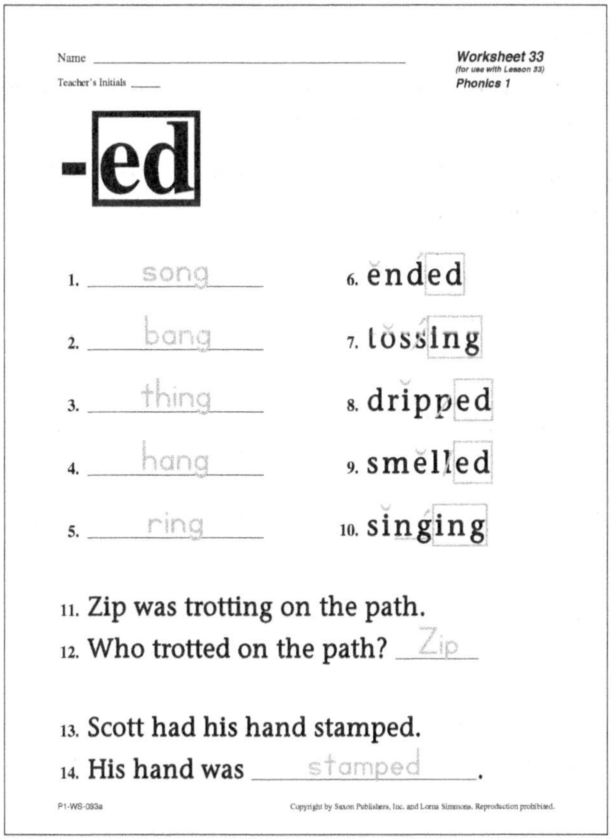

Name ______ Worksheet 33 (for use with Lesson 33) Phonics 1

Teacher's Initials ____

-ed

1. song
2. bang
3. thing
4. hang
5. ring
6. ended
7. tossing
8. dripped
9. smelled
10. singing
11. Zip was trotting on the path.
12. Who trotted on the path? Zip
13. Scott had his hand stamped.
14. His hand was stamped.

P1-WS-033a Copyright by Saxon Publishers, Inc. and Lorna Simmons. Reproduction prohibited.

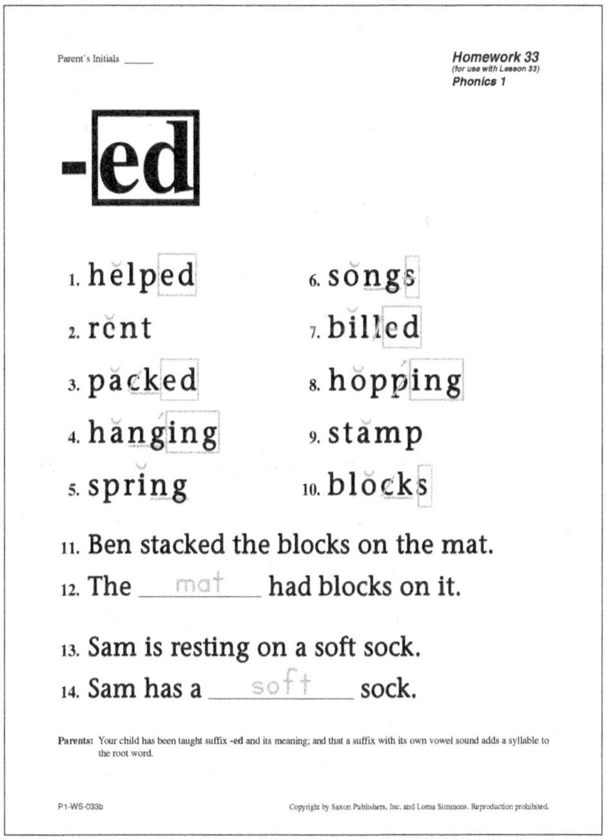

Parent's Initials ____ Homework 33 (for use with Lesson 33) Phonics 1

-ed

1. helped
2. rent
3. packed
4. hanging
5. spring
6. songs
7. billed
8. hopping
9. stamp
10. blocks
11. Ben stacked the blocks on the mat.
12. The mat had blocks on it.
13. Sam is resting on a soft sock.
14. Sam has a soft sock.

Parents: Your child has been taught suffix -ed and its meaning; and that a suffix with its own vowel sound adds a syllable to the root word.

P1-WS-033b Copyright by Saxon Publishers, Inc. and Lorna Simmons. Reproduction prohibited.

LESSON 34 — Digraph *ee*

Lesson 34

> ***lesson preparation***
>
> ***materials***
>
> Review Decks
>
> Spelling Sound Sheet 27
>
> Letter Card 23
>
> Picture Card 29
>
> Worksheet 34
>
> Sight Word Cards 9–11
>
> Reader 10 (*Who Sleeps Where?*)
>
> colored pencils

ALPHABET ACTIVITY

- The student should be seated with the alphabet strip.
- Have available the letter cards *a*, *b*, *c*, *d*, *e*, *f*, and *g*.

"Let's try some more alphabetizing today."

- Place the letter cards along the chalk tray (or anywhere else the student can see them). Deliberately place them in non-alphabetical order.

"We are going to recite the alphabet slowly. Each time we say a letter, we will quickly scan these cards to see if that letter is here."

"Let's start. A."

- Quickly scan the cards with your eyes and your index finger.

"Is there an a?" *yes*

"Let's pull the 'a' card and place it at the beginning of our new row of letters. This row will be in alphabetical order when we finish."

- Move the *a* card to a new location with enough room for the rearranged cards.

"Is there a b?" *yes*

- Pull the *b* card and place it to the right of the *a* card.

"Is there a c?" *yes*

- Pull the *c* card and place it to the right of the *b* card.
- Continue with letter cards *d*, *e*, *f*, and *g*.

"Now our letters are in ABC, or alphabetical, order."

"Let's check to see if we are right."

- Quickly recite the alphabet from *a* to *g*, touching each new card in the sequence as you say it. The student should see that your hand will move progressively to the right if the letters are in the correct order.
- Mix up the cards and alphabetize them again.

Phonemic Awareness

- **Objective:** To identify compound words.

"A compound word is two words that come together to form one new word."

"Say that with me."

- Repeat the definition slowly as the student says it with you.

"I'll say a compound word. Listen for the two words that make the compound word."

"The first word is 'popcorn.' "

"What are the two words?" *"pop" and "corn"*

"Say it without 'pop.' " *corn*

"The next word is 'beehive.' "

"What are the two words?" *"bee" and "hive"*

"Say it without 'hive.' " *bee*

"The next word is 'bathrobe.' "

"What are the two words?" *"bath" and "robe"*

"Say it without 'bath.' " *robe*

"Say 'fireplace.' " *fireplace*

"What are the two words?" *"fire" and "place"*

"Say it without 'place.' " *fire*

- Continue with additional compound words as time permits.

Review of Decks

- The student should be seated where he/she can write comfortably.
- Show the student **Letter Cards 1–22** in random order. The student should name the letter on each letter card.
- Review **Affix Cards 1–3.**
- Show the student **Picture Cards 1–28** in random order. The student should name the keyword and sound for each picture card.
- Review **Sight Word Cards 1–8.**

- Give the student **Spelling Sound Sheet 27.**
- Call out the sounds on **Spelling Cards 1–25** in random order. The student should echo each sound and name the letter or letters that make the sound as he/she writes the letter(s) on the spelling sound sheet.
- Have the student set the spelling sound sheet aside for use later in the lesson.

NEW LEARNING

"I'm going to say some words. Echo them back to me and listen for the sound in the medial, or middle, position."

- Point to your mouth as you say each word.

"Echo after me. Teeth." *teeth* ***"Beet."*** *beet* ***"Keep."*** *keep*

"What sound do you hear in the medial position?" */ē/*

"That's right. The sound you hear in the medial position is /ē/."

"Put your fingertips on the front of your neck and say /ē/. See if you can feel any vibration."

"Is this sound voiced or unvoiced?" *voiced*

- Write the following words on the chalkboard: teeth, beet, keep.

"Look at these words. What letters might be making the /ē/ sound?" *two e's*

"There is an ee in all of these words, so we can see that the letters ee must be making the /ē/ sound."

"How many sounds do you hear?" *one*

"How many letters are making that one sound?" *two*

- Use the hand signals described in Lesson 28 as you say the following:

"What do we call two letters that come together to make one sound?" *a digraph*

"Is digraph ee a vowel or consonant digraph?" *a vowel digraph, because it contains only vowels*

NEW DECK CARDS

- Pull **Spelling Card 22** from the Review Deck.
- Show the student **Letter Card 23.**

"What do we call this?" *digraph ee*

- Hold up **Picture Card 29** but keep the picture covered with your hand (or the letter card).

"Our keyword contains the /ē/ sound today."

"Let's try something different to figure out our keyword."

"Have you ever played 'Twenty Questions'?"

- Explain the game to the student. The student may ask you twenty questions in order to discover the keyword. The questions must be ones that can be answered with "yes" or "no."
- Remind the student that the answer will contain the /ē/ sound and is spelled with digraph *ee*.
- The initial questions may be haphazard or repetitive, but as the student continues to play, he/she will develop a more organized approach. Feel free to guide the questions to the extent needed to determine the keyword.

"What is our keyword?" *sheep*

- Show the student **Picture Card 29.**

"The word 'sheep' helps us remember the /ē/ sound since it contains the /ē/ sound."

- **Note:** The digraph and its picture are also shown in the Rule Book on page 21.

"Find your spelling sound sheet. Put your finger by #26."

- Hold up **Spelling Card 22** so only you can see what is written.

"Echo this sound: /ē/." */ē/*

"How do we spell the /ē/ sound?" *e or digraph ee*

"That's right. Now we know two ways to spell the /ē/ sound."

"In one-syllable words, digraph ee can be found in any of the three positions: initial, medial, or final. In two-syllable words, it's best to spell with just e, as in 'equal.' These are the best ways to spell the /ē/ sound if you're not sure."

- Write "ee, e || ee" on the chalkboard. Point to it as you ask:

"What will you say when I give you the /ē/ sound?" *digraph ee comma e final digraph ee*

"Write your new response on line #26."

- **Note:** This will be the proper response to **Spelling Card 22** until Lesson 62.
- Check the spelling sound sheet for accuracy.
- **Note:** Add the new letter and picture cards to the Review Decks (and re-insert **Spelling Card 22**).

Lesson 34

BOARDWORK

"Let's practice coding some words like the ones you'll have on your worksheet."

- Write the word "speeding" on the chalkboard.

"Let's code this word. What's the first thing we need to do?" *box the suffix -ing*

- Box suffix *-ing*: speed[ing].

"How will we code digraph ee?" *underline it*

- Underline digraph *ee*: sp<u>ee</u>d[ing].

"What sound does digraph ee make?" /ē/

"That's right. We'll put a macron over the first e and cross out the second e to show that digraph ee only makes one sound."

- Put a macron over the first *e* and mark out the second: spēed[ing].

"Where will the accent be?" *the root word*

"That's right. When you add a suffix, the accent usually stays on the root word."

- Add the accent: spēed´[ing].
- Repeat with the following word and sentence:

răn´|dŏm
v c |c v

Dăd nēed´[ed] å hĕlp´[ing] hănd.

WORKSHEET

- The student should be seated where he/she can write comfortably.
- Give the student **Worksheet 34.** Make sure the student turns to the correct side.

"Let's spell with the /ē/ sound using digraph ee today."

"Put your finger by #1. The first word is 'feel.' "

"How many syllables are in the word 'feel'?" *one*

"What is the best way to spell the /ē/ sound in a one-syllable word?" *ee*

"Unblend 'feel' with me." */f/ /ē/ /l/*

- Hold up one finger for each sound.

"Let's spell those sounds." *f ... digraph ee ... l*

- Point to each finger as you spell a sound.

"Now spell the word again and write the letters as you say them."

- Allow time for the student to do this.

"What word did you write?" *feel*

- Repeat the procedure with #2 (keep), #3 (tree), #4 (feed), and #5 (sleet).

"Now you're ready to code and read the words on your paper."

"Code the words by #6 through #10. After you have coded all the words, try to read them."

- Assist the student as necessary.

"We have three new sight words today."

- Write "to," "two," and "into" on the chalkboard.

"Do you know these sight words?" *expect various answers*

"The first word is 'to,' which means 'in the direction of.' For example, 'I went to the store.' "

"The second word is 'two,' which means the number two."

"The third word is 'into.' Can you use the word 'into' in a sentence?" *expect various answers*

"These words will always be sight words. Circle them whenever you see them."

"See if you can find these words on the sight word charts."

- Help the student locate the words in the Irregular Spelling Booklet.
- Show the student **Sight Word Cards 9–11.**

"We'll add these cards to our sight word deck."

- Draw a comma on the chalkboard.

"You'll see a comma on today's worksheet. We've been using commas in our spelling sound activities. We write them to show that we pause slightly before saying the next letter. It means the same thing in a sentence."

"At the bottom of the page are some sentences. Two of the sentences have a word missing. If you find any words you can't read, code them. Don't forget to circle the sight words. Then see if you can fill in the missing words."

- As the student works, provide help as needed. Help the student correct any incorrect answers. Then initial the worksheet in the space provided.
- Some time during the day, ask the student to read from the worksheet or homework. Although coding is important, the ultimate goal is reading, so the student, especially if he/she is having difficulty blending, should read to someone every day.
- **Note:** Always make sure the worksheet is corrected before the student begins the homework. The worksheet serves as a guide to help complete the homework.
- Add **Sight Word Cards 9–11** to the Sight Word Deck.

HOMEWORK

"Turn your paper over to the homework side."

"Do you think you know what to do on the homework paper?"

"Watch for suffixes. Always box suffixes before coding the rest of the word. Also, watch for words with a 'vccv' pattern that need to be divided."

"When you finish your paper, I will check it for you and initial it in the space provided."

- Either now or later in the day, the student should complete the homework independently (if possible). Help the student correct any incorrect answers. Then initial the homework in the space provided.

Reader

- Give the student **Reader 10 (*Who Sleeps Where?*)** and some colored pencils.

  "We're going to make another book today."

  "What is this book's title?" *Who Sleeps Where?*

- Assist the student as necessary as he/she completes the following steps:

  "Hold up your page so that the tree is facing you."

  "Now put your finger on the top dotted line."

  "Carefully fold the paper along this dotted line toward you so that it lines up with the bottom dotted line."

  "Now fold the top half of the sheet back along the dotted line."

  "Hold your book so the tree is facing you again. Then put your finger on the dotted line down the center of the page."

  "Fold the book backward along this dotted line so that the tree will still be facing you when you're finished."

- When the student completes this last step, either put a rubber band around the book's spine or staple the spine.

  "Next, carefully separate the pages along the perforated lines at the top and bottom."

- Demonstrate how to separate the pages.

  "Let's check the page numbers to see if they are in the correct order."

- Demonstrate how to check that the book's page numbers are in order.

  "The title of this book is __________?" *Who Sleeps Where?*

  "I want you to read your book to yourself. When you are finished reading, color the pictures. Write your name on the book so I will know who colored it."

  "Keep your book handy because I will be asking you to read it for me."

- Some time during the day, have the student read the reader to you.
- If possible, take time to play the Kid Card games listed in Lesson 30. Try to see that the student is prepared for tomorrow's assessment.

Name _____

Teacher's Initials _____

Worksheet 34
(for use with Lesson 34)
Phonics 1

ē é

1. _feel_ 6. strēet

2. _keep_ 7. sĕldŏm
 v c c v

3. _tree_ 8. hĭnted

4. _feed_ 9. thĭng

5. _sleet_ 10. slăck

11. The deer fed on the grass.

12. Deer feed on _grass_ .

13. Ted was sent to class to sing a song.

14. Ted sang the song in _class_ .

Parent's Initials _____

Homework 34
(for use with Lesson 34)
Phonics 1

ē é

1. slēep 6. răndŏm
 v c c v

2. snăck 7. sĭfted

3. păth 8. flĭng

4. frēe 9. sēe

5. mĕnd 10. sēed

11. Bill lost three teeth in class.

12. What was lost in class? _three teeth_

13. Dan ran to the pen to get his fat, black pig.

14. Dan's pig is _fat_ and _black_ .

Parents: Your child has been taught **digraph ee**; and that a suffix with its own vowel sound adds a syllable to the root word.

Lesson 34

Lesson 35 — Assessment

lesson preparation

materials

ball
Review Decks
Assessment 6
Spelling Test 4
Assessment 6 Recording Form
Kid Cards
tokens

the night before

- Separate the Kid Cards marked "Lesson 35."

Alphabet Activity

- Have the student stand where he/she can toss the ball back and forth to you.

  "Let's say the alphabet as we toss this ball."

  "I'll begin with 'A' and toss the ball to you. After you catch the ball, say 'B' and toss the ball back to me. We'll continue until we complete the alphabet."
- Recite the alphabet as you and the student toss the ball back and forth.
- Have the student return to his/her seat.

Phonemic Awareness

- **Objective:** To identify compound words.

  "Echo this word: fireplace." *fireplace*

  "Say it without 'fire.' " *place*
- Repeat with more words as time permits, using the list of words that follows:

afternoon	applesauce	babysit	backrest	campfire
countdown	daydream	daredevil	earmuff	evergreen
fingernail	flashlight	grapevine	gumdrop	hayloft
horseback	infield	keyhole	ladybug	lifeboat
mailbox	moonlight	newspaper	nosebleed	oatmeal
pancake	quicksand	playground	rosebush	scoreboard
snowball	thunderstorm	underground	waterproof	zigzag

Review of Decks

"Let's play 'Twenty Questions' again today."

"You know these decks very well, so I am going to choose a card and see if you can ask me questions and guess which card I have selected."

- Do not let the student see which deck or which card you select.

"You may ask me any question you like as long as I can answer 'yes' or 'no.' "

- If the student has difficulty, help him/her by suggesting questions such as "Is it a letter card?", "Is it a vowel?", "Is it a digraph?", etc.

Written Assessment

- Seat the student where he/she can write comfortably.
- Give the student **Assessment 6.**
- **Section I:**

"Today we are going to write some words for our assessment."

"I'm going to say a word. Write the letter that makes each sound in that word on the lines by #1."

"Look at the rule charts if you need to."

"Here's the first word: beg."

- Repeat with the following words in the order shown: #2 (rock), #3 (sticks), #4 (skip), and #5 (clam). Point to **Rule Charts 3** and **4** to remind the student how to spell the /k/ sound in each word.
- **Section II:**

"Look at the letter by #6."

"Find the picture of the keyword for this sound."

"Draw a line from the letter to the keyword."

- Repeat with #7 and #8. Allow a few minutes for the student to work.
- The pictures (from top to bottom) are as follows: egg, mask, lock.
- **Section III:**

"Put your finger on #9."

"Code the words by #9, #10, #11, and #12."

- Allow a few minutes for the student to work.
- **Section IV:**
- Have the student name the sound of each blend in #13–#17.
- Help identify each picture and then ask the student to name the blend each picture begins with and to draw a line from the picture to the blend. The pictures (from top to bottom) are as follows: bread, splinter, straw, scarf, block.
- **Section V:**

"Look at the sentences by #18 and #19."

"Read the sentences. If you find any words you can't read, code them to help you figure them out. Then see if you can fill in the missing words."

- **Note:** If the student absolutely cannot read the sentences, read them to the student to see if he or she can answer the questions.

"When you are finished, show your paper to me."

- This paper will be used during the oral portion of the assessment.

Spelling Test

- Give the student **Spelling Test 4.**
- Call out the following words (in the order shown). Sound them out, if necessary.

 #1 (dig), #2 (hat), #3 (ran), #4 (go), #5 (had), #6 (got), #7 (has), #8 (dog), #9 (pig), #10 (fast)

- Grade and record the test in any manner that suits your needs.

Oral Assessment

- Oral assessments are short interviews that occur during independent work time. It is important to complete them promptly (today, if possible) in order to identify any areas of weakness and begin remediation.
- Use the assessment and the following dialogue to complete the oral portion.
- **Section VI:**
- Point to the sight word by #20.

"Read this sight word for me."

- Record the student's response by placing a check mark by each word he/she reads correctly.
- Repeat with #21 and #22.
- **Section VII:**
- Show the student the letter by #23.

"Tell me the name of this letter and the sound it makes."

- Write the student's response on the adjacent line.
- Repeat with #24 and #25.

Assessment Evaluation

- Grade the assessment and record the results on **Assessment 6 Recording Form.** Check off the boxes to indicate mastery (i.e., the section was completed with 100% accuracy).
- **Reminder:** Try to give as many points as possible for work attempted. Do not grade the coding marks too severely, especially secondary marks like accents, voice lines, and k-backs. The most important coding marks to look for are breves, macrons, and syllable division lines.

- See the introductory material for detailed information regarding grading and recording procedures.
- Use the assessment results to identify those skills in which the student is weak. Practice those skills by playing Kid Card games.
- Add the Kid Cards marked "Lesson 35" to the existing decks. Listed below are games appropriate for remediation in selected areas. See "Games and Activities" for the directions for each game.
- **Section I:** Play "Spelling Deck Perfection," "Sound Scamper," "Spell Out #1," or have the student use the letter tiles to spell words you give from the Spelling Word List.
- **Section II:** Play "Keyword and Sound" or "Letter/Sound Identification."
- **Section III:** Play "Chalkboard Challenge."
- **Section IV:** Play "Blend It."
- **Section V:** Have the student read the controlled readers. Ask questions for comprehension.
- **Section VI:** Play "At First Sight."
- **Section VII:** Play "Letter Deck Data" or "Letter/Sound Identification."
- When the student seems more secure in areas that had previously proven difficult, retest him/her (in those areas only) and indicate on the recording form any sections the student has subsequently mastered.
- Try to help the student achieve mastery of all the sections before the next assessment.
- If the student is having difficulty with a particular skill, keep his or her practice activities at the most basic level so the chance of success is greater.

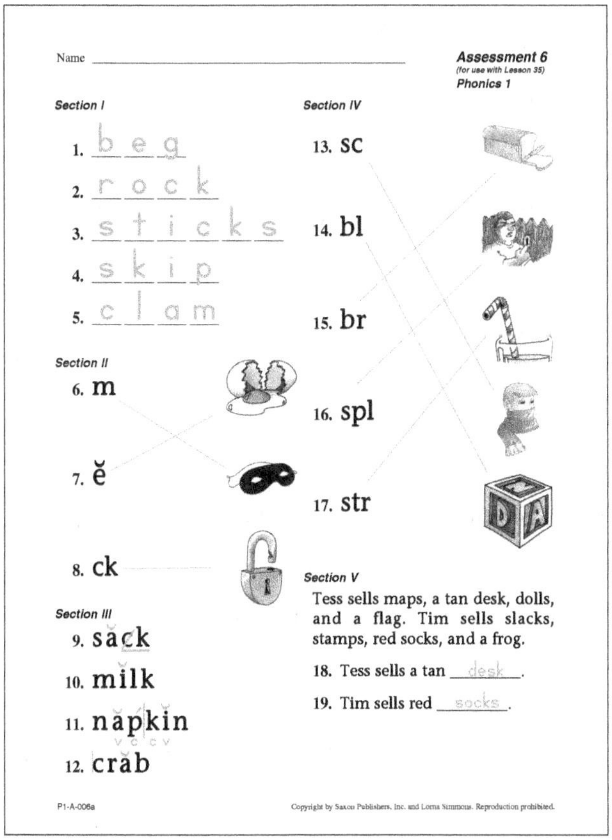
Name ______________________

Assessment 6
(for use with Lesson 35)
Phonics 1

Section I

1. b e g
2. r o c k
3. s t i c k s
4. s k i p
5. c l a m

Section II

6. m
7. ĕ
8. ck

Section III

9. săck
10. mĭlk
11. năpkĭn
12. crăb

Section IV

13. sc
14. bl
15. br
16. spl
17. str

Section V

Tess sells maps, a tan desk, dolls, and a flag. Tim sells slacks, stamps, red socks, and a frog.

18. Tess sells a tan ___desk___.
19. Tim sells red ___socks___.

P1-A-006a

Assessment 6
(for use with Lesson 35)
Phonics 1

Section VI

20. put ________
21. are ________
22. where ________

Section VII

23. m ___m, /m/___
24. e ___e, /ĕ/, /ē/___
25. ck ___digraph ck, /k/___

P1-A-006b

LESSON 36 — Spelling with Final *k*

lesson preparation

materials

Review Decks

Spelling Sound Sheet 28

Sight Word Card 12

Worksheet 36

Spelling List 5

ALPHABET ACTIVITY

- The student should be seated with the alphabet strip.

"How many letters are in the alphabet?" *26*

"What two kinds of letters make up our alphabet?" *vowels and consonants*

"Name the vowels." *a, e, i, o, and u*

"All of the other letters are called _________?" *consonants*

"The initial letter of the alphabet is _____?" *a*

"The final letter of the alphabet is _____?" *z*

"Let's point to each letter and say the whole alphabet."

"Put your index finger on 'a' and say the names with me."

PHONEMIC AWARENESS

- **Objective:** To identify the number of words in sentences.

"Let's try something new today."

"A sentence is made up of words. For example, I can put some words together and make a sentence like 'I can jump.' "

"Can you show me with your fingers how many words are in my sentence?" *three fingers, three words*

"What are the three words?" *I, can, jump*

"Let's try another one. Are your fingers ready? Listen for the number of words in this sentence."

" 'The bus is late.' How many words are in my sentence?" *four fingers, four words*

"Here's the next one. 'I would like a drink.' How many words are in my sentence?" *five fingers, five words*

"Can you think of a sentence? If you can, we'll count the words in it."

- Have the student tell you a sentence or two to see if he/she can form sentences. Count the words in each sentence with the student.

REVIEW OF DECKS

- The student should be seated where he/she can write comfortably.
- Show the student **Letter Cards 1–23** in random order. The student should name the letter on each letter card.
- Review **Affix Cards 1–3.**
- Show the student **Picture Cards 1–29** in random order. The student should name the keyword and sound for each picture card.
- Review **Sight Word Cards 1–11.**
- Give the student **Spelling Sound Sheet 28.**
- Call out the sounds on **Spelling Cards 1–25** in random order. The student should echo each sound and name the letter or letters that make the sound as he/she writes the letter(s) on the spelling sound sheet.
- Have the student set the spelling sound sheet aside for use later in the lesson.

NEW LEARNING

- Pull **Spelling Card 18** from the Review Deck.

"We have learned several rules for spelling the /k/ sound."

"At the beginning or middle of the word, we use k or c."

- Refer to **Rule Chart 3.**

"Can you tell me when we use k?" *before e, i, and y*

"Can you tell me when we use c?" *before anything else (a, o, u, or any consonant)*

"About a week ago, we learned how to spell the /k/ sound at the end of a word."

"Do you remember what digraph we use to spell /k/ at the end of a word?" *digraph ck*

"What is it that always comes before digraph ck?" *a short vowel*

"Today we are going to learn another way to spell the /k/ sound at the end of a word."

- Write the following words on the chalkboard in two columns:

tank	peek
silk	sleek
bank	seek
hulk	meek

"How have we spelled the /k/ sound in these two lists of words?" *k*

"Did the /k/ sound come right after a short vowel?" *no*

"So we couldn't use digraph ck, could we? Look at these words carefully. I think you can tell me two times when we end a word with k by itself instead of digraph ck." *after a consonant or digraph ee*

"That's right, but not just digraph ee. As we learn more vowel digraphs, this rule will apply to them as well."

- Refer to **Rule Chart 4.**

"Now we know that ck comes after a short vowel, but k comes after a consonant, as in 'milk' or 'tank,' or a vowel digraph, as in 'peek' or 'seek.' "

"Find your spelling sound sheet. Put your finger by #26."

- Hold up **Spelling Card 18.**

"We need to add another spelling response to our /k/ spelling card."

"What have we been saying for /k/?" *k comma c final digraph ck*

- Write "k, c || ck" on the chalkboard.

"Now we know how to spell with k in the final position, so we need to add k after the final line."

- Add *k* to the response: k, c || ck, k.

"Now we will say 'k comma c final digraph ck comma k.' "

"Write the new response on line #26."

- **Note:** This will be the proper response to **Spelling Card 18** until Lesson 44.
- Check the spelling sound sheet for accuracy.
- **Note:** Be sure to re-insert **Spelling Card 18** in the Review Decks.

Boardwork

"Let's practice coding some words like the ones you'll have on your worksheet."

"The rule charts are in your Rule Book if you need to look at them."

- Write the following words and sentence (without the coding marks) on the chalkboard, one at a time. Ask the student to help you code them. The correct coding is as follows:

risǩ' ing

milǩ ed

Dăn pēek ed (into) the căn (of) ănt s.

- When you reach the word "of" in the sentence, point it out to the student.

"We have a new sight word in this sentence. Do you see it?"

- Show the student **Sight Word Card 12.**

"This word is 'of.' Can you use the word 'of' in another sentence?" *expect various answers*

- Help the student locate the word in the Irregular Spelling Booklet.

"Circle this word each time you see it."

"We'll add this card to our sight word deck."

"Let's practice spelling some words like the ones you'll have on your worksheet."

- Write the following on the chalkboard: slee___, stǐ___, clŏ___, lee___.

"All of these words end with the /k/ sound. You'll need to decide if the word should end with digraph ck or just k by itself."

- Refer to **Rule Chart 4** to help the student determine whether to use *k* or *ck*: sleek, stick, clock, leek.
- Define the word "leek" for the student (as opposed to "leak"), if desired.
- Add **Sight Word Card 12** to the Sight Word Deck.

Lesson 36

Worksheet

- The student should be seated where he/she can write comfortably.
- Give the student **Worksheet 36.** Make sure the student turns to the correct side.

"Look at the word by #1. Use the rule at the top of the page to finish spelling the word with k or digraph ck."

- Repeat with #2 through #5.

"Now you're ready to code and read the words on your paper."

"Code the words by #6 through #10. After you have coded all the words, try to read them."

- Assist the student as necessary.

"At the bottom of the page are some sentences. If you find any words you can't read, code them. Don't forget to circle the sight words. Then see if you can answer the questions."

- As the student works, provide help as needed. Help the student correct any incorrect answers. Then initial the worksheet in the space provided.
- Some time during the day, ask the student to read from the worksheet or homework. Although coding is important, the ultimate goal is reading, so the student, especially if he/she is having difficulty blending, should read to someone every day.
- **Note:** Always make sure the worksheet is corrected before the student begins the homework. The worksheet serves as a guide to help complete the homework.

Homework

"Turn your paper over to the homework side."

"Do you know what to do on the rest of the homework paper?"

"Watch for suffixes. Always box suffixes before coding the rest of the word. Also, watch for words with a 'vccv' pattern that need to be divided."

"When you finish your paper, I will check it for you and initial it in the space provided."

- Either now or later in the day, the student should complete the homework independently (if possible). Help the student correct any incorrect answers. Then initial the homework in the space provided.

Spelling List

- Fold **Spelling List 5** in half lengthwise (with the printed side facing out).

"Leave your paper just like I give it to you."

- Give the student **Spelling List 5,** folded with the blank lines facing up.

"Let's spell some more words."

- Call out the following words (in the order shown). Sound them out, if necessary.

  #1 (cat), #2 (clip), #3 (skip), #4 (raft), #5 (kid), #6 (glad), #7 (skid), #8 (cast), #9 (milk), #10 (cost), #11 (oh), #12 (what)

"Now unfold your paper and check your words."

- Check the student's work to see if he/she needs extra help with spelling.

"I want you to practice these words. We'll have a spelling test in a few days."

- If possible, take time to play the Kid Card games listed in Lesson 35.

Name ______________________

Teacher's Initials _____

Worksheet 36
(for use with Lesson 36)
Phonics 1

k

ck is found after a short vowel.
k is found after a consonant or vowel digraph.

1. mil k
2. ră ck
3. see k
4. ban k
5. lŏ ck
6. hĕlpíng
7. păssed
8. three
9. zing
10. traffic (v c c v)

11. Pam missed the last step and fell on top of Kim.
12. Who missed the step? Pam
13. Mom is going to let Zack and Dad go camping.
14. Who is going camping? Dad and Zack

P1-WS-036a

Parent's Initials _____

Homework 36
(for use with Lesson 36)
Phonics 1

k

ck is found after a short vowel.
k is found after a consonant or vowel digraph.

1. deep
2. stŏmpíng
3. spĕlled
4. ring
5. smăck
6. pĕt
7. speed
8. sĕtting
9. bŏng
10. flĭck

11. Deb sang the song and the class clapped.
12. Who clapped? the class
13. The test was a mess but Lee passed the class.
14. What was a mess? the test

Parents: Your child has been taught that when spelling the "k" sound at the end of a word, k follows a consonant or vowel digraph and ck follows a short vowel.

P1-WS-036b

Lesson 36

LESSON 37 — The Letter *U*

lesson preparation

materials

Review Decks
Spelling Sound Sheet 29
container of letter tiles
Letter Card 24
Picture Cards 30–31
Spelling Cards 26–27
Worksheet 37
Sight Word Card 13
Reader 11 (*Zip's Mess*)
colored pencils

the night before

- **Optional:** Select a piece of music appropriate for a marching activity.
- Add the *u* letter tile to the student's container.

ALPHABET ACTIVITY

"Today we're going to have an alphabet march."

"Let's stand up and form a line. Say the alphabet together as we march around the room. Each time we take a step, we will say a letter."

- Lead the student in a march. Let the student take a turn leading, if desired. Marching music can be played, if desired.
- **Optional:** Have the student march as he/she sings the alphabet song.
- Have the student return to his/her seat.

PHONEMIC AWARENESS

- **Objective:** To identify the number of words in sentences.

"Yesterday we counted the number of words in some sentences. Let's try some more of those today."

"Show me with your fingers how many words are in this sentence. 'Ice cream tastes good.' " *four fingers, four words*

"What are the words?" *ice, cream, tastes, good*

"Let's try another one. Are your fingers ready? Listen to the number of words in this sentence."

" 'Books teach us so much.' How many words are in my sentence?" *five fingers, five words*

"Here's the next one. 'Grandma lives in the country.' How many words are in my sentence?" *five fingers, five words*

"Can you think of a sentence to tell me? We'll count the words in it together."

- Have the student tell you a sentence or two to see if he/she can form sentences. Count the words in each sentence with the student.

REVIEW OF DECKS

- The student should be seated where he/she can write comfortably.
- Show the student **Letter Cards 1–23** in random order. The student should name the letter on each letter card.
- Review **Affix Cards 1–3.**
- Show the student **Picture Cards 1–29** in random order. The student should name the keyword and sound for each picture card.
- Review **Sight Word Cards 1–12.**
- Give the student **Spelling Sound Sheet 29.**
- Call out the sounds on **Spelling Cards 1–25** in random order. The student should echo each sound and name the letter or letters that make the sound as he/she writes the letter(s) on the spelling sound sheet.
- Check the student's response after each card.
- Have the student set the spelling sound sheet aside for use later in the lesson.

NEW LEARNING

"I'm going to say some words. Echo them back to me and listen for the sound in the initial position."

- Point to your mouth as you say each word.

"Echo after me. Up." *up* ***"Under."*** *under* ***"Umpire."*** *umpire*

"What sound do you hear in the initial position?" */ŭ/*

"That's right. The sound you hear in the initial position is /ŭ/."

"Put your fingertips on the front of your neck and say /ŭ/. See if you feel any vibration."

"Is this sound voiced or unvoiced?" *voiced*

"Since /ŭ/ vibrates, it is a voiced sound."

- Write the following words on the chalkboard: rust, fun, bug.

"What letter do you see that might be making the /ŭ/ sound?" *u*

- If the student does not know the name of the letter, say it for him/her.

"There is a u in all of these words, so we can see that the letter u must be making the /ŭ/ sound. Is u a vowel or a consonant?" *a vowel*

Handwriting/Letter Tiles

- The student should be seated where he/she can write comfortably.
- Write a capital *U* on the chalkboard.

"This is a capital U. Let's practice skywriting capital U's before we write them on our paper."

- Have the student practice skywriting capital *U*'s.

"Find your spelling sound sheet."

- Draw handwriting lines on the chalkboard. Write a capital *U* on the handwriting lines in the handwriting you want the student to learn.

"Find the first handwriting line on your paper and practice writing capital U's like I wrote this one on the chalkboard. Say the name of the letter each time you write it."

- Allow a few minutes for the student to practice writing capital *U*'s.
- Write a lowercase *u* on the handwriting lines in the handwriting you want the student to learn.

"This is a lowercase u."

- Have the student practice skywriting lowercase *u*'s.

"Now practice writing lowercase u's on the second handwriting line. Say the name of the letter each time you write it."

- Have the student set the spelling sound sheet aside for use later in the lesson.
- Leave the handwriting lines and letters on the chalkboard for the remainder of the lesson.
- Give the student the container of letter tiles.

"Today I've given you another new letter tile."

"Find your u letter tile and look at it. One side has a capital U and the other side has a lowercase u."

"Hold your letter tile up in the air. Turn it so I can see the capital U."

"Now turn it so I can see the lowercase u."

"Spell the word 'us' with your letter tiles."

"This time, spell the word 'up.' "

"Now add one letter to make the word 'cup.' "

- Watch to see if the student refers to **Rule Chart 3.**
- Choose additional words from the Spelling Word List, if desired.
- Have the student replace the tiles in the container and put it away.
- Reinforce the name, sound, and shape of the letter *u* throughout the day.

New Deck Cards

- Show the student **Letter Card 24.**

  "What is the name of this letter?" *u*

- Hold up **Picture Card 30** but keep the picture covered.

  "I have a card with a picture on it that begins with the /ŭ/ sound."

  "I am going to describe it for you. See if you can guess what the picture is."

  "You might find this in a closet, on a beach, or in a rainstorm. This can be very colorful. It is used for protection against sun and rain. What do you think the picture is?" *umbrella*

  "That's right. The keyword is 'umbrella' and the sound we have learned is /ŭ/."

- Show the student **Picture Card 30,** and then point to the picture of an umbrella on the alphabet strip.

  "The word 'umbrella' helps us remember the /ŭ/ sound because it begins with /ŭ/."

  "I have another riddle for you today. Why would we have two riddles for the letter u?" *u is a vowel and vowels have at least two sounds*

- Hold up **Picture Card 31** but keep the picture covered.

  "I have a card with a picture on it that begins with the long sound of u. See if you can guess what the picture is."

  "This is an animal that isn't real. We read about it in stories that are make-believe. It looks like a horse with a horn coming out of its forehead. What do you think the picture is?" *unicorn*

  "That's right. The keyword is 'unicorn' and the sound we have learned is /ū/."

- Show the student **Picture Card 31.**

  "The word 'unicorn' helps us remember the /ū/ sound because it begins with the /ū/ sound."

"We will keep these cards together in our review deck to help us remember that the letter u can make two sounds."

"Find your spelling sound sheet. Find #26 and put your finger on it."

- Hold up **Spelling Cards 26** and **27** (one at a time) so only you can see what is written. Follow the instructions on each card.
- Check the spelling sound sheet for accuracy.
- **Note:** Add the new letter, picture, and spelling cards to the Review Decks. Always keep **Picture Card 31** behind **Picture Card 30** to help the student remember that the letter *u* has two sounds.

BOARDWORK

"Let's practice coding some words like the ones you'll have on your worksheet."

"The rule charts are in your Rule Book if you need to look at them."

- Write the following word, phrase, and sentence (without the coding marks) on the chalkboard, one at a time. Ask the student to help you code them. The correct coding is as indicated:

hŭnt´[ing]

căp~~p~~[ed] tē~~e~~th

Mĕg kĭs~~s~~[ed] Mŏm ănd lĕft.

WORKSHEET

- The student should be seated where he/she can write comfortably.
- Give the student **Worksheet 37.** Make sure the student turns to the correct side.

"Today, let's spell with the /ŭ/ sound."

"Put your finger by #1. The first word is 'hug.'"

"Unblend 'hug' with me." */h/ /ŭ/ /g/*

- Hold up one finger for each sound.

"Let's spell those sounds." **h ... u ... g**

- Point to each finger as you spell a sound.

"Now spell the word again and write the letters as you say them."

- Allow time for the student to do this.

"What word did you write?" ***hug***

- Repeat the procedure with #2 (stuck), #3 (thump), #4 (peek), and #5 (sunk).

"Now you're ready to code and read the words on your paper."

"Code the words by #6 through #10. After you have coded all the words, try to read them."

- Assist the student as necessary.

  "At the bottom of the page are some sentences. If you find any words you can't read, code them. Don't forget to circle the sight words. Then see if you can fill in the missing words."

- As the student works, provide help as needed. Help the student correct any incorrect answers. Then initial the worksheet in the space provided.
- Some time during the day, ask the student to read from the worksheet or homework.
- **Note:** Always make sure the worksheet is corrected before the student begins the homework. The worksheet serves as a guide to help complete the homework.

HOMEWORK

"Turn your paper over to the homework side."

"Put your finger on the top row of handwriting lines. Write your best capital U on these lines so I will know what a capital U should look like."

- Have the student write a lowercase letter *u* on the second handwriting line. Make sure that the student has written the letters correctly (to the best of his or her ability). He/She will use them as guides when completing the homework.

  "Do you know what to do on the rest of the homework paper?"

  "When you finish your paper, I will check it for you and initial it in the space provided."

- Either now or later in the day, the student should complete the homework independently (if possible). Help the student correct any incorrect answers. Then initial the homework in the space provided.

READER

"We have a new book today and our book has a new sight word."

- Show the student **Sight Word Card 13.**

  "Do you know what this word is?" *expect various answers*

  "This word is 'come.' Can you use the word 'come' in a sentence?" *expect various answers*

- Write the word "comes" on the chalkboard.

  "If I add an s to it, what is the word?" *comes*

  "You will see this word in your book. Circle it to help you remember that it is a sight word."

  "We will add this card to our sight word deck."

- Give the student **Reader 11 (*Zip's Mess*)** and some colored pencils.

"We're going to make another book today."

"What is this book's title?" *Zip's Mess*

- Assist the student as necessary as he/she completes the following steps:

"Hold up your page so that the tree is facing you."

"Now put your finger on the top dotted line."

"Carefully fold the paper along this dotted line toward you so that it lines up with the bottom dotted line."

"Now fold the top half of the sheet back along the dotted line."

"Hold your book so the tree is facing you again. Then put your finger on the dotted line down the center of the page."

"Fold the book backward along this dotted line so that the tree will still be facing you when you're finished."

- When the student completes this last step, either put a rubber band around the book's spine or staple the spine.

"Next, carefully separate the pages along the perforated lines at the top and bottom."

- Demonstrate how to separate the pages.

"Let's check the page numbers to see if they are in the correct order."

- Demonstrate how to check that the book's page numbers are in order.

"The title of this book is ___________?" *Zip's Mess*

"Turn to page 8."

"Do you see the contraction?"

- Point out the contraction "it's."

"Do you remember what a contraction is?" *a short way of saying two words*

"That's right. The contraction 'it's' is short for 'it is.' Which letter has been replaced by an apostrophe?" *i*

"I want you to read your book to yourself. When you are finished reading, color the pictures. Write your name on the book so I will know who colored it."

"Keep your book handy because I will be asking you to read it for me."

- Some time during the day, have the student read the reader to you.
- Add **Sight Word Card 13** to the Sight Word Deck.
- If possible, take time to play the Kid Card games listed in Lesson 35.

Name ______________________

Teacher's Initials ____

Worksheet 37
(for use with Lesson 37)
Phonics 1

Uu

1. hug
2. stuck
3. thump
4. peek
5. sunk
6. green
7. limped
8. planted
9. thinking
10. scrub
11. Sam's feet sank in the mud.
12. Sam's feet are stuck.
13. Bees are buzzing in the deep grass.
14. The grass is deep.

P1-WS-037a

Parent's Initials ____

Homework 37
(for use with Lesson 37)
Phonics 1

Uu

1. tub
2. keeping
3. bulbs
4. track
5. tilted
6. stuff
7. trusted
8. pumping
9. Tess asked Ron to get a coffee mug.
10. What did Ron get? a coffee mug
11. Beth hummed and Pam skipped.
12. Who was skipping? Pam

Parents: Your child has been taught the name, shape, and short and long sounds of the letter u.

P1-WS-037b

LESSON 38 — The Letter *W*

lesson preparation

materials

ball
Activity Sheet 1
Review Decks
Spelling Sound Sheet 30
container of letter tiles
Letter Card 25
Picture Card 32
Spelling Card 28
Sight Word Card 14
Worksheet 38

new concepts

paragraph

the night before

- Cut apart the word slips on Activity Sheet 1.
- Add the *w* letter tile to the student's container.

ALPHABET ACTIVITY

- You and the student should be seated on the floor with the ball.

  "How many letters are in the alphabet?" *26*

  "What two kinds of letters make up our alphabet?" *vowels and consonants*

  "Name the vowels." *a, e, i, o, and u*

  "All of the other letters are called _________?" *consonants*

  "The initial letter of the alphabet is _____?" *a*

  "The final letter of the alphabet is _____?" *z*

  "Let's say the alphabet while we roll this ball back and forth."

  "I'll begin with 'A' and roll the ball to you. After you catch the ball, say 'B' and roll the ball back to me. We'll continue until we complete the alphabet."

- Recite the alphabet as you and the student roll the ball back and forth.

Phonemic Awareness

- **Objective:** To establish word order in sentences.

  "This week, we have counted the number of words in sentences. What we're going to do today should be fun."

  "I have some words written on slips of paper. I want you to arrange the words into a sentence that makes sense."
- Lay the following slips of paper from **Activity Sheet 1** randomly on the table or floor: The, fan, is, going, fast.
- Let the student put the words in an order that makes sense. (If necessary, read the words aloud.) When the student is through, read the sentence aloud and let the student determine if the sentence makes sense.
- Repeat with the following sentences:

  I see a big cat.

  The pond has grass in it.

  Frank was standing on the rug.

  I can't go swimming in the cold.

  Who asked this ant to the picnic?

Review of Decks

- The student should be seated where he/she can write comfortably.
- Show the student **Letter Cards 1–24** in random order. The student should name the letter on each letter card.
- Review **Affix Cards 1–3.**
- Show the student **Picture Cards 1–31** in random order. The student should name the keyword and sound for each picture card.
- Review **Sight Word Cards 1–13.**
- Give the student **Spelling Sound Sheet 30.**
- Call out the sounds on **Spelling Cards 1–27** in random order. The student should echo each sound and name the letter or letters that make the sound as he/she writes the letter(s) on the spelling sound sheet.
- Have the student set the spelling sound sheet aside for use later in the lesson.

New Learning

"I'm going to say some words. Echo them back to me and listen for the sound in the initial position."

- Point to your mouth as you say each word.

"Echo after me. Wind." *wind* ***"West."*** *west* ***"Wag."*** *wag*

"What sound do you hear in the initial position?" */w/*

- **Note:** Make sure the student is giving the pure sound of *w* and not pronouncing it with a short *u* sound, as in /wŭh/.

"That's right. The sound you hear in the initial position is /w/."

"Put your fingertips on the front of your neck and say /w/. See if you feel any vibration."

"Is this sound voiced or unvoiced?"

- The student will probably answer that /w/ is voiced. However, there is some controversy surrounding the /w/ sound. Some think that the sound is voiced, while others say there is no sound, only a rounding of the lips. Choose whichever sound suits you and continue with that sound.
- Write the following words on the chalkboard: wind, wet, wag.

"What letter do you see that might be making the /w/ sound?" *w*

- If the student does not know the name of the letter, say it for him/her.

"W is the first letter in all of these words, so we can see that w must be the letter used to spell the /w/ sound."

"Is w a vowel or a consonant?" *a consonant*

Handwriting/Letter Tiles

- The student should be seated where he/she can write comfortably.
- Write a capital *W* on the chalkboard.

"This is a capital W. Let's practice skywriting capital W's before we write them on our paper."

- Have the student practice skywriting capital *W*'s.

"Find your spelling sound sheet."

- Draw handwriting lines on the chalkboard. Write a capital *W* on the handwriting lines in the handwriting you want the student to learn.

"Find the first handwriting line on your paper and practice writing capital W's like I wrote this one on the chalkboard."

"Say the name of the letter each time you write it."

- Allow a few minutes for the student to practice writing capital *W*'s.
- Write a lowercase *w* on the handwriting lines in the handwriting you want the student to learn.

"This is a lowercase w."

- Have the student practice skywriting lowercase *w*'s.

"Now practice writing lowercase w's on the second handwriting line. Say the name of the letter each time you write it."

- Have the student set the spelling sound sheet aside for use later in the lesson.
- Leave the handwriting lines and letters on the chalkboard for the remainder of the lesson.
- Give the student the container of letter tiles.

"Today I've given you another letter tile."

"Find your w letter tile and look at it. One side has a capital W and the other side has a lowercase w."

"Hold your letter tile up in the air. Turn it so I can see the capital W."

"Now turn it so I can see the lowercase w."

"Spell the word 'wit' with your letter tiles."

"Now change one letter to make the word 'win.' "

"Now add one letter to make the word 'wink.' "

- Watch to see if the student refers to **Rule Chart 4.**
- Choose additional words from the Spelling Word List, if desired.
- Have the student replace the tiles in the container and put it away.
- Reinforce the name, sound, and shape of the letter *w* throughout the day.

NEW DECK CARDS

- Show the student **Letter Card 25.**

"What is the name of this letter?" *w*

- Hold up **Picture Card 32** but keep the picture covered with your hand (or the letter card).

"I have a card with a picture on it that begins with the /w/ sound."

"I am going to describe it for you. See if you can guess what the picture is."

"Most small children want one of these. They are fun to ride in or to pull your little brother or sister in. They used to be red but now they come in many colors. What do you think the picture is?" *wagon*

"That's right. The keyword is 'wagon' and the sound we have learned is /w/."

- Show the student **Picture Card 32,** and then point to the picture of a wagon on the alphabet strip.

"The word 'wagon' helps us remember the /w/ sound because it begins with /w/."

"Find your spelling sound sheet. Put your finger on line #28."

- Hold up **Spelling Card 28** so only you can see what is written. Using the hand signals, follow the instructions on the card.

- Check the spelling sound sheet for accuracy.
- **Note:** Add the new letter, picture, and spelling cards to the Review Decks.

BOARDWORK

"Today we have a new sight word and a new blend."

- Show the student **Sight Word Card 14.**

"This is our new sight word. Can you tell me what this word is?"

"This word is 'do.' It will always be a sight word. Circle it whenever you see it."

"We'll add this card to our sight word deck."

- Write "tw" on the chalkboard.

"We also have a new blend. Can you give me a word that has this new blend in the initial position?"

- Examples include the following: twin, twirl, twinkle, tweezers, tweed, tweet, twelve, twenty, twilight, twill, twine, twister, twitch, twig, twitter.

"Let's practice coding some words like the ones you'll have on your worksheet."

"The rule charts are in your Rule Book if you need to look at them."

- Write the following word, phrase, and sentence (without the coding marks) on the chalkboard, one at a time. Ask the student to help you code them. The correct coding is as indicated:

$$w\bar{e}\cancel{e}d'\boxed{ing}$$

$$tw\breve{i}n\ r\breve{a}b'\boxed{\cancel{b}\breve{i}t\boxed{s}}$$
$$\phantom{tw\breve{i}n\ }v\ c\ |\ c\ v$$

$$W\bar{e}'\ dr\breve{o}p\cancel{p}\boxed{ed}\ \cancel{the}\ cl\breve{o}\cancel{c}k.$$

- Add **Sight Word Card 14** to the Sight Word Deck.

WORKSHEET

- The student should be seated where he/she can write comfortably.
- Give the student **Worksheet 38.** Make sure the student turns to the correct side.

"Today, let's spell with the /w/ sound."

"Put your finger by #1. The first word is 'wig.' "

"Unblend 'wig' with me." /w/ /ĭ/ /g/

- Hold up one finger for each sound.

"Let's spell those sounds." w … i … g

- Point to each finger as you spell a sound.

"Now spell the word again and write the letters as you say them."

- Allow time for the student to do this.

  "What word did you write?" *wig*

- Repeat the procedure with #2 (we), #3 (twig), #4 (week), and #5 (wing).

  "Now you're ready to code and read the words on your paper."

  "Code the words by #6 through #10. After you have coded these words, try to read them."

- Assist the student as necessary.

  "Numbers 11 and 12 are questions about the paragraph just above them. A paragraph is a group of sentences. If you find any words you can't read, code them. Don't forget to circle the sight words. Then see if you can answer the questions."

- As the student works, provide help as needed. Help the student correct any incorrect answers. Then initial the worksheet in the space provided.
- Some time during the day, ask the student to read from the worksheet or homework.
- **Note:** Always make sure the worksheet is corrected before the student begins the homework. The worksheet serves as a guide to help complete the homework.

HOMEWORK

"Turn your paper over to the homework side."

"Put your finger on the top row of handwriting lines. Write your best capital W on these lines so I will know what a capital W should look like."

- Have the student write a lowercase letter *w* on the second handwriting line. Make sure that the student has written the letters correctly (to the best of his or her ability). He/She will use them as guides when completing the homework.

  "Do you know what to do on the rest of the homework paper?"

  "Watch for suffixes and words with a 'vccv' pattern that need to be divided."

  "When you finish your paper, I will check it for you and initial it in the space provided."

- Either now or later in the day, the student should complete the homework independently (if possible). Help the student correct any incorrect answers. Then initial the homework in the space provided.
- If possible, take time to play the Kid Card games listed in Lesson 35.

Name ______________________

Teacher's Initials ____

Worksheet 38
(for use with Lesson 38)
Phonics 1

Ww

1. wig
2. we
3. twig
4. week
5. wing
6. click
7. tablet
8. then
9. twisted
10. sleeting

Zack is sweeping the truck bed. He will help pack the tent so he and Dad can go camping.

11. What is Zack sweeping? the truck bed

12. What will he help pack? the tent

P1-WS-038a

Parent's Initials ____

Homework 38
(for use with Lesson 38)
Phonics 1

Ww

1. wink
2. with
3. seeded
4. stuffing
5. flock
6. thank
7. thud
8. sudden
9. swimming
10. fled

Zack will pack the tent so he and Dad can sleep in it. The tent will be on the creek bank with the rest of the camping stuff.

11. Who is going camping on the creek bank? Zack and Dad

12. Where will Zack and Dad sleep? in the tent

13. Where is the camping stuff? on the creek bank

Parents: Your child has been taught the name, shape, and sound of the letter w; and that a paragraph is a group of sentences.

P1-WS-038b

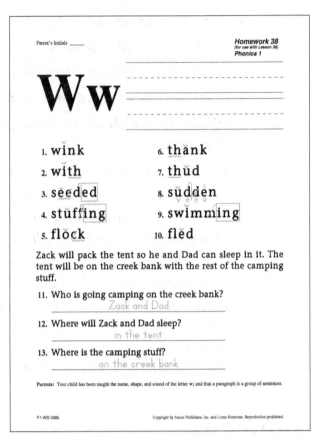

LESSON 39 — The Rule vc|cv´

lesson preparation

materials

container of letter tiles

Review Decks

Worksheet 39

Reader 12 (*Spilled Milk*)

colored pencils

new concepts

vc|cv´ pattern

ALPHABET ACTIVITY

- The student should be seated with the container of letter tiles.

  "Today we are going to alphabetize letters again."

  "I want you to pick any five letter tiles out of your container and put them in alphabetical order."

  "Tell me when you think you have them in alphabetical order."

- Check the student's work when he/she is finished. If the student is having difficulty alphabetizing, give him/her extra practice.
- Have the student replace the tiles in the container and put it away.

PHONEMIC AWARENESS

- **Objective:** To identify the number of words in sentences.
- Give the student a piece of scratch paper.

  "Today I am going to say some extra long sentences. See if you can tell me how many words are in each one."

  "You might want to make a mark for each word you hear because these are very long sentences."

  "Here is the first sentence. 'My dad works at the hospital in the city and he leaves for work at seven.' " *(16)*

  "We work at home to learn how to read, do math, spell, and write." *(14)*

  "When it is freezing, water turns to ice, and the animals have a hard time getting drinks of water." *(19)*

REVIEW OF DECKS

"Let's play 'Twenty Questions' again today."

"I'm going to choose a card. See if you can ask me questions and guess which card I have selected."

- Do not let the student see which deck or which card you select.

"You may ask me any question you like as long as I can answer 'yes' or 'no.' "

- If the student has difficulty, help him/her by suggesting questions such as "Is it a letter card?", "Is it a vowel?", "Is it a digraph?", etc.

NEW LEARNING

- Write the word "until" on the chalkboard.

"What should I do to code this word?"

- Code the word as the student instructs: ŭn´|tĭl. (vc|cv)

"Can you read this word the way it is coded?" *expect various responses*

- If necessary, say the word yourself to emphasize the accent on the first syllable.

"Do we say 'un´|til'?" *no*

"Sometimes when we have a 'vccv' word, the accent will be on the second syllable."

- Put the accent on the second syllable: un|til´.
- Say the word again with the accent on the second syllable.

"Doesn't that sound better?"

"If you are trying to code the accent on a word and you can't decide where the accent is, you can look the word up in the dictionary."

"I have a chart that shows the two 'vccv' syllable divisions we will use this year."

"Get out your Rule Book and turn to page 17."

- Point to the two division methods on **Syllable Division Chart 2** as you say the following:

"Look at this chart if you forget how to divide words."

"Dividing big words makes them easier to read."

WORKSHEET

- The student should be seated where he/she can write comfortably.
- Give the student **Worksheet 39.** Make sure the student turns to the correct side.

"All of the 'vccv' words on today's worksheet will have the accent on the second syllable."

"Let's see if you can code the first word."

- Allow time for the student to do this. Provide assistance as necessary.
- If the student seems to understand the new coding, ask him/her to code #2 and #3 independently. If the student seems unsure, code the words together on the chalkboard.
- When the student has finished coding (either independently or with you), continue:

"Read the paragraph and answer questions four and five."

- As the student works, provide help as needed. Help the student correct any incorrect answers. Then initial the worksheet in the space provided.
- Some time during the day, ask the student to read from the worksheet or homework.
- **Note:** Always make sure the worksheet is corrected before the student begins the homework. The worksheet serves as a guide to help complete the homework.

HOMEWORK

"Turn your paper over to the homework side."

"Do you know what to do on the rest of the homework paper?"

"When you finish your paper, I will check it for you and initial it in the space provided."

- Either now or later in the day, the student should complete the homework independently (if possible). Help the student correct any incorrect answers. Then initial the homework in the space provided.

READER

"We have another new book today."

- Give the student **Reader 12 (*Spilled Milk*)** and some colored pencils.

"Can you tell me this book's title?" *Spilled Milk*

- Assist the student as necessary as he/she completes the following steps:

"Hold up your page so that the tree is facing you."

"Now put your finger on the top dotted line."

"Carefully fold the paper along this dotted line toward you so that it lines up with the bottom dotted line."

"Now fold the top half of the sheet back along the dotted line."

"Hold your book so the tree is facing you again. Then put your finger on the dotted line down the center of the page."

"Fold the book backward along this dotted line so that the tree will still be facing you when you're finished."

- When the student completes this last step, either put a rubber band around the book's spine or staple the spine.

  "Next, carefully separate the pages along the perforated lines at the top and bottom."

- Demonstrate how to separate the pages.

  "Let's check the page numbers to see if they are in the correct order."

- Demonstrate how to check that the book's page numbers are in order.

  "The title of this book is ________?" *Spilled Milk*

  "I want you to read your book to yourself. When you are finished reading, color the pictures. Write your name on the book so I will know who colored it."

  "Keep your book handy because I will be asking you to read it for me."

- Some time during the day, have the student read the reader to you.
- If possible, take time to play the Kid Card games listed in Lesson 35. Try to see that the student is prepared for tomorrow's assessment.

Name ______________________

Teacher's Initials ____

Worksheet 39
(for use with Lesson 39)
Phonics 1

vc|cv´

1. ŭn|lĕss
   v c|c v
2. cŏn|fĕss
   v c|c v
3. ĭn|dĕnt
   v c|c v

Mom said to sweep the rug and dust the lamps. If I pick up the mess on the desk, I will be a big help.

4. What do we sweep? the rug
5. Who said to dust? Mom

P1-WS-039a

Parent's Initials ____

Homework 39
(for use with Lesson 39)
Phonics 1

vc|cv´

1. ăd|mĭt
   v c|c v
2. ĭn|fĕct
   v c|c v
3. dĭs|cŭss
   v c|c v

Mack the dog gets drinks at the well. He licks the bucket and gets wet. He is a mess.

4. Who gets drinks at the well? Mack
5. Mack licks the bucket.

Parents: Your child has been taught the syllable division rule vc|cv.

P1-WS-039b

LESSON 40 — Assessment

lesson preparation

materials

Review Decks

Assessment 7

Spelling Test 5

Assessment 7 Recording Form

Kid Cards

tokens

the night before

- Separate the Kid Cards marked "Lesson 40."

ALPHABET ACTIVITY

- The student should be seated.

  "As we say the alphabet, let's snap on the consonants and clap on the vowels."

- **Note:** This is more difficult than it seems. Do not expect the student (or yourself) to do it without a few mistakes.

PHONEMIC AWARENESS

- Today's phonemic awareness activity is part of the assessment.

REVIEW OF DECKS

- The student should be seated where he/she can write comfortably.
- Show the student **Letter Cards 1–25** in random order. The student should name the letter on each letter card.
- Review **Affix Cards 1–3.**
- Show the student **Picture Cards 1–32** in random order. The student should name the keyword and sound for each picture card.
- Review **Sight Word Cards 1–14.**

WRITTEN ASSESSMENT

- Seat the student where he/she can write comfortably.
- Give the student **Assessment 7.**
- **Section I:**

  "Today we are going to write some words for our assessment."

  "I'm going to say a word. Write the letter that makes each sound in that word on the lines by #1."

  "Look at the rule charts if you need to."

  "Here's the first word: seen."
- Repeat with the following words in the order shown: #2 (rested), #3 (ringing), #4 (thick), and #5 (that).
- **Reminder:** While the student spells, be ready to point to appropriate rule charts as necessary. For example, point to **Rule Chart 4** while the student spells #4.
- **Section II:**

  "Look at the letters by #6."

  "Find the picture of the keyword for this sound."

  "Draw a line from the letters to the keyword."
- Repeat with #7, #8, and #9. Allow a few minutes for the student to work.
- The pictures (from top to bottom) are as follows: feather, thimble, sheep, lung.
- **Section III:**

  "Put your finger on #10."

  "Code the words by #10 through #15."
- Allow a few minutes for the student to work.
- **Section IV:**
- Have the student name the sound of each blend in #16–#18.
- Help identify each picture and then ask the student to name the blend each picture begins with and to draw a line from the picture to the blend. The pictures (from top to bottom) are as follows: spray, scratch, straw.
- **Section V:**

  "Read the paragraph. If you find any words you can't read, code them to help you figure them out."

  "Look at the sentences by #19 and #20. See if you can answer the questions."
- **Note:** If the student absolutely cannot read the paragraph, read it to the student to see if he or she can answer the questions.

  "When you are finished, show your paper to me."
- This paper will be used during the oral portion of the assessment.

Spelling Test

- Give the student **Spelling Test 5.**
- Call out the following words (in the order shown). Sound them out, if necessary.

  #1 (kid), #2 (cast), #3 (milk), #4 (cost), #5 (cat), #6 (skid), #7 (glad), #8 (clip), #9 (skip), #10 (raft), #11 (oh), #12 (what)
- Grade and record the test in any manner that suits your needs.

Oral Assessment

- Oral assessments are short interviews that occur during independent work time. It is important to complete them promptly (today, if possible) in order to identify any areas of weakness and begin remediation.
- Use the assessment and the following dialogue to complete the oral portion.
- **Section VI:**
- Point to the sight word by #21.

  "Read this sight word for me."
- Record the student's response by placing a check mark by each word he/she reads correctly.
- Repeat with #22.
- **Section VII:**
- Show the student the digraph by #23.

  "Tell me the name of this digraph and the sound it makes."
- Write the student's response on the adjacent line.
- Repeat with #24 and #25.

Assessment Evaluation

- Grade the assessment and record the results on **Assessment 7 Recording Form.** Check off the boxes to indicate mastery (i.e., the section was completed with 100% accuracy).
- **Reminder:** Try to give as many points as possible for work attempted. Do not grade the coding marks too severely, especially secondary marks like accents, voice lines, and k-backs. The most important coding marks to look for are breves, macrons, and syllable division lines.
- See the introductory material for detailed information regarding grading and recording procedures.
- Use the assessment result to identify those skills in which the student is weak. Practice those skills by playing Kid Card games.

- Add the Kid Cards marked "Lesson 40" to the existing decks. Listed below are games appropriate for remediation in selected areas. See "Games and Activities" for the directions for each game.
- **Section I:** Play "Spelling Deck Perfection," "Sound Scamper," "Spell Out #1," or have the student use the letter tiles to spell words you give from the Spelling Word List.
- **Section II:** Play "Keyword and Sound" or "Letter/Sound Identification."
- **Section III:** Play "Chalkboard Challenge."
- **Section IV:** Play "Blend It."
- **Section V:** Have the student read the controlled readers. Ask questions for comprehension.
- **Section VI:** Review the Sight Word Deck, or lay the sight words out with a token on each one and let the student try to get as many tokens as possible for the sight words he/she can read.
- **Section VII:** Play "Letter Deck Data" or "Letter/Sound Identification."
- When the student seems more secure in areas that had previously proven difficult, retest him/her (in those areas only) and indicate on the recording form any sections the student has subsequently mastered.
- Try to help the student achieve mastery of all the sections before the next assessment.
- If the student is having difficulty with a particular skill, keep his or her practice activities at the most basic level so the chance of success is greater.

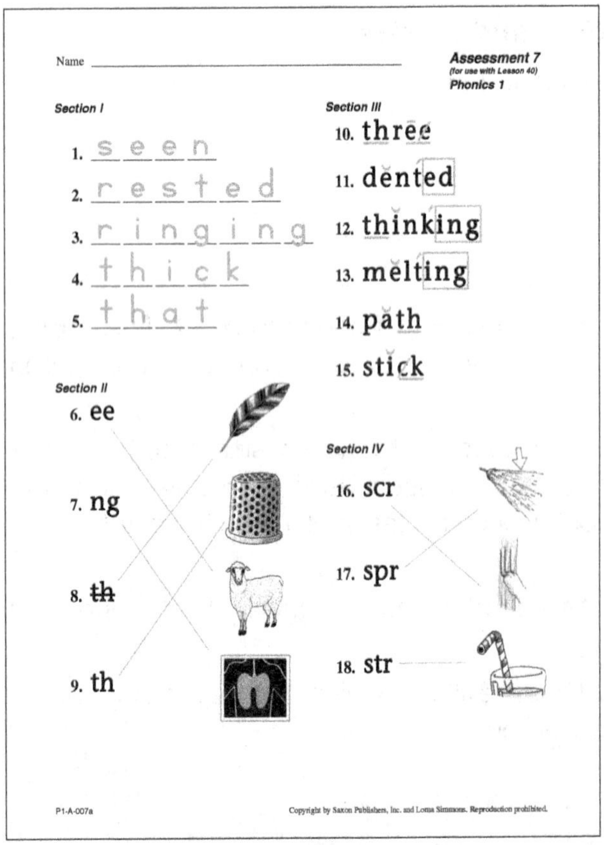
Name ______________________

Assessment 7
(for use with Lesson 40)
Phonics 1

Section I

1. seen
2. rested
3. ringing
4. thick
5. that

Section II

6. ee
7. ng
8. th
9. th

Section III

10. three
11. dented
12. thinking
13. melting
14. path
15. stick

Section IV

16. scr
17. spr
18. str

P1-A-007a

Copyright by Saxon Publishers, Inc. and Lorna Simmons. Reproduction prohibited.

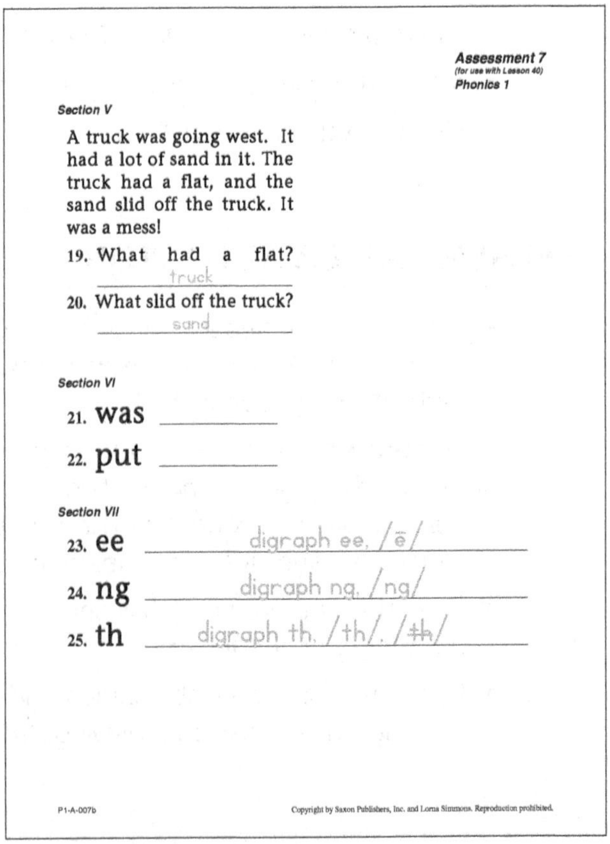
Assessment 7
(for use with Lesson 40)
Phonics 1

Section V

A truck was going west. It had a lot of sand in it. The truck had a flat, and the sand slid off the truck. It was a mess!

19. What had a flat? truck
20. What slid off the truck? sand

Section VI

21. was ______
22. put ______

Section VII

23. ee digraph ee, /ē/
24. ng digraph ng, /ng/
25. th digraph th, /th/, /t͟h/

P1-A-007b

Copyright by Saxon Publishers, Inc. and Lorna Simmons. Reproduction prohibited.

LESSON 41 — *a* consonant *e*

lesson preparation

materials

Review Decks

Spelling Sound Sheet 31

3 index cards (see *the night before*)

Letter Card 26

Picture Card 33

Sight Word Card 15

Worksheet 41

Spelling List 6

new concepts

sneaky *e*

quotation marks

the night before

- Write the letter *a* on one index card, a long dash (—) on another index card, and the letter *e* with a slash mark through it (ɇ) on the third index card.

ā	—	ɇ

- The "New Learning" activity requires the assistance of two people. Therefore, complete the activity whenever two playmates, siblings, or other people are available to help. You and the helpers should prepare yourselves to do a little "acting."

ALPHABET ACTIVITY

- The student should be seated with the alphabet strip.

"How many letters are in the alphabet?" *26*

"What two kinds of letters make up our alphabet?" *vowels and consonants*

"Name the vowels." *a, e, i, o, and u*

"All of the other letters are called _________?" *consonants*

"The initial letter of the alphabet is _____?" *a*

"The final letter of the alphabet is _____?" *z*

"Let's point to each letter and say the whole alphabet."

"Put your index finger on 'a' and say the names with me."

PHONEMIC AWARENESS

- **Objective:** To distinguish between words that are the same and words that are different.

  "Listen to these two words. Let's see if you can tell me if they are the same word or different words."

  "Mat, top. Are they the same or are they different?" *different*

  "Sit, sit." *same*

  "Boy, less." *different*

  "Give, plan." *different*

  "Man, man." *same*

- If the exercise goes quickly, continue with additional words. If the student has auditory discrimination difficulties, some sounds will be difficult, such as /m/ and /n/, /p/ and /b/, /t/ and /d/, and /k/ and /g/.

REVIEW OF DECKS

- The student should be seated where he/she can write comfortably.
- Show the student **Letter Cards 1–25** in random order. The student should name the letter on each letter card.
- Review **Affix Cards 1–3.**
- Show the student **Picture Cards 1–32** in random order. The student should name the keyword and sound for each picture card.
- Review **Sight Word Cards 1–14.**
- Give the student **Spelling Sound Sheet 31.**
- Call out the sounds on **Spelling Cards 1–28** in random order. The student should echo each sound and name the letter or letters that make the sound as he/she writes the letter(s) on the spelling sound sheet.
- Check the student's response after each card.
- Have the student set the spelling sound sheet aside for use later in the lesson.

NEW LEARNING

"I'm going to say some words. Echo them back to me and listen for the sound in the medial, or middle, position."

- Point to your mouth as you say each word.

  "Echo after me. Sale." *sale* ***"Face."*** *face* ***"Gate."*** *gate*

  "What sound do you hear in the medial position?" */ā/*

  "That's right. The sound you hear in the medial position is /ā/."

  "Put your fingertips on the front of your neck and say /ā/. See if you feel any vibration."

"Is this sound voiced or unvoiced?" *voiced*

- **Note:** The following skit was used in *Phonics K Individualized Study*. If this skit was used with the student previously *and* the student understands sneaky *e*, you may wish to omit the activity. Please note, however, that some students will benefit from the additional review.
- For the next section, you will need two extra people and the three index cards. The two "helpers" should stand in front of the student, who should be seated on the floor. Helper 1 should stand so that, when facing the student, he/she appears to the student's left.
- Hand the card with the letter *a* on it to Helper 1 and say:

"I want you to hold this card with the letter a on it. In a few minutes, I'm going to sneak up behind you and say 'Boo!' When I do this, say /ā/."

- Make sure Helper 1 understands what he/she is supposed to do. Then hand the card with the long dash on it to Helper 2 and say:

"I want you to hold this card with the long dash on it. When (Helper 1) says /ā/, I want you to ask 'Why did you say /ā/? You're supposed to say /ă/!' "

- When Helper 2 understands what he/she is supposed to do, turn to Helper 1 again and say:

"When (Helper 2) asks why you said /ā/, say 'Something just snuck up and scared me!' "

- Position Helper 2 to the right of Helper 1 (so the student reads the cards as "ā—").
- Then ask the student the following questions:

"What does the letter a say when it is followed by a consonant?" */ă/*

- Point to the "—" card.

"This line stands for any consonant."

"What would this word be if that line were the letter t?" *at*

"What would this word be if that line were the letter m?" *am*

"What would this word be if that line were the letter n?" *an*

- Continue until you feel confident that the student understands that the line stands for any consonant.
- Quietly pick up the "e̸" card and begin moving around the room acting "sneaky": tiptoe, snoop through papers while occasionally glancing over your shoulder, peer out from behind a door, glance furtively from side to side, etc.
- When you have the student's complete attention, walk over beside Helper 2 (the consonant) and hold up your card (e̸). Stand there a moment so the student can see the "e̸" card in the final position (ā—e̸).
- Then tiptoe behind Helper 2 (the consonant) to stand behind Helper 1 (the *a*) and say "Boo!"
- Helpers 1 and 2 should deliver their respective lines. Prompt, if necessary. Then continue.

"I am 'Sneaky E.' I'm so sneaky that I don't make any sound. The a doesn't know I'm here, so I can sneak behind the consonant, say 'boo!', and scare the vowel into making its long sound, /ā/."

- Repeat the previous demonstration, if necessary. Then the helpers may sit down.
- Write the letter *a* on the chalkboard.

"What does this letter say if it is followed by a consonant?" */ă/*

- Write the letter *t* beside the *a*.

"What is this word?" *at*

- Write the letter *e* beside the *t*. Point to the *e*.

"This is sneaky e. Sneaky e's are so sneaky that they don't make any sound, so we'll cross them out whenever we see them."

- Cross out the *e*: atȩ̸.

"When a sneaky e is on the end of a word, it sneaks up behind the vowel and scares it into making its long sound."

"Do you remember how we code long vowel sounds?" *with macrons*

- Put a macron over the *a*: ātȩ̸.

"So what does this word say?" *ate*

"Good! Let's try another word."

- Write the following word on the chalkboard: bake.

"Echo this word: bake." *bake*

"Look at this word and tell me what letter you see that might be making the /ā/ sound." *a*

"Do you see a sneaky e?" *yes*

"How do we code sneaky e's?" *cross them out*

"What do sneaky e's do?" *make vowels say their long sounds*

"That's right! Let's code the word 'bake' and see if we can read it."

- Code the word: bākȩ̸. Have the student read it. Leave the word on the chalkboard for use later in the lesson.

"What does the sneaky e do to the a?" *expect variations on the "sneaky e" story*

"That's right. It sneaks behind the consonant and scares the a so it says its long sound."

"Whenever an a is followed by a consonant and a silent e …"

- Write "ā–ȩ̸" on the chalkboard.

"… we call it 'a consonant e.' The line can stand for any consonant."

- Some people call this "*a* consonant sneaky *e*." Either name is acceptable.
- Point to the *a*.

"Is this a vowel sound or a consonant sound?" *vowel sound*

- Keep the "sneaky *e*" and "long dash" signs for use during the next two lessons.

Lesson 41

NEW DECK CARDS

- Pull **Spelling Card 10** from the Review Deck.
- Show the student **Letter Card 26.**

  "What do we call this?" *a consonant e (or sneaky e)*

  "Our keyword contains the /ā/ sound today. This word will have an a in it, but it will also have a sneaky letter on the end. What letter do we know can be sneaky?" *sneaky e*
- Hold up **Picture Card 33** but keep the picture covered with your hand (or the letter card).

  "I'm going to describe the picture on this card for you. See if you can guess what it is."

  "Someone who has a sweet tooth likes to eat this. It can come in any flavor or shape. It is used for celebrating special events like weddings, anniversaries, and birthdays. What do you think the picture is?" *cake*
- Show the student **Picture Card 33.**
- Write the word "cake" on the chalkboard.

  "The word 'cake' helps us remember the /ā/ sound since it contains that sound. It also has something special on the end. What is it?" *sneaky e*

  "How do you think we will code the word 'cake'?"

  "Since the sneaky e is silent, we'll mark it out."
- Mark out the "e": cakø.

  "Then we'll sneak past the consonant and put a macron over the a."
- Put a macron over the "a": cākø.

  "Does this word need any other coding?" *yes, k-back on the c*
- Put a k-back on the "c": cākø.

  "Can you read this word?" *cake*

  "Find your spelling sound sheet. Find #29 and put your finger on it."
- Hold up **Spelling Card 10** so only you can see what is written

  "Echo this sound: /ā/."

  "Before today, how have we been spelling /ā/?" *a*

  "Now we know a new way to spell /ā/."
- Write "a–e" on the chalkboard.

  "This means 'a consonant e.' The line stands for any consonant."
- Add a comma and the letter *a*: a–e, a.

  "Our new response is 'a consonant e comma a.' Say that with me." *a consonant e comma a*

  "Write the new response on line #29."

Lesson 41

- **Note:** The new response to **Spelling Card 10** (a–e, a) is the first response that requires the student to re-order the spellings (rather than simply adding the new one to the end of the list). The spelling card responses for individual long vowel sounds will always be in the following order:
    1. the most common way(s) to spell the sound in the initial or medial position in one-syllable words
    2. the most common way(s) to spell the sound in the initial or medial position in two-syllable words
    3. the most common way(s) to spell the sound in the final position in one-syllable words
    4. the most common way(s) to spell the sound in the final position in two-syllable words

  Example: The final response to **Spelling Card 10** (after Lesson 71) will be:

  "a–e, a || ay"
- Check the spelling sound sheet for accuracy.
- **Note:** Add the new letter and picture cards to the Review Decks (and re-insert **Spelling Card 10**).

BOARDWORK

"Today we have a new sight word."

- Show the student **Sight Word Card 15.**

"Can you tell me what this word is?" *you*

"This word is 'you.' Does it follow the rules we've learned so far?" *no*

- Help the student locate the word in the Irregular Spelling Booklet.

"How do we code a sight word?" *draw a circle around it*

"We'll add this card to our sight word deck."

"We have a new vowel rule today. It's the rule for sneaky e."

"Get out your Rule Book and turn to page 5."

- Point to **Rule Chart 5** as you say the following:

"This rule tells us that a vowel followed by a consonant and sneaky e is long; code the vowel with a macron and cross out the e. Why is the vowel long?" *sneaky e sneaks up on it and scares it*

"Let's practice coding some words like the ones you'll have on your worksheet."

"The vowel charts are in your Rule Book if you need to look at them."

- Write the word "crane" on the chalkboard.

"Can you help me code this word?"

- Code the word as the student instructs: crān~~e~~.
- Write the following sentence on the chalkboard: Miss Pate said, "You are late!"

"How will we code this sentence?"

- Code the sentence as the student instructs:

  Mis̆s̸ Pāte̸ (said), "(You) (are) lāte̸!"

- Point to the quotation marks.

  "These are called quotation marks. Do you know what they mean?"

  "They show us exactly what Miss Pate said. When we see quotation marks, it means someone is talking."

- Have the student help you identify each of the items coded as either a word, a phrase, or a sentence.
- Add **Sight Word Card 15** to the Sight Word Deck.

WORKSHEET

- The student should be seated where he/she can write comfortably.
- Give the student **Worksheet 41.** Make sure the student turns to the correct side.

  "Today, let's spell with the /ā/ sound. When we spell with sneaky e, we must hear a consonant because sneaky e only sneaks up behind consonants."

- As you teach a–e (o–e, u–e, etc.), the student may question you about words with long vowel sounds but no sneaky *e* (e.g., *baby*). The v|cv syllable division pattern will be presented in Lesson 81. The student has learned that the letter *a*, when open and accented, will say /ā/. In the a–e pattern, the consonant and the long vowel sound must be heard in the same syllable for the sneaky *e* rule to apply. Remember that the student will become very aware of letters, sounds, and spellings and will look for exceptions. Praise the student for being so alert.

  "Put your finger by #1. The first word is 'tape.' "

  "Do you hear an /ā/ sound?" *yes*

  "Do you hear a consonant that sneaky e could sneak behind to scare that a?" *yes, a p*

  "Let's unblend 'tape.' " */t/ /ā/ /p/*

- Hold up one finger for each sound.

  "Let's spell those sounds." *t … a … p*

- Point to a finger as you say each letter.

  "And what sneaky thing goes on the end?" *sneaky e*

  "Now spell the word again and write the letters as you say them."

- Allow time for the student to do this. He/She may say "*T* … *a* … *p* … sneaky *e*."

  "What word did you write?" *tape*

- Quickly check to see if the student included the final *e*. If he/she has failed to do so, help by saying, "I'm afraid sneaky *e* snuck up on you instead of the vowel. Isn't there something missing on the end of your word?"
- Repeat the procedure with #2 (wade), #3 (came), #4 (mane), and #5 (name).
- Check each word for accuracy after the student has spelled it.

"Now you're ready to code and read the words on your paper."

"Using the rules we just practiced on the chalkboard, code the words by #6 through #10. After you have coded these words, try to read them."

- Assist the student as necessary.

"Now read the paragraph in the middle of the page. If you find any words you can't read, code them. Then answer the questions by #11 and #12."

- As the student works, provide help as needed. Help the student correct any incorrect answers. Then initial the worksheet in the space provided.
- Some time during the day, ask the student to read from the worksheet, a controlled reader, your basal reader, or other material of your choice.
- **Note:** Always make sure the worksheet is corrected before the student begins the homework. The worksheet serves as a guide to help complete the homework.

HOMEWORK

"Turn your paper over to the homework side."

"Do you know what to do on the homework paper?"

"Watch for suffixes and words with a 'vccv' pattern in the paragraph."

"Don't let sneaky e sneak up on you at home. As a matter of fact, you should tell (someone at home) about sneaky e so it doesn't sneak up on them!"

"When you finish your paper, I will check it for you and initial it in the space provided."

- Either now or later in the day, the student should complete the homework independently (if possible). Help the student correct any incorrect answers. Then initial the homework in the space provided.

SPELLING LIST

- Fold **Spelling List 6** in half lengthwise (with the printed side facing out).

"Leave your paper just like I give it to you."

- Give the student **Spelling List 6,** folded with the blank lines facing up.

"Today I'm going to let you try your spelling words without ever seeing them."

- Call out the following words (in the order shown). Sound them out, if necessary.

  #1 (lamp), #2 (man), #3 (crab), #4 (skin), #5 (rock), #6 (neck), #7 (sock), #8 (clock), #9 (napkin), #10 (insect), #11 (who),
  #12 (was)

"Now unfold your paper and check your words."

- Check the student's work to see if he/she needs extra help with spelling.

"I want you to practice these words. We'll have a spelling test in a few days."

- If possible, take time to play the Kid Card games listed in Lesson 40.

Name ______________________

Teacher's Initials _____

Worksheet 41
(for use with Lesson 41)
Phonics 1

ā–e̸

1. tape
2. wade
3. came
4. mane
5. name
6. game
7. cane
8. snake
9. grade
10. frame

Kate is fond of sweets. Kate asked Bess, "Will you bake me a cake?" Bess said, "I will be glad to bake you a cake if you will help me."

11. Kate is fond of what? sweets

12. What did Kate ask Bess to bake? a cake

P1-WS-041a

Parent's Initials _____

Homework 41
(for use with Lesson 41)
Phonics 1

ā–e̸

1. cake
2. same
3. ate
4. safe
5. gate
6. fade
7. state
8. plane
9. grape
10. plate

Kate got the pans and handed them to Bess. Bess cracked the eggs as Kate added the milk. Kate asked, "Can I frost the cake?" Bess hugged Kate and said, "You are so fond of sweets!"

11. Who cracked the eggs? Bess

12. What did Kate add? milk

Parents: Your child has been taught that a vowel is long when followed by a consonant and a **silent e**; and that silent e's are coded by crossing them out.

P1-WS-041b

LESSON 42 *o* consonant *e*; *u* consonant *e*

lesson preparation

materials

Review Decks

Spelling Sound Sheet 32

2 index cards (see *the night before*)

Letter Cards 27–28

Picture Cards 34–35

cube in a sack (see *the night before*)

Worksheet 42

Reader 13 (*Zip Gets a Beef Bone*)

colored pencils

the night before

- Prepare two index cards. Write a large *o* on one and a large *u* on the other. Put them with the "long dash" and "e̸" cards from yesterday's lesson. If possible, locate two "helpers" for the "New Learning" demonstration.
- Put a "cube" in a sack for the student to use to "discover" the new keyword. Possible items include children's blocks, dice, sugar cubes, or ice cubes.

ALPHABET ACTIVITY

- The student should be standing.

  "Let's say the alphabet as we touch our toes."

  "We'll say a letter each time we bend over."
- Say the alphabet; then have the student return to his/her seat.

PHONEMIC AWARENESS

- **Objective:** To distinguish between words that are the same and words that are different.

  "Listen to the final sound in these two words. Let's see if you can tell me if they are the same word or different words."

  "Hat, ham. Are they the same or are they different?" *different*

"Fin, fin." same

"Bet, bell." different

"Rig, rim." different

"Rot, rot." same

"Lap, lag." different

"Mat, mat." same

- Continue with additional words, if desired.

REVIEW OF DECKS

- The student should be seated where he/she can write comfortably.
- Show the student **Letter Cards 1–26** in random order. The student should name the letter on each letter card.
- Review **Affix Cards 1–3.**
- Show the student **Picture Cards 1–33** in random order. The student should name the keyword and sound for each picture card.
- Review **Sight Word Cards 1–15.**
- Give the student **Spelling Sound Sheet 32.**
- Call out the sounds on **Spelling Cards 1–28** in random order. The student should echo each sound and name the letter or letters that make the sound as he/she writes the letter(s) on the spelling sound sheet.
- Have the student set the spelling sound sheet aside for use later in the lesson.

NEW LEARNING

"I'm going to say some words. Echo them back to me and listen for the sound in the medial, or middle, position."

- Point to your mouth as you say each word.

"Echo after me. Tone." tone ***"Hope."*** hope ***"Code."*** code

"What sound do you hear in the medial position?" /ō/

"That's right. The sound you hear in the medial position is /ō/."

"Put your fingertips on the front of your neck and say /ō/. See if you feel any vibration."

"Is this sound voiced or unvoiced?" voiced

- You will need two helpers to repeat yesterday's demonstration of "sneaky e." Call them aside and instruct them as you did yesterday's "actors." (See Lesson 41.) Give the *o* card to Helper 1 and the long dash card to Helper 2.
- Position Helper 2 to the right of Helper 1 (so the student reads the cards as "ō—").

"What does the letter o say when it is followed by a consonant?" /ŏ/

- Point to the card with the long dash.

  "This line stands for any consonant."

  "What would this word be if that line were the letter n?" *on*

  "What would the word be if that line were the letter z?" *Oz*

- Begin your "sneaky" act, and then repeat yesterday's skit.
- When Helper 1 and Helper 2 have finished their lines, continue.

  "Sneaky e is back! I'm so sneaky that I don't make any sound at all. The o doesn't know I'm here, so I can sneak behind the consonant, say 'boo!', and scare that vowel and make it say its long sound, /ō/."

- Repeat the previous demonstration, if necessary. Then the helpers may sit down.
- Write the following words on the chalkboard: tone, hope, code.

  "Look at these words on the chalkboard. What letter do you see that might be making the /ō/ sound?" *o*

  "Do you see any sneaky e's?" *yes*

  "When you see a sneaky e, cross it out because it makes no sound."

  "What does the sneaky e do to the o?" *expect variations on the "sneaky e" story*

  "That's right. It sneaks behind the o and scares it so it says its long sound."

  "Whenever an o is followed by a consonant and a silent e ..."

- Write "ō–e̸" on the chalkboard.

  "... we call it 'o consonant e.' The line stands for any consonant."

- Some people call this "*o* consonant sneaky *e*." Either name is acceptable.
- Point to the *o*.

  "Is this a vowel sound or a consonant sound?" *vowel sound*

- Repeat any or all of this portion to introduce ū–e̸. For auditory and visual discovery, use the following words: cute, fuse, mule.
- Keep the "sneaky *e*" and "long dash" cards for use during the next lesson.

Lesson 42

NEW DECK CARDS

- Pull **Spelling Cards 3** and **27** from the Review Deck.
- Show the student **Letter Card 27.**

  "What do we call this?" *o consonant e (or sneaky e)*

  "Our keyword contains the /ō/ sound today. This word will have an o in it, but it will also have a sneaky letter on the end. What letter do we know that can be sneaky?" *sneaky e*

- Hold up **Picture Card 34** but keep the picture covered with your hand (or the letter card).

  "I'm going to describe the picture on this card for you. See if you can guess what it is."

"This is something you would find outside someone's home or in a garage. Many of them are green, but they come in other colors. They are very long and very skinny. If you have a swimming pool, you need one to fill the pool with water. What do you think the picture is?" *hose*

- Show the student **Picture Card 34.**

"We have two sounds today, so we have two sets of cards."

- Show the student **Letter Card 28.**

"What do we call this?" *u consonant e (or sneaky e)*

"Our next keyword contains the /ū/ sound. This word will have a u in it, but it will also have a sneaky letter on the end."

"This sack contains a clue to our new keyword. Don't look in the sack, but put your hand inside and see if you can guess what is inside the sack."

- Allow the student a chance to feel inside the sack.

"I'm going to count to three. On three, whisper what you think is in the sack."

"One, two, three." *cube*

- **Optional:** You may have to lead the student from the object to the shape. Use the following riddle:

"This is a shape. It's a type of square. Dice and children's blocks come in this shape. Ice can also be this shape. What do you think the picture is?" *cube*

"That's right! Our keyword is 'cube.' "

- Show the student **Picture Card 35.**
- Write the words "hose" and "cube" on the chalkboard.

"The words 'hose' and 'cube' help us remember the /ō/ and /ū/ sounds, since they contain those sounds. Also, they both have something special on the end. What is it?" *sneaky e*

"How will we code the word 'hose'?"

- Code the word as the student instructs: hōsø.

"How will we code the word 'cube'?"

- Code the word as the student instructs: cūbø.

" 'U consonant e' can be tricky because it has two sounds. When we see 'u consonant e,' we usually pronounce the u as /yōō/, as in the words 'cube' or 'cute.' But look at this!"

- Write the word "rule" on the chalkboard.

"What is this word?"

- If the student does not know, pronounce it for him/her.

"This word is 'rule.' Do we read the u as /yōō/ in this word?" *no, it says /ōō/*

"Why don't we read the u as /yōō/?" *expect various answers*

"Try to say this word with the /yōō/ sound."

- Allow the student to experiment with the two different sounds of /ū/.

Lesson 42

"Can you say 'rule' with the /yo͞o/ sound?" *no (or yes, but it sounds wrong)*

"It's almost impossible for our mouths to pronounce the /yo͞o/ sound right after the /r/ sound. When you see a word with 'u consonant e,' try the /yo͞o/ sound first. If your mouth doesn't want to say it that way, use the /o͞o/ sound instead."

- The student will have a clearer understanding of this when digraph *oo* is taught (in Lesson 49).

"Find your spelling sound sheet. Find #29 and put your finger on it."

- Hold up **Spelling Card 3** so only you can see what is written. Using the hand signals, follow the instructions on the card.
- Repeat with **Spelling Card 27.**
- Check the spelling sound sheet for accuracy.
- **Note:** Add the new letter and picture cards to the Review Decks (and re-insert **Spelling Cards 3** and **27**).

BOARDWORK

"Let's practice coding some words like the ones you'll have on your worksheet."

"The rule charts are in your Rule Book if you need to look at them."

- Point to **Rule Chart 5.**

"This rule tells us that a vowel followed by a consonant and sneaky (or silent) e is long; code the vowel with a macron and cross out the e. Why is the vowel long?" *sneaky e sneaks up and scares it*

- Write the following word, phrase, and sentence (without the coding marks) on the chalkboard, one at a time. Ask the student to help you code them. The correct coding is as indicated:

nōs̶e̸

flŏss̸ [ed] tē̸eth

Dăd wĭll̸ rāke̸ th̶e stĭc̸k [s].

- Have the student help you identify each of the items coded as either a word, a phrase, or a sentence.

WORKSHEET

- The student should be seated where he/she can write comfortably.
- Give the student **Worksheet 42.** Make sure the student turns to the correct side.

"Let's spell today with the /ō/ and /ū/ sounds. Remember, when we spell with sneaky e, we must hear a consonant because sneaky e only sneaks behind consonants."

"Put your finger by #1. The first word is 'mule.'"

"Do you hear a /ū/ sound?" *yes*

Lesson 42

"Do you hear a consonant that sneaky e could sneak behind to scare that u?" *yes, an l*

"Let's unblend 'mule.' " */m/ /ū/ /l/*

- Hold up one finger for each sound.

"Let's spell those sounds." *m ... u ... l*

- Point to each finger as you say each letter.

"And what sneaky thing goes on the end?" *sneaky e*

"Now spell the word again and write the letters as you say them."

- Allow time for the student to do this. He/She may say "*M* ... *u* ... *l* ... sneaky *e*."

"What word did you write?" *mule*

- Quickly check to see if the student included the final *e*. If he/she has failed to do so, help by saying "I'm afraid sneaky *e* snuck up on you instead of the vowel. Isn't there something missing on the end of your word?"
- Repeat the procedure with #2 (cone), #3 (fume), #4 (rope), and #5 (globe).
- Check each word for accuracy after the student spells it.

"Now we're ready to code and read the words on your paper."

"Using the rules we just practiced on the chalkboard, code the words by #6 through #10. After you have coded these words, try to read them."

- Assist the student as necessary.

"Now read the word by #11. If you have trouble reading the word, code it. Then draw a line from the word to the picture it matches."

- Repeat with #12 through #14.
- As the student works, provide help as needed. Help the student correct any incorrect answers. Then initial the worksheet in the space provided.
- Some time during the day, ask the student to read from the worksheet, a controlled reader, your basal reader, or other material of your choice.
- **Note:** Always make sure the worksheet is corrected before the student begins the homework. The worksheet serves as a guide to help complete the homework.

HOMEWORK

"Turn your paper over to the homework side."

"Do you know what to do on the homework paper?"

"Watch for suffixes and words with a 'vccv' pattern."

"Remember, don't let sneaky e sneak up on you. Make sure everyone at home knows about sneaky e so it doesn't sneak up on them!"

- Discuss the pictures to make sure the student understands the word each one represents: #11 (lake), #12 (rabbit), #13 (twin), and #14 (tree).

"When you finish your paper, I will check it for you and initial it in the space provided."

- Either now or later in the day, the student should complete the homework independently (if possible). Help the student correct any incorrect answers. Then initial the homework in the space provided.

READER

"We have another new book today."

- Give the student **Reader 13 (*Zip Gets a Beef Bone*)** and some colored pencils.

  "Can you tell me this book's title?" *Zip Gets a Beef Bone*
- Assist the student as necessary as he/she constructs the book.
- When the student finishes, staple or put a rubber band around the book's spine.
- If necessary, demonstrate how to separate the pages and check the page order.

  "The title of this book is __________?" *Zip Gets a Beef Bone*

  "I want you to read your book to yourself. When you are finished reading, color the pictures. Write your name on the book so I will know who colored it."

  "Keep your book handy because I will be asking you to read it for me."
- Some time during the day, have the student read the reader to you.
- If possible, take time to play the Kid Card games listed in Lesson 40.

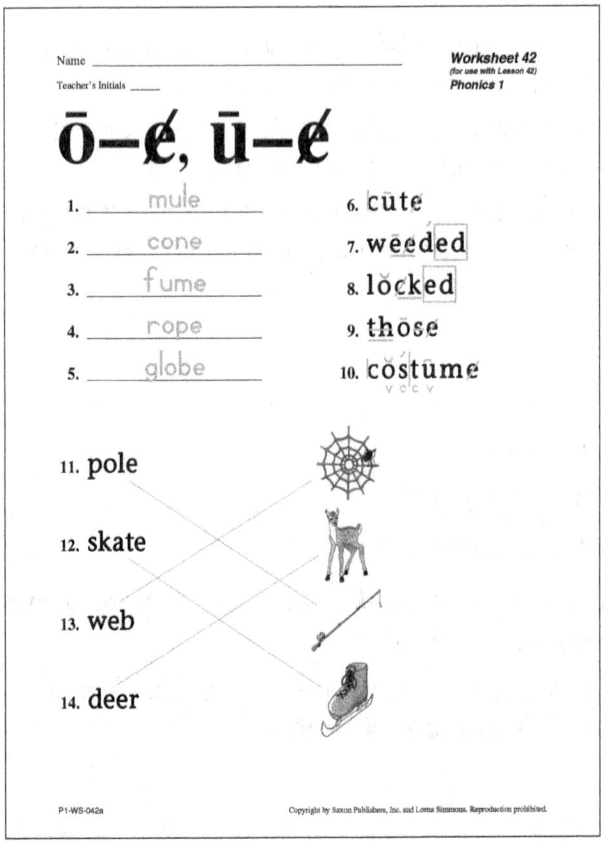
Name __________
Teacher's Initials ____

Worksheet 42
(for use with Lesson 42)
Phonics 1

ō–e, ū–e

1. mule
2. cone
3. fume
4. rope
5. globe
6. cute
7. weeded
8. locked
9. those
10. costume

11. pole
12. skate
13. web
14. deer

P1-WS-042a

Copyright by Saxon Publishers, Inc. and Lorna Simmons. Reproduction prohibited.

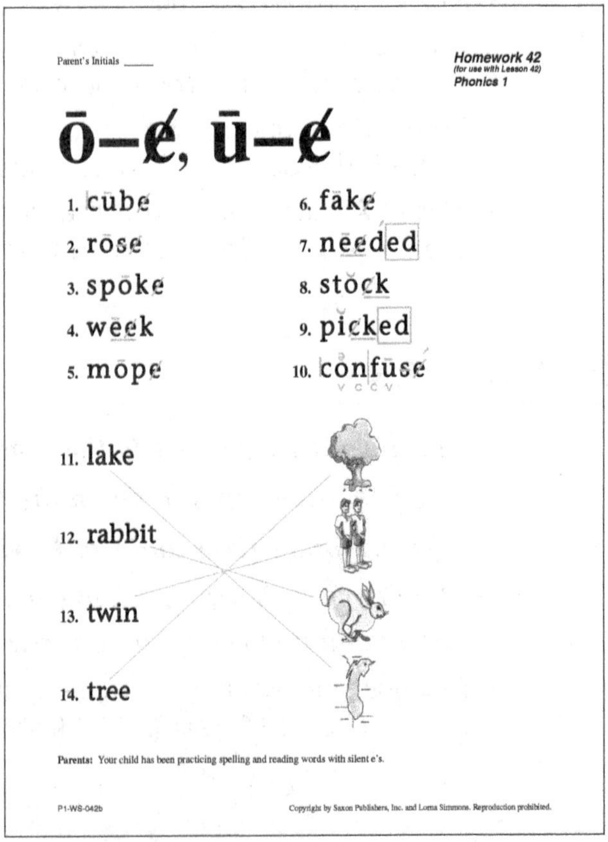
Parent's Initials ____

Homework 42
(for use with Lesson 42)
Phonics 1

ō–e, ū–e

1. cube
2. rose
3. spoke
4. week
5. mope
6. fake
7. needed
8. stock
9. picked
10. confuse

11. lake
12. rabbit
13. twin
14. tree

Parents: Your child has been practicing spelling and reading words with silent e's.

P1-WS-042b

Copyright by Saxon Publishers, Inc. and Lorna Simmons. Reproduction prohibited.

LESSON 43 *i* consonant *e*; *e* consonant *e*

lesson preparation

materials

ball
Review Decks
Spelling Sound Sheet 33
tokens or colored pencil
2 index cards (see *the night before*)
Letter Cards 29–30
dime in a sack (see *the night before*)
Picture Cards 36–37
Sight Word Card 16
Worksheet 43

new concepts

silent *e*

the night before

- Prepare two more index cards. Write a large *i* on one and a large *e* on the other. Put them with the "long dash" and "ɇ" cards from yesterday's lesson. If possible, locate two "helpers" to demonstrate the "New Learning" activity.
- Put a dime in a sack for the student to use to "discover" the new keyword.

ALPHABET ACTIVITY

- You and the student should be standing with the ball.

  "Let's say the alphabet while we toss this ball."

  "I'll begin with 'A' and toss the ball to you. After you catch the ball, say 'B' and toss the ball back to me. We'll continue until we complete the alphabet."
- Recite the alphabet as you and the student toss the ball back and forth.
- Have the student return to his/her seat.

PHONEMIC AWARENESS

- **Objective:** To distinguish between words that are the same and words that are different.

  "Yesterday we listened to the final sounds of words to decide if they were the same or different. Today, let's listen to the initial sound. Where is the initial sound in a word?" *at the beginning*

"Tell me if these words are the same or different."

"Lip, hip. Are they the same or different?" *different*

"Tin, bin." *different* ***"Let, let."*** *same*

"Fig, jig." *different* ***"Rate, rate."*** *same*

"Time, dime." *different* ***"Lamb, lamb."*** *same*

- Continue with additional words, if desired.
- Take note if the student is having difficulty distinguishing between words. Children who are weak in this area are likely to have more difficulty reading as well. Provide the student with additional practice by repeating this activity (using different words).

REVIEW OF DECKS

- Seat the student at a table or a desk.
- Show the student **Letter Cards 1–28** in random order. The student should name the letter on each letter card.
- Review **Affix Cards 1–3.**
- Show the student **Picture Cards 1–35** in random order. The student should name the keyword and sound for each picture card.
- Review **Sight Word Cards 1–15.**
- Give the student **Spelling Sound Sheet 33** and at least twelve tokens (or a colored pencil).

"Let's play Bingo!"

"When I call out the spelling sounds today, I want you to cover (or X out) the space that contains the letter(s) that spell that sound."

"When you cover (or X out) all of the letters on one line, either up and down, across, or from corner to corner, call out Bingo!"

- Demonstrate, if necessary.

"Don't forget to refer to your rule charts if you need to."

"Are you ready?"

"Cover (or X out) the letters that spell the final sound in 'math.' " *th*

"Cover (or X out) the letter that spells the initial sound in 'candy.' " *c*

"Cover (or X out) the letter that spells the final sound in 'dim.' " *m*

"Cover (or X out) the letter that spells the initial sound in 'rice.' " *r*

"Cover (or X out) the letter that spells the initial sound in 'elephant.' " *e*

"Cover (or X out) the letter that spells the final sound in 'hard.' " *d*

"Cover (or X out) the letters that spell the final sound in 'rock.' " *ck*

"Cover (or X out) the letter that spells the initial sound in 'willow.' " *w*

- The student should Bingo by the time all the sounds have been called out.
- Collect the tokens (or colored pencil) and the spelling sound sheet. If you used tokens and the spelling sound sheet is unmarked, keep it available for practice.

NEW LEARNING

"I'm going to say some words. Echo them back to me and listen for the sound in the medial, or middle, position."

- Point to your mouth as you say each word.

"Echo after me. Tide." *tide* ***"Line."*** *line* ***"Mile."*** *mile*

"What sound do you hear in the medial position?" */ī/*

"That's right. The sound you hear in the medial position is /ī/."

"Put your fingertips on the front of your neck and say /ī/. See if you feel any vibration."

"Is this sound voiced or unvoiced?" *voiced*

- You will need two helpers to repeat the demonstration of "sneaky *e*." Call them aside and instruct them as you did the previous "actors." (See Lesson 41.) Give the *i* card to Helper 1 and the long dash card to Helper 2.
- Position Helper 2 to the right of Helper 1 (so the student reads the signs as "ī—").

"What does the letter i say when it is followed by a consonant?" */ĭ/*

- Point to the sign with the long dash.

"This line stands for any consonant."

"What would this word be if that line were the letter n?" *in*

"What would the word be if that line were the letter t?" *it*

- Begin your "sneaky" act; then repeat the skit.
- When Helper 1 and Helper 2 have finished their lines, continue.

"Sneaky e is here once more! I'm so sneaky that I don't make any sound at all. The i doesn't know I'm here, so I can sneak behind the consonant, say 'boo!', and scare that vowel and make it say its long sound, /ī/."

- Repeat the previous demonstration, if necessary. Then the helpers may sit down.
- Write the following words on the chalkboard: tide, line, mile.

"Look at these words on the chalkboard. What letter do you see that might be making the /ī/ sound?" *i*

"Do you see any sneaky e's?" *yes*

"When you see a sneaky e, cross it out because it makes no sound."

"What does the sneaky e do to the i?" *expect variations on the "sneaky e" story*

"That's right. It sneaks behind the i and scares it so it says its long sound."

Lesson 43

"Whenever an i is followed by a consonant and a sneaky e ..."

- Write "ī–ɇ" on the chalkboard.

"... we call it 'i consonant e.' The line stands for any consonant."

- Some people call this "*i* consonant sneaky *e*." Either name is acceptable.
- Point to the *i*.

"Is this a vowel sound or a consonant sound?" *vowel sound*

- Repeat as much of this lesson as you think necessary to introduce ē–ɇ. There are very few one-syllable words containing ē–ɇ, so you need not devote a great deal of time to it. For auditory and visual discovery, use the following words: theme, complete.

"Sometimes we will have a word like this."

- Write the word "horse" on the chalkboard.

"How many sounds are between the e and the o?" *two*

"What are they?" */r/ and /s/*

"The sneaky e is too far away and can't kick the vowel to make it long, so you just cross the e out."

"We'll just call this a 'silent e' since it doesn't make any sound."

"Let's code this word and see if we can read it. How should I do this?"

- Code the word as the student instructs: horsɇ.
- Have the student read the word and use it in a sentence.
- Leave the words on the chalkboard for the student to refer to when completing the worksheet.

NEW DECK CARDS

- Pull **Spelling Cards 7** and **22** from the Review Deck.
- Show the student **Letter Card 29.**

"What do you call this?" *i consonant e (or sneaky e)*

"I have a sack that contains a clue to our new keyword. Don't look in the sack, but put your hand inside and see if you can guess what is inside the sack. Remember, the keyword contains the /ī/ sound."

- Allow the student a chance to feel inside the sack.

"I'm going to count to three. On three, whisper what you think is in the sack."

"One, two, three." *dime*

"That's right! Our keyword is 'dime.'"

- Show the student **Picture Card 36.**

"We have two sounds today, so we have two sets of cards."

- Show the student **Letter Card 30.**

  "What do we call this?" *e consonant e (or sneaky e)*

- Hold up **Picture Card 37** but keep the picture covered with your hand (or the letter card.)

  "This keyword contains the /ē/ sound. This is a two-syllable word with an /ē/ sound in it, but it also has a sneaky e on the end."

  "I'm going to describe the picture on this card for you. See if you can guess what it is."

  "This is mixed in huge trucks. Part of the truck goes round and round to mix it. It is poured out on top of dirt to make sidewalks, driveways, slabs to build houses on, and other things. It is not cement. What do you think the picture is?" *concrete*

- Show the student **Picture Card 37.** You may have to explain that concrete is sometimes poured into block shapes and left to harden to build walls, fences, etc.

- Write the words "dime" and "concrete" on the chalkboard.

  "The words 'dime' and 'concrete' help us remember the /ī/ and /ē/ sounds since they contain those sounds. Also, they both have something special on the end. What is it?" *sneaky e*

  "How will we code the word 'dime'?"

- Code the word as the student instructs: dīmɇ.

  "The word 'concrete' follows a syllable division pattern that we haven't learned yet, so I'll code it for you."

- Code the word as follows:

  ꝁŏn′|ꝁrētɇ
  vc|ccv

- Hold up **Spelling Card 7** so only you can see what is written. Using the hand signals, follow the instructions on the card.

- Have the student write the response with his/her finger on the desktop.

- Hold up **Spelling Card 22** so only you can see what is written. Using the hand signals, follow the instructions on the card. (This is *not* a new response.)

- **Note:** The response to **Spelling Card 22** remains "digraph *ee* comma *e* final digraph *ee*." Because digraph *ee* is a much more common spelling than ē–ɇ, the /ē/ card will not include the response "*e* consonant *e*." Explain this as much as you think necessary to help the student understand the discrepancy.

- Have the student write the response with his/her finger on the desktop.

- **Note:** Add the new letter and picture cards to the Review Decks (and re-insert **Spelling Cards 7** and **22**).

Lesson 43

BOARDWORK

"Let's practice coding some words like the ones you'll have on your worksheet."

"The vowel charts are in your Rule Book if you need to look at them."

- Point to **Rule Chart 5.**

"Remember the 'sneaky e' rule: 'A vowel followed by a consonant and sneaky e is long; code the vowel with a macron and cross out the e.' "

"Why is the vowel long?" *sneaky e sneaks up on it and scares it*

- Write the following phrase and sentence (without the coding marks) on the chalkboard, one at a time. Ask the student to help you code them. The correct coding is as indicated:

thrēē kīte[s]

Pēte ĭs sĭng′ [ing].

- Have the student help you identify each item as a word, a phrase, or a sentence.

"We have another new sight word today."

- Show the student **Sight Word Card 16.**

"Can you tell me what this word is?"

"This word is 'one,' as in the number one. Does it follow the rules we've learned so far?" *no*

"Can you use the word 'one' in a sentence?"

- Make sure the student uses the word to mean "one" (as opposed to "won").
- Help the student locate the word in the Irregular Spelling Booklet.

"How do we code a sight word?" *draw a circle around it*

"We'll add this card to our sight word deck."

- Add **Sight Word Card 16** to the Sight Word Deck.

WORKSHEET

- The student should be seated where he/she can write comfortably.
- Give the student **Worksheet 43.** Make sure the student turns to the correct side.

"Let's spell today with the /ī/ sound. Remember, when we spell with sneaky e, we must hear a consonant because sneaky e only sneaks behind consonants."

"Put your finger by #1. The first word is 'life.' "

"Do you hear an /ī/ sound?" *yes*

"Do you hear a consonant that sneaky e could sneak behind to scare that i?" *yes, an f*

"Let's unblend 'life.' " */l/ /ī/ /f/*

- Hold up one finger for each sound.

"Let's spell those sounds." *l ... i ... f*

- Point to a finger as you say each letter.

"And what sneaky thing goes on the end?" *sneaky e*

"Now spell the word again and write the letters as you say them."

- Allow time for the student to do this. He/She may say "*L* ... *i* ... *f* ... sneaky *e*."

"What word did you write?" *life*

- Quickly check to see if the student included the final *e*. If he/she has failed to do so, help correct him/her by saying "I'm afraid sneaky *e* snuck up on you instead of the vowel. Isn't there something missing on the end of your word?"
- Repeat the procedure with #2 (fine), #3 (here), #4 (ripe), and #5 (smile).
- The word "here" is included because it is a word commonly used by the student, although the ē–ɇ spelling is not. (Because the /r/ sound alters the /ē/ sound slightly, the student may need your help to hear the individual sounds.)
- Check each word for accuracy after the student spells it.

"Now you're ready to code and read the words on your paper."

"Using the rules we just practiced on the chalkboard, code the words by #6 through #10. After you have coded these words, try to read them."

- Assist the student as necessary.

"Now read the paragraph in the middle of the page. If you find any words you can't read, code them. Then answer the questions by #11 and #12."

- As the student works, provide help as needed. Help the student correct any incorrect answers. Then initial the worksheet in the space provided.
- Some time during the day, ask the student to read from the worksheet, a controlled reader, your basal reader, or other material of your choice.
- **Note:** Always make sure the worksheet is corrected before the student begins the homework. The worksheet serves as a guide to help complete the homework.

HOMEWORK

"Turn your paper over to the homework side."

"Do you know what to do on the homework paper?"

"Don't let sneaky e sneak up on you. Make sure everyone at home knows about it, too!"

"When you finish your paper, I will check it for you and initial it in the space provided."

- Either now or later in the day, the student should complete the homework independently (if possible). Help the student correct any incorrect answers. Then initial the homework in the space provided.
- If possible, take time to play the Kid Card games listed in Lesson 40.

43

Name _____

Teacher's Initials _____

Worksheet 43
(for use with Lesson 43)
Phonics 1

ī–é, ē–é

1. _____life_____ 6. mīne
2. _____fine_____ 7. swēet
3. _____here_____ 8. thēse
4. _____ripe_____ 9. slīdes
5. _____smile_____ 10. flinging

Miss Smith said, "It's time to go to the bake sale." We are going to take nine cakes. We hope to sell them so we can go on a fun trip.

11. Where is Miss Smith going? _____

_____to the bake sale_____

12. We will take _____nine cakes_____ to the bake sale.

P1-WS-043a

Parent's Initials _____

Homework 43
(for use with Lesson 43)
Phonics 1

ī–é, ē–é

1. stōne 6. thēme
2. dīme 7. līnes
3. wīse 8. rŭsting
4. bēef 9. fūse
5. rĭnging 10. blāme

We went to the bake sale with Miss Smith's nine cakes. Nine of them had pink frosting, three had red ribbons, and one had stripes. The striped cake was the best.

11. _____Nine_____ cakes had pink frosting.

12. The best cake was _____striped_____.

Parents: Your child has been practicing spelling and reading words with silent e's.

P1-WS-043b

LESSON 44 — Spelling with Final *ke*

lesson preparation

materials

container of letter tiles

Review Decks

Spelling Sound Sheet 34

Worksheet 44

Reader 14 (*Huck's Raft*)

colored pencils

ALPHABET ACTIVITY

- The student should be seated with the alphabet strip.
- Have available the letter cards *b*, *d*, *e*, and *h*.

  "Let's try alphabetizing some more letters today. Watch closely because it's going to be a little different this time."

- Place the letter cards along the chalk tray (or anywhere else the student can see them). Deliberately place them in non-alphabetical order.

  "When we alphabetize, we recite the alphabet and put the letters in order as we say them. Watch as I alphabetize this group of letters. Each time we say a letter, we will quickly scan these cards to see if that letter is here."

  "Let's start. A."

- Quickly scan the cards with your eyes and your index finger.

  "Is there an a?" *no*

  "B."

- Quickly scan the cards with your eyes and your index finger.

  "Is there a b?" *yes*

  "Let's pull the b card and place it at the beginning of our new row of letters. This row will be in alphabetical order when we finish."

- Move the *b* card to a new location with enough room for the rearranged cards.

  "C."

- Quickly scan the cards with your eyes and your index finger.

  "Is there a c?" *no*

"D."

- Quickly scan the cards with your eyes and your index finger.

  "Is there a d?" *yes*

- Pull the *d* card and place it to the right of the *b* card.
- Continue, calling out the letters *e, f, g,* and *h.*

  "Now our letters should be in ABC, or alphabetical, order."

  "Let's check to see if we are right."

- Quickly recite the alphabet from *a* to *h*, touching each new card in the sequence as you say it. The student should see that your hand will move progressively to the right if the letters are in the correct order.

  "We did it right, didn't we? The letters are in alphabetical order."

  "You get to try this with your letter tiles today."

- Give the student the container of letter tiles.

  "Take any four letters out of your container. It doesn't matter which ones."

  "Line up the four letters in front of you."

  "Put your finger under your first letter tile, the one on the left side. When you scan, move your finger under the row of letters to make sure you look at every letter."

  "We will say the alphabet slowly, and when we say one of your letters, pull it down to start a new row. This will be the row that will be in ABC order."

  "Listen carefully and watch for the letters in front of you."

- Begin reciting the alphabet. Encourage the student to say it with you. Make sure the student is using his/her finger to scan the letters.
- If time permits, have the student trade the letters for four new ones and try the procedure again.
- Allow the student to work independently, but take note if he/she is having difficulty. Provide the student with additional practice by repeating this activity, if necessary.
- Have the student replace the tiles in the container and put it away.

PHONEMIC AWARENESS

- **Objective:** To distinguish between words that are the same and words that are different.

  "Yesterday we listened to the initial sounds of the words to decide if they were the same or different. Today let's listen to the medial sound. Where is the medial sound in a word?" *in the middle*

  "Tell me if these words are the same or different."

  "Hat, hot. Are they the same or different?" *different*

"Tub, tab." different

"Lace, lace." same

"Pin, pan." different

"Beg, beg." same

"Sack, sock." different

"Rim, rim." same

- Continue with additional words, if desired.
- Take note if the student is having difficulty distinguishing between words. Children who are weak in this area are likely to have difficulty reading as well. Provide the student with additional practice by repeating this activity (using different words).

REVIEW OF DECKS

- The student should be seated where he/she can write comfortably.
- Show the student **Letter Cards 1–30** in random order. The student should name the letter on each letter card.
- Review **Affix Cards 1–3.**
- Show the student **Picture Cards 1–37** in random order. The student should name the keyword and sound for each picture card.
- Review **Sight Word Cards 1–16.**
- Give the student **Spelling Sound Sheet 34.**
- Call out the sounds on **Spelling Cards 1–28** in random order. The student should echo each sound and name the letter or letters that make the sound as he/she writes the letter(s) on the spelling sound sheet.
- Have the student set the spelling sound sheet aside for use later in the lesson.

NEW LEARNING

"We have learned several rules for spelling the /k/ sound."

"At the beginning or middle of a word, we use k or c."

- Point to **Rule Chart 3.**

"Can you tell me when we use k?" before e, i, and y

"Can you tell me when we use c?" before anything else (a, o, u, and any consonant)

"We have also learned two ways to spell /k/ at the end of a word."

"Do you remember what digraph we use after a short vowel sound?" digraph ck

"What spelling do we use for /k/ after a consonant or a vowel digraph?" k by itself

Lesson 44

"Today we are going to learn another way to spell /k/ at the end of a word."

- Write the following words on the chalkboard: take, like, hike, make.

"How have we spelled the /k/ sound in these words?" *ke*

"Do you see anything in these words that we learned this week?" *yes, sneaky e*

"What happens to the vowel when we have a sneaky e on the end of the word?" *it sneaks up on the vowel and scares it; the vowel says its long sound*

"So this is a long vowel sound."

"Do you know why we need 'ke' after a long vowel sound?" *the e is the sneaky e*

"We know that digraph ck comes after a short vowel, and that k follows a consonant, as in 'milk' or 'tank,' or a vowel digraph, as in 'peek' or 'seek.' Now we know that 'ke' follows a long vowel sound."

"The next time we review our spelling deck, we will have a really long response when we get to the /k/ sound."

"I am going to see if you can say all of the responses for that sound. I will be amazed if you can remember that much!"

- Convince the student that you think it is too hard. The student will consider it a challenge and will do what he/she can to prove you wrong.

"Our new response is 'k comma c final digraph ck comma k comma ke.' "

- Write the new response on the chalkboard: k, c || ck, k, ke.

"Let's practice this together before we have to say it tomorrow." *k comma c final digraph ck comma k comma ke*

- Say it with the student two or three times.

"Find your spelling sound sheet. Write the new response on the line by #29."

- Check the spelling sound sheet for accuracy.

BOARDWORK

"Let's practice spelling the final /k/ sound in some words like the ones you'll have on your worksheet."

"The rule chart for spelling with final /k/ is in your Rule Book. Look at it if you need to."

- Write the following on the chalkboard, one at a time:

cl$\breve{\text{i}}$__ h$\bar{\text{i}}$__ m$\breve{\text{i}}$l__ see__

- Ask the student to help you decide whether to use *ck*, *k*, or *ke*. (The words are "click," "hike," "milk," and "seek.")

Worksheet

- The student should be seated where he/she can write comfortably.
- Give the student **Worksheet 44.** Make sure the student turns to the correct side.

"Let's practice spelling some more words with the final /k/ sound. I'll say a word. You will need to decide if the word should end with digraph ck, k by itself, or ke. Refer to the rule charts if you need to."

"Put your finger by #1. The first word is 'like.' "

"Let's unblend 'like.' " /l/ /ī/ /k/

"Now spell the word and write it on the line by #1."

- Repeat with #2 (bake), #3 (hike), #4 (flake), #5 (smoke), #6 (milk), #7 (lick), #8 (take), #9 (meek), and #10 (kick).
- Make sure the student has not failed to include the final *e*'s.

"Now you're ready to spell the final /k/ sound in the words on your paper."

"Find #11 on your paper. Using the rules we just practiced on the chalkboard, fill in the blank with ck, k or ke."

- Repeat with #12 through #20.
- As the student works, provide help as needed. Help the student correct any incorrect answers. Then initial the worksheet in the space provided.
- Some time during the day, ask the student to read from the worksheet, a controlled reader, your basal reader, or other material of your choice.
- **Note:** Always make sure the worksheet is corrected before the student begins the homework. The worksheet serves as a guide to help complete the homework.

Homework

"Turn your paper over to the homework side."

"Do you know what to do on the homework paper?"

"Look at the two boxes beside the list of words."

"As you do your homework, you need to think of two words that end with the /k/ sound. Each word should have only one syllable."

"In the first box, draw a picture of one of the words. Then write the word on the line under the picture. You'll need to decide the correct way to spell the final /k/ sound in your word. Then do the same thing for the second word you chose."

- Discuss the activity further, if necessary.

"Remember, you'll need to think of words that you can draw."

"When you finish your paper, I will check it for you and initial it in the space provided."

- Either now or later in the day, the student should complete the homework independently (if possible). Help the student correct any incorrect answers. Then initial the homework in the space provided.

READER

"We have another new book today."

- Give the student **Reader 14 (*Huck's Raft*)** and some colored pencils.

"Can you tell me this book's title?" ***Huck's Raft***

- Assist the student as necessary as he/she constructs the book.
- When the student finishes, staple or put a rubber band around the book's spine.
- If necessary, demonstrate how to separate the pages and check the page order.

"The title of this book is __________?" ***Huck's Raft***

"I want you to read your book to yourself. When you are finished reading, color the pictures. Write your name on the book so I will know who colored it."

"Keep your book handy because I will be asking you to read it for me."

- Some time during the day, have the student read the reader to you.
- If possible, take time to play the Kid Card games listed in Lesson 40. Try to see that the student is prepared for tomorrow's assessment.

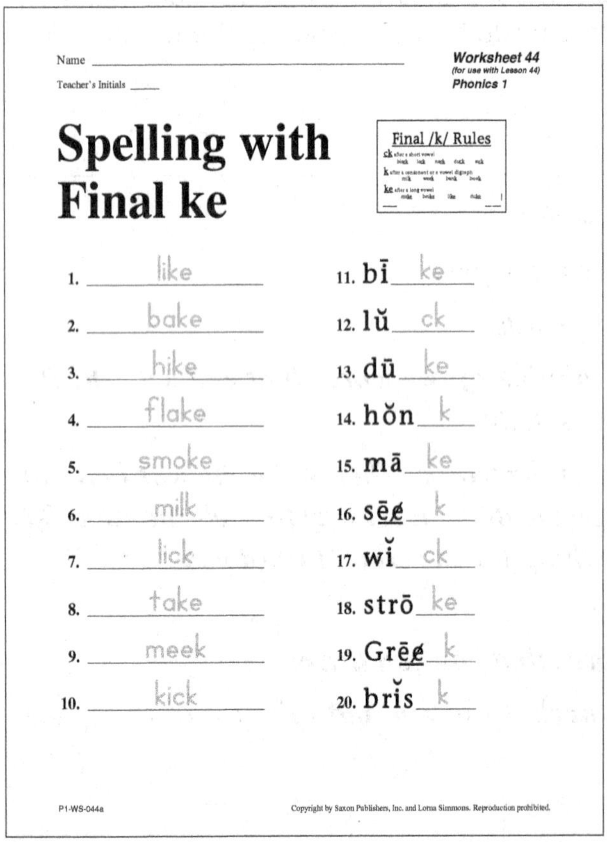
Name ________________
Teacher's Initials ____

Worksheet 44
(for use with Lesson 44)
Phonics 1

Spelling with Final ke

Final /k/ Rules
ck after a short vowel: black lock neck duck sick
k after a consonant or a vowel digraph: milk week bank book
ke after a long vowel: make broke like duke

1. like
2. bake
3. hike
4. flake
5. smoke
6. milk
7. lick
8. take
9. meek
10. kick
11. bī ke
12. lŭ ck
13. dū ke
14. hŏn k
15. mā ke
16. sēe̸ k
17. wĭ ck
18. strō ke
19. Grēe̸ k
20. brĭs k

P1-WS-044a
Copyright by Saxon Publishers, Inc. and Lorna Simmons. Reproduction prohibited.

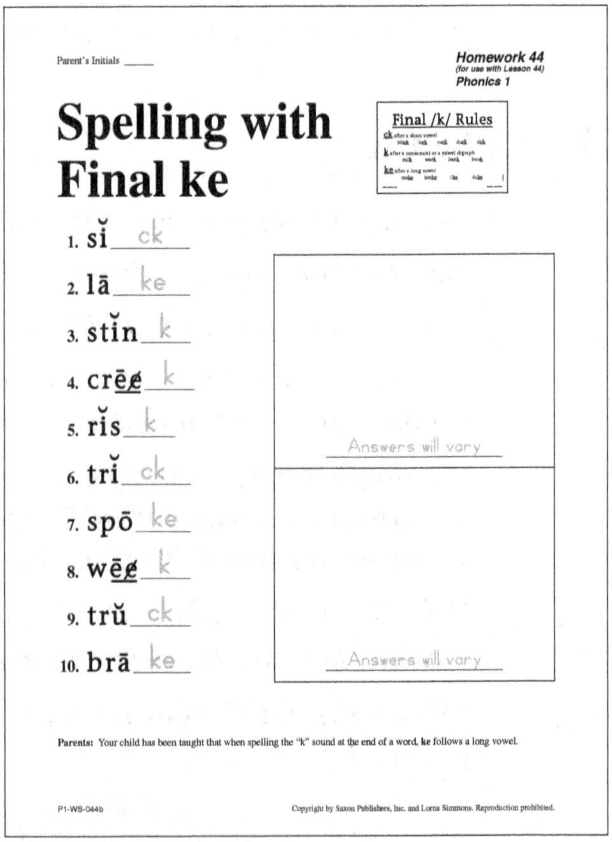
Parent's Initials ____

Homework 44
(for use with Lesson 44)
Phonics 1

Spelling with Final ke

Final /k/ Rules
ck after a short vowel: black lock neck duck sick
k after a consonant or a vowel digraph: milk week bank book
ke after a long vowel: make broke like duke

1. sĭ ck
2. lā ke
3. stĭn k
4. crēe̸ k
5. rĭs k
6. trĭ ck
7. spō ke
8. wēe̸ k
9. trŭ ck
10. brā ke

Answers will vary

Answers will vary

Parents: Your child has been taught that when spelling the "k" sound at the end of a word, **ke** follows a long vowel.

P1-WS-044b
Copyright by Saxon Publishers, Inc. and Lorna Simmons. Reproduction prohibited.

LESSON 45 Assessment

lesson preparation

materials

Review Decks

Assessment 8

Spelling Test 6

Assessment 8 Recording Form

Kid Cards

tokens

the night before

- Separate the Kid Cards marked "Lesson 45."

ALPHABET ACTIVITY

- The student should be seated.

  "Today I want to see if you can say the alphabet from beginning to end."

- Allow the student to recite as much of the alphabet as possible; then help him/her complete it.
- If the student needs extra motivation, give a token (cereal, poker chip, small candy) for each letter.

PHONEMIC AWARENESS

- **Objective:** To distinguish between words that are the same and words that are different.

  "Today let's listen to these words to see if they are the same or if they are different. Sit down if they are the same, but stand up if they are different."

  "Bit, sit. Are they the same or different?" *different (stand up)*

  "Cat, Cap." *different (remain standing)*

  "Tap, Tap." *same (sit down)*

  "Pig, pin." *different (stand up)*

  "Seat, seat." *same (sit down)*

"Snack, snap." *different (stand up)*

"Rip, rip." *same (sit down)*

- Continue with additional words, if desired.
- Take note if the student is having difficulty distinguishing between words. Children who are weak in this area are likely to have difficulty reading as well. Provide the student with additional practice by repeating this activity (using different words).

REVIEW OF DECKS

- The student should be seated where he/she can write comfortably.
- Show the student **Letter Cards 1–30** in random order. The student should name the letter on each letter card.
- Review **Affix Cards 1–3.**
- Show the student **Picture Cards 1–37** in random order. The student should name the keyword and sound for each picture card.
- Review **Sight Word Cards 1–16.**

WRITTEN ASSESSMENT

- Seat the student where he/she can write comfortably.
- Give the student **Assessment 8.**
- **Section I:**

  "Today we are going to write some words for our assessment."

  "I'm going to say a word. Write the letter that makes each sound in that word on the lines by #1."

  "Look at the rule charts if you need to."

  "Here's the first word: weep."
- Repeat with the following words in the order shown: #2 (twist), #3 (gust), #4 (brisk), and #5 (peek).
- **Reminder:** While the student spells, be ready to point to appropriate rule charts as necessary. For example, point to **Rule Chart 4** while the student spells #4.
- **Section II:**

  "Look at the letter by #6."

  "Find the picture of the keyword for this sound."

  "Draw a line from the letter to the keyword."
- Repeat with #7, #8, and #9. Allow a few minutes for the student to work.
- The pictures (from top to bottom) are as follows: umbrella, wagon, ivy, unicorn.

- **Section III:**

  "Put your finger on #10."

  "Code the words by #10 through #14."
- Allow a few minutes for the student to work.
- **Section IV:**
- Have the student name the sound of each blend in #15–#17.
- Help identify each picture and then ask the student to name the blend each picture begins with and to draw a line from the picture to the blend. The pictures (from top to bottom) are as follows: swing, twins, splinter.
- **Section V:**

  "Read the paragraph. If you find any words you can't read, code them to help you figure out the words."

  "Look at the sentences by #18 and #19 and answer the questions."
- **Note:** If the student absolutely cannot read the paragraph, read it to the student to see if he or she can answer the questions.

  "When you are finished, show your paper to me."
- This paper will be used during the oral portion of the assessment.

SPELLING TEST

- Give the student **Spelling Test 6.**
- Call out the following words (in the order shown). Sound them out, if necessary.

  #1 (sock), #2 (man), #3 (neck), #4 (rock), #5 (lamp), #6 (crab), #7 (skin), #8 (clock), #9 (insect), #10 (napkin), #11 (was), #12 (who)
- Grade and record the test in any manner that suits your needs.

ORAL ASSESSMENT

- Oral assessments are short interviews that occur during independent work time. It is important to complete it promptly (today, if possible) in order to identify any areas of weakness and begin remediation.
- Use the assessment and the following dialogue to complete the oral portion.
- **Section VI:**
- Point to the sight word by #20.

  "Read this sight word for me."
- Record the student's response by placing a check mark by each word he/she reads correctly.
- Repeat with #21, #22, and #23.

- **Section VII:**
- Show the student the letter by #24.

  "Tell me the name of this letter and the sound it makes."
- Write the student's response on the adjacent line.
- Repeat with #25.

ASSESSMENT EVALUATION

- Grade the assessment and record the results on **Assessment 8 Recording Form.** Check off the boxes to indicate mastery (i.e., the section was completed with 100% accuracy).
- **Reminder:** Try to give as many points as possible for work attempted. Do not grade the coding marks too severely. The most important coding marks to look for are breves, macrons, and syllable division lines.
- See the introductory material for detailed information regarding grading and recording procedures.
- Use the assessment results to identify those skills in which the student is weak. Practice those skills by playing Kid Card games.
- Add the Kid Cards marked "Lesson 45" to the existing decks. Listed below are games appropriate for remediation in selected areas. See "Games and Activities" for the directions for each game
- **Section I:** Play "Spelling Deck Perfection," "Sound Scamper," "Spell Out #1," or have the student use the letter tiles to spell words you give from the Spelling Word List.
- **Section II:** Play "Keyword and Sound" or "Letter/Sound Identification."
- **Section III:** Play "Chalkboard Challenge." Check the daily work carefully.
- **Section IV:** Play "Blend It."
- **Section V:** Have the student read the controlled readers. Ask questions for comprehension.
- **Section VI:** Play "At First Sight."
- **Section VII:** Play "Letter/Sound Identification."
- When the student seems more secure in areas that had previously proven difficult, retest him/her (in those areas only) and indicate on the recording form any sections the student has subsequently mastered.
- Try to help the student achieve mastery of all the sections before the next assessment.
- If the student is having difficulty with a particular skill, keep his or her practice activities at the most basic level so the chance of success is greater.

Name ______________________

Assessment 8
(for use with Lesson 45)
Phonics 1

Section I

1. w e e p
2. t w i s t
3. g u s t
4. b r i s k
5. p e e k

Section II

6. w
7. ū
8. ŭ
9. ī

Section III

10. wĕb
11. swēep
12. stŭmp
13. hŭgging
14. drŭm

Section IV

15. tw
16. sw
17. spl

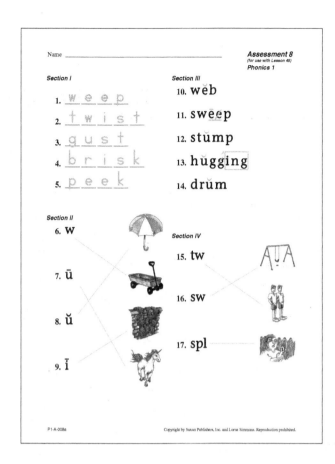

P1-A-008a

Assessment 8
(for use with Lesson 45)
Phonics 1

Section V

This week the bug club is going on a trip. Seth will be going with Smith. Seth and Smith will trap bugs. Seth will feed them and then Smith will let them go.

18. Who is going on a trip?
the bug club, or
Seth and Smith

19. What will Seth do to the bugs? feed them

Section VI

20. into ______
21. two ______
22. of ______
23. come ______

Section VII

24. w ______ w, /w/
25. u ______ u, /ŭ/, /ū/

P1-A-008b

Lesson 45

LESSON 46 — The Letter *X*

lesson preparation

materials

Review Decks
Spelling Sound Sheet 35
container of letter tiles
Letter Card 31
Picture Card 38
Spelling Card 29
Worksheet 46
Spelling List 7

the night before

- Add the *x* letter tile to the student's container.

ALPHABET ACTIVITY

- The student should be seated with the alphabet strip.

  "How many letters are in the alphabet?" *26*

  "What two kinds of letters make up our alphabet?" *vowels and consonants*

  "Name the vowels." *a, e, i, o, and u*

  "All of the other letters are called _________?" *consonants*

  "The initial letter of the alphabet is _____?" *a*

  "The final letter of the alphabet is _____?" *z*

  "Let's point to each letter and say the whole alphabet."

  "Put your index finger on 'a' and say the names with me."

PHONEMIC AWARENESS

- **Objective:** To identify the number of syllables in words.

  "I'm going to say a word and clap as I say it. Listen to the word and the claps and see if you can tell me how many claps or parts you hear."

- Say "Sep·tem·ber" and clap on each syllable.

  "How many parts did you hear?" *three*

"Each of those parts is a syllable. If it has three parts, how many syllables are there?" *three*

"Let's try the word 'kitten.' Clap and say it with me." *kit … ten*

"How many parts does this word have?" *two*

"So how many syllables are in this word?" *two*

"Try 'elephant.' Clap with me." *el … e … phant*

"How many parts does this word have?" *three*

"How many syllables are in this word?" *three*

"Try the word 'dime.' Clap with me." *dime*

"How many parts does this word have?" *one*

"How many syllables are in this word?" *one*

REVIEW OF DECKS

- The student should be seated where he/she can write comfortably.
- Show the student **Letter Cards 1–30** in random order. The student should name the letter on each letter card.
- Review **Affix Cards 1–3.**
- Show the student **Picture Cards 1–37** in random order. The student should name the keyword and sound for each picture card.
- Review **Sight Word Cards 1–16.**
- Give the student **Spelling Sound Sheet 35.**
- Call out the sounds on **Spelling Cards 1–28** in random order. The student should echo each sound and name the letter or letters that make the sound as he/she writes the letter(s) on the spelling sound sheet.
- Check the student's response after each card.
- Have the student set the spelling sound sheet aside for use later in the lesson.

NEW LEARNING

"I'm going to say some words. Echo them back to me and listen for the sound in the final position."

- Point to your mouth as you say each word.

"Echo after me. Box." *box* ***"Ax."*** *ax* ***"Fix."*** *fix*

"What sound do you hear in the final position?" */ks/ (the sound of x)*

- **Note:** Make sure the student is giving the pure sound of *x* and not pronouncing it with a short *e* sound, as in /ěks/.

"That's right. The sound you hear in the final position is /ks/."

"How many sounds do you hear in /ks/?" *two*

"What are they?" */k/ and /s/*

"Put your fingertips on the front of your neck and say /ks/. See if you feel any vibration."

"Is this sound voiced or unvoiced?" *unvoiced*

- Write the following words on the chalkboard: box, ax, fix.

"What letter do you see that might be making the /ks/ sound?" *x*

- If the student does not know the name of the letter, say it for him/her.

"X is the last letter in all of these words, so we can see that x must be the letter used to spell the /ks/ sound."

"Is x a vowel or a consonant?" *consonant*

HANDWRITING/LETTER TILES

- The student should be seated where he/she can write comfortably.
- Draw handwriting lines on the chalkboard. Write a capital *X* on the handwriting lines in the handwriting you want the student to learn.

"This is a capital X. Let's practice skywriting capital X's."

- Have the student practice skywriting capital *X*'s.

"Say the name of the letter each time you write it."

- Allow a few minutes for the student to practice writing capital *X*'s.
- Now write a lowercase *x* on the handwriting lines in the handwriting you want the student to learn.

"This is a lowercase x."

- Have the student practice skywriting lowercase *x*'s.

"Now practice writing lowercase x's on the second handwriting line. Say the name of the letter each time you write it."

- Leave the handwriting lines and letters on the chalkboard for the remainder of the lesson.
- Give the student the container of letter tiles.

"I've given you a new letter tile today. What do you think it is?" *x*

"Find your x letter tile and look at it. One side has a capital X and the other side has a lowercase x."

"Hold your letter tile up in the air. Turn it so I can see the capital X."

"Now turn it so I can see the lowercase x."

"Spell the word 'ox' with your letter tiles."

"Now spell the word 'mix.' "

"Now change one letter to make the word 'six.' "

- Choose additional words from the Spelling Word List, if desired.
- Have the student replace the tiles in the container and put it away.
- Reinforce the name, sound, and shape of the letter *x* throughout the day.

NEW DECK CARDS

- Show the student **Letter Card 31.**

  "What is the name of this letter?" x

- Hold up **Picture Card 38** but keep the picture covered with your hand (or the letter card).

  "I have a card with a picture on it that ends with the /ks/ sound."

  "I am going to describe it for you. See if you can guess what the picture is."

  "This animal lives in the woods. It has a bushy red tail and a reputation for being sly. Its name rhymes with 'box.' What do you think the picture is?" fox

  "That's right. The keyword is 'fox' and the sound we have learned is /ks/."

- Show the student **Picture Card 38,** and then point to the picture of a fox on the alphabet strip.

  "The word 'fox' helps us remember the /ks/ sound because it ends with /ks/."

  "Find your spelling sound sheet. Put your finger on line #29."

- Hold up **Spelling Card 29** so only you can see what is written. Using the hand signals, follow the instructions on the card.
- Check the spelling sound sheet for accuracy.
- **Note:** Add the new letter, picture, and spelling cards to the Review Decks.

Lesson 46

BOARDWORK

"Let's practice coding some words like the ones you'll have on your worksheet."

"The vowel charts are in your Rule Book if you need to look at them."

- Write the following word and phrases (without the coding marks) on the chalkboard, one at a time. Ask the student to help you code them. The correct coding is as indicated:

clăsp′ing

fĭxed the snăcks

gĕtt′ing the kĭt′|tĕn s ĭn the trēes
vc | c v

- Have the student help you identify each of the items coded as a word, a phrase, or a sentence.

WORKSHEET

- The student should be seated where he/she can write comfortably.
- Give the student **Worksheet 46.** Make sure the student turns to the correct side.

"Today, let's spell with the /ks/ sound."

"Put your finger by #1. The first word is 'box.' "

"Unblend 'box' with me." */b/ /ŏ/ /ks/*

- Hold up one finger for each sound.

"Let's spell those sounds." ***b … o … x***

- Point to each finger as you spell a sound.

"Now spell the word again and write the letters as you say them."

- Allow time for the student to do this.

"What word did you write?" ***box***

- Repeat the procedure with #2 (six), #3 (wax), #4 (nine), and #5 (hope).

"Now you're ready to code and read the words on your paper."

"Code the words by #6 through #10. After you've coded all the words, try to read them."

- Assist the student as necessary.

"Numbers 11 and 12 are questions about the paragraph just above them. If you find any words you can't read, code them. Then see if you can answer the questions."

- As the student works, provide help as needed. Help the student correct any incorrect answers. Then initial the worksheet in the space provided.
- Some time during the day, ask the student to read from the worksheet, a controlled reader, your basal reader, or other material of your choice.
- **Note:** Always make sure the worksheet is corrected before the student begins the homework. The worksheet serves as a guide to help complete the homework.

HOMEWORK

"Turn your paper over to the homework side."

"Put your finger on the top row of handwriting lines. Write your best capital X on these lines so I will know what a capital X should look like."

- Have the student write a lowercase letter *x* on the second handwriting line. Make sure that the student has written the letters correctly (to the best of his or her ability). He/She will use them as guides when completing the homework.

"Do you know what to do on the rest of the homework paper?"

"Remember to look for suffixes and words with a 'vccv' pattern that need to be divided."

"When you finish your paper, I will check it for you and initial it in the space provided."

- Either now or later in the day, the student should complete the homework independently (if possible). Help the student correct any incorrect answers. Then initial the homework in the space provided.

SPELLING LIST

- Fold **Spelling List 7** in half lengthwise (with the printed side facing out).

  "Leave your paper just like I give it to you."

- Give the student **Spelling List 7,** folded with the blank lines facing up.

  "Let's spell some more words."

- Call out the following words (in the order shown). Sound them out, if necessary.

  #1 (deep), #2 (camping), #3 (honk), #4 (thick), #5 (packing), #6 (singing), #7 (rested), #8 (helped), #9 (speed), #10 (sticks), #11 (put), #12 (are)

  "Now unfold your paper and check your words."

- Check the student's work to see if he/she needs extra help with spelling.

  "I want you to practice these words. We'll have a spelling test in a few days."

- If possible, take time to play the Kid Card games listed in Lesson 45.

Lesson 46

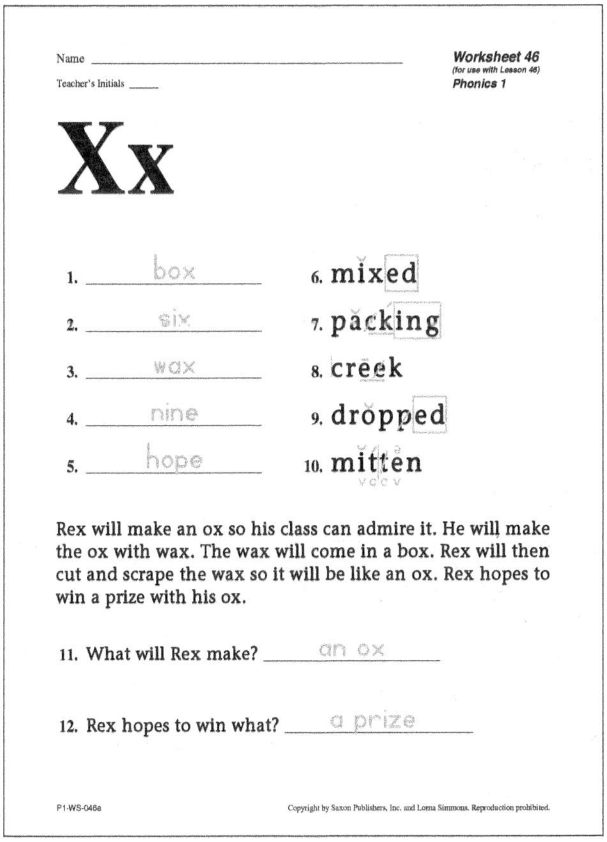

Name ______

Teacher's Initials ____

Worksheet 46
(for use with Lesson 46)
Phonics 1

Xx

1. box
2. six
3. wax
4. nine
5. hope
6. mixed
7. packing
8. creek
9. dropped
10. mitten

Rex will make an ox so his class can admire it. He will make the ox with wax. The wax will come in a box. Rex will then cut and scrape the wax so it will be like an ox. Rex hopes to win a prize with his ox.

11. What will Rex make? an ox
12. Rex hopes to win what? a prize

P1-WS-046a

Copyright by Saxon Publishers, Inc. and Lorna Simmons. Reproduction prohibited.

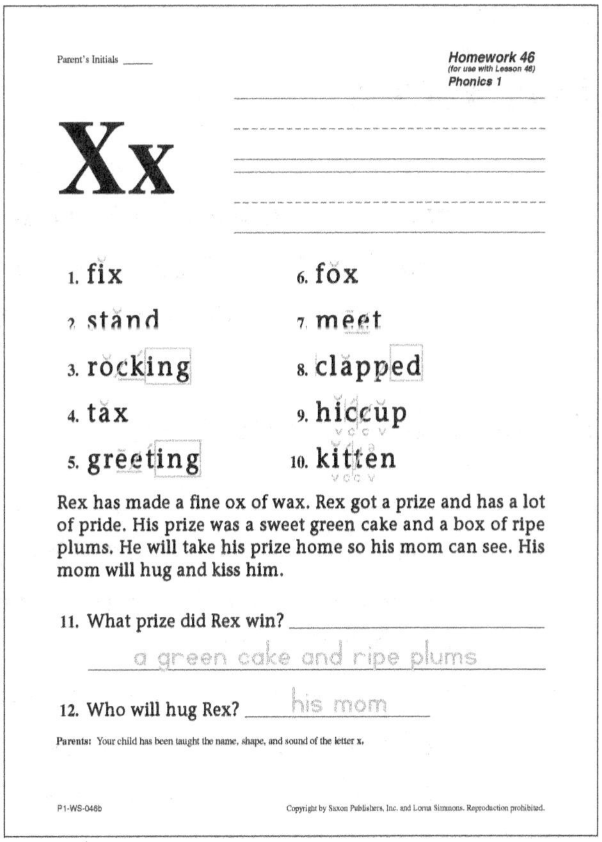

Parent's Initials ____

Homework 46
(for use with Lesson 46)
Phonics 1

Xx

1. fix
2. stand
3. rocking
4. tax
5. greeting
6. fox
7. meet
8. clapped
9. hiccup
10. kitten

Rex has made a fine ox of wax. Rex got a prize and has a lot of pride. His prize was a sweet green cake and a box of ripe plums. He will take his prize home so his mom can see. His mom will hug and kiss him.

11. What prize did Rex win? a green cake and ripe plums
12. Who will hug Rex? his mom

Parents: Your child has been taught the name, shape, and sound of the letter x.

P1-WS-046b

Copyright by Saxon Publishers, Inc. and Lorna Simmons. Reproduction prohibited.

LESSON 47 — The Letter *Y*

lesson preparation

materials

Review Decks
Spelling Sound Sheet 36
container of letter tiles
Letter Card 32
yarn in a sack (see *the night before*)
Picture Card 39
Spelling Card 30
Worksheet 47
Reader 15 (*A Flat On Bill's Bus*)
colored pencils

the night before

- Add the *y* letter tile to the student's container.
- Put some yarn in a sack for the student to use to "discover" the new keyword.

ALPHABET ACTIVITY

- The student should be seated with the alphabet strip.

  "Let's point to each letter and say the whole alphabet."

  "Put your index finger on 'a' and say the names with me."

- Try to set a steady pace so the student cannot sing the alphabet.

PHONEMIC AWARENESS

- **Objective:** To identify the number of syllables in words.

  "Let's try counting the number of syllables in words again today."

  "As I say the word, clap it or tap it on the table with your fingertips to count the number of syllables."

  "Let's try the word 'chalkboard.' Clap or tap with me."

- Demonstrate tapping the table top with your fingertips to count the syllables.

  "How many syllables are in this word?" *two*

- Repeat with the following words: lockers (2), education (4), eraser (3), cafeteria (5), music (2).
- Continue with additional words, if time permits.

"Tomorrow we will be finding out how many syllables are in your name. Be thinking about your name and how many syllables it has."

REVIEW OF DECKS

- The student should be seated where he/she can write comfortably.
- Show the student **Letter Cards 1–31** in random order. The student should name the letter on each letter card.
- Review **Affix Cards 1–3.**
- Show the student **Picture Cards 1–38** in random order. The student should name the keyword and sound for each picture card.
- Review **Sight Word Cards 1–16.**
- Give the student **Spelling Sound Sheet 36.**
- Call out the sounds on **Spelling Cards 1–29** in random order. The student should echo each sound and name the letter or letters that make the sound as he/she writes the letter(s) on the spelling sound sheet.
- Have the student set the spelling sound sheet aside for use later in the lesson.

NEW LEARNING

"I'm going to say some words. Echo them back to me and listen for the sound in the initial position."

- Point to your mouth as you say each word.

"Echo after me. Yes." *yes* ***"Yellow."*** *yellow* ***"Yam."*** *yam*

"What sound do you hear in the initial position?" */y/*

- **Note:** Make sure the student is giving the pure sound of *y* and not pronouncing it with a short *u* sound, as in /yŭh/.

"That's right. The sound you hear in the initial position is /y/."

"Put your fingertips on the front of your neck and say /y/. See if you feel any vibration."

"Is this sound voiced or unvoiced?" *voiced*

- Write the following words on the chalkboard: yes, yet, yam.

"What letter do you see that might be making the /y/ sound?" *y*

- If the student does not know the name of the letter, say it for him/her.

"Y is the first letter in all of these words, so we can see that y must be the letter used to spell the /y/ sound. Is y a vowel or a consonant?" *a consonant*

- If the student points out that *y* is also a vowel, say, "You are so smart! We are going to learn about *y* as a vowel in a couple of weeks. Today we are learning about *y* as a consonant."

HANDWRITING/LETTER TILES

- The student should be seated where he/she can write comfortably.
- Write a capital *Y* on the chalkboard.

  "This is a capital Y. Let's practice skywriting capital Y's before we write them on our papers."

- Have the student practice skywriting capital *Y*'s.

  "Find your spelling sound sheet."

- Draw handwriting lines on the chalkboard. Write a capital *Y* on the handwriting lines in the handwriting you want the student to learn.

  "Find the first handwriting line on your paper and practice writing capital Y's like I wrote this one on the chalkboard. Say the name of the letter each time you write it."

- Allow a few minutes for the student to practice writing capital *Y*'s.
- Write a lowercase *y* on the handwriting lines in the handwriting you want the student to learn.

  "This is a lowercase y."

- Have the student practice skywriting lowercase *y*'s.

  "Now practice writing lowercase y's on the second handwriting line. Say the name of the letter each time you write it."

- Have the student set the spelling sound sheet aside for use later in the lesson.
- Leave the handwriting lines and letters on the chalkboard for the remainder of the lesson.
- Give the student the container of letter tiles.

  "Today I've given you the y letter tile."

  "Find your y letter tile and look at it. One side has a capital Y and the other side has a lowercase y."

  "Hold your letter tile up in the air. Turn it so I can see the capital Y."

  "Now turn it so I can see the lowercase y."

  "Spell the word 'yet' with your letter tiles."

  "Now change one tile to spell the word 'yes.' "

  "Now spell the word 'yams.' "

- Choose additional words from the Spelling Word List, if desired.
- Have the student replace the tiles in the container and put it away.
- Reinforce the name, sound, and shape of the letter *y* throughout the day.

New Deck Cards

- Show the student **Letter Card 32.**

  "What is the name of this letter?" *y*

  "I have another sack today. It contains a clue to our new keyword. Don't look in the sack, but put your hand inside and see if you can guess what it is. Remember that the object in the sack starts with the /y/ sound."
- Allow the student a chance to feel inside the sack.

  "I'm going to count to three. On three, whisper what you think is in the sack."

  "One, two, three." *yarn*

  "That's right. The keyword is 'yarn' and the sound is /y/."
- Show the student **Picture Card 39,** and then point to the picture of yarn on the alphabet strip.

  "The word 'yarn' helps us remember the /y/ sound because it begins with /y/."

  "Find your spelling sound sheet. Put your finger on #30."
- Hold up **Spelling Card 30** so only you can see what is written. Using the hand signals, follow the directions on the card.
- Check the spelling sound sheet for accuracy.
- **Note:** Add the new letter, picture, and spelling cards to the Review Decks.

Boardwork

Lesson 47

"Let's practice coding some words like the ones you'll have on your worksheet."

"The vowel charts are in your Rule Book if you need to look at them."

- Write the following words and phrase (without the coding marks) on the chalkboard, one at a time. Ask the student to help you code them. The correct coding is as indicated:

trād~~e~~

ĭn´|sĕct
vc | cv

thrē~~e~~ skāt~~e~~[s]

- Have the student help you identify each of the items coded as a word, a phrase, or a sentence.

Worksheet

- The student should be seated where he/she can write comfortably.
- Give the student **Worksheet 47.** Make sure the student turns to the correct side.

  "Let's spell today with the /y/ sound."

  "Put your finger by #1. The first word is 'yes.'"

"Unblend 'yes' with me." /y/ /ĕ/ /s/

- Hold up one finger for each sound.

"Let's spell those sounds." y ... e ... s

- Point to each finger as you spell a sound.

"Now spell the word again and write the letters as you say them."

- Allow time for the student to do this.

"What word did you write?" yes

"We are also going to spell some words with 'sneaky e.' Make sure 'sneaky e' sneaks up on the consonant and not on you."

- Repeat the procedure with #2 (line), #3 (tube), #4 (flame), and #5 (swept).

"Now you're ready to code and read the words on your paper."

"Code the words by #6 through #10. After you have coded all the words, try to read them."

- Assist the student as necessary.

"Now read the word by #11. If you have trouble reading the word, code it. Then draw a line from the word to the picture it matches."

- Repeat with #12 through #14.
- As the student works, provide help as needed. Help the student correct any incorrect answers. Then initial the worksheet in the space provided.
- Some time during the day, ask the student to read from the worksheet, a controlled reader, your basal material, or other material of your choice.
- **Note:** Always make sure the worksheet is corrected before the student begins the homework. The worksheet serves as a guide to help complete the homework.

HOMEWORK

"Turn your paper over to the homework side."

"Put your finger on the top row of handwriting lines. Write your best capital Y on these lines so I will know what a capital Y should look like."

- Have the student write a lowercase letter *y* on the second handwriting line. Make sure that the student has written the letters correctly (to the best of his or her ability). He/She will use them as guides when completing the homework.

"Do you know what to do on the rest of the homework paper?"

"Remember to look for suffixes and words with a 'vccv' pattern that need to be divided."

- Discuss the pictures to make sure the student understands the word each one represents: #11 (tape), #12 (bone), #13 (lime), and #14 (globe).

"When you finish your paper, I will check it for you and initial it in the space provided."

- Either now or later in the day, the student should complete the homework independently (if possible). Help the student correct any incorrect answers. Then initial the homework in the space provided.

READER

"We have another new book today."

- Give the student **Reader 15 (*A Flat on Bill's Bus*)** and some colored pencils.

"Can you tell me this book's title?" *A Flat on Bill's Bus*

- Assist the student as necessary as he/she constructs the book.
- When the student finishes, staple or put a rubber band around the book's spine.
- If necessary, demonstrate how to separate the pages and check the page order.

"The title of this book is __________?" *A Flat on Bill's Bus*

"I want you to read your book to yourself. When you are finished reading, color the pictures. Write your name on the book so I will know who colored it."

"Keep your book handy because I will be asking you to read it for me."

- Some time during the day, have the student read the reader to you.
- If possible, take time to play the Kid Card games listed in Lesson 45.

Lesson 47

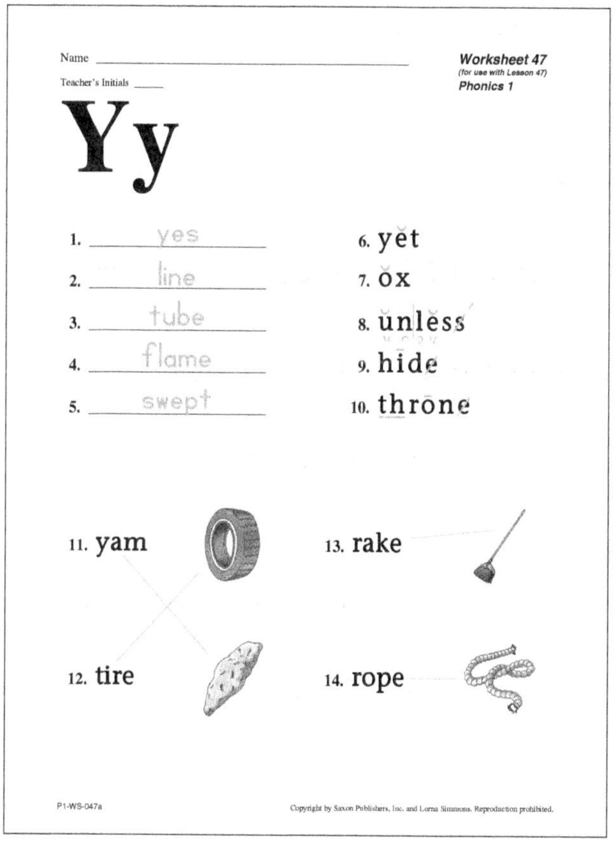

Name __________

Teacher's Initials ____

Worksheet 47
(for use with Lesson 47)
Phonics 1

Yy

1. yes
2. line
3. tube
4. flame
5. swept
6. yet
7. ox
8. unless
9. hide
10. throne

11. yam
12. tire
13. rake
14. rope

P1-WS-047a

Copyright by Saxon Publishers, Inc. and Lorna Simmons. Reproduction prohibited.

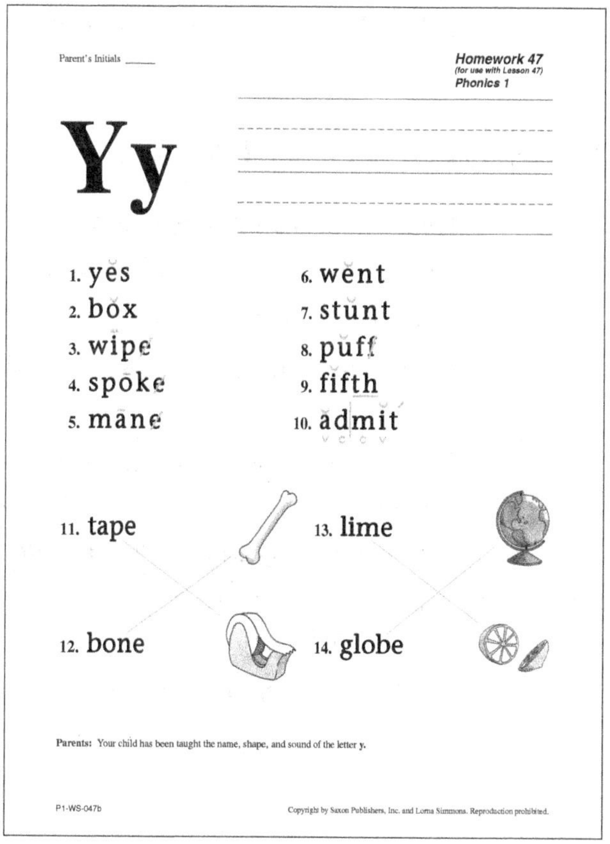

Parent's Initials ____

Homework 47
(for use with Lesson 47)
Phonics 1

Yy

1. yes
2. box
3. wipe
4. spoke
5. mane
6. went
7. stunt
8. puff
9. fifth
10. admit

11. tape
12. bone
13. lime
14. globe

Parents: Your child has been taught the name, shape, and sound of the letter y.

P1-WS-047b

Copyright by Saxon Publishers, Inc. and Lorna Simmons. Reproduction prohibited.

LESSON 48 — Digraph *sh*

lesson preparation

materials

Review Decks

Letter Card 33

Picture Card 40

Spelling Card 31

Worksheet 48

ALPHABET ACTIVITY

- The student should be seated.

  "Let's work again with the words 'before' and 'after.'"

  "I'll name a letter, and then I'll ask you to give me the letter before or after the letter I name."

- Name letters at random and ask the student to name a letter that comes either before or after yours. Continue as long as time permits.

PHONEMIC AWARENESS

- **Objective:** To identify the number of syllables in words.

  "Yesterday, we talked about syllables. Every word has at least one syllable and some have many syllables."

  "Do you know how many syllables are in my name? Today we are going to find out."

- Say and clap your name with the student and determine the correct number of syllables. (Use your first or last name.)

  "How many syllables are in your name?"

- Allow a moment for the student to count the number of syllables in his/her name. Provide help if necessary.

  "Let's think of some other names and see how many syllables they have."

- Play as long as time permits.

REVIEW OF DECKS

- Show the student **Letter Cards 1–32** in random order. The student should name the letter on each letter card.
- Review **Affix Cards 1–3.**
- Show the student **Picture Cards 1–39** in random order. The student should name the keyword and sound for each picture card.
- Review **Sight Word Cards 1–16.**

"Let's do something a little different with our spelling cards today."

"You'll play 'teacher' and I'll play 'student.' "

- Allow the student to call out the sounds on **Spelling Cards 1–30,** one at a time, while you write the responses (on a scrap piece of paper, on the chalkboard, or with your finger).

NEW LEARNING

"I'm going to say some words. Echo them back to me and listen for the sound in the initial position."

- Point to your mouth as you say each word.

"Echo after me. Shell." *shell* ***"Ship."*** *ship* ***"Shock."*** *shock*

"What sound do you hear in the initial position?" */sh/*

"That's right. The sound you hear in the initial position is /sh/."

"Put your fingertips on the front of your neck and say /sh/. See if you feel any vibration."

"Is this sound voiced or unvoiced?" *unvoiced*

- Write the following words on the chalkboard: shell, ship, shock.

"What do you see that might be making the /sh/ sound?" *sh*

" 'Sh' are the first letters in all of these words, so we can see that 'sh' must be the letters used to spell the /sh/ sound."

"How many sounds do you hear?" *one*

"How many letters are making that one sound?" *two*

- Use the hand signals described in Lesson 28 as you say the following:

"What do we call two letters that come together to make one sound?" *a digraph*

"Is 'digraph sh' a vowel digraph or a consonant digraph?" *a consonant digraph, because it contains only consonants*

NEW DECK CARDS

- Show the student **Letter Card 33.**

  "What do we call this?" *digraph sh*

- Hold up **Picture Card 40** but keep the picture covered with your hand (or the letter card).

  "Our keyword contains the /sh/ sound today."

  "Let's play 'Twenty Questions' to figure out our keyword."

  "Do you remember how to play 'Twenty Questions'?"

- Remind the student how the game is played. The student may ask you twenty questions in order to discover the keyword. The questions must be ones that can be answered with "yes" or "no."
- Remind the student that the answer will contain the /sh/ sound.
- The initial questions may be nonproductive, but as the student continues to play, he/she will develop a more organized approach. Feel free to guide the student's questions to the extent needed to determine the keyword.

  "What is our keyword?" *shark*

- Show the student **Picture Card 40.**

  "The word 'shark' helps us remember the /sh/ sound since it contains the /sh/ sound."

- **Note:** The digraph and its picture are also shown in the Rule Book on page 21.
- Hold up **Spelling Card 31** so only you can see what is written. Using the hand signals, follow the directions on the card.
- Have the student write the response on the desktop with his/her finger.
- **Note:** Add the new letter, picture, and spelling cards to the Review Decks.

Lesson 48

BOARDWORK

"Let's practice coding some words like the ones you'll have on your worksheet."

"The vowel charts are in your Rule Book if you need to look at them."

- Write the following words and sentence (without the coding marks) on the chalkboard, one at a time. Ask the student to help you code them. The correct coding is as indicated:

shāke

shrĕdd′ing

The wīre shŏcked mē′.

- Have the student help you identify each of the items coded as a word, a phrase, or a sentence.

WORKSHEET

- The student should be seated where he/she can write comfortably.
- Give the student **Worksheet 48.** Make sure the student turns to the correct side.

"Let's spell with the /sh/ sound using digraph sh today."

"Digraph sh is used for spelling in all three positions: initial, medial, and final."

"Put your finger by #1. The first word is 'shut.' "

"Unblend 'shut' with me." */sh/ /ŭ/ /t/*

- Hold up one finger for each sound.

"Let's spell those sounds." *digraph sh ... u ... t*

- Point to each finger as you spell a sound.

"Now spell the word again and write the letters as you say them."

- Allow time for the student to do this.

"What word did you write?" *shut*

- Repeat the procedure with #2 (dish), #3 (brush), #4 (tide), and #5 (sweep).

"Now you're ready to code and read the words on your paper."

"Code the words by #6 through #10. After you have coded all the words, try to read them."

- Assist the student as necessary.

"Numbers 11 and 12 are questions about the paragraph just above them. If you find any words you can't read, code them. Then see if you can answer the questions."

- As the student works, provide help as needed. Help the student correct any incorrect answers. Then initial the worksheet in the space provided.
- Some time during the day, ask the student to read from the worksheet, a controlled reader, your basal reader, or other material of your choice.
- **Note:** Always make sure the worksheet is corrected before the student begins the homework. The worksheet serves as a guide to help complete the homework.

HOMEWORK

"Turn your paper over to the homework side."

"Do you know what to do on the rest of the homework paper?"

"Remember to look for suffixes and words with a 'vccv' pattern that need to be divided."

"When you finish your paper, I will check it for you and initial it in the space provided."

- Either now or later in the day, the student should complete the homework independently (if possible). Help the student correct any incorrect answers. Then initial the homework in the space provided.
- If possible, take time to play the Kid Card games listed in Lesson 45.

Lesson 48

Name ______________________

Teacher's Initials ____

Worksheet 48
(for use with Lesson 48)
Phonics 1

sh

1. shut
2. dish
3. brush
4. tide
5. sweep
6. căsh
7. shāpe
8. shē
9. shipping
10. smăshed

Dan is a stunt man. Stunt men must do lots of things. Dan must get in a lake and swim with big fish where it is deep. Then he will get on a ship that will crash into the shore. Then he must take a big risk. He will trap a snake with big fangs.

11. Where will Dan swim? a lake

12. What will crash? a ship

P1-WS-048a

Parent's Initials ____

Homework 48
(for use with Lesson 48)
Phonics 1

sh

1. rŭsh
2. splăshing
3. shīne
4. smăsh
5. wĭshing
6. fĭsh
7. shŏt
8. slăshed
9. trăsh
10. shĕlf

Dan is seeking a red rose in the brush. A bee stings him on the neck. Dan slips on a slick rock and lands on a cactus. Dan is feeling sick and is wishing he was home. Then he sees a red rose. Dan picks the rose and takes it home.

11. What stung Dan? a bee

12. What did Dan see? a rose

Parents: Your child has been taught digraph sh.

P1-WS-048b

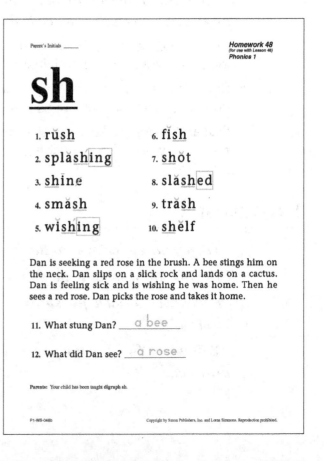

LESSON 49 — Digraph *oo*

lesson preparation

materials

container of letter tiles
Review Decks
Spelling Sound Sheet 37
Letter Card 34
Picture Cards 41–42
Spelling Cards 32–33
Worksheet 49
Sight Word Card 17
Reader 16 (*A Picnic in the Woods*)
colored pencils

ALPHABET ACTIVITY

- The student should be seated with the container of letter tiles.

  "Let's try alphabetizing some more letters today."

  "Take any five letter tiles out of your container. It doesn't matter which ones."

  "Line up the five letters in front of you."

  "Put your finger under your first letter tile, the one on the left side. When you scan, move your finger under the row of letters to make sure you look at every letter."

  "We will say the alphabet slowly, and when we say one of your letters, move it to start a new row. This will be the row that will be in ABC order."

  "Listen carefully and watch for your letters."

- Begin reciting the alphabet. Encourage the student to say it with you. Make sure the student is using his/her finger to scan the letters.
- If time permits, have the student trade the letters for five new ones and try the procedure again.
- Allow the student to work independently, but take note if he/she is having difficulty. Provide the student with additional practice by repeating this activity, if necessary.
- Have the student replace the tiles in the containers and put it away.

PHONEMIC AWARENESS

- **Objective:** To identify the number of syllables in words.

  "We've been talking this week about syllables in words and names."

  "To show you how important vowels are, not only must every word contain a vowel, every syllable must contain a vowel sound. A word can have more vowels than syllables, but it can't have fewer vowel sounds than syllables."

  "Let's check this rule on a few words."

  "Let's try the word 'napkin.' How many syllables are in 'napkin'?"

- Clap and say "nap·kin."

  "How many syllables are in this word? Hold up that many fingers." *two*

  "Let's look at it and see if it has two or more vowels."

- Write "napkin" on the chalkboard.

  "How many vowels are in 'napkin'?" *two*

  "Did the rule work?" *yes*

  "What about the word 'school'?"

- Have the student clap and hold up that many fingers (one).

  "How many syllables are in the word 'school'?" *one*

- Write "school" on the chalkboard.

  "How many vowels are in the word 'school'?" *two*

  "Does the rule work?" *yes*

  "It sure does. The word can have more vowels than syllables, but not fewer vowels than syllables."

  "Let's try a hard one and see if it still works. Let's clap the word 'rhinoceros.' "

- Clap and say "rhi·noc·er·os" with the student.

  "How many syllables are in this word?" *four*

- Write "rhinoceros" on the chalkboard.

  "How many vowels are in the word 'rhinoceros'?" *four*

  "Did the rule work?" *yes*

  "Wow! That's pretty exciting! The rule is working on all of our words."

REVIEW OF DECKS

- The student should be seated where he/she can write comfortably.
- Show the student **Letter Cards 1–33** in random order. The student should name the letter on each letter card.
- Review **Affix Cards 1–3.**

- Show the student **Picture Cards 1–40** in random order. The student should name the keyword and sound for each picture card.
- Review **Sight Word Cards 1–16.**
- Give the student **Spelling Sound Sheet 37.**
- Call out the sounds on **Spelling Cards 1–31** in random order. The student should echo each sound and name the letter or letters that make the sound as he/she writes the letter(s) on the spelling sound sheet.
- Have the student set the spelling sound sheet aside for use later in the lesson.

NEW LEARNING

- Breves will be used on all of the words containing the /o͝o/ sound, as in "foot," and macrons on the /o͞o/ sound, as in "boot," in order for you to distinguish between the two. The student will code digraph *oo* simply by underlining it. If you would like the student to code the two sounds of digraph *oo*, be sure to point out that, in this case, a breve doesn't really mean "short" and a macron doesn't really mean "long."

"I'm going to say some words. Echo them back to me and listen for the sound in the medial position."

- Point to your mouth as you say each word.

"Echo after me. Hook." *hook* ***"Wood."*** *wood* ***"Foot."*** *foot*

"What sound do you hear in the medial position?" */o͝o/*

"That's right. The sound you hear in the medial position is /o͝o/."

"Put your fingertips on the front of your neck and say /o͝o/. See if you feel any vibration."

"Is this sound voiced or unvoiced?" *voiced*

- Write the following words on the chalkboard: hook, wood, foot.

"What do you see that might be making the /o͝o/ sound?" *oo*

" 'Oo' are the middle letters in all of these words, so we can see that 'oo' must be the letters used to spell the /o͝o/ sound."

"I'm going to say some more words. Echo them back to me and listen for the sound in the medial position."

"Echo after me. Scoot." *scoot* ***"Room."*** *room* ***"Boot."*** *boot*

"What sound do you hear in the medial position?" */o͞o/*

"How many sounds do you hear?" *one*

- Write the following words on the chalkboard: scoot, room, boot.

"How many letters are making that one sound?" *two*

- Use the hand signals described in Lesson 28 as you say the following:

  "Do we have two letters that come together to make one sound?" *yes*

  "What is that called?" *a digraph*

  "Both of these are called 'digraph oo,' but now we know that digraph oo has two sounds ... /ŏŏ/ and /ōō/."

  "How do we code digraphs?" *underline them*

- Underline each digraph *oo.*

  "Is digraph oo a vowel or a consonant digraph?" *a vowel digraph because it contains only vowels*

New Deck Cards

- Show the student **Letter Card 34.**

  "What do we call this?" *digraph oo*

- Hold up **Picture Card 41** but keep the picture covered with your hand (or the letter card).

  "I have a card with a picture on it that contains the /ŏŏ/ sound."

  "I am going to describe it for you. See if you can guess what the picture is. Remember, this keyword contains the /ŏŏ/ sound."

  "This is something people use when they go fishing. It is very sharp. In the story about Peter Pan, there was a pirate who had one of these in place of his hand. What do you think the picture is?" *hook*

  "That's right. The keyword is 'hook' and the sound we have learned is /ŏŏ/."

- Show the student **Picture Card 41.**

  "The word 'hook' helps us remember the /ŏŏ/ sound since it contains that sound."

- Hold up **Picture Card 42** but keep the picture covered with your hand (or the letter card).

  "I have another card with a picture on it that contains the /ōō/ sound."

  "I'm going to describe it for you. See if you can guess what the picture is. Remember, this keyword contains the /ōō/ sound."

  "This is something that begins growing when we are babies. Then we lose or pull our first one when we are about five years old. A new one grows in its place for us to use as adults. What do you think the picture is?" *tooth*

  "That's right. The keyword is 'tooth' and the sound we have learned is /ōō/."

- Show the student **Picture Card 42.**

  "The word 'tooth' helps us remember the /ōō/ sound since it contains that sound."

- **Note:** The digraphs and pictures are also shown in the Rule Book on page 21.

"Find your spelling sound sheet. Put your finger on #32."

- Hold up **Spelling Card 32** so only you can see what is written. Using the hand signals, follow the instructions on the card.

"Now put your finger on #33."

- Repeat with **Spelling Card 33.**
- Check the spelling sound sheet for accuracy.
- **Note:** Add the new letter, picture, and spelling cards to the Review Decks.

BOARDWORK

"Let's practice coding some words like the ones you'll have on your worksheet."

"The rule charts are in your Rule Book if you need to look at them."

- Write the following words and sentence (without the coding marks) on the chalkboard, one at a time. Ask the student to help you code them. The correct coding is as indicated:

zoom

lāne

The slănt'ed cŭt ŏn his foot wĭll blēed.

- Have the student help you identify each of the items coded as a word, a phrase, or a sentence.

Lesson 49

WORKSHEET

- The student should be seated where he/she can write comfortably.
- Give the student **Worksheet 49.** Make sure the student turns to the correct side.

"Let's spell with the two sounds of digraph oo today."

"Put your finger by #1. The first word is 'cool.'"

"Unblend 'cool' with me." /k/ /o͞o/ /l/

- Hold up one finger for each sound.

"Let's spell those sounds." c … digraph oo … l

- Point to each finger as you spell a sound.

"Now spell the word again and write the letters as you say them."

- Allow time for the student to do this.

"What word did you write?" cool

- Repeat the procedure with #2 (moon), #3 (good), #4 (look), and #5 (shook).

"Now you're ready to code and read the words on your paper."

"Code the words by #6 through #10. After you have coded all the words, try to read them."

- Assist the student as necessary.

"Now read the word by #11. If you have trouble reading the word, code it. Then draw a line from the word to the picture it matches."

- Repeat with #12 through #14.
- As the student works, provide help as needed. Help the student correct any incorrect answers. Then initial the worksheet in the space provided.
- Some time during the day, ask the student to read from the worksheet, a controlled reader, your basal reader, or other material of your choice.
- **Note:** Always make sure the worksheet is corrected before the student begins the homework. The worksheet serves as a guide to help complete the homework.

HOMEWORK

"Turn your paper over to the homework side."

"Do you know what to do on the homework paper?"

"Remember to look for suffixes, digraphs, and sneaky e's."

- Discuss the pictures to make sure the student understands the word each one represents: #11 (spoon), #12 (book), #13 (broom), and #14 (ship).

"When you finish your paper, I will check it for you and initial it in the space provided."

- Either now or later in the day, the student should complete the homework independently (if possible). Help the student correct any incorrect answers. Then initial the homework in the space provided.

READER

"We have another new book today and the book has a new sight word in it."

- Show the student **Sight Word Card 17.**

"Do you know this word?" *expect various answers*

"This word is 'some.' Can you use the word 'some' in a sentence?"

- Make sure the student uses the word to mean "some" rather than "sum."
- Help the student locate the word in the Irregular Spelling Booklet.

"When you see this word, you can circle it as a reminder that we can't sound it out."

"We will add this card to our sight word deck."

- Give the student **Reader 16 (*A Picnic in the Woods*)** and some colored pencils.

"Can you tell me this book's title?" *A Picnic in the Woods*

- Assist the student as necessary as he/she constructs the book.
- When the student finishes, staple or put a rubber band around the book's spine.
- If necessary, demonstrate how to separate the pages and check the page order.

  "The title of this book is __________?" *A Picnic in the Woods*

  "I want you to read your book to yourself. When you are finished reading, color the pictures. Write your name on the book so I will know who colored it."

  "Keep your book handy because I will be asking you to read it for me."
- Some time during the day, have the student read the reader to you.
- Add **Sight Word Card 17** to the Sight Word Deck.
- If possible, take time to play the Kid Card games listed in Lesson 45. Try to see that the student is prepared for tomorrow's assessment.

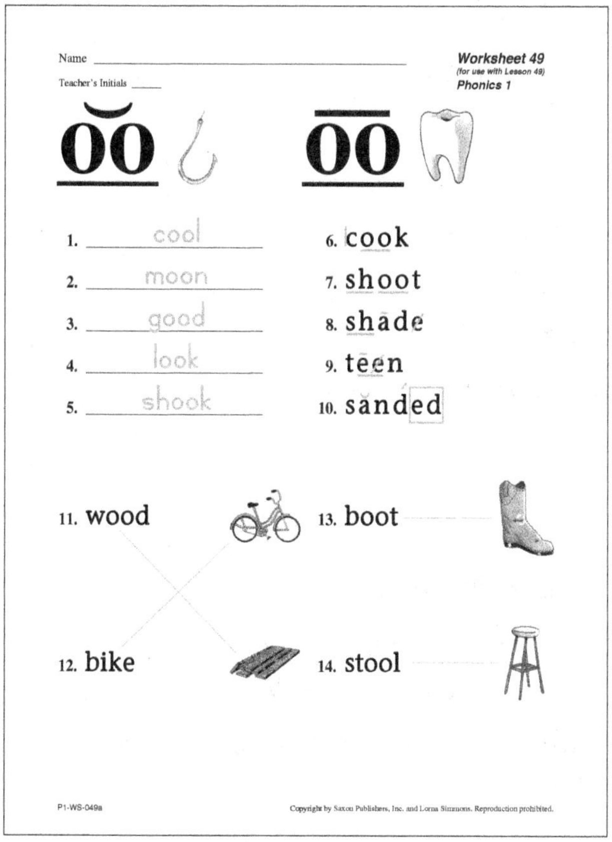

Name ______________________

Teacher's Initials ____

Worksheet 49
(for use with Lesson 49)
Phonics 1

oo̯ oo

1. cool
2. moon
3. good
4. look
5. shook

6. cook
7. shoot
8. shade
9. teen
10. sănded

11. wood
12. bike
13. boot
14. stool

P1-WS-049a

Copyright by Saxon Publishers, Inc. and Lorna Simmons. Reproduction prohibited.

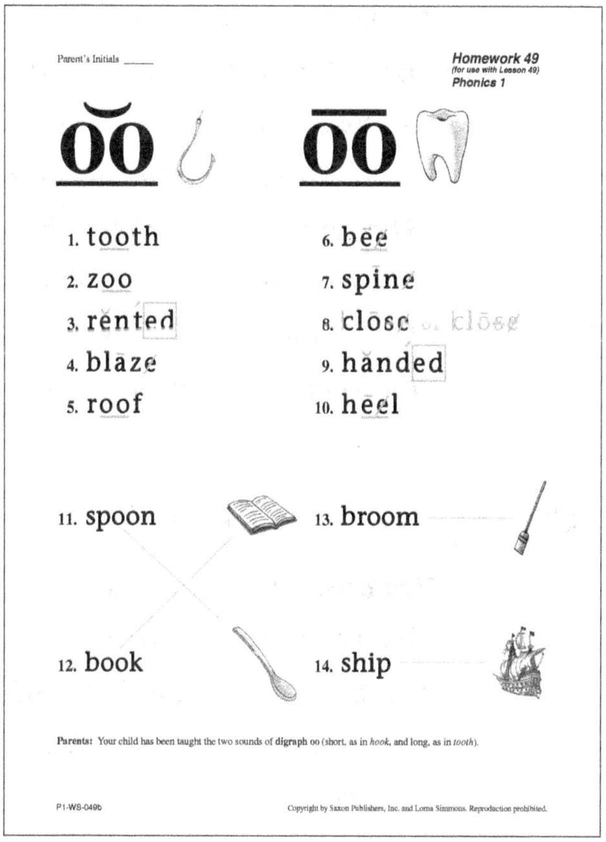

Parent's Initials ____

Homework 49
(for use with Lesson 49)
Phonics 1

oo̯ oo

1. tooth
2. zoo
3. rĕnted
4. blaze
5. roof

6. bee
7. spine
8. close or clōse
9. hănded
10. heel

11. spoon
12. book
13. broom
14. ship

Parents: Your child has been taught the two sounds of **digraph oo** (short, as in *hook*, and long, as in *tooth*).

P1-WS-049b

Copyright by Saxon Publishers, Inc. and Lorna Simmons. Reproduction prohibited.

LESSON 50 Assessment

lesson preparation

materials

Review Decks

Assessment 9

Spelling Test 7

Assessment 9 Recording Form

Kid Cards

tokens

the night before

- Separate the Kid Cards marked "Lesson 50."

ALPHABET ACTIVITY

- The student should be seated with the alphabet strip.

  "How many letters are in the alphabet?" *26*

  "What two kinds of letters make up our alphabet?" *vowels and consonants*

  "Name the vowels." *a, e, i, o, and u*

  "All of the other letters are called _________?" *consonants*

  "The initial letter of the alphabet is _____?" *a*

  "The final letter of the alphabet is _____?" *z*

  "Let's point to each letter and say the whole alphabet."

  "Put your index finger on 'a' and say the names with me."

PHONEMIC AWARENESS

- **Objective:** To identify the number of syllables in words.

  "We've been counting the number of syllables in words this week."

  "Today, let's do something different as we work with syllables."

  "I'm going to say some syllables. You put them together to form a word."

  "At·lan·tic."

- Pause briefly between each syllable.

  "Can you tell me what this word is?" Atlantic
- Repeat with the following syllables:

  2. re·mem·ber
  3. fuzz·y
  4. car·na·tion
  5. grand·fa·ther
  6. gi·ant
  7. ham·bur·ger
  8. oc·cu·pa·tion
  9. re·cord
  10. his·tor·i·an
- Continue with additional words, if time permits.

REVIEW OF DECKS

"Let's play 'Twenty Questions' again today."

"You know these decks very well, so I am going to choose a card and see if you can ask me questions and guess which card I have selected."

- Do not let the student see which deck or which card you select.

  "You may ask me any question you like as long as I can answer 'yes' or 'no.' "
- If the student has difficulty, help him/her by suggesting questions such as "Is it a letter card?", "Is it a vowel?", "Is it a digraph?", etc.

WRITTEN ASSESSMENT

- Seat the student where he/she can write comfortably.
- Give the student **Assessment 9.**
- **Section I:**

  "Today we are going to write some words for our assessment."

  "I'm going to say a word. Write the letter that makes each sound in that word on the lines by #1."

  "Look at the rule charts if you need to."

  "Here's the first word: make."
- Repeat with the following words in the order shown: #2 (came), #3 (nine), #4 (use), and #5 (smoke).
- **Reminder:** While the student spells, be ready to point to appropriate rule charts as necessary.

- **Section II:**

  "Look at the letters by #6."

  "Find the picture of the keyword for this sound."

  "Draw a line from the letters to the keyword."
- Repeat with #7, #8, #9, and #10. Allow a few minutes for the student to work.
- The pictures (from top to bottom) are as follows: hose, dime, cake, cube, concrete.
- **Section III:**

  "Put your finger on #11."

  "Code the words by #11 through #15."
- Allow a few minutes for the student to work.
- **Section IV:**

  "Look at #16. Fill in the blanks to make the letters in ABC order."
- Repeat with #17.
- **Section V:**

  "Read the paragraph. If you find any words you can't read, code them to help you figure them out. Then answer the question by filling in the blanks by #18, #19, and #20."
- **Reminder:** If the student absolutely cannot read the paragraph, read it to the student to see if he or she can answer the questions.

  "When you are finished, show your paper to me."
- This paper will be used during the oral portion of the assessment.

SPELLING TEST

- Give the student **Spelling Test 7.**
- Call out the following words (in the order shown). Sound them out, if necessary.

  #1 (honk), #2 (singing), #3 (deep), #4 (speed), #5 (camping), #6 (packing),
  #7 (sticks), #8 (helped), #9 (thick), #10 (rested),
  #11 (are), #12 (put)
- Grade and record the paper in any manner that suits your needs.

ORAL ASSESSMENT

- It is important to complete the oral assessment promptly (today, if possible) in order to identify any areas of weakness and begin remediation.
- Use the assessment and the following dialogue to complete the oral portion.

- **Section VI:**
- Show the student the letters by #21.

  "Tell me the name for these letters and the sound they make."
- Write the student's response on the adjacent line.
- Repeat with #22, #23, #24, and #25.

ASSESSMENT EVALUATION

- Grade the assessment and record the results on **Assessment 9 Recording Form.** Check off the boxes to indicate mastery (i.e., the section was completed with 100% accuracy).
- **Reminder:** Try to give as many points as possible for work attempted. Do not grade the coding marks too severely. The most important coding marks to look for are breves, macrons, and syllable division lines.
- See the introductory material for detailed information regarding grading and recording procedures.
- Use the assessment results to identify those skills in which the student is weak. Practice those skills by playing Kid Card games.
- Add the Kid Cards marked "Lesson 50" to the existing decks. Listed below are games appropriate for remediation in selected areas. See "Games and Activities" for the directions for each game.
- **Section I:** Play "Spelling Deck Perfection," "Sound Scamper," "Spell Out #1," or have the student use the letter tiles to spell words you give from the Spelling Word List.
- **Section II:** Play "Keyword and Sound" or "Letter/Sound Identification."
- **Section III:** Play "Chalkboard Challenge."
- **Section IV:** Play "Alphabet Add On," "Alphabetizing Objects," or "Alphabet Roll."
- **Section V:** Either have the student read the controlled readers and then ask questions for comprehension, or play "Acting Out" with the green Kid Cards.
- **Section VI:** Play "Letter/Sound Identification."
- When the student seems more secure in areas that had previously proven difficult, retest him/her (in those areas only) and indicate on the recording form any sections the student has subsequently mastered.
- Try to help the student achieve mastery of all the sections before the next assessment.
- If the student is having difficulty with a particular skill, keep his or her practice activities at the most basic level so the chance of success is greater.

Name ____________________

Assessment 9
(for use with Lesson 50)
Phonics 1

Section I

1. m a k e
2. c a m e
3. n i n e
4. u s e
5. s m o k e

Section II

6. ī–e̸

7. ō–e̸

8. ē–e̸

9. ā–e̸

10. ū–e̸

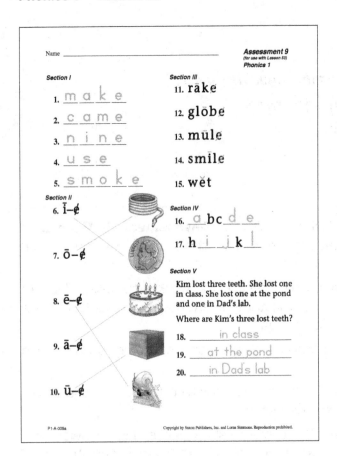

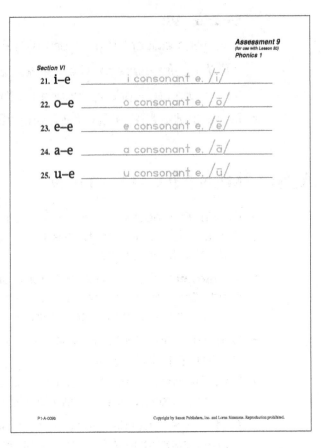

Section III

11. rāke̸
12. glōbe̸
13. mūle̸
14. smīle̸
15. wĕt

Section IV

16. a bc d e
17. h i j k l

Section V

Kim lost three teeth. She lost one in class. She lost one at the pond and one in Dad's lab.

Where are Kim's three lost teeth?

18. in class
19. at the pond
20. in Dad's lab

P1-A-009a

Assessment 9
(for use with Lesson 50)
Phonics 1

Section VI

21. i–e i consonant e, /ī/
22. o–e o consonant e, /ō/
23. e–e e consonant e, /ē/
24. a–e a consonant e, /ā/
25. u–e u consonant e, /ū/

P1-A-009b

Lesson 50

LESSON 51 — The Letter *J*

lesson preparation

materials

Review Decks

Spelling Sound Sheet 38

container of letter tiles

Letter Card 35

Picture Card 43

Spelling Card 34

Sight Word Card 18

Worksheet 51

Spelling List 8

new concepts

accent

the night before

- Add the *j* letter tile to the student's container.

ALPHABET ACTIVITY

- The student should be seated with the alphabet strip.

"I am going to mix up the alphabet questions today to see if you can still answer them."

"What is the final letter of the alphabet?" *z*

"How many letters are in the alphabet?" *26*

"What two kinds of letters make up our alphabet?" *vowels and consonants*

"What do we call the letters that are not vowels?" *consonants*

"Name the vowels." *a, e, i, o, and u*

"What is the initial letter of the alphabet?" *a*

"Let's point to each letter and say the whole alphabet."

"Put your index finger on 'a' and say the names with me."

PHONEMIC AWARENESS

- **Objective:** To hear and identify the accents on syllables.

  "Listen to this word: teach … er."

- Be sure to exaggerate the accent on the first syllable.

  "How many syllables are in this word? Hold up your fingers." *two*

  "That's right, two syllables. Listen to the first syllable and see if you notice anything different about the way I say the first syllable."

- Repeat the word "teach·er," again exaggerating the accent on the first syllable.

  "Did you notice anything different about the way I said the first syllable?"

- Ideally, the student will answer that it was longer, louder, and/or at a higher pitch. If he/she does not indicate any of these things, prompt as follows:

  "Listen to the first syllable again and tell me if I say it longer or shorter."

- Exaggerate the length of the first syllable. The student should say "longer."

  "Now, listen to see if I say it louder or softer."

- Exaggerate the loudness of the first syllable. The student should say "louder."

  "One more time, listen to see if I say the first syllable with a higher or lower pitch." *higher pitch*

  "So I said it longer, louder, and higher. When we say one syllable longer, louder, and higher than the other syllables, we are accenting that syllable."

  "There is a special little mark we use to show accent."

- Put an accent mark on the chalkboard.

  "It looks like this. It is the same mark we use on our long vowel rule. An open, accented vowel is long; code it with a macron."

- Write the symbols for this rule on the chalkboard (v̄′→) and point out the accent mark.

  "Almost every word in our language has an accent on it. Even little one-syllable words like 'me' and 'so' are accented. We don't hear the accent on those words because it's the whole word that is accented. But, if the word has two or more syllables, we hear the accent because one syllable is longer, louder, and higher than the rest of the word."

  "Let's try another word. See if you can hear the accent. Hold up one finger if you hear the accent on the first syllable and two fingers if you hear the accent on the second syllable."

- Say "sum·mer." Remember to exaggerate the first syllable. The student should hold up one finger.
- Repeat with "mu·sic." The student should hold up one finger.

REVIEW OF DECKS

- The student should be seated where he/she can write comfortably.
- Show the student **Letter Cards 1–34** in random order. The student should name the letter on each letter card.
- Review **Affix Cards 1–3.**
- Show the student **Picture Cards 1–42** in random order. The student should name the keyword and sound for each picture card.
- Review **Sight Word Cards 1–17.**
- Give the student **Spelling Sound Sheet 38.**
- Call out the sounds on **Spelling Cards 1–33** in random order. The student should echo each sound and name the letter or letters that make the sound as he/she writes the letter(s) on the spelling sound sheet.
- Check the student's response after each card.
- Have the student set the spelling sound sheet aside for use later in the lesson.

NEW LEARNING

"I'm going to say some words. Echo them back to me and listen for the sound in the initial position."

- Point to your mouth as you say each word.

"Echo after me. Jelly." *jelly* ***"Jump."*** *jump* ***"Joke."*** *joke*

"What sound do you hear in the initial position?" */j/*

- **Note:** Make sure the student is giving the pure sound of *j* and not pronouncing it with a short *u* sound, as in /jŭh/.

"That's right. The sound you hear in the initial position is /j/."

"Put your fingertips on the front of your neck and say /j/. See if you feel any vibration."

"Is this sound voiced or unvoiced?" *voiced*

- Write the following words on the chalkboard: jelly, jump, joke.

"What letter do you see that might be making the /j/ sound?" *j*

- If the student does not know the name of the letter, say it for him/her.

"J is the first letter in all of these words, so we can see that j must be the letter used to spell the /j/ sound."

"Is j a vowel or a consonant?" *consonant*

HANDWRITING/LETTER TILES

- The student should be seated where he/she can write comfortably.
- Write a capital *J* on the chalkboard.

  "This is a capital J. Let's practice skywriting capital J's before we write them on our papers."
- Have the student practice skywriting capital *J*'s.

  "Find your spelling sound sheet."
- Draw handwriting lines on the chalkboard. Write a capital *J* on the handwriting lines in the handwriting you want the student to learn.

  "Find the first handwriting line on your paper and practice writing capital J's like I wrote this one on the chalkboard. Say the name of the letter each time you write it."
- Allow a few minutes for the student to practice writing capital *J*'s.
- Write a lowercase *j* on the handwriting lines in the handwriting you want the student to learn.

  "This is a lowercase j."
- Have the student practice skywriting lowercase *j*'s.

  "Now practice writing lowercase j's on the second handwriting line. Say the name of the letter each time you write it."
- Have the student set the spelling sound sheet aside for use later in the lesson.
- Leave the handwriting lines and letters on the chalkboard for the remainder of the lesson.
- Give the student the container of letter tiles.

  "Today I've given you the j letter tile."

  "Find your j letter tile and look at it. One side has a capital J and the other side has a lowercase j. Hold your letter tile up in the air. Turn it so I can see the capital J."

  "Now turn it so I can see the lowercase j."

  "Spell the word 'jam' with your letter tiles."

  "Now spell the word 'job.' "

  "Now change one letter to spell the word 'jab.' "
- Choose additional words from the Spelling Word List, if desired.
- Have the student replace the tiles in the container and put it away.
- Reinforce the name, sound, and shape of the letter *j* throughout the day.

NEW DECK CARDS

- Show the student **Letter Card 35.**

  "What is the name of this letter?" *j*

- Hold up **Picture Card 43** but keep the picture covered with your hand (or the letter card).

  "I have a card with a picture on it that begins with the /j/ sound."

  "I am going to describe it to you. See if you can guess what the picture is. Remember, our new keyword starts with the /j/ sound."

  "It is something that is huge. You usually see them high in the sky. They are used to take people from one place to another quickly. A ticket to travel on one of these is rather expensive. What do you think the picture is?" *jet*

  "That's right. The keyword is 'jet' and the sound we have learned is /j/."

- Show the student **Picture Card 43,** and then point to the picture of a jet on the alphabet strip.

  "The word 'jet' helps us remember the /j/ sound since it begins with /j/."

  "Find your spelling sound sheet. Put your finger on #34."

- Hold up **Spelling Card 34** so only you can see what is written. Using the hand signals, follow the instructions on the card.
- Check the spelling sound sheet for accuracy.
- **Note:** Add the new letter, picture, and spelling cards to the Review Decks.

BOARDWORK

"We have a new sight word today."

- Show the student **Sight Word Card 18.**

  "Can you tell me what this word is?"

  "This word is 'friend.' It doesn't follow our rules, so we must memorize it. How do we mark sight words since we can't code them?" *circle them*

- Help the student locate the word in the Irregular Spelling Booklet.

  "We will add this card to our sight word deck."

  "Let's practice coding some words like the ones you'll have on your worksheet."

  "The rule charts are in your Rule Book if you need to look at them."

- Write the following words and phrase (without the coding marks) on the chalkboard, one at a time. Ask the student to help you code them. The correct coding is as indicated:

hook[ed]

thǐng

bloom′[ing] rōse (to) å (friend)

- Have the student help you identify each of the items coded as a word, a phrase, or a sentence.
- Add **Sight Word Card 18** to the Review Decks.

WORKSHEET

- The student should be seated where he/she can write comfortably.
- Give the student **Worksheet 51.** Make sure the student turns to the correct side.

"Today, let's spell with the /j/ sound."

"Put your finger by #1. The first word is 'just.' "

"Unblend 'just' with me." */j/ /ŭ/ /s/ /t/*

- Hold up one finger for each sound.

"Let's spell those sounds." ***j … u … s … t***

- Point to a finger each time the student spells a sound.

"Now spell the word again and write the letters as you say them."

- Allow time for the student to do this.

"What word did you write?" ***just***

- Repeat the procedure with #2 (joke), #3 (jumping), #4 (soon), and #5 (hood).

"Now you're ready to code and read the words on your paper."

"Code the words by #6 through #10. After you have coded all the words, try to read them."

- Assist the student as necessary.

"Numbers 11 and 12 are questions about the paragraph just above them. If you find any words you can't read, code them. Then see if you can answer the questions."

- As the student works, provide help as needed. Help the student correct any incorrect answers. Then initial the worksheet in the space provided.
- Some time during the day, ask the student to read from the worksheet, a controlled reader, your basal reader, or other material of your choice.
- **Note:** Always make sure the worksheet is corrected before the student begins the homework. The worksheet serves as a guide to help complete the homework.

HOMEWORK

"Turn your paper over to the homework side."

"Put your finger on the top row of handwriting lines. Write your best capital J on these lines so I will know what a capital J should look like."

- Have the student write a lowercase letter *j* on the second row of handwriting lines. Make sure that each student has written the letters correctly (to the best of his or her ability). They will use them as guides when completing the homework.

"Do you know what to do on the rest of the homework paper?"

"Watch for digraphs, suffixes, and words with a 'vccv' pattern that need to be divided."

"When you finish your paper, I will check it for you and initial it in the space provided."

- Either now or later in the day, the student should complete the homework independently (if possible). Help the student correct any incorrect answers. Then initial the homework in the space provided.

SPELLING LIST

- Fold **Spelling List 8** in half lengthwise (with the printed side facing out).

"Leave your paper just like I give it to you."

- Give the student **Spelling List 8,** folded with the blank lines facing up.

"Let's spell some more words."

- Call out the following words (in the order shown). Sound them out, if necessary.

    #1 (teeth), #2 (disk), #3 (creek), #4 (swim), #5 (duck), #6 (snack), #7 (locking), #8 (needed), #9 (hunting), #10 (tricked), #11 (where), #12 (said)

"Now unfold your paper and check your words."

- Check the student's work to see if he/she needs extra help with spelling.

"I want you to practice these words. We'll have a spelling test in a few days."

- If possible, take time to play the Kid Card games listed in Lesson 50.

Name ____________________

Teacher's Initials ____

Worksheet 51
(for use with Lesson 51)
Phonics 1

Jj

1. just
2. joke
3. jumping
4. soon
5. hood
6. looked
7. jŏgging
8. shāke
9. smooth
10. strings

Deb was jogging in the woods. She met a skunk and stopped to pet it. The skunk's leg had a cut. Deb took the skunk home. Deb kept the skunk until it was well. The skunk was Deb's friend.

11. Where did Deb meet the skunk? in the woods

12. Deb took the skunk home.

P1-WS-051a

Parent's Initials ____

Homework 51
(for use with Lesson 51)
Phonics 1

Jj

1. jĕt
2. books
3. zōne
4. jămmed
5. brōke
6. jŭmping
7. roost
8. shāme
9. jŏb
10. rīse

Deb has a friend. Deb's friend likes roots. He has a stripe on his back. Deb's friend can smell if he is upset. Deb's friend has a name. His name is Jack. Jack is a skunk.

11. What is Deb's friend? a skunk

12. What is on Jack's back? a stripe

Parents: Your child has been taught the name, shape, and sound of the letter j.

P1-WS-051b

Lesson 51

LESSON 52 — Floss Rule

lesson preparation

materials	***new concepts***
Review Decks	floss words
Spelling Sound Sheet 39	irregular floss words
Worksheet 52	
Reader 17 (*Fig Jam*)	
colored pencils	
fig cookies	

ALPHABET ACTIVITY

"Let's play 'Follow the Leader.' We will skip around the room as we say the alphabet together. Do you want to be the leader?"

- If the student wants to be the leader, line up behind the student and skip around the room. If the student does not wish to be the leader, have him/her line up behind you. In either case, try to set a steady pace as you skip and recite the alphabet.

PHONEMIC AWARENESS

- **Objective:** To hear and identify the accent on syllables.

"Let's see how well you can hear an accent today. When a syllable is accented, how does it sound different from the others?" *it is louder, longer, and higher*

"I'll say a word. You listen carefully. If you hear the accent on the first syllable, hold up one finger. If you hear the accent on the second syllable, hold up two fingers. Ready?"

- Say the following words, exaggerating the accented syllables slightly.

ti´·ger	1st syllable	1 finger
el´·e·phant	1st syllable	1 finger
hy·e´·na	2nd syllable	2 fingers
spi´·der	1st syllable	1 finger
an´·te·lope	1st syllable	1 finger
rhi·noc´·er·os	2nd syllable	2 fingers

"Tomorrow, we will play an accenting game with a new deck called the Alphabet/Accent Deck."

Review of Decks

- The student should be seated where he/she can write comfortably.
- Show the student **Letter Cards 1–35** in random order. The student should name the letter on each letter card.
- Review **Affix Cards 1–3.**
- Show the student **Picture Cards 1–43** in random order. The student should name the keyword and sound for each picture card.
- Review **Sight Word Cards 1–18.**
- Give the student **Spelling Sound Sheet 39.**
- Call out the sounds on **Spelling Cards 1–34** in random order. The student should echo each sound and name the letter or letters that make the sound as he/she writes the letter(s) on the spelling sound sheet.
- Have the student set the spelling sound sheet aside for use later in the lesson.

New Learning

- Pull **Spelling Cards 8, 12,** and **14** from the Review Deck.
- Write the following words on the chalkboard in three columns, as shown:

off	fill	pass
staff	shell	boss
stuff	doll	less
sniff	dull	miss

"Can you tell me something that is alike in all of these words?" *all the words end with double consonants f, l, or s; all of the vowels are short vowels; all of the words are one-syllable words; every word is a root word*

- Point out any similarities the student has missed.

"We have a new spelling rule today. You'll be able to spell many new words with this rule."

"Here is what the new rule says: In a one-syllable root word with a short vowel sound, the letters f, l, and s usually double when they are at the end of the word."

"Our new rule is called the 'floss rule' because the rule name helps us remember the parts of the rule."

- Write the word "floss" on the chalkboard.

"Is this a one-syllable word?" *yes*

"Is this a root word?" *yes*

"Does this word have a short vowel sound?" *yes*

"Does it end with f, l, or s?" *yes*

"The word 'floss' is a floss word."

"The trick is learning to recognize floss words."

"I will put a word on the chalkboard. Look at it and tell me if you think it is a floss word."

- Write the word "class" on the chalkboard.

  "Is this a floss word?" *yes*

  "How do you know?" *it is one syllable; it is a root word; it has a short vowel; it ends with s*

- Repeat the procedure with a few more words. If desired, use the following: fluff, mess, toss, smell, gull, buff. Be sure to insert two or three words that are not floss words (e.g., cat, tip, beg).
- **Note:** Obviously, these words are easier to recognize visually than aurally. The first step to being aware of floss words is recognizing them in print. The student will practice "hearing" floss words later. (Words such as "ball," "mall," and "small" are also floss words, but will not be introduced until the student has learned the /ŏ/ sound of *a*.)

  "Get out your Rule Book and turn to page 6."

- Point to **Rule Chart 6** as you say the following:

  "This is our floss rule chart and you can refer to it anytime."

  "This is a very special rule we have learned today."

- Whisper to the student:

  "But, whatever you do, don't tell (older brother, sister, etc.) about this rule or (he/she) will think you're too smart."

- Such tactics create a fun atmosphere and encourage the student to listen more carefully in hopes being able to tell a big brother or sister.

  "Find your spelling sound sheet. Put your finger on #35."

- Hold up **Spelling Card 8** so only you can see what is written. Using the hand signals, follow the instructions on the card.
- Repeat with **Spelling Cards 12** and **14.**
- As with any rule, there are exceptions to the floss rule, such as "tough," "rough," "gas," and "bus." These words will be taught as sight words.

  "There are some words that sound like floss words, but don't follow the rules. We must memorize these words."

  "There is a list of floss words in your Irregular Spelling Booklet."

  "Look in your booklet and see if you can tell me where to find irregular floss words."

- Allow time for the student to do this.

  "The irregular floss words are on page 32. Let's turn to page 32 and look at them."

- Allow time for the student to examine the list of irregular floss words.
- **Note:** Because the student may not be able to read the words, you may wish to read and briefly define some or all of the words.
- Check the spelling sound sheet for accuracy.
- Erase the words on the chalkboard. Put **Spelling Cards 8, 12,** and **14** back into the Review Deck.

BOARDWORK

"Now we're going to have a special spelling practice with floss words."

"I'll say a word and I want you to try to spell it."

"Your first word is 'miss.' Let's unblend it together. What sounds do we hear? /M/..."

- Hold up one finger.

"... /ĭ/ ..."

- Hold up a second finger.

"... /s/ ..."

- Hold up a third finger.

"Can you spell 'miss'?"

- Point to each of the fingers you are holding up as the student gives the letters. In the beginning, repeat a sound if the student has difficulty with it. Write the word on the chalkboard after the student spells it.

"We can check this word to see if it is correct. Let's code and read it to see if it is the word I gave you."

- Point to the *i*.

"A vowel followed by a consonant is short; code it with a breve."

- Code the *i* with a breve.

"We have two s's. We need to mark through one of them."

"What does this word say?" ***miss***

"Were you right?"

- Continue giving words to the student until he/she is consistently correct. Use these words, if desired: moss, gill, glass, tell, bill, brass, doll, staff, off, skill, smell, sniff.
- Occasionally throw in a word that is not a floss word to see if the student is really paying attention (e.g., bug, fit, sat).
- **Optional:** Deliberately misspell a word on the chalkboard. Let the student help you correct it. (This should be done only if the student has the ability to catch your "error.")

WORKSHEET

- The student should be seated where he/she can write comfortably.
- Give the student **Worksheet 52.** Make sure the student turns to the correct side.

"Let's practice spelling some floss words."

"Put your finger by #1. Echo the word after I say it and then spell it."

"The word is 'tell.' Unblend 'tell' with me." /t/ /ĕ/ /l/

- Hold up one finger for each sound.

"Let's spell those sounds." *t ... e ... l*

- Point to a finger each time the student spells a sound.

"Now spell the word again and write the letters as you say them."

- Allow time for the student to do this.

"What word did you write?" *tell*

"It is a floss word. Did you spell it with two l's?"

"Try another one. Cuff."

- Allow the student time to write. Check to see that he/she doubled the *f*.
- Repeat the procedure with #3 (smell), #4 (toss), #5 (pass), #6 (sniff), #7 (muff), and #8 (yell).

"At the bottom of your worksheet are some pictures in boxes. Some of the names of the items are floss words. Let's see if we can determine what these pictures are."

- Discuss the pictures to make sure the student understands the word each one represents: #9 (class), #10 (doll), and #11 (bed).

"On the line below each picture, write the word that picture represents."

"Remember, the rule chart for spelling floss words is in your Rule Book if you need to look at it."

- As the student works, provide help as needed. Help the student correct any incorrect answers. Then initial the worksheet in the space provided.
- Some time during the day, ask the student to read from the worksheet, a controlled reader, your basal reader, or other material of your choice.
- **Note:** Always make sure the worksheet is corrected before the student begins the homework. The worksheet serves as a guide to help complete the homework.

HOMEWORK

"Turn your paper over to the homework side."

"Do you know what to do on the homework paper?"

- Discuss the pictures to make sure the student understands the word each one represents: #1 (shell), #2 (dress), #3 (dog), #4 (bell), #5 (map), #6 (kiss), #7 (glass), #8 (box), and #9 (frog).

"When you finish your paper, I will check it for you and initial it in the space provided."

- Either now or later in the day, the student should complete the homework independently (if possible). Help the student correct any incorrect answers. Then initial the homework in the space provided.

READER

- Give the student **Reader 17 (*Fig Jam*)** and some colored pencils.

  "We're going to make another book today."

  "What is this book's title?" *Fig Jam*

  "Have you ever heard of a fig before?" *expect various answers*

  "I've brought something to help you understand what figs are."
- Show the student the fig cookies.

  "These are cookies made with figs. Have you eaten these before?"

  "When you finish making your book, you may have a cookie if you would like one."
- Assist the student as necessary as he/she constructs the book.
- When the student finishes, staple or put a rubber band around the book's spine.
- If necessary, demonstrate how to separate the pages and check the page order.

  "The title of this book is _________?" *Fig Jam*

  "I want you to read your book to yourself. When you are finished reading, color the pictures. Write your name on the book so I will know who colored it."

  "Keep your book handy because I will be asking you to read it for me."
- Some time during the day, have the student read the reader to you.
- Offer a fig cookie to the student when he/she finishes reading.
- If possible, take time to play the Kid Card games listed in Lesson 50.

Lesson 52

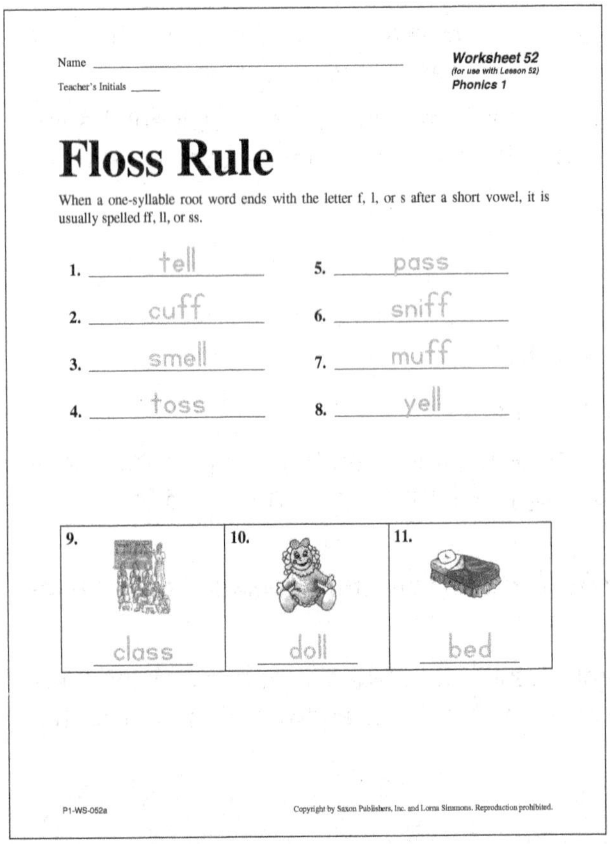

Name ____________________
Teacher's Initials _____

Worksheet 52
(for use with Lesson 52)
Phonics 1

Floss Rule

When a one-syllable root word ends with the letter f, l, or s after a short vowel, it is usually spelled ff, ll, or ss.

1. tell
2. cuff
3. smell
4. toss
5. pass
6. sniff
7. muff
8. yell

9.	10.	11.
class	doll	bed

P1-WS-052a

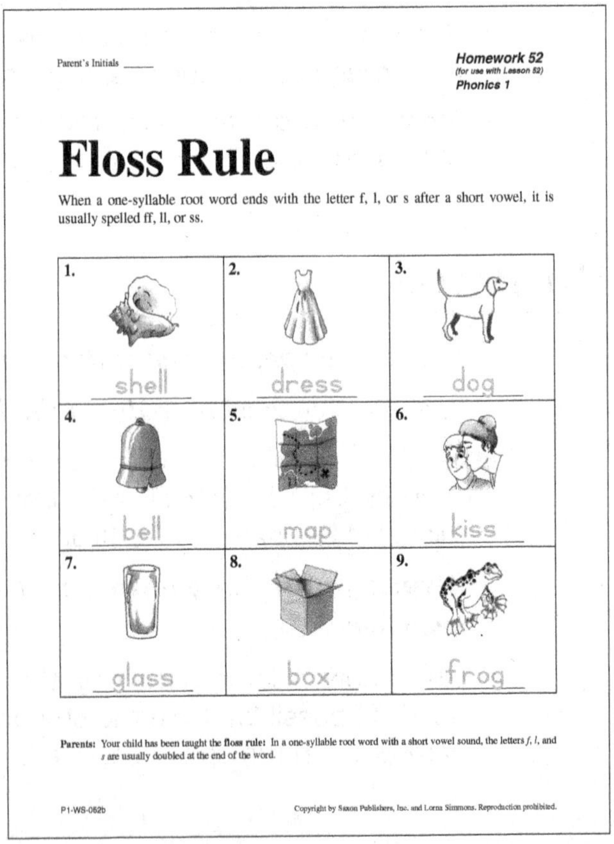

Parent's Initials _____

Homework 52
(for use with Lesson 52)
Phonics 1

Floss Rule

When a one-syllable root word ends with the letter f, l, or s after a short vowel, it is usually spelled ff, ll, or ss.

1.	2.	3.
shell	dress	dog
4. bell	5. map	6. kiss
7. glass	8. box	9. frog

Parents: Your child has been taught the **floss rule:** In a one-syllable root word with a short vowel sound, the letters *f*, *l*, and *s* are usually doubled at the end of the word.

P1-WS-052b

LESSON 53 — The Letter *V*; Final *ve*

lesson preparation

materials

Alphabet/Accent Deck (Section 1)
Review Decks
Spelling Sound Sheet 40
tokens or colored pencil
Letter Card 36
Picture Card 44
Spelling Card 35
Sight Word Card 19
Worksheet 53

the night before

- Add the *v* letter tile to the student's container.

ALPHABET ACTIVITY

- The student should be seated.

  "Today we're going to work with the Alphabet/Accent Deck."

- Show the student **Alphabet/Accent Card 1.**

  "Look at this card. We're going to pretend that this is a two-syllable word. The straight line in the middle separates the first syllable from the second syllable. Instead of using words, we're going to use letters for our syllables. Where is the accent mark? Is it on the first or second syllable?" *second*

  "When we read this card, we will read the first syllable as 'A' and the second syllable as 'B.' "

  "The accent mark tells us to accent the second syllable, so how will we say the second syllable?" *longer, louder, and higher*

  "We're going to do something fun to help us feel the accent. Push your chair back from your (desk or table) just enough so you can stand up without bumping it."

"For the first card, we will say the 'A' softly, sitting down. Then we will stand and say the 'B' longer, louder, and higher. Let's practice."

- Have the student say "A" (softly and sitting down) and then "B" (louder, longer, higher, and standing).

"Sit back down. Let's try the next card."

- Show the student **Alphabet/Accent Card 2.**

"If 'B' is now the first syllable, what is the second syllable?" *c*

"How will we say this card?"

- The student should say "B" (softly and sitting down) and then "C" (louder, longer, higher, and standing).
- Continue with **Alphabet/Accent Cards 3–25,** moving as quickly as possible.

Phonemic Awareness

- **Objective:** To hear and identify the accent on syllables.

"Let's listen for accents again today. When a syllable is accented, how does it sound different from the others?" *it is louder, longer, and higher*

"I'll say a word. Listen carefully. I want you to tell me where you hear the accent. Ready?"

- Say the following words, exaggerating the accented syllable slightly.

bas′·ket	1st syllable
dis·cov′·er	2nd syllable
of′·fice	1st syllable
cray′·on	1st syllable
cel′·e·brate	1st syllable
in·vent′·ed	2nd syllable

- Continue with additional words, if time permits.

Lesson 53

Review of Decks

- The student should be seated where he/she can write comfortably.
- Show the student **Letter Cards 1–35** in random order. The student should name the letter on each letter card.
- Review **Affix Cards 1–3.**
- Show the student **Picture Cards 1–43** in random order. The student should name the keyword and sound for each picture card.
- Review **Sight Word Cards 1–18.**
- Give the student **Spelling Sound Sheet 40** and at least 12 tokens (or a colored pencil).

"Let's play Bingo!"

"When I call out the spelling sounds today, I want you to put a token on (or draw a big X in) the space that spells that sound."

"When you have covered (or X'd out) all of the letters on one line, either up and down, across, or from corner to corner, call out Bingo!"

"Don't forget to refer to your rule charts if you need to."

"Are you ready?"

"Cover (or X out) the letters that spell the final sound in 'brick.' " *ck*

"Cover (or X out) the letter that spells the initial sound in 'yellow.' " *y*

"Cover (or X out) the letters that spell the vowel sound in 'tape.' " *a–e*

"Cover (or X out) the letters that spell the initial sound in 'shoes.' " *sh*

"Cover (or X out) the letters that spell the final sound in 'boss.' " *ss*

"Cover (or X out) the letters that spell the vowel sound in 'bike.' " *i–e*

"Cover (or X out) the letter that spells the initial sound in 'jiggle.' " *j*

"Cover (or X out) the letters that spell the vowel sound in 'home.' " *o–e*

"Cover (or X out) the letter that spells the final sound in 'mix.' " *x*

"Cover (or X out) the letters that spell the vowel sound in 'sleep.' " *ee*

- The student should Bingo by the time all the sounds have been called out.
- Collect the tokens (or colored pencil) and the spelling sound sheet. If you used tokens and the spelling sound sheet is unmarked, keep it available for practice.

NEW LEARNING

"I'm going to say some words. Echo them back to me and listen for the sound that is the same in each word."

- Point to your mouth as you say each word.

"Echo after me. Dove." *dove* ***"Van."*** *van* ***"Have."*** *have* ***"Very."*** *very*

"What sound do you hear that is the same in all of these words?" */v/*

- **Note:** Make sure the student is giving the pure sound of *v* and not pronouncing it with a short *u* sound, as in /vŭh/.

"That's right. The sound you hear in all of these words is /v/."

"Put your fingertips on the front of your neck and say /v/. See if you feel any vibration."

"Is this sound voiced or unvoiced?" *voiced*

- Write the following words on the chalkboard: dove, van, have, very, save, vent.

"What letter do you see in all of these words that might be making the /v/ sound?" *v*

- If the student does not know the name of the letter, say it for him/her.

  "Do you notice anything special about the way the /v/ is spelled in the final position?" *it always has an e after it*

  "That is exactly right. English words don't end with v, so we always need to add an e after the v when we hear /v/ at the end of a word. It doesn't matter if it's a long vowel or a short vowel. There is always an e."

  "I have a rule chart to help us remember the 'final v' rule."

  "Get out your Rule Book and turn to page 7."

- Briefly discuss **Rule Chart 7.**

  "Look at this chart any time you need help spelling the final /v/ sound."

  "Is v a vowel or a consonant?" *consonant*

- Give the student the container of letter tiles.

  "Today I've given you the v letter tile."

  "Find your v letter tile and look at it. One side has a capital V and the other side has a lowercase v."

  "Hold your letter tile up in the air. Turn it so I can see the capital V."

  "Now turn it so I can see the lowercase v."

  "Spell the word 'van' with your letter tiles."

  "Now add one letter to spell the word 'vane.' "

  "Now spell the word 'give.' "

- Choose additional words from the Spelling Word List, if desired.
- Have the student replace the tiles in the container and put it away.
- Reinforce the name, sound, and shape of the letter *v* throughout the day.

NEW DECK CARDS

- Show the student **Letter Card 36.**

  "What is the name of this letter?" *v*

- Hold up **Picture Card 44** but keep the picture covered with your hand (or the letter card).

  "I have a card with a picture on it that begins with the /v/ sound."

  "I am going to describe it to you. See if you can guess what the picture is. Remember, our new keyword starts with the /v/ sound."

  "This is a piece of clothing. Most people wear them over their shirts. It doesn't have sleeves, but it usually has a few buttons. What do you think the picture is?" *vest*

  "That's right. The keyword is 'vest' and the sound we have learned is /v/."

- Show the student **Picture Card 44,** and then point to the picture of a vest on the alphabet strip.

  "The word 'vest' helps us remember the /v/ sound since it begins with /v/."

- Hold up **Spelling Card 35** so that only you can see what is written.

  "We have a special response for this spelling card. Since the /v/ sound on the end of the word always has an e with it, we are going to say 'v final ve' while we write this."

- Write the following on the chalkboard: v || ve.
- Follow the instructions on the card and have the student write the response with his/her finger on the desk or tabletop.
- **Note:** Add the new letter, picture, and spelling cards to the Review Decks.

BOARDWORK

"We have a new sight word today."

- Show the student **Sight Word Card 19.**

  "Can you tell me what this word is?"

  "This word is 'their.' Spelled this way, 'their' means 'belonging to them,' as in 'people and their cars.' "

- Help the student locate the word in the Irregular Spelling Booklet.

  "How do we code sight words?" *circle them*

  "We will add this card to our sight word deck."

  "Let's practice coding some words like the ones you'll have on your worksheet."

  "The rule charts are in your Rule Book if you need to look at them."

- Write the following word and sentence (without the coding marks) on the chalkboard, one at a time. Ask the student to help you code them. The correct coding is as indicated:

  crăsh

  The răb'|bĭt hăd å thĭn rĭb'|bŏn ŏn hĭs foot.
  (vc | cv ... vc | cv)

- Have the student help you identify each of the items coded as a word, a phrase, or a sentence.
- Add **Sight Word Card 19** to the Sight Word Deck.

Lesson 53

WORKSHEET

- The student should be seated where he/she can write comfortably.
- Give the student **Worksheet 53.** Make sure the student turns to the correct side.

  "Today, let's spell with the /v/ sound."

"Remember, if a word ends with the /v/ sound, an e will be added whether the vowel is long or short."

"Put your finger by #1. The first word is 'live.' "

- Pronounce this word as /lĭv/.

"Unblend 'live' with me." */l/ /ĭ/ /v/*

- Hold up one finger for each sound.

"Let's spell those sounds." *l ... i ... v*

- Point to a finger each time the student spells a sound.

"English words don't end with v by itself, so what must we add?" *an e*

"Now spell the word again and write the letters as you say them."

- Allow time for the student to do this.

"What word did you write?" *live*

"What would you have written if I had said /līv/?" *l-i-v-e*

"That's right. /Lĭv/ and /līv/ are spelled exactly the same way."

- Repeat the procedure with #2 (have), #3 (cave), #4 (brave), and #5 (solve).

"Now you're ready to code and read the words on your paper."

"Code the words by #6 through #10. After you have coded all the words, try to read them."

- Assist the student as necessary.

"Numbers 11 and 12 are questions about the paragraph just above them. If you find any words you can't read, code them. Then see if you can answer the questions."

- As the student works, provide help as needed. Help the student correct any incorrect answers. Then initial the worksheet in the space provided.
- Some time during the day, ask the student to read from the worksheet, the controlled reader, your basal reader, or other material of your choice.
- **Note:** Always make sure the worksheet is corrected before the student begins the homework. The worksheet serves as a guide to help complete the homework.

HOMEWORK

"Turn your paper over to the homework side."

"Put your finger on the top row of handwriting lines. Write your best capital V on these lines so I will know what a capital V should look like."

- Have the student write a lowercase letter *v* on the second handwriting line. Make sure that the student has written the letters correctly (to the best of his or her ability). He/She will use them as guides when completing the homework.

"Do you know what to do on the rest of the homework paper?"

"Watch for digraphs, suffixes, and words with a 'vccv' pattern that need to be divided."

"When you finish your paper, I will check it for you and initial it in the space provided."

- Either now or later in the day, the student should complete the homework independently (if possible). Help the student correct any incorrect answers. Then initial the homework in the space provided.
- If possible, take time to play the Kid Card games listed in Lesson 50.

Name ______________________

Teacher's Initials ____

Worksheet 53
(for use with Lesson 53)
Phonics 1

Vv

1. live
2. have
3. cave
4. brave
5. solve
6. vĕt
7. vĕlvĕt (v c c v)
8. booth
9. cook
10. hŭsh

Jeff lives with his sis, Tish. Tish has a job at a plant. The plant makes vans. Jeff likes vans and likes to go to the plant with Tish.

11. Jeff lives with Tish.
12. Vans are made at the plant.

P1-WS-053a

Parent's Initials ____

Homework 53
(for use with Lesson 53)
Phonics 1

Vv

1. vĕnt
2. skill
3. jŭst
4. ships
5. blăst
6. vĕst
7. boost
8. took
9. shĕd
10. vĭctĭm (v c c v)

Tish makes vans at a plant. The vans are green, red, and tan. The vans cost a lot and Tish can't have one yet. She hopes to get one if she saves some cash. It will take a long time to save the cash.

11. The vans are green, red, and tan.
12. What will Tish save? cash

Parents: Your child has been taught the name, shape, and sound of the letter v; and that the "v" sound at the end of a word is spelled ve.

P1-WS-053b

Lesson 53

LESSON 54 Spelling with Final *c*

lesson preparation

materials

container of letter tiles

Review Decks

Spelling Sound Sheet 41

Worksheet 54

Reader 18 (*Deb's Dogs*)

colored pencils

ALPHABET ACTIVITY

- The student should be seated with the alphabet strip.

  "Today we are going to alphabetize letters again."

  "When we alphabetize, we recite the alphabet from a to z and put the letters in order as we say them. Then they should be in alphabetical order, but we can check it. Here's how."

- Demonstrate, using the alphabet strip.

  "I put my finger on the first letter and begin reciting the alphabet."

  "As soon as I say the name of the letter I am touching, I move my finger to the next letter and leave it there until I say that letter; then my finger moves to the right again."

- Remember that when facing the student, the student's right is your left.
- Give the student the container of letter tiles.

  "Take any six letters out of your container. It doesn't matter which ones."

  "Line up the six letters in front of you."

  "Put your finger under your first letter tile, the one on the left side. When you scan, move your finger under the row of letters to make sure that you look at every letter."

  "We will say the alphabet slowly, and when we say one of your letters, move it to start a new row. This will be the row that is in ABC order."

  "Listen carefully and watch for your letters."

- Begin reciting the alphabet. Encourage the student to say it with you. Make sure the student uses his/her finger to scan under the letters.
- If time permits, have the student trade the letters for six new ones and try the procedure again.
- Allow the student to work independently, but take note if he/she is having difficulty. Provide the student with additional practice by repeating this activity, if necessary.
- Have the student replace the tiles in the container and put it away.

PHONEMIC AWARENESS

- **Objective:** To hear and identify the accent on syllables.

  "Let's listen for accent today."

  "I'll say a word. I want you to listen very carefully and decide if the word is accented on the first syllable or the second syllable."

  "Let's try this."

  "The first word is 'in … fant.' "
- Be sure to exaggerate the first syllable.

  "Do you hear the accent on the first syllable or the second?" *first syllable*
- Continue with the following words: mas′·cot, ta′·ble, re·duce′, or′·der, be·tween′.
- Continue with additional words, if desired.

REVIEW OF DECKS

- The student should be seated where he/she can write comfortably.
- Show the student **Letter Cards 1–36** in random order. The student should name the letter on each letter card.
- Review **Affix Cards 1–3.**
- Show the student **Picture Cards 1–44** in random order. The student should name the keyword and sound for each picture card.
- Review **Sight Word Cards 1–19.**
- Give the student **Spelling Sound Sheet 41.**
- Call out the sounds on **Spelling Cards 1–35** in random order. The student should echo each sound and name the letter or letters that make the sound as he/she writes the letter(s) on the spelling sound sheet.
- Have the student set the spelling sound sheet aside for use later in the lesson.

NEW LEARNING

- Pull **Spelling Card 18** from the Review Deck.

  "We have learned several rules for spelling the /k/ sound."

"At the beginning or middle of the word, we use k or c."

- Point to **Rule Chart 3.**

"Can you tell me when we use k?" *before e, i, or y*

"Can you tell me when we use c?" *before anything else (a, o, u, or any consonant)*

"We have also learned three ways to spell /k/ at the end of a word."

- Point to **Rule Chart 4.**

"What digraph do we use after a short vowel sound?" *digraph ck*

"What spelling do we use for /k/ after a consonant or a vowel digraph?" *k by itself*

"What spelling do we use after a long vowel sound?" *ke*

"Today we are going to learn another way to spell /k/ at the end of a word."

- Write the following words on the chalkboard and then read them aloud:

plastic	sonic
rustic	majestic

"How have we spelled the final /k/ sound in these words?" *c*

"When we used the other rules for spelling /k/ at the end of the word, the words were one-syllable words."

"Are these one-syllable words?" *no*

"A few days ago, we learned that sometimes we can count the vowels to find out how many syllables the word has."

"Let's see how many syllables are in these words."

- Point to "plastic."

"What about the word 'plastic'? How many vowels are in this word?" *two*

"So, this might be a two-syllable word."

- Have the student help you with the remaining words: sonic (2), rustic (2), majestic (3).

"If all of our other rules only work on one-syllable words, then what is it about these words that tells us to use a 'c' on the end?" *they have more than one syllable*

"That's right. When a word with two or more syllables ends with the /k/ sound, we spell the /k/ sound with a 'c.' "

"Find your spelling sound sheet. Put your finger by #36."

- Hold up **Spelling Card 18** so only you can see what is written.

"We have to change our spelling card response once more, but this is the last time. It won't change again after this."

"Our new response is 'k comma c, final digraph ck, comma k, comma ke, comma c.' "

- Write the new response on the chalkboard: k, c || ck, k, ke, c.

"Let's practice it together before we have to say it tomorrow."

"Take a deep breath! Ready?" *k comma c final digraph ck comma k comma ke comma c*

"Write the new response on the line by #36."

- Check the spelling sound sheet for accuracy.
- Put **Spelling Card 18** back into the Review Deck.

BOARDWORK

- Write the following sentence (without the coding marks) on the chalkboard:

  The ____ is hŏt ănd the moon is cool.

  "Can you help me code this sentence?"

- Code the sentence as the student instructs. If the student mentions that the sentence is missing a word, whisper: "Yes, I noticed that, too."

  "Can you read this sentence?"

- If he/she hasn't already, the student will probably tell you that the sentence is missing a word (or will read the sentence without the missing word).

  "There's something funny about this sentence. It doesn't make sense, does it? But I think I know how we can fix it."

WORKSHEET

- Give the student **Worksheet 54.** Make sure the student turns to the correct side.

  "Do you see the long, skinny box in the middle of your worksheet? Look at the words in that box. Do you see a word that would go into our sentence on the chalkboard and help it make sense?" *sun*

- Write the word "sun" in the blank. Have the student come to the chalkboard and code the word: sŭn.

  "Now let's read the sentence together."

- Read the sentence with the student.

  "Does it make sense?" *yes*

  "We filled in the blank with a word that made the sentence make sense."

  "You'll get to fill in all those blanks on your worksheet in a few minutes. First, let's spell some words with our new final k rule."

  "Remember to look at the rule charts to help you decide if the word should end with digraph ck, k by itself, ke, or c."

- Review **Rule Chart 4:** *ck* follows a short vowel sound, *k* follows a consonant or a vowel digraph, *ke* follows a long vowel sound, and *c* goes on the end of a word that has more than one syllable.

"Look at #1 through #5. All of these words end with the /k/ sound. For each word, check the rule chart and decide whether you will spell it with digraph ck, k, ke, or c."

"The first word is 'silk.' What kind of letter comes before the /k/ sound?" *a consonant*

"Which /k/ spelling do we use after a consonant?" *k*

"Write a 'k' in the space to finish spelling the word."

- Repeat with #2 (pluck), #3 (plastic), #4 (take), and #5 (picnic), helping the student determine the correct /k/ spelling in each word.

"Now you're ready to code and read the words on your paper."

"Code the words by #6 through #10. After you've coded all the words, try to read them."

- Assist the student as necessary.

"At the bottom of the page are sentences with some words missing. All of the missing words are in the box above the sentences. Use each word once."

"Read the sentence by #11. Then decide which of the words in the box makes that sentence make sense. Write that word in the blank space."

- Repeat with #12, #13, #14, and #15.
- As the student works, provide help as needed. Help the student correct any incorrect answers. Then initial the worksheet in the space provided.
- Some time during the day, ask the student to read from the worksheet, a controlled reader, your basal reader, or other material of your choice.
- **Note:** Always make sure the worksheet is corrected before the student begins the homework. The worksheet serves as a guide to help complete the homework.

HOMEWORK

"Turn your paper over to the homework side."

"Do you know what to do on the homework paper?"

- Discuss the activities, if necessary.

"When you finish your paper, I will check it for you and initial it in the space provided."

- Either now or later in the day, the student should complete the homework independently (if possible). Help the student correct any incorrect answers. Then initial the homework in the space provided.

READER

- Give the student **Reader 18 (*Deb's Dogs*)** and some colored pencils.

  "We're going to make another book today."

  "What is this book's title?" *Deb's Dogs*
- Assist the student as necessary as he/she constructs the book.
- When the student finishes, staple or put a rubber band around the book's spine.
- If necessary, demonstrate how to separate the pages and check the page order.

  "The title of this book is _________?" *Deb's Dogs*

  "I want you to read your book to yourself. Fill in the blanks with the correct answers. When you are finished reading, color the pictures. Write your name on the book so I will know who colored it."

  "Keep your book handy because I will be asking you to read it for me."
- Some time during the day, have the student read the reader to you.
- If possible, take time to play the Kid Card games listed in Lesson 50. Try to see that the student is prepared for tomorrow's assessment.

Name ____________________

Teacher's Initials ____

Worksheet 54
(for use with Lesson 54)
Phonics 1

llc

Final /k/ Rules

1. sĭl k
2. plŭ ck
3. plastĭ c
4. tā ke
5. picnĭ c
6. swoop
7. rode
8. slŭmped
9. greeting
10. sack

sun	deep	pool	fifteen	cool

11. Splash! Jan jumped into the pool.
12. It felt cool on Jan's skin.
13. The sun was hot so it felt good.
14. Jan can dive in the deep end.
15. She swims fifteen laps and feels pooped.

P1-WS-054a

Parent's Initials ____

Homework 54
(for use with Lesson 54)
Phonics 1

llc

Final /k/ Rules

1. mĭl k
2. frantĭ c
3. pō ke
4. loo k
5. thĭn k
6. see k
7. attĭ c
8. boo k
9. tā ke
10. lī ke

name	friends	dog	some	woods

11. Deb has a black dog.
12. Deb's dog ate some dog food.
13. The dog's name is Rex.
14. Rex likes to hunt in the woods.
15. Rex and Deb are good friends.

Parents: Your child has been taught that the "k" sound at the end of a word with two or more syllables is spelled with a c.

P1-WS-054b

Lesson 54

LESSON 55 Assessment

lesson preparation

materials

ball

Review Decks

Assessment 10

Spelling Test 8

Assessment 10 Recording Form

Kid Cards

tokens

the night before

- Separate the Kid Cards marked "Lesson 55."

ALPHABET ACTIVITY

- You and the student should be standing with the ball.

  "Let's play 'Alphabet Toss' again."

  "I am going to change the rules today. I'll say a letter of the alphabet and toss the ball to you. After you catch the ball, you must say a word that begins with the letter I said. Then say another letter and toss the ball back to me."

  "I will then say a word that begins with the letter you said."

  "Keep your eye on the ball!"

- Play as long as time permits; then have the student return to his/her seat.

PHONEMIC AWARENESS

- **Objective:** To hear and identify the accent on syllables within words.

  "Let's see how well you can hear an accent today. When a syllable is accented, how does it sound different from the others?" *it is louder, longer, and higher*

  "I'll say a word. Listen carefully. If you hear the accent on the first syllable, hold up one finger. If you hear the accent on the second syllable, hold up two fingers. Ready?"

- Say the following words, exaggerating the accented syllables slightly:

bea´·ver	1st syllable	1 finger
ba·nan´·a	2nd syllable	2 fingers
ca·nar´·y	2nd syllable	2 fingers
der´·by	1st syllable	1 finger
fire´·place	1st syllable	1 finger
kook´·a·bur·ra	1st syllable	1 finger

REVIEW OF DECKS

- The student should be seated where he/she can write comfortably.
- Show the student **Letter Cards 1–36** in random order. The student should name the letter on each letter card.
- Review **Affix Cards 1–3.**
- Show the student **Picture Cards 1–44** in random order. The student should name the keyword and sound for each picture card.
- Review **Sight Word Cards 1–19.**

WRITTEN ASSESSMENT

- The student should be seated where he/she can write comfortably.
- Give the student **Assessment 10.**
- **Section I:**

  "Today we are going to write some words for our assessment."

  "I'm going to say a word. Write the letter or letters that make each sound in that word on the lines by #1."

  "Look at the rule charts if you need to."

  "Here's the first word: zoom."
- Repeat with the following words in the order shown: #2 (good), #3 (shake), #4 (yet), and #5 (mix).
- **Reminder:** While the student spells, be ready to point to appropriate rule charts as necessary.
- **Section II:**

  "Look at the letters by #6."

  "Find the pictures of the keywords for this sound."

  "Draw lines from the letters to the keywords."
- Repeat with #7, #8, and #9. Allow a few minutes for the student to work.
- The pictures (from top to bottom) are as follows: hook/tooth, shark, fox, yarn.

- **Section III:**

  "Put your finger on #10."

  "Code the words by #10 through #14."
- Allow a few minutes for the student to work.
- **Section IV:**

  "Read the paragraph. If you find any words you can't read, code them to help you figure them out. Then answer the questions by #15, #16, and #17."
- **Reminder:** If the student absolutely cannot read the paragraph, read it to the student to see if he or she can answer the questions.

  "When you are finished, show your paper to me."
- This paper will be used during the oral portion of the assessment.

Spelling Test

- Give the student **Spelling Test 8.**
- Call out the following words (in the order shown). Sound them out, if necessary.

  #1 (snack), #2 (duck), #3 (teeth), #4 (disk), #5 (swim), #6 (creek), #7 (hunting), #8 (needed), #9 (tricked), #10 (locking), #11 (said), #12 (where)
- Grade and record the test in any manner that suits your needs.

Oral Assessment

- It is important to complete the oral assessment promptly (today, if possible) in order to identify any areas of weakness and begin remediation.
- Use the assessment and the following dialogue to complete the oral portion.
- **Section V:**
- Point to the sight word by #18.

  "Read this sight word for me."
- Record the student's response by placing a check mark by each word he/she reads correctly.
- Repeat with #19, #20, and #21.
- **Section VI:**
- Show the student the letters by #22.

  "Tell me the name of these letters and the sounds they make."
- Write the student's response on the adjacent line.
- Repeat with #23, #24, and #25.

Assessment Evaluation

- Grade the assessment and record the results on **Assessment 10 Recording Form.** Check off the boxes to indicate mastery (i.e., the section was completed with 100% accuracy).
- **Reminder:** Try to give as many points as possible for work attempted. Do not grade the coding marks too severely. The most important coding marks to look for are breves, macrons, and syllable division lines.
- See the introductory material for detailed information regarding grading and recording procedures.
- Use the assessment results to identify those skills in which the student is weak. Practice those skills by playing Kid Card games.
- Add the Kid Cards marked "Lesson 55" to the existing decks. Listed below are games appropriate for remediation in selected areas. See "Games and Activities" for the directions for each game.
- **Section I:** Play "Spelling Deck Perfection," "Sound Scamper," "Spell Out #1," or have the student use the letter tiles to spell words you give from the Spelling Word List.
- **Section II:** Play "Keyword and Sound" or "Letter/Sound Identification."
- **Section III:** Play "Chalkboard Challenge."
- **Section IV:** Either have the student read the controlled readers and then ask questions for comprehension, or play "Acting Out" with the green Kid Cards.
- **Section V:** Play "At First Sight."
- **Section VI:** Play "Letter/Sound Identification."
- When the student seems more secure in areas that had previously proven difficult, retest him/her (in those areas only) and indicate on the recording form any sections the student has subsequently mastered.
- Try to help the student achieve mastery of all the sections before the next assessment.
- If the student is having difficulty with a particular skill, keep his or her practice activities at the most basic level so the chance of success is greater.

Name ______________________

Assessment 10
(for use with Lesson 55)
Phonics 1

Section I

1. z o o m
2. g o o d
3. s h a k e
4. y e t
5. m i x

Section II

6. oo 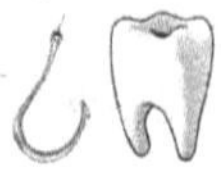

7. x 

8. sh 

9. y 

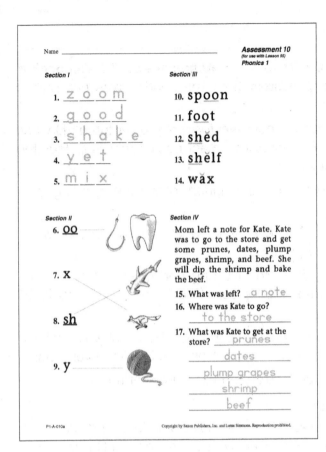

Section III

10. spoon
11. foot
12. shĕd
13. shĕlf
14. wăx

Section IV

Mom left a note for Kate. Kate was to go to the store and get some prunes, dates, plump grapes, shrimp, and beef. She will dip the shrimp and bake the beef.

15. What was left? a note
16. Where was Kate to go? to the store
17. What was Kate to get at the store? prunes / dates / plump grapes / shrimp / beef

P1-A-010a

Assessment 10
(for use with Lesson 55)
Phonics 1

Section V

18. you ________
19. one ________
20. some ________
21. do ________

Section VI

22. oo digraph oo, /ŏŏ/, /ōō/
23. x x, /ks/
24. sh digraph sh, /sh/
25. y y, /y/

P1-A-010b

Lesson 55

LESSON 56 — Final, Stable Syllable *-ble*

lesson preparation

materials

container of letter tiles

Review Decks

Spelling Sound Sheet 42

Letter Card 37

Picture Card 45

liquid bubbles and bubble maker

Spelling Card 36

Worksheet 56

Spelling List 9

new concepts

final, stable syllable

the night before

- Punch out the *q* letter tile but do not add it to the student's container at this time.

ALPHABET ACTIVITY

- The student should be seated with the container of letter tiles.

  "You are going to enjoy our alphabet activity today."

- Give the following instructions one at a time, allowing time for the student to accomplish each task before giving the next instruction.

  "Take all of the letter tiles out of your container."

  "Flip all of the letters over so that you are looking at the capital letters. If they are flipped correctly, they will all be green."

  "Before we start, let's say the alphabet together so it is fresh in our minds."

- Recite the alphabet with the student.

  "I want you to start putting your letter tiles in ABC order. See if you can find the letter that is missing."

- The student will probably call out "missing" letters when he/she does not find them immediately. Just say, "No, that is not the missing letter."
- When the student discovers that *q* is the missing letter, continue:

  "That's right! The missing letter is q. The only time q is found by itself is when we alphabetize."

- Give the student the *q* letter tile.

  "Now we're ready to put all of the letters in alphabetical order. If you recite the alphabet and move each letter to the right place as you say it, it won't be difficult. It will be just like when we put a few letters into alphabetical order."
- If the desk or table is not wide enough to accommodate the letter tiles placed end to end, demonstrate how to arrange the tiles in an arc.
- Assist the student as necessary as he/she alphabetizes the letter tiles.
- When the student has finished, replace the tiles in the container and put it away.

Phonemic Awareness

- **Objective:** To manipulate sounds within words.

  "Echo this word. Seat." *seat*

  "What is the initial sound in 'seat'?" */s/*

  "Can you say it out loud without the initial sound?" *eat*
- Repeat the procedure with the following words: land...and; gone...on; sit...it; rat...at; fin...in; bus...us.

Review of Decks

- The student should be seated where he/she can write comfortably.
- Show the student **Letter Cards 1–36** in random order. The student should name the letter on each letter card.
- Review **Affix Cards 1–3.**
- Show the student **Picture Cards 1–44** in random order. The student should name the keyword and sound for each picture card.
- Review **Sight Word Cards 1–19.**
- Give the student **Spelling Sound Sheet 42.**
- Call out the sounds on **Spelling Cards 1–35** in random order. The student should echo each sound and name the letter or letters that make the sound as he/she writes the letter(s) on the spelling sound sheet.
- Have the student set the spelling sound sheet aside for use later in the lesson.

New Learning

"I'm going to say some words. Echo them back to me and listen for the sound that is the same at the end of each word."

- Point to your mouth as you say each word.

  "Echo after me. Table." *table* ***"Thimble."*** *thimble* ***"Stubble."*** *stubble*

"What sound do you hear in the final position?" /bəl/

"This sound is different from the sounds we have been learning because it contains two sounds, the /b/ and the /l/."

- If necessary, repeat the words, exaggerating the final syllable.

"Let's look at these words and see what is making that sound."

- Write the following words on the chalkboard: table, thimble, stubble.

"What is the same in all of these words that is making the /bəl/ sound?" *ble*

"That's right! Ble is making the /bəl/ sound."

"How many syllables do you hear in the word 'table'?" *two*

"The word 'table' needs to be divided, but one of the syllables does not follow our rules. We must treat it differently."

"We call 'ble' a final, stable syllable."

"Why do you think it is called 'final'?" *because it is in the final position*

"Why do you think we call it a syllable?" *it has its own vowel sound*

"We say it is stable because it doesn't change. We can count on it having the /bəl/ sound whenever we see it in the final position even though it does not follow the rules."

"The strange thing about it being a syllable is that we don't hear or see the vowel in the place where we hear the sound. We hear the schwa vowel sound between the b and the l, but the syllable has a silent e on the end."

- Cross out the *e*'s on each word.

"We code a final, stable syllable by placing a bracket in front of it."

"The bracket actually divides the word into syllables. The bracket tells us that this two-syllable word is different."

- Add brackets to the three words: ta[blø, thim[blø, stub[blø.
- When you divide the word "stubble," point out that only one *b* goes inside the bracket.

"How have we been coding twin consonants?" *we cross them out*

"I think you know by now that we don't say the sound twice when we have twin consonants. I don't think we need to code them anymore."

- **Note:** If the student depends heavily on coding, feel free to continue coding twin consonants.

"We marked out the e's because they were silent. Now we mark the accent on the syllable right before the bracket."

- Place the accent mark in the first word: ta´[blø.

"When a word has a final, stable syllable, the accent usually falls on the syllable before the bracket."

"The bracket separates the word into syllables. When we code the vowel, we look only at the letters in the syllable containing the vowel."

Lesson 56

"How do we code an 'a' that is open and accented?" *with a macron*

"That's right. The syllable here is 'tā.' The 'a' is not followed by a consonant and the syllable is accented."

- Code the *a* with a macron: tā´[blɇ.

"Can you read this word?" *table*

"Can you use this word in a sentence?"

- Allow time for the student to use the word in a sentence.
- Finish coding the remaining words: <u>th</u>ĭm´[blɇ, stŭb´[blɇ.
- Have the student read the words and use them in sentences.
- Leave the words on the chalkboard for the remainder of the lesson.

NEW DECK CARDS

- Hold up **Letter Card 37.**

"When we see this card, we will say 'final, stable syllable ble.' What is this card called?" *final, stable syllable ble*

- Hold up **Picture Card 45** but keep the picture covered with your hand (or the letter card).

"You are going to try to guess our new keyword. Close your eyes and hold out your hands with your palms facing me so I can give you a clue."

- Quietly get the jar of liquid bubbles. Begin blowing bubbles toward the student's palms. Blow hard enough for the bubbles to pop on the student's palms.

"Now, can you tell me the keyword for final, stable syllable ble?"

- Provide more clues as necessary for the student to guess the keyword "bubble."
- Show the student **Picture Card 45.**

"What will we say when we see this card?" *bubble, /bəl/*

- **Note:** The final, stable syllable and its picture are also shown in the Rule Book on page 22.

"Find your spelling sound sheet. Put your finger on line #36."

- Hold up **Spelling Card 36** so only you can see what is written.

"Echo this sound: /bəl/." */bəl/*

"How do we spell the /bəl/ sound in the final syllable?" *ble*

"That's right. Now when I say /bəl/, you will respond 'final, stable syllable ble' and write 'ble' on your paper."

- Write "ble" on the chalkboard.

"Write the response on the line by #36."

- Check the spelling sound sheet for accuracy.
- **Note:** Add the new letter, picture, and spelling cards to the Review Decks.

Boardwork

"Let's practice coding some words like the ones you'll have on your worksheet."

"The rule charts are in your Rule Book if you need to look at them."

- Write the following sentences (without the coding marks) on the chalkboard, one at a time. Ask the student to help you code them. The correct coding is as indicated:

The răc|coon′ scoot′ed ŭp the trēe.

The shēep (are) ĭn the stā′[ble.

- Have the student help you identify each of the items coded as a word, a phrase, or a sentence.

Worksheet

- The student should be seated where he/she can write comfortably.
- Give the student **Worksheet 56.** Make sure the student turns to the correct side.

"Today, let's spell with final, stable syllable ble."

"Before we start, let's practice with a word. Can you help me spell 'stubble'?"

- If the student spells the word with only one *b*, which is not uncommon, do not correct the spelling immediately. Instead, say the following:

"Let's code this word and see if it is spelled correctly."

- Code the word as shown: stū′[ble.

"How will we read this word?"

- Read it as it is coded: styōō′[bəl.

"Is this the word we wanted to spell?" *no*

- Point to the *u*.

"This vowel needs to be short. What must follow the 'u' to make it short?" *a consonant*

"What consonant should I use?"

- Let the student try to help. Read the word with each letter suggested until the student realizes that the consonant must be another *b*.
- Refer to the words written on the chalkboard during "New Learning."

"Why didn't we double the b in 'table'?" *the vowel is supposed to be long*

"Why didn't we double the b in 'thimble'?" *the consonant m is there to keep the vowel short*

"Some of the words I give you may need a double consonant. After you spell a word, code it and see if the word says what you meant it to say."

"Put your finger by #1. The first word is 'bumble.'"

"Unblend the first syllable with me." */b/ /ŭ/ /m/*

- Hold up one finger for each sound.

"The last syllable is /bəl/. Spell /bəl/." *final, stable syllable ble*

"Let's spell the whole word. B … u … m … b … l … e."

"Now spell the word again and write the letters as you say them."

- Allow time for the student to do this.

"What word did you write?" *bumble*

- Repeat the procedure with #2 (cable), #3 (dribble), #4 (pebble), and #5 (stable).

"Now you're ready to code and read the words on your paper."

"Code the words by #6 through #10. After you have coded all the words, try to read them."

- Assist the student as necessary.

"Numbers 11 and 12 are questions about the paragraph just above them. If you find any words you can't read, code them. Then see if you can answer the questions."

- As the student works, provide help as needed. Help the student correct any incorrect answers. Then initial the worksheet in the space provided.
- Some time during the day, ask the student to read from the worksheet, a controlled reader, your basal reader, or other material of your choice.
- **Note:** Always make sure the worksheet is corrected before the student begins the homework. The worksheet serves as a guide to help complete the homework.

HOMEWORK

"Turn your paper over to the homework side."

"Do you know what to do on the homework paper?"

"Watch for final, stable syllables and always bracket the ble. Remember, only one b goes behind the bracket. Then mark the e silent, and accent the syllable before the bracket."

"When you finish your paper, I will check it for you and initial it in the space provided."

- Either now or later in the day, the student should complete the homework independently (if possible). Help the student correct any incorrect answers. Then initial the homework in the space provided.

Spelling List

- Fold **Spelling List 9** in half lengthwise (with the printed side facing out).

  "Leave your paper just like I give it to you."
- Give the student **Spelling List 9,** folded with the blank lines facing up.

  "Let's spell some more words."
- Call out the following words (in the order shown). Sound them out, if necessary.

  #1 (green), #2 (plus), #3 (bake), #4 (spoke), #5 (wink), #6 (make),
  #7 (like), #8 (upset), #9 (brushing), #10 (admit), #11 (do), #12 (to)

  "Now unfold your paper and check your words."
- Check the student's work to see if he/she needs extra help with spelling.

  "I want you to practice these words. We'll have a spelling test in a few days."
- If possible, take time to play the Kid Card games listed in Lesson 55.

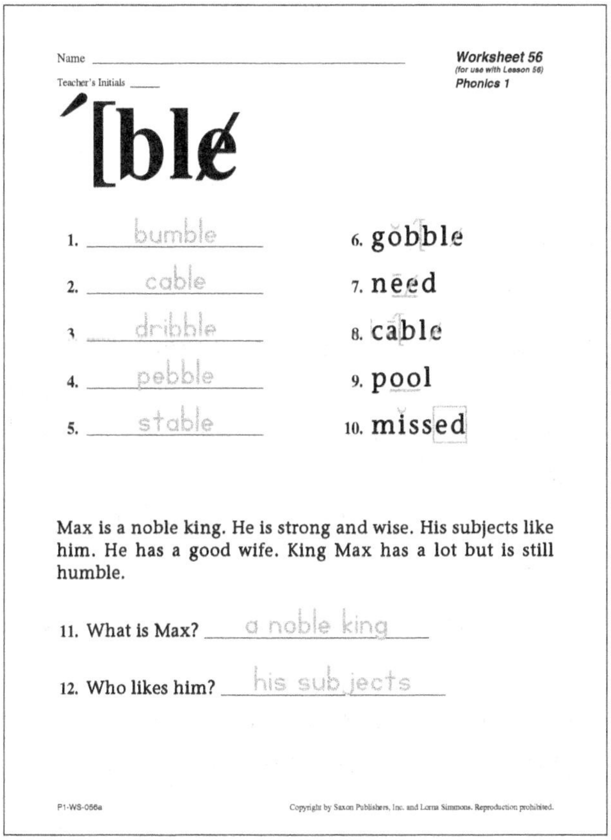

Name ______________________

Teacher's Initials ____

Worksheet 56
(for use with Lesson 56)
Phonics 1

[blé

1. bumble
2. cable
3. dribble
4. pebble
5. stable
6. gobble
7. need
8. cable
9. pool
10. missed

Max is a noble king. He is strong and wise. His subjects like him. He has a good wife. King Max has a lot but is still humble.

11. What is Max? a noble king
12. Who likes him? his subjects

P1-WS-056a

Copyright by Saxon Publishers, Inc. and Lorna Simmons. Reproduction prohibited.

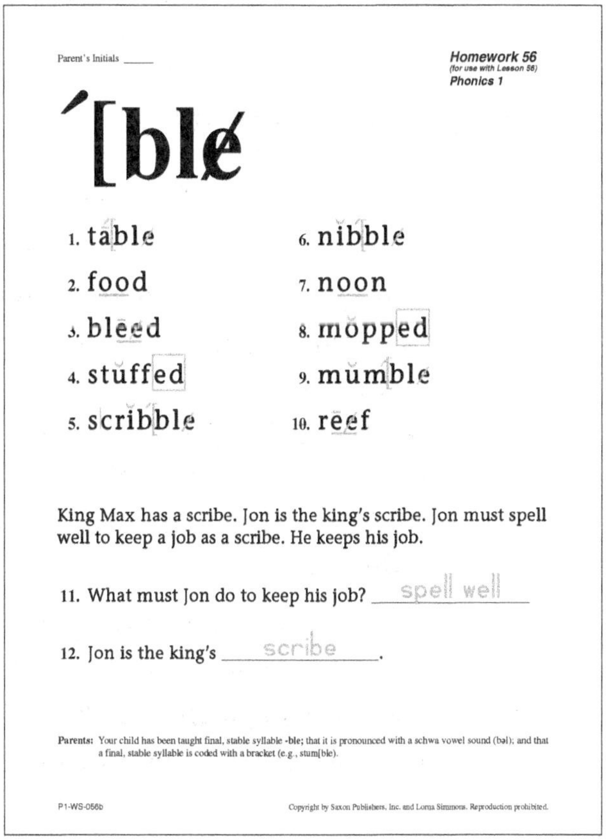

Parent's Initials ____

Homework 56
(for use with Lesson 56)
Phonics 1

[blé

1. table
2. food
3. bleed
4. stuffed
5. scribble
6. nibble
7. noon
8. mopped
9. mumble
10. reef

King Max has a scribe. Jon is the king's scribe. Jon must spell well to keep a job as a scribe. He keeps his job.

11. What must Jon do to keep his job? spell well
12. Jon is the king's scribe.

Parents: Your child has been taught final, stable syllable -ble; that it is pronounced with a schwa vowel sound (bəl); and that a final, stable syllable is coded with a bracket (e.g., stum[ble).

P1-WS-056b

Copyright by Saxon Publishers, Inc. and Lorna Simmons. Reproduction prohibited.

Lesson 56

Lesson 57

Final, Stable Syllables *-fle, -ple, -dle*

lesson preparation

materials

Alphabet/Accent Deck (Section 1)

Review Decks

Spelling Sound Sheet 43

Letter Cards 38–40

Picture Cards 46–48

candles in a sack (see *the night before*)

Worksheet 57

Sight Word Card 20

Reader 19 (*Jogging Josh*)

colored pencils

the night before

- Put some candles in a sack for the student to use to "discover" the new keyword. Birthday candles work well and are inexpensive.

Alphabet Activity

- The student should be seated.

  "Let's play the Alphabet/Accent game again today."

- Show the student **Alphabet/Accent Card 1.**

  "Look at this card. We're going to pretend that this is a two-syllable word. The straight line in the middle separates the first syllable from the second syllable. Instead of using words, we're going to use letters for our syllables. Where is the accent mark? Is it on the first or second syllable?" *second*

  "When we read this card, we will read the first syllable as 'A' and the second syllable as 'B.' "

  "The accent mark tells us to accent the second syllable, so how will we say the second syllable?" *longer, louder, and higher*

  "We're going to do something fun to help us feel the accent. Push your chair back from the (desk or table) just enough so you can stand up without bumping it."

"For the first card, we will say the 'A' softly, sitting down. Then we will stand and say the 'B' longer, louder, and higher. Let's practice."

- Have the student say "A" (softly and sitting down) and then "B" (louder, longer, higher, and standing).

"Sit back down. Let's try the next card."

- Show the student **Alphabet/Accent Card 2.**

"If 'B' is now the first syllable, what is the second syllable?" *C*

"How will we say this card?"

- The student should say "B" (softly and sitting down) and then "C" (louder, longer, higher, and standing).
- Continue with **Alphabet/Accent Cards 3–25,** moving as quickly as possible.

PHONEMIC AWARENESS

- **Objective:** To manipulate sounds within words.

"Echo this word. Cup." *cup*

"What is the initial sound in 'cup'?" */k/*

"Can you say it without the initial sound?" *up*

- Repeat the procedure with the following words: cough...off; fill...ill; his...is; tape...ape; soak...oak; gate...ate.

REVIEW OF DECKS

- The student should be seated where he/she can write comfortably.
- Show the student **Letter Cards 1–37** in random order. The student should name the letter on each letter card.
- Review **Affix Cards 1–3.**
- Show the student **Picture Cards 1–45** in random order. The student should name the keyword and sound for each picture card.
- Review **Sight Word Cards 1–19.**
- Give the student **Spelling Sound Sheet 43.**
- Call out the sounds on **Spelling Cards 1–36** in random order. The student should echo each sound and name the letter or letters that make the sound as he/she writes the letter(s) on the spelling sound sheet.
- Have the student set the spelling sound sheet aside for use later in the lesson.

NEW LEARNING

"I'm going to say some words. Echo them back to me and listen for the sound that is the same at the end of each word."

- Point to your mouth as you say each word.

"Echo after me. Baffle." *baffle* ***"Ruffle."*** *ruffle* ***"Stifle."*** *stifle*

"What sound do you hear in the final position?" */fəl/*

"Look at these words and see what is making that sound."

- Write the following in a column on the chalkboard: baffle, ruffle, stifle.

"What is the same in all of these words that is making the /fəl/ sound?" *fle*

"That's right. Fle is making the /fəl/ sound."

"Listen and echo these words. Dimple." *dimple* ***"Apple."*** *apple* ***"Simple."*** *simple*

"What do you hear at the end of these words?" */pəl/*

"What do you think is making the /pəl/ sound/?"

- The student may or may not already know that it is *ple*.

"Look at these words and see what is making that sound."

- Write the following in a second column on the chalkboard: dimple, apple, simple.

"What is the same in all of these words that is making the /pəl/ sound?" *ple*

"Listen once more and echo these words. Bundle." *bundle* ***"Cradle."*** *cradle* ***"Fiddle."*** *fiddle*

"What do you hear on the end of these words?" */dəl/*

"What do you think is making the /dəl/ sound?"

"Look at these words and see what is making that sound."

- Write the following in a third column on the chalkboard: bundle, cradle, fiddle.

"What is the same in all of these words that is making the /dəl/ sound?" *dle*

"Does this remind you of something we learned yesterday?" *yes, final, stable syllable ble*

"These are all final, stable syllables, too."

"Why are they called final?" *they are in the final position*

"Why are they called syllables?" *they have their own vowel sounds*

"They are stable because they don't change. We can count on them having the /fəl/, /pəl/, or /bəl/ sound whenever we see them in the final position, even though they don't follow the rules we know."

"How do we code a final, stable syllable?" *put a bracket in front of it*

"We'll put a bracket in front of the final, stable syllable."

- Put brackets in all of the words on the chalkboard. Continue to code the words as you explain each step.

  "Then we mark out the e because it is silent, and we mark the accent on the syllable right before the bracket. The accent usually falls on the syllable before the bracket."

- Code the remaining vowels. The words should be coded as shown:

băf´[flé̸	dĭm´[plé̸	bŭn´[dlé̸
rŭf´[flé̸	ăp´[plé̸	cră̄´[dlé̸
stī´[flé̸	sĭm´[plé̸	fĭd´[dlé̸

  "Let's read these words."

- Have the student read the words and use them in sentences.
- Leave the words on the chalkboard for the remainder of the lesson.

New Deck Cards

- Pull **Spelling Card 36** from the Review Deck.
- Hold up **Letter Card 38.**

  "What do we call this?" *final, stable syllable fle*

- Hold up **Picture Card 46** but keep the picture covered with your hand (or the letter card).

  "I have a card with a picture on it that ends with the /fəl/ sound."

  "I am going to describe it to you. See if you can guess what the picture is. Remember, our new keyword ends with the /fəl/ sound."

  "This is something you would find on a girl's dress or blouse. It is usually at the edges to make the dress look fancier. Sometimes men wear them on shirts that go with tuxedos. Ladies who square dance might have rows and rows of them on their skirts. What do you think the picture is?" *ruffle*

- Show the student **Picture Card 46.**

  "What do you think we will say when we see this card?" *ruffle, /fəl/*

- Hold up **Letter Card 39.**

  "What do we call this?" *final, stable syllable ple*

- Hold up **Picture Card 47** but keep the picture covered with your hand (or the letter card).

  "I have a card with a picture on it that ends with the /pəl/ sound."

  "I am going to describe it to you. See if you can guess what the picture is."

  "This is something you would find in an office or school room. They are tiny metal things that fit inside a hand-operated or electric machine. They are used to hold stacks of papers together. What do you think the picture is?" *staple*

- Show the student **Picture Card 47.**

  "What do you think we will say when we see this card?" *staple, /pəl/*

  "Our third keyword has the /dəl/ sound at the end."

- Hold up **Letter Card 40.**

  "What do we call this?" *final, stable syllable dle*

  "This sack contains a clue to our new keyword. Don't look in the sack, but put your hand inside and see if you can feel what is inside the sack."

- Allow the student a chance to feel inside the sack.

  "I'm going to count to three. On three, whisper what you think is in the sack."

  "One, two, three." *candle*

  "Can you tell me the keyword for final, stable syllable dle?"

- Show the student **Picture Card 48.**
- **Note:** The final, stable syllables and their pictures are also shown in the Rule Book on page 22.

  "Find your spelling sound sheet. Put your finger by #37."

- Hold up **Spelling Card 36** so only you can see what is written.

  "Echo this sound: /fəl/." */fəl/*

  "How do we spell the /fəl/ sound in the final position?" *final, stable syllable fle*

- Write "fle" on the chalkboard.

  "Write your response on the line by #37."

  "How do we spell the /pəl/ sound in the final position?" *final, stable syllable ple*

  "How do we spell the /dəl/ sound in the final position?" *final, stable syllable dle*

  "Now you know how to spell all of these final, stable syllables."

- Check the spelling sound sheet for accuracy.
- **Note:** Add the new letter and picture cards to the Review Decks (and re-insert **Spelling Card 36**).

Lesson 57

BOARDWORK

"Let's practice coding some words like the ones you'll have on your worksheet."

"The rule charts are in your Rule Book if you need to look at them."

- Write the following sentence (without the coding marks) on the chalkboard. Ask the student to help you code it. The correct coding is as indicated:

  Brĭng thė noo´[dlės sō´ wē´ căn cook thĕm.

Worksheet

- The student should be seated where he/she can write comfortably.
- Give the student **Worksheet 57.** Make sure the student turns to the correct side.

"Today, let's spell with our new final, stable syllables."

"Before we start, let's practice with a word. Can you help me spell 'huddle'?"

- If the student spells the word with only one *d*, which is not uncommon, do not correct the spelling immediately. Instead, say the following:

"Let's code this word and see if it is spelled correctly."

- Code the word as shown: hū′[dlé̸.

"How will we read this word?"

- Read it as it is coded: hyōō′[dəl.

"Is that the word we wanted to spell?" *no*

- Point to the *u*.

"This vowel needs to be short. What needs to follow the 'u' to make it short?" *a consonant*

"What consonant should I use?"

- Let the student try to help. Read the word with each letter suggested until the student realizes that the consonant must be another *d*.

"Put your finger by #1. The first word is 'puddle.'"

"Unblend the first syllable with me." */p/ /ŭ/ (The student may hear the /d/ sound in the first syllable.)*

- Hold up one finger for each sound.

"The last syllable is /dəl/. Spell /dəl/." *final, stable syllable dle*

"Let's spell it. P … u … d … d … l … e."

"Now spell the word again and write the letters as you say them."

- Allow time for the student to do this.

"What word did you write?" *puddle*

- Repeat the procedure with #2 (ample), #3 (spindle), #4 (fable), and #5 (ripple).

"Now you're ready to code and read the words on your paper."

"Code the words by #6 through #10. After you have coded all the words, try to read them."

- Assist the student as necessary.

"Now read the word by #11. If you have trouble reading the word, code it. Then draw a line from the word to the picture it matches."

- Repeat with #12, #13, and #14.
- As the student works, provide help as needed. Help the student correct any incorrect answers. Then initial the worksheet in the space provided.

- Some time during the day, ask the student to read from the worksheet, a controlled reader, your basal reader, or other material of your choice.
- **Note:** Always make sure the worksheet is corrected before the student begins the homework. The worksheet serves as a guide to help complete the homework.

HOMEWORK

"Turn your paper over to the homework side."

"Do you know what to do on the homework paper?"

"Watch out for final, stable syllables. Always bracket them, mark out the silent e, and accent the syllable before the bracket."

- Discuss the homework pictures to make sure the student understands the word each one represents: #11 (candle), #12 (bubbles), #13 (broom), and #14 (table).

"When you finish your paper, I will check it for you and initial it in the space provided."

- Either now or later in the day, the student should complete the homework independently (if possible). Help the student correct any incorrect answers. Then initial the homework in the space provided.

READER

"We have a new sight word today."

- Show the student **Sight Word Card 20.**

"Can you tell me what this word is?"

"This word is 'does.' It doesn't follow our rules, so we must memorize it. How do we mark sight words since we can't code them?" *circle them*

"Can you use the word 'does' in a sentence?" *expect various answers*

- Help the student locate the word in the Irregular Spelling Booklet.

"We will add this card to our sight word deck."

"We have another new book today."

- Give the student **Reader 19 (*Jogging Josh*)** and some colored pencils.

"Can you tell me this book's title?" *Jogging Josh*

- Assist the student as necessary as he/she constructs the book.
- When the student finishes, staple or put a rubber band around the book's spine.
- If necessary, demonstrate how to separate the pages and check the page order.

"The title of this book is ________?" *Jogging Josh*

"I want you to read your book to yourself. When you are finished reading, color the pictures. Write your name on the book so I will know who colored it."

Lesson 57

"Keep your book handy because I will be asking you to read it for me."

- Some time during the day, have the student read the reader to you.
- Add **Sight Word Card 20** to the Sight Word Deck.
- If possible, take time to play the Kid Card games listed in Lesson 55.

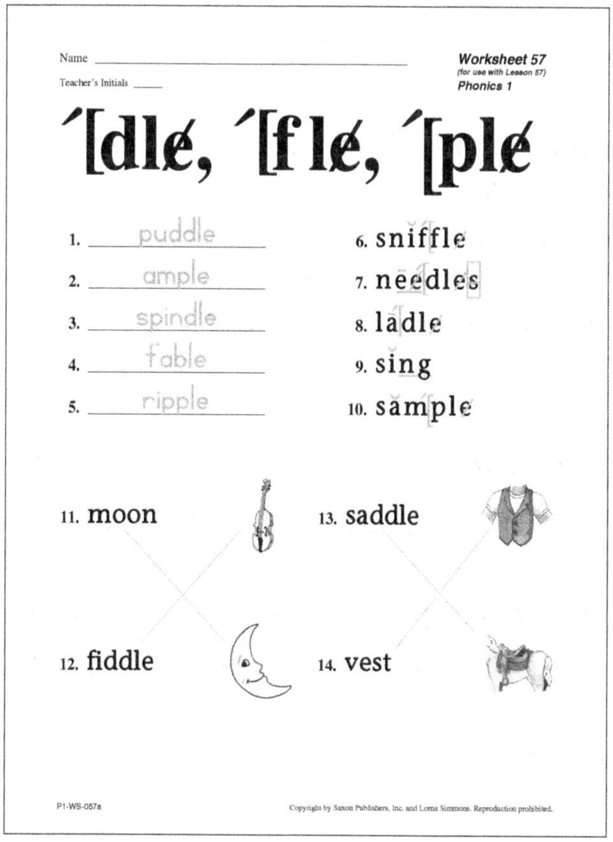
Name ______________________ **Worksheet 57**
(for use with Lesson 57)
Teacher's Initials ____ Phonics 1

´dle, ´fle, ´ple

1. puddle
2. ample
3. spindle
4. table
5. ripple
6. sniffle
7. needles
8. ladle
9. sing
10. sămple
11. moon
12. fiddle
13. saddle
14. vest

P1-WS-057a

Parent's Initials ____ **Homework 57**
(for use with Lesson 57)
Phonics 1

´dle, ´fle, ´ple

1. pŭddle
2. sămple
3. tŏng
4. noodles
5. dŭst
6. rŭffle
7. hăndle
8. lŏng
9. maple
10. bĕst
11. candle
12. bubbles
13. broom
14. table

Parents: Your child has been taught final, stable syllables -fle, -ple, and -dle.

P1-WS-057b

Lesson 57

LESSON 58 Final, Stable Syllables -*tle*, -*gle*

lesson preparation

materials

4 index cards (see *the night before*)

Review Decks

Letter Cards 41–42

bottle in a sack (see *the night before*)

Picture Cards 49–50

Sight Word Card 21

Worksheet 58

the night before

- Write the following words on index cards (one word per card): ask, big, can, dog. Write the words as large as possible.
- Put a bottle in a sack for the student to use to "discover" the new keyword.

ALPHABET ACTIVITY

- The student should be seated.

  "Today, let's try alphabetizing some words instead of letters. Since you can now alphabetize letters easily, this won't be too difficult."

- Place the four word cards (ask, big, can, dog) in the chalk tray (or anywhere else the student can see them). Deliberately place them in non-alphabetical order.

  "When we alphabetize words, we use the first letter of each word as the 'guide letter.' "

- Underline the first letter in each word.

  "Are the first letters of these words all different?" *yes*

  "So the first letter can be our guide letter. We can put them in order using just the first letters. It doesn't matter what the other letters in the words are."

  "We will recite the alphabet slowly. Each time we say a letter, we will quickly scan the guide letters in these words to see if the letter we are reciting is here and needs to be pulled."

  "You can say the alphabet with me. Let's start. 'A.' "

- Quickly scan the guide letters with your index finger.

"Is there an a?" *yes*

"Let's pull the word that has a as its guide letter and place it at the beginning of our new row of words. This row will be in alphabetical order when we finish."

- Move "ask" to a new location with enough room for the rearranged words.

"B."

- Quickly scan the cards again with your index finger.

"Is there a b?" *yes*

- Pull "big" and place it to the right of "ask."

"C."

"Is there a c?" *yes*

- Pull "can" and place it to the right of "big."

"D."

"Is there a d?" *yes*

- Pull "dog" and place it to the right of "can."

"All the cards have been used, so we can stop."

"Now our words should be in ABC, or alphabetical, order. We can quickly check them just like we did with letters to see if we are right."

- Quickly recite the alphabet from *a* to *d*, touching each new word in the sequence as you say it. The student should see that your hand will move progressively to the right if the words are in the correct order.
- Mix up the words and alphabetize them again.

"Alphabetizing words is easy once you know the guide letters."

PHONEMIC AWARENESS

- **Objective:** To manipulate sounds within words.

"Echo this word. Train." *train*

"What is the final sound in 'train'?" */n/*

"Can you say it without the final sound?" *tray*

- Repeat the procedure with the following words: pail...pay; beet...be; join...joy; soak...so; paint...pain; role...row.

REVIEW OF DECKS

- Show the student **Letter Cards 1–40** in random order. The student should name the letter on each letter card.
- Review **Affix Cards 1–3.**

- Show the student **Picture Cards 1–48** in random order. The student should name the keyword and sound for each picture card.
- Review **Sight Word Cards 1–20.**

"When we review the spelling cards today, I'll let you play 'teacher' again and I'll play 'student.' "

- Let the student call out the sounds on **Spelling Cards 1–36** in random order while you write the responses (on a scrap piece of paper, on the chalkboard, or with your finger).

NEW LEARNING

"I'm going to say some words. Echo them back to me and listen for the sound that is the same at the end of each word."

- Point to your mouth as you say each word.

"Echo after me. Beetle." *beetle* ***"Little."*** *little* ***"Rattle."*** *rattle*

"What sound do you hear in the final position?" */təl/*

"Look at these words and see what is making that sound."

- Write the following words in a column on the chalkboard: beetle, little, rattle.

"What is the same in all of these words that is making the /təl/ sound?" *tle*

"That's right. Tle is making the /təl/ sound."

"Listen and echo these words. Jingle." *jingle* ***"Struggle."*** *struggle* ***"Jiggle."*** *jiggle*

"What do you hear at the end of these words?" */gəl/*

"What is making the /gəl/ sound?"

- The student may or may not already know that it is *gle*.

"Look at these words and see what is making that sound."

- Write the following words in a second column on the chalkboard: jingle, struggle, jiggle.

"What is the same in all of these words that is making the /gəl/ sound?" *gle*

"What are these called?" *final, stable syllables*

"These are all final, stable syllables."

"Why are they called final?" *they are in the final position*

"Why are they called syllables?" *they have their own vowel sounds*

"They are stable because they don't change. We can count on them having the /təl/ or /gəl/ sound whenever we see them in the final position, even though they don't follow the rules we know."

"How do we code a final, stable syllable?" *put a bracket in front of it*

- Put brackets in all of the words on the chalkboard. Continue to code the words as you explain each step.

  "We mark out the e because it is silent. Then we mark the accent on the syllable right before the bracket. The accent usually falls on the syllable before the bracket."

- Code the remaining vowels. The words should be coded as shown:

bē̸e′[tle̸	jĭn′[gle̸
lĭt′[tle̸	strŭg′[gle̸
răt′[tle̸	jĭg′[gle̸

  "Let's read these words."

- Have the student read the words and use them in sentences.
- Leave the words on the chalkboard for the remainder of the lesson.

NEW DECK CARDS

- Pull **Spelling Card 36** from the Review Deck.
- Hold up **Letter Card 41.**

  "What do we call this?" *final, stable syllable tle*

  "This sack contains a clue to our new keyword. Don't look in the sack, but put your hand inside and see if you can feel what is inside the sack."

- Allow the student a chance to feel inside the sack.

  "Can you tell me the keyword for final, stable syllable tle?" *bottle*

- Show the student **Picture Card 49.**

  "What do you think we will say when we see this card?" *bottle, /təl/*

- Hold up **Letter Card 42.**

  "What do we call this?" *final, stable syllable gle*

- Hold up **Picture Card 50** but keep the picture covered with your hand (or the letter card).

  "I have a card with a picture on it that ends with the /gəl/ sound."

  "I am going to describe it to you. See if you can guess what the picture is."

  "This is a musical instrument that is used in the army to wake the soldiers. It looks and sounds like a trumpet. Remember, it ends with the /gəl/ sound. What do you think the picture is?" *bugle*

- Show the student **Picture Card 50.**

  "What do you think we will say when we see this card?" *bugle, /gəl/*

- **Note:** The final, stable syllables and their pictures are also shown in the Rule Book on page 22.
- Hold up **Spelling Card 36** so only you can see what is written.

  "Echo this sound: /təl/." */təl/*

"How do we spell the /təl/ sound in the final position?" *final, stable syllable tle*

"Echo this sound: /gəl/." */gəl/*

"How do we spell the /gəl/ sound in the final position?" *final, stable syllable gle*

"Now you know how to spell two more final, stable syllables."

- **Note:** Add the new letter and picture cards to the Review Decks (and re-insert **Spelling Card 36**).

BOARDWORK

"We have a new sight word today."

- Show the student **Sight Word Card 21.**

"Can you tell me what this word is?"

"This word is 'from.' It doesn't follow our rules, so we must memorize it. Can you use the word 'from' in a sentence?" *expect various answers*

- Help the student locate the word in the Irregular Spelling Booklet.

"We will add this card to our sight word deck."

"Let's practice coding some words like the ones you'll have on your worksheet."

"The rule charts are in your Rule Book if you need to look at them."

- Write the following sentence (without the coding marks) on the chalkboard. Ask the student to help you code it. The correct coding is as indicated:

The lĭt´[tle pĕt snāke wĭg´[gles (from) hĭs hōle.

- Add **Sight Word Card 21** to the Sight Word Deck.

Lesson 58

WORKSHEET

- The student should be seated where he/she can write comfortably.
- Give the student **Worksheet 58.** Make sure the student turns to the correct side.

"Today, let's spell with our new final, stable syllables."

"Before we start, let's practice with a word. Can you help me spell 'settle'?"

- The student may spell the word with only one *t*, which is not uncommon. (If the student spells the word correctly, praise him/her. Then quickly review the spelling of final, stable syllables and move to #1 on the worksheet.)

"Let's code this word and see if it is spelled correctly."

- Code the word as shown: sē´[tle.

"How will we read this word?"

- Read it as it is coded: see´[təl.

"Is this the word we wanted to spell?" *no*

- Point to the *e*.

"This vowel needs to be short. What needs to follow the e to make it short?" *a consonant*

"Which consonant should I use?"

- Let the student try to help. Read the word with each letter suggested until the student realizes that the consonant must be another *t*.

"Put your finger by #1. The first word is 'little.' "

"Unblend the first syllable with me." */l/ /ĭ/*

- Hold up one finger for each sound.

"The last syllable is /təl/. Spell /təl/." *final, stable syllable tle*

"Let's spell the whole word. L … i … t … t … l … e."

"Now spell the word again and write the letters as you say them."

- Allow time for the student to do this.

"What word did you write?" *little*

- Repeat the procedure with #2 (title), #3 (bugle), #4 (middle), and #5 (tumble).

"Now you're ready to code and read the words on your paper."

"Code the words by #6 through #10. After you have coded all the words, try to read them."

- Assist the student as necessary.

"Numbers 11 and 12 are questions about the paragraph just above them. If you find any words you cannot read, code them. Then see if you can answer the questions."

- As the student works, provide help as needed. Help the student correct any incorrect answers. Then initial the worksheet in the space provided.
- Some time during the day, ask the student to read from the worksheet, a controlled reader, your basal reader, or other material of your choice.
- **Note:** Always make sure the worksheet is corrected before the student begins the homework. The worksheet serves as a guide to help complete the homework.

HOMEWORK

"Turn your paper over to the homework side."

"Do you know what to do on the homework paper?"

"Watch for final, stable syllables and always bracket them. Then mark out the silent e, and accent the syllable before the bracket."

"When you finish your paper, I will check it for you and initial it in the space provided."

- Either now or later in the day, the student should complete the homework independently (if possible). Help the student correct any incorrect answers. Then initial the homework in the space provided.
- If possible, take time to play the Kid Card games listed in Lesson 55.

Name ______________________

Teacher's Initials ____

Worksheet 58
(for use with Lesson 58)
Phonics 1

´[tlé, ´[glé

1. little
2. title
3. bugle
4. middle
5. tumble
6. rĭddle
7. tăngle
8. wīde
9. brīdle
10. stāple

A little beetle bug fell in a puddle of mud. He tossed and struggled to free himself from the mud puddle. He struggled a long time. At last he was able to grab a twig.

11. What fell in the puddle? a beetle bug

12. What did he grab? a twig

P1-WS-058a

Parent's Initials ____

Homework 58
(for use with Lesson 58)
Phonics 1

´[tlé, ´[glé

1. băttle
2. prūne
3. kĕttle
4. tīme
5. stōne
6. ăngle
7. sĭngle
8. smīle
9. brīde
10. lāte

A beetle bug fell in a mud puddle. He grabbed a twig to free himself. The twig snapped in two and the end flipped up, hitting a rock. The beetle, gripping the end of the twig, was lifted from the puddle. He was safe at last.

11. What did the twig hit? a rock

12. What lifted the beetle from the puddle? the twig

Parents: Your child has been taught final, stable syllables -tle and -gle.

P1-WS-058b

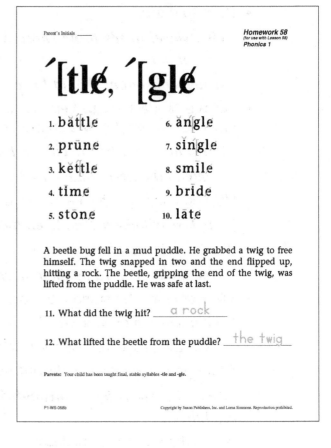

Lesson 59

Final, Stable Syllables *-cle, -zle, -sle, -kle*

lesson preparation

materials

Alphabet/Accent Deck (Section 1)
Review Decks
Spelling Sound Sheet 44
Worksheet 59
Reader 20 (*Mom's Cake*)
colored pencils

Alphabet Activity

- The student should be standing.

  "Let's work with the Alphabet/Accent Deck again today."

  "Last week, we pushed our chairs back and stood up every time we came to the accented syllable. Today, let's karate punch on the accented syllable."

- Show the student **Alphabet/Accent Card 1.**

  "On the first card, we will say 'A' standing still. Then we will punch when we say 'B.' "

- Have the student say "A" (softly), and then "B" (as he/she punches forward).
- Continue with **Alphabet/Accent Cards 2–25,** moving as quickly as possible.

Phonemic Awareness

- **Objective:** To manipulate sounds within words.

  "Echo this word. Great." *great*

  "What is the final sound in 'great'?" */t/*

  "Can you say it without the final sound?" *gray*

- Repeat the procedure with the following words: neat...knee; goat...go; treat...tree; float...flow; bloom...blue.

Review of Decks

- The student should be seated where he/she can write comfortably.
- Show the student **Letter Cards 1–42** in random order. The student should name the letter on each letter card.

- Review **Affix Cards 1–3.**
- Show the student **Picture Cards 1–50** in random order. The student should name the keyword and sound for each picture card.
- Review **Sight Word Cards 1–21.**
- Give the student **Spelling Sound Sheet 44.**
- Call out the sounds on **Spelling Cards 1–36** in random order. The student should echo each sound and name the letter or letters that make the sound as he/she writes the letter(s) on the spelling sound sheet.
- Check the student's response after each card.

NEW LEARNING

"I'm going to say some words. Echo them back to me and listen for the sound at the end of each word."

- Point to your mouth as you say each word.

"Echo after me. Uncle." *uncle* ***"Muzzle."*** *muzzle* ***"Hassle."*** *hassle* ***"Pickle."*** *pickle*

"What final, stable syllables do you hear in the final position?" */kəl/, /zəl/, /səl/*

"Look at these words and see what is making those sounds."

- Write the following on the chalkboard: uncle, muzzle, hassle, pickle.

"What are the final, stable syllables?" *cle, zle, sle, kle*

"That's right! These are all final, stable syllables."

"They are called final because ...?" *they are in the final position*

"They are called syllables because ...?" *they have their own vowel sounds*

"They are called stable because ...?" *they don't change; we can count on them having the /kəl/, /zəl/, or /səl/ sound whenever we see them in the final position, even though they don't follow the rules we know*

"How do we code a final, stable syllable?" *put a bracket in front of it*

- Put brackets in all of the words on the chalkboard. Continue to code the words as you explain each step.

"We mark out the e because it is silent. Then we mark the accent on the syllable right before the bracket. The accent usually falls on the syllable before the bracket."

- Code the remaining vowels. The words should be coded as shown:

ŭn´[cle̸ mŭz´[zle̸

hăs´[sle̸ pĭc´[kle̸

- **Note:** In the word "pickle," [kle is the final, stable syllable. We use the letter *c* to keep the vowel short because the letter *k* does not double in English words. (This resembles the rule for spelling with *ck* after a short vowel. The letters *ckle* usually follow short vowels, as in the words "pickle," "tickle," "speckle," "tackle," and "crackle.") As with twin consonants, crossing out the *c* is optional.

"Let's read these words."

- Have the student read the words and use them in sentences.

"I want you to look at another situation with final, stable syllables."

- Write the word "noodle" on the chalkboard.

"Sometimes you will see a digraph or a combination in the syllable before the final, stable syllable. All you do is bracket off the final, stable syllable, and code the digraph or combination just like you always do."

- Code the word: noo´[dlé.

"These types of words with final, stable syllables are easy to read but difficult to spell, so I'm going to show you a chart that lists some of these words so you can learn to spell them correctly."

"Get out your Irregular Spelling Booklet."

"Look in the table of contents and see if you can find the irregular spelling chart for final, stable syllables. What page is this chart on?" *page 30*

- Make sure the student is on the correct page.

"Let's look at the words on this chart."

- After allowing time for the student to examine the chart, discuss the definition and pronunciation of each word.

"Let's look at the word 'people.' "

- Write the word "people" on the chalkboard.

"This word is irregular because the letters 'eo' are making only one sound, /ē/, as in 'people.' You don't hear the letter o in this word, do you?"

"This word is easy to read, so we won't list it as a sight word, but it is listed in your Irregular Spelling Booklet in case you need to know how to spell it."

"Can you think of some more words with final, stable syllables that are not on this list?"

- If the student thinks of any appropriate words, write the words on the chalkboard and have the student add them to the chart.
- Leave the words on the chalkboard for the remainder of the lesson.

BOARDWORK

"Let's practice coding some words like the ones you'll have on your worksheet."

"The rule charts are in your Rule Book if you need to look at them."

- Write the following phrase and sentence (without the coding marks) on the chalkboard, one at a time. Ask the student to help you code them. The correct coding is as indicated:

brōké thė răt´[tlé

Thė pĭc´[klé (was) măsh[ed] ŏn thė stool.

- Have the student help you identify each of the items coded as a word, a phrase, or a sentence.

WORKSHEET

- The student should be seated where he/she can write comfortably.
- Give the student **Worksheet 59.** Make sure the student turns to the correct side.

  "Today, let's spell with our new final, stable syllables. Before we start, let's practice with a word."
- Write "kettle" on the chalkboard, but spell it "ketle."

  "Is this how we would spell the word 'kettle'?" *no*

  "What do I need to do with it?" *double the first t to make the vowel short*

  "Put your finger by #1. The first word is 'puzzle.'"

  "Unblend the first syllable with me." */p/ /ŭ/*
- Hold up one finger for each sound.

  "The last syllable is /zəl/. Spell /zəl/." *final, stable syllable zle*

  "Let's spell the whole word. P ... u ... z ... z ... l ... e."

  "Now spell the word again and write the letters as you say them."
- Allow time for the student to do this.

  "What word did you write?" *puzzle*
- Repeat the procedure with #2 (scribble), #3 (maple), #4 (smuggle), and #5 (paddle).

  "Now you're ready to code and read the words on your paper."

  "Code the words by #6 through #10. After you have coded all the words, try to read them."
- Assist the student as necessary.

  "Now read the word by #11. If you have trouble reading the word, code it. Then read the word and draw a line from the word to the picture it matches."
- Repeat with #12, #13, and #14.
- As the student works, provide help as needed. Help the student correct any incorrect answers. Then initial the worksheet in the space provided.
- Some time during the day, ask the student to read from the worksheet, a controlled reader, your basal reader, or other material of your choice.
- **Note:** Always make sure the worksheet is corrected before the student begins the homework. The worksheet serves as a guide to help complete the homework.

HOMEWORK

"Turn your paper over to the homework side."

"Do you know what to do on the homework paper?"

"Watch for final, stable syllables. Always bracket them. Mark out the silent e, and accent the syllable before the bracket."

- Discuss the homework pictures to make sure the student understands the word each one represents: #11 (pickles), #12 (juggle), #13 (apple), and #14 (bugle).

"When you finish your paper, I will check it for you and initial it in the space provided."

- Either now or later in the day, the student should complete the homework independently (if possible). Help the student correct any incorrect answers. Then initial the homework in the space provided.

READER

"We have another new book today."

- Give the student **Reader 20 (*Mom's Cake*)** and some colored pencils.

"Can you tell me this book's title?" *Mom's Cake*

- Assist the student as necessary as he/she constructs the book.
- When the student finishes, staple or put a rubber band around the book's spine.
- If necessary, demonstrate how to separate the pages and check the page order.

"The title of this book is __________?" *Mom's Cake*

"I want you to read your book to yourself. When you are finished reading, color the pictures. Write your name on the book so I will know who colored it."

"Keep your book handy because I will be asking you to read it for me."

- Some time during the day, have the student read the reader to you.
- If possible, take time to play the Kid Card games listed in Lesson 55. Try to see that the student is prepared for tomorrow's assessment.

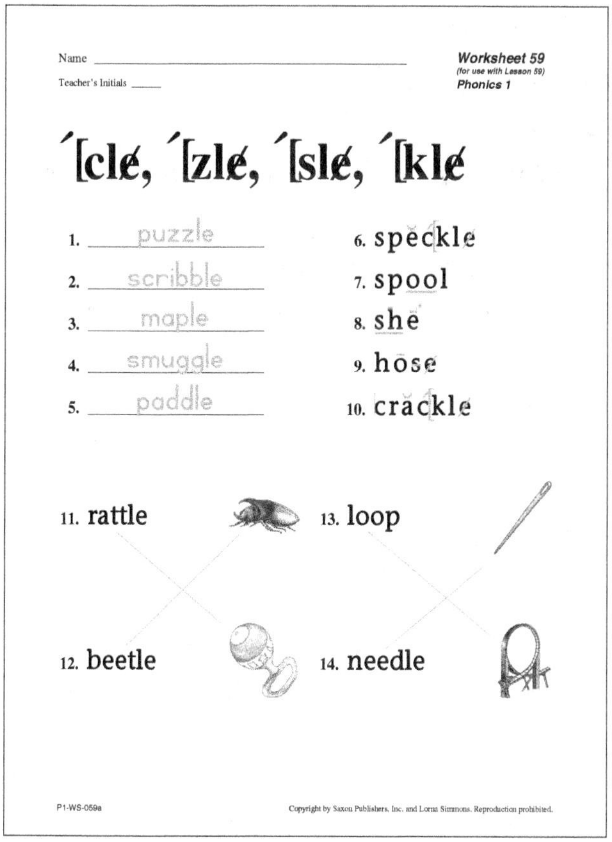
Name __________
Teacher's Initials ____
Worksheet 59
(for use with Lesson 59)
Phonics 1

´[cle, ´[zle, ´[sle, ´[kle

1. puzzle
2. scribble
3. maple
4. smuggle
5. paddle
6. speckle
7. spool
8. she
9. hose
10. crackle
11. rattle
12. beetle
13. loop
14. needle

P1-WS-059a
Copyright by Saxon Publishers, Inc. and Lorna Simmons. Reproduction prohibited.

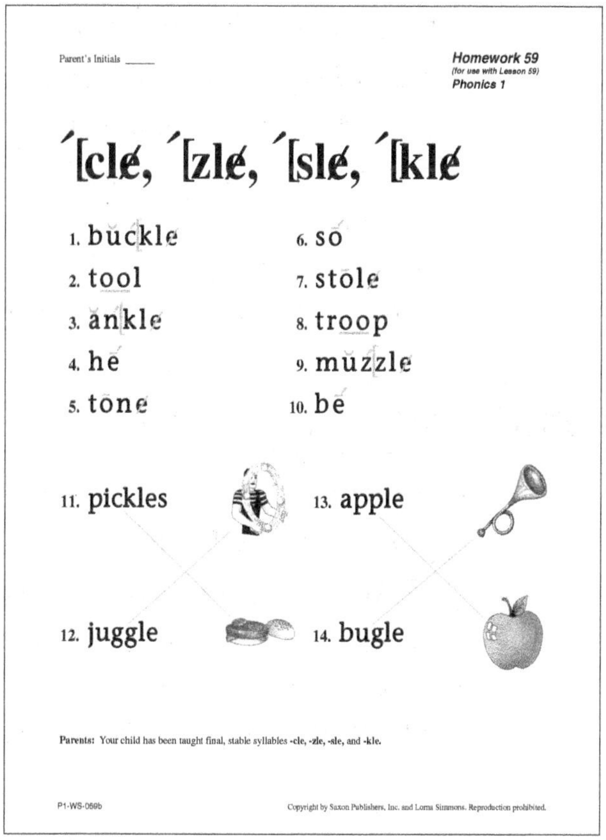
Parent's Initials ____
Homework 59
(for use with Lesson 59)
Phonics 1

´[cle, ´[zle, ´[sle, ´[kle

1. buckle
2. tool
3. ankle
4. he
5. tone
6. so
7. stole
8. troop
9. muzzle
10. be
11. pickles
12. juggle
13. apple
14. bugle

Parents: Your child has been taught final, stable syllables **-cle, -zle, -sle,** and **-kle.**

P1-WS-059b
Copyright by Saxon Publishers, Inc. and Lorna Simmons. Reproduction prohibited.

Lesson 59

LESSON 60 Assessment

lesson preparation

materials

Alphabet/Accent Deck (Section 1)

Review Decks

Assessment 11

Spelling Test 9

Assessment 11 Recording Form

Kid Cards

tokens

the night before

- Separate the Kid Cards marked "Lesson 60."

ALPHABET ACTIVITY

- The student should be standing.

  "Let's work with the Alphabet/Accent Deck again today."

  "Let's karate punch on the accented syllable again."

- Show the student **Alphabet/Accent Card 1.**

  "On the first card, we will say 'A' standing still. Then we will punch when we say 'B.' "

- Have the student say "A" (softly), and then "B" (as he/she punches forward).
- Continue with **Alphabet/Accent Cards 2–25,** moving as quickly as possible.

PHONEMIC AWARENESS

- **Objective:** To manipulate sounds within words.

  "Echo this word. Card." *card*

  "What is the final sound in 'card'?" */d/*

  "Can you say it without the final sound?" *car*

- Repeat the procedure with the following words: beat...bee; skeet...ski; seam... see; throat...throw; slope...slow.

REVIEW OF DECKS

- The student should be seated where he/she can write comfortably.
- Show the student **Letter Cards 1–42** in random order. The student should name the letter on each letter card.
- Review **Affix Cards 1–3.**
- Show the student **Picture Cards 1–50** in random order. The student should name the keyword and sound for each picture card.
- Review **Sight Word Cards 1–21.**

ASSESSMENT

- Have the student sit where he/she can write comfortably.
- Give the student **Assessment 11.**
- **Section I:**

  "Today we are going to write some words for our assessment."

  "I'm going to say a word. Write the letter that makes each sound in that word on the lines by #1."

  "Look at the rule charts if you need to."

  "Here's the first word: van."
- Repeat with the following words in the order shown: #2 (picnic), #3 (smell), #4 (joke), and #5 (glass).
- **Reminder:** While the student spells, be ready to point to appropriate rule charts as necessary.
- **Section II:**

  "Look at the letter by #6."

  "Find the picture of the keyword for this sound."

  "Draw a line from the letter to the keyword."
- Repeat with #7, #8, #9, and #10. Allow a few minutes for the student to work.
- The pictures (from top to bottom) are as follows: equal, vest, acorn, open, jet.
- **Section III:**

  "Put your finger on #11."

  "Code the words by #11 through #15."
- Allow a few minutes for the student to work.
- **Section IV:**

  "Look at #16."

  "How do you spell the /k/ sound in this situation?"
- Repeat with #17 and #18.

- **Section V:**

  "Read the paragraph. If you find any words you can't read, code them to help you figure them out. Then answer the questions by #19 and #20."
- **Reminder:** If the student absolutely cannot read the paragraph, read it to the student to see if he or she can answer the questions.

  "When you are finished, show your paper to me."
- This paper will be used during the oral portion of the assessment.

Spelling Test

- Give the student **Spelling Test 9.**
- Call out the following words (in the order shown). Sound them out, if necessary.

  #1 (spoke), #2 (like), #3 (wink), #4 (upset), #5 (plus), #6 (make), #7 (bake), #8 (admit), #9 (brushing), #10 (green), #11 (to), #12 (do)
- Grade and record the test in any manner that suits your needs.

Oral Assessment

- It is important to complete the oral assessment promptly (today, if possible) in order to identify any areas of weakness and begin remediation.
- Use the assessment and the following dialogue to complete the oral portion.
- **Section VI:**
- Point to the sight word by #21.

  "Read this sight word for me."
- Record the student's response by placing a check mark by each word he/she reads correctly.
- Repeat with #22 and #23.
- **Section VII:**
- Show the student the letter by #24.

  "Tell me the name of this letter and the sound it makes."
- Write the student's response on the adjacent line.
- Repeat with #25.

Assessment Evaluation

- Grade the assessment and record the results on **Assessment 11 Recording Form.** Check off the boxes to indicate mastery (i.e., the section was completed with 100% accuracy).
- **Reminder:** Try to give as many points as possible for work attempted. Do not grade the coding marks too severely. The most important coding marks to look for are breves, macrons, and syllable division lines.

- See the introductory material for detailed information regarding grading and recording procedures.
- Use the assessment results to identify those skills in which the student is weak. Practice those skills by playing Kid Card games.
- Add the Kid Cards marked "Lesson 60" to the existing decks. Listed below are games appropriate for remediation in selected areas. See "Games and Activities" for the directions for each game.
- **Section I:** Play "Spelling Deck Perfection," "Sound Scamper," "Spell Out #1," or have the student use the letter tiles to spell words you give from the Spelling Word List.
- **Section II:** Play "Keyword and Sound" or "Letter/Sound Identification."
- **Section III:** Play "Chalkboard Challenge."
- **Section IV:** Play "Spell Out #1." Use words that contain the /k/ sound.
- **Section V:** Either have the student read the controlled readers and then ask questions for comprehension, or play "Acting Out" with the green Kid Cards.
- **Section VI:** Play "At First Sight."
- **Section VII:** Play "Letter/Sound Identification."
- When the student seems more secure in areas that had previously proven difficult, retest him/her (in those areas only) and indicate on the recording form any sections the student has subsequently mastered.
- Try to help the student achieve mastery of all the sections before the next assessment.
- If the student is having difficulty with a particular skill, keep his or her practice activities at the most basic level so the chance of success is greater.

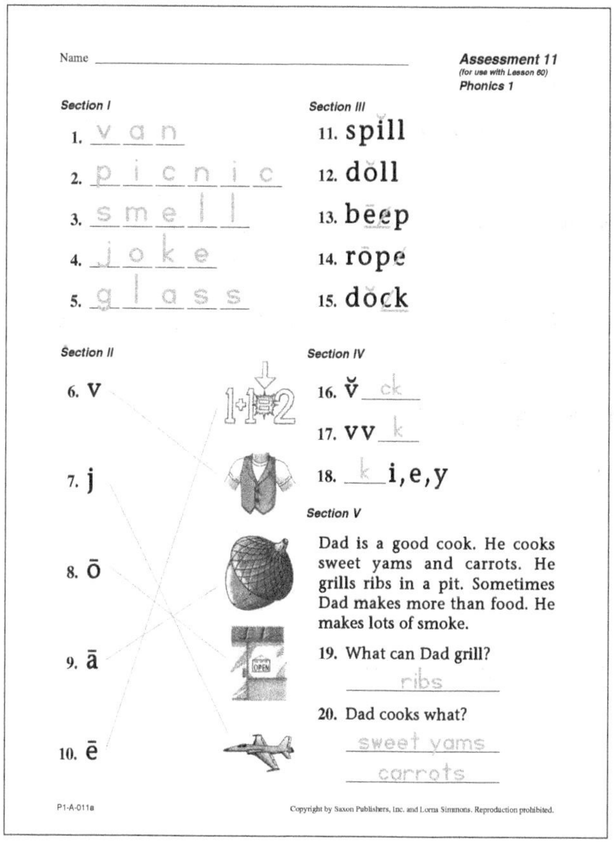
Name

Assessment 11
(for use with Lesson 60)
Phonics 1

Section I
1. van
2. picnic
3. smell
4. joke
5. glass

Section III
11. spill
12. doll
13. beep
14. rope
15. dock

Section II
6. v
7. j
8. ō
9. ā
10. ē

Section IV
16. v̆ ck
17. vv k
18. k i,e,y

Section V
Dad is a good cook. He cooks sweet yams and carrots. He grills ribs in a pit. Sometimes Dad makes more than food. He makes lots of smoke.

19. What can Dad grill?
ribs

20. Dad cooks what?
sweet yams
carrots

P1-A-011a

Copyright by Saxon Publishers, Inc. and Lorna Simmons. Reproduction prohibited.

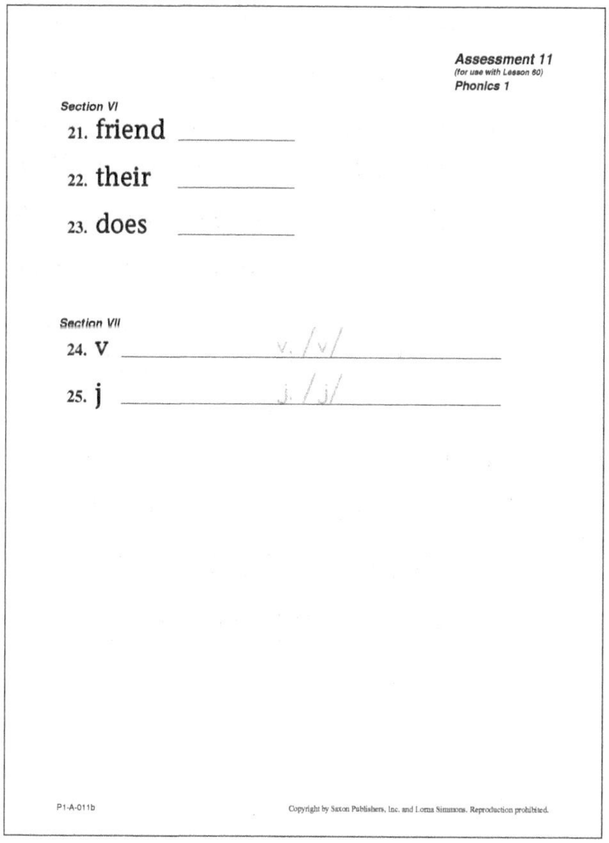
Assessment 11
(for use with Lesson 60)
Phonics 1

Section VI
21. friend
22. their
23. does

Section VII
24. v v, /v/
25. j j, /j/

P1-A-011b

Copyright by Saxon Publishers, Inc. and Lorna Simmons. Reproduction prohibited.

Lesson 60

LESSON 61 — Vowel ȳ′

lesson preparation

materials

container of letter tiles
Review Decks
Spelling Sound Sheet 45
Letter Card 43
Picture Card 51
Sight Word Card 22
Worksheet 61
Spelling List 10

new concepts

vowel *y*

ALPHABET ACTIVITY

- The student should be seated with the container of letter tiles.
- Give the following instructions one at a time, allowing time for the student to accomplish each task before giving the next instruction.

  "Take all of the letter tiles out of your container."

  "Flip all of the letters over so that you are looking at the lowercase letters. If they are flipped correctly, they will all be blue."

  "Before we start, let's say the alphabet together so it is fresh in our minds."
- Recite the alphabet with the student.

  "Now we're ready. See if you can put all of your letters in ABC order. If you need help, please ask me."
- If necessary, help the student alphabetize the letter tiles.
- When the student has finished, continue.

  "Point to the initial letter."

  "Point to the final letter."

  "Quickly pull down the vowels."
- Have the student replace the tiles in the container and put it away.

Phonemic Awareness

- **Objective:** To manipulate sounds within words.

  "Echo this word. Boast." *boast*

  "What is the final blend in 'boast'?" */st/*

  "Can you say it without the final blend?" *bō*

- Repeat the procedure with the following words: risk...rǐ; trust...trŭ; tusk...tŭ; toast...tō; best...bĕ.
- The word fragment that remains after dropping the blend does not have to be a complete word. It is more difficult, however, when only a fragment remains.

Review of Decks

- The student should be seated where he/she can write comfortably.
- Show the student **Letter Cards 1–42** in random order. The student should name the letter on each letter card.
- Review **Affix Cards 1–3.**
- Show the student **Picture Cards 1–50** in random order. The student should name the keyword and sound for each picture card.
- Review **Sight Word Cards 1–21.**
- Give the student **Spelling Sound Sheet 45.**
- Call out the sounds on **Spelling Cards 1–36** in random order. The student should echo each sound and name the letter or letters that make the sound as he/she writes the letter(s) on the spelling sound sheet.
- Have the student set the spelling sound sheet aside for use later in the lesson.

New Learning

"I'm going to say some words. Echo them back to me and listen for the sound that is the same in the final position of each word."

- Point to your mouth as you say each word.

  "Echo after me. Shy." *shy* ***"Try."*** *try* ***"Sky."*** *sky* ***"Reply."*** *reply*

  "What sound do you hear in the final position?" */ī/*

  "That's right. The sound you hear in the final position is /ī/."

  "Put your fingertips on the front of your neck and say /ī/. See if you feel any vibration."

  "Is this sound voiced or unvoiced?" *voiced*

  "Since /ī/ vibrates, it is a voiced sound."

- Write the following on the chalkboard: shy, try, sky, reply.

  "What letter do you see that might be making the /ī/ sound?" *y*
- If the student does not know the name of the letter, say it for him/her.

  "Do you see a vowel in any of these three words?"
- The student may or may not know that *y* can sometimes be a vowel.

  "We learned at the first of the year that every word must have a vowel. Sometimes y becomes a vowel. A long time ago, someone must have decided that English words didn't look right when they ended with an i. So they changed the i to a y. It has the same sound as i. You'll see it on the end of lots of words."

  "Let's put a dot over these y's to help us remember that these are vowel y's."
- Dot the *y*'s: shẏ, trẏ, skẏ, replẏ.

  "Is there a consonant after any of these y's?" *no*

  "Let's put macrons over them since they are not followed by consonants."
- Put macrons over the *y*'s: shȳ, trȳ, skȳ, replȳ.

  "Let's check the accent on these words."
- Help the student understand that the first three words ("shy," "try," and "sky") are accented because all words, even one-syllable words, have accents. When you pronounce the word "reply," exaggerate the accent on the second syllable.
- Accent the words to demonstrate: shȳ′, trȳ′, skȳ′, replȳ′.

  "Does the vowel y that says /ī/ appear in an accented syllable or an unaccented syllable?" *an accented syllable*

  "This follows our long vowel rule: 'An open, accented vowel is long; code it with a macron.' "

  "So, is this y a vowel or a consonant?" *a vowel*

  "Whenever you see a y at the end of a word, it will most likely be a vowel."
- **Note:** Don't be surprised if the student questions you about words that end with the letter *i*, such as "ski." Praise the student for being so observant. Explain that sometimes the English language takes words directly from other languages without changing the spelling. These words follow the rules of the languages from which they came and must therefore be taught as sight words. The word "ski" (derived from "skith") came into our language in the 19th century from the Norwegian language. The word "hi" is considered slang (which may or may not follow the rules).

New Deck Cards

- Pull **Spelling Card 7** from the Review Deck.
- Hold up **Letter Card 43.**

  "What is the special name of this letter?" *vowel y*
- Hold up **Picture Card 51** but keep the picture covered with your hand (or the letter card).

"I have a card with a picture on it that ends with the /ī/ sound."

"I'm going to describe it for you. See if you can guess what the picture is."

"This is something babies and young children do more often than grown people. We do this when we are upset or sad. Sometimes tears come out of our eyes when we do this. What do you think the picture is?" *cry*

"That's right. The keyword is 'cry' and the sound we have learned is /ī/."

▪ Show the student **Picture Card 51.**

"What will we say when we see this card?" *cry, /ī/*

"Find your spelling sound sheet. Put your finger on #37."

▪ Write the following on the chalkboard: i–e, i ‖ y.

▪ Hold up **Spelling Card 7** so only you can see what is written.

"Our new response to this card is 'i consonant e comma i final vowel y.'"

▪ Point to the written response on the chalkboard.

"Write the new response on the line by #37."

▪ Check the spelling sound sheet for accuracy.

▪ **Note:** Add the new letter and picture cards to the Review Decks (and re-insert **Spelling Card 7**).

BOARDWORK

"We have a new sight word today."

▪ Show the student **Sight Word Card 22.**

"This word is 'were.' It doesn't follow our rules, so we must memorize it. Circle it whenever you see it."

"Can you use the word 'were' in a sentence?" *expect various answers*

"Let's find the word on our sight word charts."

▪ Help the student locate the word in the Irregular Spelling Booklet.

"We will add this card to our sight word deck."

"Let's practice coding some words like the ones you'll have on your worksheet."

"The rule charts are in your Rule Book if you need to look at them."

▪ Write the following phrase and sentence (without the coding marks) on the chalkboard, one at a time. Ask the student to help you code them. The correct coding is as indicated:

dr̄y̆′|ing| w<u>oo</u>d

T̶h̶ĕ pĭc′[kl∉|s̶| (were) smă<u>sh</u>|ed| ŏn t̶h̶ĕ tā′[bl∉.

▪ Have the student determine whether each of the items coded is a word, a phrase, or a sentence.

▪ Add **Sight Word Card 22** to the Sight Word Deck.

WORKSHEET

- The student should be seated where he/she can write comfortably.
- Give the student **Worksheet 61.** Make sure the student turns to the correct side.

  "Today, let's spell with final y."

  "Put your finger by #1. The first word is 'sky.' "

  "Unblend 'sky' with me." */s/ /k/ /ī/*
- Hold up one finger for each sound.

  "Let's spell those sounds." *s ... k ... y*
- Point to a finger as the student spells each sound.

  "Look at Rule Chart 3. What do we use before a 'y'?" *k*

  "Now spell the word again and write the letters as you say them."
- Allow time for the student to do this.

  "What word did you write?" *sky*
- Repeat the procedure with #2 (cry) and #3 (shy).

  "Before we do #4, you need to know that when we add suffix -ing to a word that ends with y, we just add it to the root word."

  "Word #4 is 'frying.' What is the root word?" *fry*

  "Write that on the line by #4."
- Allow time for the student to spell the word.

  "Now add 'ing.' "
- Repeat with #5 (flying).

  "Now you're ready to code and read the words on your paper."

  "Code the words by #6 through #10. After you have coded all the words, try to read them."
- Assist the student as necessary.

  "Numbers 11 and 12 are questions about the paragraph just above them. If you find any words you can't read, code them. Then see if you can answer the questions."
- As the student works, provide help as needed. Help the student correct any incorrect answers. Then initial the worksheet in the space provided.
- Some time during the day, ask the student to read from the worksheet, a controlled reader, your basal reader, or other material of your choice.
- **Note:** Always make sure the worksheet is corrected before the student begins the homework. The worksheet serves as a guide to help complete the homework.

HOMEWORK

"Turn your paper over to the homework side."

"Do you know what to do on the homework paper?"

"Remember to look for vowel y. Watch out for final, stable syllables, too. Always bracket them, mark out the silent e, and accent the syllable before the bracket."

"When you finish your paper, I will check it for you and initial it in the space provided."

- Either now or later in the day, the student should complete the homework independently (if possible). Help the student correct any incorrect answers. Then initial the homework in the space provided.

SPELLING LIST

- Fold **Spelling List 10** in half lengthwise (with the printed side facing out).

  "Leave your paper just like I give it to you."

- Give the student **Spelling List 10,** folded with the blank lines facing up.

  "Let's spell some more words."

- Call out the following words (in the order shown). Sound them out, if necessary.

  #1 (state), #2 (those), #3 (rule), #4 (box), #5 (six), #6 (smile), #7 (fun), #8 (sweeping), #9 (boost), #10 (room), #11 (two), #12 (of)

  "Now unfold your paper and check your words."

- Check the student's work to see if he/she needs extra help with spelling.

  "I want you to practice these words. We'll have a spelling test in a few days."

- If possible, take time to play the Kid Card games listed in Lesson 60.

Name ______________________

Teacher's Initials ____

Worksheet 61
(for use with Lesson 61)
Phonics 1

ȳ

1. sky
2. cry
3. shy
4. frying
5. flying
6. trying
7. by
8. freckles
9. able
10. cooked

"Let's have a fish fry," said Mom. "We can invite Pam and Fred," she said. "I will get Ann to dry the spoons and plates. Jo can help set the table and I will get the fish."

11. What is Mom going to have? a fish fry

12. Who will help set the table? Jo

P1-WS-061a

Parent's Initials ____

Homework 61
(for use with Lesson 61)
Phonics 1

ȳ

1. fry
2. drying
3. buckles
4. ladle
5. stuffed
6. lifted
7. booked
8. sly
9. spry
10. tossed

The table was set with plates and napkins for the fish fry. Pam and Fred came with a cake. We ate until we were stuffed. We had fun!

11. What was on the table? plates and napkins

12. What did Pam and Fred bring? a cake

Parents: Your child has been taught the long sound of vowel y (as in *cry*); that vowel y is coded by placing a dot over it; and that the long sound of vowel y occurs in accented syllables only.

P1-WS-061b

Lesson 62

Vowel ẏ

lesson preparation

materials

Alphabet/Accent Deck (Section 1)

Review Decks

Spelling Sound Sheet 46

Affix Card 4

wrapped candy in a sack (see *the night before*)

Picture Card 52

Worksheet 62

Reader 21 (*The Tale of Rex Rabbit*)

colored pencils

the night before

- Put wrapped candy in a sack for the student to use to "discover" the new keyword. If the student has dietary restrictions, use the optional riddle.

Alphabet Activity

- The student should be seated.

  "Let's work with the Alphabet/Accent Deck again today."

  "A few days ago, we stood up and every time we came to the accented syllable, we got to karate punch. Today, let's say it in the normal way, but raise the pitch of our voices on the accented syllable."

- Show the student **Alphabet/Accent Card 1.**
- Have the student say "A" (softly), and then "B" (with a higher pitch).
- Continue with **Alphabet/Accent Cards 2–25,** moving as quickly as possible.

Phonemic Awareness

- **Objective:** To manipulate sounds within words.

  "Echo this word. Sly." *sly*

  "What is the initial blend in 'sly'?" */sl/*

"Can you say it without the initial blend?" /ī/

- Repeat the procedure with the following words: skim...ĭm; snake...āk~~e~~; flop...ŏp; drum...ŭm; trace...āc~~e~~.
- The word fragment that remains after dropping the blend does not have to be a complete word. It is more difficult, however, when only a fragment remains.

REVIEW OF DECKS

- The student should be seated where he/she can write comfortably.
- Show the student **Letter Cards 1–43** in random order. The student should name the letter on each letter card.
- Review **Affix Cards 1–3.**
- Show the student **Picture Cards 1–51** in random order. The student should name the keyword and sound for each picture card.
- Review **Sight Word Cards 1–22.**
- Give the student **Spelling Sound Sheet 46.**
- Call out the sounds on **Spelling Cards 1–36** in random order. The student should echo each sound and name the letter or letters that make the sound as he/she writes the letter(s) on the spelling sound sheet.
- Have the student set the spelling sound sheet aside for use later in the lesson.

NEW LEARNING

- **Note:** The sound of vowel *y* on the end of a word varies somewhat in different parts of the country. The following dialogue teaches the long *e* sound. If the sound is different where you live, make any adjustments you feel are necessary.

"I'm going to say some words. Echo them back to me and listen for the sound that is the same in the final position of each word."

- Point to your mouth as you say each word.

"Echo after me. Happy." *happy* ***"Silly."*** *silly* ***"Sandy."*** *sandy* ***"Dirty."*** *dirty*

"What sound do you hear in the final position?" /ē/

"That's right. The sound you hear in the final position is /ē/."

"Put your fingertips on the front of your neck and say /ē/. See if you feel any vibration."

"Is this sound voiced or unvoiced?" *voiced*

"Since /ē/ vibrates, it is a voiced sound."

- Write the following words on the chalkboard: happy, silly, sandy, dirty.

"What letter do you see that might be making the /ē/ sound?" *y*

"Is the y making a vowel sound or a consonant sound?" *vowel sound*

Lesson 62

"Let's put a dot over these y's to help us remember that these are vowel y's."

- Dot the *y*'s.

"Are there consonants after these y's?" *no*

"Let's check the accent on these words."

- Help the student see that in all of these words, the *y* says /ē/ in an unaccented syllable.

"Does the vowel y that says /ē/ appear in an accented syllable or an unaccented syllable?" *an unaccented syllable*

"In Great Britain, vowel y acts just like vowel i. When it is followed by a consonant, it says its short sound, /ĭ/, as in 'symbol.' "

- Write the word "symbol" on the chalkboard and code as indicated:

sy̆m′ | bȯl
v c | c v

- Point out the position of the *y*.

"This follows our short vowel rule: 'A vowel followed by a consonant is short; code it with a breve.' "

"When vowel y is open and accented, it says its long sound, /ī/, as in 'cry.' "

"When vowel y is open and unaccented, it usually says /ē/, as in 'penny.' "

- Write the word "penny" on the chalkboard and point out the position of the *y*.

"In some places, people pronounce this y with its short sound. They would say 'pennĭ.' But in most places, the unaccented vowel y is pronounced /ē/."

"Since neither a breve nor a macron will indicate that the y says /ē/, we will leave the vowel coding off and only put the dot."

- Some people put a tiny *e* above the vowel *y*. You may have a different idea. Anything that helps the student remember the /ē/ sound is acceptable.

"Remember, when you see 'y' at the end of a word, it will most likely be a vowel."

- Point to "sandy" and "dirty."

"These words are slightly different. If I cover the 'y' on 'sandy,' what do I have left?" *sand (a root word)*

"If I cover the 'y' in 'dirty', I also have a root word left."

"Y can also be a suffix at the end of a word."

"When 'y' is a suffix, it will be boxed, of course."

- Suffix -*y* has numerous meanings. They are easier to demonstrate than to explain:

full of	(dirty)
like	(homey)
having the quality of	(slangy)
somewhat	(sleepy)
apt to	(runny)

- Use whatever examples you like to help the student gain some understanding of the meanings of suffix *-y*, but remember that the most important thing is that he/she is able to read it.
- Show the student **Affix Card 4.**

  "We have a new affix card for suffix -y. We will add it to our review decks to help us remember that y can also be a suffix."
- Add **Affix Card 4** to the Affix Deck.

New Deck Cards

- Pull **Spelling Card 22** and **Letter Card 43** from the Review Decks.
- Show the student **Letter Card 43.**

  "What is the special name of this letter?" *vowel y*

  "I have another sack today. It contains a clue to our new keyword. Don't look in the sack, but put your hand inside and see if you can guess what it is. Keep in mind that the object in the sack ends with the /ē/ sound."
- Allow the student a chance to feel inside the sack.
- If candy is impractical, use the following riddle instead:

  "This is something most people really like to eat. It is usually very sweet. There are lots of different kinds, but none of them are very nutritious. If you eat too much, you can get a stomachache. What is the keyword?" *candy*

  "That's right. The keyword is 'candy' and the sound is /ē/."
- Show the student **Picture Card 52.**

  "What will we say when we see this card?" *candy, /ē/*

  "Find your spelling sound sheet. Put your finger on the line by #37."
- Hold up **Spelling Card 22** so only you can see what is written.

  "Echo this sound: /ē/." */ē/*

  "How have we been spelling the /ē/ sound?" *digraph ee comma e final digraph ee*
- Write "ee, e || ee, y" on the chalkboard. Point to it as you ask:

  "What will be our new response when I give you the /ē/ sound?" *digraph ee comma e final digraph ee comma vowel y*

  "Write your new response on line #37."
- **Note:** This will be the proper response to **Spelling Card 22** for the rest of the year.
- If you provided candy, allow the student to eat the candy when it is convenient.
- Check the spelling sound sheet for accuracy.
- **Note:** Add the new picture card to the Review Decks (and re-insert **Spelling Card 22** and **Letter Card 43**).

BOARDWORK

"Let's practice coding some words like the ones you'll have on your worksheet."

"The rule charts are in your Rule Book if you need to look at them."

- Write the following phrase and sentence (without the coding marks) on the chalkboard, one at a time. Ask the student to help you code them. The correct coding is as indicated:

dry̅′ trăsh′y wēeds

Hē′ ăcts līke å sĭl′ly fool.
vc | cv

- Have the student determine whether each of the items coded is a word, a phrase, or a sentence.

WORKSHEET

- The student should be seated where he/she can write comfortably.
- Give the student **Worksheet 62.** Make sure the student turns to the correct side.

"Today, all of the words we spell will have a final y."

"For now, we won't use y to spell the /ī/ or /ē/ sounds unless it's in the final position."

"Put your finger by #1. The first word is 'candy.' "

"Unblend 'candy' with me." */k/ /ă/ /n/ /d/ /ē/*

- Hold up one finger for each sound.

"Let's spell those sounds." *c ... a ... n ... d ... y*

- Point to each finger as the student spells a sound.

"Now spell the word again and write the letters as you say them."

- Allow time for the student to do this.

"What word did you write?" *candy*

- Repeat the procedure with #2 (fifty), #3 (crispy), #4 (mushy), and #5 (sleepy).

"Now you're ready to code and read the words on your paper."

"Code the words by #6 through #10. After you have coded all the words, try to read them."

- Assist the student as necessary.

"Now read the word by #11. If you have trouble reading the word, code it. Then draw a line from the word to the picture it matches."

- Repeat with #12, #13, and #14.
- As the student works, provide help as needed. Help the student correct any incorrect answers. Then initial the worksheet in the space provided.

Lesson 62

- Some time during the day, ask the student to read from the worksheet, a controlled reader, your basal reader, or other material of your choice.
- **Note:** Always make sure the worksheet is corrected before the student begins the homework. The worksheet serves as a guide to help complete the homework

HOMEWORK

"Turn your paper over to the homework side."

"Do you know what to do on the homework paper?"

"Be sure to look for vowel y, digraphs, suffixes, and final, stable syllables."

- Discuss the homework pictures to make sure the student understands the word each one represents: #11 (messy), #12 (candy), #13 (cry), and #14 (puzzle).

"When you finish your paper, I will check it for you and initial it in the space provided."

- Either now or later in the day, the student should complete the homework independently (if possible). Help the student correct any incorrect answers. Then initial the homework in the space provided.

READER

"We have another new book today."

- Give the student **Reader 21 (*The Tale of Rex Rabbit*)** and some colored pencils.

"Can you tell me this book's title?" *The Tale of Rex Rabbit*

- Assist the student as necessary as he/she constructs the book.
- When the student finishes, staple or put a rubber band around the book's spine.
- If necessary, demonstrate how to separate the pages and check the page order.

"The title of this book is __________?" *The Tale of Rex Rabbit*

"I want you to read your book to yourself. When you are finished reading, color the pictures. Write your name on the book so I will know who colored it."

"Keep your book handy because I will be asking you to read it for me."

- Some time during the day, have the student read the reader to you.
- If possible, take time to play the Kid Card games listed in Lesson 60.

Name ______________________ **Worksheet 62** *(for use with Lesson 62)* **Phonics 1**

Teacher's Initials _____

ẏ or -[y]

1. candy
2. fifty
3. crispy
4. mushy
5. sleepy
6. fishy
7. needy
8. silly
9. sty
10. hike

11. puppy
12. fly
13. buckle
14. flute

P1-WS-062a

Parent's Initials _____ **Homework 62** *(for use with Lesson 62)* **Phonics 1**

ẏ or -[y]

1. pride
2. pine
3. sandy
4. beefy
5. sly
6. my
7. mole
8. Rome
9. guppy
10. lumpy

11. messy  13. cry 

12. candy  14. puzzle 

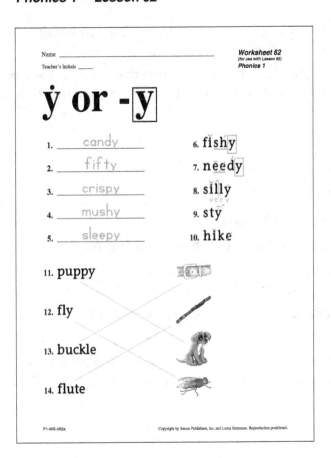

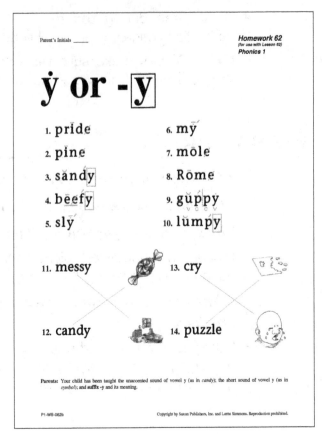

Parents: Your child has been taught the unaccented sound of vowel y (as in *candy*); the short sound of vowel y (as in *symbol*); and **suffix -y** and its meaning.

P1-WS-062b

LESSON 63 Combination *er*

lesson preparation

materials

6 index cards (see *the night before*)

Review Decks

Spelling Sound Sheet 47

tokens or colored pencil

Letter Card 44

Picture Card 53

Spelling Card 37

Sight Word Cards 23–24

Worksheet 63

new concepts

combination

the night before

- Write the following words on index cards (one word per card): bird, duck, egg, kiss, lamp, nut. Write the words as large as possible.

ALPHABET ACTIVITY

- The student should be seated.

  "Let's try alphabetizing some words again today."

- Place the six word cards (bird, duck, egg, kiss, lamp, nut) in the chalk tray (or anywhere else the student can see them). Deliberately place them in non-alphabetical order.

  "When we alphabetize words, we use the first letter of each word as the 'guide letter.' "

- Underline the first letter in each word.

  "Are the first letters of these words all different?" *yes*

  "So the first letter can be our guide letter. We can put these words in order using just the first letters. It doesn't matter what the other letters in the words are."

  "We will recite the alphabet slowly. Each time we say a letter, we will quickly scan the guide letters in these words to see if the letter we are reciting is here and needs to be pulled."

  "You can say the alphabet with me. Let's start. 'A.' "

- Quickly scan the guide letters with your index finger.

  "Is there an a?" *no*

  "B."

- Quickly scan the cards again with your index finger.

  "Is there a b?" *yes*

  "Let's pull the word that has b as its guide letter and place it at the beginning of our new row of words. This row will be in alphabetical order when we finish."

- Move "bird" to the new location with enough room for the rearranged words.

  "C."

  "Is there a c?" *no*

  "D."

  "Is there a d?" *yes*

- Pull "duck" and place it to the right of "bird."

  "E."

  "Is there an e?" *yes*

- Pull "egg" and place it to the right of "duck."
- Continue with the letters *f* through *n*, pulling "kiss," "lamp," and "nut" accordingly.

  "All the cards have been used, so we can stop."

  "Now our words should be in ABC, or alphabetical, order. We can quickly check them just like we did with letters only to see if we are right."

- Quickly recite the alphabet from *a* to *n*, touching each new word in the sequence as you say it. The student should see that your hand will move progressively to the right if the words are in the correct order.
- Mix up the words and alphabetize them again.

  "Alphabetizing words is easy once you know the guide letters."

Phonemic Awareness

- **Objective:** To manipulate sounds within words.

  "Echo this blend: /st/." */st/*

  "Echo this blend: /ŏp/." */ŏp/*

  "Now put /st/ with /ŏp/ and tell me the word." *stop*

- Repeat the procedure with the following words:

  /sk/ + /ē/ = ski
  /sl/ + /ēp/ = sleep
  /fl/ + /ī t/ = flight
  /tw/ + /ĭst/ = twist

- Continue with additional blends/words, if desired.

Review of Decks

- Seat the student at a table or a desk.
- Show the student **Letter Cards 1–43** in random order. The student should name the letter on each letter card.
- Review **Affix Cards 1–4.**
- Show the student **Picture Cards 1–52** in random order. The student should name the keyword and sound for each picture card.
- Review **Sight Word Cards 1–22.**
- Give the student **Spelling Sound Sheet 47** and at least 12 tokens (or a colored pencil).

"Let's play Bingo!"

"When I call out the spelling sounds today, I want you to put a token on (or draw a big X in) the space that spells that sound."

"When you have covered (or X'ed out) all of the letters on one line, either up and down, across, or from corner to corner, call out Bingo!"

"Don't forget to refer to your rule charts if you need to."

"Are you ready?"

"Cover (or X out) the letters that spell the final sound in 'stumble.' " *ble*

"Cover (or X out) the letters that spell the final sound in 'save.' " *ve*

"Cover (or X out) the letters that spell the vowel sound in 'spoon.' " *oo*

"Cover (or X out) the letters that spell the final sound in 'brittle.' " *tle*

"Cover (or X out) the letters that spell the initial sound in 'shake.' " *sh*

"Cover (or X out) the letter that spells the final sound in 'fry.' " *ȳ*

"Cover (or X out) the letter that spells the initial sound in 'jiggle.' " *j*

"Cover (or X out) the letters that spell the vowel sound in 'tame.' " *a–e*

"Cover (or X out) the letters that spell the final sound in 'spangle.' " *gle*

"Cover (or X out) the letter that spells the final sound in 'plastic.' " *c*

"Cover (or X out) the letters that spell the final sound in 'bundle.' " *dle*

- The student should Bingo by the time all the sounds have been called out.
- Collect the tokens (or colored pencil) and the spelling sound sheet. If you used tokens and the spelling sound sheet is unmarked, keep it available for practice.

New Learning

"I'm going to say some words. Echo them back to me and listen for the sound that is the same in each word."

- Point to your mouth as you say each word.

"Echo after me. Her." *her* ***"Fern."*** *fern* ***"Tern."*** *tern*

"What sound do you hear that is the same in each word?" */er/*

"That's right. The sound you hear in these words is /er/."

"Put your fingertips on the front of your neck and say /er/. See if you feel any vibration."

"Is this sound voiced or unvoiced?" *voiced*

"Since /er/ vibrates, it is a voiced sound."

- Write the following words on the chalkboard: her, fern, tern.

"What do you see that might be making the /er/ sound?" *er*

"There is an 'er' in all of these words, so we can see that the letters 'er' must be making the /er/ sound."

"Let's try coding these words."

"A vowel followed by a consonant is __________?" *short; code it with a breve*

- Put a breve on the *e* in "her."

"Let's read this with a short e."

- Pronounce the word as "hair."

"Is this word 'hair'?" *no*

"You're right. This word isn't 'hair,' but 'her.' This is something new."

"Er is a combination. A combination is two letters that come together and make an unexpected sound. We expect this e to say /ĕ/, as in 'egg,' but it doesn't. It says /er/, as in 'her.'"

"Combination er makes the sound /er/, as in 'her,' not the /r/ sound, as in 'rat.'"

"We code a combination by drawing an arc underneath it, like this."

- Put an arc under the *er*: her.
- Code and read the remaining words with the student: fern, tern.

New Deck Cards

- Hold up **Letter Card 44.**

"What do we call this?" *combination er*

- Hold up **Picture Card 53** but keep the picture covered with your hand (or the letter card).

"I have a card with a picture on it that ends with the /er/ sound."

"I am going to describe it for you. See if you can guess what the picture is."

"This is something you might use on toast. It is usually stored in the refrigerator. It is almost pure fat and comes from a cow. What do you think the picture is?" *butter*

"That's right. The keyword is 'butter' and the sound we have learned is /er/."

- Show the student **Picture Card 53.**

  "The word 'butter' helps us remember the /er/ sound since it contains that sound."

- **Note:** The combination and its picture are also shown in the Rule Book on page 22.
- Hold up **Spelling Card 37** so only you can see what is written. Follow the instructions on the card. Have the student write the response on the desk or table top with his/her finger.
- **Note:** Add the new letter, picture, and spelling cards to the Review Decks.

BOARDWORK

"We have some new sight words today."

- Show the student **Sight Word Cards 23** and **24.**

  "These words are 'again' and 'against.' They don't follow our rules. We must memorize them. Circle them when you see them."

- Help the student locate the words in the Irregular Spelling Booklet.

  "Can you use these words in sentences?" *expect various answers*

  "We will add these cards to our sight word deck."

  "Let's practice coding some words like the ones you'll have on your worksheet."

  "The rule charts are in your Rule Book if you need to look at them."

- Write the following sentences (without the coding marks) on the chalkboard, one at a time. Ask the student to help you code them. The correct coding is as indicated:

  The greed′y lĭt′tle măn bŭt′ter|ed his mŭf′fĭn|s.
  (VC | CV in but|ter and muf|fins)

  Tĕr′ry ĭs fry′ing ĭn bŭt′ter.
  (VC | CV in Ter|ry and but|ter)

  "We have a special situation in the last sentence."

- Point to the name "Terry."

  "This is a name, but it's not 'T-/er/-ry' (rhymes with 'worry'). When er is followed by another r, it is not a combination. The e is coded short and says /ĕ/. This name is 'Terry' (pronounced to rhyme with 'berry')."

- Have the student determine whether each of the items coded is a word, a phrase, or a sentence.
- Add **Sight Word Cards 23** and **24** to the Sight Word Deck.

Lesson 63

WORKSHEET

- The student should be seated where he/she can write comfortably.
- Give the student **Worksheet 63.** Make sure the student turns to the correct side.

  "Today, let's spell with the /er/ sound using combination er."

  "Combination er is used for spelling in all three positions of a word: initial, medial, or final."

  "Put your finger by #1. The first word is 'her.' "

  "Unblend 'her' with me." */h/ /er/*
- Hold up one finger for each sound.

  "Let's spell those sounds." *h … combination er*
- Point to a finger as the student spells a sound.

  "Now spell the word again and write the letters as you say them."
- Allow time for the student to do this.

  "What word did you write?" *her*
- Repeat the procedure with #2 (serve), #3 (verb), #4 (clerk), and #5 (shelter).

  "Now you're ready to code and read the words on your paper."

  "Code the words by #6 through #10. After you have coded all the words, try to read them."
- Assist the student as necessary.

  "Numbers 11 and 12 are questions about the paragraph just above them. If you find any words you can't read, code them. Then see if you can answer the questions."
- As the student works, provide help as needed. Help the student correct any incorrect answers. Then initial the worksheet in the space provided.
- Some time during the day, ask the student to read from the worksheet, a controlled reader, your basal reader, or other material of your choice.
- **Note:** Always make sure the worksheet is corrected before the student begins the homework. The worksheet serves as a guide to help complete the homework.

HOMEWORK

"Turn your paper over to the homework side."

"Do you know what to do on the homework paper?"

"Watch for suffixes and final, stable syllables and code them first. Also, watch for combination er, digraphs, and words with a 'vccv' pattern that need to be divided."

"When you finish your paper, I will check it for you and initial it in the space provided."

- Either now or later in the day, the student should complete the homework independently (if possible). Help the student correct any incorrect answers. Then initial the homework in the space provided.
- If possible, take time to play the Kid Card games listed in Lesson 60.

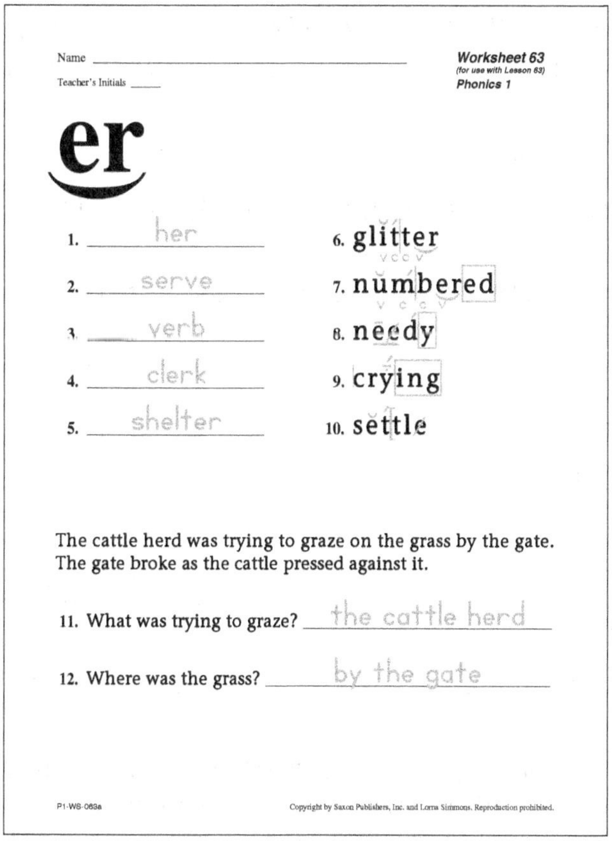

Name ______________

Teacher's Initials ____

Worksheet 63
(for use with Lesson 63)
Phonics 1

er

1. her
2. serve
3. verb
4. clerk
5. shelter
6. glitter
7. numbered
8. needy
9. crying
10. settle

The cattle herd was trying to graze on the grass by the gate. The gate broke as the cattle pressed against it.

11. What was trying to graze? the cattle herd

12. Where was the grass? by the gate

P1-WS-063a

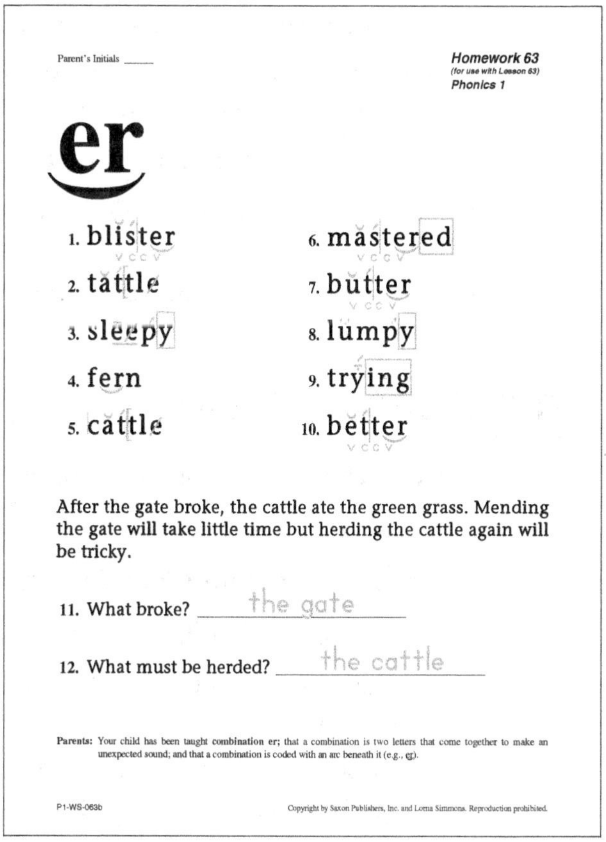

Parent's Initials ____

Homework 63
(for use with Lesson 63)
Phonics 1

er

1. blister
2. tattle
3. sleepy
4. fern
5. cattle
6. mastered
7. butter
8. lumpy
9. trying
10. better

After the gate broke, the cattle ate the green grass. Mending the gate will take little time but herding the cattle again will be tricky.

11. What broke? the gate

12. What must be herded? the cattle

Parents: Your child has been taught **combination er;** that a combination is two letters that come together to make an unexpected sound; and that a combination is coded with an arc beneath it (e.g., er).

P1-WS-063b

Lesson 63

LESSON 64 — Trigraph *igh*

lesson preparation

materials	***new concepts***
Alphabet/Accent Deck (Section 1)	trigraph
Review Decks	
Spelling Sound Sheet 48	
Letter Card 45	
Picture Card 54	
Worksheet 64	
Sight Word Card 25	
Reader 22 (*What Will Uncle Dave Make?*)	
colored pencils	

ALPHABET ACTIVITY

"Let's work with the Alphabet/Accent Deck again today."

"Let's try something different when we say the accented syllable. Let's stand up. Start with your arms at your sides. When you say the accented syllable, raise your arms high over your head."

- Show the student **Alphabet/Accent Card 1.**
- Have the student say "A" (with arms down), and then "B" (with arms raised overhead).
- Continue with **Alphabet/Accent Cards 2–25,** moving as quickly as possible.

PHONEMIC AWARENESS

- **Objective:** To manipulate sounds within words.

  "Echo this word. Blue." *blue*

  "What is the initial blend in 'blue'?" */bl/*

  "Can you say it without the initial blend?" */o͞o/*

- Repeat the procedure with the following words: stick...ĭck; plan...ăn; frog...ŏg; green...een; slice...īce.
- The word fragment that remains after dropping the blend does not have to be a complete word. It is more difficult, however, when only a fragment remains.

Review of Decks

- The student should be seated where he/she can write comfortably.
- Show the student **Letter Cards 1–44** in random order. The student should name the letter on each letter card.
- Review **Affix Cards 1–4.**
- Show the student **Picture Cards 1–53** in random order. The student should name the keyword and sound for each picture card.
- Review **Sight Word Cards 1–24.**
- Give the student **Spelling Sound Sheet 48.**
- Call out the sounds on **Spelling Cards 1–37** in random order. The student should echo each sound and name the letter or letters that make the sound as he/she writes the letter(s) on the spelling sound sheet.
- Check the student's response after each card.

New Learning

"I'm going to say some words to you. Echo them back to me and listen for the sound that is the same in each word."

- Point to your mouth as you say each word.

"Echo after me. Night." *night* ***"Thigh."*** *thigh* ***"Bright."*** *bright*

"What sound do you hear that is the same in all of these words?" */ī/*

"That's right. The sound you hear in all of these words is /ī/."

"Put your fingertips on the front of your neck and say /ī/. See if you feel any vibration."

"Is this sound voiced or unvoiced?" *voiced*

"Since /ī/ vibrates, it is a voiced sound."

- Write the following on the chalkboard: night, thigh, bright.

"What do you see that might be making the /ī/ sound?" *igh*

"There is an igh in all of these words, so we can see that the letters igh are making the /ī/ sound."

"How many sounds do you hear?" *one*

"How many letters are making the /ī/ sound?" *three*

"We call three letters that come together to make one sound a 'trigraph.' "

- Demonstrate three fingers coming together, two dropping to leave one.

"So 'igh' will be called 'trigraph igh.' Does the word 'trigraph' remind you of another word we have learned?" *digraph*

"That's right. A digraph is made when two letters come together. A trigraph uses three letters, just like a tricycle has three wheels."

"Since a trigraph is similar to a digraph, do you want to guess how we code a trigraph?" *draw a line underneath the three letters*

"Very good! We are going to draw a line underneath the three letters of the trigraph, just as we do under the two letters of a digraph."

"Can you hear the g and the h?" *no*

"How should we code them?" *mark them out because they are silent*

"How should we code the i?" *with a macron*

"Does this trigraph make a vowel sound or a consonant sound?" *vowel sound*

New Deck Cards

- Hold up **Letter Card 45.**

  "What do we call this?" *trigraph igh*

- Hold up **Picture Card 54** but keep the picture covered with your hand (or the letter card).

  "I have a card with a picture on it that contains the /ī/ sound in the middle."

  "I am going to describe it for you. See if you can guess what the picture is."

  "This is found everywhere in the world, inside and outside. It can be very bright or very soft, natural or electric. Usually you turn it off in your bedroom before you go to sleep at night. What do you think the picture is?" *light*

- **Alternate clue:** Tell the student that he/she is to sit very still while you change something in the room. Turn the lights off and then on again. Ask the student what changed.

  "That's right. The keyword is 'light' and the sound we have learned is /ī/."

- Show the student **Picture Card 54.**

  "The word 'light' helps us remember the /ī/ sound spelled with trigraph igh."

- **Note:** The trigraph and its picture are also shown in the Rule Book on page 22.

  " 'Igh' doesn't follow our rules for spelling, so we will not add that response to our spelling card for the /ī/ sound."

- **Note:** Add the new letter and picture cards to the Review Decks.

Boardwork

"Let's practice coding some words like the ones you'll have on your worksheet."

"The rule charts are in your Rule Book if you need to look at them."

- Write the following word and phrases (without the coding marks) on the chalkboard, one at a time. Ask the student to help you code them. The correct coding is as indicated:

$$s\breve{u}m´|m\,\underline{er}\;n\overline{i\cancel{gh}}t|s$$
$$\mathbf{v\;\;c}\;|\;\mathbf{c\;\;v}$$

$$st\overline{i}´[fl\cancel{e}$$

$$\mathring{a}\;m\breve{i}s|t\overline{a}ke´\;\breve{i}n\;t\breve{e}ll´|\boxed{ing}\;\cancel{th}\mathring{e}\;r\breve{i}d´[dl\cancel{e}$$
$$\mathbf{vc|c\,v}$$

- Have the student determine whether each of the items coded is a word, a phrase, or a sentence.

WORKSHEET

- The student should be seated where he/she can write comfortably.

- Give the student **Worksheet 64.** Make sure the student turns to the correct side.

"Today, let's spell with the /ī/ sound using trigraph igh."

"You'll find trigraph igh only in the medial or final position. 'Igh' doesn't follow our rules for spelling, but there are lots of words spelled with it. One thing to remember when spelling words containing the /ī/ sound is that when /ī/ is followed by the /t/ sound, as in 'light,' 'fight,' or 'right,' it will often be spelled with trigraph igh."

"Because of this, there is a list of these words in your Irregular Spelling Booklet. Get out your booklet and turn to page 10."

"Look at the 'igh' words at the bottom of the page. These will have to be memorized. For now, you can refer to this list any time you're spelling."

- Allow a moment for the student to examine the words; then have the student put the booklet away.

"Now see if you can write the words I'm about to give you. They all contain trigraph igh."

"Put your finger by #1. The first word is 'right.' "

"Unblend 'right' with me." /r/ /ī/ /t/

- Hold up one finger for each sound.

"Let's spell those sounds." *r ... trigraph igh ... t*

- Point to a finger as the student spells each sound.

"Now spell the word again and write the letters as you say them. Remember, when you write the words, you will have three letters making the medial /ī/ sound."

- Allow time for the student to do this.

"What word did you write?" *right*

- Repeat the procedure with #2 (fight), #3 (high), #4 (night), and #5 (might).

"Now you're ready to code and read the words on your paper."

"Code the words by #6 through #10. After you have coded all the words, try to read them."

- Assist the student as necessary.

"Now read the word by #11. If you have trouble reading the word, code it. Then draw a line from the word to the picture it matches."

- Repeat with #12, #13, and #14.
- As the student works, provide help as needed. Help the student correct any incorrect answers. Then initial the worksheet in the space provided.
- Some time during the day, ask the student to read from the worksheet, a controlled reader, your basal reader, or other material of your choice.
- **Note:** Always make sure the worksheet is corrected before the student begins the homework. The worksheet serves as a guide to help complete the homework.

HOMEWORK

"Turn your paper over to the homework side."

"Do you know what to do on the homework paper?"

"Be sure to look for vowel y, digraphs, suffixes, and final, stable syllables."

- Discuss the homework pictures to make sure the student understands the word each one represents: #11 (light), #12 (fingers), #13 (slippers), and #14 (fish).

"When you finish your paper, I will check it for you and initial it in the space provided."

- Either now or later in the day, the student should complete the homework independently (if possible). Help the student correct any incorrect answers. Then initial the homework in the space provided.

READER

"We have another new sight word today."

- Show the student **Sight Word Card 25.**

"Can you tell me what this word is?"

"This word is 'brought.' It doesn't follow our rules, so we must memorize it. How do we mark sight words since we can't code them?" *circle them*

- Help the student locate the word in the Irregular Spelling Booklet.

"Can you use the word 'brought' in a sentence?" *expect various answers*

"We will add this card to our sight word deck."

"We also have another new book today."

- Give the student **Reader 22 (*What Will Uncle Dave Make?*)** and some colored pencils.

"Can you tell me this book's title?" *What Will Uncle Dave Make?*

- Assist the student as necessary as he/she constructs the book.
- When the student finishes, staple or put a rubber band around the book's spine.
- If necessary, demonstrate how to separate the pages and check the page order.

"The title of this book is __________?" *What Will Uncle Dave Make?*

"I want you to read your book to yourself. When you are finished reading, color the pictures. Write your name on the book so I will know who colored it."

"Keep your book handy because I will be asking you to read it for me."

- Some time during the day, have the student read the reader to you.
- Add **Sight Word Card 25** to the Sight Word Deck.
- If possible, take time to play the Kid Card games listed in Lesson 60. Try to see that the student is prepared for tomorrow's assessment.

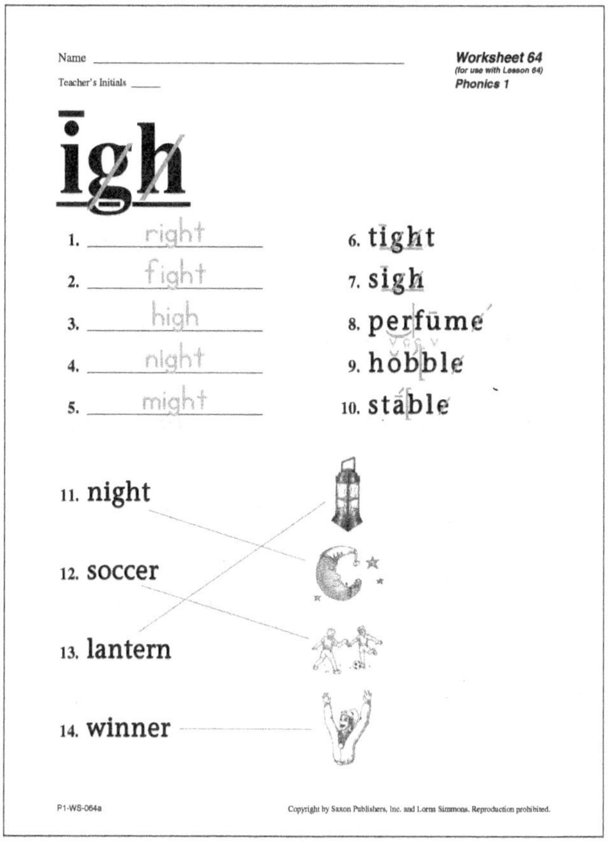
Name __________
Teacher's Initials _____
Worksheet 64
(for use with Lesson 64)
Phonics 1

igh

1. right
2. fight
3. high
4. night
5. might
6. tight
7. sigh
8. perfume
9. hobble
10. stable

11. night
12. soccer
13. lantern
14. winner

P1-WS-064a
Copyright by Saxon Publishers, Inc. and Lorna Simmons. Reproduction prohibited.

Parent's Initials _____
Homework 64
(for use with Lesson 64)
Phonics 1

igh

1. bright
2. flight
3. fable
4. simple
5. bake
6. admire
7. silver
8. pure
9. life
10. ramble

11. light
12. fingers
13. slippers
14. fish

Parents: Your child has been taught **trigraph igh**; that a trigraph is three letters that come together to make one sound; and that trigraphs are coded by underlining them.

P1-WS-064b
Copyright by Saxon Publishers, Inc. and Lorna Simmons. Reproduction prohibited.

Lesson 64

Lesson 65

Assessment

lesson preparation

materials

assorted items (see *the night before*)

Review Decks

Assessment 12

Spelling Test 10

Assessment 12 Recording Form

Kid Cards

tokens

the night before

- Locate a small assortment of items, each of whose name begins with a different letter. Some examples include a **p**encil, a **r**uler, a **d**oll, **t**ape, a **c**rayon, a **b**all, etc. (See "Alphabetizing Objects" in the appendix for further suggestions.)
- Separate the Kid Cards marked "Lesson 65."

Alphabet Activity

- The student should be seated on the floor.

  "Let's alphabetize objects today."

  "I'm going to give you some items. I want you to try to put the items in alphabetical order. Refer to the alphabet strip if you need to."

- Give the student 3 or 4 objects. Ask the student to identify the letter each object begins with and then put the objects in alphabetical order.

  "See how quickly you can alphabetize the objects. Then double check to see if they really are in alphabetical order."

- If the student seems unsure about the procedure, demonstrate with a small number of objects.

  "If you work quickly and quietly, we may have time to play this game two or three times."

- As the student works, check to see that he/she is following the correct procedure.

PHONEMIC AWARENESS

- **Objective:** To manipulate sounds within words.

  "Echo this word. Tote." *tote*

  "What is the final sound in 'tote'?" */t/*

  "Can you say it without the final sound?" *toe*

- Repeat the procedure with the following words: great...gray; drive...dry; soak...so; boat...bō; note...no.
- The word fragment that remains after dropping the final sound does not have to be a complete word. It is more difficult, however, when only a fragment remains.

REVIEW OF DECKS

- The student should be seated where he/she can write comfortably.
- Show the student **Letter Cards 1–45** in random order. The student should name the letter on each letter card.
- Review **Affix Cards 1–4.**
- Show the student **Picture Cards 1–54** in random order. The student should name the keyword and sound for each picture card.
- Review **Sight Word Cards 1–25.**

WRITTEN ASSESSMENT

- Have the student sit where he/she can write comfortably.
- Give the student **Assessment 12.**
- **Section I:**

  "Today we are going to write some words for our assessment."

  "I'm going to say a word. Write the letter that makes each sound in that word on the lines by #1."

  "Look at the rule charts if you need to."

  "Here's the first word: little."

- Repeat with the following words in the order shown: #2 (handle), #3 (maple), #4 (sniff), and #5 (shop).
- **Reminder:** While the student spells, be ready to point to appropriate rule charts as necessary.
- **Section II:**

  "Look at the letters by #6."

  "Find the picture of the keyword for this sound."

"Draw a line from the letters to the keyword."

- Repeat with #7, #8, #9, and #10. Allow a few minutes for the student to work.
- The pictures (from top to bottom) are as follows: ruffle, candle, bubble, bugle, bottle.
- **Section III:**

"Put your finger on #11."

"Code the words by #11 through #15."

- Allow a few minutes for the student to work.
- **Section IV:**

"Read the paragraph. If you find any words you can't read, code them to help you figure them out. Then answer the questions by #16, #17, and #18."

- **Reminder:** If the student absolutely cannot read the paragraph, read it to the student to see if he or she can answer the questions.

"When you are finished, show your paper to me."

- This paper will be used during the oral portion of the assessment.

Spelling Test

- Give the student **Spelling Test 10.**
- Call out the following words (in the order shown). Sound them out, if necessary.

  #1 (smile), #2 (state), #3 (room), #4 (six), #5 (fun), #6 (boost), #7 (box), #8 (sweeping), #9 (those), #10 (rule), #11 (two), #12 (of)
- Grade and record the test in any manner that suits your needs.

Oral Assessment

- It is important to complete the oral assessment promptly (today, if possible) in order to identify any areas of weakness and begin remediation.
- Use the assessment and the following dialogue to complete the oral portion.
- **Section V:**
- Point to the sight word by #19.

"Read this sight word for me."

- Record the student's response by placing a check mark by each word he/she reads correctly.
- Repeat with #20.
- **Section VI:**
- Show the student the letters by #21.

"Tell me the name of these letters and the sound they make."

- Write the student's response on the adjacent line.
- Repeat with #22 through #25.

ASSESSMENT EVALUATION

- Grade the assessment and record the results on **Assessment 12 Recording Form.** Check off the boxes to indicate mastery (i.e., the section was completed with 100% accuracy).
- **Reminder:** Try to give as many points as possible for work attempted. Do not grade the coding marks too severely. The most important coding marks to look for are breves, macrons, and syllable division lines.
- See the introductory material for detailed information regarding grading and recording procedures.
- Use the assessment results to identify those skills in which the student is weak. Practice those skills by playing Kid Card games.
- Add the Kid Cards marked "Lesson 65" to the existing decks. Listed below are games appropriate for remediation in selected areas. See "Games and Activities" for the directions for each game.
- **Section I:** Play "Spelling Deck Perfection," "Sound Scamper," "Spell Out #1," or have the student use the letter tiles to spell words you give from the Spelling Word List.
- **Section II:** Play "Keyword and Sound" or "Letter/Sound Identification."
- **Section III:** Play "Chalkboard Challenge."
- **Section IV:** Either have the student read the controlled readers and then ask questions for comprehension, or play "Acting Out" with the green Kid Cards.
- **Section V:** Play "At First Sight," review the Sight Word Deck, or lay the sight words out with a token on each one and let the student try to get as many tokens as possible for the sight words he/she can read.
- **Section VI:** Play "Letter/Sound Identification."
- When the student seems more secure in areas that had previously proven difficult, retest him/her (in those areas only) and indicate on the recording form any sections the student has subsequently mastered.
- Try to help the student achieve mastery of all the sections before the next assessment.
- If the student is having difficulty with a particular skill, keep his or her practice activities at the most basic level so the chance of success is greater.

Name ______________________

Assessment 12
(for use with Lesson 65)
Phonics 1

Section I

1. l i t t l e
2. h a n d l e
3. m a p l e
4. s n i f f
5. s h o p

Section II

6. [blȩ]
7. [flȩ]
8. [dlȩ]
9. [tlȩ]
10. [glȩ]

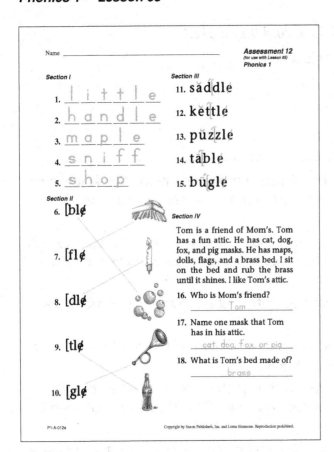

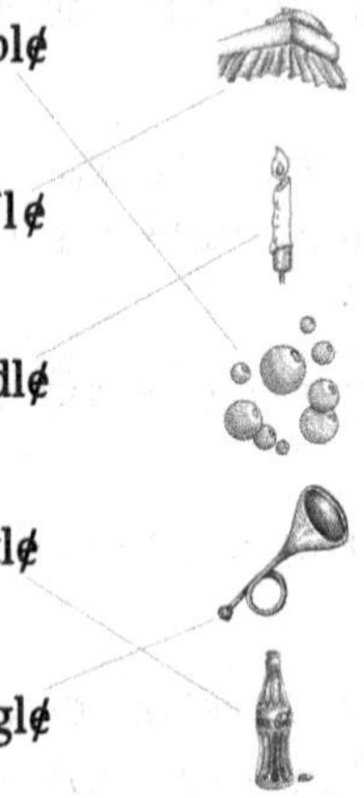

Section III

11. sǎddlȩ
12. kěttlȩ
13. pǔzzlȩ
14. tāblȩ
15. būglȩ

Section IV

Tom is a friend of Mom's. Tom has a fun attic. He has cat, dog, fox, and pig masks. He has maps, dolls, flags, and a brass bed. I sit on the bed and rub the brass until it shines. I like Tom's attic.

16. Who is Mom's friend?
Tom

17. Name one mask that Tom has in his attic.
cat, dog, fox, or pig

18. What is Tom's bed made of?
brass

P1-A-012a

Assessment 12
(for use with Lesson 65)
Phonics 1

Section V

19. from ____________
20. were ____________

Section VI

21. ble f.s.s. b-l-e, /bəl/
22. fle f.s.s. f-l-e, /fəl/
23. dle f.s.s. d-l-e, /dəl/
24. tle f.s.s. t-l-e, /təl/
25. gle f.s.s. g-l-e, /gəl/

P1-A-012b

Lesson 65

LESSON 66 — Compound Words

lesson preparation

materials

container of letter tiles

Review Decks

Spelling Sound Sheet 49

Worksheet 66

Spelling List 11

new concepts

coding compound words

ALPHABET ACTIVITY

- The student should be seated with the container of letter tiles.

  "Before we start, let's say the alphabet together so it is fresh in our minds."
- Recite the alphabet with the student.

  "Today you are going to put your letter tiles in alphabetical order."

  "When I say 'go,' dump your tiles on the (desk), turn them to the lowercase (blue) side, and begin working. We'll see how fast you can alphabetize your tiles."

  "Sometimes it's hard to tell if a lowercase letter is right side up or upside down. If you're not sure, look at the other side to see which end is up."

  "Ready, set, go!"
- Allow enough time for the student to complete the sequencing.
- If desired, time the student throughout the year so he/she can monitor any improvements.
- Have the student replace the tiles in the container and put it away.

PHONEMIC AWARENESS

- **Objective:** To manipulate sounds within words.

  "Echo this word. Back." *back*

  "What is the initial sound in 'back'?" */b/*

  "Can you change the /b/ sound to a /p/ sound and tell me the new word?" *pack*
- Repeat the procedure with the following words: tame...lame; rat...cat; roll...hole; feet...beet; soak...joke.

Review of Decks

- The student should be seated where he/she can write comfortably.
- Show the student **Letter Cards 1–45** in random order. The student should name the letter on each letter card.
- Review **Affix Cards 1–4.**
- Show the student **Picture Cards 1–54** in random order. The student should name the keyword and sound for each picture card.
- Review **Sight Word Cards 1–25.**
- Give the student **Spelling Sound Sheet 49.**
- Call out the sounds on **Spelling Cards 1–37** in random order. The student should echo each sound and name the letter or letters that make the sound as he/she writes the letter(s) on the spelling sound sheet.
- Check the student's response after each card.

New Learning

"We're going to review a certain kind of word today. Listen and echo these words after I say them. As you do this, try to think of what these words have in common."

"Echo after me. Grapevine." *grapevine* ***"Homeroom."*** *homeroom* ***"Dishcloth."*** *dishcloth*

"Do you know what these words have in common?" *each word is made up of two smaller words*

- To help the student realize that these are compound words, write the words on the chalkboard.

"Look at the words written on the chalkboard. Do you notice anything special about them?" *each word is made up of two smaller words*

"That's right. Each of the words is a longer word made up of two smaller words. Y ou probably remember that we call these 'compound words.' "

"What is a compound word?" *two smaller words put together to form one new word*

"Can you see anything in our room with a name that is a compound word?" *chalkboard, bookshelf, backpack, etc.*

- Point to "grapevine."

"If I wanted to draw a line to separate the two words in this compound word, where would I draw the line?" *between e and v*

"That's right. What are the two words?" *"grape" and "vine"*

- Draw a division line between the two words: grape|vine.

Lesson 66

- Point to "homeroom" and have the student help you determine where to separate it. Repeat the procedure with "dishcloth." Draw division lines in both words.

"Once the word is broken into parts, we can code the two little words. How do we code the first word?"

- Code the word as the student instructs: grāpe̸.

"Sneaky e is really sneaky here! It looks like it is in the middle of the word because it has another word attached to it, but it is actually at the end of one of the smaller words."

"How do we code the second little word?"

- Code the word as the student instructs: vīne̸.

"The accent usually is on the first word in a compound word."

- Place the accent mark on the first word: grāpe̸′|vīne.

"Do you know what a grapevine is?" *a vine that grapes grow on*

- Point to "homeroom."

"Can you tell me how to code the first word in this compound word?"

- Code the word as the student instructs: hōme̸.

"Can you tell me how to code the second word in this compound word?"

- Code the word as the student instructs: room.

"What is the word?" *homeroom*

"What are the two separate words?" *"home" and "room"*

"Do you know what a homeroom is?"

- Point to "dishcloth."

"Can you tell me how to code the first word in this compound word?"

- Code the word as the student instructs: dĭsh.

"Can you tell me how to code the second word in this compound word?"

- Code the word as the student instructs: clŏth.

"What is the word?" *dishcloth*

"What are the two separate words?" *"dish" and "cloth"*

"What is a dishcloth?" *a cloth for washing dishes*

"It's fun and easy to determine the meanings of compound words. You just join the meanings of the two small words, like the words themselves are joined."

BOARDWORK

"Let's practice coding some words like the ones you'll have on your worksheet."

"The rule charts are in your Rule Book if you need to look at them."

- Write the following word and phrases (without the coding marks) on the chalkboard, one at a time. Ask the student to help you code them. The correct coding is as indicated:

sŭm′|mer|tīme
vc cv

băs′|kĕt (of) loose rŭb′|ber bănds
vc cv vc cv

nŭm′|bers ănd lĕt′|ters
vc cv vc cv

- Have the student help you identify each of the items coded as a word, a phrase, or a sentence.

WORKSHEET

- The student should be seated where he/she can write comfortably.
- Give the student **Worksheet 66.** Make sure the student turns to the correct side.

"Put your finger by #1. The first word is 'bedtime.'"

"What two words do you think make up this compound word?" *"bed" and "time"*

"Unblend the first word, 'bed,' with me." */b/ /ĕ/ /d/*

- Hold up one finger for each sound.

"Let's spell those sounds and write them on your paper." *b … e … d*

"What is the second word in 'bedtime'?" *time*

"Let's unblend it." */t/ /ī/ /m/*

- Hold up one finger for each sound.

"Now spell the word again and write the letters next to 'bed' as you say them." *t … i … m … e*

- Allow time for the student to do this.

"What word did you write?" *bedtime*

- Repeat the procedure with #2 (flagpole), #3 (footprint), #4 (hatband), and #5 (candlestick).

"Now you're ready to code and read the words on your paper. Most of the words in this lesson are compound words. You will need to determine what the two small words are and draw a division line between them. Then code each small word separately. Remember that in compound words, the accent almost always stays on the first word."

"Code the words by #6 through #10. After you have coded all the words, try to read them."

- Assist the student as necessary.

"Numbers 11 and 12 are questions about the paragraph just above them. If you find any words you can't read, code them. Then see if you can answer the questions."

- As the student works, provide help as needed. Help the student correct any incorrect answers. Then initial the worksheet in the space provided.
- Some time during the day, ask the student to read from the worksheet, a controlled reader, your basal reader, or other material of your choice.
- **Note:** Always make sure the worksheet is corrected before the student begins the homework. The worksheet serves as a guide to help complete the homework.

HOMEWORK

"Turn your paper over to the homework side."

"Do you know what to do on the homework paper?"

"Remember to divide compound words. Look for suffixes and final, stable syllables and code them first. Also, watch for combination er and trigraph igh."

"When you finish your paper, I will check it for you and initial it in the space provided."

- Either now or later in the day, the student should complete the homework independently (if possible). Help the student correct any incorrect answers. Then initial the homework in the space provided.

SPELLING LIST

- Fold **Spelling List 11** in half lengthwise (with the printed side facing out).

"Leave your paper just like I give it to you."

- Give the student **Spelling List 11,** folded with the blank lines facing up.

"Let's spell some more words."

- Call out the following words (in the order shown). Sound them out, if necessary.

  #1 (five), #2 (fox), #3 (cooling), #4 (joke), #5 (jumped), #6 (street), #7 (plastic), #8 (yes), #9 (off), #10 (sniff), #11 (come), #12 (some)

"Now unfold your paper and check your words."

- Check the student's work to see if he/she needs extra help with spelling.

"I want you to practice these words. We'll have a spelling test in a few days."

- If possible, take time to play the Kid Card games listed in Lesson 65.

Name _____

Teacher's Initials _____

Worksheet 66
(for use with Lesson 66)
Phonics 1

Compound Words

1. bedtime
2. flagpole
3. footprint
4. hatband
5. candlestick

6. toothbrush
7. cŭpcakes
8. bĕehive
9. flăshlight
10. grăsshŏpper
 v c c v

Frank likes to make pancakes on the weekend. He gets up and makes the pancake batter. As we wake up he makes us fresh pancakes with butter.

11. Who likes to make pancakes? _____ Frank _____

12. What does Frank serve with his pancakes? ___ butter ___

Parent's Initials _____

Homework 66
(for use with Lesson 66)
Phonics 1

Compound Words

1. hĭlltŏp
2. bĕdroom
3. băthtŭb
4. hăndcŭffs
5. nōseblēed

6. wēekĕnd
7. păncāke
8. nĭghtlight
9. stĕplădder
 v c c v
10. ăfternoon
 v c c v

One time, Frank was making pancakes. His friend Smith came to see him. Frank and Smith were discussing the big game and the pancakes were on the stove. That weekend we had black pancakes.

11. Who is Smith? _____ Frank's friend _____

12. What was black? _____ the pancakes _____

Parents: Your child has been taught how to recognize and divide compound words.

LESSON 67 Suffixes -*ly*, -*less*, -*ness*

lesson preparation

materials

Alphabet/Accent Deck (Section 1)

Review Decks

Spelling Sound Sheet 50

Affix Cards 5–7

Sight Word Cards 26–27

Worksheet 67

Reader 23 (*Ann and the Dentist*)

colored pencils

ALPHABET ACTIVITY

- The student should be seated.

  "Let's work with the Alphabet/Accent Deck again today."

  "Let's say the first syllable in a normal voice while sitting down, and then stand and say the accented syllable louder."

- Show the student **Alphabet/Accent Card 1.**
- Have the student say "A" (seated and in a normal voice), and then "B" (standing and louder).
- Continue with **Alphabet/Accent Cards 2–25,** moving as quickly as possible.

PHONEMIC AWARENESS

- **Objective:** To substitute sounds within words.

  "Echo this word. Pat." pat

  "What is the vowel sound in 'pat'?" /ă/

  "Can you say 'pat' and change the /ă/ to /ĭ/?" pit

- Repeat the procedure with the following words: boast...best; sell...seal; sick...sack; dense...dance; tight...tote.

REVIEW OF DECKS

- The student should be seated where he/she can write comfortably.
- Show the student **Letter Cards 1–45** in random order. The student should name the letter on each letter card.
- Review **Affix Cards 1–4.**
- Show the student **Picture Cards 1–54** in random order. The student should name the keyword and sound for each picture card.
- Review **Sight Word Cards 1–25.**
- Give the student **Spelling Sound Sheet 50.**
- Call out the sounds on **Spelling Cards 1–37** in random order. The student should echo each sound and name the letter or letters that make the sound as he/she writes the letter(s) on the spelling sound sheet.
- Check the student's response after each card.

NEW LEARNING

"Echo these words and tell me what you hear at the end. Hairless." *hairless* ***"Endless."*** *endless* ***"Useless."*** *useless*

"What do you hear at the end of these words?" *less*

- Write the following on the chalkboard: hairless, endless, useless.

"What is the same at the end of all of these words?" *less*

"Look at these words. Can I cover up the 'less' and still have a root word?" *yes*

"What do we call something that is added to the end of a root word?" *a suffix*

"This is suffix -less. What do you think it means when added to a root word?" *without*

"How do we code suffixes?" *box them*

- Box the suffix *-less* on all three words: hair[less], end[less], use[less].

"Suffixes are either vowel suffixes or consonant suffixes. A suffix is named according to its first letter. What kind is this one?" *consonant suffix*

"What word can I make from the word 'color' that means 'without color'?" *colorless*

- Show the student **Affix Card 5.**

"What do we call this?" *suffix -less*

- Have the student say the word "less" rather than spell it. He/She will recognize and understand it more readily when it appears at the end of words.

"Let's try another one."

"Echo these words and tell me what you hear at the end. Softness." *softness* ***"Redness."*** *redness* ***"Weakness."*** *weakness*

"What do you hear at the end of these words?" *ness*

- Write the following on the chalkboard: softness, redness, weakness.

"What is the same at the end of all these words?" *ness*

"Can I cover up the 'ness' and still have a root word?" *yes*

"This is suffix -ness. What do you think it means when added to a root word?" *expect various answers*

"Suffix -ness describes a particular quality of something. If we talk about a blanket's softness, it means the blanket is soft. If we discuss a crayon's redness, it means the crayon is red."

- Box the suffix *-ness* on all three words: soft[ness], red[ness], weak[ness].

"Is suffix -ness a vowel suffix or a consonant suffix?" *consonant suffix*

- Show the student **Affix Card 6.**

"What do we call this?" *suffix -ness*

- Have the student say "ness" rather than spell it.

"Let's try one more."

"Echo these words and tell me what you hear at the end. Sweetly." *sweetly* ***"Slowly."*** *slowly* ***"Neatly."*** *neatly*

"What do you hear at the end of these words?" */lē/*

- Write the following on the chalkboard: sweetly, slowly, neatly.

"What is the same at the end of all of these words?" *ly*

"Can I cover up the 'ly' and still have a root word?" *yes*

"This is suffix -ly. It describes how something is done. If someone gave you a job and said 'Be quick!', how would you do the job?" *quickly*

"What if I use the words 'weekly,' 'yearly,' and 'monthly' when I talk about that job? What are the words telling me?" *when (or how often) I did the job*

"If I asked you to act like a friend to someone, how would you act?" *friendly*

"That's right. Suffix -ly also means to be like something."

- Box the suffix *-ly* on all three words: sweet[ly], slow[ly], neat[ly].

"Is suffix -ly a vowel suffix or a consonant suffix?" *consonant suffix*

- Show the student **Affix Card 7.**

"What do we call this?" *suffix -ly*

- Have the student say "ly" (lē) rather than spell it.

"Suffix -ly usually tells how, when, or like."

"Remember that when we add a suffix, the accent almost always stays on the root word."

- **Note:** Add the new affix cards to the Affix Deck.

BOARDWORK

"We have some new sight words today."

- Hold up **Sight Word Cards 26** and **27.**

"These words are 'says' and 'they.' They don't follow our rules. We must memorize them. Circle them when you see them."

- Help the student locate the words in the Irregular Spelling Booklet.

"Can you use these words in sentences?" *expect various answers*

"We will add these cards to our sight word deck."

"Let's practice coding some words like the ones you'll have on your worksheet."

"The rule charts are in your Rule Book if you need to look at them."

- Write the following words and sentences (without the coding marks) on the chalkboard, one at a time. Ask the student to help you code them. The correct coding is as indicated:

pūre′ ly

Mŏm (says) wē′ căn gō′ ĭn the lĭv′ ing room.

rĕst′ less

(They) tĕst′ ed the thĭck′ ness (of) the wood.

- Have the student help you identify each of the items coded as a word, a phrase, or a sentence.
- Add **Sight Word Cards 26** and **27** to the Sight Word Deck.

WORKSHEET

Lesson 67

- The student should be seated where he/she can write comfortably.
- Give the student **Worksheet 67.** Make sure the student turns to the correct side.

"Today, most of the words we spell will be with our new suffixes."

"Put your finger by #1. The first word is 'gladly.' "

"What is the root word?" *glad*

"What is the suffix?" *ly*

"Try to spell the word and write the letters on the line by #1."

- Allow time for the student to do this. Repeat the word a few times, if necessary, instead of guiding the student through the unblending process. By this time, the student should begin to do some unblending in his/her head.

  "What word did you write?" *gladly*

- Repeat the procedure with #2 (hatless), #3 (sadness), #4 (badly), and #5 (frosty).

  "Now you're ready to code and read the words on your paper."

  "Code the words by #6 through #10. After you have coded all the words, try to read them."

- Assist the student as necessary.

  "Now read the word by #11. If you have trouble reading the word, code it. Then draw a line from the word to the picture it matches."

- Repeat with #12, #13, and #14.
- As the student works, provide help as needed. Help the student correct any incorrect answers. Then initial the worksheet in the space provided.
- Some time during the day, ask the student to read from the worksheet, a controlled reader, your basal reader, or other material of your choice.
- **Note:** Always make sure the worksheet is corrected before the student begins the homework. The worksheet serves as a guide to help complete the homework.

HOMEWORK

"Turn your paper over to the homework side."

"Do you know what to do on the homework paper?"

"Be sure to watch for the three new suffixes."

- Discuss the homework pictures to make sure the student understands the word each one represents: #11 (fishhook), #12 (rosebud), #13 (pinecone), and #14 (bathtub).

  "When you finish your paper, I will check it for you and initial it in the space provided."

- Either now or later in the day, the student should complete the homework independently (if possible). Help the student correct any incorrect answers. Then initial the homework in the space provided.

READER

"We have another new book today."

- Give the student **Reader 23 (*Ann and the Dentist*)** and some colored pencils.

  "Can you tell me this book's title?" *Ann and the Dentist*

- Assist the student as necessary as he/she constructs the book.

- When the student finishes, staple or put a rubber band around the book's spine.
- If necessary, demonstrate how to separate the pages and check the page order.

  "The title of this book is __________?" *Ann and the Dentist*

  "I want you to read your book to yourself. When you are finished reading, color the pictures. Write your name on the book so I will know who colored it."

  "Keep your book handy because I will be asking you to read it for me."

- Some time during the day, have the student read the reader to you.
- If possible, take time to play the Kid Card games listed in Lesson 65.

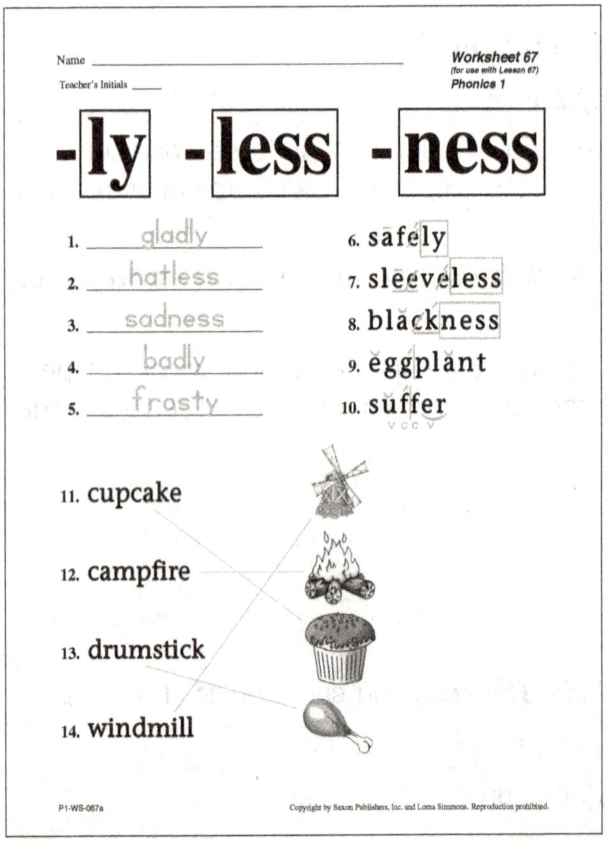
Name ________________

Teacher's Initials ____

Worksheet 67
(for use with Lesson 67)
Phonics 1

-ly -less -ness

1. gladly
2. hatless
3. sadness
4. badly
5. frosty
6. safely
7. sleeveless
8. blackness
9. eggplant
10. suffer
11. cupcake
12. campfire
13. drumstick
14. windmill

P1-WS-067a

Copyright by Saxon Publishers, Inc. and Lorna Simmons. Reproduction prohibited.

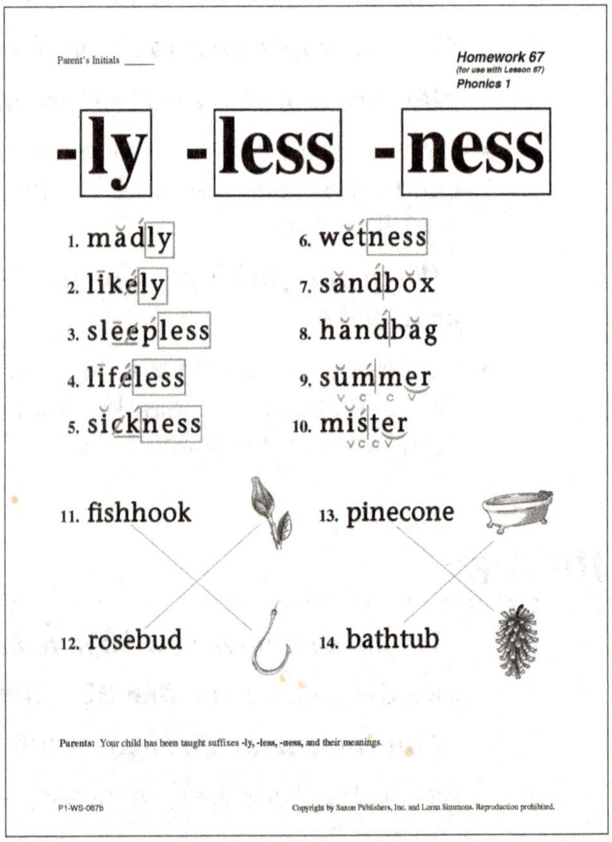
Parent's Initials ____

Homework 67
(for use with Lesson 67)
Phonics 1

-ly -less -ness

1. mădly
2. likely
3. sleepless
4. lifeless
5. sickness
6. wĕtness
7. săndbŏx
8. hăndbăg
9. sŭmmer
10. mĭster
11. fishhook
12. rosebud
13. pinecone
14. bathtub

Parents: Your child has been taught suffixes -ly, -less, -ness, and their meanings.

P1-WS-067b

Copyright by Saxon Publishers, Inc. and Lorna Simmons. Reproduction prohibited.

Lesson 67

LESSON 68 — Digraph *ai*

lesson preparation

materials

Review Decks

Letter Card 46

Picture Card 55

Sight Word Cards 28–29

Worksheet 68

ALPHABET ACTIVITY

- The student should be seated.

"We are going to alphabetize words in a list today."

"Let me show you on the chalkboard how we'll do it."

- Write the following on the chalkboard:

_____ puddle
_____ little
_____ middle
_____ boggle
_____ kettle
_____ fiddle

"Which letter will we use as our 'guide letter'?" *the first one*

"Let's underline the guide letters so we can see them easily."

- Underline the first letter in each word. Let the student help you make sure all of the first letters are different.

"We won't be able to move the words today, so the process is a little bit different. Let me show you a little trick that can help you keep your place."

"How many words are on this list?" *six*

"We are going to put numbers 1 through 6 below (or beside) our list to use as we alphabetize."

- Write the numbers 1–6 below (or beside) the list of words.

"Now we'll recite the alphabet slowly and scan the guide letters on these words each time we say a letter."

"Let's start. A."

- Quickly scan the guide letters with your index finger.

"Is there an a?" *no*

"B."

- Quickly scan the guide letters with your index finger.

"Is there a b?" *yes*

"Let's put a 1 beside 'boggle' and mark out the 1 at the bottom."

"C." *no* ***"D."*** *no* ***"E."*** *no*

"F." *yes*

"Since the number 1 has been used, we know to use a number 2 by the next word."

- Put a 2 in front of "fiddle" and mark out the 2 at the bottom.

"G." *no* ***"H."*** *no* ***"I."*** *no* ***"J."*** *no*

"K." *yes*

- Put a 3 in front of "kettle" and mark out the 3 at the bottom.

"L." *yes*

- Put a 4 in front of "little" and mark out the 4 at the bottom.

"M." *yes*

- Put a 5 in front of "middle" and mark out the 5 at the bottom.

"N." *no* ***"O."*** *no*

"P." *yes*

- Put a 6 in front of "puddle" and mark out the 6 at the bottom.

"All of the words have been used, so we can stop."

- **Optional:** Letter order can be checked, but it is more difficult. If you would like to check letter order with the student, quickly recite the alphabet, starting with your finger on number 1. As that letter is named, move your finger to the second word, and continue until that letter is named. Move your finger to the next number each time the appropriate letter is named.

PHONEMIC AWARENESS

- **Objective:** To substitute sounds within words.

"Echo this word. Snag." *snag*

"What is the final sound in 'snag'?" */g/*

"Can you say 'snag' and change the final sound to /k/?" *snack*

- Repeat the procedure with the following words: tree...true; frame...frail; băss...bag; slick...slip; real...read; voice...void.

REVIEW OF DECKS

- The student should be seated where he/she can write comfortably.
- Show the student **Letter Cards 1–45** in random order. The student should name the letter on each letter card.
- Review **Affix Cards 1–7.**
- Show the student **Picture Cards 1–54** in random order. The student should name the keyword and sound for each picture card.
- Review **Sight Word Cards 1–27.**

  "Let's review our spelling cards orally today."
- Give the sounds on **Spelling Cards 1–37** in random order. The student should echo each sound and then skywrite the letter or letters that make the sound.

NEW LEARNING

"I'm going to say some words. Echo them back to me and listen for the sound that is the same in each word."

- Point to your mouth as you say each word.

  "Echo after me. Aim." *aim* ***"Braid."*** *braid* ***"Train."*** *train*

  "What sound do you hear that is the same in each of these words?" */ā/*

  "That's right. The sound you hear is /ā/."

  "Put your fingertips on the front of your neck and say /ā/. See if you feel any vibration."

  "Is this sound voiced or unvoiced?" *voiced*

  "Since /ā/ vibrates, it is a voiced sound."
- Write the following on the chalkboard: aim, braid, train.

  "What two letters do you see that might be making the /ā/ sound?" *ai*

  "There is an 'ai' in all of these words, so we can see that 'ai' must be the letters used to spell the /ā/ sound."

  "How many sounds do you hear?" *one*

  "How many letters are making that sound?" *two*
- Use the digraph hand signals (two fingers coming together to make one) as you say the following:

  "What do we call two letters that come together to make one sound?" *a digraph*

  "How do we code digraphs?" *underline them*

  "How will we show that digraph ai makes the /ā/ sound?" *put a macron over the a, cross out the i*
- Code the words as the student instructs: āi̸m, brāi̸d, trāi̸n.

  "Is digraph ai a vowel digraph or a consonant digraph?" *a vowel digraph*

NEW DECK CARDS

- Hold up **Letter Card 46.**

  "What do we call this?" *digraph ai*
- Hold up **Picture Card 55** but keep the picture covered with your hand (or the letter card).

  "I have a card with a picture on it that contains the /ā/ sound in the middle."

  "I am going to describe it for you. See if you can guess what the picture is."

  "This is a kind of weather. It falls from the sky and makes puddles in the street. People usually carry umbrellas when it is falling. What do you think the picture is?" *rain*
- Show the student **Picture Card 55.**

  "The 'ai' spelling for the /ā/ sound is not used very often, so we won't add it to the spelling deck responses."
- **Note:** The digraph and its picture are also shown in the Rule Book on page 21.

  "Get out your Irregular Spelling Booklet."

  "Look at the table of contents. Can you find the page that shows words spelled with digraph ai?" *page 2*

  "Look at page 2. All of these words are spelled with digraph ai. They don't follow our regular rules, so we must memorize them. For now, you can refer to this booklet any time you're spelling."
- **Note:** Add the new letter and picture cards to the Review Decks.

BOARDWORK

"Let's practice coding some words like the ones you'll have on your worksheet."

"The rule charts are in your Rule Book if you need to look at them."

- Write the following word and sentence (without the coding marks) on the chalkboard, one at a time. Ask the student to help you code them. The correct coding is as indicated:

wāist′|līne

The māil′|măn căn sēe thăt ĭt ĭs rāin′|ing.

- Have the student help you identify each of the items coded as a word, a phrase, or a sentence.

Lesson 68

Worksheet

"We have two new sight words today."

- Show the student **Sight Word Cards 28** and **29.**

"These words are 'build' and 'built.' They don't follow our rules, so we must memorize them. Circle them when you see them."

"Can you use either of these words in a sentence?" *expect various answers*

"Let's find the words on our sight word charts."

- Help the student locate the words in the Irregular Spelling Booklet.

"We will add these words to our sight word deck."

- Add **Sight Word Cards 28** and **29** to the Sight Word Deck.
- The student should be seated where he/she can write comfortably.
- Give the student **Worksheet 68.** Make sure the student turns to the correct side.

"Let's spell with the /ā/ sound using digraph ai."

"Digraph ai is usually used for spelling in the initial or medial position."

"Put your finger by #1. The first word is 'rain.' "

"Unblend 'rain' with me." */r/ /ā/ /n/*

- Hold up one finger for each sound.

"Let's spell those sounds." *r … digraph ai … n*

- Point to a finger as the student spells each sound.

"Now spell the word again and write the letters as you say them."

- Allow time for the student to do this.

"What word did you write?" *rain*

- You may stop unblending each word when the student can do so without your help.
- Repeat the procedure with #2 (nail), #3 (paint), #4 (mail), and #5 (snail).

"Now you're ready to code and read the words on your paper."

"Code the words by #6 through #10. After you have coded all the words, try to read them."

- Assist the student as necessary.

"Numbers 11 and 12 are questions about the paragraph just above them. If you find any words you can't read, code them. Then see if you can answer the questions."

- As the student works, provide help as needed. Help the student correct any incorrect answers. Then initial the worksheet in the space provided.
- Some time during the day, ask the student to read from the worksheet, a controlled reader, your basal reader, or other material of your choice.
- **Note:** Always make sure the worksheet is corrected before the student begins the homework. The worksheet serves as a guide to help complete the homework.

HOMEWORK

"Turn your paper over to the homework side."

"Do you know what to do on the homework paper?"

"Watch for digraph ai. Remember to divide compound words into two smaller words before you code them. Look for suffixes and final, stable syllables and code them first."

"When you finish your paper, I will check it for you and initial it in the space provided."

- Either now or later in the day, the student should complete the homework independently (if possible). Help the student correct any incorrect answers. Then initial the homework in the space provided.
- If possible, take time to play the Kid Card games listed in Lesson 65.

Name ______________________

Teacher's Initials ____

Worksheet 68
(for use with Lesson 68)
Phonics 1

āi

1. rain
2. nail
3. paint
4. mail
5. snail
6. sāil
7. drāining
8. fāinted
9. hāirbrŭsh
10. māiled

We are going to build a home. My home will have three bedrooms, one bathroom, and a game room. I hope it will be built soon.

11. What is being built? a home

12. My home will have three bedrooms.

P1-WS-068a

Parent's Initials ____

Homework 68
(for use with Lesson 68)
Phonics 1

āi

1. māid
2. bŭs
3. spŭn
4. drāined
5. trāining
6. strāined
7. pāinting
8. toothbrŭsh
9. āided
10. will

My dad is going to help build my home. He said the bedrooms will be upstairs. The bedrooms will be painted light green and the lights will be silver. I hope my room has a rug.

11. Where will the bedrooms be? upstairs

12. What will be painted light green? the bedrooms

Parents: Your child has been taught **digraph ai**; and that it is usually found in the initial or medial position.

P1-WS-068b

Lesson 68

LESSON 69 — Digraph *ay*

lesson preparation

materials

Alphabet/Accent Deck (Section 1)
Review Decks
Spelling Sound Sheet 51
Letter Card 47
Picture Card 56
Worksheet 69
Reader 24 (*A Wet Picnic*)
colored pencils

ALPHABET ACTIVITY

"We're going to work with the Alphabet/Accent Deck again today."

"Let's stand up to go through the deck. Every time we say the accented syllable, we'll jump a little."

- Show the student **Alphabet/Accent Card 1.**
- Have the student say "A" (softly), and then "B" (as he/she jumps up).
- Continue with **Alphabet/Accent Cards 2–25,** moving as quickly as possible.

PHONEMIC AWARENESS

- **Objective:** To substitute sounds within words.

"Echo this word. Stop." *stop*

"What is the initial blend in 'stop'?" */st/*

"Can you say 'stop' and change the initial blend to /fl/?" *flop*

- Repeat the procedure with the following words: slip...flip; track...flack; bring...sling; stoop...droop; span...scan; brush...thrush; slate...freight.

Review of Decks

- The student should be seated where he/she can write comfortably.
- Show the student **Letter Cards 1–46** in random order. The student should name the letter on each letter card.
- Review **Affix Cards 1–7.**
- Show the student **Picture Cards 1–55** in random order. The student should name the keyword and sound for each picture card.
- Review **Sight Word Cards 1–29.**
- Give the student **Spelling Sound Sheet 51.**
- Call out the sounds on **Spelling Cards 1–37** in random order. The student should echo each sound and name the letter or letters that make the sound as he/she writes the letter(s) on the spelling sound sheet.
- Have the student set the spelling sound sheet aside for use later in the lesson.

New Learning

"I'm going to say some words. Echo them back to me and listen for the sound that is the same in the final position of each word."

- Point to your mouth as you say each word.

"Echo after me. Gray." *gray* ***"Play."*** *play* ***"Stay."*** *stay*

"What sound do you hear in the final position?" */ā/*

"That's right. The sound you hear in the final position is /ā/."

"Put your fingertips on the front of your neck and say /ā/. See if you feel any vibration."

"Is this sound voiced or unvoiced?" *voiced*

"Since /ā/ vibrates, it is a voiced sound."

- Write the following on the chalkboard: gray, play, stay.

"What two letters do you see that might be making the /ā/ sound?" *ay*

"There is an ay in all of these words, so we can see that ay must be the letters used to spell the /ā/ sound."

"How many sounds do you hear?" *one*

"How many letters are making that sound?" *two*

- Use the digraph hand signals (two fingers coming together to make one) as you say the following:

"What do we call two letters that come together to make one sound?" *a digraph*

"How do we code digraphs?" *underline them*

Lesson 69

"How will we show that digraph ay makes the /ā/ sound?" *put a macron over the a, cross out the y*

- Code the words as the student instructs: grā~~y~~, plā~~y~~, stā~~y~~.

"Remember, English words don't end with 'i,' so all of the ai's at the end of words were changed to ay's."

"Is digraph ay a vowel digraph or a consonant digraph?" *a vowel digraph ("y" is acting as a vowel and "a" is always a vowel)*

New Deck Cards

- Pull **Spelling Card 10** from the Review Deck.
- Hold up **Letter Card 47.**

"What do we call this?" *digraph ay*

- Hold up **Picture Card 56** but keep the picture covered with your hand (or the letter card).

"I have a card with a picture on it that contains the /ā/ sound."

"I am going to describe it for you. See if you can guess what the picture is."

"This is found in fields. When it is golden brown, farmers use tractors to form it into tight bundles. Then animals like horses and cows eat it all winter. What do you think the picture is?" *hay*

"That's right. The keyword is 'hay' and the sound we've learned is /ā/."

- Show the student **Picture Card 56.**

"The word 'hay' helps us remember the /ā/ sound, spelled with digraph ay."

- **Note:** The digraph and its picture are also shown in the Rule Book on page 21.

"Find your spelling sound sheet. Put your finger on the line by #38."

- Hold up **Spelling Card 10** so only you can see what is written.

"Echo this sound: /ā/." */ā/*

"If you hear /ā/ at the end of the word and you're not sure how to spell it, the best choice is 'ay.' So we will add this response to our spelling card."

- Write the following on the chalkboard: a–e, a || ay.

"Our new response will be 'a consonant e comma a final digraph ay.' Say that with me." *a consonant e comma a final digraph ay*

"Write the new response on the line by #38."

- Check the spelling sound sheet for accuracy.
- **Note:** Add the new letter and picture cards to the Review Decks (and re-insert **Spelling Card 10**).

BOARDWORK

"Let's practice coding some words like the ones you'll have on your worksheet."

"The rule charts are in your Rule Book if you need to look at them."

- Write the following phrase and sentence (without the coding marks) on the chalkboard, one at a time. Ask the student to help you code them. The correct coding is as indicated:

Stăck thė trāy[s].

Bŏb clāim[ed] thė bŭc'[klė hē' lŏst.

- **Note:** Crossing out the *c* in "buckle" is optional.
- Have the student help you identify each of the items coded as a word, a phrase, or a sentence.

WORKSHEET

- The student should be seated where he/she can write comfortably.
- Give the student **Worksheet 69.** Make sure the student turns to the correct side.

"Today, let's spell with the /ā/ sound using digraph ay."

"Digraph ay is usually found in the final position and is the best choice if you don't know how to spell the /ā/ sound."

"Put your finger by #1. The first word is 'day.' "

"Spell the word and write it by #1."

- Allow time for the student to do this.
- You may stop unblending each word when the student can do so without your help.

"What word did you write?" *day*

- Repeat the procedure with #2 (may), #3 (say), #4 (stay), and #5 (sway).

"Now you're ready to code and read the words on your paper."

"Code the words by #6 through #10. After you have coded all the words, try to read them."

- Assist the student as necessary.

"Now read the word by #11. If you have trouble reading the word, code it. Then draw a line from the word to the picture it matches."

- Repeat with #12, #13, and #14.
- As the student works, provide help as needed. Help the student correct any incorrect answers. Then initial the worksheet in the space provided.
- Some time during the day, ask the student to read from the worksheet, a controlled reader, your basal reader, or other material of your choice.
- **Note:** Always make sure the worksheet is corrected before the student begins the homework. The worksheet serves as a guide to help complete the homework.

HOMEWORK

"Turn your paper over to the homework side."

"Do you know what to do on the homework paper?"

"Be sure to watch for digraph ay and digraph ai."

- Discuss the homework pictures to make sure the student understands the word each one represents: #11 (tray), #12 (train), #13 (candle), and #14 (braid).

"When you finish your paper, I will check it for you and initial it in the space provided."

- Either now or later in the day, the student should complete the homework independently (if possible). Help the student correct any incorrect answers. Then initial the homework in the space provided.

READER

"We have another new book today."

- Give the student **Reader 24 (*A Wet Picnic*)** and some colored pencils.

"Can you tell me this book's title?" *A Wet Picnic*

- Assist the student as necessary as he/she constructs the book.
- When the student finishes, staple or put a rubber band around the book's spine.
- If necessary, demonstrate how to separate the pages and check the page order.

"The title of this book is __________?" *A Wet Picnic*

"I want you to read your book to yourself. When you are finished reading, color the pictures. Write your name on the book so I will know who colored it."

"Keep your book handy because I will be asking you to read it for me."

- Some time during the day, have the student read the reader to you.
- If possible, take time to play the Kid Card games listed in Lesson 65. Try to see that the student is prepared for tomorrow's assessment.

Name ______________________

Teacher's Initials _____

Worksheet 69
(for use with Lesson 69)
Phonics 1

āy

1. day
2. may
3. say
4. stay
5. sway
6. clāy
7. strāin
8. tăckle
9. strāyed
10. smŏck

11. hay
12. snail
13. tight
14. pickle

P1-WS-069a

Parent's Initials _____

Homework 69
(for use with Lesson 69)
Phonics 1

āy

1. hāy
2. cāble
3. sāying
4. tĭckle
5. plāyed
6. lăck
7. frĕckle
8. trāil
9. răck
10. răffle

11. tray 

12. train 

13. candle 

14. braid 

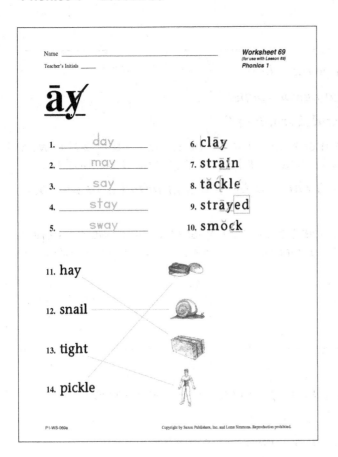

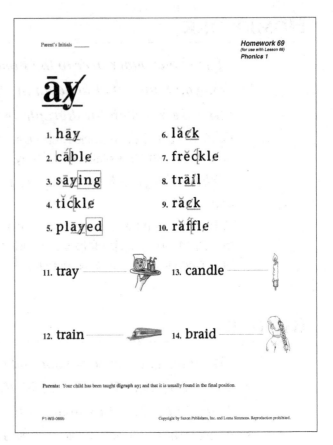

Parents: Your child has been taught **digraph ay;** and that it is usually found in the final position.

P1-WS-069b

Lesson 69

LESSON 70 — Assessment

lesson preparation

materials

ball

Review Decks

Assessment 13

Spelling Test 11

Assessment 13 Recording Form

Kid Cards

tokens

the night before

- Sort through the Review Decks and remove any of the following cards the student knows very well:

  Letter Deck: *n, t, p, l, z, s, d, f, h, r, k.*

  Picture Deck: Cards that correspond to the letter cards that are removed.

  Sight Word Deck: Cards that (based on assessment results) the student knows very well.

  Spelling Deck: Cards that correspond to any letter cards that are removed, with the exception of cards with more than one response: #12 (/s/) and #18 (/k/).
- Separate these cards from the others by placing a rubber band around each deck and labeling them "Retired Letter Deck," "Retired Picture Deck," etc. These decks will be reviewed once a week in place of the active decks so the student will not forget them.
- Throughout the year, you may evaluate and retire cards as indicated in the teacher's guide or according to the student's needs. Please remember, though, that the vowel cards should never be retired. Also, cards that were deliberately kept together within decks should remain together (in either the active deck or the retired deck).
- Separate the Kid Cards marked "Lesson 70."

ALPHABET ACTIVITY

- You and the student should be standing with the ball.

  "Let's play 'Alphabet Toss' again."

  "I am going to change the rules today. I'll say a letter of the alphabet and toss the ball to you."

"After you catch the ball, say the two letters that come after the letter I said."

"Then toss the ball back to me, and I will say the next two letters."

"Keep your eye on the ball!"

- Play as long as time permits; then have the student return to his/her seat.

REVIEW OF DECKS

- Show the student **Letter Cards 1–47** in random order. The student should name the letter on each letter card.
- Review **Affix Cards 1–7.**
- Show the student **Picture Cards 1–56** in random order. The student should name the keyword and sound for each picture card.
- Review **Sight Word Cards 1–29.**

WRITTEN ASSESSMENT

- Seat the student where he/she can write comfortably.
- Give the student **Assessment 13.**
- **Section I:**

  "Today we are going to write some words for our assessment."

  "I'm going to say a word. Write the letter or letters that make each sound in that word on the lines by #1."

  "Look at the rule charts if you need to."

  "Here's the first word: after."
- Repeat with the following words in the order shown: #2 (sleepy), #3 (crispy), #4 (my), and #5 (trying).
- **Reminder:** While the student spells, be ready to point to appropriate rule charts as necessary.
- **Section II:**

  "Look at the letters by #6."

  "Find the picture of the keyword for this sound."

  "Draw a line from the letters to the keyword."
- Repeat with #7, #8, and #9. Allow a few minutes for the student to work.
- The pictures (from top to bottom) are as follows: butter, cry, candy, light.
- **Section III:**

  "Put your finger on #10."

  "Code the words by #10 through #14."
- Allow a few minutes for the student to work.

- **Section IV:**

  "Read the paragraph. If you find any words you can't read, code them to help you figure them out. Then answer the questions by #15 through #18."
- **Reminder:** If the student absolutely cannot read the paragraph, read it to the student to see if he or she can answer the questions.

  "When you are finished, show your paper to me."
- This paper will be used during the oral portion of the assessment.

Spelling Test

- Give the student **Spelling Test 11.**
- Call out the following words (in the order shown). Sound them out, if necessary.

  #1 (joke), #2 (yes), #3 (plastic), #4 (five), #5 (street), #6 (jumped),
  #7 (cooling), #8 (off), #9 (fox), #10 (sniff), #11 (some), #12 (come)
- Grade and record the test in any manner that suits your needs.

Oral Assessment

- It is important to complete the oral assessment promptly (today, if possible) in order to identify any areas of weakness and begin remediation.
- Use the assessment and the following dialogue to complete the oral portion.
- **Section V:**
- Point to the sight word by #19.

  "Read this sight word for me."
- Record the student's response by placing a check mark by each word he/she reads correctly.
- Repeat with #20, #21, and #22.
- **Section VI:**
- Show the student the letters by #23.

  "Tell me the name of these letters and the sound they make."
- Write the student's response on the adjacent line.
- Repeat with #24 and #25.

Assessment Evaluation

- Grade the assessment and record the results on **Assessment 13 Recording Form.** Check off the boxes to indicate mastery (i.e., the section was completed with 100% accuracy).
- **Reminder:** Try to give as many points as possible for work attempted. Do not grade the coding marks too severely. The most important coding marks to look for are breves, macrons, and syllable division lines.

- See the introductory material for detailed information regarding grading and recording procedures.
- Use the assessment results to identify those skills in which the student is weak. Practice those skills by playing Kid Card games.
- Add the Kid Cards marked "Lesson 70" to the existing decks. Listed below are games appropriate for remediation in selected areas. See "Games and Activities" for the directions for each game.
- **Section I:** Play "Spelling Deck Perfection," "Sound Scamper," "Spell Out #1," or have the student use the letter tiles to spell words you give from the Spelling Word List.
- **Section II:** Play "Keyword and Sound" or "Letter/Sound Identification."
- **Section III:** Play "Chalkboard Challenge."
- **Section IV:** Either have the student read the controlled readers and then ask questions for comprehension, or play "Acting Out" with the green Kid Cards.
- **Section V:** Play "At First Sight," review the Sight Word Deck, or lay the sight words out with a token on each one and let the student try to get as many tokens as possible for the sight words he/she can read.
- **Section VI:** Play "Letter/Sound Identification."
- When the student seems more secure in areas that had previously proven difficult, retest him/her (in those areas only) and indicate on the recording form any sections the student has subsequently mastered.
- Try to help the student achieve mastery of all the sections before the next assessment.
- If the student is having difficulty with a particular skill, keep his or her practice activities at the most basic level so the chance of success is greater.

Name ______________________

Assessment 13
(for use with Lesson 70)
Phonics 1

Section I

1. after
2. sleepy
3. crispy
4. my
5. trying

Section II

6. igh
7. er
8. ȳ
9. ẏ

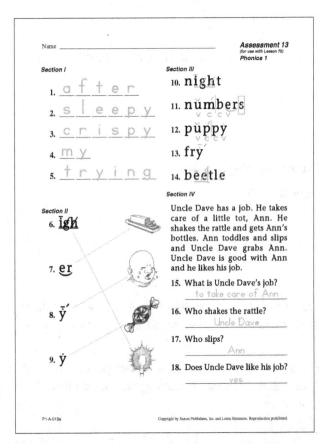

Section III

10. night
11. numbers
12. puppy
13. fry
14. beetle

Section IV

Uncle Dave has a job. He takes care of a little tot, Ann. He shakes the rattle and gets Ann's bottles. Ann toddles and slips and Uncle Dave grabs Ann. Uncle Dave is good with Ann and he likes his job.

15. What is Uncle Dave's job?
to take care of Ann
16. Who shakes the rattle?
Uncle Dave
17. Who slips?
Ann
18. Does Uncle Dave like his job?
yes

P1-A-013a

Assessment 13
(for use with Lesson 70)
Phonics 1

Section V

19. again ________
20. against ________
21. brought ________
22. says ________

Section VI

23. igh trigraph i-g-h, /ī/
24. er combination er, /er/
25. ẏ vowel y, /ī/, /ē/

P1-A-013b

LESSON 71 Combination *ar*

lesson preparation

materials

container of letter tiles

Review Decks

Spelling Sound Sheet 52

Letter Card 48

Picture Card 57

Spelling Card 38

Sight Word Card 30

Worksheet 71

Spelling List 12

ALPHABET ACTIVITY

- The student should be seated with the container of letter tiles.

  "Before we start, let's say the alphabet together so it is fresh in our minds."

- Recite the alphabet with the student.
- Give the following instructions one at a time, allowing time for the student to accomplish each task before giving the next instruction.

  "Take all of your letter tiles out of your container."

  "Flip all of the letters over so that you are looking at the lowercase letters. If they are flipped correctly, they will all be blue."

  "Now you're ready. See if you can put all your letters in alphabetical order. If you need help, let me know."

- Assist the student as necessary.
- When the student has finished, continue by saying the following:

  "Point to the initial letter."

  "Point to the final letter."

  "Pull down three voiced consonants."

  "Make a digraph with any of your letters."

- Have the student replace the tiles in the container and put it away.

Phonemic Awareness

- Starting today, phonemic awareness activities will be combined with other areas of the lesson.

Review of Decks

- The student should be seated where he/she can write comfortably.
- Show the student **Letter Cards 1–47** in random order. The student should name the letter on each letter card.
- Review **Affix Cards 1–7.**
- Show the student **Picture Cards 1–56** in random order. The student should name the keyword and sound for each picture card.
- Review **Sight Word Cards 1–29.**
- Give the student **Spelling Sound Sheet 52.**
- Call out the sounds on **Spelling Cards 1–37** in random order. The student should echo each sound and name the letter or letters that make the sound as he/she writes the letter(s) on the spelling sound sheet.
- Have the student set the spelling sound sheet aside for use later in the lesson.

New Learning

"I'm going to say some words. Echo them back to me and listen for the sound that is the same in each word."

- Point to your mouth as you say each word.

"Echo after me. Far." *far* ***"Card."*** *card* ***"Start."*** *start*

"What sound do you hear that is the same in all of these words?" */ar/*

"That's right. The sound you hear is /ar/."

"Put your fingertips on the front of your neck and say /ar/. See if you feel any vibration."

"Is this sound voiced or unvoiced?" *voiced*

"Since /ar/ vibrates, it is a voiced sound."

Lesson 71

- Write the following on the chalkboard: far, card, start.

"What do you see that might be making the /ar/ sound?" *ar*

"Let's code these words."

- Code the *a* in each word with a breve and attempt to read the words with the /ă/ sound.

"These don't sound right."

"We have two letters that come together and make an unexpected sound. Do you remember what that is called?" combination

"How many sounds do you hear?" one

"How many letters are making that sound?" two

"A combination is two letters that come together and make an unexpected sound."

"How do we code a combination?" draw an arc underneath the letters

- Erase the breves and draw an arc under each combination: far, card, start.

New Deck Cards

- Hold up **Letter Card 48.**

  "What do we call this?" combination ar

- Hold up **Picture Card 57** but keep the picture covered with your hand (or the letter card).

  "I have a card with a picture on it that contains the /ar/ sound."

  "I am going to describe it for you. See if you can guess what the picture is."

  "This is a part of your body. It begins at the top of your shoulder and ends down by your hand. It would be difficult to carry things without two of these. What do you think the picture is?" arm

  "That's right. The keyword is 'arm' and the sound we have learned is /ar/."

- Show the student **Picture Card 57.**

  "What will we say when we see this card?" arm, /ar/

- **Note:** The combination and its picture are also shown in the Rule Book on page 22.

  "Find your spelling sound sheet. Put your finger on the line by #38."

- Hold up **Spelling Card 38** so that only you can see what is written. Using the hand signals, follow the instructions on the card.
- Check the spelling sound sheet for accuracy.
- **Note:** Add the new letter, picture, and spelling cards to the Review Decks.

Lesson 71

Boardwork

- Write the following on the chalkboard:

  people /pē´ pəl/

  "We have a new sight word today. See if you can sound it out using the coding I have provided."

"Can you tell me what this word is? Remember, it's a sight word, so it won't follow all of our rules."

- Allow the student to try to pronounce the word. If necessary, say it for him/her.

  "This word is 'people.' Can you use the word 'people' in a sentence?" *expect various answers*

- Show the student **Sight Word Card 30.**

  "Let's find this word on our sight word charts."

- Help the student locate the word in the Irregular Spelling Booklet.

  "We will add this card to our sight word deck."

  "Let's practice coding some words like the ones you'll have on your worksheet."

  "The rule charts are in your Rule Book if you need to look at them."

- Write the following phrases and sentence (without the coding marks) on the chalkboard, one at a time. Ask the student to help you code them. The correct coding is as indicated:

  smart ănd swēēt

  thė sāmé căn

  Mĕg (was) lĭck´ing thė cāké spoon.

- Have the student determine whether each of the items coded is a word, a phrase, or a sentence.
- Add **Sight Word Card 30** to the Sight Word Deck.

WORKSHEET

- The student should be seated where he/she can write comfortably.
- Give the student **Worksheet 71.** Make sure the student turns to the correct side.

  "Today, let's spell with the /ar/ sound using combination ar."

  "Put your finger by #1. The first word is 'arm.' "

  "Unblend 'arm' with me." */ar/ /m/*

  "Now spell those sounds and write the word by #1."

- Allow time for the student to do this.

  "What word did you write?" *arm*

- Repeat the procedure with #2 (art), #3 (car), #4 (dark), and #5 (gargle).

  "Now you're ready to code and read the words on your paper."

  "Code the words by #6 through #10. After you have coded all the words, try to read them."

- Assist the student as necessary.

Lesson 71

"Numbers 11 and 12 are questions about the paragraph just above them. If you find any words you can't read, code them. Then see if you can answer the questions."

- As the student becomes more confident, he/she may begin to answer these written questions with complete sentences, although some children will continue to respond with single words or phrases. Any answer that shows comprehension is acceptable.
- As the student works, provide help as needed. Help the student correct any incorrect answers. Then initial the worksheet in the space provided.
- Some time during the day, ask the student to read from the worksheet, a controlled reader, your basal reader, or other material of your choice.
- **Note:** Always make sure the worksheet is corrected before the student begins the homework. The worksheet serves as a guide to help complete the homework.

HOMEWORK

"Turn your paper over to the homework side."

"Do you know what to do on the homework paper?"

"Remember to look for combination ar. Always code suffixes and final, stable syllables before coding the rest of the word."

"When you finish your paper, I will check it for you and initial it in the space provided."

- Either now or later in the day, the student should complete the homework independently (if possible). Help the student correct any incorrect answers. Then initial the homework in the space provided.

SPELLING LIST

- Fold **Spelling List 12** in half lengthwise (with the printed side facing out).

"Leave your paper just like I give it to you."

- Give the student **Spelling List 12,** folded with the blank lines facing up.

"Let's spell some more words."

- Call out the following words (in the order shown). Sound them out, if necessary.

  #1 (table), #2 (sniffle), #3 (apple), #4 (candle), #5 (little), #6 (jiggle), #7 (puzzle), #8 (title), #9 (fluff), #10 (class), #11 (friend), #12 (one)

"Now unfold your paper and check your words."

- Check the student's work to see if he/she needs extra help with spelling.

"I want you to practice these words. We'll have a spelling test in a few days."

- If possible, take time to play the Kid Card games listed in Lesson 70.

Name ____________________ Teacher's Initials ____

Worksheet 71
(for use with Lesson 71)
Phonics 1

ar

1. arm
2. art
3. car
4. dark
5. gargle
6. card
7. darkroom
8. kicking
9. home
10. tweet

Kim sells greeting cards. The cards tell people to have a happy day. She sells her cards to stores who sell them to the public.

11. What does Kim sell? greeting cards

12. Who sells cards to the public? stores

P1-WS-071a

Parent's Initials ____

Homework 71
(for use with Lesson 71)
Phonics 1

ar

1. mark
2. parking
3. creed
4. farmyard
5. buzzing
6. carp
7. yardstick
8. meek
9. roommate
10. grub

Mark parks cars. People drive up and he takes their cars and parks them. People tip him after he brings their cars back.

11. What does Mark do? He parks cars.

12. What does Mark get? He gets tips.

Parents: Your child has been taught **combination ar** (as in *arm*).

P1-WS-071b

Lesson 71

LESSON 72 Digraph *ch*, Part 1

lesson preparation

materials

Alphabet/Accent Deck (Section 1)
Retired Decks
Affix Deck
Spelling Sound Sheet 53
Letter Card 49
Picture Card 58
Spelling Card 39
Sight Word Card 31
Worksheet 72
Reader 25 (*Chester*)
colored pencils

ALPHABET ACTIVITY

"Today, we're going to work with the Alphabet/Accent Deck again."

"Let's stand up. Every time we say the accented syllable, we'll karate punch."

- Show the student **Alphabet/Accent Card 1.**
- Have the student say "A" (softly), and then "B" (as he/she punches forward).
- Continue with **Alphabet/Accent Cards 2–25,** moving as quickly as possible.

REVIEW OF DECKS

- The student should be seated where he/she can write comfortably.
- Show the student the retired letter cards in random order. The student should name the letter on each letter card.
- Review **Affix Cards 1–7.**
- Show the student the retired picture cards in random order. The student should name the keyword and sound for each picture card.
- Review the retired sight word cards.
- Give the student **Spelling Sound Sheet 53.**

- Call out the sounds on the retired spelling cards in random order. The student should echo each sound and name the letter or letters that make the sound as he/she writes the letter(s) on the spelling sound sheet.
- **Note:** The spelling sound sheet will always contain enough lines to accommodate the entire spelling deck.
- Have the student set the spelling sound sheet aside for use later in the lesson.

NEW LEARNING

"I'm going to say some words to you. Echo them back to me and listen for the sound that is the same in each word."

- Point to your mouth as you say each word.

"Echo after me. Chart." *chart* ***"Touch."*** *touch* ***"Chimp."*** *chimp*

"What sound do you hear that is the same in each of these words?" */ch/*

"That's right. The sound you hear is /ch/."

- Write the following on the chalkboard: chart, touch, chimp.

"What do you see that might be making the /ch/ sound?" *ch*

"How many sounds do you hear?" *one*

"How many letters are making that sound?" *two*

"What do you think 'ch' is?" *a digraph, because it is two letters that make one sound*

"How do we code digraphs?" *draw a line under them*

- Underline digraph *ch* in each of the words on the chalkboard.

"Is digraph ch a vowel digraph or a consonant digraph?" *consonant digraph*

NEW DECK CARDS

- Hold up **Letter Card 49.**

"What do we call this?" *digraph ch*

- Hold up **Picture Card 58** but keep the picture covered with your hand (or the letter card).

"I have a card with a picture on it that contains the /ch/ sound."

"I am going to describe it for you. See if you can guess what the picture is."

"This is a kind of food. It is made from milk and comes in many different kinds, like swiss, cheddar, or parmesan. It is a main ingredient in pizza and nachos. What do you think the picture is?" *cheese*

- Show the student **Picture Card 58.**

"The word 'cheese' helps us remember the /ch/ sound because it begins with /ch/."

- **Note:** The digraph and its picture are also shown in the Rule Book on page 21.

"Find your spelling sound sheet. Put your finger on the line by #39."

- **Note:** Because some of the spelling cards may have been retired, the next available line on the spelling sound sheet may not be #39. Glance at the student's paper to determine the correct line or simply instruct the student to use the next available line for the spelling card response.
- Hold up **Spelling Card 39** so that only you can see what is written. Using the hand signals, follow the instructions on the card.
- Check the spelling sound sheet for accuracy.
- **Note:** Add the new letter, picture, and spelling cards to the Review Decks.

BOARDWORK

- Write the following on the chalkboard:

there /~~th~~ĕr/

"We have a new sight word today. See if you can read it using the coding I've provided."

"Can you tell me what this word is? Remember, it's a sight word, so it won't follow all of our rules."

- Allow the student to try to pronounce the word. If necessary, say it for him/her.

"This word is 'there.' Can you use the word 'there' in a sentence?" *expect various answers*

- Make sure the student does not confuse "there" ("in," "at," or "to that place") with the words "their" or "they're."
- Show the student **Sight Word Card 31.**

"Let's find this word on our sight word charts."

- Help the student locate the word in the Irregular Spelling Booklet.

"We will add this card to our sight word deck."

"Let's practice coding some words like the ones you'll have on your worksheet."

"The rule charts are in your Rule Book if you need to look at them."

- Write the following phrase and sentence (without the coding marks) on the chalkboard, one at a time. Ask the student to help you code them. The correct coding is as indicated:

hăp′ | pẙ p<u>er</u>′ | sŏn
vc | cv vc | cv

~~Th~~e dŏg[~~s~~] l<u>oo</u>k[ed] ŏn ~~ăs~~ å f<u>ar</u>′ | m<u>er</u> slĕpt ĭn (their) <u>chā</u>/r.
vc | cv

- Have the student determine whether each of the items coded is a word, a phrase, or a sentence.
- Add **Sight Word Card 31** to the Sight Word Deck.

WORKSHEET

- The student should be seated where he/she can write comfortably.
- Give the student **Worksheet 72.** Make sure the student turns to the correct side.

"Today, let's spell with the /ch/ sound using digraph ch."

"Put your finger by #1. The first word is 'check.' "

"Unblend 'check' with me." */ch/ /ĕ/ /k/*

- Hold up one finger for each sound.

"Refer to Rule Chart 4 for the last sound, if you need to."

"Let's spell those sounds." *ch … e … ck*

- Point to a finger as the student spells each sound.

"Now spell the word again and write the letters as you say them."

- Allow time for the student to do this.

"What word did you write?" *check*

- Repeat the procedure with #2 (inch) and #3 (march).

"What special thing would we need to do to the word 'March' if we were spelling the name of the month?" *capitalize the m*

- Continue with #4 (such) and #5 (chill).
- After the student has written the word "chill," remind him/her that the floss rule should have been applied. If the student misspelled the word, allow him/her to correct it.

"Now you're ready to code and read the words on your paper."

"Code the words by #6 through #10. After you have coded all the words, try to read them."

- Assist the student as necessary.

"Now read the word by #11. If you have trouble reading the word, code it. Then draw a line from the word to the picture it matches."

- Repeat with #12, #13, and #14.
- As the student works, provide help as needed. Help the student correct any incorrect answers. Then initial the worksheet in the space provided.
- Some time during the day, ask the student to read from the worksheet, a controlled reader, your basal reader, or other material of your choice.
- **Note:** Always make sure the worksheet is corrected before the student begins the homework. The worksheet serves as a guide to help complete the homework.

Homework

"Turn your paper over to the homework side."

"Do you know what to do on the homework paper?"

"Be sure to look for digraph ch. Always code suffixes and final, stable syllables before coding the rest of the word."

- Discuss the homework pictures to make sure the student understands the word each one represents: #11 (car), #12 (chest), #13 (harp), and #14 (chin).

"When you finish your paper, I will check it for you and initial it in the space provided."

- Either now or later in the day, the student should complete the homework independently (if possible). Help the student correct any incorrect answers. Then initial the homework in the space provided.

Reader

"We have another new book today."

- Give the student **Reader 25 (*Chester*)** and some colored pencils.

"Can you tell me this book's title?" *Chester*

- Assist the student as necessary as he/she constructs the book.
- When the student finishes, staple or put a rubber band around the book's spine.
- If necessary, demonstrate how to separate the pages and check the page order.

"The title of this book is __________?" *Chester*

"I want you to read your book to yourself. When you are finished reading, color the pictures. Write your name on the book so I will know who colored it."

"Keep your book handy because I will be asking you to read it for me."

- Some time during the day, have the student read the reader to you.
- If possible, take time to play the Kid Card games listed in Lesson 70.

Name ______________________________

Teacher's Initials _____

Worksheet 72
(for use with Lesson 72)
Phonics 1

ch

1. check
2. inch
3. march
4. such
5. chill
6. chain
7. charming
8. perch
9. chose
10. pinched

11. artist

12. chick

13. barn

14. highchair

P1-WS-072a

Parent's Initials _____

Homework 72
(for use with Lesson 72)
Phonics 1

ch

1. bunch
2. start
3. choke
4. slanted
5. punching
6. charting
7. champ
8. lifting
9. marched
10. brunch

11. car

13. harp

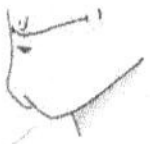

12. chest

14. chin

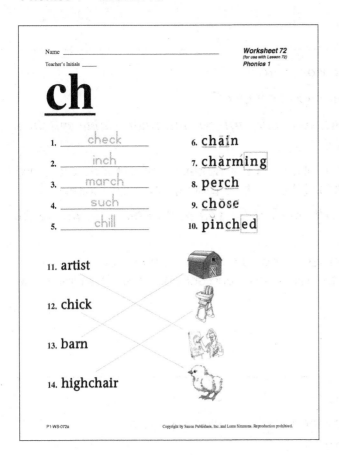

Parents: Your child has been taught **digraph ch** (as in *cheese*).

P1-WS-072b

Lesson 72

LESSON 73 Combination *or*

lesson preparation

materials

Activity Sheet 2

Review Decks

Spelling Sound Sheet 54

tokens or colored pencil

Letter Card 50

Picture Card 59

Spelling Card 40

Worksheet 73

the night before

- If possible, locate something fun to use as bingo tokens. Small wrapped candies, goldfish-shaped crackers, and cereal pieces work well.

ALPHABET ACTIVITY

- The student should be seated.

  "Let's alphabetize words in a list again today. Do you remember how we did that? I'll show you how again."

- Write the following on the chalkboard:

  _____ farmer
  _____ jar
  _____ harm
  _____ cart
  _____ barn
  _____ dart
  _____ lark

  "Which letter will we use as our 'guide letter'?" *the first one*

  "Let's underline the guide letters so we can see them easily."

- Underline the first letter in each word. Let the student help you make sure all of the first letters are different.

"When we alphabetize words in lists, we can't move the words. Let's use the little trick with numbers we tried last week."

"How many words are in this list?" *7*

"We are going to put numbers 1 through 7 below (or beside) our list to use as we alphabetize."

- Write the numbers 1–7 below (or beside) the list of words.

"Now we'll recite the alphabet slowly and scan the guide letters on these words each time we say a letter."

"Let's start. A."

- Quickly scan the guide letters with your index finger.

"Is there an a?" *no*

"B."

- Quickly scan the guide letters with your index finger.

"Is there a b?" *yes*

"Let's put a 1 beside 'barn' and mark out the 1 at the bottom. We'll know to put a 2 by the next word."

"C." *yes*

- Put a 2 in front of "cart" and mark out the 2 at the bottom.

"D." *yes*

- Put a 3 in front of "dart" and mark out the 3 at the bottom.

"E." *no*

"F." *yes*

- Put a 4 in front of "farmer" and mark out the 4 at the bottom.

"G." *no*

"H." *yes*

- Put a 5 in front of "harm" and mark out the 5 at the bottom.

"I." *no*

"J." *yes*

- Put a 6 in front of "jar" and mark out the 6 at the bottom.

"K." *no*

"L." *yes*

- Put a 7 in front of "lark" and mark out the 7 at the bottom.

"All of the words have been used, so we can stop."

"Today I'm going to let you try this yourself."

- Give the student **Activity Sheet 2.**

"Alphabetize these words just like we alphabetized the words on the chalkboard."

- Assist the student as necessary. The correct order is 3, 1, 2, 4.

- **Optional:** Letter order can be checked, but it is more difficult. If you would like to check letter order with the student, quickly recite the alphabet, starting with your finger on number 1. As the appropriate letter is named, move your finger to number 2 and continue until that letter is named. Move your finger to the next number each time the appropriate letter is named.

REVIEW OF DECKS

- The student should be seated where he/she can write comfortably.
- Show the student **Letter Cards 1–49** in random order. The student should name the letter on each letter card.
- Review **Affix Cards 1–7.**
- Show the student **Picture Cards 1–58** in random order. The student should name the keyword and sound for each picture card.
- Review **Sight Word Cards 1–31.**
- Give the student **Spelling Sound Sheet 54** and at least a dozen tokens (or a colored pencil).

"Let's play Bingo!"

"When I call out the spelling sounds, I want you to put a token on (or draw a big X in) the space that spells that sound."

"When you cover (or X out) all of the letters on one line, either up and down, across, or from corner to corner, call out Bingo!"

"Don't forget to refer to your rule charts if you need to."

"Are you ready?"

"Cover (or X out) the letters that spell the final sound in 'still.' " *ll*

"Cover (or X out) the letters that spell the suffix in 'slowly.' " *ly*

"Cover (or X out) the letters that spell the vowel sound in 'spray.' " *ay*

"Cover (or X out) the letters that spell the k sound in 'hike.' " *ke*

"Cover (or X out) the letters that spell the initial sound in 'artist.' " *ar*

"Cover (or X out) the letters that spell the suffix in 'harmless.' " *less*

"Cover (or X out) the letters that spell the final sound in 'stuff.' " *ff*

"Cover (or X out) the letters that spell the medial sound in 'term.' " *er*

"Cover (or X out) the letter that spells the final sound in 'shook.' " *k*

"Cover (or X out) the letter that spells the final sound in 'majestic.' " *c*

"Cover (or X out) the letters that spell the initial sound in 'choose.' " *ch*

- The student should Bingo by the time all the sounds have been called out.
- Collect the tokens (or colored pencil) and the spelling sound sheet. If you used tokens and the spelling sound sheet is unmarked, keep it available for practice.

NEW LEARNING

"I'm going to say some words to you. Echo them back to me and listen for the sound that is the same in each word."

- Point to your mouth as you say each word.

"Echo after me. Cork." *cork* ***"Sort."*** *sort* ***"Forget."*** *forget*

"What sound do you hear that is the same in all of these words?" */or/*

"That's right. The sound you hear is /or/."

"Put your fingertips on the front of your neck and say /or/. See if you feel any vibration."

"Is this sound voiced or unvoiced?" *voiced*

"Since /or/ vibrates, it is a voiced sound."

- Write the following words on the chalkboard: cork, sort, forget.

"What do you see that might be making the /or/ sound?" *or*

"That's right. Do you think /or/ is a digraph or a combination?" *a combination*

"Remember, a combination is two letters that come together to make an unexpected sound. The 'o' looks like it should be coded short. But if the 'o' made its short sound, the 'or' would say something like 'are.'"

"So 'or' is coded as a combination. How do we code combinations?" *put an arc underneath*

- Code the words:

cork sort for|gĕt´
vc|cv

NEW DECK CARDS

- Hold up **Letter Card 50.**

"What do we call this?" *combination or*

- Hold up **Picture Card 59** but keep the picture covered with your hand (or the letter card).

"I have a card with a picture on it that contains the /or/ sound."

"I am going to describe it for you. See if you can guess what the picture is."

"This is an eating utensil. It is made of metal and usually has three or four points for picking up food. You would not use one of these if you were eating a sandwich or a bowl of soup. This is used for eating spaghetti, green beans, or a piece of cake. What do you think the picture is?" *fork*

"That's right. The keyword is 'fork' and the sound we have learned is /or/."

- Show the student **Picture Card 59.**

- **Note:** The combination and its picture are also shown in the Rule Book on page 22.

  "Combination or is used a lot for spelling, so we are going to add a new spelling card today."

- Hold up **Spelling Card 40** so only you can see what is written. Follow the instructions on the card. Have the student write the letters with his/her finger on the desktop, or skywrite the letter.
- **Note:** Add the new letter, picture, and spelling cards to the Review Decks.

Boardwork

"Let's practice coding some words like the ones you'll have on your worksheet."

"The rule charts are in your Rule Book if you need to look at them."

- Write the following sentences (without the coding marks) on the chalkboard, one at a time. Ask the student to help you code them. The correct coding is as indicated:

  Hē´ chĕck|ed| ŏn the̊ short snāil.

  Ī´ sēe å dĕnse bŭnch (of) trēe|s| ĭn the̊ park.

- Remind the student that *e* at the end of a word is almost always silent. Sometimes it is a sneaky *e* and other times it is simply a silent *e*, as in "dense."
- Have the student determine whether each of the items coded is a word, a phrase, or a sentence.

Worksheet

- The student should be seated where he/she can write comfortably.
- Give the student **Worksheet 73.** Make sure the student turns to the correct side.

  "Today, let's spell with the /or/ sound."

  "Combination or can be used in the initial, medial, or final position."

  "Put your finger by #1. The first word is 'horn.' "

  "Unblend 'horn' with me." */h/ /or/ /n/*

- Hold up one finger for each sound.

  "Now spell the word again and write the letters as you say them."

- Allow time for the student to do this.

  "What word did you write?" *horn*

- Repeat the procedure with #2 (for), #3 (corn), #4 (north), and #5 (porch).

  "Now you're ready to code and read the words on your paper."

  "Code the words by #6 through #10. After you have coded all the words, try to read them."

- Assist the student as necessary.

"Numbers 11 and 12 are questions about the paragraph just above them. If you find any words you can't read, code them. Then see if you can answer the questions."

- As the student works, provide help as needed. Help the student correct any incorrect answers. Then initial the worksheet in the space provided.
- Some time during the day, ask the student to read from the worksheet, a controlled reader, your basal reader, or other material of your choice.
- **Note:** Always make sure the worksheet is corrected before the student begins the homework. The worksheet serves as a guide to help complete the homework.

HOMEWORK

"Turn your paper over to the homework side."

"Do you know what to do on the homework paper?"

"Remember to look for combination or. Always code suffixes and final, stable syllables before coding the rest of the word."

"When you finish your paper, I will check it for you and initial it in the space provided."

- Either now or later in the day, the student should complete the homework independently (if possible). Help the student correct any incorrect answers. Then initial the homework in the space provided.
- If possible, take time to play the Kid Card games listed in Lesson 70.

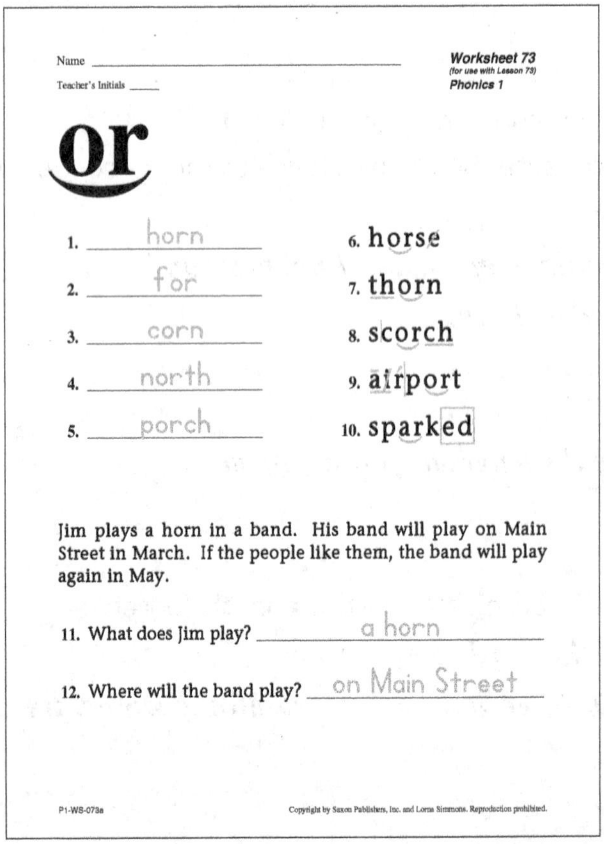

Name ____________ Teacher's Initials ____

Worksheet 73 (for use with Lesson 73) Phonics 1

or

1. horn
2. for
3. corn
4. north
5. porch
6. horse
7. thorn
8. scorch
9. airport
10. sparked

Jim plays a horn in a band. His band will play on Main Street in March. If the people like them, the band will play again in May.

11. What does Jim play? a horn

12. Where will the band play? on Main Street

P1-WS-073a Copyright by Saxon Publishers, Inc. and Lorna Simmons. Reproduction prohibited.

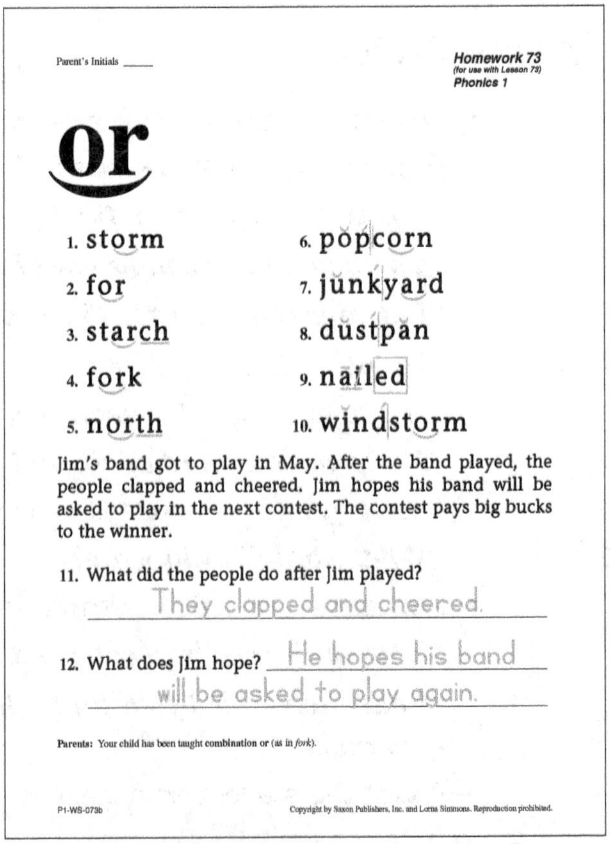

Parent's Initials ____

Homework 73 (for use with Lesson 73) Phonics 1

or

1. storm
2. for
3. starch
4. fork
5. north
6. popcorn
7. junkyard
8. dustpan
9. nailed
10. windstorm

Jim's band got to play in May. After the band played, the people clapped and cheered. Jim hopes his band will be asked to play in the next contest. The contest pays big bucks to the winner.

11. What did the people do after Jim played? They clapped and cheered.

12. What does Jim hope? He hopes his band will be asked to play again.

Parents: Your child has been taught combination or (as in *fork*).

P1-WS-073b Copyright by Saxon Publishers, Inc. and Lorna Simmons. Reproduction prohibited.

Lesson 73

LESSON 74 Combination *qu*

lesson preparation

materials

Alphabet/Accent Deck (Section 1)
Review Decks
Spelling Sound Sheet 55
container of letter tiles
Letter Card 51
Picture Card 60
Spelling Card 41
Sight Word Cards 32–33
Worksheet 74
Reader 26 (*Copper*)
colored pencils

ALPHABET ACTIVITY

- The student should be seated.

  "Let's work with the Alphabet/Accent Deck again today."

  "Let's say the first syllable in a normal voice and then say the accented syllable with a higher pitch."

- Show the student **Alphabet/Accent Card 1.**
- Have the student say "A" (in a normal voice), and then "B" (with a higher pitch).
- Continue with **Alphabet/Accent Cards 2–25,** moving as quickly as possible.

REVIEW OF DECKS

- The student should be seated where he/she can write comfortably.
- Show the student **Letter Cards 1–50** in random order. The student should name the letter on each letter card.
- Review **Affix Cards 1–7.**
- Show the student **Picture Cards 1–59** in random order. The student should name the keyword and sound for each picture card.

- Review **Sight Word Cards 1–31.**
- Give the student **Spelling Sound Sheet 55.**
- Call out the sounds on **Spelling Cards 1–40** in random order. The student should echo each sound and name the letter or letters that make the sound as he/she writes the letter(s) on the spelling sound sheet.
- Have the student set the spelling sound sheet aside for use later in the lesson.

NEW LEARNING

"I'm going to say some words. Echo them back to me and listen for the sound that is the same in each word."

- Point to your mouth as you say each word.

"Echo after me. Queen." *queen* ***"Quack."*** *quack* ***"Squint."*** *squint*

"What sound do you hear that is the same in each of these words?" */kw/*

"That's right. The sound you hear is /kw/."

"Put your fingertips on the front of your neck and say /kw/. See if you feel any vibration."

"Is this sound voiced or unvoiced?" *unvoiced*

- Write the following on the chalkboard: queen, quack, squint.

"What do you see that might be making the /kw/ sound?" *qu*

"There is a qu in all of these words, so we can see that qu must be the letters used to spell the /kw/ sound."

"How many sounds do you hear?" *one*

"How many letters are making that sound?" *two*

"Does qu look like it would make the sound of /kw/?" *no*

"So we have two letters that come together and make an unexpected sound."

"What do we call that?" *a combination*

- The letter *q* is almost always part of combination *qu*. Sometimes it will be seen alone in "invented" words (e.g., advertising copy and brand names).

Lesson 74

HANDWRITING/LETTER TILES

- The student should be seated where he/she can write comfortably.
- Write a capital *Q* on the chalkboard.

"This is a capital Q. Let's practice skywriting capital Q's before we write them on our papers."

- Have the student practice skywriting capital *Q*'s.

"Find your spelling sound sheet."

- Draw handwriting lines on the chalkboard. Write a capital *Q* on the handwriting lines in the handwriting you want the student to learn.

"Find the first handwriting line on your paper and practice writing capital Q's like I wrote this one on the chalkboard."

"Say the name of the letter each time you write it."

- Allow a few minutes for the student to practice writing capital *Q*'s.
- Write a lowercase *q* on the handwriting lines in the handwriting you want the student to learn.

"This is a lowercase q."

- Have the student practice skywriting lowercase *q*'s.

"Now practice writing lowercase q's on the second handwriting line. Say the name of the letter each time you write it."

- Have the student set the spelling sound sheet aside for use later in the lesson.
- Leave the handwriting lines and letters on the chalkboard for the remainder of the lesson.
- Give the student the container of letter tiles.

"I've already given you the q letter tile. Pour all of the tiles onto your desk and see if you can find the q."

- Allow time for the student to locate the *q* letter tile.

"Look at your q letter tile. One side has a capital Q and the other side has a lowercase q."

"Hold your letter tile up in the air. Turn it so I can see the capital Q."

"Now turn it so I can see the lowercase q."

"In order to spell words with the letter q, what other letter do we need?" *u*

"That's right. Find the u letter tile and put it next to the q."

- Allow time for the student to locate the *u* letter tile.

"Spell the word 'quiz' with your letter tiles."

"Now change one letter to make the word 'quit.'"

"Now add one letter to make the word 'quite.'"

- Choose additional words from the Spelling Word List, if desired.
- Have the student replace the tiles in the container and put it away.
- Reinforce the name and shape of the letter *q* (and the sound of combination *qu*) throughout the day.

NEW DECK CARDS

- Hold up **Letter Card 51.**

  "What do we call this?" *combination qu*
- Hold up **Picture Card 60** but keep the picture covered with your hand (or the letter card).

  "I have a card with a picture on it that contains the /kw/ sound in the initial position."

  "I am going to describe it for you. See if you can guess what the picture is."

  "This is a type of bird. It has mottled brown plumage and a short tail. Its call sounds like 'bob white.' What do you think the picture is?" *quail*

  "That's right. The keyword is 'quail' and the sound we have learned is /kw/."
- Show the student **Picture Card 60,** and then point to the picture of a quail on the alphabet strip.

  "The word 'quail' helps us remember the /kw/ sound because it begins with /kw/."
- **Note:** The combination and its picture are also shown in the Rule Book on page 22.

  "Find your spelling sound sheet. Put your finger on the line by #41."
- Hold up **Spelling Card 41** so only you can see what is written. Using the hand signals, follow the instructions on the card.
- Check the spelling sound sheet for accuracy.
- **Note:** Add the new letter, picture, and spelling cards to the Review Decks.

BOARDWORK

- Write the following on the chalkboard:

  love /lŭv/ shoe /shōō/

  "We have some new sight words today."
- Point to the first word.

  "Can you tell me what this word is? Remember, it's a sight word, so it won't follow all of our rules."
- Allow the student to try to pronounce the word. If necessary, say it for him/her.

  "This word is 'love.' Can you use the word 'love' in a sentence?" *expect various answers*
- Repeat with "shoe."
- Show the student **Sight Word Cards 32** and **33.**

  "Let's find these words on our sight word charts."
- Help the student locate the words in the Irregular Spelling Booklet.

  "We will add these cards to our sight word deck."

  "Let's practice coding some words like the ones you'll have on your worksheet."

"The rule charts are in your Rule Book if you need to look at them."

- Write the following word and sentences (without the coding marks) on the chalkboard, one at a time. Ask the student to help you code them. The correct coding is as indicated:

quĭlt′ĭng

(Put) th̶ĕ kītȩ ĭn th̶ăt c̲o̲r̲′ n e̲r̲.
 v c｜c v

Th̶ĕ sh̲ă̲c̶k (was) mād̶ȩ (to) lo̲o̲k līk̶ȩ å f̲o̲r̲t.

- Have the student determine whether each of the items coded is a word, a phrase, or a sentence.

- Add **Sight Word Cards 32** and **33** to the Sight Word Deck.

WORKSHEET

- The student should be seated where he/she can write comfortably.

- Give the student **Worksheet 74.** Make sure the student turns to the correct side.

 "Let's spell with the /kw/ sound using combination qu. Remember that q almost never comes by itself. It almost always comes with the letter u."

 "Also, combination qu is never used in the final position, only in the initial or medial position."

 "Put your finger by #1. The first word is 'quest.' "

 "Unblend 'quest' with me." */kw/ /ĕ/ /s/ /t/*

- Hold up one finger for each sound.

 "Now spell the word and write it on the line by #1."

- Allow time for the student to do this.

 "What word did you write?" *quest*

- Repeat the procedure with #2 (quit), #3 (quake), #4 (chart), and #5 (born).

 "Now you're ready to code and read the words on your paper."

 "Code the words by #6 through #10. After you have coded all the words, try to read them."

- Assist the student as necessary.

 "Now read the word by #11. If you have trouble reading the word, code it. Then draw a line from the word to the picture it matches."

- Repeat with #12 (fork), #13 (check), and #14 (horn).

- As the student works, provide help as needed. Help the student correct any incorrect answers. Then initial the worksheet in the space provided.

- Some time during the day, ask the student to read from the worksheet, a controlled reader, your basal reader, or other material of your choice.

- **Note:** Always make sure the worksheet is corrected before the student begins the homework. The worksheet serves as a guide to help complete the homework.

HOMEWORK

"Turn your paper over to the homework side."

"Put your finger on the top row of handwriting lines. Write your best capital Q on these lines so I will know what a capital Q should look like."

- Have the student write a lowercase letter *q* on the second handwriting line. Make sure that the student has written the letters correctly (to the best of his or her ability). He/She will use them as guides when completing the homework.

"Do you know what to do on the homework paper?"

"Be sure to look for combinations ar, or, and qu. Always code suffixes and final, stable syllables before coding the rest of the word."

- Discuss the homework pictures to make sure the student understands the word each one represents: #11 (quilt), #12 (horse), #13 (torch), and #14 (stork).

"When you finish your paper, I will check it for you and initial it in the space provided."

- Either now or later in the day, the student should complete the homework independently (if possible). Help the student correct any incorrect answers. Then initial the homework in the space provided.

READER

"We have another new book today."

- Give the student **Reader 26 (*Copper*)** and some colored pencils.

"Can you tell me this book's title?" *Copper*

- Assist the student as necessary as he/she constructs the book.
- When the student finishes, staple or put a rubber band around the book's spine.
- If necessary, demonstrate how to separate the pages and check the page order.

"The title of this book is __________?" *Copper*

"I want you to read your book to yourself. When you are finished reading, color the pictures. Write your name on the book so I will know who colored it."

"Keep your book handy because I will be asking you to read it for me."

- Some time during the day, have the student read the reader to you.
- If possible, take time to play the Kid Card games listed in Lesson 70. Try to see that the student is prepared for tomorrow's assessment.

Name ______________________________ **Worksheet 74**
(for use with Lesson 74)
Phonics 1

Teacher's Initials _____

qu

1. quest
2. quit
3. quake
4. chart
5. born
6. quite
7. quack
8. scorn
9. shortstop
10. hornet

11. queen
12. fork
13. check
14. horn

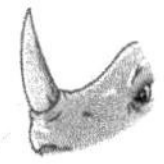

P1-WS-074a

Parent's Initials _____ **Homework 74**
(for use with Lesson 74)
Phonics 1

qu

1. quake
2. quick
3. kick
4. quest
5. slate
6. corner
7. wade
8. shortcake
9. orbit
10. absorb

11. quilt

12. horse

13. torch

14. stork

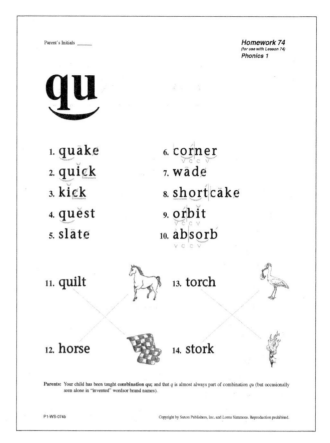

Parents: Your child has been taught **combination qu;** and that *q* is almost always part of combination *qu* (but occasionally seen alone in "invented" wordsor brand names).

P1-WS-074b

LESSON 75 — Assessment

lesson preparation

materials

Alphabet/Accent Deck (Section 1)
Review Decks
Assessment 14
Spelling Test 12
Assessment 14 Recording Form
Kid Cards
tokens

the night before

- Separate the Kid Cards marked "Lesson 75."

ALPHABET ACTIVITY

"We're going to work with the Alphabet/Accent Deck again today."

"Let's stand up. Every time we say the accented syllable, we'll karate punch."

- Show the student **Alphabet/Accent Card 1.**
- Have the student say "A" (softly), and then "B" (as he/she punches forward).
- Continue with **Alphabet/Accent Cards 2–25,** moving as quickly as possible.

REVIEW OF DECKS

- The student should be seated where he/she can write comfortably.
- Show the student **Letter Cards 1–51** in random order. The student should name the letter on each letter card.
- Review **Affix Cards 1–7.**
- Show the student **Picture Cards 1–60** in random order. The student should name the keyword and sound for each picture card.
- Review **Sight Word Cards 1–33.**

Written Assessment

- Have the student sit where he/she can write comfortably.
- Give the student **Assessment 14.**
- **Section I:**

  "Today we are going to write some words for our assessment."

  "I'm going to say a word. Write the letter that makes each sound in that word on the lines by #1."

  "Look at the rule charts if you need to."

  "Here's the first word: spray."
- Repeat with the following words in the order shown: #2 (goodness), #3 (helpless), #4 (softly), and #5 (sandbox).
- **Reminder:** While the student spells, be ready to point to appropriate rule charts as necessary.
- **Section II:**

  "Look at the letters by #6."

  "Find the picture of the keyword for this sound."

  "Draw a line from the letters to the keyword."
- Repeat with #7. Allow a few minutes for the student to work.
- The pictures (from top to bottom) are as follows: rain, hay.
- **Section III:**

  "Put your finger on #8."

  "Code the words by #8 through #12."
- Allow a few minutes for the student to work.
- **Section IV:**

  "Read the paragraph. If you find any words you can't read, code them to help you figure them out. Then answer the questions by #13 through #19."
- **Reminder:** If the student absolutely cannot read the paragraph, read it to the student to see if he or she can answer the questions.

  "When you are finished, show your paper to me."
- This paper will be used during the oral portion of the assessment.

Spelling Test

- Give the student **Spelling Test 12.**
- Call out the following words (in the order shown). Sound them out, if necessary.

  #1 (title), #2 (sniffle), #3 (class), #4 (puzzle), #5 (jiggle), #6 (little),
  #7 (candle), #8 (table), #9 (apple), #10 (fluff), #11 (friend), #12 (one)
- Grade and record the test in any manner that suits your needs.

Oral Assessment

- It is important to complete the oral assessment promptly (today, if possible) in order to identify any areas of weakness and begin remediation.
- Use the assessment and the following dialogue to complete the oral portion.
- **Section V:**
- Point to the sight word by #20.

  "Read this sight word for me."
- Record the student's response by placing a check mark by each word he/she reads correctly.
- Repeat with #21, #22, and #23.
- **Section VI:**
- Show the student the letters by #24.

  "Tell me the name of these letters and the sound they make."
- Write the student's response on the adjacent line.
- Repeat with #25.

Assessment Evaluation

- Grade the assessment and record the results on **Assessment 14 Recording Form.** Check off the boxes to indicate mastery (i.e., the section was completed with 100% accuracy).
- **Reminder:** Try to give as many points as possible for work attempted. Do not grade the coding marks too severely. The most important coding marks to look for are breves, macrons, and syllable division lines.
- See the introductory material for detailed information regarding grading and recording procedures.
- Use the assessment results to identify those skills in which the student is weak. Practice those skills by playing Kid Card games.
- Add the Kid Cards marked "Lesson 75" to the existing decks. Listed below are games appropriate for remediation in selected areas. See "Games and Activities" for the directions for each game.
- **Section I:** Play "Spelling Deck Perfection," "Sound Scamper," "Spell Out #1," or have the student use the letter tiles to spell words you give from the Spelling Word List.
- **Section II:** Play "Keyword and Sound" or "Letter/Sound Identification."
- **Section III:** Play "Chalkboard Challenge."
- **Section IV:** Either have the student read the controlled readers and then ask questions for comprehension, or play "Acting Out" with the green Kid Cards.
- **Section V:** Play "At First Sight," review the Sight Word Deck, or lay the sight words out with a token on each one and let the student try to get as many tokens as possible for the sight words he/she can read.

- **Section VI:** Play "Letter/Sound Identification."
- When the student seems more secure in areas that had previously proven difficult, retest him/her (in those areas only) and indicate on the recording form any sections the student has subsequently mastered.
- Try to help the student achieve mastery of all the sections before the next assessment.
- If the student is having difficulty with a particular skill, keep his or her practice activities at the most basic level so the chance of success is greater.

Name ______________________

Assessment 14
(for use with Lesson 75)
Phonics 1

Section I

1. s p r a y
2. g o o d n e s s
3. h e l p l e s s
4. s o f t l y
5. s a n d b o x

Section II

6. ā~~y~~

7. ā~~i~~

Section III

8. sprāy
9. snāil
10. windmill
11. flăshlight
12. footprint

Section IV

The night was cool and Jake and Dad went on a bike ride. Jake was happy that Dad trusted him to ride at night with him. Jake and Dad rode to the lake and sat by the dock. The fish jumped and Jake and Dad tossed pebbles. Soon it was time to go back. It was a fun night with Dad.

13. What was the night like?
    cool, fun
14. What did Dad trust Jake to do?
    ride at night with him
15. Where did Jake and Dad go?
    to the lake
16. What did Jake and Dad do at the lake?
    sat by the dock tossed pebbles

P1-A-014a

Assessment 14
(for use with Lesson 75)
Phonics 1

17. What jumped?
    fish
18. What did Jake and Dad toss?
    pebbles
19. Did Jake like to ride with Dad?
    yes

Section V

20. they ______
21. build ______
22. built ______
23. people ______

Section VI

24. ay digraph ay, /ā/
25. ai digraph ai, /ā/

P1-A-014b

Lesson 75

LESSON 76 — **Combination *ir***

lesson preparation

materials

container of letter tiles

Review Decks

Spelling Sound Sheet 56

Letter Card 52

Picture Card 61

Sight Word Cards 34–37

Worksheet 76

Spelling List 13

ALPHABET ACTIVITY

- The student should be seated with the container of letter tiles.

  "Before we start, let's say the alphabet together so it is fresh in our minds."

- Recite the alphabet with the student.

  "Today, I'm going to let you try to put the letter tiles in alphabetical order again. When I say 'go,' dump your tiles on the desk, turn them to the lowercase (blue) side, and begin working."

  "Sometimes it's hard to tell if a lowercase letter is right side up or upside down. If you're not sure, look at the other side to see which end is up."

  "Ready, set, go!"

- Allow enough time for the student to alphabetize the letters.
- If desired, time the student and compare it with his/her time from Lesson 66.
- Have the student replace the tiles in the container and put it away.

REVIEW OF DECKS

- The student should be seated where he/she can write comfortably.
- Show the student **Letter Cards 1–51** in random order. The student should name the letter on each letter card.
- Review **Affix Cards 1–7.**

- Show the student **Picture Cards 1–60** in random order. The student should name the keyword and sound for each picture card.
- Review **Sight Word Cards 1–33.**
- Give the student **Spelling Sound Sheet 56.**
- Call out the sounds on **Spelling Cards 1–41** in random order. The student should echo each sound and name the letter or letters that make the sound as he/she writes the letter(s) on the spelling sound sheet.
- Check the student's response after each card.

NEW LEARNING

"I'm going to say some words. Echo them back to me and listen for the sound that is the same in each word."

- Point to your mouth as you say each word.

"Echo after me. Dirt." *dirt* ***"Fir."*** *fir* ***"Girl."*** *girl*

"What sound do you hear that is the same in each of these words?" */er/*

"That's right. The sound you hear is /er/."

"Put your fingertips on the front of your neck and say /er/. See if you feel any vibration."

"Is this sound voiced or unvoiced?" *voiced*

- Write the following words on the chalkboard: dirt, fir, girl.

"What do you see that might be making the /er/ sound?" *ir*

"The letters 'ir' can make the same sound as the letters 'er.' "

"How many sounds do you hear?" *one*

"How many letters are making that sound?" *two*

"What do you think 'ir' is?" *a combination*

"That's right. If we tried to code it, it would say /ear/. It makes an unexpected sound, so it is a combination."

"How do we code combinations?" *put arcs underneath them*

- Code the words: dirt, fir, girl.
- Leave the words on the chalkboard for the remainder of the lesson.

NEW DECK CARDS

- Show the student **Letter Card 52.**

"What do we call this?" *combination ir*

- Hold up **Picture Card 61** but keep the picture covered with your hand (or the letter card).

"I have a card with a picture on it that contains the /er/ sound."

"I am going to describe it for you. See if you can guess what the picture is."

"This is a piece of clothing that you wear on the upper part of your body. It might button up the front, or it might be pulled on over your head. It can be short-sleeved or long-sleeved. What do you think the picture is?" shirt

"That's right. The keyword is 'shirt' and the sound we have learned is /er/."

- Show the student **Picture Card 61.**

"The word 'shirt' helps us remember the /er/ sound that is spelled 'ir.' "

- **Note:** The combination and its picture are also shown in the Rule Book on page 22.

"When you are spelling a word you don't know, the best choice for the /er/ sound is still 'er,' so we won't add 'ir' to our spelling deck response for the /er/ sound."

"Get out your Irregular Spelling Booklet."

"Look at the table of contents. Can you find the page that shows words spelled with combination ir?" page 22

"Turn to page 22. All of these words are spelled with combination ir. They don't follow our regular rules, so we must memorize them. For now, you can refer to this booklet any time you're spelling."

- **Note:** Add the new letter and picture cards to the Review Decks.

BOARDWORK

- Write the following on the chalkboard:

full /fo͝ol/ goes /gōz/ pull /po͝ol/ want /wŏnt/

"We have some new sight words today."

- Point to the first word.

"Can you tell me what this word is? Remember, it's a sight word, so it won't follow all of our rules."

- Allow the student to try to pronounce the word. If necessary, say it for him/her.

"This word is 'full.' Can you use the word 'full' in a sentence?" expect various answers

- Repeat with the remaining words.
- Show the student **Sight Word Cards 34–37.**

"Let's find these words on our sight word charts."

- Help the student locate the words in the Irregular Spelling Booklet.

"We will add these cards to our sight word deck."

"Let's practice coding some words like the ones you'll have on your worksheet."

"The rule charts are in your Rule Book if you need to look at them."

- Write the following sentences (without the coding marks) on the chalkboard, one at a time. Ask the student to help you code them. The correct coding is as indicated:

The squir´|rel ănd chĭp´|mŭnk răn ŭp the first tree.
VC|CV VC|CV

A dirt´|y fork stāined the tā´|ble|clŏth.

- Have the student determine whether each of the items coded is a word, a phrase, or a sentence.
- Add **Sight Word Cards 34–37** to the Sight Word Deck.

WORKSHEET

- The student should be seated where he/she can write comfortably.
- Give the student **Worksheet 76.** Make sure the student turns to the correct side.

"Today, let's spell with the /er/ sound using combination ir."

"Combination ir can be used anywhere in a word."

"Put your finger by #1. The first word is 'bird.' "

"Unblend 'bird' with me." */b/ /er/ /d/*

- Hold up one finger for each sound.

"Let's spell those sounds. B … combination ir … d."

- Point to a finger as the student spells each sound.

"Now spell the word again and write it on the line by #1."

- Allow time for the student to do this.

"What word did you write?" *bird*

- Repeat the procedure with #2 (girl), #3 (first), #4 (third), and #5 (sir).

"Now you're ready to code and read the words on your paper."

"Code the words by #6 through #10. After you have coded all the words, try to read them."

- Assist the student as necessary.

"Numbers 11 and 12 are questions about the paragraph just above them. If you find any words you can't read, code them. Then see if you can answer the questions."

- As the student works, provide help as needed. Help the student correct any incorrect answers. Then initial the worksheet in the space provided.
- Some time during the day, ask the student to read from the worksheet, a controlled reader, your basal reader, or other material of your choice.
- **Note:** Always make sure the worksheet is corrected before the student begins the homework. The worksheet serves as a guide to help complete the homework.

HOMEWORK

"Turn your paper over to the homework side."

"Do you know what to do on the homework paper?"

"Remember to look for combinations. Always code suffixes and final, stable syllables before coding the rest of the word."

"When you finish your paper, I will check it for you and initial it in the space provided."

- Either now or later in the day, the student should complete the homework independently (if possible). Help the student correct any incorrect answers. Then initial the homework in the space provided.

SPELLING LIST

- Fold **Spelling List 13** in half lengthwise (with the printed side facing out).

  "Leave your paper just like I give it to you."

- Give the student **Spelling List 13,** folded with the blank lines facing up.

  "Let's spell some more words."

- Call out the following words (in the order shown). Sound them out, if necessary.

  #1 (sky), #2 (try), #3 (puppy), #4 (thirty), #5 (lucky), #6 (after),
  #7 (sister), #8 (shelter), #9 (flying), #10 (sticky), #11 (you), #12 (their)

  "Now unfold your paper and check your words."

- Check the student's work to see if he/she needs extra help with spelling.

  "I want you to practice these words. We'll have a spelling test in a few days."

- If possible, take time to play the Kid Card games listed in Lesson 75.

Name ______________________

Teacher's Initials _____

Worksheet 76
(for use with Lesson 76)
Phonics 1

ir

1. bird
2. girl
3. first
4. third
5. sir
6. thirsty
7. squirm
8. chirping
9. corked
10. plain

A blackbird is sitting in my elm tree. He is singing songs and chattering to the red bird in the birch tree. At first he sang by himself but then the red bird sang with him.

11. Where is the red bird? in the birch tree

12. What is the blackbird doing? singing songs and chattering to the red bird

P1-WS-076a

Parent's Initials _____

Homework 76
(for use with Lesson 76)
Phonics 1

ir

1. swirl
2. squirt
3. munching
4. flirting
5. rainy
6. quacking
7. form
8. squint
9. braided
10. rail

My first class has a girl with a long braid. Her braid is so long she can sit on it. Her hair is black. We flirt with her by pulling her braid.

11. The girl with the long braid is in what class? the first class

12. What can she do with her braid? sit on it

Parents: Your child has been taught **combination ir.**

P1-WS-076b

Lesson 76

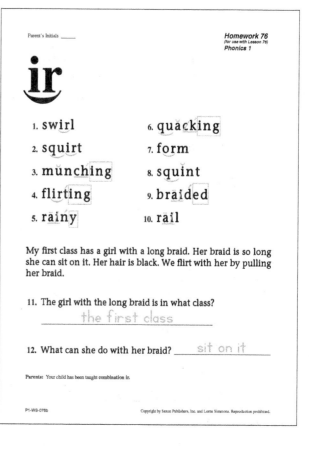

LESSON 77 — Combination *ur*

lesson preparation

materials

Alphabet/Accent Deck (Section 1)

Retired Decks

Affix Deck

Spelling Sound Sheet 57

Letter Card 53

purse in a sack (see *the night before*)

Picture Card 62

Worksheet 77

Reader 27 (*Beth Cuts a Tooth*)

colored pencils

the night before

- Put a purse in a sack for the student to use to "discover" the new keyword.

ALPHABET ACTIVITY

"Let's work with the Alphabet/Accent Deck again today."

"Today, let's say the first syllable in a normal voice while sitting down, and then stand and say the accented syllable louder."

- Show the student **Alphabet/Accent Card 1.**
- Have the student say "A" (seated and in a normal voice), and then "B" (standing and louder).
- Continue with **Alphabet/Accent Cards 2–25,** moving as quickly as possible.

REVIEW OF DECKS

- The student should be seated where he/she can write comfortably.
- Show the student the retired letter cards in random order. The student should name the letter on each letter card.
- Review **Affix Cards 1–7.**
- Show the student the retired picture cards in random order. The student should name the keyword and sound for each picture card.

- Review the retired sight word cards.
- Give the student **Spelling Sound Sheet 57.**
- Call out the sounds on the retired spelling cards in random order. The student should echo each sound and name the letter or letters that make the sound as he/she writes the letter(s) on the spelling sound sheet.
- Check the student's response after each card.

NEW LEARNING

"I'm going to say some words. Echo them back to me and listen for the sound that is the same in each word."

- Point to your mouth as you say each word.

"Echo after me. Turnip." *turnip* ***"Blur."*** *blur* ***"Curl."*** *curl*

"What sound do you hear that is the same in each of these words?" */er/*

"That's right. The sound you hear is /er/."

"Put your fingertips on the front of your neck and say /er/. See if you feel any vibration."

"Is this sound voiced or unvoiced?" *voiced*

- Write the following on the chalkboard: turnip, blur, curl.

"What do you see that might be making the /er/ sound?" *ur*

"The letters 'ur' can make the same sound as the letters 'er.' "

"How many sounds do you hear?" *one*

"How many letters are making that sound?" *two*

"What do you think ur is?" *a combination*

"What is a combination?" *two letters that come together to make an unexpected sound*

"How do we code combinations?" *put arcs underneath*

- Code the words:

tur´|nĭp (vc|cv) blur curl

- Leave the words on the chalkboard for the remainder of the lesson.

NEW DECK CARDS

- Show the student **Letter Card 53.**

"What do we call this?" *combination ur*

"I have another sack today. It contains a clue to our new keyword. Don't look in the sack, but put your hand inside and see if you can feel what is inside the sack. Keep in mind that the object in the sack contains the /er/ sound."

Lesson 77

- Allow the student a chance to feel inside the sack.

  "Can you guess the new keyword?" *purse*
- Show the student **Picture Card 62.**

  "The word 'purse' helps us remember the /er/ sound that is spelled 'ur.' "
- **Note:** The combination and its picture are also shown in the Rule Book on page 22.

  "The best choice for the /er/ sound is still 'er,' so we won't add 'ur' to our spelling deck response for the /er/ sound."
- **Note:** Add the new letter and picture cards to the Review Decks.

Boardwork

"Let's practice coding some words like the ones you'll have on your worksheet."

"The rule charts are in your Rule Book if you need to look at them."

- Write the following word and phrases (without the coding marks) on the chalkboard, one at a time. Ask the student to help you code them. The correct coding is as indicated:

  squirt´ed the cheese

  or´|biting the moon
  VC|CV

  gar´gle
- Have the student determine whether each of the items coded is a word, a phrase, or a sentence.

Worksheet

- The student should be seated where he/she can write comfortably.
- Give the student **Worksheet 77.** Make sure the student turns to the correct side.

  "Let's spell with the /er/ sound using combination ur."

  "Combination ur is like combination ir. It's not used very often for spelling. If you don't know which one to use, your best choice is still 'er.' "

  "Let's see what kinds of words are spelled with 'ur.' Get out your Irregular Spelling Booklet."

  "Look at the table of contents. Can you find the page that shows words spelled with combination ur?" *page 24*

  "That's right. Turn to page 24. All of these words are spelled with combination ur. They don't follow our regular rules, so we must memorize them. Until then, you can refer to your booklet."

  "Put your booklet away for now and let's try to spell some words."

"Put your finger by #1. The first word is 'burn.' "

"Unblend 'burn' with me." /b/ /er/ /n/

- Hold up one finger for each sound.

"Let's spell those sounds. B … combination ur … n."

- Point to a finger as the student spells each sound.

"Now spell the word and write it on the line by #1."

- Allow time for the student to do this.

"What word did you write?" burn

- Repeat the procedure with #2 (turn), #3 (hurt), #4 (curling), and #5 (sunburn).

"Now you're ready to code and read the words on your paper."

"Code the words by #6 through #10. After you have coded all the words, try to read them."

- Assist the student as necessary.

"Now read the word by #11. If you have trouble reading the word, code it. Then draw a line from the word to the picture it matches."

- Repeat with #12, #13, and #14.
- As the student works, provide help as needed. Help the student correct any incorrect answers. Then initial the worksheet in the space provided.
- Some time during the day, ask the student to read from the worksheet, a controlled reader, your basal reader, or other material of your choice.
- **Note:** Always make sure the worksheet is corrected before the student begins the homework. The worksheet serves as a guide to help complete the homework.

HOMEWORK

"Turn your paper over to the homework side."

"Do you know what to do on the homework paper?"

"Watch for combinations qu, ar, or, er, ir, and ur. Always code suffixes and final, stable syllables before coding the rest of the word. Also, watch for words with a 'vccv' pattern that need to be divided."

- Discuss the homework pictures to make sure the student understands the word each one represents: #11 (girl), #12 (shirt), #13 (church), and #14 (first).

"When you finish your paper, I will check it for you and initial it in the space provided."

- Either now or later in the day, the student should complete the homework independently (if possible). Help the student correct any incorrect answers. Then initial the homework in the space provided.

READER

"We have another new book today."

- Give the student **Reader 27 (*Beth Cuts a Tooth*)** and some colored pencils.

  "Can you tell me this book's title?" *Beth Cuts a Tooth*

- Assist the student as necessary as he/she constructs the book.
- When the student finishes, staple or put a rubber band around the book's spine.
- If necessary, demonstrate how to separate the pages and check the page order.

  "The title of this book is __________?" *Beth Cuts a Tooth*

  "I want you to read your book to yourself. When you are finished reading, color the pictures. Write your name on the book so I will know who colored it."

- **Reminder:** This reader contains the word "have." The student has already been taught that all words that end with the /v/ sound are spelled "ve," but you may have to assist with the correct pronunciation—/hăv/, not /hāv/.

  "Keep your book handy because I will be asking you to read it for me."

- Some time during the day, have the student read the reader to you.
- If possible, take time to play the Kid Card games listed in Lesson 75.

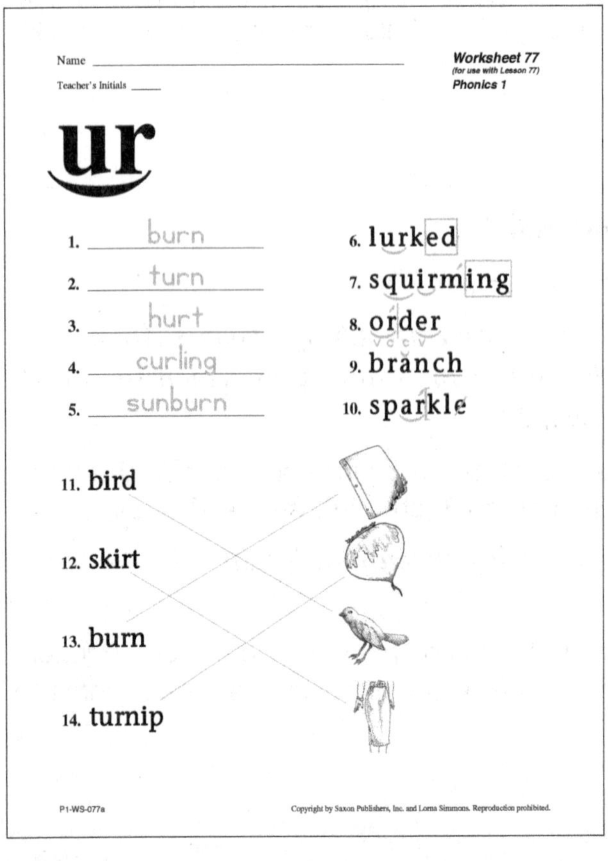

Name

Teacher's Initials

Worksheet 77
(for use with Lesson 77)
Phonics 1

ur

1. burn
2. turn
3. hurt
4. curling
5. sunburn
6. lurked
7. squirming
8. order
9. branch
10. sparkle
11. bird
12. skirt
13. burn
14. turnip

P1-WS-077a

Copyright by Saxon Publishers, Inc. and Lorna Simmons. Reproduction prohibited.

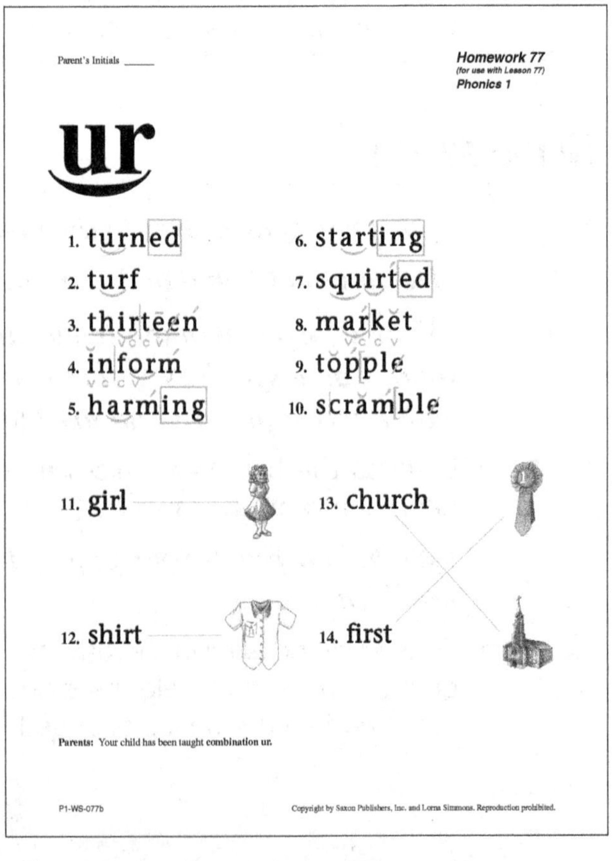

Parent's Initials

Homework 77
(for use with Lesson 77)
Phonics 1

ur

1. turned
2. turf
3. thirteen
4. inform
5. harming
6. starting
7. squirted
8. market
9. topple
10. scramble
11. girl
12. shirt
13. church
14. first

Parents: Your child has been taught combination ur.

P1-WS-077b

Copyright by Saxon Publishers, Inc. and Lorna Simmons. Reproduction prohibited.

Lesson 77

LESSON 78 — *c* That Sounds Like *s*

lesson preparation

materials

Activity Sheet 3

Review Decks

Picture Card 63

Sight Word Card 38

Worksheet 78

new concepts

soft *c*, cedilla *ç*

the night before

- Gather a few circular objects (e.g., cup, coin, plate, compact disc or record album, coaster, or jar lid) for the student to use to "discover" the new keyword.

ALPHABET ACTIVITY

- The student should be seated.

  "We're going to alphabetize letters in a list again, but you will have your own list today."

  "You will have to determine your 'guide letters' and then underline them in your words."

- Give the student **Activity Sheet 3.**

  "We can't move the words, so use the numbers at the bottom to keep track of the number you are using."

  "Tell me when you are finished, and I will check your word order."

- The correct order is 3, 4, 2, 6, 1, 5. If the student did not alphabetize the list successfully, spend some extra time practicing with him/her.

REVIEW OF DECKS

- The student should be seated where he/she can write comfortably.
- Show the student **Letter Cards 1–53** in random order. The student should name the letter on each letter card.
- Review **Affix Cards 1–7.**

- Show the student **Picture Cards 1–62** in random order. The student should name the keyword and sound for each picture card.
- Review **Sight Word Cards 1–37.**

  "Instead of writing responses for our spelling cards, let's just review them out loud today."

- Give the sounds on **Spelling Cards 1–41** in random order. The student should echo each sound and then skywrite the letter or letters that make the sound.

NEW LEARNING

"I'm going to say some words. Echo them back to me and listen for the sound that is the same in each word."

- Point to your mouth as you say each word.

  "Echo after me. Cent." *cent* ***"Cinch."*** *cinch* ***"Nice."*** *nice*

  "What sound do you hear that is the same in all of these words?" */s/*

  "That's right. The sound you hear is /s/."

  "Is this sound voiced or unvoiced?" *unvoiced*

- Write the following on the chalkboard: cent, cinch, nice.

  "What do you see in all of these words that might be making the /s/ sound? It may surprise you!" *c*

  "That's right! When we read with c before today, what sound did it make?" */k/*

  "Is c a vowel or a consonant?" *consonant*

  "Now we can see that c also makes the /s/ sound. This kind of c is called a 'soft c,' and we code it by putting a mark beneath it called a 'cedilla' (sĭ-dil-ə). The hard c sound, /k/, is sometimes called a 'k-back c.' What could we call the c that makes the /s/ sound?" *cedilla c*

  "This is a cedilla c."

- Code the appropriate *c* in each word with a cedilla: çent, çinch, niçe.
- Write the word "cedilla" on the chalkboard.

  "This is the word 'cedilla.' Do you notice anything special about this word?"

- If the student does not notice that the word "cedilla" contains the soft *c*, point it out.

  "So we have the same letter making two completely different sounds: /k/ and /s/."

  "How do we know which sound the letter c makes in a particular word?"

  "We have a rule we can use."

- Write the following rule on the chalkboard and read it to the student:

  If *c* comes before an *e*, *i*, or *y*, it makes the /s/ sound.

  If *c* comes before an *a*, *o*, *u*, or any consonant, it makes the /k/ sound.

  "Sometimes the letters e, i, and y are called 'softeners' because they cause letters that have both hard and soft sounds to make their soft sound."

- This is related to the *k* and *c* rule: the /k/ sound before *e*, *i*, or *y* is spelled with the letter *k*, so the letter *c* before *e*, *i*, or *y* must make a sound other than /k/. If you think that the student will understand this relationship, point it out.

  "This rule helps us determine which sound the letter c will make in a particular word. It also helps us spell words that have the /s/ sound in the initial or medial position."

  "But what about words that have the /s/ sound in the final position? We need a different rule, don't we?"

  "Get out your Rule Book and turn to page 8."

- Point to each rule on **Rule Chart 8** as you read it:

  "After a short vowel, we use 'ss.' This is the floss rule."

  "After a long vowel, we usually spell with 'ce,' as in the words 'ice' and 'space.' "

  "After a consonant or two adjacent vowels, we usually spell with 'se.' "

- There are a few words wherein "se" follows a long vowel (e.g., "base"), but most long vowels are followed by "ce."
- **Optional:** Print the "softener" letters (*e*, *i*, and *y*) on a fabric softener sheet or a cloud-shaped cutout of white paper and display the letters in your room to remind the student of the rule.

New Deck Cards

- Pull **Spelling Card 12** from the Review Deck.
- Hold up **Picture Card 63** but keep the picture covered with your hand (or the letter card).

  "Our new keyword begins with the soft c, or cedilla c. What sound does the soft c make?" /s/

- Bring out the objects you collected the night before. Hold them up one at a time.

  "Look at these objects. What shape do they have in common? That shape is our keyword today. Can you tell me the name of the shape?" *circle*

- Show the student **Picture Card 63.**

  "The word 'circle' helps us remember the soft sound of c, since 'circle' begins with /s/."

- Hold up **Spelling Card 12** so only you can see what is written.

"Now we know that the /s/ sound can be spelled different ways, so we need to change our spelling deck response. What two letters make the /s/ sound?" *s and c*

- Write the following on the chalkboard: s, c.

"Let's look at our new rule chart. How do we spell the /s/ sound in the final position?" *ss, se, or ce*

"That's right. Let's add them to our response."

- Complete the response: s, c || ss, se, ce.

"From now on, when I give the /s/ sound, you'll write what I've written here on the chalkboard and say 's comma c final ss comma se comma ce.' Say that with me." *s comma c final ss comma se comma ce*

- Have the student write the new response with his/her finger on the desktop.

"Get out your Irregular Spelling Booklet."

"In the initial position, the c that sounds like an s is irregular for spelling, so we have a chart that lists some of these words."

"Look in the table of contents, find the 'C That Sounds Like S' chart, and turn to that page."

- Allow time for the student to do this.

"What page is this chart on?" *page 29*

- Make sure the student is on the correct page.

"Let's look at these words."

- Discuss the definition and pronunciation of each word on the chart.
- Have the student put the booklet away.
- **Note:** Add the new picture card to the Review Decks (and re-insert **Spelling Card 12**).

BOARDWORK

- Write the following on the chalkboard:

floor /flor/

"We have a new sight word today."

"Can you tell me what this word is? Remember, it's a sight word, so it won't follow all of our rules."

- Allow the student to try to pronounce the word. If necessary, say it for him/her.

"This word is 'floor.' Can you use the word 'floor' in a sentence?" *expect various answers*

- Show the student **Sight Word Card 38.**

"Let's find this word on our sight word charts."

- Help the student locate the word in the Irregular Spelling Booklet.

"We will add this card to our sight word deck."

"Let's practice coding some words like the ones you'll have on your worksheet."

"The rule charts are in your Rule Book if you need to look at them."

- Write the following word and phrases (without the coding marks) on the chalkboard, one at a time. Ask the student to help you code them. The correct coding is as indicated:

çĭt′|rŭs
vc|c v

tur′|tle ănd quāil

stāy′|ing| ĭn spāçe

- Have the student determine whether each of the items coded is a word, a phrase, or a sentence.
- Add **Sight Word Card 38** to the Sight Word Deck.

WORKSHEET

- The student should be seated where he/she can write comfortably.
- Give the student **Worksheet 78.** Make sure the student turns to the correct side.

"Today, let's spell using the /s/ sound in the final position."

"We have a lot to remember, so be sure to refer to our new rule chart. It shows the three rules for spelling the /s/ sound in the final position."

"Let's begin. Put your finger by #1. The first word is 'brace.' "

"The a in this word is a long vowel, so we will spell the final /s/ sound with a 'ce.' We need the sneaky e to keep the vowel long and to make the c soft."

"Unblend 'brace' with me." */b/ /r/ /ā/ /s/*

- Hold up one finger for each sound.

"Let's spell those sounds. B … r … a … ce."

- Point to a finger as the student spells each sound.

"Now spell the word again and write the letters as you say them."

- Allow time for the student to do this.

"What word did you write?" *brace*

- Repeat the procedure with #2 (ice), #3 (nice), #4 (face), and #5 (race).

"Now you're ready to code and read the words on your paper."

"Using the rules we just practiced, code the words by #6 through #10. After you have coded all the words, try to read them."

- Assist the student as necessary.

Lesson 78

"Numbers 11 and 12 are questions about the paragraph just above them. If you find any words you can't read, code them. Then see if you can answer the questions."

- As the student works, provide help as needed. Help the student correct any incorrect answers. Then initial the worksheet in the space provided.
- Some time during the day, ask the student to read from the worksheet, a controlled reader, your basal reader, or other material of your choice.
- **Note:** Always make sure the worksheet is corrected before the student begins the homework. The worksheet serves as a guide to help complete the homework.

HOMEWORK

"Turn your paper over to the homework side."

"Do you know what to do on the homework paper?"

"Watch for cedilla c and k-back c. Always code suffixes and final, stable syllables before coding the rest of the word."

"When you finish your paper, I will check it for you and initial it in the space provided."

- Either now or later in the day, the student should complete the homework independently (if possible). Help the student correct any incorrect answers. Then initial the homework in the space provided.
- If possible, take time to play the Kid Card games listed in Lesson 75.

Name ______________________

Teacher's Initials ____

Worksheet 78
(for use with Lesson 78)
Phonics 1

ç

1. brace
2. ice
3. nice
4. face
5. race
6. miçe
7. çircus
8. burst
9. squint
10. graying

Shay's dad has a shed. His shed has grain in it for his horse. Mice like the grain too. They get in the shed and munch on the grain on the floor.

11. Where does Shay's dad keep his grain? in a shed

12. What gets in the grain? mice

P1-WS-078a

Parent's Initials ____

Homework 78
(for use with Lesson 78)
Phonics 1

ç

1. plaçe
2. priçe
3. succçess
4. curl
5. quill
6. saying
7. quilting
8. spaçe
9. çell
10. çent

Rattlesnakes like mice. If grain spills on the floor in Dad's shed, the shed gets lots of mice in it. If Dad forgets to pick the grain up, his shed soon has rattlesnakes too.

11. What do rattlesnakes like? mice

12. Why does Dad keep the grain off the floor?
to keep the rattlesnakes away

Parents: Your child has been taught the **soft c** (s); that this sound is also called **cedilla c**; and the **final s rules** (after a short vowel, use **ss**; after a long vowel, use **ce**; after a consonant or two vowels, use **se**).

P1-WS-078b

Lesson 78

LESSON 79 — Digraph *ow*

lesson preparation

materials

Alphabet/Accent Deck (Section 1)
Review Decks
Spelling Sound Sheet 58
Letter Card 54
Picture Card 64
Worksheet 79
Reader 28 (*Chester's Bath*)
colored pencils

ALPHABET ACTIVITY

- The student should be seated.

  "It's Alphabet/Accent Day."

  "Let's say the first syllable in a normal voice while sitting down, and then stand and say the accented syllable louder."
- Show the student **Alphabet/Accent Card 1.**
- Have the student say "A" (seated and in a normal voice), and then "B" (standing and louder).
- Continue with **Alphabet/Accent Cards 2–25,** moving as quickly as possible.

REVIEW OF DECKS

- The student should be seated where he/she can write comfortably.
- Show the student **Letter Cards 1–53** in random order. The student should name the letter on each letter card.
- Review **Affix Cards 1–7.**
- Show the student **Picture Cards 1–63** in random order. The student should name the keyword and sound for each picture card.
- Review **Sight Word Cards 1–38.**
- Give the student **Spelling Sound Sheet 58.**

- Call out the sounds on **Spelling Cards 1–41** in random order. The student should echo each sound and name the letter or letters that make the sound as he/she writes the letter(s) on the spelling sound sheet.
- Have the student set aside the spelling sound sheet for use later in the lesson.

NEW LEARNING

"I'm going to say some words. Echo them back to me and listen for the sound that is the same in the final position."

- Point to your mouth as you say each word.

"Echo after me. Grow." *grow* ***"Low."*** *low* ***"Show."*** *show*

"What sound do you hear that is the same in all of these words?" */ō/*

"That's right. The sound you hear is /ō/."

"Put your fingertips on the front of your neck and say /ō/. See if you feel any vibration."

"Is this sound voiced or unvoiced?" *voiced*

- Write the following on the chalkboard: grow, low, show.

"What do you see that might be making the /ō/ sound?" *ow*

"Where do the letters 'ow' appear in these words?" *final position*

"How many sounds do you hear?" *one*

"How many letters are making that sound?" *two*

"What do we call two letters that come together to make one sound?" *a digraph*

"That's right. Do you think digraph ow is a vowel digraph or a consonant digraph?" *vowel digraph*

"Digraph ow is a vowel digraph even though it contains the consonant w."

"It is unusual to find an English word that ends with o. If you hear the /ō/ sound at the end of a word, there's a good chance it is spelled with 'ow.' "

"How do we code digraph ow?" *underline the letters, put a macron over the o, cross out the w*

- Code the words: grōw, lōw, shōw.

"Do these words need any other coding?" *yes, underline digraph sh*

- Underline digraph *sh* and then leave the words on the chalkboard for the remainder of the lesson.

NEW DECK CARDS

- Pull **Spelling Card 3** from the Review Deck.
- Show the student **Letter Card 54.**

  "What do we call this?" *digraph ow*
- Hold up **Picture Card 64** but keep the picture covered with your hand (or the letter card).

  "I have a card with a picture on it that ends with the /ō/ sound."

  "I am going to describe it for you. See if you can guess what the picture is."

  "This is something that is found on birthday presents. It is usually made of brightly colored ribbon. Sometimes girls wear them in their hair. What do you think the picture is?" *bow*

  "That's right. The keyword is 'bow' and the sound we have learned is /ō/."
- Show the student **Picture Card 64.**

  "The word 'bow' helps us remember the /ō/ sound since it ends with that sound."
- **Note:** The digraph and its picture are also shown in the Rule Book on page 21.

  "Since digraph ow is used a lot to spell the final /ō/ sound, we will add it to our /ō/ spelling card response."
- Write the following on the chalkboard: o–e, o || ow.

  "Find your spelling sound sheet. Put your finger on the line by #42."
- Hold up **Spelling Card 3** so only you can see what is written.

  "Echo this sound: /ō/." */ō/*

  "From now on, the response to this card will be 'o consonant e comma o final digraph ow.' Say that with me." *o consonant e comma o final digraph ow*
- Point to the new response on the chalkboard.

  "Write the new response on the line by #42."
- Check the spelling sound sheet for accuracy.
- **Note:** Add the new letter and picture cards to the Review Decks (and re-insert **Spelling Card 3**).

BOARDWORK

"Let's practice coding some words like the ones you'll have on your worksheet."

"The rule charts are in your Rule Book if you need to look at them."

- Write the following phrases and sentence (without the coding marks) on the chalkboard, one at a time. Ask the student to help you code them. The correct coding is as indicated:

  slēēp′y hŏl′low
  vc cv

  tōw′ing thė trŭck

  Thė rācė car hĭt thė rāil.

- Have the student determine whether each of the items coded is a word, a phrase, or a sentence.

WORKSHEET

- The student should be seated where he/she can write comfortably.
- Give the student **Worksheet 79.** Make sure the student turns to the correct side.

  "Let's spell with the /ō/ sound using digraph ow."

  "Digraph ow is almost always used in the final position."

  "Put your finger by #1. The first word is 'blow.' "

  "Unblend 'blow' with me." */b/ /l/ /ō/*
- Hold up one finger for each sound.

  "Let's spell those sounds. B … l … digraph ow."
- Point to a finger as the student spells each sound.

  "Now spell the word on the line by #1."
- Allow time for the student to do this.

  "What word did you write?" *blow*
- Repeat the procedure with #2 (grow), #3 (mow), #4 (shadow), and #5 (slow).

  "Now you're ready to code and read the words on your paper."

  "Code the words by #6 through #10. After you have coded all the words, try to read them."
- Assist the student as necessary.

  "Now read the word by #11. If you have trouble reading the word, code it. Then draw a line from the word to the picture it matches."
- Repeat with #12, #13, and #14.
- As the student works, provide help as needed. Help the student correct any incorrect answers. Then initial the worksheet in the space provided.
- Some time during the day, ask the student to read from the worksheet, a controlled reader, your basal reader, or other material of your choice.
- **Note:** Always make sure the worksheet is corrected before the student begins the homework. The worksheet serves as a guide to help complete the homework.

HOMEWORK

"Turn your paper over to the homework side."

"Do you know what to do on the homework paper?"

"Watch for combinations qu, ar, or, er, ir, and ur. Watch for digraph ow, too. Always box suffixes before coding the rest of the word. Also, watch for words with a 'vccv' pattern that need to be divided."

- Discuss the homework pictures to make sure the student understands the word each one represents: #11 (spaceship), #12 (crow), #13 (pillow), and #14 (window).

"When you finish your paper, I will check it for you and initial it in the space provided."

- Either now or later in the day, the student should complete the homework independently (if possible). Help the student correct any incorrect answers. Then initial the homework in the space provided.

READER

"We have another new book today."

- Give the student **Reader 28 (*Chester's Bath*)** and some colored pencils.

"Can you tell me this book's title?" *Chester's Bath*

- Assist the student as necessary as he/she constructs the book.
- When the student finishes, staple or put a rubber band around the book's spine.
- If necessary, demonstrate how to separate the pages and check the page order.

"The title of this book is __________?" *Chester's Bath*

"I want you to read your book to yourself. When you are finished reading, color the pictures. Write your name on the book so I will know who colored it."

"Keep your book handy because I will be asking you to read it for me."

- Some time during the day, have the student read the reader to you.
- If possible, take time to play the Kid Card games listed in Lesson 75. Try to see that the student is prepared for tomorrow's assessment.

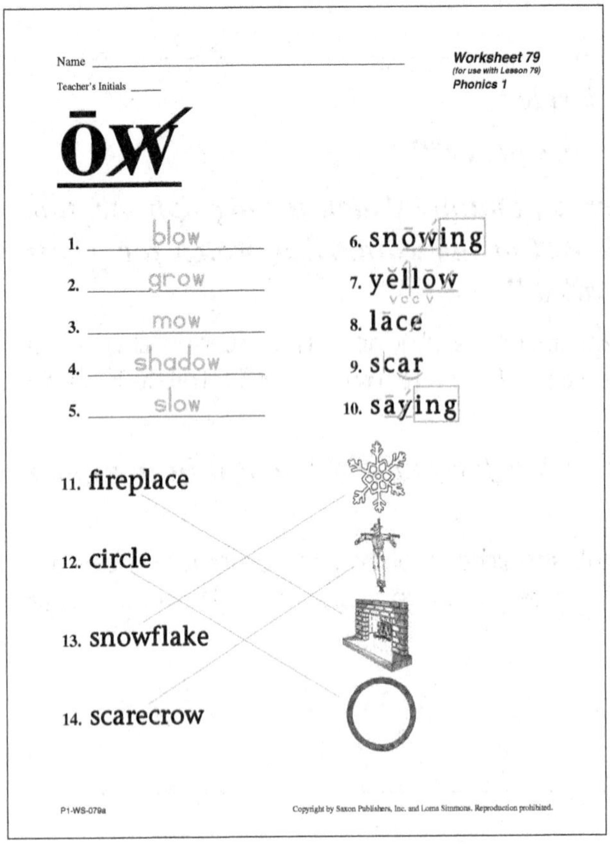

Name ____________________ **Worksheet 79**
(for use with Lesson 79)
Phonics 1

Teacher's Initials ____

ōw

1. blow	6. snowing
2. grow	7. yellow
3. mow	8. lace
4. shadow	9. scar
5. slow	10. saying

11. fireplace
12. circle
13. snowflake
14. scarecrow

P1-WS-079a

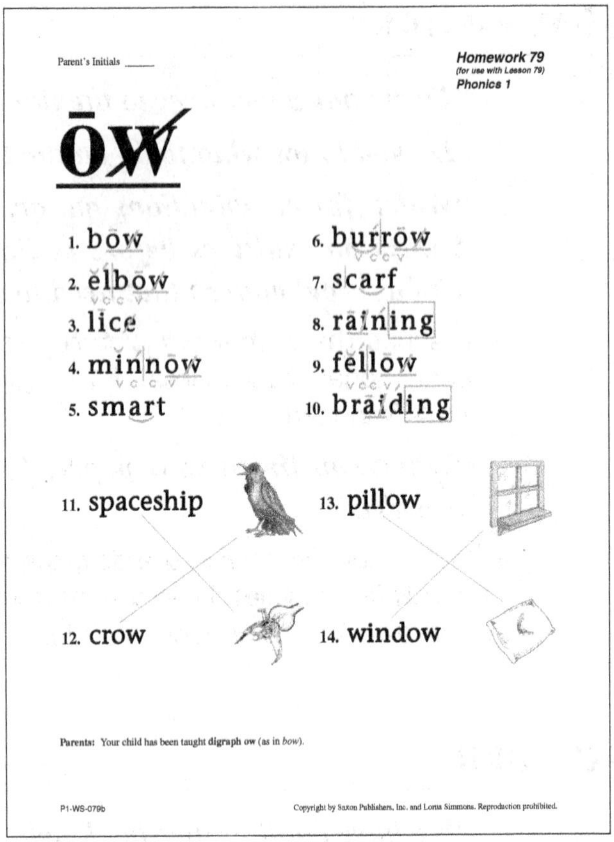

Parent's Initials ____ **Homework 79**
(for use with Lesson 79)
Phonics 1

ōw

1. bow	6. burrow
2. elbow	7. scarf
3. lice	8. raining
4. minnow	9. fellow
5. smart	10. braiding

11. spaceship
12. crow
13. pillow
14. window

Parents: Your child has been taught **digraph ow** (as in *bow*).

P1-WS-079b

Lesson 79

Lesson 80

Assessment

lesson preparation

materials

ball

Review Decks

Assessment 15

Spelling Test 13

Assessment 15 Recording Form

Kid Cards

tokens

the night before

- Sort through the Review Decks and remove any of the following cards the student knows very well:

  Letter Deck: *b, m, w, x, y.*

  Picture Deck: Cards that correspond to the letter cards that are removed.

  Sight Word Deck: Cards that (based on assessment results) the student knows very well.

  Spelling Deck: Cards that correspond to the letter cards that are removed.
- Add these cards to the retired decks.
- Separate the Kid Cards marked "Lesson 80."

Alphabet Activity

- You and the student should be seated with the ball.

  "Let's play 'Alphabet Toss' again."

  "I'll say a letter of the alphabet and toss the ball to you. After you catch the ball, say the two letters that come after the letter I said, and then toss the ball back to me."

  "I'll say the next two letters, and then toss the ball back to you."
- Play as long as time permits.

REVIEW OF DECKS

- The student should be seated where he/she can write comfortably.
- Show the student **Letter Cards 1–54** in random order. The student should name the letter on each letter card.
- Review **Affix Cards 1–7.**
- Show the student **Picture Cards 1–64** in random order. The student should name the keyword and sound for each picture card.
- Review **Sight Word Cards 1–38.**

WRITTEN ASSESSMENT

- Have the student sit where he/she can write comfortably.
- Give the student **Assessment 15.**
- **Section I:**

  "Today we are going to write some words for our assessment."

  "I'm going to say a word. Write the letter that makes each sound in that word on the lines by #1."

  "Look at the rule charts if you need to."

  "Here's the first word: quick."
- Repeat with the following words in the order shown: #2 (thorny), #3 (such), #4 (gargle), and #5 (junkyard).
- **Reminder:** While the student spells, be ready to point to appropriate rule charts as necessary.
- **Section II:**

  "Look at the letters by #6."

  "Find the picture of the keyword for this sound."

  "Draw a line from the letters to the keyword."
- Repeat with #7, #8, and #9. Allow a few minutes for the student to work.
- The pictures (from top to bottom) are as follows: arm, cheese, quail, fork.
- **Section III:**

  "Put your finger on #10."

  "Code the words by #10 through #15."
- Allow a few minutes for the student to work.
- **Section IV:**

  "Read the paragraph. If you find any words you can't read, code them to help you figure them out. Then answer the questions by #16 through #19."
- **Reminder:** If the student absolutely cannot read the paragraph, read it to the student to see if he or she can answer the questions.

"When you are finished, show your paper to me."

- This paper will be used during the oral portion of the assessment.

Spelling Test

- Give the student **Spelling Test 13.**
- Call out the following words (in the order shown). Sound them out, if necessary.
  #1 (try), #2 (sky), #3 (puppy), #4 (sister), #5 (after), #6 (lucky),
  #7 (thirty), #8 (shelter), #9 (sticky), #10 (flying), #11 (you), #12 (their)
- Grade and record the test in any manner that suits your needs.

Oral Assessment

- It is important to complete the oral assessment promptly (today, if possible) in order to identify any areas of weakness and begin remediation.
- Use the assessment and the following dialogue to complete the oral portion.
- **Section V:**
- Point to the sight word by #20.

  "Read this sight word for me."
- Record the student's response by placing a check mark by each word he/she reads correctly.
- Repeat with #21.
- **Section VI:**
- Show the student the letters by #22.

  "Tell me the name of these letters and the sound they make."
- Write the student's response on the adjacent line.
- Repeat with #23, #24, and #25.

Assessment Evaluation

- Grade the assessment and record the results on **Assessment 15 Recording Form.** Check off the boxes to indicate mastery (i.e., the section was completed with 100% accuracy).
- **Reminder:** Try to give as many points as possible for work attempted. Do not grade the coding marks too severely. The most important coding marks to look for are breves, macrons, and syllable division lines.
- See the introductory material for detailed information regarding grading and recording procedures.
- Use the assessment results to identify those skills in which the student is weak. Practice those skills by playing Kid Card games.

- Add the Kid Cards marked "Lesson 80" to the existing decks. Listed below are games appropriate for remediation in selected areas. See "Games and Activities" for the directions for each game.
- **Section I:** Play "Spelling Deck Perfection," "Sound Scamper," "Spell Out #1," or have the student use the letter tiles to spell words you give from the Spelling Word List.
- **Section II:** Play "Keyword and Sound" or "Letter/Sound Identification."
- **Section III:** Play "Chalkboard Challenge."
- **Section IV:** Either have the student read the controlled readers and then ask questions for comprehension, or play "Acting Out" with the green Kid Cards.
- **Section V:** Play "At First Sight," review the Sight Word Deck, or lay the sight words out with a token on each one and let the student try to get as many tokens as possible for the sight words he/she can read.
- **Section VI:** Play "Letter/Sound Identification."
- When the student seems more secure in areas that had previously proven difficult, retest him/her (in those areas only) and indicate on the recording form any sections the student has subsequently mastered.
- Try to help the student achieve mastery of all the sections before the next assessment.
- If the student is having difficulty with a particular skill, keep his or her practice activities at the most basic level so the chance of success is greater.

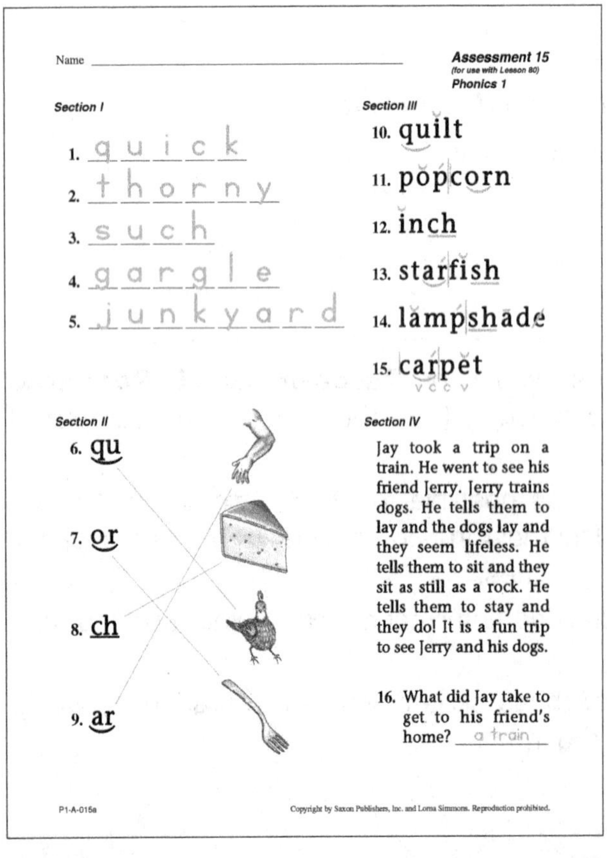

Name

Assessment 15
(for use with Lesson 80)
Phonics 1

Section I

1. quick
2. thorny
3. such
4. gargle
5. junkyard

Section II

6. qu
7. or
8. ch
9. ar

Section III

10. quilt
11. popcorn
12. inch
13. starfish
14. lampshade
15. carpet

Section IV

Jay took a trip on a train. He went to see his friend Jerry. Jerry trains dogs. He tells them to lay and the dogs lay and they seem lifeless. He tells them to sit and they sit as still as a rock. He tells them to stay and they do! It is a fun trip to see Jerry and his dogs.

16. What did Jay take to get to his friend's home? a train

P1-A-015a

Copyright by Saxon Publishers, Inc. and Lorna Simmons. Reproduction prohibited.

Assessment 15
(for use with Lesson 80)
Phonics 1

17. Who is Jay's friend? Jerry
18. What does Jerry train? dogs
19. What can the dogs do? lay sit stay

Section V

20. there
21. love

Section VI

22. qu combination qu, /kw/
23. or combination or, /or/
24. ch digraph ch, /ch/
25. ar combination ar, /ar/

P1-A-015b

Copyright by Saxon Publishers, Inc. and Lorna Simmons. Reproduction prohibited.

LESSON 81 The Rule v′|cv with *a*

lesson preparation

materials

container of letter tiles

Review Decks

Spelling Sound Sheet 59

Sight Word Card 39

Worksheet 81

Spelling List 14

new concepts

v′|cv pattern

ALPHABET ACTIVITY

- The student should be seated with the container of letter tiles.

  "Before we start, let's say the alphabet together so it is fresh in our minds."

- Recite the alphabet with the student.
- Give the following instructions one at a time, allowing time for the student to accomplish each task before giving the next instruction.

  "Take all of the letter tiles out of your container."

  "Flip all of the letters over so that you are looking at the lowercase letters. If they are flipped correctly, they will all be blue."

  "Now we're ready. See if you can put all your letters in alphabetical order."

- Assist the student as necessary. When the student has finished, continue.

  "Point to the initial letter."

  "Point to the final letter."

  "Pull down the letters that are always vowels."

  "Now point to the letter that can sometimes be a vowel." *y*

- Have the student replace the tiles in the container and put it away.

REVIEW OF DECKS

- The student should be seated where he/she can write comfortably.
- Show the student **Letter Cards 1–54** in random order. The student should name the letter on each letter card.
- Review **Affix Cards 1–7.**

- Show the student **Picture Cards 1–64** in random order. The student should name the keyword and sound for each picture card.
- Review **Sight Word Cards 1–38.**
- Give the student **Spelling Sound Sheet 59.**
- Call out the sounds on **Spelling Cards 1–41** in random order. The student should echo each sound and name the letter or letters that make the sound as he/she writes the letter(s) on the spelling sound sheet.
- Check the student's response after each card.

NEW LEARNING

- Write the word "wafer" on the chalkboard.

  "What is the first thing I should do to code this word?" *look for suffixes or final, stable syllables*

- Have the student refer to **Syllable Division Chart 1,** if necessary.

  "Are there any?" *no*

  "Does this word need to be divided?" *yes, it has two vowels*

  "What should I do next?" *find the vowels*

  "Which ones are the vowels?" *a, e*

- Write small *v*'s under the vowels:

  wafer
  v v

  "What is the next step?" *look between the vowels*

  "What do we have between the vowels?" *only one consonant*

- Write a small *c* under the consonant:

  wafer
  vcv

  "Our syllable division rule won't work on this. We need two consonants and we only have one."

  "This is a new pattern. If there is only one consonant, we divide before the consonant."

- Put the dividing line between the *a* and the *f*:

  wa|fer
  v|cv

  "It is always best to try the accent on the first syllable first."

- Put an accent on the first syllable:

  wa′|fer
  v|cv

  "Let's see what we have in each syllable now."

"The a is open and accented. How should it be coded?" *long; with a macron*

"What should we code in the second syllable?" *combination er*

- Finish coding the word:

wā´ | fer
v | cv

- Point to the *a* in the first syllable.

"What is the a in this first syllable going to say?" */ā/*

"Can you read this word the way it is coded?" *wafer*

"Can you use the word 'wafer' in a sentence?" *expect various answers*

"This pattern is shown on our new syllable division chart. We don't know all of these patterns yet, but we just learned one more."

- Show the student **Syllable Division Chart 3** in the Rule Book (on page 18). Point to the "v´|cv" pattern.

"You can see now that dividing big words makes them a lot easier to read."

"Let's try one more word with this pattern before you divide one by yourself."

- Write the word "gravy" on the chalkboard and repeat the coding procedure. The word should be coded as follows:

grā´ | vẏ
v | cv

- The vowel *y* will have the /ē/ sound because the second syllable is unaccented. For some children, the rule may be overwhelming. Ask the student to say "gravy" with both sounds of vowel *y* to determine which sound makes a word he/she knows.

BOARDWORK

- Write the following on the chalkboard:

early /er´ lē/

"We have a new sight word today."

"Can you tell me what this word is? Remember, it's a sight word, so it won't follow all of our rules."

- Allow the student to try to pronounce the word. If necessary, say it for him/her.

"This word is 'early.' Can you use the word 'early' in a sentence?" *expect various answers*

- Show the student **Sight Word Card 39.**

"Let's find this word on our sight word charts."

- Help the student locate the word in the Irregular Spelling Booklet.

"We will add this card to our sight word deck."

"Let's practice coding some words like the ones you'll have on your worksheet."

"The rule charts are in your Rule Book if you need to look at them."

- Write the following phrase and sentence (without the coding marks) on the chalkboard, one at a time. Ask the student to help you code them. The correct coding is as indicated:

grōw′ing tur′ nĭp s
vc | cv

The nīce lā′ dy̆ (was) charmed bȳ′ mȳ′ măn′ ner s.
v | cv vc | cv

- Have the student determine whether each of the items coded is a word, a phrase, or a sentence.
- Add **Sight Word Card 39** to the Sight Word Deck.

Worksheet

- The student should be seated where he/she can write comfortably.
- Give the student **Worksheet 81.** Make sure the student turns to the correct side.

"Today, let's spell with these long vowel sounds."

- When you pronounce these words, make a distinct separation between syllables. The student will be more successful if he/she spells by syllables.

"Put your finger by #1. The first word is 'gra … vy.' "

"Unblend the first syllable with me." */g/ /r/ /ā/*

"Spell and write those sounds by #1." *g … r … a*

"Unblend the second syllable with me." */v/ /ē/*

"How do we spell the /ē/ sound at the end of a word?" *vowel y*

"Finish spelling the word." *v … y*

"What word did you write?" *gravy*

- Repeat the procedure with #2 (paper) and #3 (baby).

"Before we spell the next word, think about how we learned to spell /ō/ at the end of a word. What letters did we use?" *ow*

"Spell the word 'low.' Write the letters that spell those sounds by #4."

- Repeat the procedure with #5 (order).

"Now you're ready to code and read the words on your paper."

"Using the rules we just practiced on the chalkboard, code the words by #6 through #10. After you have coded all the words, try to read them."

"All of the 'vcv' words will have the accent on the first syllable today."

- Assist the student as necessary.

"Numbers 11 and 12 are questions about the paragraph just above them. If you find any words you can't read, code them. Then see if you can answer the questions."

- As the student works, provide help as needed. Help the student correct any incorrect answers. Then initial the worksheet in the space provided.
- Some time during the day, ask the student to read from the worksheet, a controlled reader, your basal reader, or other material of your choice.
- **Note:** Always make sure the worksheet is corrected before the student begins the homework. The worksheet serves as a guide to help complete the homework.

HOMEWORK

"Turn your paper over to the homework side."

"Do you know what to do on the homework paper?"

"Watch for words with the 'vcv' pattern. Always code suffixes and final, stable syllables before coding the rest of the word."

"When you finish your paper, I will check it for you and initial it in the space provided."

- Either now or later in the day, the student should complete the homework independently (if possible). Help the student correct any incorrect answers. Then initial the homework in the space provided.

SPELLING LIST

- Fold **Spelling List 14** in half lengthwise (with the printed side facing out).

"Leave your paper just like I give it to you."

- Give the student **Spelling List 14,** folded with the blank lines facing up.

"Let's spell some more words."

- Call out the following words (in the order shown). Sound them out, if necessary.

  #1 (day), #2 (stay), #3 (blister), #4 (winter), #5 (bathtub), #6 (gumdrop), #7 (softness), #8 (helpless), #9 (saying), #10 (driveway), #11 (does), #12 (from)

"Now unfold your paper and check your words."

- Check the student's work to see if he/she needs extra help with spelling.

"I want you to practice these words. We'll have a spelling test in a few days."

- If possible, take time to play the Kid Card games listed in Lesson 80.

Name ______________________

Teacher's Initials ____

Worksheet 81
(for use with Lesson 81)
Phonics 1

á|cv

1. gravy
2. paper
3. baby
4. low
5. order
6. crazy
7. showing
8. twice
9. churn
10. started

Jill likes muffins with eggs and bacon. Kerry makes cherry muffins since Jill likes those best. The coffee has to perk and the cups need to be filled with milk. Then Kerry gets her mom.

11. Who likes cherry muffins? Jill

12. What does the coffee need to do? perk

P1-WS-081a

Parent's Initials ____

Homework 81
(for use with Lesson 81)
Phonics 1

á|cv

1. navy
2. bacon
3. price
4. fancy
5. acorn
6. darted
7. mowing
8. march
9. lady
10. blurt

Kerry likes to cook for her mom, Jill. Kerry gets up early and starts the bacon. After the bacon cooks, Kerry starts cooking eggs.

11. Who is Kerry's mom? Jill

12. What does Kerry start first? bacon

Parents: Your child has been taught the syllable division rule v́|cv with a.

P1-WS-081b

Lesson 81

LESSON 82 The Rule v′|cv with *i* and *e*

lesson preparation

materials

Alphabet/Accent Deck (Section 1)

Retired Decks

Affix Deck

Spelling Sound Sheet 60

Sight Word Cards 40–41

Worksheet 82

Reader 29 (*Jon Helps Dad*)

colored pencils

ALPHABET ACTIVITY

"We're going to work with the Alphabet/Accent Deck again today."

"Let's stand up. Every time we say the accented syllable, we'll karate punch."

- Show the student **Alphabet/Accent Card 1.**
- Have the student say "A" (softly), and then "B" (as he/she punches forward).
- Continue with **Alphabet/Accent Cards 2–25,** moving as quickly as possible.
- **Optional:** If you think the student is ready, shuffle the Alphabet/Accent Deck before the activity. Warn the student that something will be different this time and that he/she must pay very close attention to the cards.

REVIEW OF DECKS

- The student should be seated where he/she can write comfortably.
- Show the student the retired letter cards in random order. The student should name the letter on each letter card.
- Review **Affix Cards 1–7.**
- Show the student the retired picture cards in random order. The student should name the keyword and sound for each picture card.
- Review the retired sight word cards.
- Give the student **Spelling Sound Sheet 60.**

- Call out the sounds on the retired spelling cards in random order. The student should echo each sound and name the letter or letters that make the sound as he/she writes the letter(s) on the spelling sound sheet.
- Check the student's response after each card.

NEW LEARNING

"Yesterday we learned how to divide a word with a 'vcv' pattern. Let's try some more of those words."

- Write the word "fiber" on the chalkboard.

"What is the first thing I should do to code this word?" *look for suffixes or final, stable syllables*

"Are there any?" *no*

"Does this word need to be divided?" *yes, it has two vowels*

"What should I do next?" *find the vowels*

"Which ones are the vowels?" *i and e*

- Write small *v*'s under the vowels:

fiber
v v

"What is the next step?" *look at what is between the vowels*

"What do we have between the vowels?" *only one consonant*

- Write a small *c* under the *b*:

fiber
vcv

- Refer the student to **Syllable Division Chart 3.** Point to the "v́|cv" pattern.

"This is the pattern we learned yesterday. There is only one consonant, so we divide before the consonant."

- Put the dividing line between the *i* and the *b*:

fi|ber
v|cv

"Which syllable is usually accented?" *the first syllable*

- Put an accent on the first syllable:

fí|ber
v|cv

"Let's see what we have in each syllable now."

"The i is open and accented. How should it be coded?" *long; with a macron*

"What should we code in the second syllable?" *an arc under combination er*

Lesson 82

- Finish coding the word:

fī́|ber
v|cv

"What is the i in this first syllable going to say?" /ī/

"Can you read this word the way it is coded?" fiber

"Let's try one more word with this pattern."

- Write the word "minus" on the chalkboard and repeat the coding procedure. The word should be coded as follows:

mī́|nŭs
v|cv

"What is this word?" minus

"Can you tell me what the word 'minus' means, or use it in a sentence?" expect various answers

"Now we know the 'vcv' pattern using a and i. Let's work with it using e."

- Write "fever" on the chalkboard and repeat the coding procedure. The word should be coded as follows:

fḗ|ver
v|cv

"Can you read this word?" fever

- Leave the words on the chalkboard for the remainder of the lesson.

BOARDWORK

- Write the following on the chalkboard:

bush /bo͝osh/ push /po͝osh/

"We have two new sight words today."

- Point to the first word.

"Can you tell me what this word is? Remember, it's a sight word, so it won't follow all of our rules."

- Allow the student to try to pronounce the word. If necessary, say it for him/her.

"This word is 'bush.' Can you use the word 'bush' in a sentence?" expect various answers

- Repeat with "push."
- Show the student **Sight Word Cards 40** and **41.**

"Let's find these words on our sight word charts."

- Help the student locate the words in the Irregular Spelling Booklet.

"We will add these cards to our sight word deck."

"Let's practice coding some words like the ones you'll have on your worksheet."

"The rule charts are in your Rule Book if you need to look at them."

- Write the following word and sentence (without the coding marks) on the chalkboard, one at a time. Ask the student to help you code them. The correct coding is as indicated:

throw

A black spi|der bit the me|ter man.

- Have the student determine whether each of the items coded is a word, a phrase, or a sentence.
- Add **Sight Word Cards 40** and **41** to the Sight Word Deck.

WORKSHEET

- The student should be seated where he/she can write comfortably.
- Give the student **Worksheet 82.** Make sure the student turns to the correct side.

"Let's spell with long vowel sounds again today."

- When you pronounce these words, make a distinct separation between syllables. The student will be more successful if he/she spells by syllables.

"Put your finger by #1. The first word is 'fe … ver.'"

"Unblend the first syllable with me." /f/ /ē/

"Spell and write those sounds by #1." *f … e*

"Unblend the second syllable with me." /v/ /er/

"Finish spelling the word." *v … er*

"What word did you write?" *fever*

- Repeat the procedure with #2 (zero), #3 (spider), #4 (mark), and #5 (name).

"Now you're ready to code and read the words on your paper."

"Code the words by #6 through #10. After you have coded all the words, try to read them."

- Assist the student as necessary.

"Now read the word by #11. If you have trouble reading the word, code it. Then draw a line from the word to the picture it matches."

- Repeat with #12, #13, and #14.
- As the student works, provide help as needed. Help the student correct any incorrect answers. Then initial the worksheet in the space provided.
- Some time during the day, ask the student to read from the worksheet, a controlled reader, your basal reader, or other material of your choice.
- **Note:** Always make sure the worksheet is corrected before the student begins the homework. The worksheet serves as a guide to help complete the homework.

Lesson 82

Homework

"Turn your paper over to the homework side."

"Do you know what to do on the homework paper?"

"Watch for words with the new 'vcv' pattern. Always code suffixes and final, stable syllables before coding the rest of the word."

- Discuss the homework pictures to make sure the student understands the word each one represents: #11 (ladybug), #12 (spider), #13 (rainbow), and #14 (zero).

"When you finish your paper, I will check it for you and initial it in the space provided."

- Either now or later in the day, the student should complete the homework independently (if possible). Help the student correct any incorrect answers. Then initial the homework in the space provided.

Reader

"We have another new book today."

- Give the student **Reader 29 (*Jon Helps Dad*)** and some colored pencils.

"Can you tell me this book's title?" *Jon Helps Dad*

- Assist the student as necessary as he/she constructs the book.
- When the student finishes, staple or put a rubber band around the book's spine.
- If necessary, demonstrate how to separate the pages and check the page order.

"The title of this book is ________?" *Jon Helps Dad*

"I want you to read your book to yourself. When you are finished reading, color the pictures. Write your name on the book so I will know who colored it."

"Keep your book handy because I will be asking you to read it for me."

- Some time during the day, have the student read the reader to you.
- If possible, take time to play the Kid Card games listed in Lesson 80.

Name ______________________

Teacher's Initials ____

Worksheet 82
(for use with Lesson 82)
Phonics 1

í|cv, é|cv

1. fever
2. zero
3. spider
4. mark
5. name
6. silver
7. female
8. pilot
9. even
10. window

11. baby
12. circle
13. bacon
14. turnip

P1-WS-082a

Parent's Initials ____

Homework 82
(for use with Lesson 82)
Phonics 1

í|cv, é|cv

1. final
2. butter
3. item
4. willow
5. slender
6. minnow
7. glitter
8. evil or evil
9. master
10. Venus

11. ladybug 
13. rainbow 
12. spider 
14. zero 

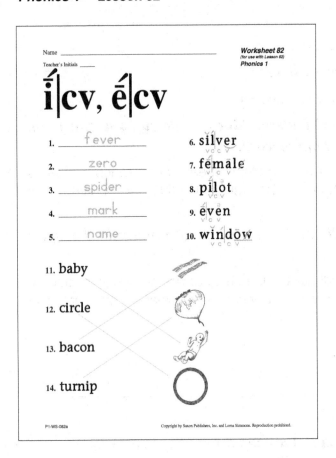

Parents: Your child has been taught the syllable division rule v'|cv with i and e.

P1-WS-082b

Lesson 82

LESSON 83 The Rule v´|cv with *o* and *u*

> ***lesson preparation***
>
> ***materials***
>
> container of letter tiles
> Review Decks
> Spelling Sound Sheet 61
> tokens or colored pencil
> Worksheet 83
>
> ***new concepts***
>
> abbreviation

ALPHABET ACTIVITY

- The student should be seated with the container of letter tiles.

  "I am going to give you four (or five) letters. Put the letters in alphabetical order and I'll time you."

  "We'll do this several times and we'll see which group of letters you can alphabetize the fastest."

  "Do not start until I say go."
- Mix up the letter tiles and give four (or five) to the student.
- Play as many rounds as possible, keeping track of how long each one took.

REVIEW OF DECKS

- The student should be seated where he/she can write comfortably.
- Show the student **Letter Cards 1–54** in random order. The student should name the letter on each letter card.
- Review **Affix Cards 1–7.**
- Show the student **Picture Cards 1–64** in random order. The student should name the keyword and sound for each picture card.
- Review **Sight Word Cards 1–41.**
- Give the student **Spelling Sound Sheet 61** and at least 12 tokens (or a colored pencil).

  "Let's play Bingo!"

  "When I call out the spelling sounds today, I want you to put a token on (or draw a big X in) the space that spells that sound."

  "When you cover (or X out) all of the letters on one line, either up and down, across, or from corner to corner, call out Bingo!"

"Don't forget to refer to your rule charts if you need to."

"Are you ready?"

"Cover (or X out) the letters that spell the initial sound in 'quick.' " *qu*

"Cover (or X out) the letters that spell the last syllable in 'tumble.' " *ble*

"Cover (or X out) the letter that spells the first vowel sound in 'April.' " *A*

"Cover (or X out) the letters that spell the combination in 'torn.' " *or*

"Cover (or X out) the letter that spells the /s/ sound in 'cent.' " *c*

"Cover (or X out) the letters that spell the combination in 'after.' " *er*

"Cover (or X out) the letters that spell the initial sound in 'champion.' " *ch*

"Cover (or X out) the letters that spell the final sound in 'flow.' " *ow*

"Cover (or X out) the letters that spell the final sound in 'stay.' " *ay*

"Cover (or X out) the letters that spell the final sound in 'serve.' " *ve*

- The student should Bingo by the time all the sounds have been called out.
- Collect the tokens (or colored pencil) and the spelling sound sheet. If you used tokens and the spelling sound sheet is unmarked, keep it available for practice.

NEW LEARNING

"We've been working this week with words that have a 'vcv' syllable division pattern."

- Write the word "focusing" on the chalkboard.

"What is the first thing I should do to code this word?" *look for suffixes or final, stable syllables*

"Are there any?" *yes, suffix -ing*

"How do we code suffix -ing?" *box it*

- Box the suffix:

focus[ing]

"Does this word need to be divided?" *yes, it has two vowels*

"What should I do next?" *find the vowels*

"Which ones are the vowels?" *o and u*

- Write small *v*'s under the vowels:

focus[ing]
 v v

"What is the next step?" *look between the vowels*

"What do we have between the vowels?" *only one consonant*

- Write a small *c* under the consonant:

focus[ing]
 v c v

"Where do we divide the word?" *between the first vowel and the consonant*

- Put the dividing line between the *o* and the *c*:

  fo|cus[ing]
  v|c v

  "Which syllable is usually accented?" *the first syllable*

- Put an accent on the first syllable:

  fo´|cus[ing]
  v|c v

  "The o is open and accented. How should it be coded?" *long; with a macron*

  "What should we code in the second syllable?" *put a breve over the u because it is followed by a consonant; put a k-back on the c because it comes before u*

- Finish coding the word:

  fō´|cŭs[ing]
  v|c v

- Point to the *o* in the first syllable.

  "What is the o going to say?" */ō/*

- Point to the *u* in the second syllable.

  "What is the u going to say?" */ŭ/*

- Cover the suffix with your hand.

  "What does the root word say?" *focus*

- Uncover the suffix.

  "What is the word when we add suffix -ing?" *focusing*

  "Can you tell me what 'focusing' means or use it in a sentence?" *expect various answers*

  "Now we know the 'vcv' pattern using an a, e, i, and o. Let's work with u and we will have done them all!"

- Write "music" on the chalkboard and repeat the coding procedure. The word should be coded as follows:

  mū´|sĭc
  v|c v

  "Can you read this word?" *music*

- Leave the words on the chalkboard for the remainder of the lesson.

BOARDWORK

"Let's practice coding some words like the ones you'll have on your worksheet."

"The rule charts are in your Rule Book if you need to look at them."

- Write the following words and sentence (without the coding marks) on the chalkboard, one at a time. Ask the student to help you code them. The correct coding is as indicated:

  Mĭs´|ter
  vc|cv

Lesson 83

burst

ă b|s̶ o r b´
v c|c v

Gĕt (some) frō´|zĕn corn ăt the sū´|per|mar´|kĕt.
v |c v v |c v | v c |c v

- For the word "supermarket," explain the following:

  "When two two-syllable words come together to make a compound word, the compound word is often accented in two places."

- Have the student determine whether each of the items coded is a word, a phrase, or a sentence.
- After the student reads the word "Mister," write the abbreviation "Mr." next to it.

  "This is the abbreviation for 'Mister.' Can you tell me what an abbreviation is?"

  "An abbreviation is a shortened form of a word or phrase. Many abbreviations use periods, but not all of them do."

  "You'll see this abbreviation on your worksheet today."

WORKSHEET

- The student should be seated where he/she can write comfortably.
- Give the student **Worksheet 83.** Make sure the student turns to the correct side.

  "Let's spell with long vowels again today."

- When you pronounce these words, make a distinct separation between syllables. The student will be more successful if he/she spells by syllables.

  "Put your finger by #1. The first word is 'clo ... ver.'"

  "Unblend the first syllable with me." */k/ /l/ /ō/*

  "How do we spell /k/ before l?" *c*

  "Spell and write those sounds by #1." *c ... l ... o*

  "Unblend the second syllable with me." */v/ /er/*

  "Finish spelling the word." *v ... er*

  "What word did you write?" *clover*

- Repeat the procedure with #2 (focus), #3 (over), #4 (music), and #5 (super).

  "Now you're ready to code and read the words on your paper."

  "All of the 'vcv' words will have the accent on the first syllable today."

  "Using the rules we just practiced on the chalkboard, code the words by #6 through #10. After you have coded all the words, try to read them."

- Assist the student as necessary.

  "Numbers 11 and 12 are questions about the paragraph just above them. If you find any words you can't read, code them. Then see if you can answer the questions."

Lesson 83

- As the student works, provide help as needed. Help the student correct any incorrect answers. Then initial the worksheet in the space provided.
- Some time during the day, ask the student to read from the worksheet, a controlled reader, your basal reader, or other material of your choice.
- **Note:** Always make sure the worksheet is corrected before the student begins the homework. The worksheet serves as a guide to help complete the homework.

HOMEWORK

"Turn your paper over to the homework side."

"Do you know what to do on the homework paper?"

"Watch for words with the 'vcv' pattern. Always code suffixes and final, stable syllables before coding the rest of the word."

"When you finish your paper, I will check it for you and initial it in the space provided."

- Either now or later in the day, the student should complete the homework independently (if possible). Help the student correct any incorrect answers. Then initial the homework in the space provided.
- If possible, take time to play the Kid Card games listed in Lesson 80.

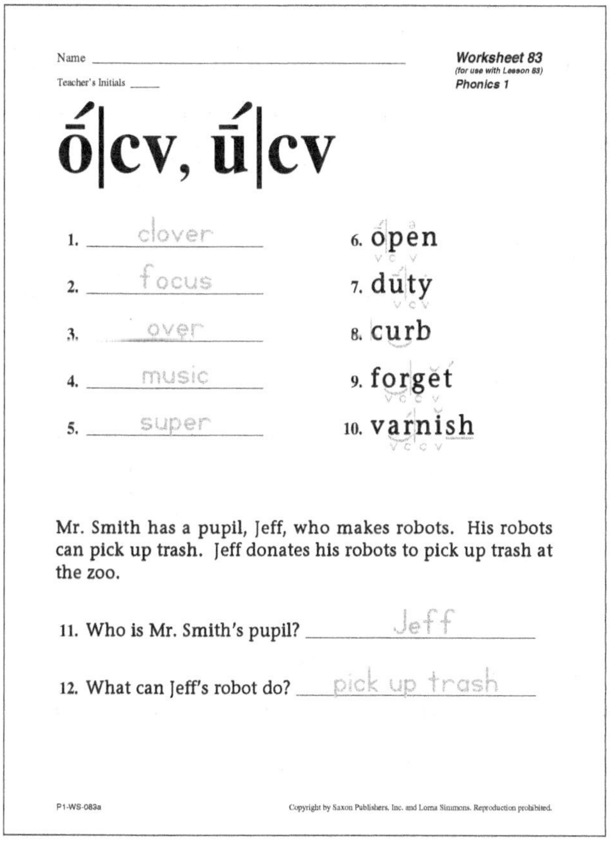

Name ____________

Teacher's Initials ____

Worksheet 83 (for use with Lesson 83) Phonics 1

ō|cv, ū|cv

1. clover
2. focus
3. over
4. music
5. super
6. open
7. duty
8. curb
9. forget
10. varnish

Mr. Smith has a pupil, Jeff, who makes robots. His robots can pick up trash. Jeff donates his robots to pick up trash at the zoo.

11. Who is Mr. Smith's pupil? Jeff

12. What can Jeff's robot do? pick up trash

P1-WS-083a

Copyright by Saxon Publishers, Inc. and Lorna Simmons. Reproduction prohibited.

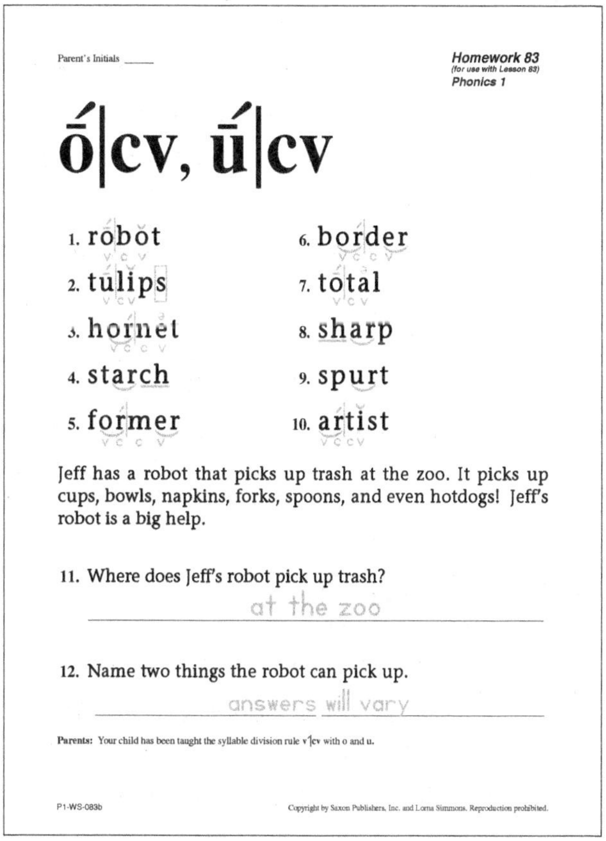

Parent's Initials ____

Homework 83 (for use with Lesson 83) Phonics 1

ō|cv, ū|cv

1. robot
2. tulips
3. hornet
4. starch
5. former
6. border
7. total
8. sharp
9. spurt
10. artist

Jeff has a robot that picks up trash at the zoo. It picks up cups, bowls, napkins, forks, spoons, and even hotdogs! Jeff's robot is a big help.

11. Where does Jeff's robot pick up trash? at the zoo

12. Name two things the robot can pick up. answers will vary

Parents: Your child has been taught the syllable division rule v|cv with o and u.

P1-WS-083b

Copyright by Saxon Publishers, Inc. and Lorna Simmons. Reproduction prohibited.

Lesson 83

LESSON 84 — The Rule v|cv′ with *a*

lesson preparation

materials

Alphabet/Accent Deck (Section 1)

Review Decks

Spelling Sound Sheet 62

banana in a sack (see *the night before*)

Picture Card 65

Worksheet 84

Reader 30 (*Kerry's Bike*)

colored pencils

new concepts

v|cv′ pattern

the night before

- Put a banana in a sack for the student to use to "discover" the new keyword.

ALPHABET ACTIVITY

"We're going to work with the Alphabet/Accent Deck again today. Let's stand."

"We'll stand with our feet flat on the floor and say the first syllable in a normal voice. When we come to the accented syllable, we'll stand on our tiptoes and say it louder."

- Show the student **Alphabet/Accent Card 1.**
- Have the student say "A" (in a normal voice with feet flat), and then "B" (louder, on tiptoes).
- Continue with **Alphabet/Accent Cards 2–25,** moving as quickly as possible.
- **Optional:** If you think the student is ready, shuffle the Alphabet/Accent Deck before the activity. Warn the student that the cards will be in random order.

REVIEW OF DECKS

- The student should be seated where he/she can write comfortably.
- Show the student **Letter Cards 1–54** in random order. The student should name the letter on each letter card.
- Review **Affix Cards 1–7.**

- Show the student **Picture Cards 1–64** in random order. The student should name the keyword and sound for each picture card.
- Review **Sight Word Cards 1–41.**
- Give the student **Spelling Sound Sheet 62.**
- Call out the sounds on **Spelling Cards 1–41** in random order. The student should echo each sound and name the letter or letters that make the sound as he/she writes the letter(s) on the spelling sound sheet.
- Have the student set the spelling sound sheet aside for use later in the lesson.

NEW LEARNING

- Write the word "awake" on the chalkboard.

"What is the first thing I should do to code this word?" *look for suffixes or final, stable syllables*

"Are there any suffixes or final, stable syllables?" *no*

"Does this word need to be divided?" *yes, it has more than one vowel*

"What should I do next?" *find the vowels*

"Which letters are the vowels?" *a, a, and silent e*

- Write small *v*'s under the first two vowels:

awake
v v

"We'll mark out the e because it is silent."

"What is the next step?" *look between the vowels*

"What do we have between the vowels?" *only one consonant*

- Write a small *c* under the *w*:

awakȩ
v c v

- Point to the "vcv" pattern under the word.

"When we see syllable division pattern 'vcv,' we divide before the consonant."

- Put the dividing line between the *a* and the *w*:

a|wakȩ
v|c v

"It's always best to try the accent on the first syllable."

- Put an accent on the first syllable:

a'|wakȩ
v|c v

"Let's see what we have in each syllable now."

"The a is open and accented. How should it be coded?" *long; with a macron*

Lesson 84

"What should we code in the second syllable?" *a macron over the a*

- Finish coding the word:

ā´|wākǿ
v | c v

- Point to the *a* in the first syllable.

"What is the a in the first syllable going to say?" /ā/

"Which syllable did we accent?" *the first syllable*

"Can you read this word the way it is coded?" *ā´|wāk*

"The way we have coded it, this word is 'ā´|wāk.' "

- Emphasize the mispronunciation.

"Have you ever heard the word 'ā´|wāk' before?"

- The student may say that he/she has heard the word, but he/she will probably pronounce it correctly.

"I have heard the word 'ŭ|wāk´' but I have never heard the word 'ā´|wāk.' Still, if we read the word the way we coded and divided it, it says 'ā´|wāk.' "

"This is not a word, so the next best thing to try is to change the accent."

- Erase the accent and macron in the first syllable and place the accent on the second syllable:

a|wākǿ´
v | c v

- Point to the *a* in the first syllable.

"Is the a still open and accented?" *no*

"That's right. The a is open but it is not accented."

"When an a is open and not accented, it is not long anymore. It becomes schwa. Let's code it with our mark for schwa."

- Put a schwa over the first *a*:

å|wākǿ´
v | c v

"What is the schwa sound?" /ŭ/

"We don't have to change the a in the second syllable because a sneaky e makes a vowel long whether it is accented or not."

"Which syllable will be accented now?" *second*

"Would you like to try and read this word?" *expect various responses*

"This word is 'ŭ|wake´.' "

"Can you use the word 'awake' in a sentence?" *expect various responses*

"Get out your Rule Book and turn to page 9."

Lesson 84

- Point to **Rule Chart 9** as you say the following:

  "We have a new rule chart today. It helps us remember the sound the a can make in an open, unaccented syllable. This chart also helps us with sounds that other vowels can make. We'll talk more about these in future lessons."

  "We have this new vowel pattern on one of our syllable division charts, too."

  "Look at your syllable division charts and see if you can find this pattern."

- After a moment, point to the "v|cv´" syllable division pattern on **Syllable Division Chart 3** (page 18).

  "This chart will help you with any of the different ways to divide."

New Deck Cards

- Pull **Letter Card 7** and **Spelling Card 26** from the Review Decks.
- Show the student **Letter Card 7.**

  "What is the name of this letter?" *a*

  "I have another sack today. It contains a clue to our new keyword. Don't look in the sack, but put your hand inside and see if you can feel what is inside the sack. Keep in mind that the object in the sack contains the /ŭ/ sound."

- Allow the student a chance to feel inside the sack.

  "Can you guess the new keyword?" *banana*

  "That's right. The keyword is 'banana.' "

- Show the student **Picture Card 65.**

  "The word 'banana' helps us remember the /ŭ/ sound since it contains that sound."

  "Find your spelling sound sheet. Put your finger on the line by #42."

- Hold up **Spelling Card 26** so only you can see what is written.

  "Echo this sound: /ŭ/." */ŭ/*

  "What do you think will be our new response to this card?" *u comma a*

  "That's right. Write 'u comma a' on the line by #42."

- Check the spelling sound sheet for accuracy.
- **Note:** Add the new picture card to the Review Deck (and re-insert **Letter Card 7** and **Spelling Card 26**).
- If desired, allow the student to eat the banana after the lesson.

Lesson 84

BOARDWORK

"Let's practice coding some words like the ones you'll have on your worksheet."

"The rule charts are in your Rule Book if you need to look at them."

- Write the following phrases (without the coding marks) on the chalkboard, one at a time. Ask the student to help you code them. The correct coding is as indicated:

mīl~~e~~[s] å|par t´
v|c v

lŏng sŭm´|mer[s]
v c | c v

- Have the student determine whether each of the items coded is a word, a phrase, or a sentence.

WORKSHEET

- The student should be seated where he/she can write comfortably.
- Give the student **Worksheet 84.** Make sure the student turns to the correct side.

"Today, let's spell with the unaccented a."

"Sometimes the /ŭ/ sound is confusing, isn't it?"

"If you hear the /ŭ/ sound by itself in a syllable, the sound is usually spelled with the letter a, as in the words 'awake,' 'about,' 'alike,' 'cola,' 'sofa,' and 'tuna.' "

"When you hear the /ŭ/ sound and it has a consonant with it in the syllable, it is spelled with the letter u, as in 'umbrella,' 'under,' 'upset,' 'fun,' 'up,' and 'truck.' "

"All of the words we will spell today have the unaccented a in them."

- When you pronounce these words, make a distinct separation between syllables. The student will be more successful if he/she spells by syllables.

"Put your finger by #1. The first word is 'a … like.' "

"Unblend the first syllable with me." */ŭ/*

"Spell and write that sound by #1." *a*

"Unblend the second syllable with me." */l/ /ī/ /k/*

"Finish spelling the word." *l … i … k … e*

"What word did you write?" *alike*

- Repeat the procedure with #2 (adapt), #3 (away), #4 (soda), and #5 (banana).

"Now you're ready to code and read the words on your paper."

"Using the rules we just practiced on the chalkboard, code the words by #6 through #10. After you have coded all the words, try to read them."

"All of the 'vcv' words will have the accent on the second syllable today."

- If the student seems to understand, let him/her code independently. If not, code each word with the student. Encourage independence as much as possible, but be ready to provide guidance for difficult concepts.

  "Look at the picture at the bottom of the page. Write a story about what is happening in the picture on the lines beside it. Don't worry about spelling. When you are finished, we will take time to check spelling and correct mistakes."

- As the student works, provide help as needed.
- Then have the student read the story silently and check for spelling errors. Help the student correct any mistakes. A perfect paper is not as important as the student putting his/her thoughts on paper and being able to recognize spelling errors that can be corrected (e.g., *k* and *c* spelling). Be sure to correct the rest of the worksheet as well. Then initial the worksheet in the space provided.
- Have the student read the story to you. It is important that children learn to feel comfortable speaking in front of others.
- **Note:** Always make sure the worksheet is corrected before the student begins the homework. The worksheet serves as a guide to help complete the homework.

HOMEWORK

"Turn your paper over to the homework side."

"Do you know what to do on the homework paper?"

"Watch for words with the new 'vcv' pattern. Always code suffixes before coding the rest of the word."

"Look at the picture at the bottom of the page. Write a story about what is about to happen in the picture."

"When you finish your paper, I will check it for you and initial it in the space provided."

- Either now or later in the day, the student should complete the homework independently (if possible). Help the student correct any incorrect answers. Then initial the homework in the space provided.

READER

"We have another new book today."

- Give the student **Reader 30 (*Kerry's Bike*)** and some colored pencils.

  "Can you tell me this book's title?" *Kerry's Bike*

- Assist the student as necessary as he/she constructs the book.
- When the student finishes, staple or put a rubber band around the book's spine.
- If necessary, demonstrate how to separate the pages and check the page order.

"The title of this book is _________?" *Kerry's Bike*

"I want you to read your book to yourself. When you are finished reading, color the pictures. Write your name on the book so I will know who colored it."

"Keep your book handy because I will be asking you to read it for me."

- Some time during the day, have the student read the reader to you.
- If possible, take time to play the Kid Card games listed in Lesson 80. Try to see that the student is prepared for tomorrow's assessment.

Name ____________________

Teacher's Initials _____

Worksheet 84
(for use with Lesson 84)
Phonics 1

ả|cv́

1. alike
2. adapt
3. away
4. soda
5. banana

6. alarm
7. abide
8. alert
9. along
10. splinter

P1-WS-084a

Parent's Initials _____

Homework 84
(for use with Lesson 84)
Phonics 1

ả|cv́

1. awake
2. alike
3. alone
4. atop
5. varmint

6. tender
7. bitter
8. chime
9. herd
10. farm

Parents: Your child has been taught the syllable division rule v | cv́ with a (the *a* becomes schwa).

P1-WS-084b

LESSON 85 — Assessment

lesson preparation

materials

container of letter tiles

Review Decks

Assessment 16

Spelling Test 14

Assessment 16 Recording Form

Kid Cards

tokens

the night before

- Separate the Kid Cards marked "Lesson 85."

ALPHABET ACTIVITY

- The student should be seated with the container of letter tiles.

  "Today we are going to alphabetize letters again."

  "I want you to pick any five letter tiles out of your container and put them in alphabetical order."

  "Tell me when you think you have them in alphabetical order."

- Check the student's work when he/she is finished. If the student is having difficulty alphabetizing, provide extra practice.
- Have the student replace the tiles in the container and put it away.

REVIEW OF DECKS

- The student should be seated where he/she can write comfortably.
- Show the student **Letter Cards 1–54** in random order. The student should name the letter on each letter card.
- Review **Affix Cards 1–7.**
- Show the student **Picture Cards 1–65** in random order. The student should name the keyword and sound for each picture card.
- Review **Sight Word Cards 1–41.**

WRITTEN ASSESSMENT

- Have the student sit where he/she can write comfortably.
- Give the student **Assessment 16.**
- **Section I:**

  "Today we are going to write some words for our assessment."

  "I'm going to say a word. Write the letter or letters that make each sound in that word on the lines by #1."

  "Look at the rule charts if you need to."

  "Here's the first word: growing."
- Repeat with the following words in the order shown: #2 (quake), #3 (scorch), #4 (march), and #5 (thunder).
- **Reminder:** While the student spells, be ready to point to appropriate rule charts as necessary.
- **Section II:**

  "Look at the letters by #6."

  "Find the picture of the keyword for this sound."

  "Draw a line from the letters to the keyword."
- Repeat with #7, #8, and #9. Allow a few minutes for the student to work.
- The pictures (from top to bottom) are as follows: circle, bow, shirt, purse.
- **Section III:**

  "Put your finger on #10."

  "Code the words by #10 through #15."
- Allow a few minutes for the student to work.
- **Section IV:**

  "Read the paragraph. If you find any words you can't read, code them to help you figure them out. Then answer the questions by #16, #17, and 18."
- **Reminder:** If the student absolutely cannot read the paragraph, read it to the student to see if he or she can answer the questions.

  "When you are finished, show your paper to me."
- This paper will be used during the oral portion of the assessment.

SPELLING TEST

- Give the student **Spelling Test 14.**
- Call out the following words (in the order shown). Sound them out, if necessary.

  #1 (day), #2 (stay), #3 (gumdrop), #4 (saying), #5 (blister), #6 (bathtub), #7 (driveway), #8 (softness), #9 (winter), #10 (helpless), #11 (from), #12 (does)
- Grade and record the test in any manner that suits your needs.

ORAL ASSESSMENT

- It is important to complete the oral assessment promptly (today, if possible) in order to identify any areas of weakness and begin remediation.
- Use the assessment and the following dialogue to complete the oral portion.
- **Section V:**
- Point to the sight word by #19.

  "Read this sight word for me."
- Record the student's response by placing a check mark by each word he/she reads correctly.
- Repeat with #20 and #21.
- **Section VI:**
- Show the student the letters by #22.

  "Tell me the name of these letters and the sound they make."
- Write the student's response on the adjacent line.
- Repeat with #23, #24, and #25.

ASSESSMENT EVALUATION

- Grade the assessment and record the results on **Assessment 16 Recording Form.** Check off the boxes to indicate mastery (i.e., the section was completed with 100% accuracy).
- **Reminder:** Try to give as many points as possible for work attempted. Do not grade the coding marks too severely. The most important coding marks to look for are breves, macrons, and syllable division lines.
- See the introductory material for detailed information regarding grading and recording procedures.
- Use the assessment results to identify those skills in which the student is weak. Practice those skills by playing Kid Card games.
- Add the Kid Cards marked "Lesson 85" to the existing decks. Listed below are games appropriate for remediation in selected areas. See "Games and Activities" for the directions for each game.
- **Section I:** Play "Spelling Deck Perfection," "Sound Scamper," "Spell Out #1," or have the student use the letter tiles to spell words you give from the Spelling Word List.
- **Section II:** Play "Keyword and Sound" or "Letter/Sound Identification."
- **Section III:** Play "Chalkboard Challenge."
- **Section IV:** Either have the student read the controlled readers and then ask questions for comprehension, or play "Acting Out" with the green Kid Cards.
- **Section V:** Play "At First Sight," review the Sight Word Deck, or lay the sight words out with a token on each one and let the student try to get as many tokens as possible for the sight words he/she can read.
- **Section VI:** Play "Letter/Sound Identification."

- When the student seems more secure in areas that had previously proven difficult, retest him/her (in those areas only) and indicate on the recording form any sections the student has subsequently mastered.
- Try to help the student achieve mastery of all the sections before the next assessment.
- If the student is having difficulty with a particular skill, keep his or her practice activities at the most basic level so the chance of success is greater.

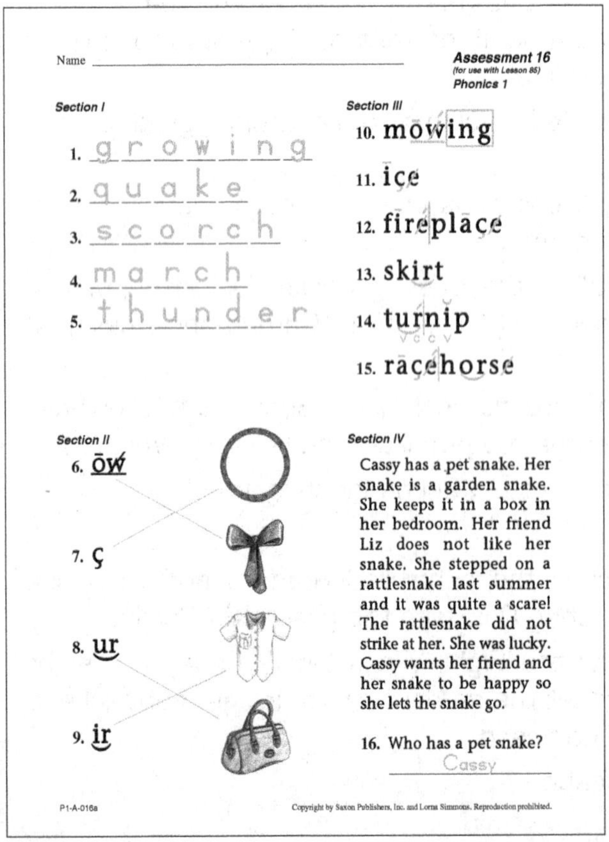

Name ______________________

Assessment 16
(for use with Lesson 85)
Phonics 1

Section I

1. growing
2. quake
3. scorch
4. march
5. thunder

Section II

6. ōw
7. ç
8. ur
9. ir

Section III

10. mowing
11. ice
12. fireplace
13. skirt
14. turnip
15. racehorse

Section IV

Cassy has a pet snake. Her snake is a garden snake. She keeps it in a box in her bedroom. Her friend Liz does not like her snake. She stepped on a rattlesnake last summer and it was quite a scare! The rattlesnake did not strike at her. She was lucky. Cassy wants her friend and her snake to be happy so she lets the snake go.

16. Who has a pet snake?
Cassy

P1-A-016a

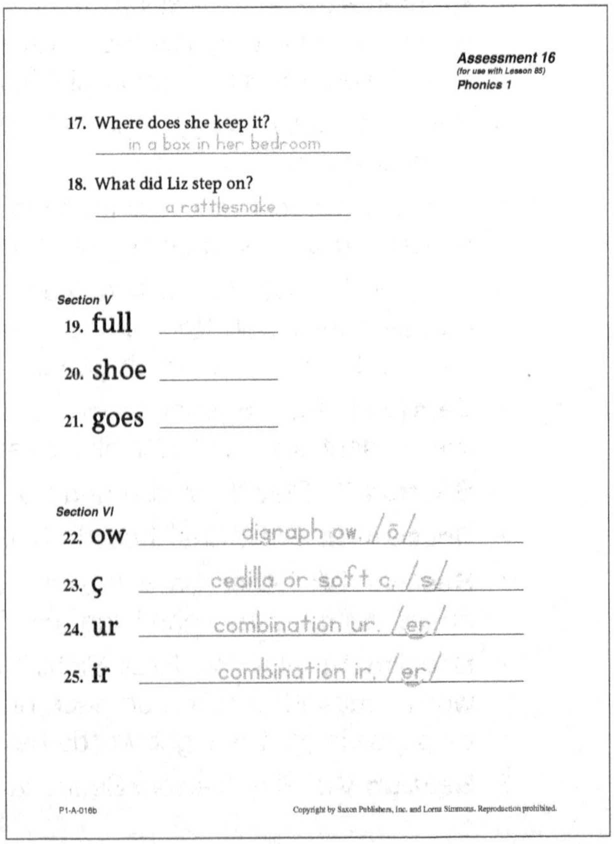

Assessment 16
(for use with Lesson 85)
Phonics 1

17. Where does she keep it?
in a box in her bedroom

18. What did Liz step on?
a rattlesnake

Section V

19. full ________
20. shoe ________
21. goes ________

Section VI

22. ow — digraph ow, /ō/
23. ç — cedilla or soft c, /s/
24. ur — combination ur, /er/
25. ir — combination ir, /er/

P1-A-016b

Lesson 85

Lesson 86

Digraph *ea*, Part 1

lesson preparation

materials

container of letter tiles

Review Decks

Spelling Sound Sheet 63

Letter Card 55

leaves in a sack (see *the night before*)

Picture Card 66

Worksheet 86

Spelling List 15

the night before

- Put some leaves in a sack for the student to use to "discover" the new keyword.

Alphabet Activity

- The student should be seated with the container of letter tiles.

  "Before we start, let's say the alphabet together so it is fresh in our minds."

- Recite the alphabet with the student.

  "Today, I'm going to let you try to put the letter tiles in alphabetical order again. When I say 'go,' dump your tiles on the desk, turn them to the lowercase (blue) side, and begin working."

  "Sometimes it's hard to tell if a lowercase letter is right side up or upside down. If you're not sure, look at the other side to see which end is up."

  "Ready, set, go!"

- Allow enough time for the student to alphabetize the letters.
- If desired, time the student and compare it with his/her times from Lessons 66 and 76.
- Have the student replace the tiles in the container and put it away.

Review of Decks

- The student should be seated where he/she can write comfortably.
- Show the student **Letter Cards 1–54** in random order. The student should name the letter on each letter card.
- Review **Affix Cards 1–7.**
- Show the student **Picture Cards 1–65** in random order. The student should name the keyword and sound for each picture card.
- Review **Sight Word Cards 1–41.**
- Give the student **Spelling Sound Sheet 63.**
- Call out the sounds on **Spelling Cards 1–41** in random order. The student should echo each sound and name the letter or letters that make the sound as he/she writes the letter(s) on the spelling sound sheet.
- Check the student's response after each card.

New Learning

"I'm going to say some words. Echo them back to me and listen for the sound that is the same in each word."

- Point to your mouth as you say each word.

"Echo after me. Seal." *seal* ***"Peach."*** *peach* ***"Bean."*** *bean*

"What sound do you hear that is the same in these words?" */ē/*

"That's right. The sound you hear is /ē/."

"Put your fingertips on the front of your neck and say /ē/. See if you feel any vibration."

"Is this sound voiced or unvoiced?" *voiced*

- Write the following on the chalkboard: seal, peach, bean.

"What do you see that might be making the /ē/ sound?" *ea*

"There is an ea in all of these words, so we can see that ea must be the letters used to spell the /ē/ sound."

"How many sounds do you hear?" *one*

"How many letters are making that sound?" *two*

- Use the digraph hand signals (two fingers coming together to make one) as you say the following:

"What do we call two letters that come together to make one sound?" *a digraph*

"How do we code digraphs?" *underline them*

"How will we show that digraph ea makes the /ē/ sound?" *put a macron over the e; cross out the a*

- Code the words on the chalkboard as the student instructs: sēal, pēach, bēan.

  "Is digraph ea a vowel digraph or a consonant digraph?" *it is a vowel digraph because it contains only vowels*

NEW DECK CARDS

- Show the student **Letter Card 55.**

  "What do we call this?" *digraph ea*

  "I have another sack today. It contains a clue to our new keyword. Don't look in the sack, but put your hand inside and see if you can feel what is inside the sack. Keep in mind that the object in the sack contains the /ē/ sound."
- Allow the student a chance to feel inside the sack.
- **Optional:** If leaves are unavailable, use the following riddle:

  "These grow on trees. They are green. In autumn they change color and fall to the ground. Then we rake them into piles in the yard."

  "Can you guess the new keyword?" *leaf*

  "That's right. The keyword is 'leaf' and the sound is /ē/."
- Show the student **Picture Card 66.**

  "What will we say when we see this card?" *digraph ea*
- **Note:** The digraph and its picture are also shown in the Rule Book on page 21.
- **Note:** Add the new letter and picture cards to the Review Decks.

BOARDWORK

"Let's practice coding some words like the ones you'll have on your worksheet."

"The rule charts are in your Rule Book if you need to look at them."

- Write the following word and sentence (without the coding marks) on the chalkboard, one at a time. Ask the student to help you code them. The correct coding is as indicated:

  squint´ing

  The sēals ăt the zoo līke pŏp´corn.
- Have the student determine whether each of the items coded is a word, a phrase, or a sentence.

WORKSHEET

- The student should be seated where he/she can write comfortably.
- Give the student **Worksheet 86.** Make sure the student turns to the correct side.

  "Let's spell with the /ē/ sound using digraph ea."

"Remember, digraph ea is not used very often for spelling. Let's see what kinds of words are spelled with digraph ea. Get out your Irregular Spelling Booklet."

"Look in the table of contents and see if you can find the page showing words that spell the /ē/ sound with digraph ea." *page 4*

"Turn to page 4. All of the words on pages 4 and 5 use digraph ea to spell the /ē/ sound. They don't follow our regular rules, so we must memorize them. Until then, you can refer to your booklet."

- Allow time for the student to examine the list of words. If time permits, discuss the definition and/or pronunciation of some or all of the words.

"Do you know any other words that belong on this list?"

- If the student offers any appropriate words, write the words on the chalkboard and have the student copy them into the booklet.

"Put your booklet away for now and let's try to spell some words."

"Put your finger by #1. The first word is 'eat.' "

"Spell the word and write it by #1."

- Allow time for the student to do this.

"What word did you write?" *eat*

- Repeat the procedure with #2 (leave), #3 (hear), #4 (reach), and #5 (speak).

"Now you're ready to code and read the words on your paper."

"Code the words by #6 through #10. After you have coded all the words, try to read them."

- Assist the student as necessary.

"Numbers 11 and 12 are questions about the paragraph just above them. If you find any words you can't read, code them. Then see if you can answer the questions."

- As the student works, provide help as needed. Help the student correct any incorrect answers. Then initial the worksheet in the space provided.
- Some time during the day, ask the student to read from the worksheet, a controlled reader, your basal reader, or other material of your choice.
- **Note:** Always make sure the worksheet is corrected before the student begins the homework. The worksheet serves as a guide to help complete the homework.

HOMEWORK

"Turn your paper over to the homework side."

"Do you know what to do on the homework paper?"

"Watch for digraph ea. Always code suffixes and final, stable syllables before coding the rest of the word."

"When you finish your paper, I will check it for you and initial it in the space provided."

- Either now or later in the day, the student should complete the homework independently (if possible). Help the student correct any incorrect answers. Then initial the homework in the space provided.

SPELLING LIST

- Fold **Spelling List 15** in half lengthwise (with the printed side facing out).

  "Leave your paper just like I give it to you."

- Give the student **Spelling List 15,** folded with the blank lines facing up.

  "Let's spell some more words."

- Call out the following words (in the order shown). Sound them out, if necessary.

  #1 (arm), #2 (sharp), #3 (bunch), #4 (chin), #5 (corn), #6 (forget), #7 (quack), #8 (quicksand), #9 (smart), #10 (squint), #11 (were), #12 (brought)

  "Now unfold your paper and check your words."

- Check the student's work to see if he/she needs extra help with spelling.

  "I want you to practice these words. We'll have a spelling test in a few days."

- If possible, take time to play the Kid Card games listed in Lesson 85.

Name ____________

Teacher's Initials ____

Worksheet 86
(for use with Lesson 86)
Phonics 1

ēa

1. eat
2. leave
3. hear
4. reach
5. speak
6. east
7. reaching
8. treated
9. squeal
10. eardrum

My grandmom cleans for a dentist. She sweeps the carpets and dusts the chairs. One time, she stepped on a tooth that fell on the floor.

11. Where does grandmom clean? at a dentist's

12. What did she step on? a tooth

P1-WS-086a

Parent's Initials ____

Homework 86
(for use with Lesson 86)
Phonics 1

ēa

1. cheap
2. teaching
3. quilt
4. nearing
5. year
6. weave
7. tea
8. speaking
9. beaded
10. seaport

My grandmom stepped on a tooth and she slipped and fell. When she fell, she hit her arm. She grabbed for the table and spilled the bleach. Her arm healed quickly, but the carpet is no longer green.

11. What did she hit? her arm

12. What spilled? bleach

Parents: Your child has been taught one sound of **digraph ea** (as in *leaf*).

P1-WS-086b

LESSON 87 — Digraph *ea*, Part 2

lesson preparation

materials

Alphabet/Accent Deck (Section 1)
Retired Decks
Affix Deck
Spelling Sound Sheet 64
spool of thread in a sack (see *the night before*)
Picture Cards 67–68
small, brittle stick
Sight Word Cards 42–43
Worksheet 87
Reader 31 (*Nubbin*)
colored pencils

the night before

- Put a spool of thread in a sack for the student to use to "discover" the new keyword.

ALPHABET ACTIVITY

"We're going to work with the Alphabet/Accent Deck again today."

"Let's say the first syllable in a normal voice while sitting down, and then stand and say the accented syllable louder."

- Show the student **Alphabet/Accent Card 1.**
- Have the student say "A" (seated and in a normal voice), and then "B" (standing and louder).
- Continue with **Alphabet/Accent Cards 2–25,** moving as quickly as possible.
- **Optional:** If you think the student is ready, shuffle the Alphabet/Accent Deck before the activity. Warn the student that the cards will be in random order.

REVIEW OF DECKS

- The student should be seated where he/she can write comfortably.
- Show the student the retired letter cards in random order. The student should name the letter on each letter card.
- Review **Affix Cards 1–7.**
- Show the student the retired picture cards in random order. The student should name the keyword and sound for each picture card.
- Review the retired sight word cards.
- Give the student **Spelling Sound Sheet 64.**
- Call out the sounds on the retired spelling cards in random order. The student should echo each sound and name the letter or letters that make the sound as he/she writes the letter(s) on the spelling sound sheet.
- Check the student's response after each card.

NEW LEARNING

"I'm going to say some words. Echo them back to me and listen for the sound that is the same in the medial position of each word."

- Point to your mouth as you say each word.

  "Echo after me. Bread." *bread* ***"Sweat."*** *sweat* ***"Head."*** *head*

  "What sound do you hear in the medial position?" */ĕ/*

- Write the following on the chalkboard: bread, sweat, head.

  "What do you see that might be making the /ĕ/ sound?" *ea*

  "Do you know what this is called?" *digraph ea*

  "How do we code a digraph?" *underline it*

- Underline the *ea*'s on the chalkboard: bread, sweat, head.

  "How can we code this digraph so it will say /ĕ/ in these words?" *put a breve on the e, mark out the a since it is silent*

- Code the words on the chalkboard: brĕad, swĕat, hĕad.

  "Can you read one of these words?"

  "Can you use the word in a sentence?" *expect various responses*

- Repeat with the remaining words.

  "Now we know that digraph ea has two sounds: /ē/ and /ĕ/."

  "Well, guess what! Digraph ea has a third sound!"

  "Echo these words and listen for the sound that is the same in the medial position of each word. Break." *break* ***"Yea."*** *yea* ***"Great."*** *great*

  "What sound do you hear in the medial position?" */ā/*

- Write the following on the chalkboard: break, yea, great.

  "What is making the /ā/ sound?" *digraph ea*

  "How do we code this digraph so it will say /ā/ in these words?" *put a macron on the a, mark out the e since it is silent*

- Code the words on the chalkboard: br~~e~~āk, y~~e~~ā, gr~~e~~āt.

  "Are the three sounds of digraph ea voiced or unvoiced?" *voiced*

  "Is digraph ea a vowel digraph or a consonant digraph?" *vowel digraph*

- Leave the words on the chalkboard for the remainder of the lesson.

New Deck Cards

- Pull **Letter Card 55** from the Review Deck.
- Show the student **Letter Card 55.**

  "What do we call this?" *digraph ea*

  "I have another sack today. It contains a clue to one of our new keywords. Don't look in the sack, but put your hand inside and see if you can guess what is inside. Keep in mind that the object in the sack contains the /ĕ/ sound."

- Allow the student a chance to feel inside the sack.

  "Can you guess the new keyword?" *thread*

  "That's right. The keyword is 'thread,' which reminds us of the /ĕ/ sound of digraph ea."

- Show the student **Picture Card 67.**

  "We have one more keyword for digraph ea. This is the keyword for digraph ea when it says /ā/."

  "Now watch me. What is it called when I do this?"

- Hold up a stick and break it in half. The student should answer "break."

  "That's right. 'Break' is our keyword for the /ā/ sound of digraph ea."

- Show the student **Picture Card 68.**
- **Note:** The digraphs and their pictures are also shown in the Rule Book on page 21.

  "There is no rule that says which sound digraph ea will make, so you'll have to try each sound until the word sounds right."

  "The sounds of /ē/, /ĕ/, and /ā/ spelled with digraph ea are irregular spelling patterns, so we won't add them to our spelling cards."

- **Note:** Add the new picture cards to the Review Deck (and re-insert **Letter Card 55**).

BOARDWORK

- Write the following on the chalkboard:

  once /wŭns/ when /hwĕn/

  "We have two new sight words today."

- Point to the first word.

  "Can you tell me what this word is? Remember, it's a sight word, so it won't follow all of our rules."

- Allow the student to try to pronounce the word. If necessary, say it for him/her.

  "This word is 'once.' Can you use the word 'once' in a sentence?" *expect various answers*

- Repeat with "when."
- Show the student **Sight Word Cards 42** and **43.**

  "Let's find these words on our sight word charts."

- Help the student locate the words in the Irregular Spelling Booklet.

  "We will add these cards to our sight word deck."

  "Let's practice coding some words like the ones you'll have on your worksheet."

  "The rule charts are in your Rule Book if you need to look at them."

- Write the following phrases (without the coding marks) on the chalkboard, one at a time. Ask the student to help you code them. The correct coding is as indicated:

  yĕl′|lōw corn′|brĕad with bŭt′|ter
  vc|cv vc|cv

  cŏf′|fēe brāak
  vc|cv

- Have the student determine whether each of the items coded is a word, a phrase, or a sentence.
- Add **Sight Word Cards 42** and **43** to the Sight Word Deck.

WORKSHEET

- The student should be seated where he/she can write comfortably.
- Give the student **Worksheet 87.** Make sure the student turns to the correct side.

  "Let's spell with the /ĕ/ and /ā/ sounds using digraph ea today."

  "Remember, digraph ea is not used very often for spelling. Let's see what kinds of words are spelled with digraph ea. Get out your Irregular Spelling Booklet."

  "Look in the table of contents and see if you can find the page showing words that spell the /ĕ/ sound with digraph ea." *page 9*

  "Turn to page 9. All of the words on page 9 use digraph ea to spell the /ĕ/ sound. They don't follow our regular rules, so we must memorize them."

- Allow time for the student to examine the list of words. If time permits, discuss the definition and/or pronunciation of some or all of the words.

  "Do you know any other words that belong on this list?"

- If the student offers any appropriate words, write the words on the chalkboard and have the student copy them into the booklet.
- Repeat with the /ā/ sound of digraph *ea* (page 3). It is unlikely that the student will be able to think of additional words.

  "Use your Irregular Spelling Booklet to help you learn how to spell the three sounds of digraph ea. For now, put your booklet away and let's try to spell some words."

- Have the student close the booklet and put it away.
- Write the word "leather" on the chalkboard.

  "Look at this word. It's a bit different for dividing, but not hard to read."

- Code the word as follows: lĕąth´|er.
- **Note:** If you choose to mark vowels and consonants, the word will be coded as follows:

  lĕą th´ | er
  v c | v

- You may choose not to teach this as it requires explaining that digraph *ea* counts as one vowel (sound) and digraph *th* counts as one consonant (sound).

  "This word and many others like it are divided after the consonant or consonant digraph. The consonant closes the syllable and maybe that's what causes the short vowel sound. When you are coding words like this, try all three sounds of digraph ea until you find a word you know."

  "Put your finger by #1. The first word is 'a … head.' "

- When you pronounce these words, make a distinct separation between syllables. The student will be more successful if he/she spells by syllables.

  "Spell the word and write it by #1."

- Allow time for the student to write the word.

  "What word did you write?" *ahead*

- Repeat the procedure with #2 (read /rĕd/), #3 (head), #4 (great), and #5 (break).

  "Now you're ready to code and read the words on your paper."

  "Code the words by #6 through #10. After you have coded all the words, try to read them."

- Assist the student as necessary.

  "Now read the word by #11. If you have trouble reading the word, code it. Then draw a line from the word to the picture it matches."

- Repeat with #12, #13, and #14.
- As the student works, provide help as needed. Help the student correct any incorrect answers. Then initial the worksheet in the space provided.

- Some time during the day, ask the student to read from the worksheet, a controlled reader, your basal reader, or other material of your choice.
- **Note:** Always make sure the worksheet is corrected before the student begins the homework. The worksheet serves as a guide to help complete the homework.

HOMEWORK

"Turn your paper over to the homework side."

"Do you know what to do on the homework paper?"

"Watch for digraph ea. Always code suffixes and final, stable syllables before coding the rest of the word."

"When you finish your paper, I will check it for you and initial it in the space provided."

- Either now or later in the day, the student should complete the homework independently (if possible). Help the student correct any incorrect answers. Then initial the homework in the space provided.

READER

"We have another new book today."

- Give the student **Reader 31 (*Nubbin*)** and some colored pencils.

"Can you tell me this book's title?" Nubbin

- Assist the student as necessary as he/she constructs the book.
- When the student finishes, staple or put a rubber band around the book's spine.
- If necessary, demonstrate how to separate the pages and check the page order.

"The title of this book is __________?" Nubbin

"I want you to read your book to yourself. When you are finished reading, color the pictures. Write your name on the book so I will know who colored it."

"Keep your book handy because I will be asking you to read it for me."

- Some time during the day, have the student read the reader to you.
- If possible, take time to play the Kid Card games listed in Lesson 85.

Name ______________________

Teacher's Initials ____

Worksheet 87
(for use with Lesson 87)
Phonics 1

ĕa, eā

1. ahead
2. read
3. head
4. great
5. break
6. dĕaf
7. yea
8. shōw
9. hĕadlight
10. wĕathervane

11. thread 

12. pea 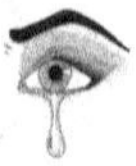

13. sweater 

14. tear 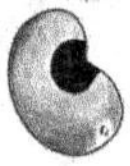

P1-WS-087a

Parent's Initials ____

Homework 87
(for use with Lesson 87)
Phonics 1

ĕa, eā

1. thrĕad
2. steak
3. break
4. swĕat
5. hĕadrĕst
6. sneak
7. flōwn
8. thīgh
9. sāle
10. sprĕad

11. bread 

13. beads 

12. leaf 

14. leak 

Parents: Your child has been taught the two additional sounds of **digraph ea** (as in *thread* and *break*).

P1-WS-087b

LESSON 88

Spelling with the Dropping Rule

lesson preparation

materials

12 index cards (see *the night before*)

Review Decks

Worksheet 88

new concepts

dropping rule

the night before

- Make two six-card sets of word cards. One set should contain the words "attic," "make," "jest," "nose," "print," and "self." The other set should contain the words "bird," "dirt," "grass," "nest," "poppy," and "tree." Write the words as large as possible. Use the first set of words for demonstration purposes.

ALPHABET ACTIVITY

- The student should be seated.

"Let's try alphabetizing some words again today."

- Place or loosely tape the six word cards from the demonstration set ("attic," "make," "jest," "nose," "print," and "self") in the chalk tray (or anywhere else the student can see them). Deliberately place them in non-alphabetical order.

"What is our guide letter?" *the first letter in each word*

"Let's underline the guide letters so we can see them easily."

- Underline the first letter in each word.

"Are the first letters of these words all different?" *yes*

"We will recite the alphabet slowly. Each time we say a letter, we will quickly scan the guide letters in these words to see if the letter we are reciting is here and needs to be pulled."

"You can say the alphabet with me. Let's start. 'A.' "

- Quickly scan the guide letters with your index finger.

"Is there an a?" *yes*

"Let's pull the word that has 'a' as its guide letter and place it at the beginning of our new row of words. This row will be in alphabetical order when we finish."

- Move "attic" to a new location with enough room for the rearranged words.

"B."

- Quickly scan the cards again with your index finger.

  "Is there a b?" *no*

  "C." *no* ***"D."*** *no* ***"E."*** *no* ***"F."*** *no*

  "G." *no* ***"H."*** *no* ***"I."*** *no* ***"J."*** *yes*

- Pull "jest" and place it to the right of "attic."
- Continue through the alphabet, pulling "make," "nose," "print," and "self" as you come to each letter. You need not recite the alphabet past *s*.

  "All the cards have been used, so we can stop."

  "Now our words should be in ABC, or alphabetical, order. Let's quickly check them to see if we are right."

- Quickly recite the alphabet from *a* to *s*, touching each new word in the sequence as you say it. The student should see that your hand will move progressively to the right if the words are in the correct order.
- Give the student the second set of word cards. Instruct the student to alphabetize the words (using the procedure just demonstrated).
- Monitor the student closely to see that he/she is following the procedure and is successful alphabetizing the words.

Review of Decks

- The student should be seated where he/she can write comfortably.
- Show the student **Letter Cards 1–55** in random order. The student should name the letter on each letter card.
- Review **Affix Cards 1–7.**
- Show the student **Picture Cards 1–68** in random order. The student should name the keyword and sound for each picture card.
- Review **Sight Word Cards 1–43.**

  "When we review the spelling cards today, I'll let you play 'teacher' and I'll be your student."

- Allow the student to give the sounds on **Spelling Cards 1–41** in random order. You should echo each sound, name the letter or letters that make the sound, and then skywrite the letter(s).

New Learning

- Write "sliding" on the chalkboard.

  "Look at this word. What do you see at the end?" *suffix -ing*

  "We have always boxed suffixes first and then coded the rest of the word. This usually makes the word easier to divide."

"But what if we decided to code the whole word at once? If we divide the word, suffix and all, into syllables, we end up with the same word. That's not the easiest way to do it, but it does work!"

"Let's try coding this word by dividing it into syllables."

"We will ignore the suffix at the end and pretend that we don't know that 'ing' is a suffix. Can you help me code this word?"

- Code the word as the student instructs: slī′|dĭng.

"What does this word say?" *sliding*

"That's right. This method worked, even though we know that 'sliding' is actually a root word with a suffix added."

"We have a special name for a root word that has a suffix added to it. We've talked about this before. It's called a 'derivative.' Say that with me." *derivative*

"What is the suffix on the word 'sliding'?" *-ing*

"If -ing is the suffix, what is the root word?" *slide*

- Cover the suffix with your hand.

"What does this root word say?" *slid*

"It is supposed to say 'slide.' What is missing?" *sneaky e*

"This is a special new rule we are about to learn."

- Write the following on the chalkboard: slide + ing.

"There are two kinds of suffixes: vowel suffixes and consonant suffixes. They are named by their first letter."

"Is -ing a vowel or consonant suffix?" *vowel suffix*

"In the word 'slide,' what sneaks up on the i to make it long?" *the e*

"Is e a vowel or a consonant?" *vowel*

- Write "slideing" on the chalkboard.

"If we just tack suffix -ing on the end of 'slide' like this, we have two vowels instead of just one sneaky e. Do we need two vowels to sneak up on that i?" *the student will probably answer no*

"That's right, we don't! Only one vowel is needed to sneak up on the i. If we leave out the i, then we won't know that it is suffix -ing. What should we do?"

- Allow the student to offer suggestions. Lead him/her to the correct answer, if necessary.

"We drop the e off 'slide' and let the i from suffix -ing sneak past the consonant d in 'slide.' Now we know the i in 'sliding' says /ī/ rather than /ĭ/."

- Write "taping" on the chalkboard.

"Does this word have a vowel suffix on it?" *yes*

"How would you say this word?" *tāping*

"Why?" *the i in suffix -ing sneaks past the consonant p and makes the a long*

"What was the word before suffix -ing was added?" *tape*

- Write the word "tapping" on the chalkboard.

"How would you say this word?" *tăpping*

"Why doesn't it happen in this word? It has a suffix -ing." *the i can only sneak past one consonant; this word has two consonants*

- Write the word "hoped" on the chalkboard.

"Let's try a different kind of word. What is this word?" *hoped*

"How do you know the o says /ō/?" *the e in suffix -ed sneaks past the consonant to make the o long*

- Write "make + ing" on the chalkboard.

"Let's try spelling this word. What if I want to add suffix -ing to the word 'make'? What should I do?" *drop the e on "make" and add -ing to the word; the word is "making"*

"There is a special checking process we use to decide when we need to drop the e."

"Let's do one more and I'll show you."

- Write the following on the chalkboard:

☐ ☐
vote + ed = ________

"First we check to see if we are adding a vowel suffix. Are we?" *yes*

- Check the second box.

☐ ☑
vote + ed = ________

"Next, we check to see if the root word ends with a sneaky e or a silent e. Silent e's work just like sneaky e's. Does the root word end with a sneaky or silent e?" *yes*

- Check the first box.

☑ ☑
vote + ed = ________

"If we have two checks, we have to do something. What do we do?" *drop the e and add the suffix to the root word*

"How will this word be spelled?" *voted*

- Write "voted" in the blank on the chalkboard.

☑ ☑
vote + ed = <u>voted</u>

"Let's try one more. Help me with this word."

- Write the following on the chalkboard:

☐ ☐

film + ing = ________

"First we check to see if we are adding a vowel suffix. Are we?" yes

- Check the second box.

☐ ☑

film + ing = ________

"Next we check to see if the root word ends with a sneaky e or a silent e. Does the root word end with a sneaky or silent e?" no

"If we have two checks we have to do something. Do we have two checks?" no

"So we can add suffix -ing to the root word without dropping anything?" yes

"How will the word be spelled if we add suffix -ing to 'film'?" filming

- Write "filming" in the blank on the chalkboard.

☐ ☑

film + ing = filming

"What we've learned today is called the 'dropping rule.' "

"Get out your Rule Book and turn to page 10."

- Point to **Rule Chart 10** as you say the following:

"We drop the sneaky or silent e on a root word before adding a vowel suffix."

"You may refer to this chart any time you need help adding a vowel suffix. We'll learn about the other rule on this chart later in the year."

- Leave the words and boxes on the chalkboard for the remainder of the lesson.

BOARDWORK

"Let's practice coding some words like the ones you'll have on your worksheet."

"The rule charts are in your Rule Book if you need to look at them."

- Write the following phrase and sentence (without the coding marks) on the chalkboard, one at a time. Ask the student to help you code them. The correct coding is as indicated:

tāk′ing å brēāk

Mȳ′ art clăss is start′ing soon.

- Have the student determine whether each of the items coded is a word, a phrase, or a sentence.

WORKSHEET

- The student should be seated where he/she can write comfortably.
- Give the student **Worksheet 88.** Make sure the student turns to the correct side.

  "Let's spell with the dropping rule today. On your worksheet there are words written with boxes, like the ones I have drawn on the chalkboard."

  "Put your finger by #1. The first root word is 'smile.' "

  "Does the root word end with a sneaky e or a silent e?" *yes*

  "Put a check in the box over the root word."

  "Is the suffix a vowel suffix?" *yes*

  "Put a check in the box over the suffix."

  "We have two checks. What should we do?" *drop the e and add the suffix*

  "Write the word on the line by #1."
- Allow time for the student to write the word.

  "What word did you write?" *smiled*
- Repeat the procedure with #2 (played), #3 (wading), #4 (caneless), #5 (bony), #6 (sadly), and #7 (hiking).

  "Now you're ready to code and read the words on your paper."

  "Code the words by #8 through #12. After you have coded all the words, try to read them."
- Assist the student as necessary.
- As the student works, provide help as needed. Help the student correct any incorrect answers. Then initial the worksheet in the space provided.
- Some time during the day, ask the student to read from the worksheet, a controlled reader, your basal reader, or other material of your choice.
- **Note:** Always make sure the worksheet is corrected before the student begins the homework. The worksheet serves as a guide to help complete the homework.

HOMEWORK

"Turn your paper over to the homework side."

"Do you know what to do on the homework paper?"

"Follow the procedure we have been working with today."

"When you finish your paper, I will check it for you and initial it in the space provided."

- Either now or later in the day, the student should complete the homework independently (if possible). Help the student correct any incorrect answers. Then initial the homework in the space provided.
- If possible, take time to play the Kid Card games listed in Lesson 85.

Name ______________________

Teacher's Initials ____

Worksheet 88
(for use with Lesson 88)
Phonics 1

Dropping Rule

1. smile + ed = smiled
2. play + ed = played
3. wade + ing = wading
4. cane + less = caneless
5. bone + y = bony
6. sad + ly = sadly
7. hike + ing = hiking

8. rising
9. drained
10. shiny
11. serving
12. sŏftness

P1-WS-088a

Parent's Initials ____

Homework 88
(for use with Lesson 88)
Phonics 1

Dropping Rule

1. tape + ing = taping
2. care + less = careless
3. rain + y = rainy
4. use + ed = used
5. bake + ing = baking
6. safe + ly = safely
7. nose + y = nosy

8. smōking
9. tāped
10. shādy
11. jōked
12. fīring

Parents: Your child has been taught the **dropping rule;** when a word ends with a silent *e*, drop the *e* before adding a vowel suffix (vowel suffixes begin with vowels, e.g., *-ed, -ing*).

P1-WS-088b

LESSON 89 Diphthongs *oi* and *oy*

lesson preparation

materials

Alphabet/Accent Deck (Section 1)
Review Decks
Spelling Sound Sheet 65
Letter Cards 56–57
Picture Cards 69–70
toy in a sack (see *the night before*)
Spelling Card 42
Sight Word Cards 44–46
Worksheet 89
Reader 32 (*Bobby*)
colored pencils

new concepts

diphthong

the night before

- Put a small toy in a sack for the student to use to "discover" the new keyword. The keyword "toy" is represented by a wind-up duck, but any small toy will do.

ALPHABET ACTIVITY

"It's Alphabet/Accent Deck day."

"Let's say the first syllable in a normal voice while sitting down, and then stand and say the accented syllable louder, longer, and higher."

- Show the student **Alphabet/Accent Card 1.**
- Have the student say "A" (seated and in a normal voice), and then "B" (standing and louder, longer, and higher).
- Continue with **Alphabet/Accent Cards 2–25,** moving as quickly as possible.
- **Optional:** If you think the student is ready, shuffle the Alphabet/Accent Deck before the activity. Warn the student that the cards will be in random order.

REVIEW OF DECKS

- The student should be seated where he/she can write comfortably.
- Show the student **Letter Cards 1–55** in random order. The student should name the letter on each letter card.
- Review **Affix Cards 1–7.**
- Show the student **Picture Cards 1–68** in random order. The student should name the keyword and sound for each picture card.
- Review **Sight Word Cards 1–43.**
- Give the student **Spelling Sound Sheet 65.**
- Call out the sounds on **Spelling Cards 1–41** in random order. The student should echo each sound and name the letter or letters that make the sound as he/she writes the letter(s) on the spelling sound sheet.
- Have the student set the spelling sound sheet aside for use later in the lesson.

NEW LEARNING

"I'm going to say some words. Echo them back to me and listen for the sound that is the same in each word."

- Point to your mouth as you say each word.

"Echo after me. Void." *void* ***"Soil."*** *soil* ***"Coin."*** *coin*

"What sound do you hear that is the same in these words?" /oi/

"That's right. The sound you hear is /oi/."

"Put your fingertips on the front of your neck and say /oi/. See if you feel any vibration."

"Is this sound voiced or unvoiced?" *voiced*

- Write the following on the chalkboard: void, soil, coin.

"What do you see that might be making the /oi/ sound?" *oi*

"This is something new. It's called a 'diphthong.'"

"A diphthong is two vowel sounds …"

- Point your index fingers toward the ceiling (about 12 inches apart).

"… that come together so quickly …"

- Bring your fingers together very quickly.

"… that they are considered to be only one syllable."

- Drop one hand; only one finger is left up.

"Watch my mouth as I say /oi/. You'll be able to see my mouth make the two vowel sounds because it changes shape as it goes from one vowel sound to the next."

- Point to your mouth and say /oi/ slowly.

  "Did you notice how my mouth started out with a round shape for the /ō/ sound and changed to a kind of smile for the /ē/ sound?"

- Have the student touch his/her mouth and make the sound. The student will feel the face muscles move.

  "Diphthongs are coded just like combinations. We put arcs under them."

- Put arcs under the diphthongs in the words: void, soil, coin.

  "Now, listen to these words and echo them back to me. Listen for the sound that is the same. Boy." *boy* ***"Soy."*** *soy* ***"Coy."*** *coy*

  "What sound did you hear?" */oi/*

  "Is this the same sound we heard before?" *yes*

- Write the following on chalkboard: boy, soy, coy.

  "What is making the /oi/ sound now?" *oy*

  "That's right. This is diphthong oy. In what position is the oy?" *final*

  "We talked about this when we learned about digraphs ai and ay."

  "Oi and oy make the exact same sound, but somebody must have decided that English words don't look right with i on the end."

- Point to the words "void," "soil," and "coin."

  "Diphthong oi is usually found in the initial or medial position."

- Point to the words "boy," "soy," and "coy."

  "When the /oi/ sound is at the end of the word, the i changes to a y."

  "When we spell the /oi/ sound, we need to use 'oi' in the initial or medial position and 'oy' in the final position."

NEW DECK CARDS

- Show the student **Letter Card 56.**

  "What do we call this?" *diphthong oi*

- Hold up **Picture Card 69** but keep the picture covered with your hand (or the letter card).

  "I have a card with a picture on it that contains the /oi/ sound."

  "I am going to describe it for you. See if you can guess what the picture is."

  "This is a slick, liquid substance. It is used in cars to keep the engine running smoothly. We use a different kind when we are baking or frying foods like french fries. It is also used in hand lotions to keep skin soft."

  "I am going to count to three. When I say 'three,' I want you to whisper what you think the keyword is. One ... two ... three." *oil*

- Show the student **Picture Card 69.**

  "What will we say when we see this card?" *oil, diphthong oi*
- Show the student **Letter Card 57.**

  "What do we call this?" *diphthong oy*

  "I also have a sack today. It contains a clue to another new keyword. Don't look in the sack, but put your hand inside and see if you can guess what is inside. Keep in mind that the object in the sack contains the /oi/ sound."
- Allow the student a chance to feel inside the sack.

  "Can you guess the new keyword?" *toy*

  "That's right. The keyword is 'toy' and the sound is /oi/."
- Show the student **Picture Card 70.**

  "What will we say when we see this card?" *toy, diphthong oy*
- **Note:** The diphthongs and their pictures are also shown in the Rule Book on page 22.

  "Find your spelling sound sheet. Put your finger on #42."
- Hold up **Spelling Card 42** so only you can see what is written.

  "How do we spell /oi/ at the beginning or middle of words?" *oi*

  "Write that on the line by #42."
- Write the following on the chalkboard: oi.

  "How do we spell /oi/ at the end of words?" *oy*
- Complete the written response on the chalkboard: oi || oy.

  "This says 'diphthong oi final diphthong oy.' Say that with me." *diphthong oi final diphthong oy*

  "Finish writing the response on the line by #42."
- Check the spelling sound sheet for accuracy.
- **Note:** Add the new letter, picture, and spelling cards to the Review Decks.

BOARDWORK

- Write the following on the chalkboard:

  any /ĕn′ ē/ learn /lern/ many /mĕn′ ē/

  "We have three new sight words today."
- Point to the first word.

  "Can you tell me what this word is? Remember, it's a sight word, so it won't follow all of our rules."
- Allow the student to try to pronounce the word. If necessary, say it for him/her.

"This word is 'any.' Can you use the word 'any' in a sentence?" *expect various answers*

- Repeat with the remaining words.
- Show the student **Sight Word Cards 44–46.**

"Let's find these words on our sight word charts."

- Help the student locate the words in the Irregular Spelling Booklet.

"We will add these cards to our Sight Word Deck."

"Let's practice coding some words like the ones you'll have on your worksheet."

"The rule charts are in your Rule Book if you need to look at them."

- Write the following words and sentence (without the coding marks) on the chalkboard, one at a time. Ask the student to help you code them. The correct coding is as indicated:

rīd´ing

thrĕad´ed

That ănt farm is mȳ´ prīde ănd joy.

- Have the student determine whether each of the items coded is a word, a phrase, or a sentence.
- Add **Sight Word Cards 44–46** to the Sight Word Deck.

WORKSHEET

- The student should be seated where he/she can write comfortably.
- Give the student **Worksheet 89.** Make sure the student turns to the correct side.

"Let's spell with the /oi/ sound today."

"Put your finger by #1. The first word is 'boil.' "

"Unblend 'boil' with me." */b/ /oi/ /l/*

"Where do you hear the /oi/ sound?" *in the middle (medial) position*

"How do we usually spell the /oi/ sound in the middle position?" *oi*

"Spell the word 'boil' and write it by #1."

- Allow time for the student to write the word.

"What word did you write?" *boil*

- Repeat the procedure with #2 (join), #3 (toy), #4 (foil), and #5 (avoided).

"Now you're ready to code and read the words on your paper."

"Code the words by #6 through #10. After you have coded all the words, try to read them."

- Assist the student as necessary.

"Numbers 11 and 12 are questions about the paragraph just above them. If you find any words you can't read, code them. Then see if you can answer the questions."

- As the student works, provide help as needed. Help the student correct any incorrect answers. Then initial the worksheet in the space provided.
- Some time during the day, ask the student to read from the worksheet, a controlled reader, your basal reader, or other material of your choice.
- **Note:** Always make sure the worksheet is corrected before the student begins the homework. The worksheet serves as a guide to help complete the homework.

HOMEWORK

"Turn your paper over to the homework side."

"Do you know what to do on the homework paper?"

"Watch for diphthongs oi and oy. Always code suffixes and final, stable syllables before coding the rest of the word. Remember to use the dropping rule if you need to."

"When you finish your paper, I will check it for you and initial it in the space provided."

- Either now or later in the day, the student should complete the homework independently (if possible). Help the student correct any incorrect answers. Then initial the homework in the space provided.

READER

"We have another new book today."

- Give the student **Reader 32 (*Bobby*)** and some colored pencils.

"Can you tell me this book's title?" *Bobby*

- Assist the student as necessary as he/she constructs the book.
- When the student finishes, staple or put a rubber band around the book's spine.
- If necessary, demonstrate how to separate the pages and check the page order.

"The title of this book is _________?" *Bobby*

"I want you to read your book to yourself. When you are finished reading, color the pictures. Write your name on the book so I will know who colored it."

"Keep your book handy because I will be asking you to read it for me."

- Some time during the day, have the student read the reader to you.
- If possible, take time to play the Kid Card games listed in Lesson 85. Try to see that the student is prepared for tomorrow's assessment.

Name ______________________ **Worksheet 89**
(for use with Lesson 89)
Teacher's Initials ____ *Phonics 1*

oi and oy

1. boil
2. join
3. toy
4. foil
5. avoided
6. coin
7. poisoned
8. avoiding
9. bread
10. baking

Jimmy wants a pet. He wants a puppy or a kitten. He asks Dad if he can get a pet, but Dad says pets are too much work. This makes Jimmy sad. But Dad sees that Jimmy is sad, and plans a party. Dad brings Jimmy a toy dog. Jimmy wanted a real pet, but this one is just as good. Jimmy named his dog Roy. Jimmy enjoys having Roy, and he's not sad anymore.

11. Why does Jimmy's dad say Jimmy can't have a pet?
They are too much work.

12. Is Jimmy still sad? no

P1-WS-089a

Parent's Initials ____ **Homework 89**
(for use with Lesson 89)
Phonics 1

oi and oy

1. coil
2. moist
3. pointed
4. soiled
5. mining
6. joyless
7. saving
8. trading
9. jointed
10. bellboy

A girl lives next door. Her name is Joy. She has long red hair. She got a new (nōō) green bike Sunday. This bike is faster than her purple one was. She doesn't show off her bike. Her mom says it is not nice. Joy is a good friend!

11. When did Joy get the green bike? Sunday

12. Is the purple bike or the green bike faster?
the green bike

Parents: Your child has been taught **diphthongs oi** and **oy**; that a diphthong is two vowel sounds that come together so quickly that they are considered to be only one syllable; and that a diphthong is coded with an arc beneath it.

P1-WS-089b

LESSON 90 — Assessment

lesson preparation

materials

assorted items (see *the night before*)

Review Decks

Assessment 17

Spelling Test 15

Assessment 17 Recording Form

Kid Cards

tokens

the night before

- Locate a small assortment of items, each of whose name begins with a different letter. (See "Alphabetizing Objects" in the appendix for some suggestions.)
- Sort through the Review Decks and remove any of the following cards the student knows very well:
  - Letter Deck: *j, v.*
  - Picture Deck: Cards that correspond to the letter cards that are removed.
  - Sight Word Deck: Cards that (based on assessment results) the student knows very well.
  - Spelling Deck: Cards that correspond to the letter cards that are removed.
- Add these cards to the retired decks.
- Separate the Kid Cards marked "Lesson 90."

ALPHABET ACTIVITY

- The student should be seated.

  "Today our alphabet activity is going to be really fun. We're going to alphabetize some objects again."

- Give the student 3 or 4 objects. Ask the student to identify the letter each object begins with and then put the objects in alphabetical order.

  "See how quickly you can alphabetize the objects. Then double check to see if they really are in alphabetical order."

- If time permits, continue with new groups of objects after the first group is alphabetized.

Review of Decks

- The student should be seated where he/she can write comfortably.
- Show the student **Letter Cards 1–57** in random order. The student should name the letter on each letter card.
- Review **Affix Cards 1–7.**
- Show the student **Picture Cards 1–70** in random order. The student should name the keyword and sound for each picture card.
- Review **Sight Word Cards 1–46.**

Written Assessment

- Have the student sit where he/she can write comfortably.
- Give the student **Assessment 17.**
- **Section I:**

  "Today we are going to write some words for our assessment."

  "I'm going to say a word. Write the letter that makes each sound in that word on the lines by #1."

  "Look at the rule charts if you need to."

  "Here's the first word: music."
- Repeat with the following words in the order shown: #2 (clover), #3 (fever), #4 (minus), and #5 (crazy).
- **Reminder:** While the student spells, be ready to point to appropriate rule charts as necessary.
- **Section II:**

  "Look at the letter by #6."

  "Find the picture of the keyword for this sound."

  "Draw a line from the letter to the keyword."
- Repeat with #7, #8, #9, and #10. Allow a few minutes for the student to work.
- The pictures (from top to bottom) are as follows: open, ivy, unicorn, acorn, equal.
- **Section III:**

  "Put your finger on #11."

  "Code the words by #11 through #15."
- Allow a few minutes for the student to work.
- **Section IV:**

  "Read the paragraph. If you find any words you can't read, code them to help you figure them out. Then answer the questions by #16, #17, and #18."
- **Reminder:** If the student absolutely cannot read the paragraph, read it to the student to see if he or she can answer the questions.

"When you are finished, show your paper to me."

- This paper will be used during the oral portion of the assessment.

Spelling Test

- Give the student **Spelling Test 15.**
- Call out the following words (in the order shown). Sound them out, if necessary.

  #1 (arm), #2 (smart), #3 (quack), #4 (corn), #5 (chin), #6 (squint), #7 (bunch), #8 (quicksand), #9 (sharp), #10 (forget), #11 (were), #12 (brought)
- Grade and record the test in any manner that suits your needs.

Oral Assessment

- It is important to complete the oral assessment promptly (today, if possible) in order to identify any areas of weakness and begin remediation.
- Use the assessment and the following dialogue to complete the oral portion.
- **Section V:**
- Point to the sight word by #19.

  "Read this sight word for me."
- Record the student's response by placing a check mark by each word he/she reads correctly.
- Repeat with #20.
- **Section VI:**
- Show the student the letter by #21.

  "Tell me the name of this letter and the sounds it makes."
- Write the student's response on the adjacent line.
- Repeat with #22, #23, #24, and #25.

Assessment Evaluation

- Grade the assessment and record the results on **Assessment 17 Recording Form.** Check off the boxes to indicate mastery (i.e., the section was completed with 100% accuracy).
- **Reminder:** Try to give as many points as possible for work attempted. Do not grade the coding marks too severely. The most important coding marks to look for are breves, macrons, and syllable division lines.
- See the introductory material for detailed information regarding grading and recording procedures.

- Use the assessment results to identify those skills in which the student is weak. Practice those skills by playing Kid Card games.
- Add the Kid Cards marked "Lesson 90" to the existing decks. Listed below are games appropriate for remediation in selected areas. See "Games and Activities" for the directions for each game.
- **Section I:** Play "Spelling Deck Perfection," "Sound Scamper," "Spell Out #1," or have the student use the letter tiles to spell words you give from the Spelling Word List.
- **Section II:** Play "Keyword and Sound" or "Letter/Sound Identification."
- **Section III:** Play "Chalkboard Challenge."
- **Section IV:** Either have the student read the controlled readers and then ask questions for comprehension, or play "Acting Out" with the green Kid Cards.
- **Section V:** Play "At First Sight," review the Sight Word Deck, or lay the sight words out with a token on each one and let the student try to get as many tokens as possible for the sight words he/she can read.
- **Section VI:** Play "Letter/Sound Identification."
- When the student seems more secure in areas that had previously proven difficult, retest him/her (in those areas only) and indicate on the recording form any sections the student has subsequently mastered.
- Try to help the student achieve mastery of all the sections before the next assessment.
- If the student is having difficulty with a particular skill, keep his or her practice activities at the most basic level so the chance of success is greater.

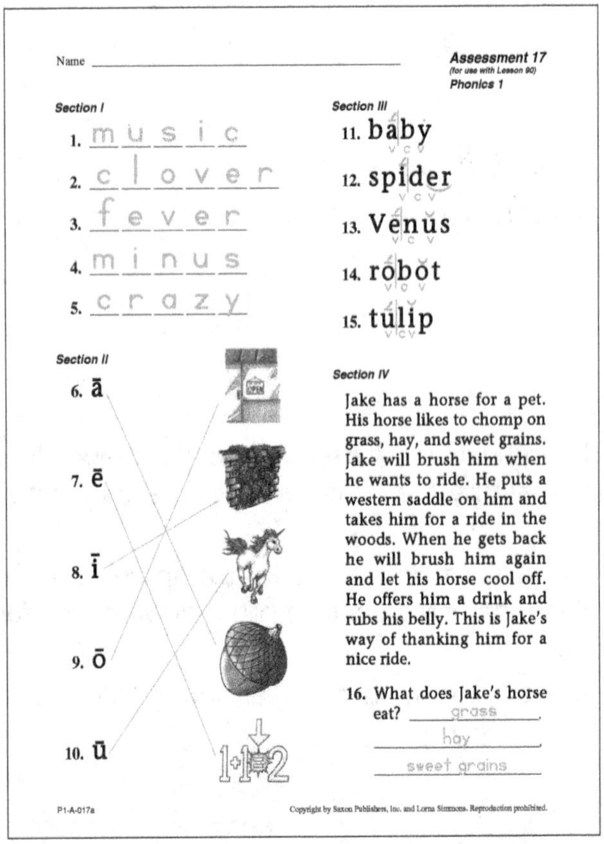

Name ______________________

Assessment 17
(for use with Lesson 90)
Phonics 1

Section I

1. music
2. clover
3. fever
4. minus
5. crazy

Section II

6. ā
7. ē
8. ī
9. ō
10. ū

Section III

11. baby
12. spider
13. Venus
14. robot
15. tulip

Section IV

Jake has a horse for a pet. His horse likes to chomp on grass, hay, and sweet grains. Jake will brush him when he wants to ride. He puts a western saddle on him and takes him for a ride in the woods. When he gets back he will brush him again and let his horse cool off. He offers him a drink and rubs his belly. This is Jake's way of thanking him for a nice ride.

16. What does Jake's horse eat? grass, hay, sweet grains.

P1-A-017a

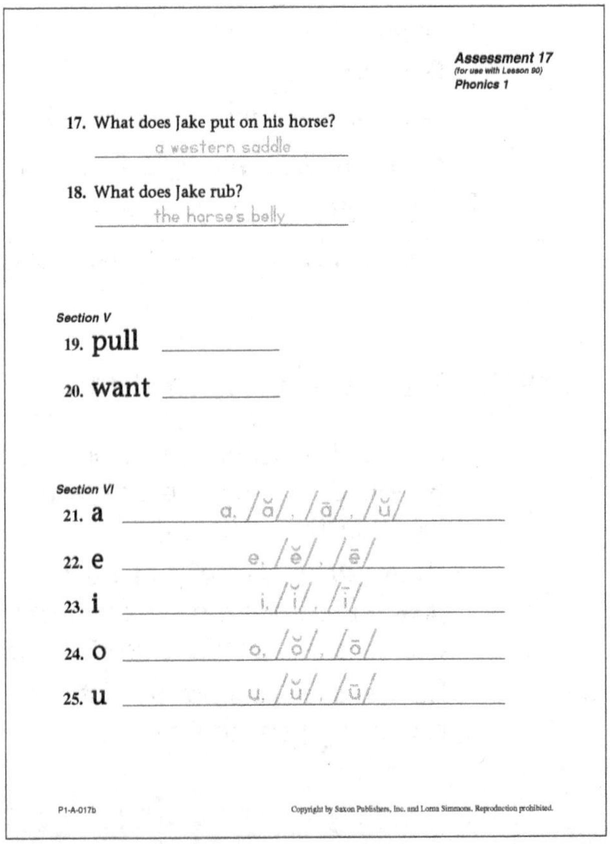

Assessment 17
(for use with Lesson 90)
Phonics 1

17. What does Jake put on his horse? a western saddle
18. What does Jake rub? the horse's belly

Section V

19. pull ____________
20. want ____________

Section VI

21. a — a, /ă/, /ā/, /ŭ/
22. e — e, /ĕ/, /ē/
23. i — i, /ĭ/, /ī/
24. o — o, /ŏ/, /ō/
25. u — u, /ŭ/, /ū/

P1-A-017b

Lesson 91

Spelling with *oi* and *oy*

lesson preparation

materials

container of letter tiles

Review Decks

Spelling Sound Sheet 66

Worksheet 91

Spelling List 16

Alphabet Activity

- The student should be seated with the container of letter tiles.

  "Before we start, let's say the alphabet together so it is fresh in our minds."

- Recite the alphabet with the student.
- Give the following instructions one at a time, allowing time for the student to accomplish each task before giving the next instruction.

  "Take all of the letter tiles out of your container."

  "Flip all of the letters over so that you are looking at the lowercase letters. If they are flipped correctly, they will all be blue."

  "Now we're ready. See if you can put all your letters in alphabetical order."

- Assist the student as necessary while he/she alphabetizes the letter tiles; however, try to let the student complete the task independently, if possible.
- When the student has finished, continue.

  "Point to the initial letter."

  "Point to the final letter."

  "Quickly pull down the vowels."

- Have the student replace the tiles in the container and put it away.

Review of Decks

- The student should be seated where he/she can write comfortably.
- Show the student **Letter Cards 1–57** in random order. The student should name the letter on each letter card.

- Review **Affix Cards 1–7.**
- Show the student **Picture Cards 1–70** in random order. The student should name the keyword and sound for each picture card.
- Review **Sight Word Cards 1–46.**
- Give the student **Spelling Sound Sheet 66.**
- Call out the sounds on **Spelling Cards 1–42** in random order. The student should echo each sound and name the letter or letters that make the sound as he/she writes the letter(s) on the spelling sound sheet.
- Have the student set the spelling sound sheet aside for use later in the lesson.

New Learning

"A few days ago we learned about reading and spelling with the /oi/ sound."

"Can you think of something to tell me about the /oi/ sound?"

- Possible responses include the keywords ("oil" and "toy"), the two spellings (*oi* and *oy*), that *oi* and *oy* are called "diphthongs," and that the /oi/ sound is really two sounds that come together so quickly that they are considered to be only one syllable.

"We know about diphthong oi. The keyword for it is 'oil.' We also know about diphthong oy. Its keyword is 'toy.' "

"When I gave you the /oi/ sound from our spelling deck just now, what did you say?" *diphthong oi final diphthong oy*

- Write the following on the chalkboard: oi || oy.

"What does this tell us?" *oi is used in the initial and medial positions; oy is used in the final position*

"That's right. If we want to spell a word with the /oi/ sound and we can't remember how it looks, our best chance is to use 'oi' in the initial or medial position and 'oy' in the final position."

- Write the following on the chalkboard: enj__.

"If I want to spell the /oi/ sound in this word, how should I spell it?" *oy, because it is at the end*

- Add "oy" to the word: enjoy.

"Can you read this word?"

- If the student cannot, have him/her help you code and then read it.
- Write the following on the chalkboard: br__l.

"If I want to spell the /oi/ sound in this word, how should I spell it?" *oi, because it is in the medial position*

- Complete the spelling of the word: broil.

"Can you read this word?"

- If the student cannot, have him/her help you code and then read it.

"Let me see if I can trick you."

- Write the following on the chalkboard: sp__led.

"How should I spell the /oi/ sound in this word?" *oi, because it is in the medial position*

"Is there something special at the end of this word?" *suffix -ed*

- Complete the word and box suffix *-ed*: spoil[ed].

"Is the /oi/ sound still in the medial position after I box the suffix?" *yes, an l comes after it*

"Can you read this word?"

- If the student cannot, have him/her help you code and then read it.
- Write the following on the chalkboard: ann__ing.

"How should I spell the /oi/ sound in this word?" *oy, because it is in the final position*

"Is there something special at the end of this word?" *suffix -ing*

- Complete the word and box suffix *-ing*: annoy[ing]

"Is the /oi/ sound still in the final position after I box the suffix?" *yes, only the suffix comes after it*

"So we spelled it correctly, didn't we?"

"Can you read this word?"

- If the student cannot, have him/her help you code and then read it.

"There are a few words with the /oi/ sound that don't follow this rule."

- Write the word "royal" on the chalkboard.

"What do you notice about this word?" *diphthong oy is in the medial position*

"That's right. The word 'royal' is an exception to the rule."

BOARDWORK

- Write the following on the chalkboard:

water /wŏ´ ter/

"We have a new sight word today. Can you tell me what this word is? Remember, it's a sight word, so it won't follow all of our rules."

- Allow the student to try to pronounce the word. If necessary, say it for him/her.

"This word is 'water.' Can you use the word 'water' in a sentence?" *expect various answers*

"This is a temporary sight word, so we don't have a card for it. By the end of the year, you'll know how to code it. Until then, you'll have to recognize it by sight."

"Let's practice coding some words like the ones you'll have on your worksheet."

"The rule charts are in your Rule Book if you need to look at them."

- Write the following phrase and sentence (without the coding marks) on the chalkboard, one at a time. Ask the student to help you code them. The correct coding is as indicated:

  cook′ing oil

  Hē′ drĕad′ed cămp′ing ŏn thė hard, rŏck′y soil.

- Have the student determine whether each of the items coded is a word, a phrase, or a sentence.
- Write the following on the chalkboard: chicken /chĭk′ ėn/.

  "Look at this word I have coded for you. Can you read it?" *chicken*

  "You'll see this word on your worksheet today."

WORKSHEET

- The student should be seated where he/she can write comfortably.
- Give the student **Worksheet 91.** Make sure the student turns to the correct side.

  "Let's spell with diphthongs oi and oy today."

  "Put your finger by #1. The first word is 'coin.'"

  "Spell the word and write it by #1."

  Allow time for the student to write the word.

  "What word did you write?" *coin*

- Repeat the procedure with #2 (boy), #3 (joy), #4 (spoil), and #5 (point).

  "Now you're ready to code and read the words on your paper."

  "Code the words by #6 through #10. After you have coded all the words, try to read them."

- Assist the student as necessary.

  "Numbers 11 and 12 are questions about the paragraphs just above them. If you find any words you can't read, code them. Then see if you can answer the questions."

- As the student works, provide help as needed. Help the student correct any incorrect answers. Then initial the worksheet in the space provided.
- Some time during the day, ask the student to read from the worksheet, a controlled reader, your basal reader, or other material of your choice.
- **Note:** Always make sure the worksheet is corrected before the student begins the homework. The worksheet serves as a guide to help complete the homework.

HOMEWORK

"Turn your paper over to the homework side."

"Do you know what to do on the homework paper?"

"Watch for words with our new digraphs and diphthongs. Always code suffixes and final, stable syllables before coding the rest of the word."

"When you finish your paper, I will check it for you and initial it in the space provided."

- Either now or later in the day, the student should complete the homework independently (if possible). Help the student correct any incorrect answers. Then initial the homework in the space provided.

SPELLING LIST

- Fold **Spelling List 16** in half lengthwise (with the printed side facing out).

"Leave your paper just like I give it to you."

- Give the student **Spelling List 16,** folded with the blank lines facing up.

"Let's spell some more words."

- Call out the following words (in the order shown). Sound them out, if necessary.

  #1 (face), #2 (ice), #3 (cent), #4 (crow), #5 (elbow), #6 (corner), #7 (startle), #8 (hard), #9 (farming), #10 (popcorn), #11 (again), #12 (against)

"Now unfold your paper and check your words."

- Check the student's work to see if he/she needs extra help with spelling.

"I want you to practice these words. We'll have a spelling test in a few days."

- If possible, take time to play the Kid Card games listed in Lesson 90.

Name ______________________

Teacher's Initials ____

Worksheet 91
(for use with Lesson 91)
Phonics 1

Spelling with oi and oy

1. coin
2. boy
3. joy
4. spoil
5. point
6. oilcăn
7. soiled
8. swĕat
9. ĕnjoying
10. băth

Ways to cook chicken:

1. Start with clean hands.
2. Take the paper off the chicken.
3. Rinse the chicken.

For boiled chicken: Place the chicken in a pot of boiling water. The hot water will cook the chicken.

For broiled chicken: Rub the chicken with butter. Place it on a pan under the broiler until it is cooked.

11. What do you take off the chicken? paper

12. What cooks the boiled chicken? water

P1-WS-091a

Parent's Initials ____

Homework 91
(for use with Lesson 91)
Phonics 1

Spelling with oi and oy

1. mĕant
2. tāil
3. ĕnjoy
4. hĕalth
5. smoothing
6. prīze
7. cūre
8. brĕath
9. lāme
10. mīle

"We can join the yearbook club," said Roy. "What fun! You can do a story and I will do the art," said Jan. Roy smiled. "Good. I'm glad you want to do that! We can see Mr. Denver on Friday."

11. Who wants to do the art for the yearbook?

Jan

12. When will Jan and Roy see Mr. Denver?

Friday

Parents: Your child has been taught that **diphthong** oi is usually found in the initial or medial position; and that **diphthong** oy is found in the final position.

P1-WS-091b

LESSON 92 — The Rule vc|cvc|cv

lesson preparation

materials

Alphabet/Accent Deck (Section 1)

Retired Decks

Affix Deck

Spelling Sound Sheet 67

Sight Word Cards 47–48

Worksheet 92

Reader 33 (*Ming and Grandmother*)

colored pencils

new concepts

vc|cvc|cv pattern

nouns; proper nouns

ALPHABET ACTIVITY

"We're going to work with the Alphabet/Accent Deck again today."

"Let's stand up. Every time we say the accented syllable, we'll karate punch."

- Show the student **Alphabet/Accent Card 1.**
- Have the student say "A" (softly), and then "B" (as he/she punches forward).
- Continue with **Alphabet/Accent Cards 2–25,** moving as quickly as possible.
- **Optional:** If you think the student is ready, shuffle the Alphabet/Accent Deck before the activity. Warn the student that the cards will be in random order.

REVIEW OF DECKS

- The student should be seated where he/she can write comfortably.
- Show the student the retired letter cards in random order. The student should name the letter on each letter card.
- Review **Affix Cards 1–7.**
- Show the student the retired picture cards in random order. The student should name the keyword and sound for each picture card.
- Review the retired sight word cards.
- Give the student **Spelling Sound Sheet 67.**

- Call out the sounds on the retired spelling cards in random order. The student should echo each sound and name the letter or letters that make the sound as he/she writes the letter(s) on the spelling sound sheet.
- Check the student's response after each card.

NEW LEARNING

- Write the word "Atlantic" on the chalkboard.

"Can you tell me what you would look for first to code this big word?" *suffixes and final, stable syllables*

"Do you see any suffixes or final, stable syllables?" *no*

"Do we need to do anything special to the c?" *put a k-back on it*

"What would you look for next?" *vowels*

"How many vowels do you see in this word?" *three*

"Let's write a small 'v' under each vowel."

- Write a *v* under each vowel and add the k-back to the *c*:

```
Atlantic
v  v  v
```

"Let's start with the first two vowels."

"How many consonants are between them?" *two*

- Write *c*'s under the first two consonants:

```
Atlantic
vccv  v
```

"Where do we divide the 'vccv' pattern?" *between the two consonants*

- Divide the word between the *t* and the *l*:

```
At|lantic
vc|cv  v
```

"We still have part of our word left, so we need to look between the next two vowels and find the consonants."

"What are the next two vowels?" *a and i*

"What consonants are between the a and the i?" *n and t*

- Write *c*'s under the next two consonants:

```
At|lantic
vc|cv ccv
```

"Where should we divide this time" *between the n and the t*

- Divide between the *n* and the *t*:

```
At|lan|tic
vc|cv c|cv
```

"Now we need to code the vowels."

- Point to the first *a*.

  "Can you tell me how to code this a?" *with a breve*
- Point to the second *a*.

  "Can you tell me how to code this a?" *with a breve*
- Point to the *i*.

  "Can you tell me how to code this i?" *with a breve*

  "Since this is new to you, I am going to tell you where this word is accented to see if you can read the word correctly."
- Code the vowels and place the accent on the second syllable:

  Ăt | lăn′ | tĭc
  vc | cvc | cv

  "Can you read this word?" *Atlantic*

  "That's a really big word to read! I am so proud of you!"

  "Let's clap to see how many syllables the word 'Atlantic' has."

  "At (clap) lan (clap) tic (clap)."

  "How many syllables did you clap?" *three*

  "We have a new syllable division chart that will help with words like these."

  "Get out your Rule Book and turn to page 19."
- Point to **Syllable Division Chart 4** as you say the following:

  "This is the pattern we just used."

  "Dividing big words makes them a lot easier to read."

  "You can always look at this chart if you need help dividing a big word."
- Leave the coding of "Atlantic" on the chalkboard for the remainder of the lesson.

BOARDWORK

- Write the following on the chalkboard:

  color /kŭ′ ler/ mother /mŭth′ er/

  "We have two new sight words today."
- Point to the first word.

  "Can you tell me what this word is? Remember, it's a sight word, so it won't follow all of our rules."
- Allow the student to try to pronounce the word. If necessary, say it for him/her.

  "This word is 'color.' Can you use the word 'color' in a sentence?" *expect various answers*
- Repeat with "mother."
- Show the student **Sight Word Cards 47** and **48.**

"Let's find these words on our sight word charts."

- Help the student locate the words in the Irregular Spelling Booklet.

"We will add these cards to our sight word deck."

"Let's practice coding some words like the ones you'll have on your worksheet."

"The rule charts are in your Rule Book if you need to look at them."

- Write the following word and sentence (without the coding marks) on the chalkboard, one at a time. Ask the student to help you code them. The correct coding is as indicated:

sŭc|çēe̸d´
v c|c v

Tāke̸ her for the̊ jŏb.

- Have the student determine whether each of the items coded is a word, a phrase, or a sentence.
- Add **Sight Word Cards 47** and **48** to the Sight Word Deck.

WORKSHEET

- The student should be seated where he/she can write comfortably.
- Give the student **Worksheet 92.** Make sure the student turns to the correct side.

"Let's practice spelling a few words."

"Find #1 on your worksheet. The first word is 'Atlantic.' Let's spell it by syllables."

"The first syllable is 'At.' Write 'At' on the line by #1."

"The second syllable is 'lan.' Write 'lan.' "

"The third syllable is 'tic.' Write 'tic.' "

- Allow time for the student to do this.

"Have you ever heard of the Atlantic Ocean?" *expect various answers*

" 'Atlantic' is the name of a specific ocean, so we need to make sure it begins with a capital letter, just like our own names. Words that name things are called 'nouns.' Words that name specific things are called 'proper nouns.' "

- Allow time for the student to correct the paper, if necessary.

"Can you tell me the final sound in 'Atlantic'?" */k/*

"How many syllables are there in 'Atlantic'?" *three*

- Point to **Rule Chart 4.**

"How do we spell the final /k/ sound in a word with two or more syllables?" *c*

- Allow time for the student to correct the paper, if necessary.
- Repeat the procedure with #2 (fantastic), #3 (sarcastic), #4 (join), and #5 (throw). (Review diphthong *oi* and digraph *ow*, if necessary.)

"Now you're ready to code and read the words on your paper."

"Code the words by #6 through #10. After you have coded all the words, try to read them."

- Assist the student as necessary.

"Now read the word by #11. If you have trouble reading the word, code it. Then draw a line from the word to the picture it matches."

- Repeat with #12, #13, and #14.
- As the student works, provide help as needed. Help the student correct any incorrect answers. Then initial the worksheet in the space provided.
- Some time during the day, ask the student to read from the worksheet, a controlled reader, your basal reader, or other material of your choice.
- **Note:** Always make sure the worksheet is corrected before the student begins the homework. The worksheet serves as a guide to help complete the homework.

HOMEWORK

"Turn your paper over to the homework side."

"Do you know what to do on the homework paper?"

"Be sure to watch for our new syllable division pattern."

- Discuss the homework pictures to make sure the student understands the word each one represents: #11 (poison), #12 (seal), #13 (feather), and #14 (coin).

"When you finish your paper, I will check it for you and initial it in the space provided."

- Either now or later in the day, the student should complete the homework independently (if possible). Help the student correct any incorrect answers. Then initial the homework in the space provided.

READER

"We have another new book today."

- Give the student **Reader 33 (*Ming and Grandmother*)** and some colored pencils.

"Can you tell me this book's title?" *Ming and Grandmother*

- Assist the student as necessary as he/she constructs the book.
- When the student finishes, staple or put a rubber band around the book's spine.
- If necessary, demonstrate how to separate the pages and check the page order.

"The title of this book is __________?" *Ming and Grandmother*

"I want you to read your book to yourself. When you are finished reading, color the pictures. Write your name on the book so I will know who colored it."

"Keep your book handy because I will be asking you to read it for me."

- Some time during the day, have the student read the reader to you.
- If possible, take time to play the Kid Card games listed in Lesson 90.

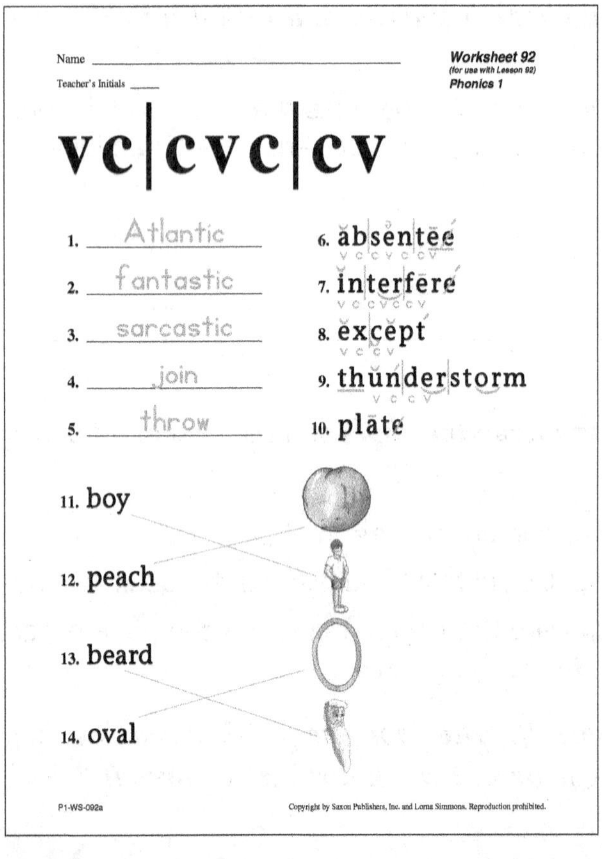

Name ____________________

Teacher's Initials ____

Worksheet 92
(for use with Lesson 92)
Phonics 1

vc|cvc|cv

1. Atlantic
2. fantastic
3. sarcastic
4. join
5. throw
6. ab|sen|tee
7. in|ter|fere
8. ex|cept
9. thun|der|storm
10. plate
11. boy
12. peach
13. beard
14. oval

P1-WS-092a

Copyright by Saxon Publishers, Inc. and Lorna Simmons. Reproduction prohibited.

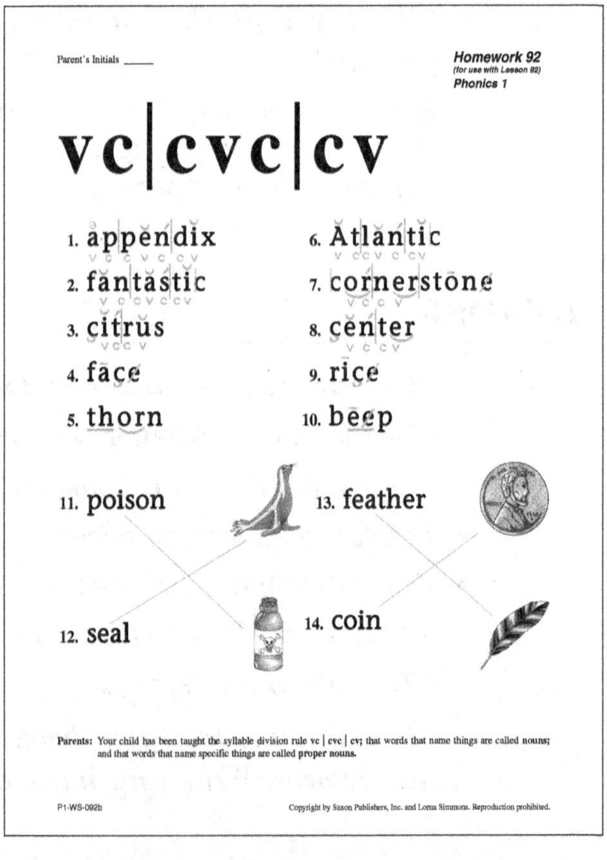

Parent's Initials ____

Homework 92
(for use with Lesson 92)
Phonics 1

vc|cvc|cv

1. ap|pen|dix
2. fan|tas|tic
3. cit|rus
4. face
5. thorn
6. At|lan|tic
7. cor|ner|stone
8. cen|ter
9. rice
10. beep
11. poison
12. seal
13. feather
14. coin

Parents: Your child has been taught the syllable division rule vc | cvc | cv; that words that name things are called nouns; and that words that name specific things are called proper nouns.

P1-WS-092b

Copyright by Saxon Publishers, Inc. and Lorna Simmons. Reproduction prohibited.

Lesson 93 — Final, Stable Syllable *-tion*

lesson preparation

materials

Activity Sheet 4

Review Decks

Spelling Sound Sheet 68

tokens or colored pencil

Letter Card 58

bottle of hand lotion in a sack (see *the night before*)

Picture Card 71

Spelling Card 43

Sight Word Cards 49–51

Worksheet 93

the night before

- Put a bottle of hand lotion in a sack for the student to use to "discover" the new keyword.

Alphabet Activity

- The student should be seated.

  "We are going to alphabetize words in a list today."

  "Watch closely so you can do a list of your own when I am finished with this one."

- Write the following on the chalkboard:

  _____ goose
  _____ crane
  _____ bluebird
  _____ flycatcher
  _____ duck
  _____ albatross
  _____ emu

"Which letter will we use as our guide letter?" *the first one*

"Let's underline the guide letters so we can see them easily."

- Underline the first letter in each word. Let the student help you make sure all of the first letters are different.

  "When we alphabetize words in lists, we can't move the words. Let's use numbers to help us like we did the last time."

  "We are going to put numbers 1 through 7 below (or beside) our list to use as we alphabetize."

- Write the numbers 1–7 below (or beside) the list of words.

  "Now we'll recite the alphabet slowly and scan the guide letters on these words each time we say a letter."

  "Let's start. A."

- Quickly scan the guide letters with your index finger.

  "Is there an a?" *yes*

  "Let's put a 1 beside 'albatross' and mark out the 1 at the bottom."

  "B."

- Quickly scan the guide letters with your index finger.

  "Is there a b?" *yes*

  "Since the number 1 has been used, we know to use a number 2 by this word."

  "Let's put a 2 beside 'bluebird' and mark out the 2 at the bottom."

- Quickly scan the guide letters with your index finger.

  "Is there a c?" *yes*

- Put a 3 in front of "crane" and mark out the 3 at the bottom.

  "D." *yes*

- Put a 4 in front of "duck" and mark out the 4 at the bottom.

  "E." *yes*

- Put a 5 in front of "emu" and mark out the 5 at the bottom.

  "F." *yes*

- Put a 6 in front of "flycatcher" and mark out the 6 at the bottom.

  "G." *yes*

- Put a 7 in front of "goose" and mark out the 7 at the bottom.

  "All of the words have been used so we can stop."

  "You get to try this by yourself again today."

- Give the student **Activity Sheet 4.**

  "Alphabetize these words. Tell me when you are finished and I will check your word order."

- The correct order is 5, 4, 3, 1, 2. If the student had difficulty, spend some extra time practicing alphabetizing.

REVIEW OF DECKS

- The student should be seated where he/she can write comfortably.
- Show the student **Letter Cards 1–57** in random order. The student should name the letter on each letter card.
- Review **Affix Cards 1–7.**
- Show the student **Picture Cards 1–70** in random order. The student should name the keyword and sound for each picture card.
- Review **Sight Word Cards 1–48.**
- Give the student **Spelling Sound Sheet 68** and at least twelve tokens (or a colored pencil).

"Let's play Bingo!"

"When I call out the spelling sounds today, I want you to place a token in (or X out) the space that spells that sound."

"When you cover (or X out) all of the letters on one line, either up and down, across, or from corner to corner, call out Bingo!"

"Don't forget to refer to your rule charts if you need to."

"Are you ready?"

"Cover (or X out) the letters that spell the final sound in 'soy.' " *oy*

"Cover (or X out) the letters that spell the initial sound in 'order.' " *or*

"Cover (or X out) the letters that spell the final sound in 'clay.' " *ay*

"Cover (or X out) the letters that spell the final sound in 'grow.' " *ow*

"Cover (or X out) the letter that spells the final /s/ sound in 'space.' " *ç*

"Cover (or X out) the letter that spells the first vowel sound in 'famous.' " *a*

"Cover (or X out) the letters that spell the medial sound in 'soil.' " *oi*

"Cover (or X out) the letter that spells the final sound in 'drafty.' " *ẏ*

"Cover (or X out) the letters that spell the initial sound in 'queen.' " *qu*

"Cover (or X out) the letter that spells the first vowel sound in 'even.' " *e*

- The student should Bingo by the time all the sounds have been called out.
- Collect the tokens (or colored pencil) and the spelling sound sheet. If you used tokens and the spelling sound sheet is unmarked, keep it available for practice.

NEW LEARNING

"I'm going to say some words. Echo them back to me and listen for the sound that is the same in each word."

- Point to your mouth as you say each word.

"Echo after me. Motion." *motion* ***"Section."*** *section* ***"Mention."*** *mention*

"What sound do you hear that is the same in all of these words?" */shŭn/*

"That's right. The sound you hear is /shŭn/."

- Write the following on the chalkboard: motion, section, mention.

"What do you see that might be making the /shŭn/ sound?" *t-i-o-n*

"There is a 't-i-o-n' in all of these words, so 't-i-o-n' must be the letters used to spell the /shŭn/ sound."

"How many syllables do you hear in the word 'motion'?" *two*

"The word 'motion' must be divided, but the last syllable, /shŭn/, doesn't follow our rules. We must treat it specially."

"Ble, tle, and fle did not follow our rules. What did we call them?" *final, stable syllables*

"This is also a final, stable syllable."

"Do you remember why it is called final?" *because it is in the final position*

"Why is it called a syllable?" *it has its own vowel sound*

"It is stable because it doesn't change. We can count on it having the /shŭn/ sound whenever we see it in the final position even though it's spelled 't-i-o-n.' "

"How do we code a final, stable syllable?" *put a bracket before it and accent the syllable before the bracket*

"The bracket actually divides the word into syllables."

- Put a bracket in the words on the chalkboard: mo[tion, sec[tion, men[tion.

"Then we mark the accent on the syllable right before the bracket."

- Mark the accent in the words: mo´[tion, sec´[tion, men´[tion.

"When a word has a final, stable syllable, the accent usually falls on the syllable before the bracket."

"Now we have two syllables. Look at the vowel in the first syllable."

- Point to "motion."

"How do we code an o that is open and accented?" *with a macron*

"That's right. The syllable here is /mō/."

"Can you read this word?"

"Can you tell me what the word 'motion' means, or use it in a sentence?" *expect various answers*

- Finish the coding procedure with the remaining two words. Have the student read the words and use them in sentences.
- Leave the words on the chalkboard for the remainder of the lesson.

NEW DECK CARDS

- Pull **Spelling Card 36** from the Review Deck.
- Hold up **Letter Card 58.**

"What will we say when we see this card?" *final, stable syllable tion*

"I have another sack today. It contains a clue to our new keyword. Don't look in the sack, but see if you can guess what is inside. Keep in mind that the object in the sack contains the /shŭn/ sound."

- Allow the student a chance to feel inside the sack.

"Can you guess the new keyword?" *lotion*

"That's right. The keyword is 'lotion' and the sound is /shŭn/."

- Show the student **Picture Card 71.**

"What will we say when we see this card?" *lotion, /shŭn/*

- **Note:** The final, stable syllable and its picture are also shown in the Rule Book on page 22.
- Hold up **Spelling Card 43** so only you can see what is written.

"We are going to add this to our spelling deck because spelling it is tricky."

"Echo this final, stable syllable sound: /shŭn/." */shŭn/*

"How do we spell the /shŭn/ sound in the final position?" *t-i-o-n*

"That's right. Now when I say /shŭn/, you will respond 'final, stable syllable t-i-o-n' and write 't-i-o-n' on your paper."

- Write "tion" on the chalkboard.

"We can also spell /shŭn/ 's-h-u-n,' but when you hear it at the end of a word, it will almost always be final, stable syllable t-i-o-n."

"Let's practice our other final, stable syllables."

- Hold up **Spelling Card 36** so only you can see what is written.
- Follow the instructions on the card and have the student write the answer with his/her finger on the desktop.
- **Note:** Add the new letter, picture, and spelling cards to the Review Decks (and re-insert **Spelling Card 36**).

BOARDWORK

- Write the following on the chalkboard:

could /ko͝od/ should /sho͝od/ would /wo͝od/

"We have three new sight words today."

- Point to the first word.

"Can you tell me what this word is? Remember, it's a sight word, so it won't follow all of our rules."

- Allow the student to try to pronounce the word. If necessary, say it for him/her.

"This word is 'could.' Can you use the word 'could' in a sentence?" *expect various answers*

- Repeat with the remaining words.
- Show the student **Sight Word Cards 49–51.**

"Let's find these words on our sight word charts."

- Help the student locate the words in the Irregular Spelling Booklet.

"We will add these cards to our sight word deck."

"Let's practice coding some words like the ones you'll have on your worksheet."

"The rule charts are in your Rule Book if you need to look at them."

- Write the following sentences and phrase (without the coding marks) on the chalkboard, one at a time. Ask the student to help you code them. The correct coding is as indicated:

Åt|tĕn′[tion, stū′|dĕnt[s]!
v c|c v v|c v

Plēase bē′ stĭll ăt the fīre drĭll.

spĭll′[ing] corn

- Have the student determine whether each of the items coded is a word, a phrase, or a sentence.
- Add **Sight Word Cards 49–51** to the Sight Word Deck.

WORKSHEET

- The student should be seated where he/she can write comfortably.
- Give the student **Worksheet 93.** Make sure the student turns to the correct side.

"Today, let's spell with final, stable syllable t-i-o-n."

"Put your finger by #1. The first word is 'nation.' "

"The first syllable is /nā/. Spell the first syllable and write it on the line by #1."

"The last syllable is /shŭn/. Spell final, stable syllable /shŭn/ and write it after /nā/ on the line by #1."

- Allow time for the student to write the word.

"What word did you write?" *nation*

- Repeat the procedure with #2 (station), #3 (section), #4 (fraction), and #5 (friction).
- Be sure to pronounce the two separate syllables distinctly.

"Now you're ready to code and read the words on your paper."

"Code the words by #6 through #10. After you have coded all the words, try to read them."

- Assist the student as necessary.

  "Numbers 11 and 12 are questions about the paragraph just above them. If you find any words you can't read, code them. Then see if you can answer the questions."

- As the student works, provide help as needed. Help the student correct any incorrect answers. Then initial the worksheet in the space provided.
- Some time during the day, ask the student to read from the worksheet, a controlled reader, your basal reader, or other material of your choice.
- **Note:** Always make sure the worksheet is corrected before the student begins the homework. The worksheet serves as a guide to help complete the homework.

HOMEWORK

"Turn your paper over to the homework side."

"Do you know what to do on the homework paper?"

"Watch for final, stable syllable t-i-o-n. Bracket it, and then accent the syllable before the bracket."

"When you finish your paper, I will check it for you and initial it in the space provided."

- Either now or later in the day, the student should complete the homework independently (if possible). Help the student correct any incorrect answers. Then initial the homework in the space provided.
- If possible, take time to play the Kid Card games listed in Lesson 90.

Name __________

Teacher's Initials ____

Worksheet 93
(for use with Lesson 93)
Phonics 1

´[tion

1. nation
2. station
3. section
4. fraction
5. friction
6. portion
7. function
8. dictation
9. wealth
10. feasting

Zack had a great invention. He invented an alarm clock that would ring again and again when no one turned it off. This clock was great for people who did not wake up when their alarm clock was ringing.

11. What was Zack's invention?
    an alarm clock
12. What did the alarm clock do?
    ring again and again when no one turned it off

P1-WS-093a

Parent's Initials ____

Homework 93
(for use with Lesson 93)
Phonics 1

´[tion

1. traction
2. fraction
3. interruption
4. information
5. threat
6. dreaming
7. heating
8. clearing
9. nŏd
10. so

Zack's alarm clock would ring for a short time. If no one turned it off, it would stop ringing, wait, and then start ringing again. It would keep ringing off and on until the alarm clock was turned off. Zack's friends were happy when they woke up and made it to class on time.

11. If no one turned the alarm clock off, what would happen?
    it would stop, then start ringing again
12. Why were Zack's friends happy?
    They made it to class on time.

Parents: Your child has been taught **final, stable syllable -tion.**

P1-WS-093b

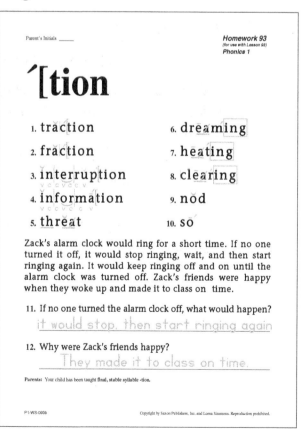

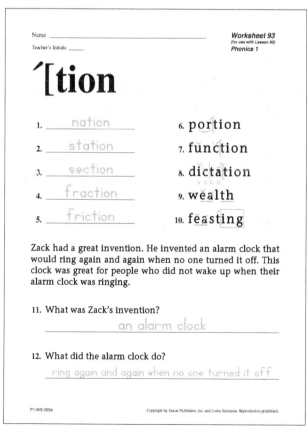

Lesson 94

Digraph *ue*

lesson preparation

materials

Alphabet/Accent Deck (Section 1)

Review Decks

Spelling Sound Sheet 69

Letter Card 59

bottle of glue in a sack (see *the night before*)

Picture Card 72

Worksheet 94

Reader 34 (*Jordan and Morgan*)

colored pencils

the night before

- Put a bottle of glue in a sack for the student to use to "discover" the new keyword.

Alphabet Activity

"Let's work with the Alphabet/Accent Deck again today. Stand up."

"We'll stand with our feet flat on the floor and say the first syllable in a normal voice. When we come to the accented syllable, we'll stand on our tiptoes and say it louder."

- Show the student **Alphabet/Accent Card 1.**
- Have the student say "A" (in a normal voice with feet flat), and then "B" (louder, on tiptoes).
- Continue with **Alphabet/Accent Cards 2–25,** moving as quickly as possible.
- **Optional:** If you think the student is ready, shuffle the Alphabet/Accent Deck before the activity. Warn the student that the cards will be in random order.

REVIEW OF DECKS

- The student should be seated where he/she can write comfortably.
- Show the student **Letter Cards 1–58** in random order. The student should name the letter on each letter card.
- Review **Affix Cards 1–7.**
- Show the student **Picture Cards 1–71** in random order. The student should name the keyword and sound for each picture card.
- Review **Sight Word Cards 1–51.**
- Give the student **Spelling Sound Sheet 69.**
- Call out the sounds on **Spelling Cards 1–43** in random order. The student should echo each sound and name the letter or letters that make the sound as he/she writes the letter(s) on the spelling sound sheet.
- Have the student set the spelling sound sheet aside for use later in the lesson.

NEW LEARNING

"I'm going to say some words. Echo them back to me and listen for the sound that is the same in the final position of each word."

- Point to your mouth as you say each word.

"Echo after me. Glue." *glue* ***"Blue."*** *blue* ***"Clue."*** *clue*

"What sound do you hear that is the same in all of these words?" */ū/ (/o͞o/)*

"That's right. The sound you hear in the final position is /ū/."

"Is this sound voiced or unvoiced?" *voiced*

- Write the following on the chalkboard: glue, blue, clue.

"What do you see in all of these words that might be making the /ū/ sound?" *ue*

"How many sounds do you hear in /ū/?" *one*

"So what do you think 'ue' is?" *a digraph*

"Now echo these words. Cue." *cue* ***"Statue."*** *statue* ***"Value."*** *value*

"What sound do you hear that is the same in all of these words?" */ū/ (/yo͞o/)*

- Write the following on the chalkboard: cue, statue, value.

"What do you see in all of these words that might be making the /yo͞o/ sound?" *digraph ue*

"That's right. Sometimes digraph ue says /yo͞o/ and other times it says /o͞o/."

"When we learned the long sound of u, as in 'unicorn,' we found the same situation. A long u could say /yo͞o/ or /o͞o/. It all depends on the sound that comes right before it. It's the same with digraph ue."

"Let's look at the words 'clue' and 'value.' If the letter l comes before it, digraph ue might say /o͞o/, as in 'clue,' because our mouths would have a hard time saying 'clyoo.' But other times, digraph ue will follow an l and say /yo͞o/, as

in 'value.' The best way to choose is to try both sounds and decide which sounds better."

"How will we code digraph ue?" *underline the letters, put a macron over the u, cross out the e because it is silent*

"Is digraph ue a vowel digraph or a consonant digraph?" *a vowel digraph because it contains only vowels*

NEW DECK CARDS

- Pull **Spelling Card 27** from the Review Deck.
- Show the student **Letter Card 59.**

  "What do we call this?" *digraph ue*

  "I have another sack today. It contains a clue to our new keyword. Don't look in the sack, but put your hand inside and see if you can guess what is inside. Keep in mind that the object in the sack contains the /ū/ sound."
- Allow the student a chance to feel inside the sack.
- **Optional:** If glue is unavailable, use the following riddle:

  "This makes things stick together. We use it to paste paper and other things together when we make art. It can come in a bottle or as a stick."

  "Can you guess the new keyword?" *glue*

  "That's right. The keyword is 'glue' and the sound is /ū/ (/o͞o/)."
- Show the student **Picture Card 72.**

  "The word 'glue' helps us remember the /ū/ (/o͞o/) sound since it contains that sound."
- **Note:** The digraph and its picture are also shown in the Rule Book on page 21.

  "Find your spelling sound sheet. Put your finger on #44."
- Hold up **Spelling Card 27** so only you can see what is written.

  "When we hear /ū/ at the end of a word, digraph ue is a very good choice. It will be correct most of the time, so we will add it to the responses on our /ū/ spelling deck card. Our full response from now on will be 'u consonant e comma u final digraph ue.' Say that with me." *u consonant e comma u final digraph ue*

  "Our written response looks like this."
- Write the following on the chalkboard: u–e, u || ue.

  "Write that on the line by #44."
- Check the spelling sound sheet for accuracy.
- **Note:** Add the new letter and picture cards to the Review Decks (and re-insert **Spelling Card 27**).

BOARDWORK

"Let's practice coding some words like the ones you'll have on your worksheet."

"The rule charts are in your Rule Book if you need to look at them."

- Write the following phrase and sentence (without the coding marks) on the chalkboard, one at a time. Ask the student to help you code them. The correct coding is as indicated:

fǐx′ing blūe′ber|ry mŭf′|fins
vccv vc|cv

Hē′ looked ǐn the purse for a clūe.

- Have the student determine whether each of the items coded is a word, a phrase, or a sentence.

WORKSHEET

- The student should be seated where he/she can write comfortably.
- Give the student **Worksheet 94.** Make sure the student turns to the correct side.

"Let's spell with the /ōō/ and /yōō/ sounds using digraph ue."

"Digraph ue is usually only used for spelling in the final position."

"Put your finger by #1. The first word is 'argue.' "

"The first syllable is 'ar.' Write that on the line by #1."

"The second syllable is 'gue.' Write that after 'ar' on the line by #1."

- Allow time for the student to do this.

"What word did you write?" *argue*

- Repeat the procedure with #2 (blue), #3 (clue), #4 (glue), and #5 (rescue).

"Now you're ready to code and read the words on your paper."

"Code the words by #6 through #10. After you have coded all the words, try to read them."

- Assist the student as necessary.

"Look at the picture at the bottom of the page. Write a story about the picture on the lines beside it. Don't worry about spelling. When you are finished, we will take time to check spelling and correct mistakes."

- As the student works, provide help as needed.
- Then have the student read the story silently and check for spelling errors. Help the student correct any mistakes. A perfect paper is not as important as the student putting his/her thoughts on paper and being able to recognize spelling errors that can be corrected (e.g., *k* and *c* spelling). Be sure to correct the rest of the worksheet as well. Then initial it in the space provided.

- Have the student read the story to you. It is important that children learn to feel comfortable speaking in front of others.
- **Note:** Always make sure the worksheet is corrected before the student begins the homework. The worksheet serves as a guide to help complete the homework.

HOMEWORK

"Turn your paper over to the homework side."

"Do you know what to do on the homework paper?"

"Watch for suffixes. Always box suffixes before coding the rest of the word. Also, watch for words that need to be divided."

"Tonight, write a story about the picture near the bottom of the page."

"When you finish your paper, I will check it for you and initial it in the space provided."

- Either now or later in the day, the student should complete the homework independently (if possible). Help the student correct any incorrect answers. Then initial the homework in the space provided.

READER

"We have another new book today."

- Give the student **Reader 34 (*Jordan and Morgan*)** and some colored pencils.

"Can you tell me this book's title?" *Jordan and Morgan*

- Assist the student as necessary as he/she constructs the book.
- When the student finishes, staple or put a rubber band around the book's spine.
- If necessary, demonstrate how to separate the pages and check the page order.

"The title of this book is __________?" *Jordan and Morgan*

"I want you to read your book to yourself. When you are finished reading, color the pictures. Write your name on the book so I will know who colored it."

"Keep your book handy because I will be asking you to read it for me."

- Some time during the day, have the student read the reader to you.
- If possible, take time to play the Kid Card games listed in Lesson 90. Try to see that the student is prepared for tomorrow's assessment.

Name ______________________

Teacher's Initials _____

Worksheet 94
(for use with Lesson 94)
Phonics 1

ūe

1. argue
2. blue
3. clue
4. glue
5. rescue
6. cue
7. blueberry
8. motion
9. pursue
10. joining

P1-WS-094a

Parent's Initials _____

Homework 94
(for use with Lesson 94)
Phonics 1

ūe

1. miscue
2. due
3. lotion
4. burden
5. spur
6. boiling
7. merry
8. grassy
9. rafting
10. romping

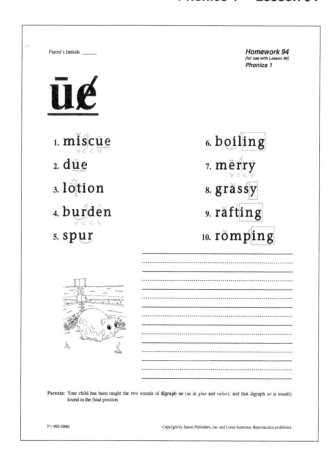

Parents: Your child has been taught the two sounds of **digraph ue** (as in *glue* and *value*); and that digraph *ue* is usually found in the final position.

P1-WS-094b

LESSON 95 — Assessment

lesson preparation

materials

ball

Review Decks

Assessment 18

Spelling Test 16

Assessment 18 Recording Form

Kid Cards

tokens

the night before

- Separate the Kid Cards marked "Lesson 95."

ALPHABET ACTIVITY

- You and the student should be standing with the ball.

  "Let's play 'Alphabet Toss' again."

  "I'll say a letter of the alphabet and toss the ball to you. After you catch the ball, say the two letters that come after the letter I said, and then toss the ball back to me."

  "I'll say the next two letters, and then toss the ball back to you."

- Play as long as time permits.

REVIEW OF DECKS

- The student should be seated where he/she can write comfortably.
- Show the student **Letter Cards 1–59** in random order. The student should name the letter on each letter card.
- Review **Affix Cards 1–7.**
- Show the student **Picture Cards 1–72** in random order. The student should name the keyword and sound for each picture card.
- Review **Sight Word Cards 1–51.**

WRITTEN ASSESSMENT

- Have the student sit where he/she can write comfortably.
- Give the student **Assessment 18.**
- **Section I:**

  "Today we are going to write some words for our assessment."

  "I'm going to say a word. Write the letter that makes each sound in that word on the lines by #1."

  "Look at the rule charts if you need to."

  "Here's the first word: point."
- Repeat with the following words in the order shown: #2 (boy), #3 (making), #4 (show), and #5 (parked).
- **Reminder:** While the student spells, be ready to point to appropriate rule charts as necessary.
- **Section II:**

  "Look at the letters by #6."

  "Find the picture of the keyword for this sound."

  "Draw a line from the letters to the keyword."
- Repeat with #7, #8, #9, and #10. Allow a few minutes for the student to work.
- The pictures (from top to bottom) are as follows: toy, oil, thread, break, leaf.
- **Section III:**

  "Put your finger on #11."

  "Code the words by #11 through #14."
- Allow a few minutes for the student to work.
- **Section IV:**

  "Read the paragraph. If you find any words you can't read, code them to help you figure them out. Then answer the questions by #15 through #18."
- **Reminder:** If the student absolutely cannot read the paragraph, read it to the student to see if he or she can answer the questions.

  "When you are finished, show your paper to me."
- This paper will be used during the oral portion of the assessment.

Spelling Test

- Give the student **Spelling Test 16.**
- Call out the following words (in the order shown). Sound them out, if necessary.

  #1 (hard), #2 (ice), #3 (crow), #4 (face), #5 (elbow), #6 (corner), #7 (popcorn), #8 (cent), #9 (startle), #10 (farming), #11 (again), #12 (against)
- Grade and record the test in any manner that suits your needs.

Oral Assessment

- It is important to complete the oral assessment promptly (today, if possible) in order to identify any areas of weakness and begin remediation.
- Use the assessment and the following dialogue to complete the oral portion.
- **Section V:**
- Point to the sight word by #19.

  "Read this sight word for me."
- Record the student's response by placing a check mark by each word he/she reads correctly.
- Repeat with #20 through #24.
- **Section VI:**
- Show the student the letters by #25.

  "Tell me the name of these letters and the sound they make."
- Write the student's response on the adjacent line.
- Repeat with #26 and #27.

Assessment Evaluation

- Grade the assessment and record the results on **Assessment 18 Recording Form.** Check off the boxes to indicate mastery (i.e., the section was completed with 100% accuracy).
- **Reminder:** Try to give as many points as possible for work attempted. Do not grade the coding marks too severely. The most important coding marks to look for are breves, macrons, and syllable division lines.
- See the introductory material for detailed information regarding grading and recording procedures.
- Use the assessment results to identify those skills in which the student is weak. Practice those skills by playing Kid Card games.

- Add the Kid Cards marked "Lesson 95" to the existing decks. Listed below are games appropriate for remediation in selected areas. See "Games and Activities" for the directions for each game.
- **Section I:** Play "Spelling Deck Perfection," "Sound Scamper," "Spell Out #1," or have the student use the letter tiles to spell words you give from the Spelling Word List.
- **Section II:** Play "Keyword and Sound" or "Letter/Sound Identification."
- **Section III:** Play "Chalkboard Challenge."
- **Section IV:** Either have the student read the controlled readers and then ask questions for comprehension, or play "Acting Out" with the green Kid Cards.
- **Section V:** Play "At First Sight."
- **Section VI:** Play "Letter/Sound Identification."
- When the student seems more secure in areas that had previously proven difficult, retest him/her (in those areas only) and indicate on the recording form any sections the student has subsequently mastered.
- Try to help the student achieve mastery of all the sections before the next assessment.
- If the student is having difficulty with a particular skill, keep his or her practice activities at the most basic level so the chance of success is greater.

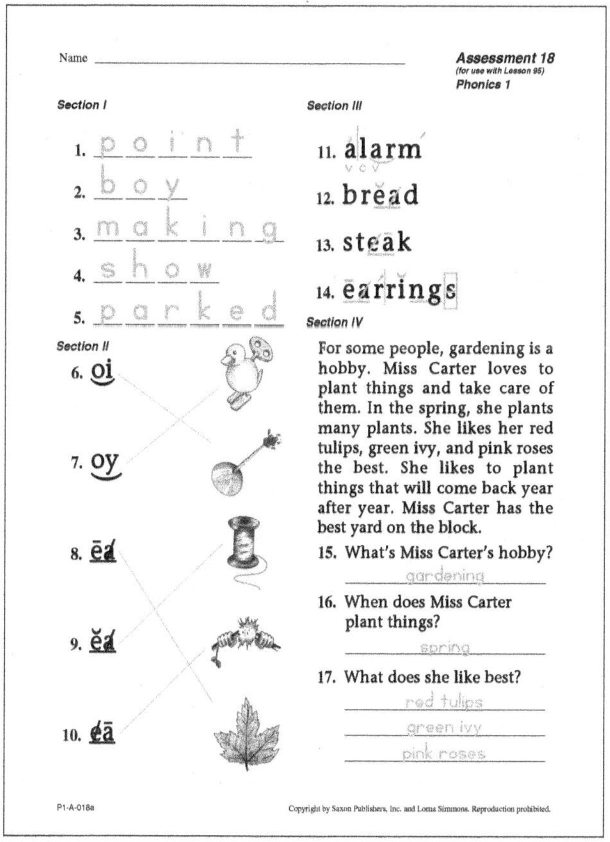

Name ______________________

Assessment 18
(for use with Lesson 95)
Phonics 1

Section I

1. point
2. boy
3. making
4. show
5. parked

Section II

6. oi
7. oy
8. ēa
9. ĕa
10. eā

Section III

11. alarm
12. bread
13. steak
14. earrings

Section IV

For some people, gardening is a hobby. Miss Carter loves to plant things and take care of them. In the spring, she plants many plants. She likes her red tulips, green ivy, and pink roses the best. She likes to plant things that will come back year after year. Miss Carter has the best yard on the block.

15. What's Miss Carter's hobby?
gardening
16. When does Miss Carter plant things?
spring
17. What does she like best?
red tulips
green ivy
pink roses

P1-A-018a

Copyright by Saxon Publishers, Inc. and Lorna Simmons. Reproduction prohibited.

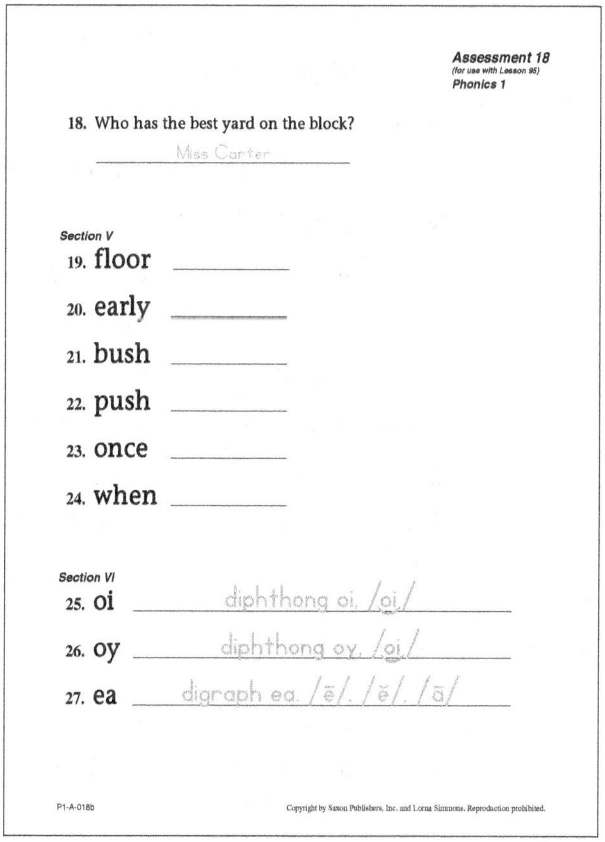

Assessment 18
(for use with Lesson 95)
Phonics 1

18. Who has the best yard on the block?
Miss Carter

Section V

19. floor ________
20. early ________
21. bush ________
22. push ________
23. once ________
24. when ________

Section VI

25. oi diphthong oi, /oi/
26. oy diphthong oy, /oi/
27. ea digraph ea, /ē/, /ĕ/, /ā/

P1-A-018b

Copyright by Saxon Publishers, Inc. and Lorna Simmons. Reproduction prohibited.

LESSON 96

Suffix *-es*

lesson preparation

materials

container of letter tiles

Review Decks

Spelling Sound Sheet 70

Affix Card 8

Worksheet 96

Spelling List 17

new concepts

sibilant sounds

ALPHABET ACTIVITY

- The student should be seated with the container of letter tiles.

  "Before we start, let's say the alphabet together so it is fresh in our minds."
- Recite the alphabet with the student.

  "Today I'm going to let you try to put the letter tiles in alphabetical order again. When I say 'go,' dump your tiles on the desk, turn them to the lowercase (blue) side, and begin working."

  "Sometimes it's hard to tell if a lowercase letter is right side up or upside down. If you're not sure, look at the other side to see which end is up."

  "Ready, set, go!"
- Allow enough time for the student to complete the sequencing.

  "Now spell the word 'true' with your letter tiles."
- Allow time for the student to work.

  "Now change two letters to spell the word 'blue.' "
- Repeat with "boy," "boil," "spider," and "tiger."
- Have the student replace the tiles in the container and put it away.

REVIEW OF DECKS

- The student should be seated where he/she can write comfortably.
- Show the student **Letter Cards 1–59** in random order. The student should name the letter on each letter card.

- Review **Affix Cards 1–7.**
- Show the student **Picture Cards 1–72** in random order. The student should name the keyword and sound for each picture card.
- Review **Sight Word Cards 1–51.**
- Give the student **Spelling Sound Sheet 70.**
- Call out the sounds on **Spelling Cards 1–43** in random order. The student should echo each sound and name the letter or letters that make the sound as he/she writes the letter(s) on the spelling sound sheet.
- Check the student's response after each card.

NEW LEARNING

"I'm going to say some words. Echo them back to me and listen for the sound that is the same in the final position of each word."

- Point to your mouth as you say each word.

"Echo after me. Dishes." *dishes* ***"Branches."*** *branches* ***"Fizzes."*** *fizzes* ***"Boxes."*** *boxes* ***"Messes."*** *messes*

"What do you hear at the end of these words?" */ĕz/ or /ŭz/*

- Write the following on the chalkboard: dishes, branches, fizzes, boxes, messes.

"What is the same at the end of all these words?" *es*

"Look at these words. Can I cover up the -es on them and still have a root word?" *yes*

"What do we call something that is added to the end of a root word?" *a suffix*

"This is suffix -es. What do you think it means when added to a root word?" *more than one*

"Suffix -es means exactly the same thing as suffix -s. The difference is in the root word that suffix -es is attached to. It has to do with the final sound in the root word. Let's check the final sound in all of these root words and see if anything is alike."

- Say each root word's final sound. Help the student see that all of the final sounds end with a hissing noise.

"The hissing sounds you hear in /s/, /ch/, /sh/, and other sounds like them are called 'sibilant sounds.' 'Sibilant' means 'hissing,' so these are hissing sounds."

"Suffix -es is added to root words that end with sibilant sounds."

"Suffixes are either vowel suffixes or consonant suffixes. They are named according to their first letter. What kind is this one?" *a vowel suffix*

- Show the student **Affix Card 8.**

"What do we call this?" *suffix -es*

- Have the student say the sound /ĕz/ rather than spell it. He/She will recognize and understand it more readily when it appears at the end of words.
- **Note:** Add the new affix card to the Affix Deck.

BOARDWORK

"Let's practice coding some words like the ones you'll have on your worksheet."

"The rule charts are in your Rule Book if you need to look at them."

- Write the following phrase and sentence (without the coding marks) on the chalkboard, one at a time. Ask the student to help you code them. The correct coding is as indicated:

pēach´es ănd crēam

Wē´ (should) mĕn´tion thė brō´|kėn stāirs.

- Have the student determine whether each of the items coded is a word, a phrase, or a sentence.

WORKSHEET

- The student should be seated where he/she can write comfortably.
- Give the student **Worksheet 96.** Make sure the student turns to the correct side.

"On the worksheet today, we will be spelling with suffixes -s and -es."

- Write the following on the chalkboard and read it:

Sibilant (hissing) sounds: *ch, j, s, sh, x, z*

1. desk ☐ ________

"If we make a word plural, we make it mean 'more than one.'"

"Put your finger by #1. The first word we want to make plural is 'desk.'"

"What suffixes can be added to make a word mean more than one?" -s or -es

"We need to check the end of the root word to see if it ends with a hissing, or sibilant, sound. There is a box to check if you hear a sibilant sound."

"What is the last sound in 'desk'?" /k/

"Is that a hissing, or sibilant, sound?" no

"Are we going to check the box?" no

"What do we use after a sound that does not hiss, -s or -es?" -s

"Spell 'desks' and write the word on the line by #1."

- As the student works, write the word on the line on the chalkboard.

"What word did you write?" desks

- Repeat the procedure with #2 (bush), #3 (book), #4 (six), #5 (boss), #6 (cupcake), #7 (rich), #8 (friend), #9 (fact), and #10 (fox).
- Assist the student as necessary.
- As the student works, provide help as needed. Help the student correct any incorrect answers. Then initial the worksheet in the space provided.
- Some time during the day, ask the student to read from the worksheet, a controlled reader, your basal reader, or other material of your choice.
- **Note:** Always make sure the worksheet is corrected before the student begins the homework. The worksheet serves as a guide to help complete the homework.

Homework

"Turn your paper over to the homework side."

"Do you know what to do on the homework paper?"

"When you finish your paper, I will check it for you and initial it in the space provided."

- Either now or later in the day, the student should complete the homework independently (if possible). Help the student correct any incorrect answers. Then initial the homework in the space provided.

Spelling List

- Fold **Spelling List 17** in half lengthwise (with the printed side facing out).

"Leave your paper just like I give it to you."

- Give the student **Spelling List 17,** folded with the blank lines facing up.

"Let's spell some more words."

- Call out the following words (in the order shown). Sound them out, if necessary.

  #1 (baby), #2 (even), #3 (over), #4 (minus), #5 (super), #6 (focus), #7 (quiz), #8 (born), #9 (tracc), #10 (clover), #11 (says), #12 (they)

"Now unfold your paper and check your words."

- Check the student's work to see if he/she needs extra help with spelling.

"I want you to practice these words. We'll have a spelling test in a few days."

- If possible, take time to play the Kid Card games listed in Lesson 95.

Name ______________________

Teacher's Initials _____

Worksheet 96
(for use with Lesson 96)
Phonics 1

Suffix -es

1. desk	☐	desks
2. bush	☑	bushes
3. book	☐	books
4. six	☑	sixes
5. boss	☑	bosses
6. cupcake	☐	cupcakes
7. rich	☑	riches
8. friend	☐	friends
9. fact	☐	facts
10. fox	☑	foxes

P1-WS-096a

Parent's Initials _____

Homework 96
(for use with Lesson 96)
Phonics 1

Suffix -es

1. dish	☑	dishes
2. cat	☐	cats
3. kite	☐	kites
4. mix	☑	mixes
5. student	☐	students
6. glass	☑	glasses
7. inch	☑	inches
8. mistake	☐	mistakes
9. splash	☑	splashes
10. seed	☐	seeds

Parents: Your child has been taught **suffix -es** and its meaning; that a **sibilant sound** is a hissing sound (*s*, *sh*, *ch*, *x*, *j*, *z*); and that suffix *-es* is added to form the plural of words that end with sibilant sounds.

P1-WS-096b

LESSON 97 Diphthongs *ou* and *ow*

lesson preparation

materials

Alphabet/Accent Deck (Section 2)
Retired Decks
Affix Deck
Spelling Sound Sheet 71
Letter Card 60
toy mouse in a sack (see *the night before*)
Picture Cards 73–74
Spelling Card 44
Sight Word Card 52
Worksheet 97
Reader 35 (*Mike on a Jet*)
colored pencils

new concepts

ou and *ow* can also be diphthongs

the night before

- Put a toy mouse in a sack for the student to use to "discover" the new keyword.

ALPHABET ACTIVITY

"It's Alphabet/Accent Deck day and we are going to work with a new deck."

- Show the student **Alphabet/Accent Card 1.**

"How do you think this card will be read?" *the middle letter (b) is missing and accented; the missing letter will be named and accented*

"Let's sit and say the first syllable with a normal voice, then stand and say the accented syllable louder, and then sit and say the last syllable with a normal voice."

- Have the student say "A" (sitting), then "B" (standing and louder), and then "C" (sitting again).
- Continue with **Alphabet/Accent Cards 2–24,** moving as quickly as possible.

REVIEW OF DECKS

- The student should be seated where he/she can write comfortably.
- Show the student the retired letter cards in random order. The student should name the letter on each letter card.
- Review **Affix Cards 1–8.**
- Show the student the retired picture cards in random order. The student should name the keyword and sound for each picture card.
- Review the retired sight word cards.
- Give the student **Spelling Sound Sheet 71.**
- Call out the sounds on the retired spelling cards in random order. The student should echo each sound and name the letter or letters that make the sound as he/she writes the letter(s) on the spelling sound sheet.
- Have the student set the spelling sound sheet aside for use later in the lesson.

NEW LEARNING

"I'm going to say some words. Echo them back to me and listen for the sound that is the same in each word."

- Point to your mouth as you say each word.

"Echo after me. Out." *out* ***"Pound."*** *pound* ***"Couch."*** *couch*

"What sound do you hear that is the same in all of these words?" */ou/*

"Is this sound voiced or unvoiced?" *voiced*

- Write the following on the chalkboard: out, pound, couch.

"What do you see in all of these words that might be making the /ou/ sound?" *ou*

"That's right. This is diphthong ou. A diphthong is two vowel sounds ..."

- Point your index fingers toward the ceiling (about 12 inches apart).

"... that come together so quickly ..."

- Bring your fingers together very quickly.

"... that they are considered to be only one syllable."

- Drop one hand; only one finger is left up.

"What are the other two diphthongs we know?" *oi and oy*

"Watch my mouth as I say /ou/. You'll be able to see my mouth make two different vowel sounds because it changes shape as it changes from one vowel sound to the next."

- Say /ou/ slowly.

"Did you notice how my mouth started out open for the /ă/ sound and closed for the /oo/ sound?"

- Have the student touch his/her mouth and make the sound. The student will feel the face muscles move.

"Diphthong ou is coded like the other diphthongs. It has an arc under it."

- Code the words: out, pound, couch.

"Now, listen and echo two more words."

"Wow." *wow* ***"Plow."*** *plow*

"What sound did you hear?" */ou/*

"Is this the same sound we heard before?" *yes*

- Write the following on the chalkboard: wow, plow.

"What is making the /ou/ sound now?" *ow*

"That's right. We know that 'ow' can be a digraph, but 'ow' can also be a diphthong."

"In what position is diphthong ow?" *final*

- Code the words: wow, plow.

"We talked about this when we learned about diphthongs oi and oy."

" 'Ou' and 'ow' make the same exact sound, just like 'oi' and 'oy' make the same exact sound. But whoever decided that English words don't look right with the letter i on the end didn't think the letter u looked right either."

"Diphthong ou is usually found in the initial or medial position."

- Point to the words "out," "pound," and "couch."

"When the /ou/ sound is at the end of the word, the u changes to a w."

- Point to the words "wow" and "plow."

"When we spell, we need to use diphthong ou in the initial or medial position and diphthong ow in the final position."

"We will see some words with 'ow' in the middle. But when you spell a word, we need to use 'ow' at the end of words and 'ou' in the initial or medial position. It's our best chance of being correct."

NEW DECK CARDS

- Show the student **Letter Card 60.**

"What do we call this?" *diphthong ou*

"I have another sack today. It contains a clue to our new keyword. Don't look in the sack, but put your hand inside and see if you can guess what is inside. Keep in mind that the object in the sack contains the /ou/ sound."

- Allow the student a chance to feel inside the sack.
- **Optional:** If a toy mouse is unavailable, use the following riddle:

  "In a famous nursery rhyme, this little animal runs up the clock. People have been known to scream when they see them, although they are very small. These animals particularly like to eat cheese."

  "Can you guess the new keyword?" *mouse*

  "That's right. The keyword is 'mouse' and the sound is /ou/."
- Show the student **Picture Card 73.**

  "What will we say when we see this card?" *mouse, diphthong ou*
- Hold up **Picture Card 74** but keep the picture covered with your hand (or the letter card).

  "I have another card with a picture on it that contains the /ou/ sound."

  "I am going to describe it for you. See if you can guess what the picture is."

  "This is a rather large animal. It lives on a farm or ranch. It eats grass and hay. The black and white spotted ones are very popular right now. It is our biggest source of milk. What do you think the picture is?" *cow*

  "That's right. This keyword is 'cow' and the sound is /ou/."
- Show the student **Picture Card 74.**

  "What will we say when we see this card?" *cow, diphthong ow*
- **Note:** The diphthongs and their pictures are also shown in the Rule Book on page 22.

  "Find your spelling sound sheet. Put your finger on #44."
- Hold up **Spelling Card 44** so only you can see what is written.

  "What is the best way to spell /ou/ in the initial or medial position?" *ou*

  "Write that on the line by #44."
- Write the following on the chalkboard: ou.

  "How do we spell /ou/ at the end of a word?" *ow*
- Complete the written response on the chalkboard: ou || ow.

  "This says 'diphthong ou final diphthong ow.' Say that with me." *diphthong ou final diphthong ow*

  "Finish writing the response on the line by #44."

  "We now have two sounds for ow. The first sound is /ō/, as in 'bow.' The second sound is /ou/, as in 'cow.' "
- Check the spelling sound sheet for accuracy.
- **Note:** Add the new letter, picture, and spelling cards to the Review Decks.

BOARDWORK

- Write the following on the chalkboard:

father /fŏ´ ther/

"We have a new sight word today."

- Point to the word.

"Can you tell me what this word is? Remember, it's a sight word, so it won't follow all of our rules."

- Allow the student to try to pronounce the word. If necessary, say it for him/her.

"This word is 'father.' Can you use the word 'father' in a sentence?" *expect various answers*

- Show the student **Sight Word Card 52.**

"Let's find this word on our sight word charts."

- Help the student locate the word in the Irregular Spelling Booklet.

"We will add this card to our sight word deck."

"Let's practice coding some words like the ones you'll have on your worksheet."

"The rule charts are in your Rule Book if you need to look at them."

- Write the following phrase and sentence (without the coding marks) on the chalkboard, one at a time. Ask the student to help you code them. The correct coding is as indicated:

stāined thĕ car´pĕting
vc | cv

Thĕ hāir´y dŏg lĕft his bōne ĭn thĕ town´house.

- Have the student determine whether each of the items coded is a word, a phrase, or a sentence.
- Add **Sight Word Card 52** to the Sight Word Deck.

WORKSHEET

- The student should be seated where he/she can write comfortably.
- Give the student **Worksheet 97.** Make sure the student turns to the correct side.

"Let's spell with the /ou/ sound today. We need to remember that 'ow' is best to use at the end of the word and 'ou' is best to use in the initial and medial positions."

"Put your finger by #1. The first word is 'pound.'"

"Spell the word and write it by #1."

- Allow time for the student to write the word.

"What word did you write?" *pound*

- Repeat the procedure with #2 (cloud), #3 (about), #4 (now), and #5 (cow).
- The student may need some guidance with #3 (about). Remind him/her of the /ŭ/ sound that comes by itself in the beginning syllable.

"Now you're ready to code and read the words on your paper."

"Code the words by #6 through #10. After you have coded all the words, try to read them."

- Assist the student as necessary.

"Now read the word by #11. If you have trouble reading the word, code it. Then draw a line from the word to the picture it matches."

- Repeat with #12, #13, and #14.
- As the student works, provide help as needed. Help the student correct any incorrect answers. Then initial the worksheet in the space provided.
- Some time during the day, ask the student to read from the worksheet, a controlled reader, your basal reader, or other material of your choice.
- **Note:** Always make sure the worksheet is corrected before the student begins the homework. The worksheet serves as a guide to help complete the homework.

HOMEWORK

"Turn your paper over to the homework side."

"Do you know what to do on the homework paper?"

"Watch for diphthongs ou and ow. Always code suffixes and final, stable syllables before coding the rest of the word."

- Discuss the homework pictures to make sure the student understands the word each one represents: #11 (crown), #12 (cowboy), #13 (birdhouse), and #14 (couch).

"When you finish your paper, I will check it for you and initial it in the space provided."

- Either now or later in the day, the student should complete the homework independently (if possible). Help the student correct any incorrect answers. Then initial the homework in the space provided.

READER

"We have another new book today."

- Write the words "Washington, D.C." on the chalkboard.

"This says 'Washington, D.C.' "

"Can you tell me what's special about Washington, D.C.?" *expect various answers*

"Washington, D.C., is our nation's capital."

- If desired, allow a few minutes for discussion about Washington, D.C.
- Write the word "travel" on the chalkboard.

"This is the word 'travel.' What does it mean when we travel?"

- Allow a few minutes to define the word "travel."

"You'll see these words in your new reader today."

- Give the student **Reader 35 (*Mike on a Jet*)** and some colored pencils.

"Can you tell me this book's title?" *Mike on a Jet*

- Assist the student as necessary as he/she constructs the book.
- When the student finishes, staple or put a rubber band around the book's spine.
- If necessary, demonstrate how to separate the pages and check the page order.

"The title of this book is __________?" *Mike on a Jet*

"I want you to read your book to yourself. When you are finished reading, color the pictures. Write your name on the book so I will know who colored it."

"Keep your book handy because I will be asking you to read it for me."

- Some time during the day, have the student read the reader to you.
- If possible, take time to play the Kid Card games listed in Lesson 95.

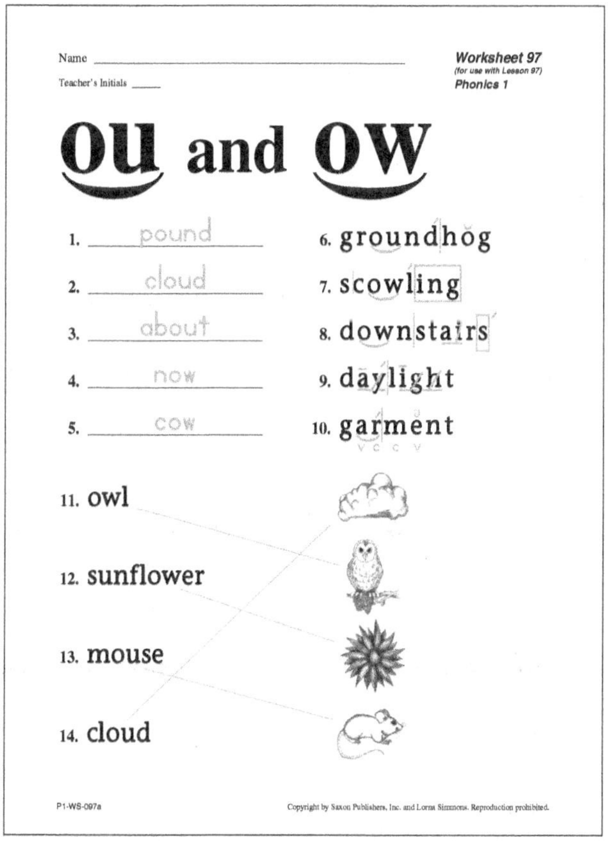
Name __________ Teacher's Initials ____

Worksheet 97 (for use with Lesson 97) Phonics 1

ou and ow

1. pound
2. cloud
3. about
4. now
5. cow
6. groundhog
7. scowling
8. downstairs
9. daylight
10. garment
11. owl
12. sunflower
13. mouse
14. cloud

P1-WS-097a

Copyright by Saxon Publishers, Inc. and Lorna Simmons. Reproduction prohibited.

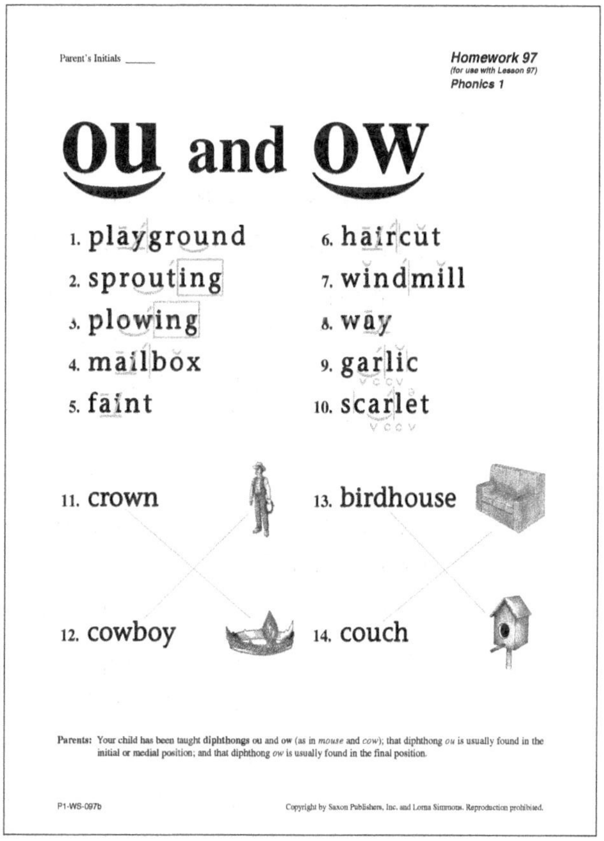
Parent's Initials ____

Homework 97 (for use with Lesson 97) Phonics 1

ou and ow

1. playground
2. sprouting
3. plowing
4. mailbox
5. faint
6. haircut
7. windmill
8. way
9. garlic
10. scarlet
11. crown
12. cowboy
13. birdhouse
14. couch

Parents: Your child has been taught diphthongs ou and ow (as in *mouse* and *cow*); that diphthong *ou* is usually found in the initial or medial position; and that diphthong *ow* is usually found in the final position.

P1-WS-097b

Copyright by Saxon Publishers, Inc. and Lorna Simmons. Reproduction prohibited.

LESSON 98 Spelling with *ou* and *ow*

lesson preparation

materials

Activity Sheet 5

Review Decks

Worksheet 98

ALPHABET ACTIVITY

- The student should be seated.

  "Let's alphabetize words in a list again today. Do you remember how we did that? I'll show you how again."

- Write the following on the chalkboard:

  ____ dimple
  ____ lip
  ____ brow
  ____ nose
  ____ head
  ____ chin
  ____ face

  "Which letter will we use as our guide letter?" *the first one*

  "Let's underline the guide letters so we can see them easily."

- Underline the first letter in each word. Let the student help you make sure all of the first letters are different.

  "When we alphabetize words in lists, we can't move the words. Let's use the numbers trick."

  "How many words are on this list?" *seven*

  "We are going to put numbers 1 through 7 below (or beside) our list to use as we alphabetize."

- Write the numbers 1–7 below (or beside) the list of words.

  "Now we'll recite the alphabet slowly and scan the guide letters on these words each time we say a letter."

  "Let's start. A."

- Quickly scan the guide letters with your index finger.

"Is there an a?" *no*

"B."

- Quickly scan the guide letters with your index finger.

"Is there a b?" *yes*

"Let's put a 1 beside 'brow' and mark out the 1 at the bottom. We'll know to put a 2 by the next word."

"C." *yes*

- Put a 2 in front of "chin" and mark out the 2 at the bottom.

"D." *yes*

- Put a 3 in front of "dimple" and mark out the 3 at the bottom.

"E." *no*

"F." *yes*

- Put a 4 in front of "face" and mark out the 4 at the bottom.

"G." *no*

"H." *yes*

- Put a 5 in front of "head" and mark out the 5 at the bottom.

"I." *no*

"J." *no*

"K." *no*

"L." *yes*

- Put a 6 in front of "lip" and mark out the 6 at the bottom.

"M." *no*

"N." *yes*

- Put a 7 in front of "nose" and mark out the 7 at the bottom.

"All of the words have been used, so we can stop."

"I'm going to let you try this yourself again."

- Give the student **Activity Sheet 5.**

"Alphabetize the words on this list."

- The correct order is 1, 5, 4, 2, 3.
- **Optional:** Letter order can be checked, but it is more difficult. Quickly recite the alphabet, starting with your finger on number 1. Move your finger to the next number each time the appropriate letter is named.

REVIEW OF DECKS

- Show the student **Letter Cards 1–60** in random order. The student should name the letter on each letter card.
- Review **Affix Cards 1–8.**

- Show the student **Picture Cards 1–74** in random order. The student should name the keyword and sound for each picture card.
- Review **Sight Word Cards 1–52.**

  "Instead of writing the spelling card responses today, let's just review them orally."
- Give the sounds on **Spelling Cards 1–44** in random order. The student should echo each sound, name the letter or letters that make the sound, and then skywrite it.

NEW LEARNING

"Yesterday, we learned about reading and spelling with the /ou/ sound."

"Can you tell me anything about the /ou/ sound?"

- Give the student a chance to respond with some or all of the following: 1. The /ou/ sound can be spelled two ways, diphthong *ou* and diphthong *ow*; 2. The keywords for these diphthongs are "mouse" and "cow," respectively; 3. Diphthongs are coded with arcs.
- Write "mouse" and "cow" on the chalkboard. Code diphthongs *ou* and *ow*.

  "We are going to talk about spelling with these two diphthongs today. They often make the same sound, so it can be confusing to know which one to write."

  "Yesterday, we learned that if a word says /ou/ in the medial position, as in 'mouse,' it will most often be spelled using diphthong ou. If the /ou/ sound comes at the end of the word, as in 'cow,' it will always be spelled with diphthong ow."
- Write "ou || ow" on the chalkboard.

  "This is our written response to the spelling card for the /ou/ sound. What does it tell us?" *ou is used in the medial position, ow in the final position*
- Write the following on the chalkboard: m__th, n__.

  "If we wanted to spell the word 'mouth,' which diphthong would we use?" *ou, because it is in the medial position*

  "What about the word 'now'?" *ow, because it is in the final position*
- Fill in the missing letters in each word: mouth, now.
- Write the following on the chalkboard: p_ting.

  "How should I spell /ou/ in this word?" *ou, because it is in the medial position*

  "Is there something special at the end of this word?" *yes, suffix -ing*
- Fill in the missing letters and box the suffix: pout[ing].

  "Is the 'ou' still in the medial position after I box the suffix?" *yes, there is a "t" after the "ou" in the root word*
- Write the following on the chalkboard: pl_ed.

"How should I spell /ou/ in this word?" *ow, because it is in the final position of the root word*

"Is there something special at the end of this word?" *yes, suffix -ed*

- Fill in the missing letters and box the suffix: plowed.

"Is the 'ow' still in the final position after I box the suffix?" *yes, only the suffix comes after it*

"If we want to spell a word with the /ou/ sound but can't remember how it looks, our best chance of being correct is to use 'ou' in the medial position and 'ow' in the final position."

"There are words that are exceptions to this rule. Some words say /ou/ in the medial position but are spelled using 'ow.' These are irregular words. They are easy to read, but you will need to memorize them in order to spell them. One of these irregular words is 'brown.' "

- Write "brown" on the chalkboard.

"Get out your Irregular Spelling Booklet."

"Look at the table of contents. Can you find the page that shows words spelled with diphthong ow in the initial or medial position?" *page 25*

"That's right. Turn to page 25. All of these words are spelled with diphthong ow. They don't follow our regular rules, so we must memorize them. For now, you can refer to this booklet any time you're spelling."

- Have the student put the booklet away.

BOARDWORK

"Let's practice coding some words like the ones you'll have on your worksheet."

"The rule charts are in your Rule Book if you need to look at them."

- Write the following word, phrase, and sentence (without the coding marks) on the chalkboard, one at a time. Ask the student to help you code them. The correct coding is as indicated:

found´ing fathers

car|nā´|tion
vc|cv

Wē´ jōk´ed å|bout´ our ăf´|ter|noon chōres ŏn the bŭs.
v|cv vc|cv

- Have the student determine whether each of the items coded is a word, a phrase, or a sentence.

Worksheet

- The student should be seated where he/she can write comfortably.
- Give the student **Worksheet 98.** Make sure the student turns to the correct side.

  "Let's spell with diphthongs ou and ow today."

  "Put your finger by #1. The first word is 'round.' "

  "Think about where the /ou/ sound comes in this word. Then spell and write 'round' by #1."
- Allow time for the student to write the word.

  "What word did you write?" *round*
- Repeat the procedure with #2 (shout), #3 (grouch), #4 (how), #5 (cow), #6 (out), #7 (mouth), #8 (count), #9 (sprout), and #10 (lookout).

  "Look at the box on the right-hand side of your worksheet. In that box is a list of irregular spelling words that use diphthong ow to spell the /ou/ sound in the medial position. Read all of these irregular words and then rewrite them on the blank lines below."
- As the student works, provide help as needed. Help the student correct any incorrect answers. Then initial the worksheet in the space provided.
- Some time during the day, ask the student to read from the worksheet, a controlled reader, your basal reader, or other material of your choice.
- **Note:** Always make sure the worksheet is corrected before the student begins the homework. The worksheet serves as a guide to help complete the homework.

Homework

"Turn your paper over to the homework side. Let's read the directions together."

- Read the directions aloud to the student.

  "Do you know what to do on the homework paper?"

  "The first thing you need to do is look for irregular spelling words. Find the words that use 'ow' in the medial position and circle them. Then code and read all of the words."

  "When you finish your paper, I will check it for you and initial it in the space provided."
- Either now or later in the day, the student should complete the homework independently (if possible). Help the student correct any incorrect answers. Then initial the homework in the space provided.
- If possible, take time to play the Kid Card games listed in Lesson 95.

Name ______________________

Teacher's Initials _____

Worksheet 98
(for use with Lesson 98)
Phonics 1

Spelling with ou and ow

1. round
2. shout
3. grouch
4. how
5. cow
6. out
7. mouth
8. count
9. sprout
10. lookout

Irregular words:

brown
down
clown
town
howl
owl

Rewrite the irregular words:

brown
down
clown
town
howl
owl

P1-WS-098a

Parent's Initials _____

Homework 98
(for use with Lesson 98)
Phonics 1

Spelling with ou and ow

When spelling with *ou* and *ow*, the most common spelling of /ou/ in the initial or medial position is *ou*. The most common spelling of /ou/ in the final position is *ow*. It is irregular to find *ou* in the final position or *ow* in the initial or medial position.

Circle the irregular spelling words, then code and read all of the words.

round	shout	howl
down	cow	around
how	town	found
brown	ground	clown

Parents: Your child has been taught to recognize the **irregular spelling** of words that use diphthong *ow* in the medial position.

P1-WS-098b

LESSON 99 The Rules vc|ccv or vcc|cv

lesson preparation

materials

Alphabet/Accent Deck (Section 1)

Review Decks

Spelling Sound Sheet 72

Sight Word Card 53

Worksheet 99

Reader 36 (*Chester and Hudson*)

colored pencils

new concepts

vc|ccv or vcc|cv pattern

ALPHABET ACTIVITY

"Let's work with the first Alphabet/Accent Deck again today. Let's stand up."

"We'll stand with our feet flat on the floor and say the first syllable in a normal voice. When we come to the accented syllable, we'll jump up and say it louder."

- Show the student **Alphabet/Accent Card 1.**
- Have the student say "A" (in a normal voice with feet flat), and then "B" (louder, jumping up).
- Continue with **Alphabet/Accent Cards 2–25,** moving as quickly as possible.
- **Optional:** If you think the student is ready, shuffle the Alphabet/Accent Deck before the activity. Warn the student that the cards will be in random order.

REVIEW OF DECKS

- Show the student **Letter Cards 1–60** in random order. The student should name the letter on each letter card.
- Review **Affix Cards 1–8.**
- Show the student **Picture Cards 1–74** in random order. The student should name the keyword and sound for each picture card.
- Review **Sight Word Cards 1–52.**
- Give the student **Spelling Sound Sheet 72.**
- Call out the sounds on **Spelling Cards 1–44** in random order. The student should echo each sound and name the letter or letters that make the sound as he/she writes the letter(s) on the spelling sound sheet.
- Check the student's response after each card.

NEW LEARNING

- Write the word "inspect" on the chalkboard.

"Can you tell me what to look for first to code this big word?" *suffixes and final, stable syllables*

"Do you see any suffixes or final, stable syllables?" *no*

"What would you look for next?" *vowels*

"How many vowels do you see in this word?" *two*

"Let's write a small v under each vowel."

- Write a small *v* under each vowel:

inspect
v v

"How many consonants are between the two vowels?" *three*

- Write a small *c* under each consonant:

inspect
vcccv

"We have a new pattern. There are three consonants between the two vowels. We need to look for digraphs or blends first, and then divide either between the first two consonants or the last two consonants."

"Do any of the three consonants between the vowels make a digraph or a blend?" *no digraphs, but sp is a blend*

"Let's try leaving 'sp' together in the same syllable, since it is a blend."

- Divide the word between *n* and *s*:

in|spect
vc|ccv

"Now we need to code the vowels in each syllable."

- Have the student help you code the remainder of the word:

ĭn|spĕct′
vc|ccv

"Sometimes words with 'vcccv' patterns divide between the last two consonants. Let's try one like that."

- Write "athletes" on the chalkboard.

"Are there any suffixes or final, stable syllables in this word?" *yes, suffix -s*

- If the student answers "suffix *-es*," point out that there must always be a root word left after the suffix is boxed.

"First we need to box the suffix. Next we need to look for the _______?" *vowels*

- Label the first two vowels (and box the suffix, if you have not already):

athlete[s]
v v

"We'll mark out the second e because it's a sneaky e."

"How many consonants are between the vowels?" *three*

- Write a small *c* under each consonant:

athletes
vcccv

"Is there a digraph or a blend among these three consonants?" *yes, digraph th*

"Let's leave 'th' together in the same syllable and divide between the h and the l. When there is a digraph in the word, we can be pretty sure about where to divide the word. Also, let's put the accent on the first syllable."

- Place the dividing line between the *h* and *l* and accent the first syllable. Code the word as follows:

ăth'|lētes
vcc|cv

"Let's read this word." *athletes*

"When we divide 'vcccv' words without digraphs, you will have to experiment with the accent on both syllables to see which one is right."

"I have a chart that will help you remember how to divide these kinds of words."

"Get out your Rule Book and turn to page 20."

- Point to **Syllable Division Chart 5** as you say the following:

"Refer to this chart any time you need help coding words with this pattern."

BOARDWORK

- Write the following on the chalkboard:

through /thrōō/

"We have a new sight word today."

- Point to the word.

"Can you tell me what this word is? Remember, it's a sight word, so it won't follow all of our rules."

- Allow the student to try to pronounce the word. If necessary, say it for him/her.

"This word is 'through.' Can you use the word 'through' in a sentence?" *expect various answers*

- Show the student **Sight Word Card 53.**

"Let's find this word on our sight word charts."

- Help the student locate the word in the Irregular Spelling Booklet.

"We will add this card to our sight word deck."

"Let's practice coding some words like the ones you'll have on your worksheet."

"The rule charts are in your Rule Book if you need to look at them."

- Write the following phrase and sentence (without the coding marks) on the chalkboard, one at a time. Ask the student to help you code them. The correct coding is as indicated:

clēar´ing thė dĭsh´es

Sort thė hĕalth´y cȧr|nā´tions.
vc|cv

- Have the student determine whether each of the items coded is a word, a phrase, or a sentence.
- Add **Sight Word Card 53** to the Sight Word Deck.

WORKSHEET

- The student should be seated where he/she can write comfortably.
- Give the student **Worksheet 99.** Make sure the student turns to the correct side.

"Today, let's spell with words that have a 'vcccv' pattern."

- When you pronounce these words, make a distinct separation between syllables. The student will be more successful if he/she spells by syllables.

"Put your finger by #1. The first word is 'arctic.' "

"The first syllable is 'arc.' Spell and write the first syllable by #1."

"The last syllable is 'tic.' Spell 'tic' and write it after 'arc' on line #1."

- Allow time for the student to do this.

"What word did you write?" *arctic*

- Repeat the procedure with #2 (partner), #3 (pumpkin), #4 (district), and #5 (lobster).

"Now you're ready to code and read the words on your paper."

"Try coding #6. You will need to decide whether the dividing line goes between the first two consonants or the last two consonants."

- Allow time for the student to do this.
- If the student understands the procedure, let him/her continue independently.

"Look at the picture at the bottom of the page. Write a story about the picture on the lines beside it. Don't worry about spelling. When you are finished, we will take time to check spelling and correct mistakes."

- As the student works, provide help as needed.
- Then have the student read the story silently and check for spelling errors. Help the student correct any mistakes. A perfect paper is not as important as the student putting his/her thoughts on paper and being able to recognize spelling errors that can be corrected (e.g., *k* and *c* spelling). Be sure to correct the rest of the worksheet as well. Then initial it in the space provided.

- Have the student read the story to you. It is important that children learn to feel comfortable speaking in front of others.
- **Note:** Always make sure the worksheet is corrected before the student begins the homework. The worksheet serves as a guide to help complete the homework.

HOMEWORK

"Turn your paper over to the homework side."

"Do you know what to do on the homework paper?"

"Be sure to look for our new syllable division pattern."

"Draw your own picture in the box at the bottom of the page. Then write a story about it."

"When you finish your paper, I will check it for you and initial it in the space provided."

- Either now or later in the day, the student should complete the homework independently (if possible). Help the student correct any incorrect answers. Then initial the homework in the space provided.

READER

"We have another new book today."

- Write the word "ever" on the chalkboard.

"This is the word 'ever.' We haven't learned the syllable division pattern for this word yet, but you'll see this word in your new reader today."

- If desired, allow a few minutes to discuss the word's definition.
- Give the student **Reader 36 (*Chester and Hudson*)** and some colored pencils.

"Can you tell me this book's title?" *Chester and Hudson*

- Assist the student as necessary as he/she constructs the book.
- When the student finishes, staple or put a rubber band around the book's spine.
- If necessary, demonstrate how to separate the pages and check the page order.

"The title of this book is __________?" *Chester and Hudson*

"I want you to read your book to yourself. When you are finished reading, color the pictures. Write your name on the book so I will know who colored it."

"Keep your book handy because I will be asking you to read it for me."

- Some time during the day, have the student read the reader to you.
- If possible, take time to play the Kid Card games listed in Lesson 95. Try to see that the student is prepared for tomorrow's assessment.

Name ______________________

Teacher's Initials ____

Worksheet 99
(for use with Lesson 99)
Phonics 1

vcccv

1. arctic
2. partner
3. pumpkin
4. district
5. lobster
6. employ
7. ointment
8. headrest
9. slowness
10. blackbird

P1-WS-099a

Parent's Initials ____

Homework 99
(for use with Lesson 99)
Phonics 1

vcccv

1. instant
2. athlete
3. address or address
4. subtract
5. boil
6. tomboy
7. snowman
8. follow
9. stir
10. pickup

Pictures will vary

Parents: Your child has been taught the syllable division rules vc | ccv and vcc | cv.

P1-WS-099b

LESSON 100 — Assessment

lesson preparation

materials

assorted items (see *the night before*)

Review Decks

Assessment 19

Spelling Test 17

Assessment 19 Recording Form

Kid Cards

tokens

the night before

- Locate a small assortment of items, each of whose name begins with a different letter. (See "Alphabetizing Objects" in the appendix for some suggestions.)
- Sort through the Review Decks and remove any of the following cards the student knows very well:

  Letter Deck: *ck, th, ~~th~~, ng, ee, sh, oo.*

  Picture Deck: Cards that correspond to the letter cards that are removed.

  Sight Word Deck: Cards that (based on assessment results) the student knows very well.

  Spelling Deck: Cards that correspond to the letter cards that are removed (except for /ē/).
- Add these cards to the retired decks.
- Separate the Kid Cards marked "Lesson 100."

ALPHABET ACTIVITY

- The student should be seated.

  "Today our alphabet activity is going to be really fun. We're going to alphabetize some objects again."
- Give the student 3 or 4 objects. Ask the student to identify the letter each object begins with and then put the objects in alphabetical order.

  "See how quickly you can alphabetize the objects. Then double check to see if they really are in alphabetical order."
- If time permits, continue with new groups of objects after the first group is alphabetized.

Review of Decks

- The student should be seated where he/she can write comfortably.
- Show the student **Letter Cards 1–60** in random order. The student should name the letter on each letter card.
- Review **Affix Cards 1–8.**
- Show the student **Picture Cards 1–74** in random order. The student should name the keyword and sound for each picture card.
- Review **Sight Word Cards 1–53.**

Written Assessment

- Have the student sit where he/she can write comfortably.
- Give the student **Assessment 19.**
- **Section I:**

  "Today we are going to write some words for our assessment."

  "I'm going to say a word. Write the letter that makes each sound in that word on the lines by #1."

  "Look at the rule charts if you need to."

  "Here's the first word: argue."
- Repeat with the following words in the order shown: #2 (station), #3 (chill), #4 (expert), and #5 (stumble).
- **Reminder:** While the student spells, be ready to point to appropriate rule charts as necessary.
- **Section II:**

  "Look at the letters by #6."

  "Find the picture of the keyword for this sound."

  "Draw a line from the letters to the keyword."
- Repeat with #7. Allow a few minutes for the student to work.
- The pictures (from top to bottom) are as follows: lotion, glue.
- **Section III:**

  "Put your finger on #8."

  "Code the words by #8 through #12."
- Allow a few minutes for the student to work.
- **Section IV:**

  "Read the paragraph. If you find any words you can't read, code them to help you figure them out. Then answer the questions by #13 through #17."
- **Reminder:** If the student absolutely cannot read the paragraph, read it to the student to see if he or she can answer the questions.

"When you are finished, show your paper to me."

- This paper will be used during the oral portion of the assessment.

Spelling Test

- Give the student **Spelling Test 17.**
- Call out the following words (in the order shown). Sound them out, if necessary.

  #1 (quiz), #2 (born), #3 (baby), #4 (focus), #5 (minus), #6 (trace), #7 (born), #8 (even), #9 (super), #10 (clover), #11 (they), #12 (says)
- Grade and record the test in any manner that suits your needs.
- Send the spelling test home with the student.

Oral Assessment

- It is important to complete the oral assessment promptly (today, if possible) in order to identify any areas of weakness and begin remediation.
- Use the assessment and the following dialogue to complete the oral portion.
- **Section V:**
- Point to the sight word by #18.

  "Read this sight word for me."
- Record the student's response by placing a check mark by each word he/she reads correctly.
- Repeat with #19 through #23.
- **Section VI:**
- Show the student the letters by #24.

  "Tell me the name of these letters and the sound (or sounds) they make."
- Write the student's response on the adjacent line.
- Repeat with #25.

Assessment Evaluation

- Grade the assessment and record the results on **Assessment 19 Recording Form.** Check off the boxes to indicate mastery (i.e., the section was completed with 100% accuracy).
- **Reminder:** Try to give as many points as possible for work attempted. Do not grade the coding marks too severely. The most important coding marks to look for are breves, macrons, and syllable division lines.
- See the introductory material for detailed information regarding grading and recording procedures.

- Use the assessment results to identify those skills in which the student is weak. Practice those skills by playing Kid Card games.
- Add the Kid Cards marked "Lesson 100" to the existing decks. Listed below are games appropriate for remediation in selected areas. See "Games and Activities" for the directions for each game.
- **Section I:** Play "Spelling Deck Perfection," "Sound Scamper," "Spell Out #1 or #2," or have the student use the letter tiles to spell words you give from the Spelling Word List.
- **Section II:** Play "Keyword and Sound" or "Letter/Sound Identification."
- **Section III:** Play "Chalkboard Challenge."
- **Section IV:** Either have the student read the controlled readers and then ask questions for comprehension, or play "Acting Out" with the green Kid Cards.
- **Section V:** Play "At First Sight," review the Sight Word Deck, or lay the sight words out with a token on each one and let the student try to get as many tokens as possible for the sight words he/she can read.
- **Section VI:** Play "Letter/Sound Identification."
- When the student seems more secure in areas that had previously proven difficult, retest him/her (in those areas only) and indicate on the recording form any sections the student has subsequently mastered.
- Try to help the student achieve mastery of all the sections before the next assessment.
- If the student is having difficulty with a particular skill, keep his or her practice activities at the most basic level so the chance of success is greater.

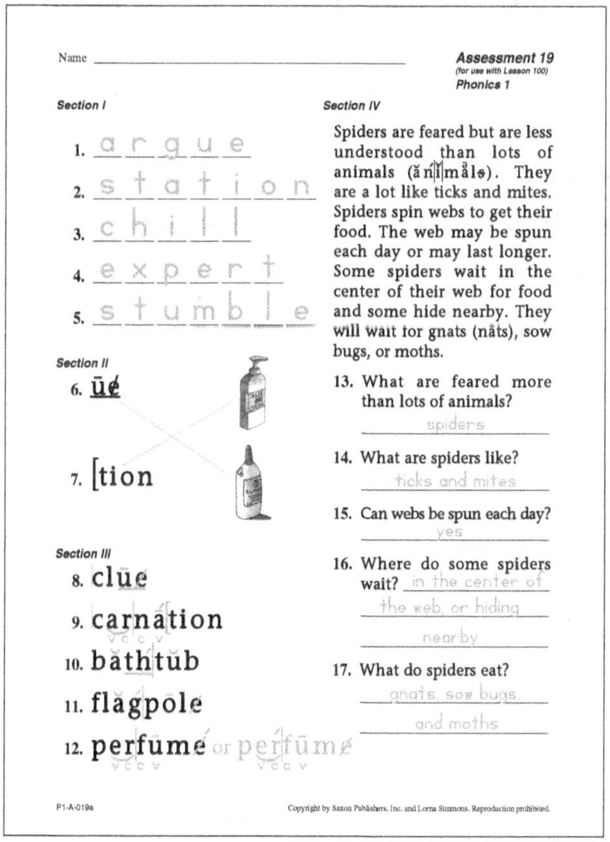

Name ______________________

Assessment 19
(for use with Lesson 100)
Phonics 1

Section I

1. a r g u e
2. s t a t i o n
3. c h i l l
4. e x p e r t
5. s t u m b l e

Section II

6. ūe
7. tion

Section III

8. clūe
9. carnation
10. băthtŭb
11. flăgpōle
12. perfūme or perfūme

Section IV

Spiders are feared but are less understood than lots of animals (ăn|ĭ|măls). They are a lot like ticks and mites. Spiders spin webs to get their food. The web may be spun each day or may last longer. Some spiders wait in the center of their web for food and some hide nearby. They will wait for gnats (năts), sow bugs, or moths.

13. What are feared more than lots of animals? spiders
14. What are spiders like? ticks and mites
15. Can webs be spun each day? yes
16. Where do some spiders wait? in the center of the web, or hiding nearby
17. What do spiders eat? gnats, sow bugs, and moths

P1-A-019a

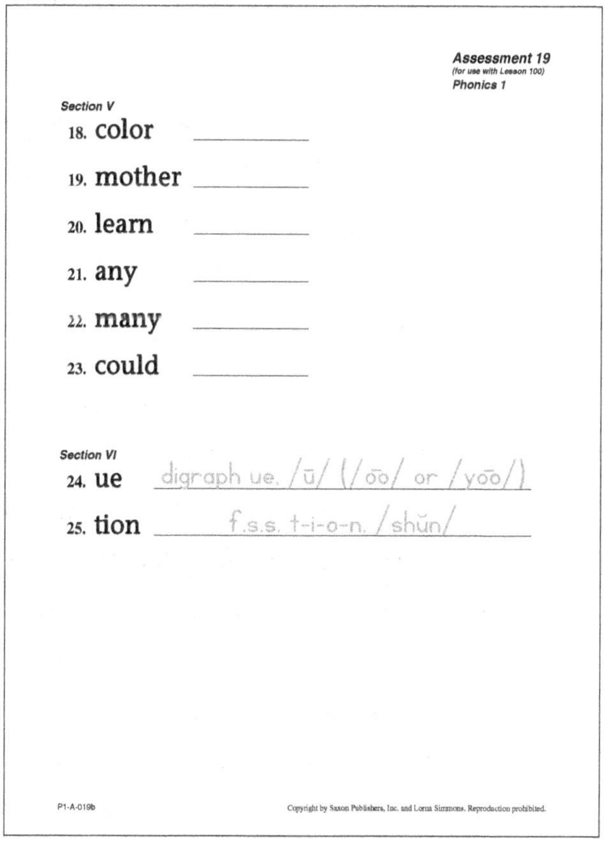

Assessment 19
(for use with Lesson 100)
Phonics 1

Section V

18. color
19. mother
20. learn
21. any
22. many
23. could

Section VI

24. ue digraph ue, /ū/ (/o͞o/ or /yo͞o/)
25. tion f.s.s. t-i-o-n, /shŭn/

P1-A-019b

LESSON 101 — Digraph *au*

lesson preparation

materials

container of letter tiles

Review Decks

Spelling Sound Sheet 73

Letter Card 61

Picture Card 75

Spelling Card 45

Sight Word Card 54

Worksheet 101

Spelling List 18

ALPHABET ACTIVITY

- The student should be seated with the container of letter tiles.

  "Before we start, let's say the alphabet together so it is fresh in our minds."

- Recite the alphabet with the student.
- Give the following instructions one at a time, allowing time for the student to accomplish each task before giving the next instruction.

  "Take all of the letter tiles out of your container."

  "Flip all of the letters over so that you are looking at the lowercase letters. If they are flipped correctly, they will all be blue."

  "Now we're ready. See if you can put all your letters in alphabetical order."

- Assist the student as necessary.
- When the student has finished, continue by saying the following:

  "Pull down the letters that are always vowels."

  "Put together two letters that make a diphthong." *oi, oy, ou, ow*

  "How many other diphthongs can you make?" *three others (as listed above)*

  "Spell the word 'soil' with your letter tiles."

  "Now change the word to 'soy.' "

  "Change one letter to make the word 'toy.' "

  "Now change the word to 'toil.' "

- Have the student replace the tiles in the container and put it away.

REVIEW OF DECKS

- Show the student **Letter Cards 1–60** in random order. The student should name the letter on each letter card.
- Review **Affix Cards 1–8.**
- Show the student **Picture Cards 1–74** in random order. The student should name the keyword and sound for each picture card.
- Review **Sight Word Cards 1–53.**
- Give the student **Spelling Sound Sheet 73.**
- Call out the sounds on **Spelling Cards 1–44** in random order. The student should echo each sound and name the letter or letters that make the sound as he/she writes the letter(s) on the spelling sound sheet.
- Have the student set the spelling sound sheet aside for use later in the lesson.

NEW LEARNING

"I'm going to say some words. Echo them back to me and listen for the sound that is the same in each word."

- Point to your mouth as you say each word.

"Echo after me. Pause." *pause* ***"Auto."*** *auto* ***"Faucet."*** *faucet*

"What sound do you hear that is the same in each of these words?" */au/*

"That's right. The sound you hear is /au/."

"Put your fingers on the front of your neck and say /au/. See if you feel any vibration."

"Is this sound voiced or unvoiced?" *voiced*

- Write the following on the chalkboard: pause, auto, faucet.

"What do you see that might be making the /au/ sound?" *au*

"There is an 'au' in all of these words, so we can see that 'au' must be the letters used to spell the /au/ sound."

"How many sounds do you hear?" *one*

"How many letters are making that sound?" *two*

"What do you think 'au' is?" *a digraph*

"How do we code a digraph?" *draw a line under it*

- Code digraph *au* in each of the words: p<u>au</u>se, <u>au</u>to, f<u>au</u>cet.

"Is 'au' a vowel digraph or a consonant digraph?" *a vowel digraph because it contains only vowels*

New Deck Cards

- Show the student **Letter Card 61.**

  "What do we call this?" *digraph au*

- Hold up **Picture Card 75** but keep the picture covered with your hand (or the letter card).

  "I have a card with a picture on it that contains the /au/ sound."

  "I am going to describe it for you. See if you can guess what the picture is."

  "This is something that you put on top of food. It can be made of tomatoes and put on spaghetti. It can be hot and spicy and put on food that is barbecued. It can be made of cheese and put on vegetables. What do you think the picture is?" *sauce*

  "That's right. The keyword is 'sauce' and the sound we have learned is /au/."

- Show the student **Picture Card 75.**

  "The word 'sauce' helps us remember the /au/ sound since it contains that sound."

- **Note:** The digraph and its picture are also shown in the Rule Book on page 21.
- **Note:** The use of **Spelling Card 45** is optional. *Au* is pronounced in various ways depending on where you live. If the sound of *au* in your area is distinctly different from the /ŏ/ sound, use Spelling Card 45. If the typical pronunciation of *au* in your area is /ŏ/, treat *au* as an irregular spelling of the /ŏ/ sound.
- **If Spelling Card 45 will be used,** use the following dialogue:

  "Find your spelling sound sheet. Put your finger on line #45."

- Hold up **Spelling Card 45** so only you can see what is written.

  "Echo this sound: /au/." */au/*

  "How do we spell the /au/ sound?" *digraph au*

  "Write that on the line by #45."

- Check the spelling sound sheet for accuracy.
- **If digraph au will be treated as an irregular spelling,** use the following dialogue:

  "The best choice for spelling the /ŏ/ sound is still o, so we won't add digraph au to our spelling deck."

  "Let's see what kinds of words are spelled with 'au.' Get out your Irregular Spelling Booklet."

  "Look at the table of contents. Can you find the page that shows words spelled with digraph au?" *page 16*

  "Turn to page 16. All of these words are spelled with digraph au. They are easy to read, but since they don't follow our regular rules, we must memorize them in order to spell them. For now, you can refer to this booklet any time you're spelling."

- **Note:** Add the new letter and picture cards (and spelling card, if used) to the Review Decks.

Lesson 101

BOARDWORK

- Write the following on the chalkboard:

sure /shŏŏr/

"We have a new sight word today. Can you tell me what this word is? Remember, it's a sight word, so it won't follow all of our rules."

- Allow the student to try to pronounce the word. If necessary, say it for him/her.

"This word is 'sure.' Can you use the word 'sure' in a sentence?" *expect various answers*

- Show the student **Sight Word Card 54.**

"Let's find this word on our sight word charts."

- Help the student locate the word in the Irregular Spelling Booklet.

"We will add this card to our sight word deck."

"Let's practice coding some words like the ones you'll have on your worksheet."

"The rule charts are here in your Rule Book if you need to look at them."

- Write the following word, phrase, and sentence (without the coding marks) on the chalkboard, one at a time. Ask the student to help you code them. The correct coding is as indicated:

fault´less

sweet, stick´y, chĕr´|rў shāke
vc|cv

Lō´|cāte the farm´|house.
v|cv

- Have the student determine whether each of the items coded is a word, a phrase, or a sentence.
- Add **Sight Word Card 54** to the Sight Word Deck.

WORKSHEET

- The student should be seated where he/she can write comfortably.
- Give the student **Worksheet 101.** Make sure the student turns to the correct side.

"Today, let's spell with the /au/ sound using digraph au."

"Digraph au is most often used for spelling in the initial or medial position."

"Put your finger by #1. The first word is 'auto.' "

"Spell the word and write the letters on the line by #1 as you say them."

- Allow time for the student to do this.

"What word did you write?" *auto*

- Repeat the procedure with #2 (laundry), #3 (haul), #4 (fault), and #5 (August). Remind the student that "August" is a proper noun and the first letter should be capitalized.

"Now you're ready to code and read the words on your paper."

"Code the words by #6 through #10. After you have coded all the words, try to read them."

- Assist the student as necessary.

"Numbers 11 and 12 are questions about the paragraph just above them. If you find any words you can't read, code them. Then see if you can answer the questions."

- As the student works, provide help as needed. Help the student correct any incorrect answers. Then initial the worksheet in the space provided.
- Some time during the day, ask the student to read from the worksheet, a controlled reader, your basal reader, or other material of your choice.
- **Note:** Always make sure the worksheet is corrected before the student begins the homework. The worksheet serves as a guide to help complete the homework.

HOMEWORK

"Turn your paper over to the homework side."

"Do you know what to do on the homework paper?"

"Watch for digraph au. Always code suffixes and final, stable syllables before coding the rest of the word."

"When you finish your paper, I will check it for you and initial it in the space provided."

- Either now or later in the day, the student should complete the homework independently (if possible). Help the student correct any incorrect answers. Then initial the homework in the space provided.

SPELLING LIST

- Fold **Spelling List 18** in half lengthwise (with the printed side facing out).

"Leave your paper just like I give it to you."

- Give the student **Spelling List 18,** folded with the blank lines facing up.

"Let's spell some more words."

- Call out the following words (in the order shown). Sound them out, if necessary.

  #1 (silent), #2 (order), #3 (farmyard), #4 (checking), #5 (year),
  #6 (teacher), #7 (seat), #8 (hiding), #9 (mice), #10 (space),
  #11 (build), #12 (built)

"Now unfold your paper and check your words."

- Check the student's work to see if he/she needs extra help with spelling.

"I want you to practice these words. We'll have a spelling test in a few days."

- If possible, take time to play the Kid Card games listed in Lesson 100.

Name ______________________

Teacher's Initials _____

Worksheet 101
(for use with Lesson 101)
Phonics 1

au

1. auto
2. laundry
3. haul
4. fault
5. August
6. cause
7. launchpad
8. rotate
9. oversleep
10. spicy

One August day, the sun was shining and my friend Terry and I were playing outside. We were riding our bikes and having a great time. Terry was not looking ahead and ran into a curb. She went flying over her handlebars. I was so scared! I was sure she was hurt.

11. What did Terry hit? a curb

12. What did Terry fly over? her handlebars

P1-WS-101a

Parent's Initials _____

Homework 101
(for use with Lesson 101)
Phonics 1

au

1. sauce
2. bonus
3. pause
4. ace
5. vault
6. donate
7. crater
8. lacy
9. succeed
10. gauze

Terry landed in the grass by the curb she hit. At first she seemed dazed. She didn't get up and she didn't speak. I ran over to her side thinking she was really hurt. Just as I got to her side she said, "Boo! Did I scare you?" I was scared but I was sure happy that she was not hurt.

11. How did Terry act at first?
She seemed dazed.

12. What did Terry say?
"Boo! Did I scare you?"

Parents: Your child has been taught **digraph au;** and that it is usually found in the initial or medial position.

P1-WS-101b

Lesson 101

LESSON 102 — Digraph *aw*

lesson preparation

materials

Alphabet/Accent Deck (Section 2)

Retired Decks

Affix Deck

Spelling Sound Sheet 74

Letter Card 62

straws in a sack (see *the night before*)

Picture Card 76

Sight Word Cards 55–56

Worksheet 102

Reader 37 (*Frank Goes Camping*)

colored pencils

the night before

- Put a few drinking straws in a sack for the student to use to "discover" the new keyword.

ALPHABET ACTIVITY

"We're going to work with the second of our Alphabet/Accent Decks today."

- Show the student **Alphabet/Accent Card 1.**

"Do you remember how this card is read?" *the middle letter (b) is missing and accented; the missing letter will be named and accented*

"That's right. Let's stand up. Every time we say the accented syllable, we'll karate punch."

- Have the student say "A" (standing, in a normal voice), then "B" (as he/she punches forward), and then "C" (standing, in a normal voice).
- Continue with **Alphabet/Accent Cards 2–24,** moving as quickly as possible.

Review of Decks

- The student should be seated where he/she can write comfortably.
- Show the student the retired letter cards in random order. The student should name the letter on each letter card.
- Review **Affix Cards 1–8.**
- Show the student the retired picture cards in random order. The student should name the keyword and sound for each picture card.
- Review the retired sight word cards.
- Give the student **Spelling Sound Sheet 74.**
- Call out the sounds on the retired spelling cards in random order. The student should echo each sound and name the letter or letters that make the sound as he/she writes the letter(s) on the spelling sound sheet.
- If **Spelling Card 45** was used in the previous lesson, have the student set the spelling sound sheet aside for use later in the lesson.
- If **Spelling Card 45** was not used in the previous lesson, have the student put the spelling sound sheet away.

New Learning

"I'm going to say some words. Echo them back to me and listen for the sound that is the same in the final position of each word."

- Point to your mouth as you say each word.

"Echo after me. Straw." *straw* ***"Paw."*** *paw* ***"Thaw."*** *thaw*

"What sound do you hear in the final position in each of these words?" */au/*

"That's right. The sound you hear is /au/."

"Put your fingers on the front of your neck and say /au/. See if you feel any vibration."

"Is this sound voiced or unvoiced?" *voiced*

- Write the following on the chalkboard: straw, paw, thaw.

"What do you see that might be making the /au/ sound?" *aw*

"There is an 'aw' in all of these words, so we can see that 'aw' must be the letters used to spell the /au/ sound."

"How many sounds do you hear?" *one*

"How many letters are making that sound?" *two*

"What do you think 'aw' is?" *a digraph*

"How do we code a digraph?" *draw a line under it*

- Code digraph *aw* in each of the words: str<u>aw</u>, p<u>aw</u>, th<u>aw</u>.

"Did you notice that in all of these words, digraph aw is in the final position? Digraphs au and aw make the same sound, but in the final position of a word, the letter w takes the place of the u. This is just like when digraph ou becomes 'ow' in the final position."

NEW DECK CARDS

- Show the student **Letter Card 62.**

  "What do we call this?" *digraph aw*

  "I have another sack today. It contains a clue to our new keyword. Don't look in the sack, but put your hand inside and see if you can guess what is inside. Keep in mind that the object in the sack contains the /au/ sound."
- Allow the student a chance to feel inside the sack.

  "Can you guess the new keyword?" *straw*

  "That's right. The keyword is 'straw' and the sound we have learned is /au/."
- Show the student **Picture Card 76.**

  "The word 'straw' helps us remember the /au/ sound that is spelled 'aw.' "
- **Note:** The digraph and its picture are also shown in the Rule Book on page 21.
- **If Spelling Card 45 was used in the previous lesson,** use the following dialogue:

  "Find your spelling sound sheet. Put your finger on line #46."
- Hold up **Spelling Card 45** so only you can see what is written.

  "Echo this sound: /au/." */au/*

  "How do we spell the /au/ sound?" *digraph au*

  "Write that on the line by #46."

  "How do we spell the /au/ sound in the final position?" *digraph aw*
- Write the following on the chalkboard: au || aw.

  "What does this say?" *digraph au final digraph aw*

  "That's right. Finish the response on line #46."
- Have the student put the spelling sound sheet away.
- **If digraph au was treated as an irregular spelling,** use the following dialogue:

  "Since digraph aw isn't used very often, we don't have a spelling card for it. But there are some words that use it."

  "Let's see what kinds of words are spelled with digraph aw. Get out your Irregular Spelling Booklet."

  "Look at the table of contents. Can you find the page that shows words spelled with digraph aw?" *page 17*

"Turn to page 17. All of these words are spelled with digraph aw. They are easy to read, but since they don't follow our regular rules, we must memorize them in order to spell them. For now, you can refer to this booklet any time you're spelling."

- **Note:** Add the new letter and picture cards to the Review Decks. Also, **Spelling Card 45** (if used) should be re-inserted.

BOARDWORK

- Write the following on the chalkboard:

earth /er th/ other /ŭth′ er/

"We have two new sight words today."

- Point to the first word.

"Can you tell me what this word is? Remember, it's a sight word, so it won't follow all of our rules."

- Allow the student to try to pronounce the word. If necessary, say it for him/her.

"This word is 'earth.' Can you use the word 'earth' in a sentence?" *expect various answers*

- Repeat with "other."
- Show the student **Sight Word Cards 55** and **56.**

"Let's find these words on our sight word charts."

- Help the student locate the words in the Irregular Spelling Booklet.

"We will add these cards to our sight word deck."

"Let's practice coding some words like the ones you'll have on your worksheet."

"The rule charts are in your Rule Book if you need to look at them."

- Write the following sentences (without the coding marks) on the chalkboard, one at a time. Ask the student to help you code them. The correct coding is as indicated:

Straw′|bĕr|rÿ sēa′|sŏn wĭll bē′ hērе soon.
v c|c v v|c v

Ī′ found hĭm yawn′ing ăt thė auc′tion.

- Have the student determine whether each of the items coded is a word, a phrase, or a sentence.
- Add **Sight Word Cards 55** and **56** to the Sight Word Deck.

WORKSHEET

- The student should be seated where he/she can write comfortably.
- Give the student **Worksheet 102.** Make sure the student turns to the correct side.

"Let's spell some words with the /au/ sound using digraph aw today."

"Remember, digraph aw is usually found in the final position."

"Put your finger by #1. The first word is 'draw.' "

"Unblend 'draw' with me." */d/ /r/ /au/*

- Hold up one finger for each sound.

"Let's spell those sounds. D ... r ... digraph aw."

- Point to a finger as the student spells each sound.

"Now spell the word again and write the letters as you say them."

- Allow time for the student to do this.

"What word did you write?" *draw*

- Repeat the procedure with #2 (claw), #3 (law), #4 (saw), and #5 (thaw).

"Now you're ready to code and read the words on your paper."

"Code the words by #6 through #10. After you have coded all the words, try to read them."

- Assist the student as necessary.

"Now read the word by #11. If you have trouble reading the word, code it. Then draw a line from the word to the picture it matches."

- Repeat with #12, #13, and #14.
- As the student works, provide help as needed. Help the student correct any incorrect answers. Then initial the worksheet in the space provided.
- Some time during the day, ask the student to read from the worksheet, a controlled reader, your basal reader, or other material of your choice.
- **Note:** Always make sure the worksheet is corrected before the student begins the homework. The worksheet serves as a guide to help complete the homework.

HOMEWORK

"Turn your paper over to the homework side."

"Do you know what to do on the homework paper?"

"Watch for digraphs au and aw. Always code suffixes and final, stable syllables before coding the rest of the word."

- Discuss the homework pictures to make sure the student understands the word each one represents: #11 (faucet), #12 (clown), #13 (lobster), and #14 (paw).

"When you finish your paper, I will check it for you and initial it in the space provided."

- Either now or later in the day, the student should complete the homework independently (if possible). Help the student correct any incorrect answers. Then initial the homework in the space provided.

READER

"We have another new book today."

- Give the student **Reader 37 (*Frank Goes Camping*)** and some colored pencils.

  "Can you tell me this book's title?" *Frank Goes Camping*
- Assist the student as necessary as he/she constructs the book.
- When the student finishes, staple or put a rubber band around the book's spine.

  "The title of this book is __________?" *Frank Goes Camping*

  "I want you to read your book to yourself. When you are finished reading, color the pictures. Write your name on the book so I will know who colored it."

  "Keep your book handy because I will be asking you to read it for me."
- Some time during the day, have the student read the reader to you.
- If possible, take time to play the Kid Card games listed in Lesson 100.

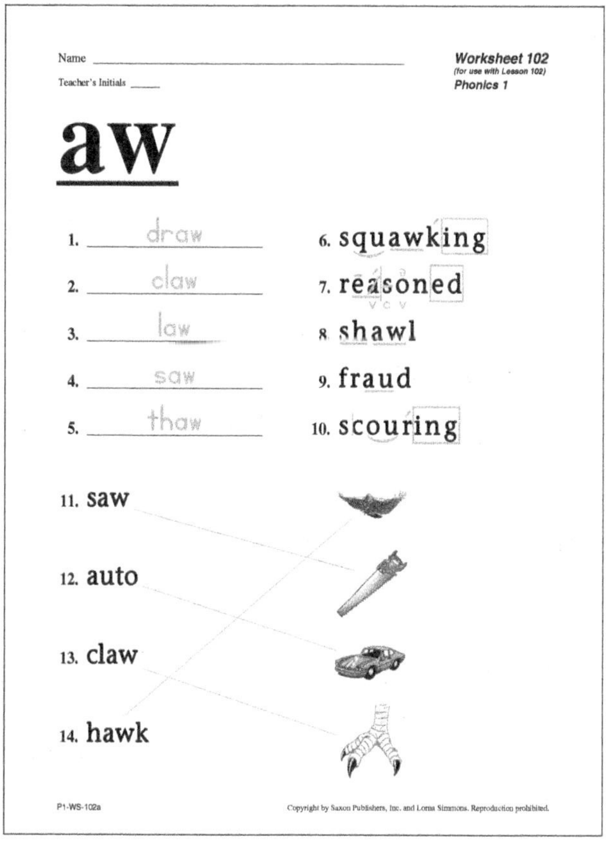
Name ________________________

Teacher's Initials ____

Worksheet 102
(for use with Lesson 102)
Phonics 1

aw

1. draw
2. claw
3. law
4. saw
5. thaw
6. squawking
7. reasoned
8. shawl
9. fraud
10. scouring

11. saw
12. auto
13. claw
14. hawk

P1-WS-102a

Copyright by Saxon Publishers, Inc. and Lorna Simmons. Reproduction prohibited.

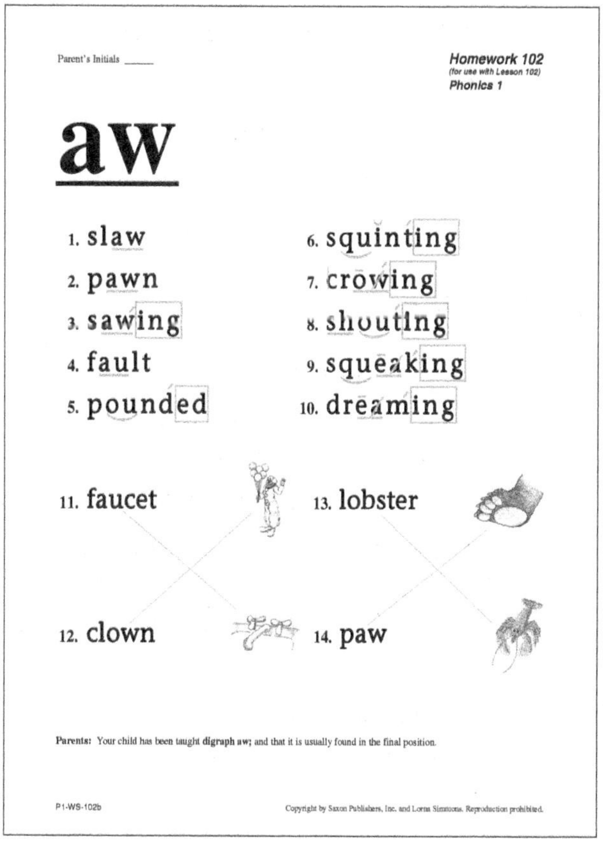
Parent's Initials ____

Homework 102
(for use with Lesson 102)
Phonics 1

aw

1. slaw
2. pawn
3. sawing
4. fault
5. pounded
6. squinting
7. crowing
8. shouting
9. squeaking
10. dreaming

11. faucet
12. clown
13. lobster
14. paw

Parents: Your child has been taught **digraph aw;** and that it is usually found in the final position.

P1-WS-102b

Copyright by Saxon Publishers, Inc. and Lorna Simmons. Reproduction prohibited.

LESSON 103 "Wild Colt" Words

lesson preparation

materials

container of letter tiles

Review Decks

Spelling Sound Sheet 75

tokens or colored pencil

Worksheet 103

new concepts

"wild colt" words

ALPHABET ACTIVITY

- The student should be seated with the container of letter tiles.

  "Let's see how fast you can alphabetize."

  "I want you to put your hand in your container of letter tiles."

  "When I say 'go,' I want you to pull out eight tiles and put them in alphabetical order. We are going to see how fast you can get them in order."

  "Raise your hand when you have them in order."

- Time the student.

  "Ready, set, go!"

- Repeat with eight more tiles if time permits.

REVIEW OF DECKS

- The student should be seated where he/she can write comfortably.
- Show the student **Letter Cards 1–62** in random order. The student should name the letter on each letter card.
- Review **Affix Cards 1–8.**
- Show the student **Picture Cards 1–76** in random order. The student should name the keyword and sound for each picture card.
- Review **Sight Word Cards 1–56.**
- Give the student **Spelling Sound Sheet 75** and at least twelve tokens (or a colored pencil).
- If you can use "fun" markers, such as goldfish-shaped crackers or cereal pieces, it is much more enjoyable for the student.

"Let's play Bingo!"

"When I call out the spelling sounds today, I want you to place a token on (or draw a big X in) the space that spells that sound on your spelling sound sheet."

"When you cover (or X out) all of the letters on one line, either up and down, across, or from corner to corner, call out Bingo!"

"Don't forget to refer to your rule charts if you need to."

"Are you ready?"

"Cover (or X out) the letters that spell the initial sound in 'ouch.' " *ou*

"Cover (or X out) the letters that spell the initial sound in 'organdy.' " *or*

"Cover (or X out) the letters that spell the final sound in 'continue.' " *ue*

"Cover (or X out) the letter that spells the final sound in 'majestic.' " *c*

"Cover (or X out) the letters that spell the initial sound in 'Chihuahua.' " *ch*

"Cover (or X out) the letters that spell the final, stable syllable in 'tradition.' " *tion*

"Cover (or X out) the letters that spell the final sound in 'plow.' " *ow*

"Cover (or X out) the letter that spells the final sound in 'cola.' " *a*

"Cover (or X out) the letter that spells the first vowel sound in 'evening.' " *e*

"Cover (or X out) the letters that spell the final sound in 'tomboy.' " *oy*

- The student should Bingo by the time all the sounds have been called out.
- Collect the tokens (or colored pencil) and the spelling sound sheet. If you used tokens and the spelling sound sheet is unmarked, keep it available for practice.

NEW LEARNING

- Write the word "told" on the chalkboard.

"How should we code this word?" *with a breve*

- Code the word with a breve: tŏld.

"Why is o coded with a breve?" *it is followed by a consonant*

- Point to "told."

"Can you read this word?"

- If the student reads the word as coded, he/she should say "tŏld" (talled).

"Have you ever heard the word 'tŏld'?" *no*

- **Note:** Most first graders will have some kind of definition for any word (real or not) that you give them.
- Erase the breve and replace it with a macron: tōld.

"Now what does it say?" *tōld*

"Have you ever heard the word 'told'?" *yes*

"This word does not follow the rules of the English language."

"English has many words where an i or an o is followed by two consonants and the vowel is long instead of short."

"There are enough of these words that they have been put in a category all by themselves. They are called 'Wild Colt' words. We will go ahead and code 'Wild Colt' words with macrons."

"Look at these words. Do you have any idea why they have that name?"

"The words 'wild' and 'colt' are examples of 'Wild Colt' words; they remind us of a wild colt because they misbehave. They also contain the letters i and o, the only two letters that act this way."

"Get out your Irregular Spelling Booklet."

"Look at the table of contents. Can you find the page that shows 'Wild Colt' words?" *page 34*

"Look at page 34. All of these words are 'Wild Colt' words. They don't follow our regular rules, so we must memorize them. If we think of some more 'Wild Colt' words during the year, we can add them to this list. For now, you can refer to this booklet any time you're spelling."

BOARDWORK

"Let's practice coding some words like the ones you'll have on your worksheet."

"The rule charts are in your Rule Book if you need to look at them."

- Write the following word and phrase (without the coding marks) on the chalkboard, one at a time. Ask the student to help you code them. The correct coding is as indicated:

bŏr´|rōw̸ ed
vc|cv

cōld lō´[tion

- Have the student determine whether each of the items coded is a word, a phrase, or a sentence.

WORKSHEET

- The student should be seated where he/she can write comfortably.
- Give the student **Worksheet 103.** Make sure the student turns to the correct side.
- Point to the word "words" at the top of the worksheet.

"We've learned that combination or makes the /or/ sound, but in this word, it makes the /er/ sound. We'll be learning more about this in a later lesson."

"If the combination makes the /er/ sound, can you read this word?" *word*

"Good! Now let's spell some 'Wild Colt' words."

"Put your finger by #1. The first word is 'wild.'"

- Hold up one finger for each sound.

"Let's spell those sounds." *w ... i ... l ... d*

- Point to a finger as the student spells each sound.

"Now spell the word again and write the letters as you say them."

- Allow time for the student to do this.

"What word did you write?" *wild*

- Repeat the procedure with #2 (colt) and #3 (sold).

"The fourth word is 'posted.' What is the root word of 'posted'?" *post*

"What is the suffix?" */ĕd/ (or suffix -ed)*

"Spell the sounds in 'posted' and write the word on the line by #4."

- Continue with #5 (child).

"Now you're ready to code and read the words on your paper."

"Using the rules we just practiced on the chalkboard, code the words by #6 through #10. After you have coded all the words, try to read them."

- Assist the student as necessary.

"Numbers 11 and 12 are questions about the paragraph just above them. If you find any words you can't read, code them. Then see if you can answer the questions."

- As the student works, provide help as needed. Help the student correct any incorrect answers. Then initial the worksheet in the space provided.
- Some time during the day, ask the student to read from the worksheet, a controlled reader, your basal reader, or other material of your choice.
- **Note:** Always make sure the worksheet is corrected before the student begins the homework. The worksheet serves as a guide to help complete the homework.

HOMEWORK

"Turn your paper over to the homework side."

"Do you know what to do on the homework paper?"

"The first thing you want to do is watch for 'Wild Colt' words. Ordinarily, you might have to try the short vowel sound and then the long one. But we know this paragraph contains many 'Wild Colt' words, so it will be a bit easier. Code any of the words you can't read."

"When you finish your paper, I will check it for you and initial it in the space provided."

- Either now or later in the day, the student should complete the homework independently (if possible). Help the student correct any incorrect answers. Then initial the homework in the space provided.
- If possible, take time to play the Kid Card games listed in Lesson 100.

Name ______________________

Teacher's Initials ____

Worksheet 103
(for use with Lesson 103)
Phonics 1

"Wild Colt" Words

1. wild
2. colt
3. sold
4. posted
5. child
6. gold
7. pint
8. auction
9. owning
10. yellow

"Wild Colt" Words

"Wild Colt" words are just like a real wild colt. No matter how hard you try to tame them, they do not do what they are supposed to. I guess (gĕs) they just have minds of their own. You can't hold them down. You can't scold them. These words must not see that they have a vowel followed by two consonants.

11. What do these words act like?
a real wild colt

12. "Wild Colt" words don't sound like they should.

P1-WS-103a

Parent's Initials ____

Homework 103
(for use with Lesson 103)
Phonics 1

"Wild Colt" Words

1. both
2. find
3. kind
4. most
5. told
6. motion
7. snow
8. follow
9. scolded
10. mind

"Wild Colt" words are bold and do not follow our short vowel rule. There are even some that follow both rules: We wind the clock but the cold wind is blowing. We can't forget about words like *sold, post, fold, grind,* and *gold*; we really need them! So I guess we will let them be the way they are ... "Wild Colt" words!

11. Write three "Wild Colt" words.
various answers

12. Write one "Wild Colt" word that follows both rules.
various answers

Parents: Your child has been taught to recognize **"Wild Colt" words** (*i* or *o* is followed by two consonants and the vowel is long instead of short, as in *wild, colt, pint, roll,* etc.).

P1-WS-103b

LESSON 104 — Digraph *oa*

lesson preparation

materials

Alphabet/Accent Deck (Section 1)
Review Decks
Spelling Sound Sheet 76
Letter Card 63
bar of soap in a sack (see *the night before*)
Picture Card 77
Sight Word Cards 57–58
Worksheet 104
Reader 38 (*The Apartment Building*)
colored pencils

the night before

- Put a bar of soap in a sack for the student to use to "discover" the new keyword.

ALPHABET ACTIVITY

"Let's work with the first Alphabet/Accent Deck again today. Stand up."

"We'll stand with our feet flat on the floor and say the first syllable in a normal voice. When we come to the accented syllable, we'll stand on our tiptoes and say it louder."

- Show the student **Alphabet/Accent Card 1.** The student should say "A" (in a normal voice with feet flat), and then "B" (louder, on tiptoes).
- Continue with **Alphabet/Accent Cards 2–25,** moving as quickly as possible.
- **Optional:** If you think the student is ready, shuffle the Alphabet/Accent Deck before the activity. Warn the student that the cards will be in random order.

REVIEW OF DECKS

- The student should be seated where he/she can write comfortably.
- Show the student **Letter Cards 1–62** in random order. The student should name the letter on each letter card.

- Review **Affix Cards 1–8.**
- Show the student **Picture Cards 1–76** in random order. The student should name the keyword and sound for each picture card.
- Review **Sight Word Cards 1–56.**
- Give the student **Spelling Sound Sheet 76.**
- Call out the sounds on **Spelling Cards 1–44** (or **45,** if used) in random order. The student should echo each sound and name the letter or letters that make the sound as he/she writes the letter(s) on the spelling sound sheet.
- Have the student put the spelling sound sheet away.

NEW LEARNING

"I'm going to say some words. Echo them back to me and listen for the sound that is the same in each word."

- Point to your mouth as you say each word.

"Echo after me. Toad." *toad* ***"Roast."*** *roast* ***"Coal."*** *coal*

"What sound do you hear that is the same in all of these words?" /ō/

"That's right. The sound you hear in all of these words is /ō/."

"Put your fingers on the front of your neck and say /ō/. See if you feel any vibration."

"Is this sound voiced or unvoiced?" *voiced*

- Write the following on the chalkboard: toad, roast, coal.

"What do you see that might be making the /ō/ sound?" *oa*

"How many sounds do you hear?" *one*

"How many letters are making that sound?" *two*

"What do you think 'oa' is?" *a digraph*

"How do we code a digraph?" *draw a line under it*

"Since digraph oa makes the /ō/ sound, we'll put a macron over the o and mark out the a."

- Code digraph *oa* in each of the words: tōad, rōast, cōal.

"Do these words need any other coding?" *yes, k-back on the c in "coal"*

- Finish coding the word "coal."

"Is digraph oa a vowel digraph or a consonant digraph?" *it is a vowel digraph because it contains two vowels*

NEW DECK CARDS

- Show the student **Letter Card 63.**

  "What do we call this?" *digraph oa*

  "I have another sack today. It contains a clue to our new keyword. Don't look in the sack, but put your hand inside and see if you can guess what is inside. Keep in mind that the object in the sack contains the /ō/ sound."

- Allow the student a chance to feel inside the sack.
- If soap is unavailable, use the following riddle:

  "This is something we use to clean ourselves in the bathtub. When you rub it between your hands, it forms lather and bubbles. It can be made in many shapes and colors but often it comes as a rectangular white bar."

  "Can you guess the new keyword?" *soap*

  "That's right. The keyword is 'soap' and the sound we have learned is /ō/."

- Show the student **Picture Card 77.**

  "The word 'soap' helps us remember the /ō/ sound that is spelled 'oa.'"

- **Note:** The digraph and its picture are also shown in the Rule Book on page 21.

  "Digraph oa is an irregular spelling for the /ō/ sound, so we won't add it to the response to our /ō/ spelling card."

  "Get out your Irregular Spelling Booklet."

  "Look in the table of contents and see if you can find the page showing words that spell the /ō/ sound with digraph oa." *page 12*

  "Turn to page 12. All of the words on page 12 use digraph oa to spell the /ō/ sound. They don't follow our regular rules, so we must memorize them."

- Allow time for the student to examine the list of words. If time permits, discuss the definition and/or pronunciation of some or all of the words.

  "Do you know any other words that belong on this list?"

- If the student offers any appropriate words, write the words on the chalkboard and have the student copy them into the booklet.

  "Look at page 13. A few words even use 'oe' to spell the /ō/ sound. There aren't very many words like this, but if you've looked everywhere else for a word that says /ō/ in the final position, try checking here."

  "Use your Irregular Spelling Booklet to help you learn how to spell with digraph oa. For now, put your booklet away and let's try to spell some words."

- **Note:** Add the new letter and picture cards to the Review Decks.

Lesson 104

Boardwork

- Write the following on the chalkboard:

  climb /klīm/ door /dor/

  "We have two new sight words today."
- Point to the first word.

  "Can you tell me what this word is? Remember, it's a sight word, so it won't follow all of our rules."
- Allow the student to try to pronounce the word. If necessary, say it for him/her.

  "This word is 'climb.' Can you use the word 'climb' in a sentence?" *expect various answers*
- Repeat with "door."
- Show the student **Sight Word Cards 57** and **58.**

  "Let's find these words on our sight word charts."
- Help the student locate the words in the Irregular Spelling Booklet.

  "We will add these cards to our sight word deck."

  "Let's practice coding some words like the ones you'll have on your worksheet."

  "The rule charts are in your Rule Book if you need to look at them."
- Write the following phrase and sentence (without the coding marks) on the chalkboard, one at a time. Ask the student to help you code them. The correct coding is as indicated:

  lōad′ing zōne

  The child pĭcked ŭp her cōat.
- **Note:** The word "child" is a "Wild Colt" word.
- Have the student determine whether each of the items coded is a word, a phrase, or a sentence.
- Add **Sight Word Cards 57** and **58** to the Sight Word Deck.

Worksheet

- The student should be seated where he/she can write comfortably.
- Give the student **Worksheet 104.** Make sure the student turns to the correct side.

  "Today, let's spell with the /ō/ sound using digraph oa. Since it does not follow our rules for spelling, I will tell you ahead of time that every /ō/ sound will be spelled with digraph oa."

  "Put your finger by #1. The first word is 'boat.'"

  "Unblend 'boat' with me." */b/ /ō/ /t/*

- Hold up one finger for each sound.

  "Let's spell those sounds. B … digraph oa … t."

- Point to a finger as the student spells each sound.

  "Now spell the word again and write the letters as you say them."

- Allow time for the student to write the word.

  "What word did you write?" *boat*

- Repeat the procedure with #2 (float), #3 (foal), #4 (coat; as you give this word, refer to **Rule Chart 3,** if necessary), and #5 (groan).

  "Now you're ready to code and read the words on your paper."

  "Code the words by #6 through #10. After you have coded all the words, try to read them."

- Assist the student as necessary.

  "Look at the picture at the bottom of the page. Write a story about what has happened in the picture. Don't worry about spelling. When you are finished, we will take time to check spelling and correct mistakes."

- As the student works, provide help as needed.
- Then have the student read the story silently and check for spelling errors. Help the student correct any mistakes. A perfect paper is not as important as the student putting his/her thoughts on paper and being able to recognize spelling errors that can be corrected (e.g., *k* and *c* spelling). Be sure to correct the rest of the worksheet as well. Then initial it in the space provided.
- Have the student read the story to you. It is important that children learn to feel comfortable speaking in front of others.
- **Note:** Always make sure the worksheet is corrected before the student begins the homework. The worksheet serves as a guide to help complete the homework.

HOMEWORK

"Turn your paper over to the homework side."

"Do you know what to do on the homework paper?"

"Watch for digraph oa. Always code suffixes and final, stable syllables before coding the rest of the word. Also, watch for words that need to be divided."

"Look at the picture at the bottom of the page. Write a story that tells what's happening in the picture."

"When you finish your paper, I will check it for you and initial it in the space provided."

- Either now or later in the day, the student should complete the homework independently (if possible). Help the student correct any incorrect answers. Then initial the homework in the space provided.

READER

"We have another new book today."

- Give the student **Reader 38 (*The Apartment Building*)** and some colored pencils.

  "Can you tell me this book's title?" *The Apartment Building*

- Assist the student as necessary as he/she constructs the book.
- When the student finishes, staple or put a rubber band around the book's spine.

  "The title of this book is _________?" *The Apartment Building*

  "I want you to read your book to yourself. When you are finished reading, color the pictures. Write your name on the book so I will know who colored it."

  "Keep your book handy because I will be asking you to read it for me."

- Some time during the day, have the student read the reader to you.
- If possible, take time to play the Kid Card games listed in Lesson 100. Try to see that the student is prepared for tomorrow's assessment.

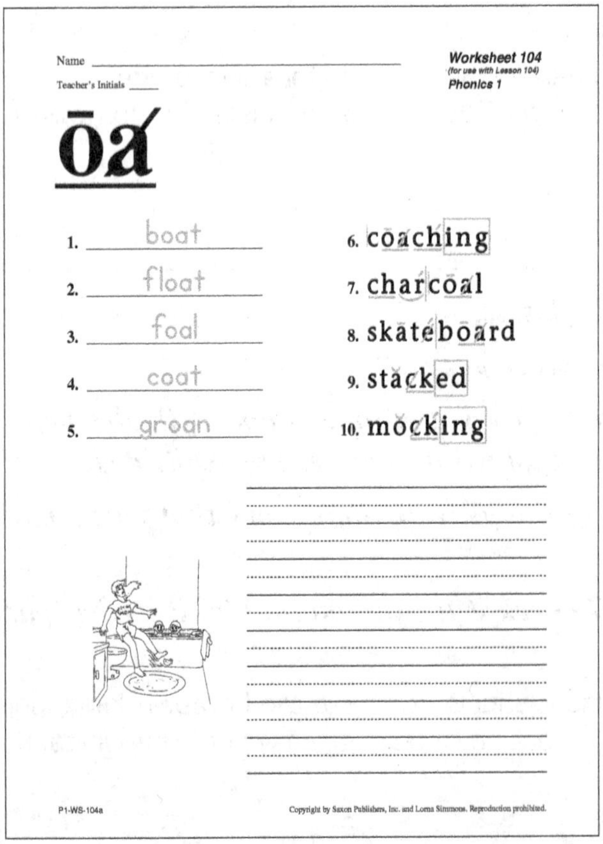
Name ______________
Teacher's Initials ____
Worksheet 104
(for use with Lesson 104)
Phonics 1

ōa

1. boat
2. float
3. foal
4. coat
5. groan

6. coaching
7. charcoal
8. skateboard
9. stacked
10. mocking

P1-WS-104a
Copyright by Saxon Publishers, Inc. and Lorna Simmons. Reproduction prohibited.

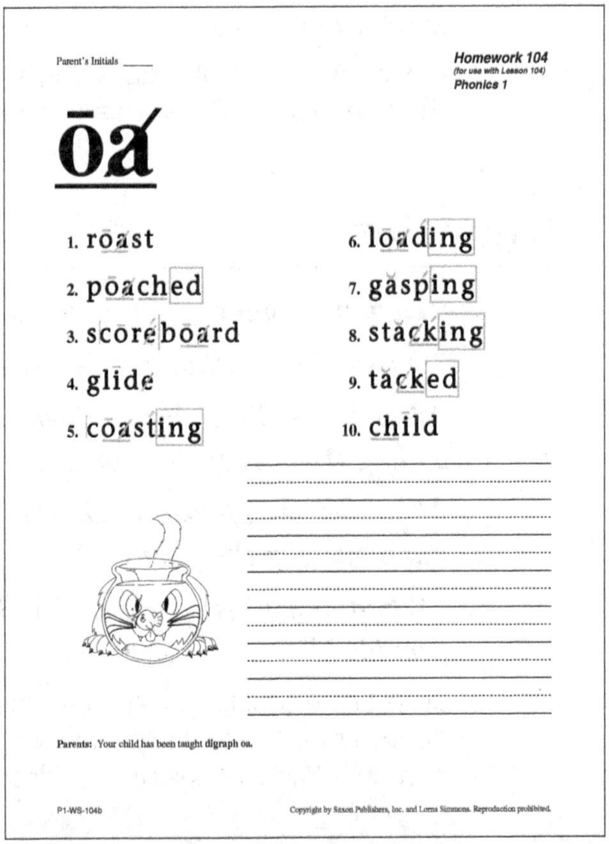
Parent's Initials ____
Homework 104
(for use with Lesson 104)
Phonics 1

ōa

1. roast
2. poached
3. scoreboard
4. glide
5. coasting

6. loading
7. gasping
8. stacking
9. tacked
10. child

Parents: Your child has been taught digraph oa.

P1-WS-104b
Copyright by Saxon Publishers, Inc. and Lorna Simmons. Reproduction prohibited.

LESSON 105 **Assessment**

lesson preparation

materials

container of letter tiles
Review Decks
Assessment 20
Spelling Test 18
Assessment 20 Recording Form
Kid Cards
tokens

the night before

- Separate the Kid Cards marked "Lesson 105."

ALPHABET ACTIVITY

- The student should be seated with the container of letter tiles.

  "Let's see how fast you can alphabetize again."

  "I want you to put your hand in your container of letter tiles."

  "When I say 'go,' I want you to pull out eight tiles and put them in alphabetical order. We are going to see how fast can get them in order."

  "Raise your hand when you have them in order."
- Time the student.

  "Ready, set, go!"
- Repeat with eight more tiles if time permits.

REVIEW OF DECKS

- The student should be seated where he/she can write comfortably.
- Show the student **Letter Cards 1–63** in random order. The student should name the letter on each letter card.
- Review **Affix Cards 1–8.**
- Show the student **Picture Cards 1–77** in random order. The student should name the keyword and sound for each picture card.
- Review **Sight Word Cards 1–58.**

WRITTEN ASSESSMENT

- Have the student sit where he/she can write comfortably.
- Give the student **Assessment 20.**
- **Section I:**

  "Today we are going to write some words for our assessment."

  "I'm going to say a word. Write the letter that makes each sound in that word on the lines by #1."

  "Look at the rule charts if you need to."

  "Here's the first word: partner."
- Repeat with the following words in the order shown: #2 (shout), #3 (now), #4 (hoping), and #5 (liked).
- **Reminder:** While the student spells, be ready to point to appropriate rule charts as necessary.
- **Section II:**

  "Look at the letters by #6."

  "Find the picture of the keyword for this sound."

  "Draw a line from the letters to the keyword."
- Repeat with #7. Allow a few minutes for the student to work.
- The pictures (from top to bottom) are as follows: cow, mouse.
- **Section III:**

  "Put your finger on #8."

  "Code the words by #8 through #12."
- Allow a few minutes for the student to work.
- **Section IV:**

  "Read the paragraph. If you find any words you can't read, code them to help you figure them out. Then answer the questions by #13 through #17."
- **Reminder:** If the student absolutely cannot read the paragraph, read it to the student to see if he or she can answer the questions.

  "When you are finished, show your paper to me."
- This paper will be used during the oral portion of the assessment.

SPELLING TEST

- Give the student **Spelling Test 18.**
- Call out the following words (in the order shown). Sound them out, if necessary.

  #1 (hiding), #2 (space), #3 (checking), #4 (farmyard), #5 (seat), #6 (teacher), #7 (year), #8 (silent), #9 (mice), #10 (order), #11 (built), #12 (build)
- Grade and record the test in any manner that suits your needs.

ORAL ASSESSMENT

- It is important to complete the oral assessment promptly (today, if possible) in order to identify any areas of weakness and begin remediation.
- Use the assessment and the following dialogue to complete the oral portion.
- **Section V:**
- Point to the sight word by #18.

  "Read this sight word for me."
- Record the student's response by placing a check mark by each word he/she reads correctly.
- Repeat with #19 through #23.
- **Section VI:**
- Show the student the letters by #24.

  "Tell me the name of these letters and the sound they make."
- Write the student's response on the adjacent line.
- Repeat with #25.

ASSESSMENT EVALUATION

- Grade the assessment and record the results on **Assessment 20 Recording Form.** Check off the boxes to indicate mastery (i.e., the section was completed with 100% accuracy).
- **Reminder:** Try to give as many points as possible for work attempted. Do not grade the coding marks too severely. The most important coding marks to look for are breves, macrons, and syllable division lines.
- See the introductory material for detailed information regarding grading and recording procedures.
- Use the assessment results to identify those skills in which the student is weak. Practice those skills by playing Kid Card games.
- Add the Kid Cards marked "Lesson 105" to the existing decks. Listed below are games appropriate for remediation in selected areas. See "Games and Activities" for the directions for each game.
- **Section I:** Play "Spelling Deck Perfection," "Sound Scamper," "Spell Out #1 or #2," or have the student use the letter tiles to spell words you give from the Spelling Word List.
- **Section II:** Play "Keyword and Sound" or "Letter/Sound Identification."
- **Section III:** Play "Chalkboard Challenge."
- **Section IV:** Either have the student read the controlled readers and then ask questions for comprehension, or play "Acting Out" with the green Kid Cards.
- **Section V:** Play "At First Sight."
- **Section VI:** Play "Letter/Sound Identification."

- When the student seems more secure in areas that had previously proven difficult, retest him/her (in those areas only) and indicate on the recording form any sections the student has subsequently mastered.
- Try to help the student achieve mastery of all the sections before the next assessment.
- If the student is having difficulty with a particular skill, keep his or her practice activities at the most basic level so the chance of success is greater.

Name ______________________

Assessment 20
(for use with Lesson 105)
Phonics 1

Section I

1. partner
2. shout
3. now
4. hoping
5. liked

Section II

6. ou
7. ow

Section III

8. owl
9. cowboy
10. lighthouse
11. mouth
12. birdhouse

Section IV

Last week my cat, Libby, had three kittens. One is black with tan feet and is a boy. The two girls are both striped. The tiny kittens snuggle up to Libby most of the time. They drink lots of milk and are getting fat. It will be fun when they can see. When they are older and can run and jump we will play together. When they get to be six weeks old, they will go to homes with people who will love them and take good care of them.

13. What is my cat's name?
Libby
14. How many kittens did she have?
three
15. How many kittens were girls?
two
16. What is making them fat?
milk

P1-A-020a

Assessment 20
(for use with Lesson 105)
Phonics 1

17. How old do they have to be to leave Libby?
six weeks old

Section V

18. through ________
19. would ________
20. sure ________
21. earth ________
22. should ________
23. father ________

Section VI

24. ou — diphthong ou, /ou/
25. ow — diphthong ow, /ou/

P1-A-020b

LESSON 106 — Digraph *ey*

lesson preparation

materials

container of letter tiles
Review Decks
Spelling Sound Sheet 77
Letter Card 64
keys in a sack (see *the night before*)
Picture Card 78
Worksheet 106
Spelling List 19

the night before

- Put some keys in a sack for the student to use to "discover" the new keyword.

ALPHABET ACTIVITY

- The student should be seated with the container of letter tiles.

  "Before we start, let's say the alphabet together so it is fresh in our minds."

- Recite the alphabet with the student.

  "Today, I'm going to let you try to put the letter tiles in alphabetical order again. When I say 'go,' dump your tiles on the desk, turn them to the capital (green) side, and begin working."

  "Ready, set, go!"

- Allow enough time for the student to complete the sequencing. Then have the student replace the tiles in the container and put it away.

REVIEW OF DECKS

- The student should be seated where he/she can write comfortably.
- Show the student **Letter Cards 1–63** in random order. The student should name the letter on each letter card.
- Review **Affix Cards 1–8.**
- Show the student **Picture Cards 1–77** in random order. The student should name the keyword and sound for each picture card.
- Review **Sight Word Cards 1–58.**

- Give the student **Spelling Sound Sheet 77.**
- Call out the sounds on **Spelling Cards 1–44** (or **45,** if used) in random order. The student should echo each sound and name the letter or letters that make the sound as he/she writes the letter(s) on the spelling sound sheet.
- Have the student put the spelling sound sheet away.

New Learning

"I'm going to say some words. Echo them back to me and listen for the sound that is the same in each word."

- Point to your mouth as you say each word.

"Echo after me. Monkey." *monkey* ***"Alley."*** *alley* ***"Trolley."*** *trolley*

"What sound do you hear that is the same in all of these words?" */ē/*

"That's right. The sound you hear in all of these words is /ē/."

"Put your fingers on the front of your neck and say /ē/. See if you feel any vibration."

"Is this sound voiced or unvoiced?" *voiced*

- Write the following on the chalkboard: monkey, alley, trolley.

"What letters do you see that might be making the /ē/ sound?" *ey*

"Where does 'ey' appear in all of these words?" *final position*

"How many sounds do you hear?" *one*

"How many letters are making that sound?" *two*

"What do you think 'ey' is?" *a digraph*

"How will we code digraph ey?" *draw a line under the letters, put a macron over the e, mark out the y*

- Code digraph *ey* in the words: monkēy̸, allēy̸, trollēy̸.

"What other coding do these words need?"

- Code the words as the student instructs:

mŏn´ | kēy̸	ăl´ | lēy̸	trŏl´ | lēy̸
v c | cv	vc | cv	vc | cv

"Is digraph ey a vowel digraph or a consonant digraph?" *a vowel digraph because e is a vowel and in this case y is acting as a vowel*

"If the letter y is making a vowel sound, where will it usually be?" *at the end of the word*

New Deck Cards

- Show the student **Letter Card 64.**

"What do we call this?" *digraph ey*

"I have another sack today. It contains a clue to our new keyword. Don't look in the sack, but put your hand inside and see if you can guess what is inside. Keep in mind that the object in the sack contains the /ē/ sound."

- Allow the student a chance to feel inside the sack.

"Can you guess the new keyword?" *key*

"That's right. The keyword is 'key' and the sound we have learned is /ē/."

- Show the student **Picture Card 78.**

"The word 'key' helps us remember the /ē/ sound that is spelled 'ey.' "

- **Note:** The digraph and its picture are also shown in the Rule Book on page 21.

"Digraph ey is an irregular spelling for the /ē/ sound, so it will not be added to the response to our /ē/ spelling card."

"Get out your Irregular Spelling Booklet."

"Look in the table of contents and see if you can find the page that shows words that spell the /ē/ sound with digraph ey." *page 7*

"Turn to page 7. All of the words on page 7 use digraph ey to spell the /ē/ sound. They don't follow our regular rules, so we must memorize them."

- Allow time for the student to examine the list of words. If time permits, discuss the definition and/or pronunciation of some or all of the words.

"Do you know any other words that belong on this list?"

- If the student offers any appropriate words, write the words on the chalkboard and have the student copy them into the booklet.

"Use your Irregular Spelling Booklet to help you learn how to spell with digraph ey. For now, put your booklet away."

- **Note:** Add the new letter and picture cards to the Review Decks.

BOARDWORK

"Let's practice coding some words like the ones you'll have on your worksheet."

"The rule charts are in your Rule Book if you need to look at them."

- Write the following sentences (without the coding marks) on the chalkboard, one at a time. Ask the student to help you code them. The correct coding is as indicated:

Kēep food ŏff the kēy′|bōard.

Hē′ filled a crā′|ter ĭn the cĕn′|ter (of) the drīve′|wāy.

- Have the student determine whether each of the items coded is a word, a phrase, or a sentence.

WORKSHEET

- The student should be seated where he/she can write comfortably.
- Give the student **Worksheet 106.** Make sure the student turns to the correct side.

"Let's spell with the /ē/ sound using digraph ey."

"Digraph ey is almost always used in the final position. If 'ey' is not in the final position, the word is probably a compound word, like 'keychain,' or has a suffix on the end, like 'keying.' "

"Since digraph ey is not regular for spelling, I will tell you that in each word we spell on the worksheet today, the /ē/ sound is spelled with digraph ey."

- When you pronounce the spelling words, make a distinct separation between syllables. The student will be more successful if he/she spells by syllables.

"Put your finger by #1. The first word is 'parsley.' "

"Spell the word and write the letters on the line by #1 as you say them."

- Allow time for the student to write the word.

"What word did you write?" *parsley*

- Repeat the procedure with #2 (barley), #3 (chimney), #4 (keyhole), and #5 (kidney).

"Now you're ready to code and read the words on your paper."

"Code the words by #6 through #10. After you have coded all the words, try to read them."

- Assist the student as necessary.

"Numbers 11 and 12 are questions about the paragraph just above them. If you find any words you can't read, code them. Then see if you can answer the questions."

- As the student works, provide help as needed. Help the student correct any incorrect answers. Then initial the worksheet in the space provided.
- Some time during the day, ask the student to read from the worksheet, a controlled reader, your basal reader, or other material of your choice.
- **Note:** Always make sure the worksheet is corrected before the student begins the homework. The worksheet serves as a guide to help complete the homework.

HOMEWORK

"Turn your paper over to the homework side."

"Do you know what to do on the homework paper?"

"Watch for digraph ey. Always code suffixes and final, stable syllables before coding the rest of the word. Also, watch for words that need to be divided."

"When you finish your paper, I will check it for you and initial it in the space provided."

- Either now or later in the day, the student should complete the homework independently (if possible). Help the student correct any incorrect answers. Then initial the homework in the space provided.

SPELLING LIST

- Fold **Spelling List 19** in half lengthwise (with the printed side facing out).

  "Leave your paper just like I give it to you."

- Give the student **Spelling List 19,** folded with the blank lines facing up.

  "Let's spell some more words."

- Call out the following words (in the order shown). Sound them out, if necessary.

  #1 (motion), #2 (action), #3 (nation), #4 (boil), #5 (point), #6 (boy), #7 (enjoy), #8 (argue), #9 (spoil), #10 (glue), #11 (people), #12 (there)

  "Now unfold your paper and check your words."

- Check the student's work to see if he/she needs extra help with spelling.

  "I want you to practice these words. We'll have a spelling test in a few days."

- If possible, take time to play the Kid Card games listed in Lesson 105.

Name ______________________

Teacher's Initials ____

Worksheet 106
(for use with Lesson 106)
Phonics 1

ēy

1. parsley
2. barley
3. chimney
4. keyhole
5. kidney
6. turkey
7. valley
8. goalkeeping
9. concerned
10. rodent

The Landreys had a day off. "Let's take a short trip to the valley," said Dad. He went to find his keys. Mom and Tommy made turkey sandwiches to take along. Vince went to get a hockey book to read on the way. It was a long time until Dad came back. When Dad came back he said, "My car is sitting in the alley, but it's locked! We can't go until we find my keychain."

11. What was missing? Dad's keychain

12. Where did they want to go? to the valley

P1-WS-106a

Parent's Initials ____

Homework 106
(for use with Lesson 106)
Phonics 1

ēy

1. donkey
2. medley
3. roam
4. creep
5. cancel
6. moment
7. soaked
8. crossroad
9. surfboard
10. oar

The Landreys started hunting for the keys. They looked through each room in the house. They checked in Dad's pockets and under the beds. Mom looked in the trash and under the pillows on the couch. Tommy and Vince went outside to look in the yard. Dotty, their dalmation puppy, was in her doghouse. Tommy and Vince could hear a jingling sound. They snuck over to see what it was. Dotty looked up surprised to see the children peeking inside. As she did, the leather keychain fell from her mouth.

11. What did Tommy and Vince hear?
a jingling sound

12. Who had the keys? Dotty the puppy

Parents: Your child has been taught digraph ey (as in *key*); and that it is usually found in the final position.

P1-WS-106b

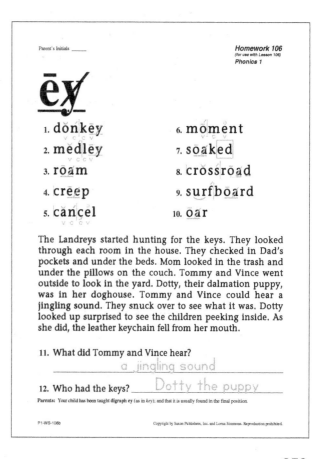

Lesson 107

The Rule vc′|v

lesson preparation

materials	new concepts
Alphabet/Accent Deck (Section 1)	vc′|v pattern
Retired Decks	
Affix Deck	
Spelling Sound Sheet 78	
Sight Word Card 59	
Worksheet 107	
Reader 39 (*Punkin Gets a Surprise*)	
colored pencils	

Alphabet Activity

"We're going to work with the first Alphabet/Accent Deck again today."

"Let's say the first syllable sitting down and with a normal voice, and then stand and say the accented syllable louder."

- Show the student **Alphabet/Accent Card 1.** The student should say "A" (sitting and in a normal voice), and then "B" (standing and louder).
- Continue with **Alphabet/Accent Cards 2–25,** moving as quickly as possible.
- **Optional:** If you think the student is ready, shuffle the Alphabet/Accent Deck before the activity. Warn the student that the cards will be in random order.

Review of Decks

- The student should be seated where he/she can write comfortably.
- Show the student the retired letter cards in random order. The student should name the letter on each letter card.
- Review **Affix Cards 1–8.**
- Show the student the retired picture cards in random order. The student should name the keyword and sound for each picture card.
- Review the retired sight word cards.
- Give the student **Spelling Sound Sheet 78.**

- Call out the sounds on the retired spelling cards in random order. The student should echo each sound and name the letter or letters that make the sound as he/she writes the letter(s) on the spelling sound sheet.
- Have the student put the spelling sound sheet away.

NEW LEARNING

- Write the word "robin" on the chalkboard.

  "What is the first thing I should do to code this word?" *look for suffixes or final, stable syllables*

  "Are there any?" *no*

  "Does this word need to be divided?" *yes, it has two vowels*

  "What should I do next?" *find the vowels*

  "Which ones are the vowels?" *o and i*

- Write small *v*'s under the vowels:

  robin
  v v

  "What is the next step?" *look between the vowels*

  "What do we have between the vowels?" *only one consonant*

- Write a small *c* under the *b*:

  robin
  vcv

  "Where do we divide a pattern like this?" *before the consonant*

- Put the dividing line between the *o* and the *b*:

  ro|bin
  v|cv

  "It's always best to try the accent on the first syllable first."

- Put an accent on the first syllable:

  ro´|bin
  v|cv

  "Let's see what we have in each syllable now."

  "How should the o be coded since it is open and accented?" *long, with a macron*

  "What should we code in the second syllable?" *code the i with a breve*

- Finish coding the word:

  rō´|bĭn
  v|cv

- Point to the *o* in the first syllable.

  "What is this long o going to say?" */ō/*

"Can you read this word the way it is coded?" *rōbin*

- If the student reads the word as "rŏbin," point out that although "rŏbin" is a word, that is not what this word is coded to say. As it is now coded, the word should be pronounced "rōbin."

"Is 'rōbin' a word we know?"

- Many first graders will tell you this (or any other non-word) is a real word. Try asking the student to explain the word, although this may prove difficult as well. (One student said he had a "rōbin" his closet!) Do what you can to explain that "rōbin" is not a word.

"I guess we need to do something different with this word. Let's rewrite it and try again."

- Write the word "robin" again beside the first coding attempt.

"Let's try dividing this word after the consonant and see what happens. We'll leave the accent on the first syllable."

- Divide the word between the *b* and the *i*. Have the student help you code the syllables:

rŏb′|ĭn
v c |v

"What does this word say now?" *robin*

"Do we know the word 'robin'?" *yes*

"Can you use the word 'robin' in a sentence?" *expect various answers*

"This is the second best way to divide a 'vcv' pattern. Try it when the first way doesn't work."

"This new pattern is shown on the syllable division chart we have in our Rule Book on page 18."

- Point to the "vc′|v" pattern on **Syllable Division Chart 3.**

"We are learning many ways to divide words. Let's try one more word with this pattern."

- Write the word "limited" on the chalkboard and repeat the coding procedure. Be sure to box the suffix first:

lĭm′|ĭt[ed]
v c |v

BOARDWORK

- Write the following on the chalkboard:

strange /strānj/

"We have a new sight word today."

- Point to the word.

"Can you tell me what this word is? Remember, it's a sight word, so it won't follow all of our rules."

- Allow the student to try to pronounce the word. If necessary, say it for him/her.

"This word is 'strange.' Can you use the word 'strange' in a sentence?" *expect various answers*

- Show the student **Sight Word Card 59.**

"Let's find this word on our sight word charts."

- Help the student locate the word in the Irregular Spelling Booklet.

"We will add this card to our sight word deck."

"Let's practice coding some words like the ones you'll have on your worksheet."

"The rule charts are in your Rule Book if you need to look at them."

- Write the following phrase and sentence (without the coding marks) on the chalkboard, one at a time. Ask the student to help you code them. The correct coding is as indicated:

å bēård´less măn

Ī´ found thə̊ cŏm´ĭc ŏn thə̊ floor.

- Have the student determine whether each of the items coded is a word, a phrase, or a sentence.
- Add **Sight Word Card 59** to the Sight Word Deck.

WORKSHEET

- The student should be seated where he/she can write comfortably.
- Give the student **Worksheet 107.** Make sure the student turns to the correct side.

"We are going to spell some words like the ones we divided today. If you spell them by syllables, they are not difficult."

- When you pronounce these words, make a distinct separation between syllables. The student will be more successful if he/she spells by syllables.

"Put your finger by #1. The first word is 'clev … er.'"

"Unblend the first syllable with me." */k/ /l/ /ĕ/ /v/*

- Remind the student to check **Rule Chart 3** for the first sound, if needed.

"Spell and write those sounds by #1."

"Unblend the second syllable with me." */er/*

"How do we spell /er/?" *combination er*

"Finish writing the word by #1."

"What word did you write?" *clever*

- Repeat the procedure with #2 (body), #3 (robin), #4 (ever), and #5 (never).

  "Now you're ready to code and read the words on your paper."

  "Code the words by #6 through #10. After you have coded all the words, try to read them."

- Assist the student as necessary.

  "Now read the word by #11. If you have trouble reading the word, code it. Then draw a line from the word to the picture it matches."

- Repeat with #12 through #14.
- As the student works, provide help as needed. Help the student correct any incorrect answers. Then initial the worksheet in the space provided.
- Some time during the day, ask the student to read from the worksheet, a controlled reader, your basal reader, or other material of your choice.
- **Note:** Always make sure the worksheet is corrected before the student begins the homework. The worksheet serves as a guide to help complete the homework.

HOMEWORK

"Turn your paper over to the homework side."

"Do you know what to do on the homework paper?"

"Watch for words with the new 'vcv' pattern. Always code suffixes and final, stable syllables before coding the rest of the word."

"When you finish your paper, I will check it for you and initial it in the space provided."

- Discuss the homework pictures to make sure the student understands the word each one represents: #11 (lily), #12 (monkey), #13 (turkey), and #14 (goldfish).
- Either now or later in the day, the student should complete the homework independently (if possible). Help the student correct any incorrect answers. Then initial the homework in the space provided.

READER

"We have another new book today."

- Give the student **Reader 39 (*Punkin Gets a Surprise*)** and some colored pencils.

  "Can you tell me this book's title?" *Punkin Gets a Surprise*

- Assist the student as necessary as he/she constructs the book.
- When the student finishes, staple or put a rubber band around the book's spine.

  "The title of this book is __________?" *Punkin Gets a Surprise*

"I want you to read your book to yourself. When you are finished reading, color the pictures. Write your name on the book so I will know who colored it."

"Keep your book handy because I will be asking you to read it for me."

- Some time during the day, have the student read the reader to you.
- If possible, take time to play the Kid Card games listed in Lesson 105.

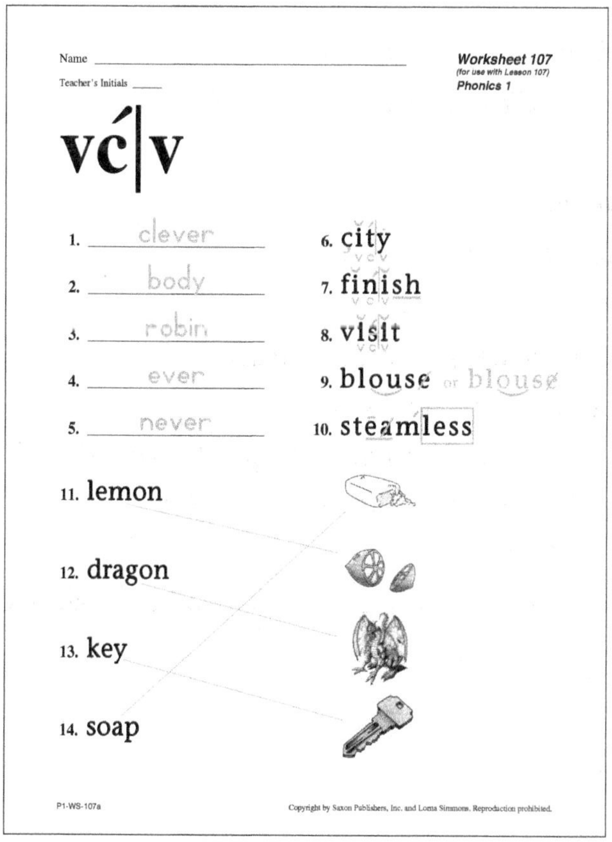

Name ______________________

Teacher's Initials ____

Worksheet 107
(for use with Lesson 107)
Phonics 1

vć|v

1. clever
2. body
3. robin
4. ever
5. never
6. city
7. finish
8. visit
9. blouse or blouse
10. steamless
11. lemon
12. dragon
13. key
14. soap

P1-WS-107a

Copyright by Saxon Publishers, Inc. and Lorna Simmons. Reproduction prohibited.

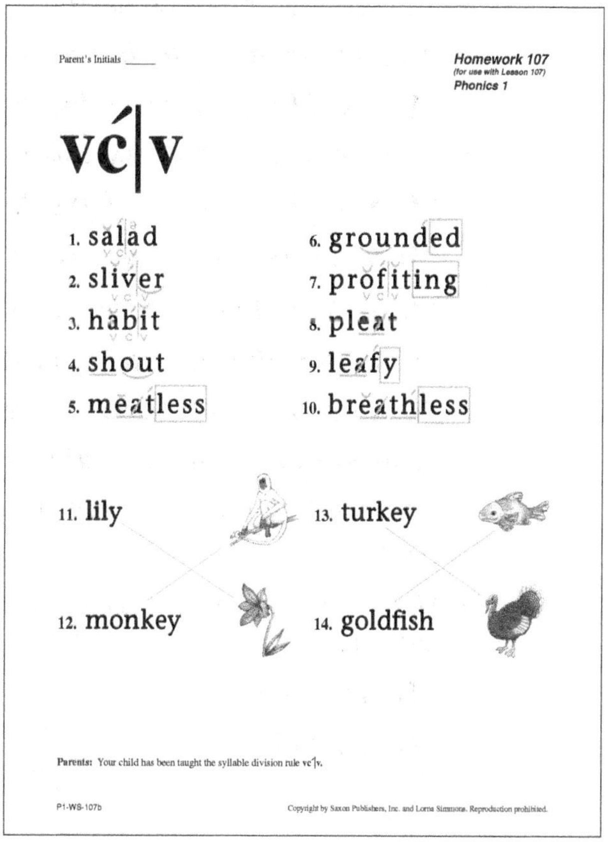

Parent's Initials ____

Homework 107
(for use with Lesson 107)
Phonics 1

vć|v

1. salad
2. sliver
3. habit
4. shout
5. meatless
6. grounded
7. profiting
8. pleat
9. leafy
10. breathless
11. lily
12. monkey
13. turkey
14. goldfish

Parents: Your child has been taught the syllable division rule vć|v.

P1-WS-107b

Copyright by Saxon Publishers, Inc. and Lorna Simmons. Reproduction prohibited.

LESSON 108 **Digraph *ph***

lesson preparation

materials

Activity Sheet 6

Review Decks

Letter Card 65

phone receiver, child's telephone, or a tape of a phone ringing (see *the night before*)

Picture Card 79

Worksheet 108

new concepts

o'clock

the night before

- Put a phone receiver or a child's telephone in a sack for the student to use to "discover" the new keyword. Or, prepare a tape recording of a phone ringing.

ALPHABET ACTIVITY

- The student should be seated.

  "We are going to alphabetize words in a list again today."

  "You will have your own list, but I will walk you through it step by step."

- Give the student **Activity Sheet 6.**

  "Look at the list on the left side of the paper."

  "Which letter will we use as our 'guide letter'?" *the first one*

  "How do we know to use that one?" *the first letter in each word is different*

  "Underline the guide letter in each of your words so you can see it."

- Allow the student time to underline the first letter in each word.

  "I want you to scan the guide letters as we slowly recite the alphabet together."

- Go through the alphabet slowly enough for the student to stay with you.

  "A."

- Have the student quickly scan the guide letters on the list with his/her eyes and index finger.

  "Is there an a?" *no*

  "Is there a b?" *yes*

"Let's put a 1 beside 'beg' and mark out the number 1 at the bottom. We will know to use a 2 by the next word."

"C." *no*

"D." *yes*

"Put a 2 beside 'drop' and mark out the number 2 at the bottom."

"E." *no*

"F." *yes*

"Put a 3 beside 'feed' and mark out the number 3 at the bottom."

"G." *no*

"H." *yes*

"Put a 4 beside 'hide' and mark out the number 4 at the bottom."

"I." *no*

"J." *yes*

"Put a 5 beside 'jump' and mark out the number 5 at the bottom."

"K." *no*

"L." *yes*

"Put a 6 beside 'list' and mark out the number 6 at the bottom."

"All of the words have been used, so we can stop."

"Try this all by yourself with the list on the right. Use the procedure we just practiced."

"Let me know if you need any help."

- Word order can be checked by using the usual procedure, but it is important that the student learns to alphabetize them correctly the first time. The correct order is 4, 2, 5, 3, 1, 6.

REVIEW OF DECKS

- The student should be seated where he/she can write comfortably.
- Show the student **Letter Cards 1–64** in random order. The student should name the letter on each letter card.
- Review **Affix Cards 1–8.**
- Show the student **Picture Cards 1–78** in random order. The student should name the keyword and sound for each picture card.
- Review **Sight Word Cards 1–59.**

"Let's review our spelling cards orally today."

- Give the sounds on **Spelling Cards 1–44** (or **45,** if used) in random order. The student should echo each response and then skywrite it.

NEW LEARNING

"I'm going to say some words. Echo them back to me and listen for the sound that is the same in the initial position of each word."

- Point to your mouth as you say each word.

"Echo after me. Phone." *phone* ***"Phonics."*** *phonics* ***"Phrase."*** *phrase*

"What sound do you hear in the initial position of these words?" */f/*

"That's right. The sound you hear in the initial position is /f/."

"Put your fingers on the front of your neck and say /f/. See if you feel any vibration."

"Is this sound voiced or unvoiced?" *unvoiced*

- Write the following on the chalkboard: phone, phonics, phrase.

"What do you see that might be making the /f/ sound?" *ph*

"How many sounds do you hear?" *one*

"How many letters are making that sound?" *two*

"What do you think 'ph' is?" *a digraph*

"How do we code a digraph?" *draw a line under it*

- Code digraph *ph* in each of the words: phone, phonics, phrase.

"Do these words need any other coding?"

- Code the words as the student instructs:

phōnę   phŏn'|ĭcs   phrāsę
vc|v

"Is digraph ph a vowel digraph or a consonant digraph?" *a consonant digraph because it contains only consonants*

NEW DECK CARDS

- Show the student **Letter Card 65.**

"What do we call this?" *digraph ph*

"I have another sack today. It contains a clue to our new keyword. Don't look in the sack, but put your hand inside and see if you can guess what is inside. Keep in mind that the object in the sack contains the /f/ sound."

- Allow the student a chance to feel inside the sack.
- If a phone is not available, use the following option:

"This is something we use to talk to someone. It makes this sound."

- Play a tape recording of a phone ringing.

"Can you guess the new keyword?" *phone*

"That's right. The keyword is 'phone' and the sound we have learned is /f/."

- Show the student **Picture Card 79.**
- **Note:** The digraph and its picture are also shown in the Rule Book on page 21.

"Digraph ph is not regular for spelling, so this response won't be added to our spelling card for the /f/ sound."

"Get out your Irregular Spelling Booklet."

"Look in the table of contents and see if you can find the page that shows words that spell the /f/ sound with digraph ph." *page 26*

"Turn to page 26. All of the words on page 26 use digraph ph to spell the /f/ sound. They don't follow our regular rules, so we must memorize them."

- Allow time for the student to examine the list of words. If time permits, discuss the definition and/or pronunciation of some or all of the words.

"Do you know any other words that belong on this list?"

- If the student offers any appropriate words, write the words on the chalkboard and have the student copy them into the booklet.

"Use your Irregular Spelling Booklet to help you learn how to spell with digraph ph. For now, put your booklet away."

- **Note:** Add the new letter and picture cards to the Review Decks.

BOARDWORK

"Let's practice coding some words like the ones you'll have on your worksheet."

"The rule charts are in your Rule Book if you need to look at them."

- Write the following sentences (without the coding marks) on the chalkboard, one at a time. Ask the student to help you code them. The correct coding is as indicated:

Lĭng căn´ | nŏt fīnd her tooth.

Kātĕ lōaned her ēar | phōnes (to) Tĕr´ | ry̆.
vc | cv

- Have the student determine whether each of the items coded is a word, a phrase, or a sentence.
- Write the word "o'clock" on the chalkboard.

"This is another contraction. Do you know what the missing letters are?"

- Allow time for the student to respond.

"This is a short cut for 'of the clock.' Let's see if we can code this word."

- Code the word as follows: o̊'clŏck.

"Can you read this word?"

- Have the student read the word and use it in a sentence.

"You'll see this word on the homework today."

Worksheet

- The student should be seated where he/she can write comfortably.
- Give the student **Worksheet 108.** Make sure the student turns to the correct side.

  "Today, let's spell with the /f/ sound using digraph ph. It is irregular for spelling, but we are going to practice some of the more common words that use digraph ph. In each of these words, the /f/ sound is spelled with digraph ph."
- When you pronounce these words, make a distinct separation between syllables. The student will be more successful if he/she spells by syllables.

  "Put your finger by #1. The first word is 'go … pher.' "

  "Unblend the first syllable with me." */g/ /ō/*

  "Now spell it and write the letters by #1 as you say them."
- Allow time for the student to write the first syllable.

  "Unblend the second syllable with me." */f/ /er/*

  "Now spell those sounds and finish writing the word."
- Allow time for the student to do this.

  "What word did you write?" ***gopher***
- Repeat the procedure with #2 (phonics), #3 (phone), #4 (dolphin), and #5 (digraph).

  "Now you're ready to code and read the words on your paper."

  "Code the words by #6 through #10. After you have coded all the words, try to read them."
- Assist the student as necessary.

  "Numbers 11 and 12 are questions about the paragraph just above them. If you find any words you can't read, code them. Then see if you can answer the questions."
- As the student works, provide help as needed. Help the student correct any incorrect answers. Then initial the worksheet in the space provided.
- Some time during the day, ask the student to read from the worksheet, a controlled reader, your basal reader, or other material of your choice.
- **Note:** Always make sure the worksheet is corrected before the student begins the homework. The worksheet serves as a guide to help complete the homework.

Homework

"Turn your paper over to the homework side."

"Do you know what to do on the homework paper?"

"Watch for digraph ph. Always code suffixes and final, stable syllables before coding the rest of the word. Also, watch for words that need to be divided."

"When you finish your paper, I will check it for you and initial it in the space provided."

- Either now or later in the day, the student should complete the homework independently (if possible). Help the student correct any incorrect answers. Then initial the homework in the space provided.
- If possible, take time to play the Kid Card games listed in Lesson 105.

Name ____________________

Teacher's Initials ____

Worksheet 108
(for use with Lesson 108)
Phonics 1

ph

1. gopher
2. phonics
3. phone
4. dolphin
5. digraph
6. orphan
7. phrase
8. toadstool
9. lash
10. molded

Our phonics class got to go to the zoo today for doing so well on our spelling test! We stayed most of the day. I loved the big, strong elephants with the long trunks. They had gophers living inside the fence with them. The best show we saw was the dolphins. They had so much talent.

11. Why did the phonics class go to the zoo?
They did well on their spelling test.

12. Who lived with the elephants? gophers

P1-WS-108a

Parent's Initials ____

Homework 108
(for use with Lesson 108)
Phonics 1

ph

1. phase
2. hole
3. topcoat
4. rush
5. hosted
6. rolled
7. side
8. bloomed
9. boasted
10. zoom

There was a male dolphin, Phil, and a female dolphin, Hazel. Hazel could speak on the phone. She looked so smart. Phil had learned his alphabet and could point to the letters the trainer named. Phil and Hazel could both jump over a rope. They had gotten a trophy for this trick. They even sang for us at the end. We had to leave at two o'clock but our teacher, Miss Jones, said that someday we could go back again.

11. Who was Hazel? a dolphin

12. What tricks could Phil do? sing, jump over a rope, point to the letters

Parents: Your child has been taught digraph ph.

P1-WS-108b

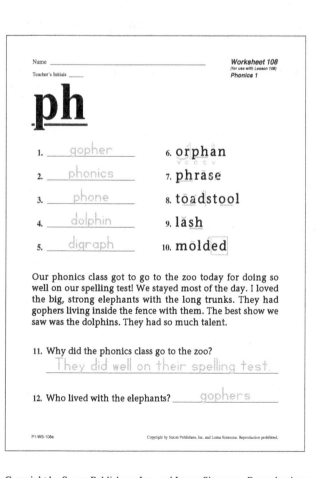

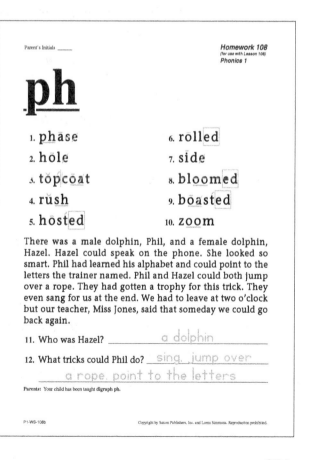

LESSON 109 — *g* That Sounds Like *j*

lesson preparation

materials

Alphabet/Accent Deck (Section 2)

Review Decks

Spelling Sound Sheet 79

Picture Card 80

Worksheet 109

Reader 40 (*Roger the Rat*)

colored pencils

ALPHABET ACTIVITY

"Let's work with the second Alphabet/Accent Deck again today."

"Stand up. We'll stand with our feet flat on the floor and say the first and third syllables in a normal voice. When we say the accented syllable, we'll jump up and say it louder."

- Show the student **Alphabet/Accent Card 1.** The student should say "A" (in a normal voice with feet flat), then "B" (louder, jumping up), and then "C" (in a normal voice with feet flat).
- Continue with **Alphabet/Accent Cards 2–24,** moving as quickly as possible.

REVIEW OF DECKS

- The student should be seated where he/she can write comfortably.
- Show the student **Letter Cards 1–65** in random order. The student should name the letter on each letter card.
- Review **Affix Cards 1–8.**
- Show the student **Picture Cards 1–79** in random order. The student should name the keyword and sound for each picture card.
- Review **Sight Word Cards 1–59.**
- Give the student **Spelling Sound Sheet 79.**

- Call out the sounds on **Spelling Cards 1–44** (or **45,** if used) in random order. The student should echo each sound and name the letter or letters that make the sound as he/she writes the letter(s) on the spelling sound sheet.
- Have the student put the spelling sound sheet away.

NEW LEARNING

"I'm going to say some words. Echo them back to me and listen for the sound that is the same in each word."

- Point to your mouth as you say each word.

"Echo after me. Giant." *giant* ***"Gentle."*** *gentle* ***"Magic."*** *magic*

"What sound do you hear that is the same in all of these words?" /j/

"That's right. The sound you hear in all of these words is /j/."

- Write the following on the chalkboard: giant, gentle, magic.

"What letter do you see that might be making the /j/ sound?" *g*

"That's right. When we had the letter g before, what sound did it make?" /g/

"The letter g also makes the /j/ sound. This kind of g is called a 'soft g,' and we code it by putting a dot on top of it so it looks like a letter j."

- Code the *g* in each of the words: ġiant, ġentle, maġic.

"So we have the same letter making two different sounds: /j/ and /g/. How do we know which sound the letter g makes in a particular word?" *expect various answers*

"Do you remember when we studied the soft c? There were three letters that acted as softeners when they appeared after the letter c. They are going to do the same thing to the letter g."

"Do you remember what the three softener letters are?" *e, i, and y*

- If you made a "softener" display in Lesson 78, refer to it now.

"So now we know that a soft g is always followed by an e, i, or y."

"Look at the words on the chalkboard. In every one of them, the g is followed by an e or an i."

"Get out your Rule Book and turn to page 11."

- Point to **Rule Chart 11** as you say the following:

"This chart will help us remember how to spell the /j/ sound. If the /j/ sound is followed by an e, i, or y, it is spelled with the letter g. If the /j/ sound is followed by an a, o, or u, it is spelled with the letter j."

NEW DECK CARDS

- Pull **Letter Card 13** and **Spelling Card 34** from the Review Decks.
- Show the student **Letter Card 13.**

  "The name of this letter is still _____?" *g*

  "Is g a vowel or a consonant?" *a consonant*

- Hold up **Picture Card 80** but keep the picture covered with your hand (or the letter card).

  "I have a card with a picture on it that begins with the /j/ sound."

  "I am going to describe it for you. See if you can guess what the picture is."

  "This is a very tall animal. It is tan with brown square-shaped spots. It eats leaves from the tops of trees. It has a very long neck."

  "I am going to count to three. When I say three, whisper what you think the new keyword is. One ... two ... three." *giraffe*

  "G is regular for spelling when it comes before e, i, and y, so we will add it to the response on our /j/ spelling card."

- Hold up **Spelling Card 34** so only you can see what is written.

  "Echo this sound: /j/." */j/*

  "Our new response to this card will be 'j comma g.' Say that with me." *j comma g*

- Write the following on the chalkboard: j, g.

  "There are some words that don't follow the rules. Let's look at them."

  "Get out your Irregular Spelling Booklet."

  "Look in the table of contents and see if you can find the page that shows words that use the irregular /g/ spelling." *page 27*

  "Turn to page 27. In all of the words on page 27, the g says its hard sound, /g/, even though it is followed by an e or i. These words don't follow our regular rules, so we must memorize them."

- Allow time for the student to examine the list of words. If time permits, discuss the definition and/or pronunciation of some or all of the words.

  "Do you know any other words that belong on this list?"

- If the student offers any appropriate words, write the words on the chalkboard and have the student copy them into the booklet.

  "Use your Irregular Spelling Booklet to help you learn how to spell with the irregular g. For now, put your booklet away."

- **Note:** Add the new picture card to the Review Deck (and re-insert **Letter Card 13** and **Spelling Card 34**).

BOARDWORK

"Let's practice coding some words like the ones you'll have on your worksheet."

"The rule charts are in your Rule Book if you need to look at them."

- Write the following phrase and sentence (without the coding marks) on the chalkboard, one at a time. Ask the student to help you code them. The correct coding is as indicated:

sĕv′|ėn pōach|ed| ĕgg|s|
vc|v

Ăn ur′|ġėnt nōte came say′|ing| (they) hăd found (some) ōld ġĕm|s|.
vc|c v

- Have the student determine whether each of the items coded is a word, a phrase, or a sentence.

WORKSHEET

- The student should be seated where he/she can write comfortably.
- Give the student **Worksheet 109.** Make sure the student turns to the correct side.

"Let's spell today using the soft g."

- Point to the words coded with a dot on the chalkboard.

"Remember that soft g will always have an e, i, or y after it."

"Put your finger by #1. The first word is 'mag ... ic.' "

"Unblend the first syllable with me." */m/ /ă/ /j/*

"The /j/ sound comes before an /ĭ/ sound, so we will use the letter g."

"Now spell it and write the letters as you say them."

- Allow time for the student to write the letters.

"Unblend the second syllable with me." */ĭ/ /k/*

- Remind the student to check **Rule Chart 4** for the final *k* sound, if needed.

"Now spell the last syllable and write it after the first one."

- Allow time for the student to finish writing the word.

"What word did you write?" *magic*

- Repeat the procedure with #2 (germ), #3 (ginger), #4 (margin), and #5 (plunger).

"Now you're ready to code and read the words on your paper."

"Code the words by #6 through #10. After you have coded all the words, try to read them."

- Assist the student as necessary.

"Look at the picture at the bottom of the page. Write a story that tells what's happening in the picture. Don't worry about spelling. When you are finished, we will take time to check spelling and correct mistakes."

- As the student works, provide help as needed.
- Then have the student read the story silently and check for spelling errors. Help the student correct any mistakes. A perfect paper is not as important as the student putting his/her thoughts on paper and being able to recognize spelling errors that can be corrected (e.g., *k* and *c* spelling). Be sure to correct the rest of the worksheet as well. Then initial it in the space provided.
- Have the student read the story to you. It is important that children learn to feel comfortable speaking in front of others.
- **Note:** Always make sure the worksheet is corrected before the student begins the homework. The worksheet serves as a guide to help complete the homework.

HOMEWORK

"Turn your paper over to the homework side."

"Do you know what to do on the homework paper?"

"Watch for soft g, suffixes, and words that need to be divided."

"Look at the picture at the bottom of the page. Tonight, write a story that tells what's happening in the picture."

"When you finish your paper, I will check it for you and initial it in the space provided."

- Either now or later in the day, the student should complete the homework independently (if possible). Help the student correct any incorrect answers. Then initial the homework in the space provided.

READER

"We have another new book today."

- Give the student **Reader 40 (*Roger the Rat*)** and some colored pencils.

"Can you tell me this book's title?" *Roger the Rat*

- Assist the student as necessary as he/she constructs the book.
- When the student finishes, staple or put a rubber band around the book's spine.

"The title of this book is __________?" *Roger the Rat*

"I want you to read your book to yourself. When you are finished reading, color the pictures. Write your name on the book so I will know who colored it."

"Keep your book handy because I will be asking you to read it for me."

- Some time during the day, have the student read the reader to you.
- If possible, take time to play the Kid Card games listed in Lesson 105. Try to see that the student is prepared for tomorrow's assessment.

Name ______________________________

Teacher's Initials _____

Worksheet 109
(for use with Lesson 109)
Phonics 1

ġ

1. magic
2. germ
3. ginger
4. margin
5. plunger
6. gĕl
7. lawyer
8. digit
9. chīld
10. roads

P1-WS-109a

Parent's Initials _____

Homework 109
(for use with Lesson 109)
Phonics 1

ġ

1. clăssic
2. stĭlt
3. outlaw
4. chŏp
5. foam
6. slĭd
7. germs
8. rōach
9. mīld
10. tragic

Parents: Your child has been taught the **soft g** (/j/); that it is always followed by an *e*, *i*, or *y*; and that it is coded by placing a dot over it.

P1-WS-109b

LESSON 110 — Assessment

lesson preparation

materials

Alphabet/Accent Deck (Section 2)

Review Decks

Assessment 21

Spelling Test 19

Assessment 21 Recording Form

Kid Cards

tokens

the night before

- Sort through the Review Decks and remove any of the following cards the student knows very well:

  Letter Deck: Final, stable syllables *-ble, -fle, -ple, -dle, -tle, -gle.*

  Picture Deck: Cards that correspond to the letter cards that are removed.

  Sight Word Deck: Cards that (based on assessment results) the student knows very well.

  Spelling Deck: Cards that correspond to the letter cards that are removed.
- Add these cards to the retired decks.
- Separate the Kid Cards marked "Lesson 110."

ALPHABET ACTIVITY

"We're going to work with the second Alphabet/Accent Deck again today."

"Let's stand up. Every time we say the accented syllable, we'll karate punch."

- Show the student **Alphabet/Accent Card 1.** The student should say "A" (in a normal voice), then "B" (as he/she punches forward), and then "C" (in a normal voice).
- Continue with **Alphabet/Accent Cards 2–24,** moving as quickly as possible.

Review of Decks

- The student should be seated where he/she can write comfortably.
- Show the student **Letter Cards 1–65** in random order. The student should name the letter on each letter card.
- Review **Affix Cards 1–8.**
- Show the student **Picture Cards 1–80** in random order. The student should name the keyword and sound for each picture card.
- Review **Sight Word Cards 1–59.**

Written Assessment

- Have the student sit where he/she can write comfortably.
- Give the student **Assessment 21.**
- **Section I:**

  "Today we are going to write some words for our assessment."

  "I'm going to say a word. Write the letter that makes each sound in that word on the lines by #1."

  "Look at the rule charts if you need to."

  "Here's the first word: faking."
- Repeat with the following words in the order shown: #2 (spoiled), #3 (rescue), #4 (lotion), and #5 (telling).
- **Reminder:** While the student spells, be ready to point to appropriate rule charts as necessary.
- **Section II:**

  "Look at the letters by #6."

  "Find the picture of the keyword for this sound."

  "Draw a line from the letters to the keyword."
- Repeat with #7 and #8. Allow a few minutes for the student to work.
- The pictures (from top to bottom) are as follows: sauce, soap, straw.
- **Section III:**

  "Put your finger on #9."

  "Code the words by #9 through #12."
- Allow a few minutes for the student to work.
- **Section IV:**

  "Read the paragraph. If you find any words you can't read, code them to help you figure them out. Then answer the questions by #13, #14, and #15."
- **Reminder:** If the student absolutely cannot read the paragraph, read it to the student to see if he or she can answer the questions.

"When you are finished, show your paper to me."

- This paper will be used during the oral portion of the assessment.

Spelling Test

- Give the student **Spelling Test 19.**
- Call out the following words (in the order shown). Sound them out, if necessary.
  #1 (nation), #2 (motion), #3 (action), #4 (glue), #5 (spoil), #6 (boy), #7 (point), #8 (enjoy), #9 (argue), #10 (boil), #11 (people), #12 (there)
- Grade and record the test in any manner that suits your needs.

Oral Assessment

- It is important to complete the oral assessment promptly (today, if possible) in order to identify any areas of weakness and begin remediation.
- Use the assessment and the following dialogue to complete the oral portion.
- **Section V:**
- Point to the sight word by #16.

  "Read this sight word for me."
- Record the student's response by placing a check mark by each word he/she reads correctly.
- Repeat with #17.
- **Section VI:**
- Show the student the letters by #18.

  "Tell me the name of these letters and the sound they make."
- Write the student's response on the adjacent line.
- Repeat with #19 and #20.
- **Section VII:**
- Show the student the coded word by #21.

  "Read this word for me."
- Write the student's response on the adjacent line.
- Repeat with #22 through #24.

Assessment Evaluation

- Grade the assessment and record the results on **Assessment 21 Recording Form.** Check off the boxes to indicate mastery (i.e., the section was completed with 100% accuracy).
- **Reminder:** Try to give as many points as possible for work attempted. Do not grade the coding marks too severely. The most important coding marks to look for are breves, macrons, and syllable division lines.

- See the introductory material for detailed information regarding grading and recording procedures.
- Use the assessment results to identify those skills in which the student is weak. Practice those skills by playing Kid Card games.
- Add the Kid Cards marked "Lesson 110" to the existing decks. Listed below are games appropriate for remediation in selected areas. See "Games and Activities" for the directions for each game.
- **Section I:** Play "Spelling Deck Perfection," "Sound Scamper," "Spell Out #1 or #2," or have the student use the letter tiles to spell words you give from the Spelling Word List.
- **Section II:** Play "Keyword and Sound" or "Letter/Sound Identification."
- **Section III:** Play "Chalkboard Challenge."
- **Section IV:** Either have the student read the controlled readers and then ask questions for comprehension, or play "Acting Out" with the green Kid Cards.
- **Section V:** Play "At First Sight."
- **Section VI:** Play "Letter/Sound Identification."
- **Section VII:** Play "Blend It."
- When the student seems more secure in areas that had previously proven difficult, retest him/her (in those areas only) and indicate on the recording form any sections the student has subsequently mastered.
- Try to help the student achieve mastery of all the sections before the next assessment.
- If the student is having difficulty with a particular skill, keep his or her practice activities at the most basic level so the chance of success is greater.

Name ______________________

Assessment 21
(for use with Lesson 110)
Phonics 1

Section I

1. faking
2. spoiled
3. rescue
4. lotion
5. telling

Section II

6. oa

7. au

8. aw

Section III

9. toast
10. goldfish
11. faucet
12. seesaw

Section IV

Amy wanted to hear a bedtime story. "What story do you want me to read?" asked Mom. "Well, I like the one about the three little pigs," said Amy. "They each build a house. One builds his house with straw, one builds his house with sticks, and the third builds his house with bricks." "That's the one with the big bad wolf (wo͝olf) who blows all the houses down except the brick house," said Mom. "You know what I'm thinking, Mom?" said Amy. "I'm glad that a wolf can't really blow a house down."

13. Who wanted to hear a bedtime story?
Amy
14. What story did Amy want her mom to read?
the three little pigs
15. With what three things did the pigs build their houses?
straw, sticks, bricks

P1-A-021a

Assessment 21
(for use with Lesson 110)
Phonics 1

Section V

16. other ________
17. climb ________

Section VI

18. oa digraph oa, /ō/
19. au digraph au, /au/
20. aw digraph aw, /au/

Section VII

21. (ĕl|ĕ|phănt) ________
22. (hĭp|pŏ|pŏt|ă|mŭs) ________
23. (gō|pher) ________
24. (ăn|tĕ|lōpe) ________

P1-A-021b

Lesson 111

Spelling with the Doubling Rule

lesson preparation

materials

container of letter tiles

Review Decks

Worksheet 111

Spelling List 20

new concepts

doubling rule

Alphabet Activity

- The student should be seated with the container of letter tiles.

  "Before we start, let's say the alphabet together so it is fresh in our minds."

- Recite the alphabet with the student.
- Give the following instructions one at a time, allowing time for the student to accomplish each task before giving the next instruction.

  "Take all of the letter tiles out of your container."

  "Flip all of the letters over so that you are looking at the lowercase letters. If they are flipped correctly, they will all be blue."

  "Now we're ready. See if you can put all your letters in alphabetical order."

- When the student has finished, continue by saying the following:

  "Pull down the letters that are always vowels."

  "Put together two letters that make a diphthong." *oi, oy, ou, ow*

  "How many other diphthongs can you make?" *three others (as listed above)*

  "Spell the word 'rag' with your letter tiles."

  "Now change the word to 'rage.' "

  "Change one letter to make the word 'cage.' "

  "Now change the word to 'cave.' "

- Have the student replace the tiles in the container and put it away.

REVIEW OF DECKS

- Let the student select a review deck (or decks) and play "teacher" with you as the student. (For the spelling card review, skywrite the letters.)

NEW LEARNING

- Write the word "sitting" on the chalkboard.

  "Look at this word. What do you see at the end?" *suffix -ing*

- Box the suffix: sitt[ing].

  "What is left after we box the suffix?" *sitt*

  "Is this the way we spell 'sit'?" *no*

  "What was done to the root word before the suffix was added?" *the final consonant was doubled (another t was added)*

  "This is a rule like the dropping rule. What kind of suffix was added to 'sitting,' a vowel suffix or a consonant suffix?" *vowel suffix*

  "This is called the doubling rule. When a vowel suffix is added to a root word that ends with one vowel and one consonant and is accented, like 'sit,' the final consonant is doubled before adding the suffix."

  "We had a special checking process for the dropping rule. We can use it on the doubling rule, too."

  "Let's try some words."

- Write the following on the chalkboard:

  ☐ ☐
  tip + ed = ________

  ☐ ☐
  jump + ing = ________

  ☐ ☐
  red + ness = ________

  ☐ ☐
  slip + ing = ________

- Point to "tip + ed = ________."

  "First we check to see if we are adding a vowel suffix. Are we?" *yes*

  "Let's put a check in the box over the suffix."

  ☐ ☑
  tip + ed = ________

  "Next, we check to see if the root word ends with one vowel, one consonant, and is accented. Does it?" *yes*

Lesson 111

"We can call this 'accented vowel-consonant' for short. We'll put a check in the box over the root word."

☑ ☑
tip + ed = ________

"If we have two checks, we have to do something. What do we do?" *double the consonant before adding the suffix*

"How will the word be spelled if we add suffix -ed to 'tip'?" *tipped*

- Write the word on the adjacent line as the student spells it.
- Point to "jump + ing = ____________."

"Help me with this word."

"Are we adding a vowel suffix?" *yes*

- Put a check in the box above the suffix.

"Does our root word end with an accented vowel-consonant?" *no*

"Do we have two checks?" *no*

"How will the word be spelled if we add suffix -ing to 'jump'?" *jumping*

- Write the word on the adjacent line as the student spells it.
- Repeat the procedure with the remaining words:

☐ ☑
jump + ing = jumping

☑ ☐
red + ness = redness

☑ ☑
slip + ing = slipping

BOARDWORK

"Let's practice coding some words like the ones you'll have on your worksheet."

"The rule charts are in your Rule Book if you need to look at them."

- Write the following sentences (without the coding marks) on the chalkboard, one at a time. Ask the student to help you code them. The correct coding is as indicated:

Ī´ ăm plănn´ing to rēad sĕv´ĕn books this sŭm´mer.

The soap slipped out of her hănd.

- As you code the word "planning," say the following:

"I know we stopped marking twin consonants a while ago. But when we're coding consonants that have been doubled by the doubling rule, let's go ahead and mark out the second consonant. That will remind us that the second consonant isn't part of the root word. It's there for a particular reason—so the suffix could be added."

- Have the student determine whether each of the items coded is a word, a phrase, or a sentence.

WORKSHEET

- The student should be seated where he/she can write comfortably.
- Give the student **Worksheet 111.** Make sure the student turns to the correct side.

"On your worksheet you'll find words written with boxes like the ones we did on the chalkboard."

"Put your finger by #1. The first root word is 'rub.' "

"Are we adding a vowel suffix?" *yes*

"Put a check in the box above it."

"Does the root word end with an accented vowel-consonant?" *yes*

"Put a check in the box above it."

"We have two checks. What should we do?" *double the final consonant (b) and add the suffix*

- Allow time for the student to write the word.

"What word did you write?" *rubbing*

"Continue with the rest of the words."

"Remember, the rule charts are in your Rule Book if you need to look at them."

- As the student works, provide help as needed. Help the student correct any incorrect answers. Then initial the worksheet in the space provided.
- Some time during the day, ask the student to read from the worksheet, a controlled reader, your basal reader, or other material of your choice.
- **Note:** Always make sure the worksheet is corrected before the student begins the homework. The worksheet serves as a guide to help complete the homework.

HOMEWORK

"Turn your paper over to the homework side."

"Do you know what to do on the homework paper?"

"Follow the procedure we've been working with today."

"When you finish your paper, I will check it for you and initial it in the space provided."

- Either now or later in the day, the student should complete the homework independently (if possible). Help the student correct any incorrect answers. Then initial the homework in the space provided.

SPELLING LIST

- Fold **Spelling List 20** in half lengthwise (with the printed side facing out).

  "Leave your paper just like I give it to you."

- Give the student **Spelling List 20,** folded with the blank lines facing up.

  "Let's spell some more words."

- Call out the following words (in the order shown). Sound them out, if necessary.

  #1 (cloud), #2 (ground), #3 (shout), #4 (subtract), #5 (empty), #6 (how), #7 (loud), #8 (cowboy), #9 (partner), #10 (lobster), #11 (love), #12 (shoe)

  "Now unfold your paper and check your words."

  "When you finish your paper, I will check it for you and initial it in the space provided."

- Either now or later in the day, the student should complete the homework independently (if possible). Help the student correct any incorrect answers. Then initial the homework in the space provided.
- If possible, take time to play the Kid Card games listed in Lesson 110.

Name ____________________

Teacher's Initials ____

Worksheet 111
(for use with Lesson 111)
Phonics 1

Doubling Rule

1. rub + ing = rubbing
2. shell + ing = shelling
3. pat + ed = patted
4. need + less = needless
5. shut + ing = shutting
6. bad + ly = badly
7. bat + ed = batted
8. sing + ing = singing
9. look + ing = looking
10. sweet + ness = sweetness

P1-WS-111a

Parent's Initials ____

Homework 111
(for use with Lesson 111)
Phonics 1

Doubling Rule

1. belt + less = beltless
2. slap + ing = slapping
3. smell + y = smelly
4. red + ness = redness
5. lap + ing = lapping
6. cook + ing = cooking
7. grant + ed = granted
8. rot + ing = rotting
9. blot + ed = blotted
10. smooth + ly = smoothly

Parents: Your child has been taught the **doubling rule:** when the final syllable of a word is accented and ends with one vowel and one consonant, double the final consonant before adding a vowel suffix.

P1-WS-111b

LESSON 112 "Ghost Letter" Digraphs

lesson preparation

materials

Alphabet/Accent Deck (Section 1)
Retired Decks
Affix Deck
Spelling Sound Sheet 80
Letter Cards 66–68
knotted rope in a sack (see *the night before*)
Picture Cards 81–83
Sight Word Cards 60–61
Worksheet 112
Reader 41 (*Carlo Is Sick*)
colored pencils

new concepts

ghost letters

the night before

- Put a knotted rope in a sack for the student to use to "discover" the new keyword.

ALPHABET ACTIVITY

"We're going to work with the first Alphabet/Accent Deck again today."

"Let's stand up. Every time we say the accented syllable, we'll karate punch."

- Show the student **Alphabet/Accent Card 1.** Have the student say "A" (softly), and then "D" (as he/she punches forward).
- Continue with **Alphabet/Accent Cards 2–25,** moving as quickly as possible.
- **Optional:** If you think the student is ready, shuffle the Alphabet/Accent Deck before the activity. Warn the student that the cards will be in random order.

REVIEW OF DECKS

- The student should be seated where he/she can write comfortably.
- Show the student the retired letter cards in random order. The student should name the letter on each letter card.
- Review **Affix Cards 1–8.**

- Show the student the retired picture cards in random order. The student should name the keyword and sound for each picture card.
- Review the retired sight word cards.
- Give the student **Spelling Sound Sheet 80.**
- Call out the sounds on the retired spelling cards in random order. The student should echo each sound and name the letter or letters that make the sound as he/she writes the letter(s) on the spelling sound sheet.
- Have the student put the spelling sound sheet away.

New Learning

"I'm going to say some words. Echo them back to me and listen for the sound that is the same in each word."

- Point to your mouth as you say each word.

"Echo after me. Knife." *knife* ***"Knee."*** *knee* ***"Knock."*** *knock*

"What sound do you hear that is the same in each of these words?" */n/*

"That's right. The sound you hear is /n/."

- Write the following on the chalkboard: knife, knee, knock.

"What letters do you see that might be making the /n/ sound?" *kn*

"Echo these words and listen for the sound that is the same in each of these words."

- Point to your mouth as you say each word.

"Echo after me. Gnat." *gnat* ***"Gnaw."*** *gnaw* ***"Gnome."*** *gnome*

"What sound do you hear that is the same in each of these words?" */n/*

- Write the following on the chalkboard: gnat, gnaw, gnome.

"What two letters do you see that might be making the /n/ sound?" *gn*

"What do all of these words have in common?" *each has a silent letter*

"These words came into our language during the time when people called 'Vikings' lived here. For us, the g is silent, but these letters were not always silent. Hundreds of years ago, people used to actually pronounce these letters very slightly. Instead of saying 'knife,' as we do, they would say 'k-nife.' "

- Say "knife," pronouncing the *k* just loudly enough for it to be heard.

"Our language has changed so that now we never pronounce g or k when they appear before the letter n. We call them 'ghost letters.' "

"This type of word is easy to read, but remembering to add the g or k when spelling makes it tricky."

"Echo these words and listen for the sound that is the same in each of these words."

- Point to your mouth as you say each word.

"Echo after me. Wrist." wrist *"Wrap."* wrap *"Wren."* wren

"What sound do you hear that is the same in each of these words?" /r/

- Write the following on the chalkboard: wrist, wrap, wren.

"What two letters do you see that might be making the /r/ sound?" wr

"The w before the r is another 'ghost' letter. You'll see it fairly often."

- Have the student read the words on the chalkboard and define them, if necessary.
- Leave the words on the chalkboard for the rest of the lesson.

" 'Kn,' 'gn,' and 'wr' are each two letters that make one sound. What must they be?" digraphs

"That's right. We call the g, k, and w 'ghost letters' to help us remember that they used to make a sound but now are silent."

"How do you think we'll code these 'ghost letter' digraphs?" underline them, mark out the letters g, k, and w

- Code the "ghost letter" digraphs in each word. Then have the student help you finish coding the words, read them, and use them in sentences.

NEW DECK CARDS

- Show the student **Letter Cards 66, 67,** and **68** (one at a time).

"What do we call this?" ghost letters kn, gn, wr (respectively)

"Today we have three keywords to help us remember our three 'ghost letter' digraphs."

"This sack contains a clue to our first new keyword. I want you to put your hand inside the sack and see if you can guess what the keyword is. Keep in mind that the object in the sack contains the /n/ sound."

- Allow the student to feel inside the sack.

"Can you guess the new keyword?" knot

"That's right. The keyword is 'knot,' and this reminds us of the /n/ sound of 'ghost letter' digraph kn."

- Show the student **Picture Card 81.**

"I have a riddle for our next keyword. This keyword also contains the /n/ sound. Listen to this riddle and see if you can guess what it is."

"These are very small bugs. They fly around your face and drive you crazy. These bugs are a type of fly. What do you think they are?" gnats

"That's right! The keyword is 'gnat,' which reminds us of the /n/ sound of 'ghost letter' digraph gn."

- Show the student **Picture Card 82.**

  "Our last new keyword today contains the /r/ sound. Listen to the riddle and see if you can guess what this is."

  "This is something you see at Christmas time. These are made with different materials, but often are made with the limbs from Christmas trees. These are round objects that some people decorate with berries or ribbons. What do you think the keyword is?" *wreath*

  "That's right! The keyword is 'wreath,' which reminds us of the /r/ sound of 'ghost letter' digraph wr."

- Show the student **Picture Card 83.**
- **Note:** The digraphs and their pictures are also shown in the Rule Book on page 21.

  "Since these are irregular spellings, we will not add them to the spelling deck."

  "Get out your Irregular Spelling Booklet."

  "Look in the table of contents and see if you can find the page that shows words spelled with 'ghost letters.' " *page 31*

  "Turn to page 31. All of the words on page 31 use 'ghost letter' digraphs to spell the words. They don't follow our regular rules, so we must memorize them."

- Allow time for the student to examine the list of words. If time permits, discuss the definition and/or pronunciation of some or all of the words.

  "Do you know any other words that belong on this list?"

- If the student offers any appropriate words, write the words on the chalkboard and have the student copy them into the booklet.

  "Use your Irregular Spelling Booklet to help you learn how to spell with 'ghost letter' digraphs. For now, put your booklet away."

- **Note:** Add the new letter and picture cards to the Review Decks.

BOARDWORK

- Write the following on the chalkboard:

  guess /gĕs/ heart /h<u>ar</u>t/

  "We have two new sight words today."

- Point to the first word.

  "Can you tell me what this word is? Remember, it's a sight word, so it won't follow all of our rules."

- Allow the student to try to pronounce the word. If necessary, say it for him/her.

  "This word is 'guess.' Can you use the word 'guess' in a sentence?" *expect various answers*

- Repeat with "heart."

- Show the student **Sight Word Cards 60** and **61.**

  "Let's find these words on our sight word charts."

- Help the student locate the words in the Irregular Spelling Booklet.

  "We will add these cards to our sight word deck."

  "Let's practice coding some words like the ones you'll have on your worksheet."

  "The rule charts are in your Rule Book if you need to look at them."

- Write the following phrases and sentence (without the coding marks) on the chalkboard one at a time. Ask the student to help you code them. The correct coding is as indicated:

A wrĕn is a bird.

gnarled ănd with′ered hănds

sŏlv′ing the rĭd′dle

- **Note:** You may need to explain that digraph *th* counts as one consonant (sound).
- Have students determine whether each of the items coded is a word, a phrase, or a sentence.
- Add **Sight Word Cards 60** and **61** to the Sight Word Deck.

WORKSHEET

- The student should be seated where he/she can write comfortably.
- Give the student **Worksheet 112.** Make sure the student turns to the correct side.

  "Today, let's spell with the dropping rule we learned a while ago. Remember, the dropping rule tells us that when we add a vowel suffix to a root word ending with silent or sneaky e, we drop the e before adding the suffix."

  "Put your finger by #1. The first word is 'hiding.'"

  "What is the root word?" *hide*

  "What is the suffix?" *-ing*

  "Do we have a vowel suffix?" *yes*

  "Does the root word 'hide' end with silent or sneaky e?" *yes*

  "What do we need to drop before spelling the word?" *the e*

  "Write the word by #1."

- Allow time for the student to write the word.

  "What word did you write?" *hiding*

- Repeat the procedure with #2 (voted), #3 (shaky), #4 (siding), and #5 (slimy).

  "Now you're ready to code and read the words on your paper."

  "Code the words by #6 through #10. After you have coded all the words, try to read them."

- Assist the student as necessary.

  "Now read the word by #11. If you have trouble reading the word, code it. Then draw a line from the word to the picture it matches."
- Repeat with #12 through #14.
- As the student works, provide help as needed. Help the student correct any incorrect answers. Then initial the worksheet in the space provided.
- Some time during the day, ask the student to read from the worksheet, a controlled reader, your basal reader, or other material of your choice.
- **Note:** Always make sure the worksheet is corrected before the student begins the homework. The worksheet serves as a guide to help complete the homework.

HOMEWORK

"Turn your paper over to the homework side."

"Do you know what to do on the homework paper?"

- Discuss the homework pictures to make sure the student understands the word each one represents: #11 (cabin), #12 (salad), #13 (phone), and #14 (box).

  "Watch for 'ghost letter' digraphs. Always code suffixes and final, stable syllables before coding the rest of the word. Also, watch for words that need to be divided."

  "When you finish your paper, I will check it for you and initial it in the space provided."
- Either now or later in the day, the student should complete the homework independently (if possible). Help the student correct any incorrect answers. Then initial the homework in the space provided.

READER

"We have another new book today."

- Give the student **Reader 41 (*Carlo Is Sick*)** and some colored pencils.

  "Can you tell me this book's title?" *Carlo Is Sick*
- Assist the student as necessary as he/she constructs the book.
- When the student finishes, staple or put a rubber band around the book's spine.

  "The title of this book is _________?" *Carlo Is Sick*

  "I want you to read your book to yourself. When you are finished reading, color the pictures. Write your name on the book so I will know who colored it."

  "Keep your book handy because I will be asking you to read it for me."
- Some time during the day, have the student read the reader to you.
- If possible, take time to play the Kid Card games listed in Lesson 110.

Name ____________________

Teacher's Initials _____

Worksheet 112
(for use with Lesson 112)
Phonics 1

kn, gn, wr

1. hiding
2. voted
3. shaky
4. siding
5. slimy
6. songwriting
7. gnawing
8. kneaded
9. wrinkle
10. campaign

11. cage 

12. river 

13. gem 

14. dolphin 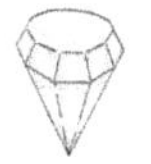

P1-WS-112a

Parent's Initials _____

Homework 112
(for use with Lesson 112)
Phonics 1

kn, gn, wr

1. knock
2. wreath
3. signing
4. toddle
5. cuddle
6. crumple
7. upstairs
8. paid
9. smeared
10. steamed

11. cabin 

12. salad 

13. phone 

14. box 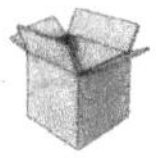

Parents: Your child has been taught the **"ghost letter" digraphs kn, gn, and wr;** and that ghost letters are letters that were originally pronounced but have become silent.

P1-WS-112b

Lesson 112

LESSON 113 Spelling with the Doubling and Dropping Rules

lesson preparation

materials

assorted items (see *the night before*)

Review Decks

Spelling Sound Sheet 81

tokens or colored pencil

Worksheet 113

the night before

- Locate a small assortment of items, each of whose name begins with a different letter. Some examples include pencils, rulers, tape, dolls, balls, crayons, etc.

ALPHABET ACTIVITY

"Today our alphabet activity is going to be really fun. We're going to alphabetize some objects again."

- Give the student 4 or 5 objects. Ask the student to identify the letter each object begins with and then put the objects in alphabetical order.
- If time permits, continue with a new group of objects after the first group is alphabetized.

REVIEW OF DECKS

- The student should be seated where he/she can write comfortably.
- Show the student **Letter Cards 1–68** in random order. The student should name the letter on each letter card.
- Review **Affix Cards 1–8.**
- Show the student **Picture Cards 1–83** in random order. The student should name the keyword and sound for each picture card.
- Review **Sight Word Cards 1–61.**
- Give the student **Spelling Sound Sheet 81** and at least twelve tokens (or a colored pencil).
- If you can use "fun" tokens, such as goldfish-shaped crackers or cereal pieces, it is much more enjoyable for the student.

"Let's play Bingo!"

"When I call out the spelling sounds, I want you to place a token on (or draw a big X in) the space that spells that sound on your spelling sound sheet."

"When you cover (or X out) all of the letters on one line, either up and down, across, or from corner to corner, call out Bingo!"

"Don't forget to refer to your rule charts if you need to."

"Are you ready?"

"Cover (or X out) the letters that spell the /au/ sound in 'fault.' " *au*

"Cover (or X out) the letters that spell the suffix meaning 'without.' " *less*

"Cover (or X out) the letters that spell the /oi/ sound in 'coin.' " *oi*

"Cover (or X out) the letters that spell the suffix meaning 'how.' " *ly*

"Cover (or X out) the letters that spell the final sound in 'flow.' " *ow*

"Cover (or X out) the letters that spell the final, stable syllable in 'motion.' " *tion*

"Cover (or X out) the letters that spell the final sound in 'annoy.' " *oy*

"Cover (or X out) the letters that spell the initial sound in 'quilting.' " *qu*

"Cover (or X out) the letters that spell the final sound in 'thaw.' " *aw*

"Cover (or X out) the letters that spell the suffix that means 'more than one' in 'bushes.' " *es*

- The student should Bingo by the time all the sounds have been called out.
- Collect the tokens (or colored pencil) and the spelling sound sheet. If you used tokens and the spelling sound sheet is unmarked, keep it available for practice.

NEW LEARNING

"When we use the dropping rule or the doubling rule to add a suffix to a word, we also use the check system to help us spell the word correctly."

"Let's work with both the dropping rule and the doubling rule today."

- Write the following on the chalkboard:

vc′ or *e*		**Vowel Suffix**		
☐		☐		
drip	+	ed	=	________
☐		☐		
trade	+	ing	=	________
☐		☐		
melt	+	ed	=	________
☐		☐		
hide	+	ing	=	________

☐		☐		
sleep	+	less	=	________
☐		☐		
fun	+	y	=	________

"Look at the first one. Are we adding a vowel suffix?" *yes*

- Put a check in the box over the suffix.

☐ ☑
drip + ed = ________

- Point to the root word.

"Does the root word end with either a silent e or an accented vowel-consonant?" *yes, accented vowel-consonant*

- Put a check in the box over the root word.

☑ ☑
drip + ed = ________

"We have two checks. We need to do something. What do we do when the word ends with the accented vowel-consonant?" *double the final consonant and add the suffix*

- Write "dripped" on the adjacent line on the chalkboard.

"What's the word?" *dripped*

"Can you give me a sentence using the word 'dripped'?" *expect various answers*

"Look at the next one. Are we adding a vowel suffix?" *yes*

- Put a check in the box over the suffix.

☐ ☑
trade + ing = ________

- Point to the root word.

"Does the root word end with either a silent e or accented vowel-consonant?" *yes, silent e*

- Put a check in the box over the root word.

☑ ☑
trade + ing = ________

"We have two checks. We need to do something. What do we do when the word ends with silent e?" *drop the silent e and add the suffix*

- Write "trading" on the adjacent line on the chalkboard.

"What's the word?" *trading*

"Can you give me a sentence using the word 'trading'?" *expect various answers*

- Repeat the procedure with the remaining words.

☐ ☑
melt + ed = melted

☑ ☑
hide + ing = hiding

☐ ☐
sleep + less = sleepless

☑ ☑
fun + y = funny

Boardwork

"Let's practice coding some words like the ones you'll have on your worksheet."

"The rule charts are in your Rule Book if you need to look at them."

- Write the following phrase and sentences (without the coding marks) on the chalkboard, one at a time. Ask the student to help you code them. The correct coding is as indicated:

fōld′ing the sheets

Ĭt seemed like a hōpe′less cause.

The phōne răng day ăf′ter day.
vc|cv

- Have the student determine whether each of the items coded is a word, a phrase, or a sentence.

Worksheet

- The student should be seated where he/she can write comfortably.
- Give the student **Worksheet 113.** Make sure the student turns to the correct side.

"On your worksheet are words written with boxes like the ones we did on the chalkboard."

"Put your finger by #1. The first root word is 'full.'"

"Are we adding a vowel suffix?" *yes*

"Does the root word end with a silent e or an accented vowel-consonant?" *no*

"We have one check. Do we need to do anything?" *no, just add the suffix to the root word*

- Allow time for the student to write the word.

"What word did you write?" *fully*

"Continue with the rest of the words and I'll check your work while you do this."

- As the student works, provide help as needed. Help the student correct any incorrect answers. Then initial the worksheet in the space provided.
- Some time during the day, ask the student to read from the worksheet, a controlled reader, your basal reader, or other material of your choice.
- **Note:** Always make sure the worksheet is corrected before the student begins the homework. The worksheet serves as a guide to help complete the homework.

HOMEWORK

"Turn your paper over to the homework side."

"Do you know what to do on the homework paper?"

"Follow the procedure we've been working with today."

"When you finish your paper, I will check it for you and initial it in the space provided."

- Either now or later in the day, the student should complete the homework independently (if possible). Help the student correct any incorrect answers. Then initial the homework in the space provided.
- If possible, take time to play the Kid Card games listed in Lesson 110.

Name ______________________

Teacher's Initials ____

Worksheet 113
(for use with Lesson 113)
Phonics 1

Doubling/Dropping

1. full + y = fully
2. slime + y = slimy
3. dig + ing = digging
4. serve + ed = served
5. tap + ing = tapping
6. plot + ed = plotted
7. soft + ness = softness
8. bake + ed = baked
9. grip + ing = gripping
10. fill + ed = filled

P1-WS-113a

Parent's Initials ____

Homework 113
(for use with Lesson 113)
Phonics 1

Doubling/Dropping

1. read + ing = reading
2. take + ing = taking
3. tumble + ed = tumbled
4. hop + ing = hopping
5. hand + y = handy
6. like + ness = likeness
7. spot + ed = spotted
8. rage + ing = raging
9. shift + less = shiftless
10. pass + ed = passed

Parents: Your child has been practicing adding suffixes according to the doubling/dropping rules.

P1-WS-113b

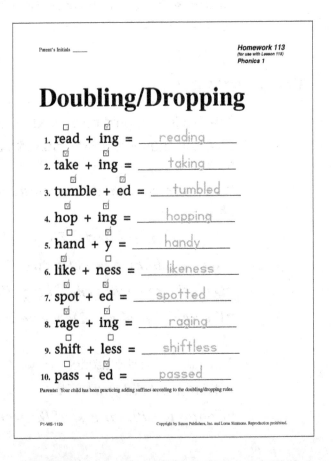

LESSON 114 The Rule v|cv′ with *e, o, u*

lesson preparation

materials

Alphabet/Accent Deck (Section 2)
Review Decks
Spelling Sound Sheet 82
Sight Word Cards 62–64
Worksheet 114
Reader 42 (*Amber at the Beach*)
colored pencils

ALPHABET ACTIVITY

"We're going to work with the second Alphabet/Accent Deck today."

"Let's stand with our feet flat and say the unaccented syllable in a normal voice. Every time we say the accented syllable, we'll stand on tiptoes and say it louder."

- Show the student **Alphabet/Accent Card 1.** The student should say "A" (in a normal voice with feet flat), then "B" (louder, on tiptoes), and then "C" (in a normal voice with feet flat).
- Continue with **Alphabet/Accent Cards 2–24,** moving as quickly as possible.

REVIEW OF DECKS

- The student should be seated where he/she can write comfortably.
- Show the student **Letter Cards 1–68** in random order. The student should name the letter on each letter card.
- Review **Affix Cards 1–8.**
- Show the student **Picture Cards 1–83** in random order. The student should name the keyword and sound for each picture card.
- Review **Sight Word Cards 1–61.**
- Give the student **Spelling Sound Sheet 82.**
- Call out the sounds on **Spelling Cards 1–44** (or **45,** if used) in random order. The student should echo each sound and name the letter or letters that make the sound as he/she writes the letter(s) on the spelling sound sheet.
- Have the student put the spelling sound sheet away.

NEW LEARNING

- Write the word "ago" on the chalkboard.

"A few weeks ago we coded a word like this."

"There are no suffixes or final, stable syllables to code."

"Do we need to divide this word?" *yes, it has two vowels*

"What are those vowels?" *a and o*

- Write small *v*'s under the vowels:

ago
v v

"What is the next step?" *look between the vowels*

"What do we have between the vowels?" *only one consonant*

- Write a small *c* under the consonant:

ago
v c v

"Let's divide before the consonant."

- Put the dividing line between the *a* and the *g* and put an accent on the second syllable:

a|go´
v|c v

"We accent this word differently. We put the accent on the second syllable instead of the first."

"What happens to this a when it is not followed by a consonant and is not accented?" *it has the schwa sound*

- Finish coding the word:

å|gō´
v|c v

"We know that this happens with the a, but what if we have an e, o, or u in the first syllable? Will it have the schwa sound, too? Let's see."

- Write the word "event" on the chalkboard.

"Are there any suffixes or final, stable syllables?" *no*

"Which letters are vowels?" *the two e's*

"What do we need to do to the two e's?" *put small v's under them*

- Write small *v*'s under the vowels:

event
v v

"How many consonants are between the vowels?" *only one consonant*

- Write a small *c* under the consonant:

event
v c v

"We will divide before the consonant, but we'll accent the last syllable."

- Put the dividing line between the *e* and the *v* and put an accent on the second syllable:

e|vent′
v|c v

"Let's try coding this word like the first one and mark the first e with a schwa."

- Put a schwa over the first *e*:

e̊|vent′
v|c v

"How is the e in the second syllable coded?" *short; with a breve*

"Why?" *it is followed by a consonant*

- Code the second *e* with a breve.

"What is the e in the first syllable going to say if it is schwa?" */ŭ/*

"Can you say this word the way it is coded?" *u … vent*

"That can't be right. This word is 'ē … vent.' When the letter e is open and unaccented, it keeps its long sound."

"Do you know what an 'event' is?" *expect various answers*

- Erase the schwa and replace it with a macron:

ē|vĕnt′
v|c v

"So e won't have the schwa sound like a did. Let's try this with the letters o and u."

- Repeat the process with "protect" and "July" to show that *o* and *u* will also retain their long sounds. (The *y* in "July" will have the /ī/ sound because the second syllable is accented.)

"So far, we have three vowel rules."

- Refer to **Rule Charts 1, 2,** and **5.**

"A vowel followed by a consonant is short; code it with a breve."

"An open, accented vowel is long; code it with a macron."

"A vowel followed by a consonant and a silent e (or sneaky e) is long; code it with a macron."

"Now we have a fourth rule. Parts of it are similar to the second rule. Here it is: When the vowels e, o, and u are open and unaccented, they keep their long sounds. When the vowel a is open and unaccented, it has the schwa sound."

- Refer to **Rule Chart 9.**

"We don't know about the vowel i yet. That will be coming soon."

"Get out your Rule Book and turn to page 18."

- Point to **Syllable Division Chart 3.** Help the student locate the "v|cv′" pattern on the chart.

"This chart helps us remember the different patterns we use for dividing longer words."

Boardwork

- Write the following on the chalkboard:

  been /bĭn/ cover /kŭv′ er/ though /thō/

  "We have three new sight words today."
- Point to the first word.

  "Can you tell me what this word is? Remember, it's a sight word, so it won't follow all of our rules."
- Allow the student to try to pronounce the word. If necessary, say it for him/her.

  "This word is 'been.' Can you use the word 'been' in a sentence?" *expect various answers*
- Repeat with the remaining words.
- Show the student **Sight Word Cards 62–64.**

  "Let's find these words on our sight word charts."
- Help the student locate the words in the Irregular Spelling Booklet.

  "We will add these cards to our sight word deck."

  "Let's practice coding some words like the ones you'll have on your worksheet."

  "The rule charts are in your Rule Book if you need to look at them."
- Write the following sentence (without the coding marks) on the chalkboard. Ask the student to help you code it. The correct coding is as indicated:

  Ā′|corns (are) tŭm′|bl|ing out (of) trēes.
  v |c v
- Add **Sight Word Cards 62–64** to the Sight Word Deck.

Worksheet

- The student should be seated where he/she can write comfortably.
- Give the student **Worksheet 114.** Make sure the student turns to the correct side.

  "Let's spell with some 'vcv' words using e, o, and u."

  "If we spell them by syllables, they will not be difficult."

  "Put your finger by #1. The first word is 'e … late.' "

  "Say the first syllable with me." */ē/*

  "Spell and write that sound by #1."

  "Unblend the second syllable with me." */l/ /ā/ /t/*

  "Finish spelling the word."

  "What word did you write?" *elate*
- Repeat the procedure with #2 (hotel), #3 (omit), #4 (protect), and #5 (superb).

  "Now you're ready to code and read the words on your paper."

"Using the rules we just practiced on the chalkboard, code the words by #6 through #10. After you have coded all the words, try to read them."

"All of the 'vcv' words will have the accent on the second syllable today."

- If the student seems to understand, let him/her code. If not, code each word with the student. Encourage independence as much as possible, but be ready to provide guidance for difficult concepts.

"Look at the picture at the bottom of the page. Write a story about the picture on the lines beside it. Don't worry about spelling. When you are finished, we will take time to check spelling and correct mistakes."

- As the student works, provide help as needed.
- Then have the student read the story silently and check for spelling errors. Help the student correct any mistakes. A perfect paper is not as important as the student putting his/her thoughts on paper and being able to recognize spelling errors that can be corrected (e.g., *k* and *c* spelling). Be sure to correct the rest of the worksheet as well. Then initial it in the space provided.
- Have the student read the story to you. It is important that children learn to feel comfortable speaking in front of others.
- **Note:** Always make sure the worksheet is corrected before the student begins the homework. The worksheet serves as a guide to help complete the homework.

HOMEWORK

"Turn your paper over to the homework side."

"Do you know what to do on the homework paper?"

"Look at the picture at the bottom of the page. Write a story about the picture on the lines beside it."

"When you finish your paper, I will check it for you and initial it in the space provided."

- Either now or later in the day, the student should complete the homework independently (if possible). Help the student correct any incorrect answers. Then initial the homework in the space provided.

READER

"We have another new book today."

- Give the student **Reader 42 (*Amber at the Beach*)** and some colored pencils.

"Can you tell me this book's title?" *Amber at the Beach*

- Assist the student as necessary as he/she constructs the book.
- When the student finishes, staple or put a rubber band around the book's spine.

"The title of this book is __________?" *Amber at the Beach*

"I want you to read your book to yourself. When you are finished reading, color the pictures. Write your name on the book so I will know who colored it."

"Keep your book handy because I will be asking you to read it for me."

- Some time during the day, have the student read the reader to you.
- If possible, take time to play the Kid Card games listed in Lesson 110. Try to see that the student is prepared for tomorrow's assessment.

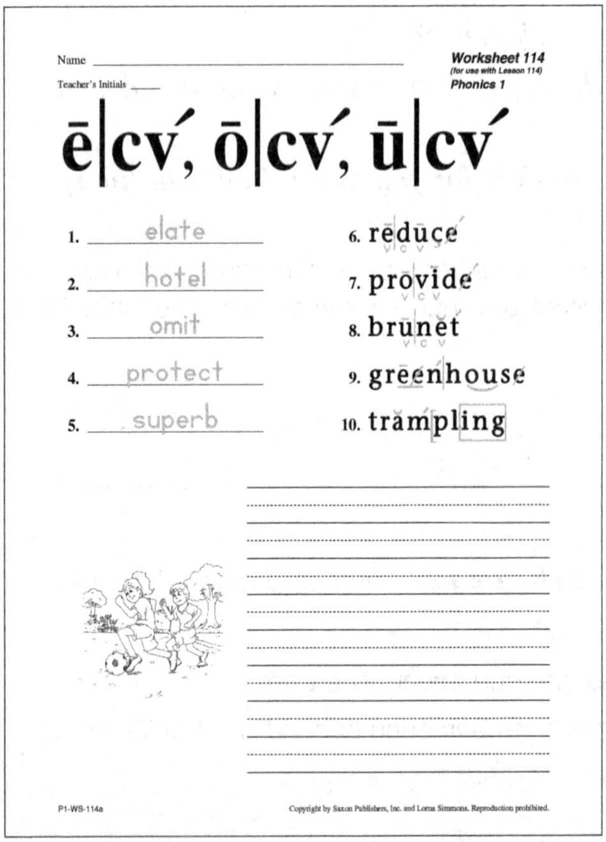
Name ______
Teacher's Initials ____
Worksheet 114
(for use with Lesson 114)
Phonics 1

ē|cv´, ō|cv´, ū|cv´

1. elate
2. hotel
3. omit
4. protect
5. superb
6. reduce
7. provide
8. brunet
9. greenhouse
10. trampling

P1-WS-114a
Copyright by Saxon Publishers, Inc. and Lorna Simmons. Reproduction prohibited.

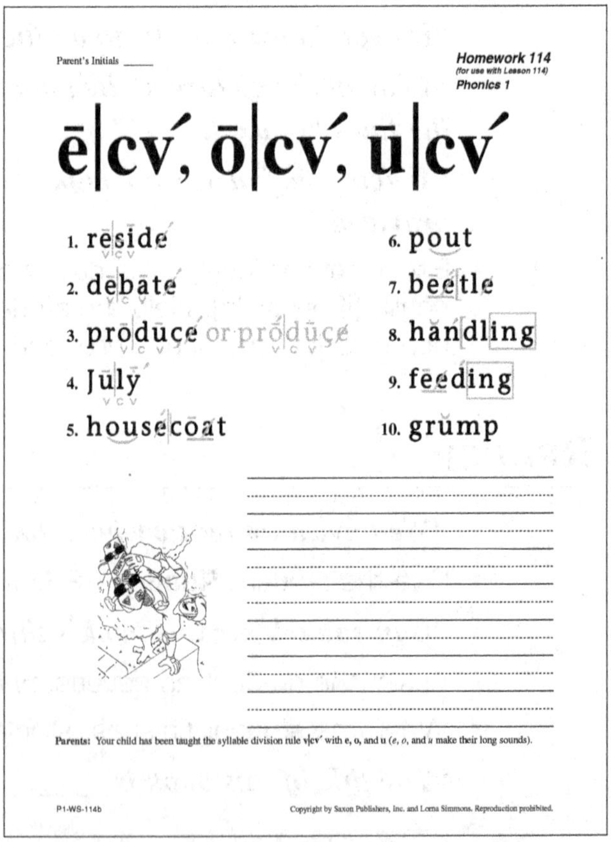
Parent's Initials ____
Homework 114
(for use with Lesson 114)
Phonics 1

ē|cv´, ō|cv´, ū|cv´

1. reside
2. debate
3. produce or produce
4. July
5. housecoat
6. pout
7. beetle
8. handling
9. feeding
10. grump

Parents: Your child has been taught the syllable division rule v|cv´ with e, o, and u (ē, ō, and ū make their long sounds).

P1-WS-114b
Copyright by Saxon Publishers, Inc. and Lorna Simmons. Reproduction prohibited.

Lesson 115 — Assessment

lesson preparation

materials

Alphabet/Accent Deck (Section 2)

Review Decks

Assessment 22

Spelling Test 20

Assessment 22 Recording Form

Kid Cards

tokens

the night before

- Separate the Kid Cards marked "Lesson 115."

Alphabet Activity

"We're going to work with the second Alphabet/Accent Deck today."

"Let's stand up. We'll stand with our feet flat on the floor and say the first and third syllables in a normal voice. When we say the accented syllable, we'll jump up and say it louder."

- Show the student **Alphabet/Accent Card 1.** The student should say "A" (in a normal voice with feet flat), then "B" (louder, jumping up), and then "C" (in a normal voice with feet flat).
- Continue with **Alphabet/Accent Cards 2–24,** moving as quickly as possible.
- **Optional:** If you think the student is ready, shuffle the Alphabet/Accent Deck before the activity. Warn the student that the cards will be in random order.

Review of Decks

- The student should be seated where he/she can write comfortably.
- Show the student **Letter Cards 1–68** in random order. The student should name the letter on each letter card.
- Review **Affix Cards 1–8.**

- Show the student **Picture Cards 1–83** in random order. The student should name the keyword and sound for each picture card.
- Review **Sight Word Cards 1–64.**

WRITTEN ASSESSMENT

- Have the student sit where he/she can write comfortably.
- Give the student **Assessment 22.**
- **Section I:**

  "Today we are going to write some words for our assessment."

  "I'm going to say a word. Write the letter that makes each sound in that word on the lines by #1."

  "Look at the rule charts if you need to."

  "Here's the first word: rattle."
- Repeat with the following words in the order shown: #2 (flying), #3 (taking), #4 (swooped), and #5 (will).
- **Reminder:** While the student spells, be ready to point to appropriate rule charts as necessary.
- **Section II:**

  "Look at the letter by #6."

  "Find the picture of the keyword for this sound."

  "Draw a line from the letter to the keyword."
- Repeat with #7 and #8. Allow a few minutes for the student to work.
- The pictures (from top to bottom) are as follows: key, phone, giraffe.
- **Section III:**

  "Put your finger on #9."

  "Code the words by #9 through #12."
- Allow a few minutes for the student to work.
- **Section IV:**

  "Read the paragraph. If you find any words you can't read, code them to help you figure them out. Then answer the questions by #13 through #17."
- **Reminder:** If the student absolutely cannot read the paragraph, read it to the student to see if he or she can answer the questions.

  "When you are finished, show your paper to me."
- This paper will be used during the oral portion of the assessment.

SPELLING TEST

- Give the student **Spelling Test 20.**
- Call out the following words (in the order shown). Sound them out, if necessary.

  #1 (empty), #2 (cowboy), #3 (cloud), #4 (subtract), #5 (shout), #6 (how), #7 (loud), #8 (ground), #9 (lobster), #10 (partner), #11 (shoe), #12 (love)
- Grade and record the test in any manner that suits your needs.

ORAL ASSESSMENT

- It is important to complete the oral assessment promptly (today, if possible) in order to identify any areas of weakness and begin remediation.
- Use the assessment and the following dialogue to complete the oral portion.
- **Section V:**
- Point to the sight word by #18.

  "Read this sight word for me."
- Record the student's response by placing a check mark by each word he/she reads correctly.
- Repeat with #19 and #20.
- **Section VI:**
- Show the student the letter by #21.

  "Tell me the name of this letter and the sounds it makes."
- Write the student's response on the adjacent line.
- Repeat with #22 and #23.

ASSESSMENT EVALUATION

- Grade the assessment and record the results on **Assessment 22 Recording Form.** Check off the boxes to indicate mastery (i.e., the section was completed with 100% accuracy).
- **Reminder:** Try to give as many points as possible for work attempted. Do not grade the coding marks too severely. The most important coding marks to look for are breves, macrons, and syllable division lines.
- See the introductory material for detailed information regarding grading and recording procedures.
- Use the assessment results to identify those skills in which the student is weak. Practice those skills by playing Kid Card games.
- Add the Kid Cards marked "Lesson 115" to the existing decks. Listed on the following page are games appropriate for remediation in selected areas. See "Games and Activities" for the directions for each game.

- **Section I:** Play "Spelling Deck Perfection," "Sound Scamper," "Spell Out #1 or #2," or have the student use the letter tiles to spell words you give from the Spelling Word List.
- **Section II:** Play "Keyword and Sound" or "Letter/Sound Identification."
- **Section III:** Play "Chalkboard Challenge."
- **Section IV:** Either have the student read the controlled readers and then ask questions for comprehension, or play "Acting Out" with the green Kid Cards.
- **Section V:** Play "At First Sight."
- **Section VI:** Play "Letter/Sound Identification."
- When the student seems more secure in areas that had previously proven difficult, retest him/her (in those areas only) and indicate on the recording form any sections the student has subsequently mastered.
- Try to help the student achieve mastery of all the sections before the next assessment.
- If the student is having difficulty with a particular skill, keep his or her practice activities at the most basic level so the chance of success is greater.

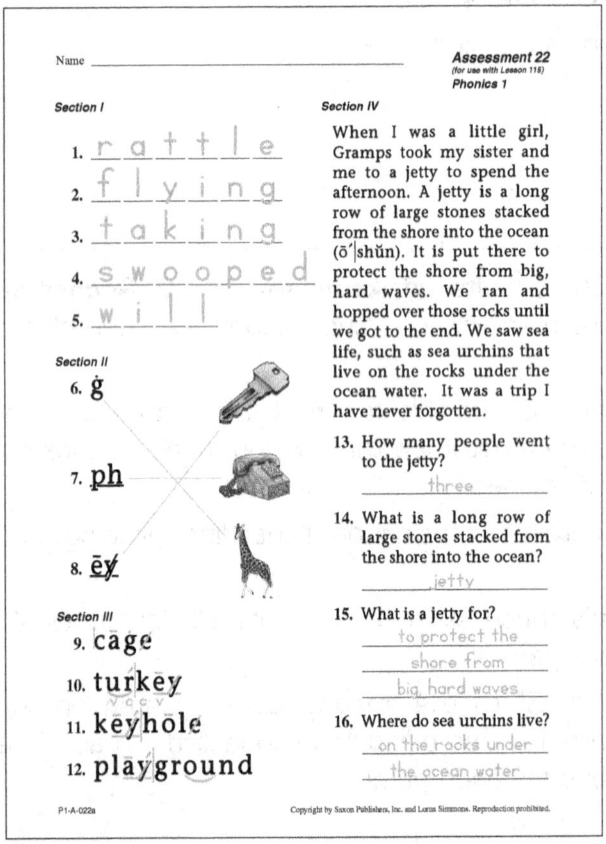
Name ____________

Assessment 22
(for use with Lesson 115)
Phonics 1

Section I

1. r a t t l e
2. f l y i n g
3. t a k i n g
4. s w o o p e d
5. w i l l

Section II

6. ġ
7. ph
8. ēy

Section III

9. cāge
10. turkey
11. keyhōle
12. playground

Section IV

When I was a little girl, Gramps took my sister and me to a jetty to spend the afternoon. A jetty is a long row of large stones stacked from the shore into the ocean (ō′|shŭn). It is put there to protect the shore from big, hard waves. We ran and hopped over those rocks until we got to the end. We saw sea life, such as sea urchins that live on the rocks under the ocean water. It was a trip I have never forgotten.

13. How many people went to the jetty?
three
14. What is a long row of large stones stacked from the shore into the ocean?
jetty
15. What is a jetty for?
to protect the shore from big, hard waves
16. Where do sea urchins live?
on the rocks under the ocean water

P1-A-022a

Copyright by Saxon Publishers, Inc. and Lorna Simmons. Reproduction prohibited.

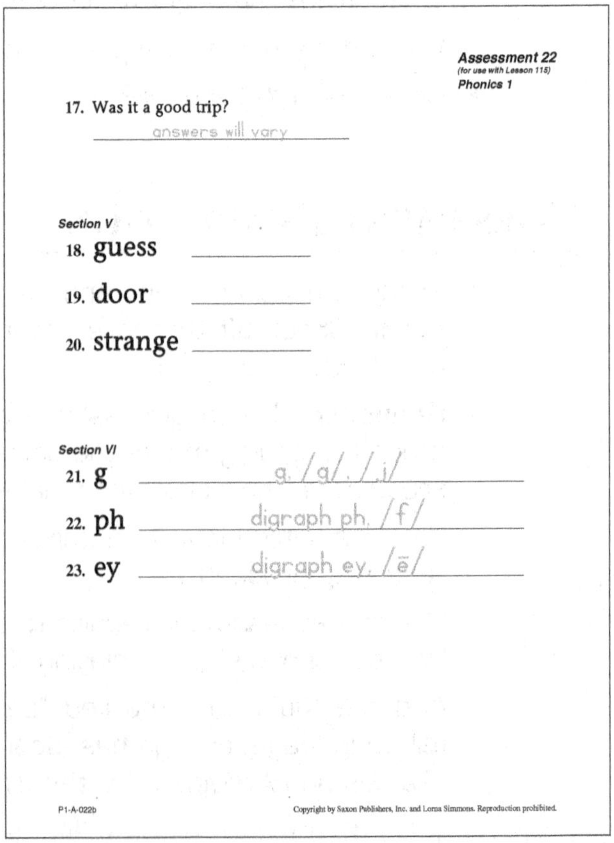
Assessment 22
(for use with Lesson 115)
Phonics 1

17. Was it a good trip?
answers will vary

Section V

18. guess ______
19. door ______
20. strange ______

Section VI

21. g   g, /g/, /j/
22. ph   digraph ph, /f/
23. ey   digraph ey, /ē/

P1-A-022b

Copyright by Saxon Publishers, Inc. and Lorna Simmons. Reproduction prohibited.

LESSON 116 Trigraph *tch*

lesson preparation

materials

container of letter tiles

Review Decks

Letter Card 69

a patch in a sack (see *the night before*)

Picture Card 84

Sight Word Card 65

Worksheet 116

Spelling List 21

the night before

- Buy or make a "patch." Put the patch in a sack for the student to use to "discover" the new keyword.

ALPHABET ACTIVITY

- The student should be seated with the container of letter tiles.

  "Before we start, let's say the alphabet together so it is fresh in our minds."

- Recite the alphabet with the student.

  "Today, I'm going to let you try to put the letter tiles in alphabetical order again. When I say 'go,' dump your tiles on the desk, turn them to the capital letter (green) side, and begin working."

  "Ready, set, go!"

- Allow enough time for the student to complete the sequencing. Then have the student replace the tiles in the container and put it away.

REVIEW OF DECKS

- Let the student select a review deck (or decks) and play "teacher" with you as the student. (For the spelling card review, skywrite the letters.)

NEW LEARNING

"I'm going to say some words. Echo them back to me and listen for the sound that is the same at the end of each word."

- Point to your mouth as you say each word.

"Echo after me. Patch." *patch* ***"Catch."*** *catch* ***"Itch."*** *itch*

"What sound do you hear at the end of these words?" */ch/*

"That's right. The sound you hear is /ch/."

"Put your fingers on the front of your neck and say /ch/. See if you feel any vibration."

"Is this sound voiced or unvoiced?" *unvoiced*

- Write the following on the chalkboard: patch, catch, itch.

"What letters do you see that might be making the /ch/ sound?" *tch*

"How many sounds do you hear?" *one*

"How many letters are making that sound?" *three*

"We had one of these before. Do you remember what this is called?" *trigraph*

"What was the name of the trigraph we learned?" *trigraph igh*

"How do you think we will code this trigraph?" *underline it*

"Can you hear the t?" *no*

"How should we code the t?" *mark it out*

- Code trigraph *tch* in each of the words: patch, catch, itch.

"Does this trigraph make a vowel sound or a consonant sound?" *consonant*

"Help me finish coding these words."

- Finish coding the words: pătch, cătch, ĭtch.

"Look at these words. What always comes before trigraph tch?" *a short vowel*

" 'Tch' is a great trigraph to use for spelling because it almost always comes after a short vowel sound, as in 'ditch,' 'batch,' and 'hutch.' "

- **Note:** "Such" and "much" are two exceptions, but there are few others.
- Write the following on the chalkboard: bunch, pouch.

"Look at these words. How is the final /ch/ sound spelled?" *ch*

"So now we have a rule for spelling with the final /ch/ sound. This rule works most of the time."

"Get out your Rule Book and turn to page 12."

- Point to **Rule Chart 12** as you say the following:

"What do we use after a short vowel?" *trigraph tch*

"What do we use after a consonant or two adjacent vowels?" *digraph ch*

"Refer to this chart when you need help spelling the /ch/ sound."

New Deck Cards

- Pull **Spelling Card 39** from the Review Deck.
- Show the student **Letter Card 69.**

  "What do we call this?" *trigraph tch*

  "I have another sack today. It contains a clue to our new keyword. Don't look in the sack, but put your hand inside and see if you can guess what is inside. Keep in mind that the object in the sack contains the /ch/ sound."
- Allow the student a chance to feel inside the sack. Since "patch" is not a word that is common with first graders, it might help to give some clues.

  "Can you guess the new keyword?" *patch*

  "That's right. The keyword is 'patch.' "
- Show the student **Picture Card 84.**

  "The word 'patch' helps us remember the /ch/ sound spelled with trigraph tch."
- **Note:** The trigraph and its picture are also shown in the Rule Book on page 22.
- Hold up **Spelling Card 39** so only you can see what is written.
- Follow the instructions on the card and have the student write the answer with his/her finger on the desktop.
- **Note:** Add the new letter and picture cards to the Review Decks (and re-insert **Spelling Card 39**).

Boardwork

- Write the following on the chalkboard:

  certain /ser´ tən/

  "We have a new sight word today."
- Point to the word.

  "Can you tell me what this word is? Remember, it's a sight word, so it won't follow all of our rules."
- Allow the student to try to pronounce the word. If necessary, say it for him/her.

  "This word is 'certain.' Can you use the word 'certain' in a sentence?" *expect various answers*
- Show the student **Sight Word Card 65.**

  "Let's find this word on our sight word charts."
- Help the student locate the word in the Irregular Spelling Booklet.

  "We will add this card to our sight word deck."

  "Let's practice coding some words like the ones you'll have on your worksheet."

  "The rule charts are in your Rule Book if you need to look at them."

- Write the following phrase and sentence (without the coding marks) on the chalkboard, one at a time. Ask the student to help you code them. The correct coding is as indicated:

reach´ing for a spoon

He´ towed the life´boat o´ver the ditch.

- Have the student determine whether each of the items coded is a word, a phrase, or a sentence.
- Add **Sight Word Card 65** to the Sight Word Deck.

WORKSHEET

- The student should be seated where he/she can write comfortably.
- Give the student **Worksheet 116.** Make sure the student turns to the correct side.

"Today, let's spell with the /ch/ sound using trigraph tch."

"Trigraph tch is used for spelling in the final position after a short vowel sound. There are many words that fit this pattern. Listen for the short vowel sound."

"Put your finger by #1. The first word is 'hatch.' "

"Unblend 'hatch' with me." */h/ /ă/ /ch/*

- Hold up one finger for each sound.

"Is there a short vowel sound?" *yes*

"How do we spell /ch/ after a short vowel sound?" *tch*

"Let's spell those sounds." *h … a … trigraph tch*

- Point to a finger as the student spells each sound.

"Now spell the word again and write the letters as you say them."

- Allow time for the student to write the word.

"What word did you write?" *hatch*

- Repeat the procedure with #2 (crutch), #3 (itch), #4 (scratch), and #5 (stretch).

"Now you're ready to code and read the words on your paper."

"Code the words by #6 through #10. After you have coded all the words, try to read them."

- Assist the student as necessary.

"Numbers 11 and 12 are questions about the paragraph just above them. If you find any words you can't read, code them. Then see if you can answer the questions."

- As the student works, provide help as needed. Help the student correct any incorrect answers. Then initial the worksheet in the space provided.

- Some time during the day, ask the student to read from the worksheet, a controlled reader, your basal reader, or other material of your choice.
- **Note:** Always make sure the worksheet is corrected before the student begins the homework. The worksheet serves as a guide to help complete the homework.

HOMEWORK

"Turn your paper over to the homework side."

"Do you know what to do on the homework paper?"

"Watch for trigraph tch. Always code suffixes and final, stable syllables before coding the rest of the word. Also, watch for words that need to be divided."

"When you finish your paper, I will check it for you and initial it in the space provided."

- Either now or later in the day, the student should complete the homework independently (if possible). Help the student correct any incorrect answers. Then initial the homework in the space provided.

SPELLING LIST

- Fold **Spelling List 21** in half lengthwise (with the printed side facing out).

"Leave your paper just like I give it to you."

- Give the student **Spelling List 21,** folded with the blank lines facing up.

"Let's spell some more words."

- Call out the following words (in the order shown). Sound them out, if necessary.

  #1 (pumpkin), #2 (show), #3 (proudly), #4 (foundation), #5 (crumple), #6 (September), #7 (making), #8 (serving), #9 (playground), #10 (portion), #11 (full), #12 (pull)

"Now unfold your paper and check your words."

- Check the student's work to see if he/she needs extra help with spelling.

"I want you to practice these words. We'll have a spelling test in a few days."

- If possible, take time to play the Kid Card games listed in Lesson 115.

Name ______________________

Teacher's Initials ____

Worksheet 116
(for use with Lesson 116)
Phonics 1

tch

1. hatch
2. crutch
3. itch
4. scratch
5. stretch
6. twitching
7. switchboard
8. stretch
9. scowled
10. teaspoon

Matt and Mitch play on a team named the Sluggers. Matt is a pitcher and can throw an excellent curve pitch. Mitch is the team's catcher. He rarely misses a pitch. Sometimes they switch places just for fun. Both boys can run really fast. They make home runs when they get hard hits.

11. What is the name of the team?

the Sluggers

12. What happens when they get hard hits?

They make home runs.

P1-WS-116a

Parent's Initials ____

Homework 116
(for use with Lesson 116)
Phonics 1

tch

1. ditch
2. switching
3. patch
4. stretching
5. coast
6. loading
7. drown
8. preaching
9. grooming
10. scoop

The team plays on a patch of ground near a deep ditch that attracts chiggers. In the springtime of the year, the boys itch and scratch from all the chigger bites they get playing on that lot. Many of their hits go into the nearby ditch if the boys can't catch them. They have been trying hard this year to be the best. If they play well this year, they are certain to win the round robin.

11. What makes the boys itch? chigger bites

12. Where do their hits go if the boys can't catch them?

into the nearby ditch

Parents: Your child has been taught **trigraph tch**; that it usually follows a short vowel; and that it is usually found in the final position.

P1-WS-116b

Lesson 116

LESSON 117 — Trigraph *dge*

lesson preparation

materials

Alphabet/Accent Deck (Section 2)
Retired Decks
Affix Deck
Spelling Sound Sheet 83
Letter Card 70
Picture Card 85
Sight Word Card 66
Worksheet 117
Reader 43 (*Butterscotch*)
colored pencils

ALPHABET ACTIVITY

"We're going to work with the second Alphabet/Accent Deck again today."

"Let's sit and say the first and third syllables in a normal voice. Every time we say the accented syllable, we'll stand and say it louder, longer, and higher."

- Show the student **Alphabet/Accent Card 1.** The student should say "A" (seated, in a normal voice), then "B" (standing, in a louder, longer, and higher voice), and then "C" (seated, in a normal voice).
- Continue with **Alphabet/Accent Cards 2–24,** moving as quickly as possible.

REVIEW OF DECKS

- The student should be seated where he/she can write comfortably.
- Show the student the retired letter cards in random order. The student should name the letter on each letter card.
- Review **Affix Cards 1–8.**
- Show the student the retired picture cards in random order. The student should name the keyword and sound for each picture card.
- Review the retired sight word cards.

- Give the student **Spelling Sound Sheet 83.**
- Call out the sounds on the retired spelling cards in random order. The student should echo each sound and name the letter or letters that make the sound as he/she writes the letter(s) on the spelling sound sheet.
- Have the student set the spelling sound sheet aside for use later in the lesson.

NEW LEARNING

"I'm going to say some words. Echo them back to me and listen for the sound that is the same at the end of each word."

- Point to your mouth as you say each word.

"Echo after me. Fudge." *fudge* ***"Badge."*** *badge* ***"Edge."*** *edge*

"What sound do you hear at the end of these words?" */j/*

"That's right. The sound you hear is /j/."

"Put your fingers on the front of your neck and say /j/. See if you feel any vibration."

"Is this sound voiced or unvoiced?" *voiced*

- Write the following on the chalkboard: fudge, badge, edge.

"What do you see that might be making the /j/ sound?" *dge*

"What do you think this is called?" *trigraph dge*

"Why is it called a trigraph?" *the three letters make one sound*

"How do you think we will code this trigraph?" *underline it*

"Can you hear the d?" *no*

"How should we code it?" *mark it out*

"Can you hear the e?" *no*

"How should we code it?" *mark it out*

"Does the g make its hard or soft sound?" *soft sound*

"How should we code it?" *put a dot on it*

- Code trigraph *dge* in each of the words: fu~~d~~ġ~~e~~, ba~~d~~ġ~~e~~, e~~d~~ġ~~e~~.

"Does the trigraph make a vowel sound or a consonant sound?" *consonant sound*

"Help me code these words."

- Code the words: fŭ~~d~~ġ~~e~~, bă~~d~~ġ~~e~~, ĕ~~d~~ġ~~e~~.

"Look at these words. Do you notice anything special that comes before 'dge' in each word?" *a short vowel*

" 'Dge' is easy to use for spelling because it almost always comes after a short vowel sound."

- Write the following on the chalkboard: bulge, hinge, cage.

"Look at these words. How is the /j/ sound spelled?" *ge*

"Why is there an e following the g?" *to keep the g soft (e is a softener); the e on "cage" is also a sneaky e*

"There is a rule for spelling the final /j/ sound that works most of the time. It tells us to use 'dge' after what?" *a short vowel*

- Point to the words "bulge," "hinge," and "cage."

"Let's code these words before we look at our new spelling rule."

- Code the words as the student instructs:

bŭlgé hĭngé cāgé

"What do we use after long vowels or after consonants?" *ge*

"We have a new rule chart for spelling with the final /j/ sound."

"Get out your Rule Book and turn to page 13."

- Point to **Rule Chart 13** as you ask the following:

"What do we use after a short vowel?" *dge*

"What do we use after anything else?" *ge*

"Refer to this chart when you need help spelling the final /j/ sound."

NEW DECK CARDS

- Pull **Spelling Card 34** from the Review Deck.
- Show the student **Letter Card 70.**

"What do we call this?" *trigraph dge*

"I have a riddle that describes our new keyword for trigraph dge. Listen to the riddle and see if you can guess what it is."

"This is something you can walk or drive on in order to cross a river or lake. Some of these are long, and some of these are short. Can you guess the new keyword?" *bridge*

- Show the student **Picture Card 85.**

"The word 'bridge' helps us remember the /j/ sound made by trigraph dge."

- **Note:** The trigraph and its picture are also shown in the Rule Book on page 22.

"We'll add trigraph dge to our spelling card for the /j/ sound because it's used a lot to spell the /j/ sound in the final position."

"Find your spelling sound sheet. Put your finger on the next free line."

- Hold up **Spelling Card 34** so only you can see what is written.
- Follow the instructions on the card and have the student write the new response on the spelling sound sheet.
- Have the student put the spelling sound sheet away.
- **Note:** Add the new letter and picture cards to the Review Decks (and re-insert **Spelling Card 34**).

Boardwork

- Write the following on the chalkboard:

heard /herd/

"We have a new sight word today."

- Point to the word.

"Can you tell me what this word is? Remember, it's a sight word, so it won't follow all of our rules."

- Allow the student to try to pronounce the word. If necessary, say it for him/her.

"This word is 'heard.' Can you use the word 'heard' in a sentence?" *expect various answers*

- If desired, discuss the difference between "heard" and "herd."
- Show the student **Sight Word Card 66.**

"Let's find this word on our sight word charts."

- Help the student locate the word in the Irregular Spelling Booklet.

"We will add this card to our sight word deck."

"Let's practice coding some words like the ones you'll have on your worksheet."

"The rule charts are in your Rule Book if you need to look at them."

- Write the following sentences (without the coding marks) on the chalkboard, one at a time. Ask the student to help you code them. The correct coding is as indicated:

Ē|rāse´ the bōard.
v|c v

Bē´ (sure) (to) chěck the trēe´|house lědge for lēav|es.

- Have the student determine whether each of the items coded is a word, a phrase, or a sentence.
- Add **Sight Word Card 66** to the Sight Word Deck.

Worksheet

- The student should be seated where he/she can write comfortably.
- Give the student **Worksheet 117.** Make sure the student turns to the correct side.

"Let's spell with the /j/ sound using trigraph dge today."

"Trigraph dge is only used for spelling in the final position after a short vowel sound, but there are many words that fit this pattern. Listen for that short vowel sound."

"Put your finger by #1. The first word is 'judge.'"

"Unblend 'judge' with me." */j/ /ŭ/ /j/*

- Hold up one finger for each sound.

"Is there a short vowel sound?" *yes*

"How do we spell /j/ after a short vowel sound?" *dge*

"Let's spell those sounds." *j … u … trigraph dge*

- Point to a finger as the student spells each sound.

"Now spell the word again and write the letters as you say them."

- Allow time for the student to write the word.

"What word did you write?" *judge*

- Repeat the procedure with #2 (smudge), #3 (bridge), #4 (pledge), and #5 (edge).

"Now you're ready to code and read the words on your paper."

"Code the words by #6 through #10. After you have coded all the words, try to read them."

- Assist the student as necessary.

"Now read the word by #11. If you have trouble reading the word, code it. Then draw a line from the word to the picture it matches."

- Repeat with #12 through #14.
- As the student works, provide help as needed. Help the student correct any incorrect answers. Then initial the worksheet in the space provided.
- Some time during the day, ask the student to read from the worksheet, a controlled reader, your basal reader, or other material of your choice.
- **Note:** Always make sure the worksheet is corrected before the student begins the homework. The worksheet serves as a guide to help complete the homework.

HOMEWORK

"Turn your paper over to the homework side."

"Do you know what to do on the homework paper?"

"Watch for trigraph dge. Always code suffixes and final, stable syllables before coding the rest of the word. Also, watch for words that need to be divided."

"When you finish your paper, I will check it for you and initial it in the space provided."

- Either now or later in the day, the student should complete the homework independently (if possible). Help the student correct any incorrect answers. Then initial the homework in the space provided.

READER

"We have another new book today."

- Give the student **Reader 43 (*Butterscotch*)** and some colored pencils.

"Can you tell me this book's title?" *Butterscotch*

- Assist the student as necessary as he/she constructs the book.
- When the student finishes, staple or put a rubber band around the book's spine.

"The title of this book is _________?" *Butterscotch*

"I want you to read your book to yourself. When you are finished reading, color the pictures. Write your name on the book so I will know who colored it."

"Keep your book handy because I will be asking you to read it for me."

- Some time during the day, have the student read the reader to you.
- If possible, take time to play the Kid Card games listed in Lesson 115.

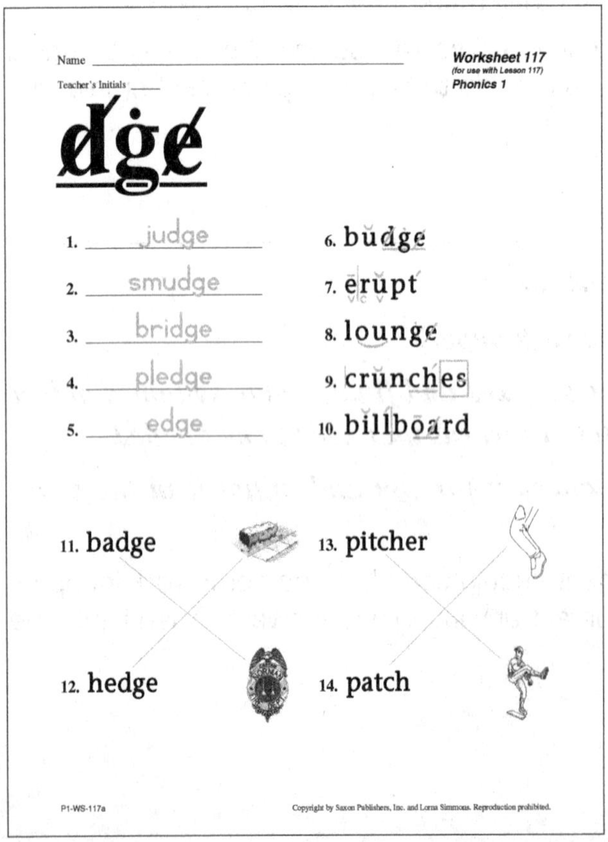
Name __________

Teacher's Initials ____

Worksheet 117 (for use with Lesson 117) Phonics 1

dge

1. judge
2. smudge
3. bridge
4. pledge
5. edge
6. budge
7. erupt
8. lounge
9. crunches
10. billboard

11. badge
12. hedge
13. pitcher
14. patch

P1-WS-117a Copyright by Saxon Publishers, Inc. and Lorna Simmons. Reproduction prohibited.

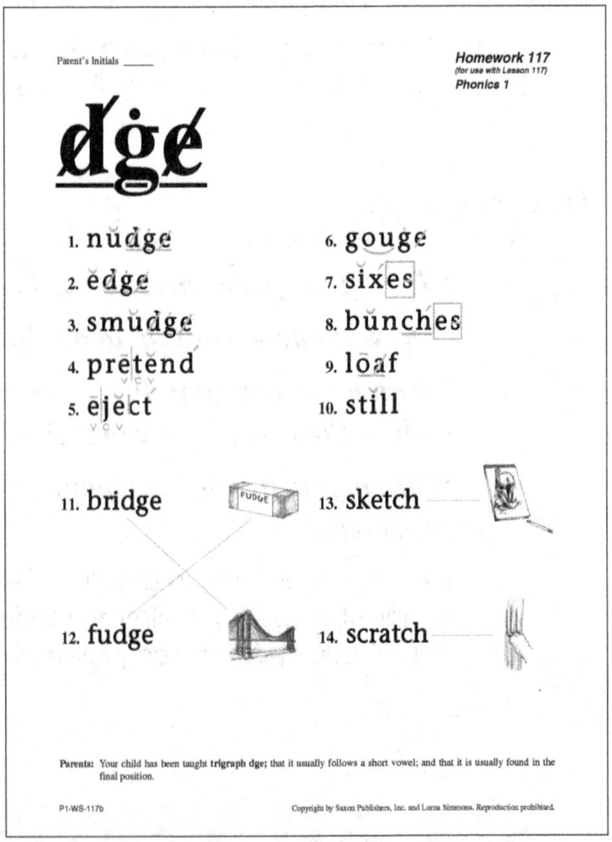
Parent's Initials ____

Homework 117 (for use with Lesson 117) Phonics 1

dge

1. nudge
2. edge
3. smudge
4. pretend
5. eject
6. gouge
7. sixes
8. bunches
9. loaf
10. still

11. bridge
12. fudge
13. sketch
14. scratch

Parents: Your child has been taught trigraph dge; that it usually follows a short vowel; and that it is usually found in the final position.

P1-WS-117b Copyright by Saxon Publishers, Inc. and Lorna Simmons. Reproduction prohibited.

LESSON 118 Spelling with /ch/ and /j/

lesson preparation

materials

Activity Sheet 7

Review Decks

Worksheet 118

ALPHABET ACTIVITY

- The student should be seated.

  "We are going to alphabetize words in a list again today. I'm going to give you your own list of words."

- Give the student **Activity Sheet 7.**

  "Alphabetize these words. Begin with 'a' and scan the list as you name each letter. Each time you use a number, mark it out at the bottom. When you're finished, we will check the list together."

- Allow time for the student to work.
- When the student has finished, recite the alphabet together to check the word order. The correct order is 5, 3, 6, 1, 4, 2.

REVIEW OF DECKS

- The student should be seated where he/she can write comfortably.
- Show the student **Letter Cards 1–70** in random order. The student should name the letter on each letter card.
- Review **Affix Cards 1–8.**
- Show the student **Picture Cards 1–85** in random order. The student should name the keyword and sound for each picture card.
- Review **Sight Word Cards 1–66.**

  "Let's review our spelling cards orally today."

- Give the sounds on **Spelling Cards 1–44** (or **45,** if used) in random order. The student should echo each response and then skywrite it.

NEW LEARNING

"We are going to practice spelling the sounds of /ch/ and /j/ today."

"Let's begin with the /ch/ sound."

- Write the following on the chalkboard:

Dŭ___	drĕn___
pŭn___	răn___
bă___	pōa̸___
ĭn___	gŭl___
pēa̸___	mă___

"Look at Rule Chart 12."

"It tells us to use trigraph tch when?" *in the final position after a short vowel sound*

"All of these words on the chalkboard end with the /ch/ sound. We need to fill in the correct spelling for the /ch/ sound."

- Point to "Dŭ___."

"The /ch/ sound comes after what kind of sound?" *a short vowel sound*

"Look at the rule chart. What will we use to spell it?" *tch*

- Complete the spelling of the word "Dutch."

"Why do you suppose this word is capitalized?" *it is a proper noun*

"That's right! It names a specific group of people from a country called 'The Netherlands.' "

- Point to "pŭn___."

"In this word, the /ch/ sound comes after what kind of sound?" *a consonant sound*

"Look at the rule chart. What will we use to spell it?" *ch*

- Complete the spelling of the word "punch."
- Repeat the procedure with the remaining words.

"Now let's spell with the /j/ sound."

- Write the following on the chalkboard:

grŭ___	plĕ___
hū___	stoo___
bŭl___	cā___
hĭn___	jŭ___

"Look at Rule Chart 13."

"It tells us to use trigraph dge when?" *in the final position after a short vowel sound*

"When do we use 'ge' in the final position?" *in all other situations*

"All of these words on the chalkboard end with the /j/ sound. We need to fill in the correct spelling for the /j/ sound."

- Point to "grŭ___."

Lesson 118

"The /j/ sound comes after what kind of sound?" *a short vowel sound*

"Look at the rule chart. What will we use to spell it?" *dge*

- Complete the spelling of the word "grudge."
- Repeat the procedure with the remaining words.

"Did you notice a similarity between the spellings we used after a short vowel?" *the longer spellings are used*

" 'Tch' and 'dge' are both three letters long, whereas the other choices for spelling are less than three letters. When we spell the /k/ sound, 'ck' is the longest spelling and it follows a short vowel also."

"If we can remember that the longer spellings ('tch' and 'dge') come after a short vowel sound, and the other spellings come after anything else, we will be better spellers."

BOARDWORK

"Let's practice coding some words like the ones you'll have on your worksheet."

"The rule charts are in your Rule Book if you need to look at them."

- Write the following phrase and sentence (without the coding marks) on the chalkboard, one at a time. Ask the student to help you code them. The correct coding is as indicated:

ĕdge the lawn

Switch the light ŏff.

- Have the student determine whether each of the items coded is a word, a phrase, or a sentence.

WORKSHEET

- The student should be seated where he/she can write comfortably.
- Give the student **Worksheet 118.** Make sure the student turns to the correct side.

"The words on the left-hand side of your worksheet all end with the /j/ sound."

"The words on the right-hand side all end with the /ch/ sound."

"Decide how to spell the final sound in each word and write the letters on the line."

- As the student works, provide help as needed. Help the student correct any incorrect answers. Then initial the worksheet in the space provided.
- Some time during the day, ask the student to read from the worksheet, a controlled reader, your basal reader, or other material of your choice.
- **Note:** Always make sure the worksheet is corrected before the student begins the homework. The worksheet serves as a guide to help complete the homework.

HOMEWORK

"Turn your paper over to the homework side."

"Do you know what to do on the homework paper?"

"The words are just like the ones we did in class today."

"When you finish your paper, I will check it for you and initial it in the space provided."

- Either now or later in the day, the student should complete the homework independently (if possible). Help the student correct any incorrect answers. Then initial the homework in the space provided.
- If possible, take time to play the Kid Card games listed in Lesson 115.

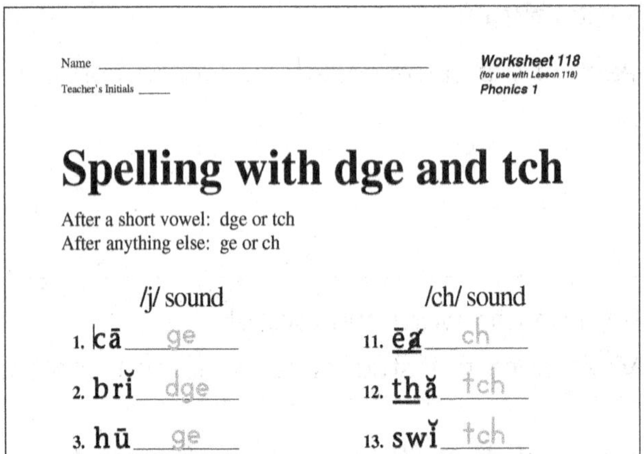

Name ______________________

Teacher's Initials ____

Worksheet 118
(for use with Lesson 118)
Phonics 1

Spelling with dge and tch

After a short vowel: dge or tch
After anything else: ge or ch

/j/ sound	/ch/ sound
1. cā ge	11. ēa ch
2. brĭ dge	12. thă tch
3. hū ge	13. swĭ tch
4. nŭ dge	14. pou ch
5. gor ge	15. scră tch
6. plŭn ge	16. bŭn ch
7. hĕ dge	17. fĕ tch
8. wĕ dge	18. hă tch
9. ver ge	19. clŭ tch
10. lŏ dge	20. bēa ch

P1-WS-118a

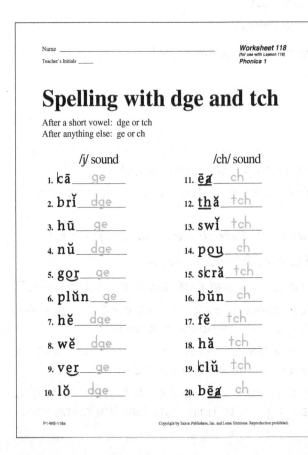

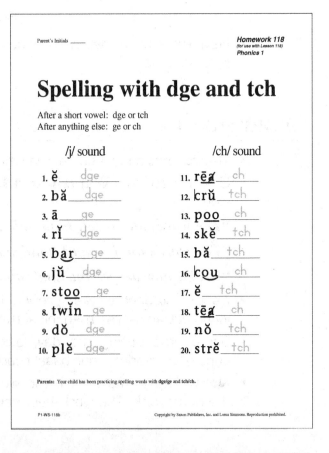

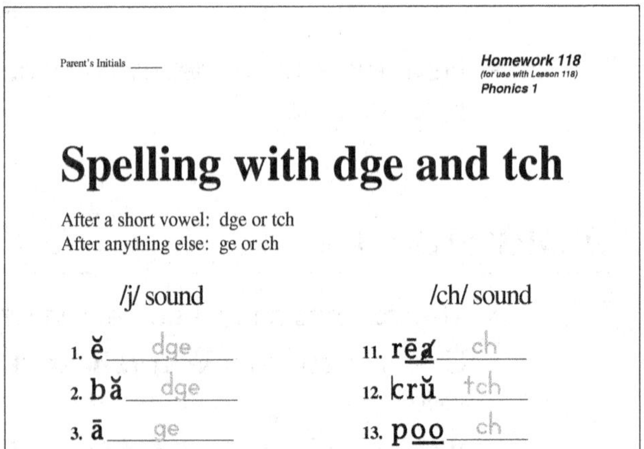

Parent's Initials ____

Homework 118
(for use with Lesson 118)
Phonics 1

Spelling with dge and tch

After a short vowel: dge or tch
After anything else: ge or ch

/j/ sound	/ch/ sound
1. ĕ dge	11. rēa ch
2. bă dge	12. crŭ tch
3. ā ge	13. poo ch
4. rĭ dge	14. skĕ tch
5. bar ge	15. bă tch
6. jŭ dge	16. cou ch
7. stoo ge	17. ĕ tch
8. twĭn ge	18. tēa ch
9. dŏ dge	19. nŏ tch
10. plĕ dge	20. strĕ tch

Parents: Your child has been practicing spelling words with **dge/ge** and **tch/ch.**

P1-WS-118b

LESSON 119 — Digraph *ie*

lesson preparation

materials

Alphabet/Accent Deck (Section 1)
Review Decks
Spelling Sound Sheet 84
Letter Card 71
Picture Cards 86–87
Sight Word Card 67
Worksheet 119
Reader 44 (*Summer and Minnie*)
colored pencils

ALPHABET ACTIVITY

"Let's work with the first Alphabet/Accent Deck again today. Stand up."

"We'll stand with our feet flat on the floor and say the first syllable in a normal voice. When we come to the accented syllable, we'll jump up."

- Show the student **Alphabet/Accent Card 1.** The student should say "A" (in a normal voice with feet flat), and then "B" (jumping up).
- Continue with **Alphabet/Accent Cards 2–25,** moving as quickly as possible.
- **Optional:** If you think the student is ready, shuffle the Alphabet/Accent Deck before the activity. Warn the student that the cards will be in random order.

REVIEW OF DECKS

- The student should be seated where he/she can write comfortably.
- Show the student **Letter Cards 1–70** in random order. The student should name the letter on each letter card.
- Review **Affix Cards 1–8.**
- Show the student **Picture Cards 1–85** in random order. The student should name the keyword and sound for each picture card.
- Review **Sight Word Cards 1–66.**
- Give the student **Spelling Sound Sheet 84.**

- Call out the sounds on **Spelling Cards 1–44** (or **45,** if used) in random order. The student should echo each sound and name the letter or letters that make the sound as he/she writes the letter(s) on the spelling sound sheet.
- Have the student put the spelling sound sheet away.

New Learning

"I'm going to say some words. Echo them back to me and listen for the sound that is the same in the medial position of each word."

- Point to your mouth as you say each word.

"Echo after me. Field." *field* ***"Thief."*** *thief* ***"Yield."*** *yield*

"What sound do you hear in the medial position?" /ē/

- Write the following on the chalkboard: field, thief, yield.

"What letters do you see that might be making the /ē/ sound?" *ie*

"Do you know what this is called?" *digraph ie*

"How do we code a digraph?" *underline it*

- Underline digraph *ie* in each of the words: field, thief, yield.

"How can we code this digraph so it will say /ē/ in these words?" *put a macron on the e, mark out the i*

"Do these words need any other coding?" *yes, underline digraph th*

- Code the words: fiēld, thiēf, yiēld.

"Can you read these words?"

- Have the student read and define each word.

"Now echo these words and listen to the sounds that are the same. Tie." *tie* ***"Lie."*** *lie*

"What sound do you hear in the final position?" /ī/

- Write the following on the chalkboard: tie, lie.

"What letters do you see that might be making the /ī/ sound?" *ie*

"How do we code this digraph so it will say /ī/ in these words?" *put a macron on the i, mark out the e*

- Code the words: tīe, līe.

"Digraph ie makes two sounds, /ē/ and /ī/."

"Are these sounds voiced or unvoiced?" *voiced*

"Is this a vowel digraph or a consonant digraph?" *vowel digraph*

- Leave the words on the chalkboard for the remainder of the lesson.

Lesson 119

New Deck Cards

- Hold up **Letter Card 71.**

  "What is this called?" *digraph ie*

- Hold up **Picture Card 86** but keep the picture covered with your hand (or the letter card).

  "I have a card with a picture on it that contains the /ī/ sound."

  "I am going to describe it for you. See if you can guess what the picture is."

  "This is a kind of dessert. It comes in a round pan. It is eaten with a fork and can be served with ice cream, whipped cream, or meringue on top. Favorite flavors of this dessert are apple, pumpkin, and lemon. What do you think the picture is?" *pie*

  "Our first keyword is 'pie.' "

- Show the student **Picture Card 86.**
- Hold up **Picture Card 87** but keep the picture covered with your hand (or the letter card).

  "Our second keyword makes the other sound of digraph ie, /ē/."

  "I have a card with a picture on it that contains that sound. See if you can guess what the picture is. "

  "This is something that knights from long ago used to carry into battle along with their swords and flags. It was usually made of metal and often had the knight's family sign painted or carved on the front. Without this object, a knight had no protection from his enemy's weapons. What do you think the picture is?" *shield*

- Do not be surprised if the student does not know this word. You might even show him/her the picture as a clue. Use this opportunity to add a new word to the student's vocabulary.

  "Our second keyword is 'shield.' "

- Show the student **Picture Card 87.**
- **Note:** The digraph and its picture are also shown in the Rule Book on page 21.

  "Digraph ie will not be added to our spelling deck since it's irregular for spelling."

  "Get out your Irregular Spelling Booklet."

  "Look in the table of contents and see if you can find the pages that show words spelled with digraph ie." *pages 8 and 10*

  "Turn to page 8. All of the words on page 8 use digraph ie to spell the /ē/ sound. They don't follow our regular rules, so we must memorize them."

- Allow time for the student to examine the list of words. If time permits, discuss the definition and/or pronunciation of some or all of the words.

"Do you know any other words that belong on this list?"

- If the student offers any appropriate words, write the words on the chalkboard and have the student copy them into the booklet.

"Turn to page 10. The words at the top of page 10 also use digraph ie, but in these words digraph ie spells the /ī/ sound. The words don't follow our regular rules, so we must memorize them."

- Repeat the procedure used for page 8.

"Use your Irregular Spelling Booklet to help you learn how to spell the two sounds of digraph ie. For now, put your booklet away."

- **Note:** Add the new letter and picture cards to the Review Decks.

BOARDWORK

- Write the following on the chalkboard:

eye /ī/

"We have a new sight word today."

- Point to the word.

"Can you tell me what this word is? Remember, it's a sight word, so it won't follow all of our rules."

- Allow the student to try to pronounce the word. If necessary, say it for him/her.

"This word is 'eye.' Can you use the word 'eye' in a sentence?" *expect various answers*

- Show the student **Sight Word Card 67.**

"Let's find this word on our sight word charts."

- Help the student locate the word in the Irregular Spelling Booklet.

"We will add this card to our sight word deck."

"Let's practice coding some words like the ones you'll have on your worksheet."

"The rule charts are in your Rule Book if you need to look at them."

- Write the following sentences (without the coding marks) on the chalkboard, one at a time. Ask the student to help you code them. The correct coding is as indicated:

The căt saw the gŭm′|drŏp ŏn the porch.

The child (wanted) ăn ouch′|less| piēce (of) tāpe.

- Have the student determine whether each of the items coded is a word, a phrase, or a sentence.
- Add **Sight Word Card 67** to the Sight Word Deck.

WORKSHEET

- The student should be seated where he/she can write comfortably.
- Give the student **Worksheet 119.** Make sure the student turns to the correct side.

  "Let's spell with the /ē/ sound using digraph ie. There aren't too many words that use digraph ie to say the /ē/ sound, but we'll do a few so you'll know about them."

  "Put your finger by #1. The first word is 'brief.' "

  "Unblend 'brief' with me." */b/ /r/ /ē/ /f/*
- Hold up a finger for each sound.

  "Let's spell those sounds." *b ... r ... digraph ie ... f*
- Point to a finger as the student spells each sound.

  "Now spell the word again and write the letters as you say them."
- Allow time for the student to write the word.

  "What word did you write?" *brief*
- Repeat the procedure with #2 (field), #3 (niece), #4 (piece), and #5 (pier).

  "Now you're ready to code and read the words on your paper."

  "Code the words by #6 through #10. After you have coded all the words, try to read them."
- Assist the student as necessary.

  "Look at the picture at the bottom of the page. Write what you think happened after the children got paint all over themselves. Don't worry about spelling. When you are finished, we will take time to check spelling and correct mistakes."
- As the student works, provide help as needed.
- Then have the student read the story silently and check for spelling errors. Help the student correct any mistakes. A perfect paper is not as important as the student putting his/her thoughts on paper and being able to recognize spelling errors that can be corrected (e.g., *k* and *c* spelling). Be sure to correct the rest of the worksheet as well. Then initial it in the space provided.
- Have the student read the story to you. It is important that children learn to feel comfortable speaking in front of others.
- **Note:** Always make sure the worksheet is corrected before the student begins the homework. The worksheet serves as a guide to help complete the homework.

Lesson 119

HOMEWORK

"Turn your paper over to the homework side."

"Do you know what to do on the homework paper?"

"Look at the picture at the bottom of the page. Use the lines beside the picture and describe how the person is making the sandwich."

"When you finish your paper, I will check it for you and initial it in the space provided."

- Either now or later in the day, the student should complete the homework independently (if possible). Help the student correct any incorrect answers. Then initial the homework in the space provided.

READER

"We have another new book today."

- Give the student **Reader 44 (*Summer and Minnie*)** and some colored pencils.

"Can you tell me this book's title?" *Summer and Minnie*

- Assist the student as necessary as he/she constructs the book.
- When the student finishes, staple or put a rubber band around the book's spine.

"The title of this book is __________?" *Summer and Minnie*

"I want you to read your book to yourself. When you are finished reading, color the pictures. Write your name on the book so I will know who colored it."

"Keep your book handy because I will be asking you to read it for me."

- Some time during the day, have the student read the reader to you.
- If possible, take time to play the Kid Card games listed in Lesson 115. Try to see that the student is prepared for tomorrow's assessment.

Name ____________________

Teacher's Initials _____

Worksheet 119
(for use with Lesson 119)
Phonics 1

ie, ie

1. brief
2. field
3. niece
4. piece
5. pier
6. cornfield
7. mouthpiece
8. tie
9. mindless
10. lampshade

P1-WS-119a

Parent's Initials _____

Homework 119
(for use with Lesson 119)
Phonics 1

ie, ie

1. yield
2. outfield
3. thornless
4. windstorm
5. pie
6. formless
7. eggnog
8. fire
9. dustpan
10. lifesize

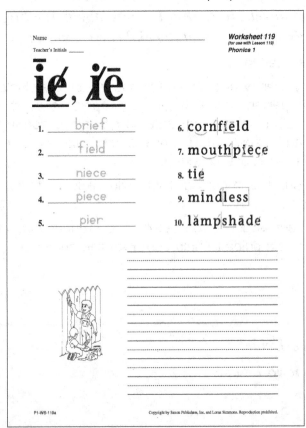

Parents: Your child has been taught the two sounds of **digraph ie** (as in *pie* and *shield*).

P1-WS-119b

LESSON 120 — Assessment

lesson preparation

materials

Alphabet/Accent Deck (Section 2)
Review Decks
Assessment 23
Spelling Test 21
Assessment 23 Recording Form
Kid Cards
tokens

the night before

- Sort through the Review Decks and remove any cards you are certain the student has mastered (not to include the vowel spelling cards; these are never retired).
- Separate the Kid Cards marked "Lesson 120."

ALPHABET ACTIVITY

"We're going to work with the second Alphabet/Accent Deck today."

"Let's stand up. We'll stand with our feet flat on the floor and say the first and third syllables in a normal voice. When we say the accented syllable, we'll karate punch."

- Show the student **Alphabet/Accent Card 1.** The student should say "A" (in a normal voice with feet flat), then "B" (as he/she punches forward), and then "C" (in a normal voice with feet flat).
- Continue with **Alphabet/Accent Cards 2–24,** moving as quickly as possible.
- **Optional:** If you think the student is ready, shuffle the Alphabet/Accent Deck before the activity. Warn the student that the cards will be in random order.

REVIEW OF DECKS

- Show the student **Letter Cards 1–71** in random order. The student should name the letter on each letter card.
- Review **Affix Cards 1–8.**
- Show the student **Picture Cards 1–87** in random order. The student should name the keyword and sound for each picture card.
- Review **Sight Word Cards 1–67.**

Written Assessment

- Have the student sit where he/she can write comfortably.
- Give the student **Assessment 23.**
- **Section I:**

  "Today we are going to write some words for our assessment."

  "I'm going to say a word. Write the letter that makes each sound in that word on the lines by #1."

  "Look at the rule charts if you need to."

  "Here's the first word: dripping."
- Repeat with the following words in the order shown: #2 (dishes), #3 (flossed), #4 (cowbell), and #5 (grouch).
- **Reminder:** While the student spells, be ready to point to appropriate rule charts as necessary.
- **Section II:**

  "Look at the letters by #6."

  "Find the picture of the keyword for this sound."

  "Draw a line from the letters to the keyword."
- Repeat with #7 and #8. Allow a few minutes for the student to work.
- The pictures (from top to bottom) are as follows: wreath, knot, gnats.
- **Section III:**

  "Put your finger on #9."

  "Code the words by #9 through #12."
- Allow a few minutes for the student to work.
- **Section IV:**

  "Read the paragraph. If you find any words you can't read, code them to help you figure them out. Then answer the questions by #13 through #16."
- **Reminder:** If the student absolutely cannot read the paragraph, read it to the student to see if he or she can answer the questions.

  "When you are finished, show your paper to me."
- This paper will be used during the oral portion of the assessment.

Spelling Test

- Give the student **Spelling Test 21.**
- Call out the following words (in the order shown). Sound them out, if necessary.

  #1 (portion), #2 (show), #3 (serving), #4 (playground), #5 (proudly),
  #6 (September), #7 (making), #8 (crumple), #9 (foundation),
  #10 (pumpkin), #11 (pull), #12 (full)
- Grade and record the test in any manner that suits your needs.

Oral Assessment

- It is important to complete the oral assessment promptly (today, if possible) in order to identify any areas of weakness and begin remediation.
- Use the assessment and the following dialogue to complete the oral portion.
- **Section V:**
- Point to the sight word by #17.

  "Read this sight word for me."
- Record the student's response by placing a check mark by each word he/she reads correctly.
- Repeat with #18.
- **Section VI:**
- Show the student the letters by #19.

  "Tell me the name of these letters and the sound they make."
- Write the student's response on the adjacent line.
- Repeat with #20 and #21.

Assessment Evaluation

- Grade the assessment and record the results on **Assessment 23 Recording Form.** Check off the boxes to indicate mastery (i.e., the section was completed with 100% accuracy).
- **Reminder:** Try to give as many points as possible for work attempted. Do not grade the coding marks too severely. The most important coding marks to look for are breves, macrons, and syllable division lines.
- See the introductory material for detailed information regarding grading and recording procedures.
- Use the assessment results to identify those skills in which the student is weak. Practice those skills by playing Kid Card games.
- Add the Kid Cards marked "Lesson 120" to the existing decks. Listed below are games appropriate for remediation in selected areas. See "Games and Activities" for the directions for each game.
- **Section I:** Play "Spelling Deck Perfection," "Sound Scamper," "Spell Out #1 or #2," or have the student use the letter tiles to spell words you give from the Spelling Word List.
- **Section II:** Play "Keyword and Sound" or "Letter/Sound Identification."
- **Section III:** Play "Chalkboard Challenge."
- **Section IV:** Either have the student read the controlled readers and then ask questions for comprehension, or play "Acting Out" with the green Kid Cards.
- **Section V:** Play "At First Sight."
- **Section VI:** Play "Letter/Sound Identification."

- When the student seems more secure in areas that had previously proven difficult, retest him/her (in those areas only) and indicate on the recording form any sections the student has subsequently mastered.
- Try to help the student achieve mastery of all the sections before the next assessment.
- If the student is having difficulty with a particular skill, keep his or her practice activities at the most basic level so the chance of success is greater.

Name ______________________

Assessment 23
(for use with Lesson 120)
Phonics 1

Section I

1. dripping
2. dishes
3. flossed
4. cowbell
5. grouch

Section II

6. kn
7. gn
8. wr

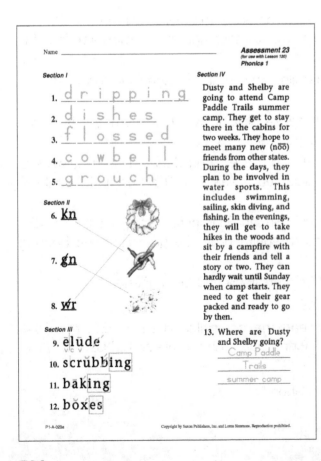

Section III

9. elude
10. scrubbing
11. baking
12. boxes

Section IV

Dusty and Shelby are going to attend Camp Paddle Trails summer camp. They get to stay there in the cabins for two weeks. They hope to meet many new (nōō) friends from other states. During the days, they plan to be involved in water sports. This includes swimming, sailing, skin diving, and fishing. In the evenings, they will get to take hikes in the woods and sit by a campfire with their friends and tell a story or two. They can hardly wait until Sunday when camp starts. They need to get their gear packed and ready to go by then.

13. Where are Dusty and Shelby going?
Camp Paddle Trails summer camp

P1-A-023a

Assessment 23
(for use with Lesson 120)
Phonics 1

14. How long will they stay?
two weeks

15. Who do they hope to meet?
new friends

16. Where do they get to sit in the evenings?
by a campfire

Section V

17. heart ______
18. been ______

Section VI

19. kn ghost letter digraph kn. /n/
20. gn ghost letter digraph gn. /n/
21. wr ghost letter digraph wr. /r/

P1-A-023b

LESSON 121 Final, Stable Syllable *-sion*

lesson preparation

materials

container of letter tiles

Review Decks

Letter Card 72

Picture Cards 88–89

Spelling Card 46

Worksheet 121

Spelling List 22

ALPHABET ACTIVITY

- The student should be seated with the container of letter tiles.

  "Before we start, let's say the alphabet together so it is fresh in our minds."

- Recite the alphabet with the student.
- Give the following instructions one at a time, allowing time for the student to accomplish each task before giving the next instruction.

  "Take all of the letter tiles out of your container."

  "Flip all of the letters over so that you are looking at the lowercase letters. If they are flipped correctly, they will all be blue."

  "Now we're ready. See if you can put all your letters in alphabetical order."

- When the student has finished, continue by saying the following:

  "Quickly pull down the vowels."

  "Put together two letters that make a diphthong." *oi, oy, ou, ow*

  "Tell me which diphthong you put together."

- Make sure the student has formed a true diphthong.

  "Spell the word 'ouch' with your letter tiles."

  "Now add one letter to make the word 'couch.' "

  "Change two letters and make the word 'mouth.' "

  "Now change two more letters to make it 'mound.' "

- Have the student replace the tiles in the container and put it away.

REVIEW OF DECKS

- Let the student select a review deck (or decks) and play "teacher" with you as the student.

NEW LEARNING

"I'm going to say some words. Echo them back to me and listen for the sound that is the same at the end of each word."

- Point to your mouth as you say each word.

"Echo after me. Conclusion." *conclusion* ***"Vision."*** *vision* ***"Decision."*** *decision*

"What sound do you hear at the end of these words?" */zhŭn/*

- Repeat and exaggerate the words, if necessary.

"That's right. The sound you hear is /zhŭn/."

- Write the following on the chalkboard: conclusion, vision, decision.

"What letters do you see that might be making the /zhŭn/ sound?" *sion*

"That's right."

- Erase the word "decision."

"How many syllables do you hear in the word 'con·clu·sion'?" *three*

"We see that in the word 'conclusion,' the third and final syllable is 's-i-o-n.' "

"What other final syllable have we studied that includes the letters 'i-o-n'?" *tion*

"What sound did it make?" */shŭn/*

"What did we call 't-i-o-n'?" *final, stable syllable -tion*

"How do we code a final, stable syllable?" *with a bracket*

"The bracket actually divides part of the word into syllables."

- Bracket the final, stable syllables: conclu[sion, vi[sion.

"Then we mark the accent on which syllable?" *the syllable before the final, stable syllable*

- Place the accent marks: conclu´[sion, vi´[sion.

"Let's code the rest of the word 'conclusion.' "

"What syllable division pattern do you think is in the word?" *vcccv*

- Label the syllable division pattern:

conclu´[sion
v c ccv

"Where do we divide words that follow the 'vcccv' syllable division pattern?" *between any two consonants*

"Let's divide this one between the first two consonants."

- Divide the word:

con|clu´[sion
v c|ccv

"We have three syllables. Look at the first one."

"How do we code an o that is followed by an n?" *with a breve*

- Point to the *c* in the first syllable.

"What sound will this c have?" */k/*

"Why?" *it is followed by the letter o*

"So how will we code it?" *with a k-back*

"The vowel in our second syllable is accented and not followed by a consonant. How should we code it?" *with a macron*

"What about the c?" *code it with a k-back since it's followed by a consonant*

- Finish coding the word:

cŏn|clū´[sion
v c|ccv

"The last syllable is final, stable syllable s-i-o-n."

"Can you tell me the sound we have learned for 's-i-o-n'?" */zhŭn/*

"Can you read this word?"

- If the word is read as coded, the first *o* should make an /ŏ/, not an /ŭ/, sound.

"The o is really making a schwa sound here, isn't it? Let's change the coding to show this."

- Erase the breve over the *o* and replace it with a schwa:

cůn|clū´[sion
v c|ccv

"Can you read this word now?" *conclusion*

"Can you define this word or use it in a sentence?" *expect various answers*

- Point to the word "vision."

"When you have an i before a final, stable syllable, it doesn't always follow the rules we have been learning."

"The letter i will often be open and accented, but will have its short sound instead of its long sound."

"This happens a lot in words with 's-i-o-n', but it can happen with almost any final, stable syllable."

"This word has that irregular i sound."

- Code the word "vision" with the student (vǐ´[sion) and discuss its meaning, if necessary.

"This short i occurs so often that you should say its short sound any time the long i sound doesn't make a word."

"I have another word I want you to look at."

- Write the word "permission" on the chalkboard.

"How should we code this word?"

- Code the word as the student instructs:

per | mis′[sion
vc | c v

"Can you read this word?" *permission*

- If the student reads "sion" as/zhŭn/, ask the student if he/she has ever heard the word "permi/zhŭn/."

"Sometimes 's-i-o-n' will sound like /shŭn/."

- Let the student read the word again.

"Final, stable syllable s-i-o-n has two sounds, /zhŭn/ and /shŭn/."

"We usually know when to use which sound, but sometimes it is hard to remember. Try both sounds. One of them should give you a word that you recognize."

- **Note:** The actual rule governing pronunciation of final, stable syllable *-sion* is as follows: After a vowel or the letter *r*, final, stable syllable *-sion* says /zhŭn/ (e.g., *lesion*, *version*). After a consonant (other than the letter *r*), final, stable syllable *-sion* says /shŭn/ (e.g., *mission*, *mansion*). Explain this to the student, if desired, although he/she will probably pronounce these words correctly without knowing the rule.

New Deck Cards

- Show the student **Letter Card 72.**

"What will we say when we see this card?" *final, stable syllable s-i-o-n*

- Hold up **Picture Card 88** but keep the picture covered with your hand (or the letter card).

"I have a card with a picture on it that contains the /zhŭn/ sound."

"I am going to describe it for you. See if you can guess what the picture is."

"This is a large, box-shaped object found in most people's homes. When it is plugged into an electrical socket and turned on, it sends out pictures and sounds. The most common names for the things shown through this electrical box are 'shows,' 'movies,' and 'commercials.' What do you think the picture is?" *television*

- Show the student **Picture Card 88.**
- Hold up **Picture Card 89** but keep the picture covered with your hand (or the letter card).

"Our second keyword makes the other sound for final, stable syllable s-i-o-n, /shŭn/. I have a card with a picture on it that contains that sound. See if you can guess what the picture is."

"This is a type of journey with a very specific purpose. The astronauts went on one when they went to the moon. Can you guess what this is?" *mission*

- Show the student **Picture Card 89.**
- **Note:** The final, stable syllable and its picture are also shown in the Rule Book on page 22.
- Hold up **Spelling Card 46** so only you can see what is written.

"Echo this sound: /zhŭn/." */zhŭn/*

"How do we spell /zhŭn/ in the final position?" *s-i-o-n*

"That's right. Now when I say /zhŭn/, you will respond 'final, stable syllable s-i-o-n' and write 's…i…o…n.'"

- Have the student write the response on the desktop with his/her finger.
- Write "sion" on the chalkboard.

"The /shŭn/ sound is regularly spelled 't-i-o-n.' Your Irregular Spelling Booklet has a list of words that contain final, stable syllable s-i-o-n that says /shŭn/."

"Get out your Irregular Spelling Booklet."

"Look in the table of contents and see if you can find the page showing words that are spelled with final, stable syllable s-i-o-n." *page 33*

"Turn to page 33. All of the words on page 33 use final, stable syllable s-i-o-n to spell /shŭn/. They don't follow our regular rules, so we must memorize them."

- Allow time for the student to examine the list of words. If time permits, discuss the definition and/or pronunciation of some or all of the words.

"Do you know any other words that belong on this list?"

- If the student offers any appropriate words, write the words on the chalkboard and have the student copy them into the booklet.

"Use your Irregular Spelling Booklet to help you learn how to spell with final, stable syllable s-i-o-n. For now, put your booklet away."

- **Note:** Add the new letter, picture, and spelling cards to the Review Decks.

BOARDWORK

"Let's practice coding some words like the ones you'll have on your worksheet."

"The rule charts are in your Rule Book if you need to look at them."

- Write the following phrase and sentence (without the coding marks) on the chalkboard, one at a time. Ask the student to help you code them. The correct coding is as indicated:

fŭn′ny ĕx|prĕs′sion
vc|ccv

Ăf′|ter (you) knŏcked, mȳ′ nēçe, Kāte, ō′|pėned thė (door).
vc|cv v|cv

- Have the student determine whether each of the items coded is a word, a phrase, or a sentence.

WORKSHEET

- The student should be seated where he/she can write comfortably.
- Give the student **Worksheet 121.** Make sure the student turns to the correct side.

"Today, let's spell with final, stable syllable s-i-o-n. We know that final, stable syllable s-i-o-n can also make the /shŭn/ sound when it follows another s, but today we will only spell with the /zhŭn/ sound."

"Put your finger by #1. The first word is 'invasion.' "

"The first syllable is /ĭn/. Spell and write the first syllable by #1."

"The second syllable is /vā/. Spell and write the second syllable by #1."

"The last syllable is /zhŭn/. Spell final, stable syllable /zhŭn/ and write it after /vā/ on the line by #1."

- Allow time for the student to write the word.

"What word did you write?" *invasion*

- Repeat the procedure with #2 (version), #3 (confusion), #4 (explosion), and #5 (vision).
- When you pronounce these words, make a distinct separation between syllables. The student will be more successful if he/she spells by syllables.

"Now you're ready to code and read the words on your paper."

"Code the words by #6 through #10. After you have coded all the words, try to read them."

- Assist the student as necessary.

"Numbers 11 and 12 are questions about the paragraph just above them. If you find any words you can't read, code them. Then see if you can answer the questions."

- As the student works, provide help as needed. Help the student correct any incorrect answers. Then initial the worksheet in the space provided.
- Some time during the day, ask the student to read from the worksheet, a controlled reader, your basal reader, or other material of your choice.
- **Note:** Always make sure the worksheet is corrected before the student begins the homework. The worksheet serves as a guide to help complete the homework.

HOMEWORK

"Turn your paper over to the homework side."

"Do you know what to do on the homework paper?"

"Watch for final, stable syllable s-i-o-n. Always bracket it and accent the syllable before the bracket."

"Read the paragraph on the front again and then continue reading on the homework side before you answer the questions."

"When you finish your paper, I will check it for you and initial it in the space provided."

- Either now or later in the day, the student should complete the homework independently (if possible). Help the student correct any incorrect answers. Then initial the homework in the space provided.

SPELLING LIST

- Fold **Spelling List 22** in half lengthwise (with the printed side facing out).

"Leave your paper just like I give it to you."

- Give the student **Spelling List 22,** folded with the blank lines facing up.

"Let's spell some more words."

- Call out the following words (in the order shown). Sound them out, if necessary.

  #1 (germ), #2 (river), #3 (finish), #4 (seven), #5 (broken), #6 (sanding), #7 (slipped), #8 (sliding), #9 (sound), #10 (glasses), #11 (goes), #12 (want)

"Now unfold your paper and check your words."

- Check the student's work to see if he/she needs extra help with spelling.

"I want you to practice these words. We'll have a spelling test in a few days."

- If possible, take time to play the Kid Card games listed in Lesson 120.

Name ______________________________ **Worksheet 121** *(for use with Lesson 121)* **Phonics 1**

Teacher's Initials _____

´[sion

1. invasion
2. version
3. confusion
4. explosion
5. vision
6. permission
7. impression
8. fierce
9. erase
10. knocked

Rod and Zack were playing a game when they heard a really loud noise. They jumped up, eager to see what the noise was. In their confusion, Rod and Zack got out the door without their coats on a day when they wished they had them. They looked every direction, but did not see anything. Perhaps it was an invasion by a space ship. Their vision blurred as they looked for space men.

11. What did Rod and Zack forget at home?
their coats

12. What did Rod and Zack think made the loud noise?
a space ship

P1-WS-121a

Parent's Initials _____ **Homework 121** *(for use with Lesson 121)* **Phonics 1**

´[sion

1. admission
2. expression
3. priest
4. recite
5. smack
6. knife
7. brief
8. unite
9. hotel
10. reserve

Rod and Zack came to the conclusion that it must have been an explosion at the gas plant. An explosion could make a noise that loud. They rushed home feeling really chilly. They could tell their version of the story to their friends as soon as they got home.

11. What made the loud noise? an explosion

12. What could they do when they got home?
tell the story

Parents: Your child has been taught the two sounds of final, stable syllable -**sion** (as in *television* and *mission*).

P1-WS-121b

Lesson 121

LESSON 122 Final, Stable Syllable *-ture*

lesson preparation

materials

Alphabet/Accent Deck (Section 3)
Retired Decks
Affix Deck
Spelling Sound Sheet 85
Letter Card 73
Picture Card 90
Spelling Card 47
Sight Word Cards 68–69
Worksheet 122
Reader 45 (*Stan and Steve*)
colored pencils

ALPHABET ACTIVITY

- The student should be seated.

  "We're going to work with a new section of the Alphabet/Accent Deck today."

- Show the student **Alphabet/Accent Card 1.**

  "What is different about this deck?" *the first letter is missing*

  "This deck is very hard!"

  "If you don't know the answer, where can you find it?" *alphabet strip*

  "When you say the accented letter, I want you to raise your hands high up in the air. Then drop them back in your lap as you say the unaccented letter."

- Have the student say "A" (raise hands high in the air), and then "B" (drop hands back in lap).
- Continue with **Alphabet/Accent Cards 2–25,** moving as quickly as possible.

REVIEW OF DECKS

- The student should be seated where he/she can write comfortably.
- Show the student the retired letter cards in random order. The student should name the letter on each letter card.
- Review **Affix Cards 1–8.**
- Show the student the retired picture cards in random order. The student should name the keyword and sound for each picture card.
- Review the retired sight word cards.
- Give the student **Spelling Sound Sheet 85.**
- Call out the sounds on the retired spelling cards in random order. The student should echo each sound and name the letter or letters that make the sound as he/she writes the letter(s) on the spelling sound sheet.
- Have the student set the spelling sound sheet aside for use later in the lesson.

NEW LEARNING

"I'm going to say some words. Echo them back to me and listen for the sound that is the same at the end of each word."

- Point to your mouth as you say each word.

"Echo after me. Posture." *posture* ***"Culture."*** *culture*

"What sound do you hear that is the same at the end of each of these words?" */cher/*

- **Note:** This pronunciation is considered standard. Pronunciation may differ in your area.
- Write the following on the chalkboard: posture, culture.

"What letters do you see that might be making the /cher/ sound?" *t-u-r-e*

"That's right. How many syllables do you hear in the word 'posture'?" *two*

"What do you think 'ture' might be?" *a final, stable syllable*

"How do we code a final, stable syllable?" *bracket it*

"The bracket helps us divide the word into syllables."

- Put brackets on the words: pos[ture, cul[ture.

"Then we mark the accent on which syllable?" *on the syllable before the final, stable syllable*

- Place the accents on the words: pos´[ture, cul´[ture.

"Let's code the rest of the word 'posture.' "

"How do we code the first vowel in this word?" *short; breve*

- Code the *o* with a breve: pŏs´[ture.

"Can you read this word?" *posture*

"Can you define 'posture' or use it in a sentence?" *expect various answers*

- Point to "culture."

"How do we code the vowel in this word?" *short; breve*

"Does this word need any other coding?" *k-back on the c*

- Finish coding the word: cŭl´[ture.

"Can you read this word?" *culture*

"Can you define 'culture' or use it in a sentence?" *expect various answers*

- Leave the words on the chalkboard for the rest of the lesson.

NEW DECK CARDS

- Hold up **Letter Card 73.**

"What is this called?" *final, stable syllable t-u-r-e*

- Hold up **Picture Card 90** but keep the picture covered with your hand (or the letter card).

"I have a card with a picture on it that contains the /cher/ sound."

"I am going to describe it for you. See if you can guess what the picture is."

"This is something that can come in many different forms. You can draw one of these yourself, you can use a camera to take one, or you may find one hanging on a wall in a frame. It can represent something you see in front of you, or it can be made up completely from your own imagination. What do you think the picture is?" *picture*

- Show the student **Picture Card 90.**
- **Note:** The final, stable syllable and its picture are also shown in the Rule Book on page 22.

"We are going to add this to our spelling deck because this spelling of the /cher/ sound is found in many English words."

"Find your spelling sound sheet. Put your finger on #47."

- Hold up **Spelling Card 47** so only you can see what is written.

"Echo this final, stable syllable: /cher/." */cher/*

"How do we spell the /cher/ sound in the final position?" *t-u-r-e*

"That's right. Now when I say /cher/, you will respond 'final, stable syllable t-u-r-e' and write 't-u-r-e' on your paper. Say that with me." *final, stable syllable t-u-r-e*

"Write the response on the line by #47."

- Have the student put the spelling sound sheet away.
- **Note:** Add the new letter, picture, and spelling cards to the Review Decks.

Boardwork

- Write the following on the chalkboard:

  brother /brŭth´ er/   chocolate /chŏk´ ə lət/

  "We have two new sight words today."

- Point to the first word.

  "Can you tell me what this word is? Remember, it's a sight word, so it won't follow all of our rules."

- Allow the student to try to pronounce the word. If necessary, say it for him/her.

  "This word is 'brother.' Can you use the word 'brother' in a sentence?" *expect various answers*

- Repeat with "chocolate."
- Show the student **Sight Word Cards 68** and **69.**

  "Let's find these words on our sight word charts."

- Help the student locate the words in the Irregular Spelling Booklet.

  "We will add these cards to our sight word deck."

  "Let's practice coding some words like the ones you'll have on your worksheet."

  "The rule charts are in your Rule Book if you need to look at them."

- Write the following words and phrase (without the coding marks) on the chalkboard, one at a time. Ask the student to help you code them. The correct coding is as indicated:

  yi̸ēld

  crēa̸´|ture

  dĭsh´|es ănd năp´|kĭns
  (v c | c v)

- Have the student determine whether each of the items coded is a word, a phrase, or a sentence.
- Add **Sight Word Cards 68** and **69** to the Sight Word Deck.

Worksheet

- The student should be seated where he/she can write comfortably.
- Give the student **Worksheet 122.** Make sure the student turns to the correct side.

  "Today, let's spell with final, stable syllable t-u-r-e."

  "Put your finger by #1. The first word is 'future.'"

  "The first syllable is /fū/. Spell and write the first syllable by #1."

"The second syllable is /cher/. Spell the final, stable syllable that says /cher/ and finish the word on the line by #1."

- Allow time for the student to write the word.

"What word did you write?" *future*

- Repeat the procedure with #2 (mixture) and #3 (nature).
- When you pronounce these words, make a distinct separation between syllables. The student will be more successful if he/she spells by syllables.
- Refer to **Rule Chart 3** before giving the next two words: #4 (picture) and #5 (capture).

"Now you're ready to code and read the words on your paper."

"Code the words by #6 through #10. After you have coded all the words, try to read them."

- Assist the student as necessary.

"Now read the word by #11. If you have trouble reading the word, code it. Then draw a line from the word to the picture it matches."

- Repeat with #12 through #14.
- As the student works, provide help as needed. Help the student correct any incorrect answers. Then initial the worksheet in the space provided.
- Some time during the day, ask the student to read from the worksheet, a controlled reader, your basal reader, or other material of your choice.
- **Note:** Always make sure the worksheet is corrected before the student begins the homework. The worksheet serves as a guide to help complete the homework.

HOMEWORK

"Turn your paper over to the homework side."

"Do you know what to do on the homework paper?"

"Watch for final, stable syllable t-u-r-e. Always bracket the final, stable syllable, and accent the syllable before the bracket."

"When you finish your paper, I will check it for you and initial it in the space provided."

- Either now or later in the day, the student should complete the homework independently (if possible). Help the student correct any incorrect answers. Then initial the homework in the space provided.

READER

"We have another new book today."

- Give the student **Reader 45 (*Stan and Steve*)** and some colored pencils.

  "Can you tell me this book's title?" *Stan and Steve*

- Assist the student as necessary as he/she constructs the book.
- When the student finishes, staple or put a rubber band around the book's spine.

  "The title of this book is _________?" *Stan and Steve*

  "I want you to read your book to yourself. When you are finished reading, color the pictures. Write your name on the book so I will know who colored it."

  "Keep your book handy because I will be asking you to read it for me."

- Some time during the day, have the student read the reader to you.
- If possible, take time to play the Kid Card games listed in Lesson 120.

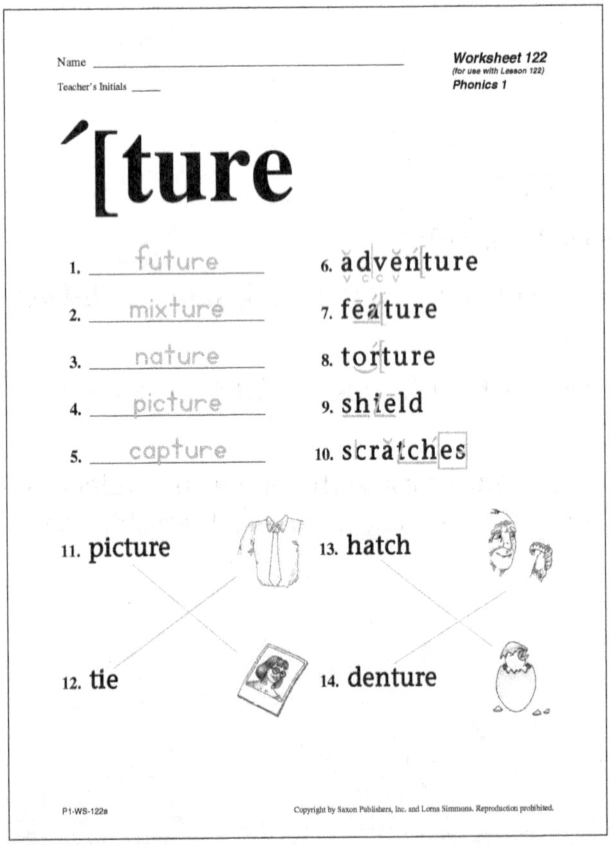

Name __________

Teacher's Initials ____

Worksheet 122
(for use with Lesson 122)
Phonics 1

´[ture

1. future
2. mixture
3. nature
4. picture
5. capture
6. adventure
7. feature
8. torture
9. shield
10. scratches

11. picture
12. tie
13. hatch
14. denture

P1-WS-122a

Parent's Initials ____

Homework 122
(for use with Lesson 122)
Phonics 1

´[ture

1. rupture
2. lecture
3. fixture
4. thief
5. grief
6. twitching
7. smashes
8. mixes
9. mascot
10. flop

11. furniture
12. pie
13. explosion
14. patch

Parents: Your child has been taught final, stable syllable **-ture.**

P1-WS-122b

LESSON 123 — Digraph *ch*, Part 2

lesson preparation

materials

purple Kid Cards
Review Decks
Spelling Sound Sheet 86
tokens or colored pencil
Sight Word Card 70
Picture Cards 91–92
Worksheet 123

ALPHABET ACTIVITY

- The student should be seated.

  "Today we are going to alphabetize some of our Kid Cards."

- Give the student four or five purple word cards. Make sure that each card begins with a different letter.

  "When I say 'go,' say the alphabet out loud."

  "The first time you say a letter that one of your cards begins with, lay that card down. Lay each card to the right of the previous one. When you finish, the words should be in alphabetical order."

  "Ready, set, go!"

- Repeat with different Kid Cards if time permits.
- Collect the Kid Cards.

REVIEW OF DECKS

- The student should be seated where he/she can write comfortably.
- Show the student **Letter Cards 1–73** in random order. The student should name the letter on each letter card.
- Review **Affix Cards 1–8.**
- Show the student **Picture Cards 1–90** in random order. The student should name the keyword and sound for each picture card.
- Review **Sight Word Cards 1–69.**

- Give the student **Spelling Sound Sheet 86** and at least twelve tokens (or a colored pencil). If you can use "fun" markers, such as goldfish-shaped crackers or cereal pieces, it is much more enjoyable for the student.

"Today, let's play Word Bingo."

"I'm going to call out a word. Then I'll tell you to change one sound in that word. I want you to cover (or X out) the space that spells the new word."

"When you cover (or X out) all of the words on one line, either up and down, across, or from corner to corner, call out Bingo!"

"Don't forget to refer to your rule charts if you need to."

"The trick is that the word is going to change. Are you ready?"

"Cover (or X out) the word that is made when you change the /ă/ vowel sound in 'hat' to /ŏ/."

- Allow the student time to cover the word.

"What word should we have covered?" *hot*

"Good job! Let's keep going."

- If the student has difficulty, give more answers before letting him/her work independently. If the student cannot do this, he/she needs more work with phonemic awareness.

"Cover (or X out) the word that is made when you change the final /t/ sound in 'hat' to /m/." *ham*

"Cover (or X out) the word that is made when you change the initial sound in 'hat' to /s/." *sat*

"Cover (or X out) the word that is made when you change the /ă/ vowel sound in 'hat' to /ŭ/." *hut*

"Cover (or X out) the word that is made when you change the initial /h/ sound in 'hat' to /p/." *pat*

"Cover (or X out) the word that is made when you change the initial /h/ sound in 'hat' to /m/." *mat*

- The student should Bingo by the time all the words have been called out.
- Collect the tokens (or colored pencil) and the spelling sound sheet. If you used tokens and the spelling sound sheet is unmarked, keep it available for practice.

NEW LEARNING

"I'm going to say some words. Echo them back to me and listen for the sound that is the same in each word."

- Point to your mouth as you say each word.

"Echo after me. Scheme." *scheme* ***"Chorus."*** *chorus* ***"Stomach."*** *stomach*

- If necessary, emphasize the /k/ sound made by the "ch."

  "What sound do you hear that is the same in all of these words?" */k/*

- Write the following on the chalkboard: scheme, chorus, stomach.

  "What letters do you see that might be making the /k/ sound?" *ch*

  "What sound have we already learned for digraph ch?" */ch/, as in "cheese"*

  "Today we are going to learn about two other sounds that digraph ch can make. The first sound is the one we just heard in 'scheme,' 'chorus,' and 'stomach.' What was that sound?" */k/*

  "This kind of 'ch' is sometimes called the 'hard ch' because it uses the hard c that sounds like k. It is also sometimes called the 'Greek ch' because these hard ch words were taken from the language of Ancient Greece and added to English. Can you repeat for me the two names of this new digraph?" *hard ch or Greek ch*

  "How do we code a digraph?" *underline it*

- Underline digraph *ch* in each of the words: s<u>ch</u>eme, <u>ch</u>orus, stoma<u>ch</u>.

  "How can we code this digraph so it will say /k/ in these words?" *put a k-back on the c, mark out the h*

- Point to the word "scheme."

  "How many syllables do you hear in the word 'scheme'?" *one*

  "Can you help me code this word?"

- Code the word as the student instructs: s<u>ch</u>ēme.

  "Now we can code the next word. What syllable division pattern is used in the word 'chorus'?" *vcv*

  "Where should we divide the 'vcv' pattern?" *either after the first vowel or after the consonant*

  "Let's divide after the consonant so we can keep combination or together."

- Divide the word after the *r*.

  "How do we code combinations?" *put arcs underneath*

  "How can we code the digraph so it will say /k/ in this word?" *put a k-back on the c, mark out the h*

  "How many syllables are there?" *two*

  "Which syllable should get the accent?" *the first syllable*

  "How should we code the u?" *breve; short*

- Finish coding the word: <u>ch</u><u>or</u>´ | ŭs.
  (vc | v)

  "Can you read this word?" *chorus*

  "The last word that we have on the chalkboard, 'stomach,' is a sight word, so we won't code it. If we did code it, we would pronounce it 'stō-măk,' but that sounds

silly, doesn't it? We all know this word but we'll have to learn it as a sight word since it doesn't follow all our rules. How do we pronounce it?" *stomach*

- Show the student **Sight Word Card 70.**

"Let's find this word on our sight word charts."

- Help the student locate the word in the Irregular Spelling Booklet.

"We will add this card to our sight word deck."

"Let's read these words together now."

- Point to each word as you read it.

"Scheme. Chorus. Stomach."

"Can you define 'scheme' or use it in a sentence?" *expect various responses*

- Have the student read and define the other words.

"This next group of words will contain another sound made by digraph ch. Echo these words and see if you can pick out the sound we are looking for. It will be the same in all three words."

Lesson 123

"Chef (/shĕf/)." *chef* ***"Charade (/shŭ rād´/)."*** *charade* ***"Crochet (/krō shā´/)."*** *crochet*

"What sound do you hear that is the same in all of these words?" */sh/*

- Write the following on the chalkboard: chef, charade, crochet.

"What do you see that might be making the /sh/ sound?" *digraph ch*

"That's right, digraph ch. How do we code a digraph?" *underline it*

- Underline the *ch* in each word, leaving enough space to mark cedillas under the *c*'s: <u>ch</u>ef, <u>ch</u>arade, cro<u>ch</u>et.

"This kind of 'ch' is sometimes called the 'soft ch' because it uses the soft c that says /s/. It is also called the 'French ch' because these soft ch words were taken from the French language. Can you repeat for me the two names of this last kind of digraph ch?" *soft ch or French ch*

"When we studied the soft c earlier this year, how did we code the c to show that it makes the /s/ sound?" *with a cedilla underneath it*

"So, how do we code this digraph so it will say /sh/ in these words?" *put a cedilla under the c*

"Very good! French ch words don't always follow our rules of coding because they usually follow French rules of pronunciation instead of English rules."

"The first two words follow our rules of coding, so we will code those."

"Can you help me code these?"

- Code the words as the student instructs: <u>çh</u>ĕf, <u>çh</u>å|rād~~e~~´ (v|cv).

"Let's read these words together."

- Point to each syllable as you say the words.

- Leave the words on the chalkboard for the rest of the lesson.
- Add **Sight Word Card 70** to the Sight Word Deck.

New Deck Cards

- Pull **Letter Card 49** from the Review Deck.
- Hold up **Letter Card 49.**

  "What is this called?" *digraph ch*
- Hold up **Picture Card 91** but keep the picture covered with your hand (or the letter card).

  "I have a card with a picture on it that contains the /k/ sound for the Greek ch."

  "I am going to describe it for you. See if you can guess what the picture is."

  "This is a sound you hear in all kinds of music. It is made when several musical notes are played at the same time on an instrument or group of instruments. These can be played in either a major or minor key, and a whole series of these make up a song. What do you think the picture is?" *chord*

  "The keyword for the Greek ch is 'chord.' That will help us remember that ch sometimes makes the /k/ sound."
- Show the student **Picture Card 91.**
- Hold up **Picture Card 92** but keep the picture covered with your hand (or the letter card).

  "Our second keyword makes the sound for the French ch, the /sh/ sound. I have a card with a picture on it that contains that sound. See if you can guess what the picture is. "

  "This is a person who does a certain kind of job. That job is cooking for a fancy restaurant and making up lots of new recipes so people will want to eat there. Sometimes this person wears a special outfit while cooking. It includes a white apron and a tall, puffy, white hat. What do you think the picture is?" *chef*

  "That's right. The keyword for the French ch is 'chef.' "
- Show the student **Picture Card 92.**
- **Note:** The digraphs and their pictures are also shown in the Rule Book on page 21.

  "These are irregular spellings for ch, so we won't add these to our spelling deck responses."
- **Note:** Add the new picture cards to the Review Deck (and re-insert **Letter Card 49**).

Lesson 123

BOARDWORK

"Let's practice coding some words like the ones you'll have on your worksheet."

"The rule charts are in your Rule Book if you need to look at them."

- Write the following word and phrases (without the coding marks) on the chalkboard, one at a time. Ask the student to help you code them. The correct coding is as indicated:

ēar´|āche

băs´|kėt (of) swēet pĭc´[tures
v c | c v

căt´[tle ĭn thė chūte

- Have the student determine whether each of the items coded is a word, a phrase, or a sentence.

Lesson 123

WORKSHEET

- The student should be seated where he/she can write comfortably.
- Give the student **Worksheet 123.** Make sure the student turns to the correct side.

"Today, let's spell two words with our new sounds."

"Put your finger by #1. The first word is 'chef.' "

"Write the word by #1."

- Allow time for the student to write the word.

"What word did you write?" *chef*

- Repeat with #2 (school).

"The rest of our words are words that you should be able to spell if you use the rules we've learned."

- Repeat with #3 (match), #4 (edge), and #5 (making).

"Now you're ready to code and read the words on your paper."

"Code the words by #6 through #10. After you have coded all the words, try to read them."

- Assist the student as necessary.

"Numbers 11 and 12 are questions about the paragraph just above them. If you find any words you can't read, code them. Then see if you can answer the questions."

- As the student works, provide help as needed. Help the student correct any incorrect answers. Then initial the worksheet in the space provided.

- Some time during the day, ask the student to read from the worksheet, a controlled reader, your basal reader, or other material of your choice.
- **Note:** Always make sure the worksheet is corrected before the student begins the homework. The worksheet serves as a guide to help complete the homework.

Homework

"Turn your paper over to the homework side."

"Do you know what to do on the homework paper?"

"When you finish your paper, I will check it for you and initial it in the space provided."

- Either now or later in the day, the student should complete the homework independently (if possible). Help the student correct any incorrect answers. Then initial the homework in the space provided.
- If possible, take time to play the Kid Card games listed in Lesson 120.

Lesson 123

Name ______________________

Teacher's Initials ____

Worksheet 123
(for use with Lesson 123)
Phonics 1

ch, ch

1. chef
2. school
3. match
4. edge
5. making
6. headache
7. chĭffŏn
8. pŭncture
9. tŏggle
10. sweetly

Dad sat by the fireplace last night and saw some good programs on the T.V. First was "The French Chef." This chef had excellent cooking skills. She made a lemon chiffon cake using eggs, flour, and other things. The cake looked so pretty when the chef was finished.

11. What did Dad watch on T.V. last night?
"The French Chef"

12. What did the chef put in the lemon chiffon cake?
eggs, flour, and other things

P1-WS-123a

Parent's Initials ____

Homework 123
(for use with Lesson 123)
Phonics 1

ch, ch

1. chĕf
2. school
3. scrĭpture
4. tĕxture
5. gŏggle
6. lŏnging
7. version
8. băffle
9. greed
10. sleet

Then Dad saw a show with a cowboy who drove a convertible rather than rode a horse. He even wore leather chaps and had a handlebar mustache. During the program, he hunted for some men who had stolen the saddles right off some horses. He looked like a real cowboy until he crawled into that convertible to chase after those men. I thought (thŏt) it was rather odd, but Dad says he enjoyed that program and the one with the chef.

11. What did the cowboy wear? chaps
12. What did the men steal? saddles

Parents: Your child has been taught the two additional sounds of *digraph ch*: the **Greek** (hard) **ch** (as in *chord*) and the **French** (soft) **ch** (as in *chef*).

P1-WS-123b

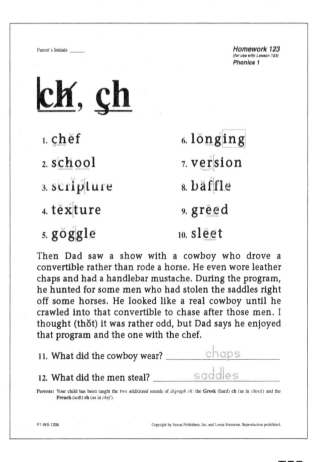

LESSON 124 Combination *wh*

lesson preparation

materials

Alphabet/Accent Deck (any section)

Review Decks

Spelling Sound Sheet 87

Letter Card 74

Picture Card 93

Spelling Card 48

Sight Word Cards 71–72

Worksheet 124

Reader 46 (*Carly's Collection*)

colored pencils

ALPHABET ACTIVITY

- The student should be seated.

  "We're going to work with the Alphabet/Accent Deck again today."

  "Let's say the unaccented syllables in a normal voice, and say the accented syllables longer, louder, and higher."

- Go through the **Alphabet/Accent Deck** (any section you choose), moving as quickly as possible.
- **Optional:** If you choose Section 1 or 2, shuffle the Alphabet/Accent Deck before the activity. Do not shuffle Section 3.

REVIEW OF DECKS

- The student should be seated where he/she can write comfortably.
- Show the student **Letter Cards 1–73** in random order. The student should name the letter on each letter card.
- Review **Affix Cards 1–8.**
- Show the student **Picture Cards 1–92** in random order. The student should name the keyword and sound for each picture card.
- Review **Sight Word Cards 1–70.**

- Give the student **Spelling Sound Sheet 87.**
- Call out the sounds on **Spelling Cards 1–47** in random order. The student should echo each sound and name the letter or letters that make the sound as he/she writes the letter(s) on the spelling sound sheet.
- Have the student set the spelling sound sheet aside for use later in the lesson.

NEW LEARNING

- **Note:** The pure sound of combination *wh* is /hw/. If it is pronounced this way, it will help the student spell correctly. In some areas of the United States, it is pronounced /w/, but this is more difficult to distinguish.

  "I'm going to say some words. Echo them back to me and listen for the sound that is the same in the initial position of each word."

- Point to your mouth as you say each word.

  "Echo after me. Wheat (/hwēt/)." *wheat* ***"Why (/hwī/)."*** *why* ***"Whip (/hwĭp/)."*** *whip*

  "What sound do you hear that is the same in all of these words?" */hw/*

  "That's right. The sound you hear is /hw/."

  "Is this sound voiced or unvoiced?" *unvoiced*

- Write the following on the chalkboard: wheat, why, whip.

  "What do you see that might be making the /hw/ sound?" *wh*

  "There is a 'wh' in all of these words, so we can see that the letters 'wh' must be making the /hw/ sound."

  "How many sounds do you hear?" *one*

  "How many letters are making that sound?" *two*

  "Is this sound what you would expect from 'wh'?" *no*

  "The unexpected thing about combination wh is that it is written as 'wh,' but we pronounce it by making the /h/ sound first. You blow air out to make the /h/ sound and then you round your lips to make the /w/ sound. You actually pronounce it backwards! This all happens very, very quickly: /hw/."

- Have the student practice making this sound until he/she is comfortable with it.

  "Do you remember how we code combinations?" *with arcs*

- Code the words:

  wh ēa̸t   whȳ′   whĭp

- Leave the words on the chalkboard for the remainder of the lesson.

Lesson 124

NEW DECK CARDS

- Show the student **Letter Card 74.**

  "What do we call this?" *combination wh*

- Hold up **Picture Card 93** but keep the picture covered with your hand (or the letter card).

  "I have a card with a picture on it that contains the /hw/ sound."

  "I am going to describe it for you. See if you can guess what the picture is."

  "These are animals that live their entire lives in oceans all over the world. Even though these animals live among the fish, they are not fish themselves; they are mammals, like us. They can survive in incredibly cold water because their thick layers of blubber keep them warm. What do you think the picture is?" *whale*

- Show the student **Picture Card 93.**

  "The word 'whale' helps us remember the /hw/ sound since it begins with that sound."

- **Note:** The combination and its picture are also shown in the Rule Book on page 22.

  "We are going to add this to our spelling deck because the spelling of the /hw/ sound is found in many English words."

  "Find your spelling sound sheet. Put your finger on #48."

- Hold up **Spelling Card 48** so only you can see what is written. Using the hand signals, follow the instructions on the card.
- Have the student put the spelling sound sheet away.
- **Note:** Add the new letter, picture, and spelling cards to the Review Decks.

BOARDWORK

- Write the following on the chalkboard:

  clothes /klōz/ don't /dōnt/

  "We have two new sight words today."

- Point to the first word.

  "Can you tell me what this word is? Remember, it's a sight word, so it won't follow all of our rules."

- Allow the student to try to pronounce the word. If necessary, say it for him/her.

  "This word is 'clothes.' Can you use the word 'clothes' in a sentence?" *expect various answers*

- Repeat with "don't."
- Show the student **Sight Word Cards 71** and **72.**

"Let's find these words on our sight word charts."

- Help the student locate the words in the Irregular Spelling Booklet.

"We will add these cards to our sight word deck."

"Let's practice coding some words like the ones you'll have on your worksheet."

"The rule charts are in your Rule Book if you need to look at them."

- Write the following sentences (without the coding marks) on the chalkboard, one at a time. Ask the student to help you code them. The correct coding is as indicated:

Mēēt the̊ first pe̲r̲′|so̊n ăt the̊ lākē.
vc|cv

Mĭng took å short′|cŭt ĭn the̊ rāçē.

- Have the student determine whether each of the items coded is a word, a phrase, or a sentence.
- Add **Sight Word Cards 71** and **72** to the Sight Word Deck.

WORKSHEET

- The student should be seated where he/she can write comfortably.
- Give the student **Worksheet 124.** Make sure the student turns to the correct side.

"Today, let's spell with the /hw/ sound using combination wh."

"Combination wh is almost always found in the initial position, so listen carefully to the beginning of each word."

"Put your finger by #1. The first word is 'whale.' "

"Unblend 'whale' with me." */hw/ /ā/ /l/*

- Hold up one finger for each sound.

"Now spell those sounds." *combination wh … a … l … e*

- Point to each finger as you spell the sounds.

"Now write 'whale' by #1."

- Allow time for the student to write the word.

"What word did you write?" *whale*

- Repeat the procedure with #2 (when), #3 (while), #4 (wheel), and #5 (which).

"Now you're ready to code and read the words on your paper."

"Code the words by #6 through #10. After you have coded all the words, try to read them."

- Assist the student as necessary.

"Look at the picture at the bottom of the page. Write a story about what's happening in the picture. Don't worry about spelling. When you are finished, we will take time to check spelling and correct mistakes."

- As the student works, provide help as needed.
- Then have the student read the story silently and check for spelling errors. Help the student correct any mistakes. A perfect paper is not as important as the student putting his/her thoughts on paper and being able to recognize spelling errors that can be corrected (e.g., *k* and *c* spelling). Be sure to correct the rest of the worksheet as well. Then initial it in the space provided.
- Have the student read the story to you. It is important that children learn to feel comfortable speaking in front of others.
- **Note:** Always make sure the worksheet is corrected before the student begins the homework. The worksheet serves as a guide to help complete the homework.

HOMEWORK

"Turn your paper over to the homework side."

"Do you know what to do on the homework paper?"

"Watch for combinations wh, ar, or, and qu. Always code suffixes and final, stable syllables before coding the rest of the word."

"Look at the picture at the bottom of the page. Write a story about what you think happened in the picture."

"When you finish your paper, I will check it for you and initial it in the space provided."

- Either now or later in the day, the student should complete the homework independently (if possible). Help the student correct any incorrect answers. Then initial the homework in the space provided.

READER

"We have another new book today."

- Give the student **Reader 46 (*Carly's Collection*)** and some colored pencils.

"Can you tell me this book's title?" Carly's Collection

- Assist the student as necessary as he/she constructs the book.
- When the student finishes, staple or put a rubber band around the book's spine.

"The title of this book is ________?" Carly's Collection

"I want you to read your book to yourself. When you are finished reading, color the pictures. Write your name on the book so I will know who colored it."

"Keep your book handy because I will be asking you to read it for me."

- Some time during the day, have the student read the reader to you.
- If possible, take time to play the Kid Card games listed in Lesson 120. Try to see that the student is prepared for tomorrow's assessment.

Lesson 124

Name ______________________

Teacher's Initials ____

Worksheet 124
(for use with Lesson 124)
Phonics 1

wh

1. whale
2. when
3. while
4. wheel
5. which
6. white
7. whirlpool
8. whisker
9. whim
10. racehorse

P1-WS-124a

Parent's Initials ____

Homework 124
(for use with Lesson 124)
Phonics 1

wh

1. whirl
2. soon
3. drool
4. swirling
5. strike
6. whimper
7. sort
8. worn
9. twice
10. ulcer

Parents: Your child has been taught **combination wh;** and that it is pronounced "hw," not "w."

P1-WS-124b

LESSON 125 Assessment

lesson preparation

materials

Alphabet/Accent Deck (Section 3)

Review Decks

Assessment 24

Spelling Test 22

Assessment 24 Recording Form

Kid Cards

tokens

the night before

- Separate the Kid Cards marked "Lesson 125."

ALPHABET ACTIVITY

- The student should be seated.

  "We're going to work with the third Alphabet/Accent Deck again today."

- Show the student **Alphabet/Accent Card 1.**

  "When you say the accented letter, I want you to raise your hands high up in the air. Then drop them back in your lap as you say the unaccented letter."

- Have the student say "A" (raise hands high in the air), and then "B" (drop hands back in lap).
- Continue with **Alphabet/Accent Cards 2–25,** moving as quickly as possible.

REVIEW OF DECKS

- The student should be seated where he/she can write comfortably.
- Show the student **Letter Cards 1–74** in random order. The student should name the letter on each letter card.
- Review **Affix Cards 1–8.**
- Show the student **Picture Cards 1–93** in random order. The student should name the keyword and sound for each picture card.
- Review **Sight Word Cards 1–72.**

WRITTEN ASSESSMENT

- Have the student sit where he/she can write comfortably.
- Give the student **Assessment 24.**
- **Section I:**

  "Today we are going to write some words for our assessment."

  "I'm going to say a word. Write the letter that makes each sound in that word on the lines by #1."

  "Look at the rule charts if you need to."

  "Here's the first word: pledge."
- Repeat with the following words in the order shown: #2 (scratch), #3 (age), #4 (inch), and #5 (cutting).
- **Reminder:** While the student spells, be ready to point to appropriate rule charts as necessary.
- **Section II:**

  "Look at the letters by #6."

  "Find the picture of the keyword for this sound."

  "Draw a line from the letters to the keyword."
- Repeat with #7 and #8. Allow a few minutes for the student to work.
- The pictures (from top to bottom) are as follows: patch, pie, bridge.
- **Section III:**

  "Put your finger on #9."

  "Code the words by #9 through #12."
- Allow a few minutes for the student to work.
- **Section IV:**

  "Read the paragraph. If you find any words you can't read, code them to help you figure them out. Then answer the questions by #13 through #16."
- **Reminder:** If the student absolutely cannot read the paragraph, read it to the student to see if he or she can answer the questions.

  "When you are finished, show your paper to me."
- This paper will be used during the oral portion of the assessment.

Spelling Test

- Give the student **Spelling Test 22.**
- Call out the following words (in the order shown). Sound them out, if necessary.

  #1 (germ), #2 (sound), #3 (broken), #4 (seven), #5 (finish), #6 (slipped), #7 (sliding), #8 (glasses), #9 (river), #10 (sanding), #11 (want), #12 (goes)
- Grade and record the test in any manner that suits your needs.

Oral Assessment

- It is important to complete the oral assessment promptly (today, if possible) in order to identify any areas of weakness and begin remediation.
- Use the assessment and the following dialogue to complete the oral portion.
- **Section V:**
- Point to the sight word by #17.

  "Read this sight word for me."
- Record the student's response by placing a check mark by each word he/she reads correctly.
- Repeat with #18 and #19.
- **Section VI:**
- Show the student the letters by #20.

  "Tell me the name of these letters and the sounds they make."
- Write the student's response on the adjacent line.
- Repeat with #21 and #22.

Assessment Evaluation

- Grade the assessment and record the results on **Assessment 24 Recording Form.** Check off the boxes to indicate mastery (i.e., the section was completed with 100% accuracy).
- **Reminder:** Try to give as many points as possible for work attempted. Do not grade the coding marks too severely. The most important coding marks to look for are breves, macrons, and syllable division lines.
- See the introductory material for detailed information regarding grading and recording procedures.
- Use the assessment results to identify those skills in which the student is weak. Practice those skills by playing Kid Card games.

- Add the Kid Cards marked "Lesson 125" to the existing decks. Listed below are games appropriate for remediation in selected areas. See "Games and Activities" for the directions for each game.
- **Section I:** Play "Spelling Deck Perfection," "Sound Scamper," "Spell Out #1 or #2," or have the student use the letter tiles to spell words you give from the Spelling Word List.
- **Section II:** Play "Keyword and Sound" or "Letter/Sound Identification."
- **Section III:** Play "Chalkboard Challenge."
- **Section IV:** Either have the student read the controlled reader and then ask questions for comprehension, or play "Acting Out" with the green Kid Cards.
- **Section V:** Play "At First Sight."
- **Section VI:** Play "Letter/Sound Identification."
- When the student seems more secure in areas that had previously proven difficult, retest him/her (in those areas only) and indicate on the recording form any sections the student has subsequently mastered.
- Try to help the student achieve mastery of all the sections before the next assessment.
- If the student is having difficulty with a particular skill, keep his or her practice activities at the most basic level so the chance of success is greater.

Name ____________________

Assessment 24
(for use with Lesson 125)
Phonics 1

Section I

1. p l e d g e
2. s c r a t c h
3. a g e
4. i n c h
5. c u t t i n g

Section II

6. ie

7. dge

8. tch

Section III

9. mouthpiece
10. thief
11. tie
12. hitch

Section IV

A long time ago, people had no cars. When they needed to go somewhere, they would walk (wŏk), ride a horse, or ride in a wagon. The wagons were big and could hold many people. Fabric was put on the top to keep sun and rain from being a problem. A team of horses pulled the wagon. When they had to travel a long way, the wagons lined up on the roads. The people felt better traveling together. At night, they formed a circle with the wagons and the people stayed in the center of the circle.

13. How did people get around a long time ago?
walk, ride a horse, ride in a wagon

14. What was on top of the wagon?
fabric

15. What pulled the wagon?
a team of horses

P1-A-024a

Assessment 24
(for use with Lesson 125)
Phonics 1

16. What did the people do at night with their wagons?
formed a circle

Section V

17. cover ________
18. though ________
19. certain ________

Section VI

20. ie digraph ie, /ī/, /ē/
21. dge trigraph dge, /j/
22. tch trigraph tch, /ch/

P1-A-024b

Lesson 126 — Quadrigraph *eigh*

lesson preparation

materials

container of letter tiles
Review Decks
Letter Card 75
Picture Card 94
Worksheet 126
Spelling List 23

new concepts

quadrigraph

Alphabet Activity

- The student should be seated with the container of letter tiles.

  "Before we start, let's say the alphabet together so it is fresh in our minds."
- Recite the alphabet with the student.
- Give the following instructions one at a time, allowing time for the student to accomplish each task before giving the next instruction.

  "Take all of the letter tiles out of your container."

  "Flip all of the letters over so that you are looking at the lowercase letters. If they are flipped correctly, they will all be blue."

  "Now we're ready. See if you can put all your letters in alphabetical order."
- When the student has finished, continue.

  "Quickly pull down the vowels."

  "Make as many three-letter words as you can until I stop you."
- As the student works, ask him/her to tell you some of the words he/she forms.
- Have the student replace the tiles in the container and put it away.

Review of Decks

- Show the student **Letter Cards 1–74** in random order. The student should name the letter on each letter card.
- Review **Affix Cards 1–8.**

- Show the student **Picture Cards 1–93** in random order. The student should name the keyword and sound for each picture card.
- Review **Sight Word Cards 1–72.**

  "Let's review our spelling cards orally today."

- Give the sounds on **Spelling Cards 1–48** in random order. The student should echo each response and then skywrite it.

NEW LEARNING

"I'm going to say some words. Echo them back to me and listen for the sound that is the same in each word."

- Point to your mouth as you say each word.

  "Echo after me. Eight." *eight* ***"Weigh."*** *weigh* ***"Neighbor."*** *neighbor*

  "What sound do you hear in all of these words?" /ā/

  "That's right. The sound you hear in all of these words is /ā/."

  "Is this sound voiced or unvoiced?" *voiced*

- Write the following on the chalkboard: eight, weigh, neighbor.

  "What do you see that might be making the /ā/ sound?" *eigh*

  "We know the word for two letters that make one sound. What is that word?" *digraph*

  "We even studied a group of three letters that make one sound: 'i-g-h.' Do you remember what we called 'i-g-h'?" *trigraph*

  "So now we see that even four letters can come together to make one sound. When that happens, those four letters are called a 'quadrigraph.' Echo that with me." *quadrigraph*

- Write the following on the chalkboard: quadrigraph.

  " 'Quad' means 'four.' There are lots of words that begin with 'quad' and they all describe something that has four parts. Like 'quadruplets,' which means four babies born at once. Or 'quadruple,' which means to make something four times as great, like quadrupling a recipe of cookies so you have four times as many cookies."

  "This quadrigraph is made up of 'e,' 'i,' 'g,' and 'h,' four letters that make one sound."

  "How do you think we code quadrigraphs?" *underline them*

  "That's right! We code quadrigraphs by underlining them, just like we code digraphs and trigraphs."

- Underline the quadrigraphs: eight, weigh, neighbor. Then have the student help you finish coding the words, and read and use them in sentences.

Lesson 126

NEW DECK CARDS

- Show the student **Letter Card 75.**

  "What will we say when we see this card?" *quadrigraph eigh*

- Hold up **Picture Card 94** but keep the picture covered with your hand (or the letter card).

  "I have a card with a picture on it that contains the /ā/ sound."

  "I am going to describe it for you. See if you can guess what the picture is."

  "This is something we sing about in holiday songs. We only bring them out when it snows. They are usually pulled by horses with big silver bells on their harnesses. What do you think the picture is?" *sleigh*

- Show the student **Picture Card 94.**

- **Note:** The quadrigraph and its picture are also shown in the Rule Book on page 22.

  "Quadrigraph eigh is an irregular spelling for the /ā/ sound, so we won't add it to our spelling deck response. Your Irregular Spelling Booklet has a list of words that contain quadrigraph eigh."

  "Get out your Irregular Spelling Booklet."

  "Look in the table of contents and see if you can find the page showing words that are spelled with quadrigraph eigh." *page 3*

  "Turn to page 3. The words at the bottom of page 3 use quadrigraph eigh, /ā/. They don't follow our regular rules, so we must memorize them."

- Allow time for the student to examine the list of words. If time permits, discuss the definition and/or pronunciation of some or all of the words.

  "Do you know any other words that belong on this list?"

- If the student offers any appropriate words, write the words on the chalkboard and have the student copy them into the booklet.

  "Use your Irregular Spelling Booklet to help you learn how to spell words with quadrigraph eigh. For now, put your booklet away."

- **Note:** Add the new letter and picture cards to the Review Decks.

BOARDWORK

"Let's practice coding some words like the ones you'll have on your worksheet."

"The rule charts are in your Rule Book if you need to look at them."

- Write the following phrase and sentences (without the coding marks) on the chalkboard, one at a time. Ask the student to help you code them. The correct coding is as indicated:

eight whoops

Lesson 126

Whȳ´ (do) wē´ spoil nā´[ture wĭth trăsh?

The bā´|bȳ (was) trȳ´ing (to) ēat the plăs´|tĭc chĭps.

- Have the student determine whether each of the items coded is a word, a phrase, or a sentence.

WORKSHEET

- The student should be seated where he/she can write comfortably.
- Give the student **Worksheet 126.** Make sure the student turns to the correct side.

"Today, let's spell with the /ā/ sound using quadrigraph eigh."

"Put your finger by #1. The first word is 'eight.' "

"Unblend 'eight' with me." */ā/ /t/*

- Hold up one finger for each sound.

"Let's spell those sounds." *quadrigraph eigh ... t*

- Point to each finger as you spell a sound.

"Now spell the word again and write it on the line by #1."

- Allow time for the student to write the word.

"What word did you write?" *eight*

- Repeat the procedure with #2 (sleigh), #3 (weigh), #4 (eighth), and #5 (freight).

"Now you're ready to code and read the words on your paper."

"Code the words by #6 through #10. After you have coded all the words, try to read them."

- Assist the student as necessary.

"Numbers 11 and 12 are questions about the paragraph just above them. If you find any words you can't read, code them. Then see if you can answer the questions."

- As the student works, provide help as needed. Help the student correct any incorrect answers. Then initial the worksheet in the space provided.
- Some time during the day, ask the student to read from the worksheet, a controlled reader, your basal reader, or other material of your choice.
- **Note:** Always make sure the worksheet is corrected before the student begins the homework. The worksheet serves as a guide to help complete the homework.

HOMEWORK

"Turn your paper over to the homework side."

"Do you know what to do on the homework paper?"

"Be sure to watch for quadrigraph eigh and words that need to be divided."

"When you finish your paper, I will check it for you and initial it in the space provided."

- Either now or later in the day, the student should complete the homework independently (if possible). Help the student correct any incorrect answers. Then initial the homework in the space provided.

SPELLING LIST

- Fold **Spelling List 23** in half lengthwise (with the printed side facing out).

  "Leave your paper just like I give it to you."

- Give the student **Spelling List 23,** folded with the blank lines facing up.

  "Let's spell some more words."

- Call out the following words (in the order shown). Sound them out, if necessary.

  #1 (saving), #2 (sending), #3 (smiled), #4 (melted), #5 (shiny), #6 (dusty), #7 (boxes), #8 (wishes), #9 (mention), #10 (marching), #11 (floor), #12 (early)

  "Now unfold your paper and check your words."

- Check the student's work to see if he/she needs extra help with spelling.

  "I want you to practice these words. We'll have a spelling test in a few days."

- If possible, take time to play the Kid Card games listed in Lesson 125.

Name ______ **Worksheet 126** (for use with Lesson 126) **Phonics 1**

Teacher's Initials ____

eigh

1. eight
2. sleigh
3. weigh
4. eighth
5. freight
6. overweight
7. moisture
8. toothache
9. whispering
10. wheat

My neighbor, Ted, drives a freight truck for his boss. This means he takes products from the people who make them to the people who want them. People who make products phone him for help getting the products to the people who need them.

11. What does my neighbor do for his boss?
    He drives a freight truck.
12. How do people tell Ted they need him?
    They phone him.

P1-WS-126a

Parent's Initials ____ **Homework 126** (for use with Lesson 126) **Phonics 1**

eigh

1. underweight
2. freight
3. sculpture
4. backache
5. screaming
6. grease or grease
7. please
8. proof
9. boom
10. lantern

Ted weighs the products and sets a price according to the total weight. For example, if someone were to send a sleigh, it might weigh eighty pounds. Ted might charge that person fifty cents to deliver it. Ted would then take his truckload of products, including the sleigh, to the people who ordered them. The sleigh might be his eighth delivery that day. The next day he starts with a load of new (noo) freight.

11. What does Ted do before he sets a price for shipping the products? He weighs them.
12. What will Ted do the next day?
    He will start with a new load.

Parents: Your child has been taught quadrigraph eigh; that a quadrigraph is four letters that come together to make one sound; and that quadrigraphs are coded by underlining them.

P1-WS-126b

LESSON 127 — *w* or *qu* before *a*

lesson preparation

materials

Alphabet/Accent Deck (any section)

Retired Decks

Affix Deck

Spelling Sound Sheet 88

Picture Card 95

Sight Word Cards 73–75

Worksheet 127

Reader 47 (*Bo and the Bagel*)

colored pencils

ALPHABET ACTIVITY

"We're going to work with the Alphabet/Accent Deck again today."

"Let's stand up. When you say the accented letters, I want you to stand up on your tiptoes, and then drop back down as you say the unaccented letters."

- Go through the **Alphabet/Accent Deck** (any section you choose), moving as quickly as possible.
- Have the student take his/her seat.
- **Optional:** If you use Section 1 or 2, shuffle the deck before the activity. Do not shuffle Section 3.

REVIEW OF DECKS

- The student should be seated where he/she can write comfortably.
- Show the student the retired letter cards in random order. The student should name the letter on each letter card.
- Review **Affix Cards 1–8.**
- Show the student the retired picture cards in random order. The student should name the keyword and sound for each picture card.
- Review the retired sight word cards.

- Give the student **Spelling Sound Sheet 88.**
- Call out the sounds on the retired spelling cards in random order. The student should echo each sound and name the letter or letters that make the sound as he/she writes the letter(s) on the spelling sound sheet.
- Have the student put the spelling sound sheet away.

NEW LEARNING

"I'm going to say some words. Echo them back to me and listen for the sound that is the same in the medial position of each word."

- Point to your mouth as you say each word.

"Echo after me. Wasp." *wasp* ***"Wand."*** *wand* ***"Watch."*** *watch*

"What sound do you hear in the medial position of these words?" */ä/ (similar to /ŏ/)*

"That's right. The sound you are hearing is /ä/."

- Write the following on the chalkboard: wasp, wand, watch.

"What letter is making the /ä/ sound?" *a*

"That's right. Do you see anything else that these words have in common?" *they all start with w*

"The letter w before an a makes the a take on the sound /ä/."

- Although the /ä/ sound is slightly different from the /ŏ/ sound, most people don't make the distinction.

"The letter w is a bossy letter and makes lots of letters take on different sounds when they are near it."

"Remember digraph aw? Even when w comes after the a, it makes the a say /ä/, as in 'straw.' "

"Now echo these words. Squash." *squash* ***"Quad."*** *quad* ***"Squabble."*** *squabble*

"Look at these words and see what else makes the a say this /ä/ sound."

- Write the following on the chalkboard: squash, quad, squabble.

"What else do you think can make the letter a say /ä/?" *qu*

"When 'qu' comes before a, it causes the a to make the sound of /ä/."

"We code this sound by putting two dots over the a, like this."

- Code all the a's with two dots: wäsp, wänd, wätch, squäsh, quäd, squäbble.

"Let's code the rest of these words and read them."

- Finish coding the words: wäsp, wänd, wätch, squäsh, quäd, squäb´[ble.

"Can you tell me what any of these words mean, or use them in sentences?" *expect various responses*

- Discuss the meaning of each word.
- Leave the words on the chalkboard for the rest of the lesson.

NEW DECK CARDS

- Pull **Letter Card 7** from the Review Deck.
- Hold up **Letter Card 7.**

"What do we say when we see this card?" *a*

- Hold up **Picture Card 95** but keep the picture covered with your hand (or the letter card).

"I have a card with a picture on it that contains the /ä/ sound."

"I am going to describe it for you. See if you can guess what the picture is."

"These are things that can come in many different materials, but most are made of leather. They are usually folded once or twice. Men usually carry them in their back pockets; women carry them in their purses. These might contain money, photos, or credit cards. What do you think the picture is?" *wallet*

- Show the student **Picture Card 95.**

"The word 'wallet' helps us remember the /ä/ sound since it contains that sound."

"This spelling of the /ä/ sound is irregular, so we won't add it to our spelling deck responses."

- **Note:** Add the new picture card to the Review Deck (and re-insert **Letter Card 7**).

BOARDWORK

- Write the following on the chalkboard:

bought /bŏt/ fought /fŏt/ thought /thŏt/

"We have three new sight words today."

- Point to the first word.

"Can you tell me what this word is? Remember, it's a sight word, so it won't follow all of our rules."

- Allow the student to try to pronounce the word. If necessary, say it for him/her.

"This word is 'bought.' Can you use the word 'bought' in a sentence?" *expect various answers*

- Repeat with "fought" and "thought."
- Show the student **Sight Word Cards 73–75.**

"Let's find these words on our sight word charts."

- Help the student locate the words in the Irregular Spelling Booklet.

"We will add these cards to our sight word deck."

"Let's practice coding some words like the ones you'll have on your worksheet."

"The rule charts are in your Rule Book if you need to look at them."

- Write the following phrase and sentence (without the coding marks) on the chalkboard, one at a time. Ask the student to help you code them. The correct coding is as indicated:

Wē′ wä′|ter|ed| thė plănt|s| slōw′|ly.
v | c v

pēa′|nŭt bŭt′|ter ănd jĕl′|lȳ
v | c v v c | c v v c | cv

- Have the student determine whether each of the items coded is a word, a phrase, or a sentence.

"Did you notice that we can now code 'watered'? It's no longer a temporary sight word since we've learned the /ŏ/ sound of the letter a."

- Add **Sight Word Cards 73–75** to the Sight Word Deck.

WORKSHEET

- The student should be seated where he/she can write comfortably.

"Your Irregular Spelling Booklet has a list of words that contain the /ä/ sound spelled with 'a.' "

"Get out your Irregular Spelling Booklet."

"Look in the table of contents and see if you can find the page showing words that are spelled with 'a' after 'w' or 'qu.' " *page 14*

"Turn to page 14. All of the words on page 14 have the /ŏ/ sound. They don't follow our regular rules, so we must memorize them."

- Allow time for the student to examine the list of words. If time permits, discuss the definition and/or pronunciation of some or all of the words.

"Do you know any other words that belong on this list?"

- If the student offers any appropriate words, write the words on the chalkboard and have the student copy them into the booklet.

"Use your Irregular Spelling Booklet to help you learn how to spell words with the /ä/ sound. For now, put your booklet away and let's try to spell some words."

- Give the student **Worksheet 127.** Make sure the student turns to the correct side.

"Let's spell today with the /ä/ sound of 'a.' "

"Put your finger by #1. The first word is 'wasp.' "

"Unblend 'wasp' with me." */w/ /ä/ /s/ /p/*

- Hold up one finger for each sound.

"Now spell those sounds." *w ... a ... s ... p*

- Point to a finger as the student spells each sound.

"Now write 'wasp' by #1."

- Allow time for the student to write the word.

"What word did you write?" *wasp*

- Repeat the procedure with #2 (watch), #3 (squash), #4 (squat), and #5 (squad).

"Now you're ready to code and read the words on your paper."

"Code the words by #6 through #10. After you have coded all the words, try to read them."

- Assist the student as necessary.

"Now read the word by #11. If you have trouble reading the word, code it. Then draw a line from the word to the picture it matches."

- Repeat with #12 through #14.
- As the student works, provide help as needed. Help the student correct any incorrect answers. Then initial the worksheet in the space provided.
- Some time during the day, ask the student to read from the worksheet, a controlled reader, your basal reader, or other material of your choice.
- **Note:** Always make sure the worksheet is corrected before the student begins the homework. The worksheet serves as a guide to help complete the homework.

HOMEWORK

"Turn your paper over to the homework side."

"Do you know what to do on the homework paper?"

"When you finish your paper, I will check it for you and initial it in the space provided."

- Either now or later in the day, the student should complete the homework independently (if possible). Help the student correct any incorrect answers. Then initial the homework in the space provided.

READER

"We have another new book today."

- Give the student **Reader 47 (*Bo and the Bagel*)** and some colored pencils.

"Can you tell me this book's title?" *Bo and the Bagel*

- Assist the student as necessary as he/she constructs the book.

- When the student finishes, staple or put a rubber band around the book's spine.

  "The title of this book is __________?" *Bo and the Bagel*

  "I want you to read your book to yourself. When you are finished reading, color the pictures. Write your name on the book so I will know who colored it."

  "Keep your book handy because I will be asking you to read it for me."

- Some time during the day, have the student read the reader to you.
- If possible, take time to play the Kid Card games listed in Lesson 125.

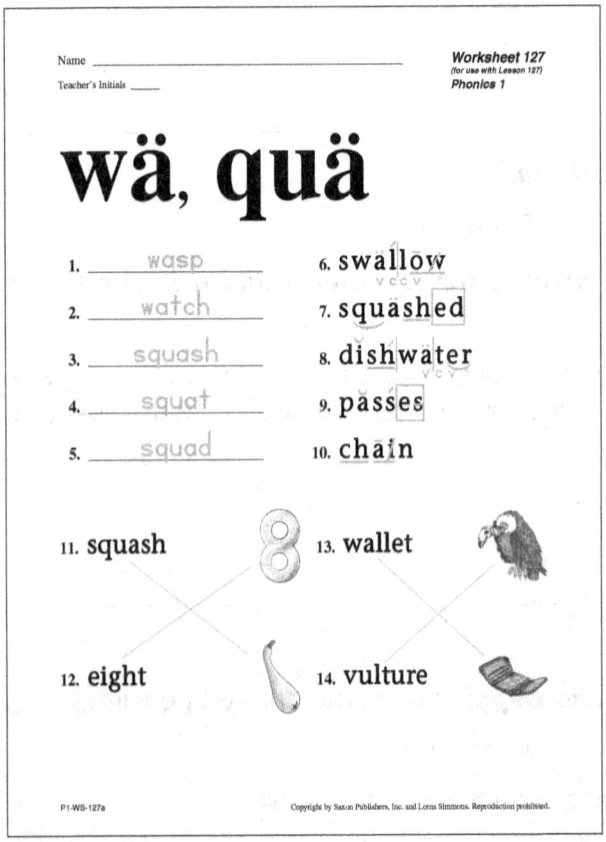

Name __________
Teacher's Initials ____

Worksheet 127
(for use with Lesson 127)
Phonics 1

wä, quä

1. wasp
2. watch
3. squash
4. squat
5. squad
6. swallow
7. squashed
8. dishwater
9. passes
10. chain

11. squash
12. eight
13. wallet
14. vulture

P1-WS-127a

Parent's Initials ____

Homework 127
(for use with Lesson 127)
Phonics 1

wä, quä

1. walk
2. wall
3. squad
4. slushes
5. taxes
6. twirl
7. chirped
8. roommate
9. hilltop
10. trailed

11. school
12. sleigh
13. wasp
14. chef

Parents: Your child has been taught that when the letter **a** follows **w** or **qu**, its sound is altered (as in *wallet* and *quantity*); and that this sound is coded by placing two dots over the *a* (*ä*).

P1-WS-127b

LESSON 128 — *a* before *l*

lesson preparation

materials

purple Kid Cards
Review Decks
Spelling Sound Sheet 89
tokens or colored pencil
Sight Word Card 76
Worksheet 128

ALPHABET ACTIVITY

- The student should be seated.

  "Today we are going to alphabetize some of our Kid Cards again."

- Give the student four or five purple word cards. Make sure that each card begins with a different letter.

  "When I say 'go,' say the alphabet out loud."

  "The first time you say a letter that one of your cards begins with, lay that card down. Lay each card to the right of the previous one. When you finish, the words should be in alphabetical order."

  "Ready, set, go!"

- Repeat with different Kid Cards if time permits.
- Collect the Kid Cards.

REVIEW OF DECKS

- The student should be seated where he/she can write comfortably.
- Show the student **Letter Cards 1–75** in random order. The student should name the letter on each letter card.
- Review **Affix Cards 1–8.**
- Show the student **Picture Cards 1–95** in random order. The student should name the keyword and sound for each picture card.
- Review **Sight Word Cards 1–75.**

- Give the student **Spelling Sound Sheet 89** and at least twelve tokens (or a colored pencil). If you can use "fun" markers, such as goldfish-shaped crackers or cereal pieces, it is much more enjoyable for the student.

  "Today, let's play Sight Word Bingo."

  "When I call out the sight words today, I want you to put a token on (or X out) the space with that word on your spelling sound sheet."

  "When you cover (or X out) all of the words on one line, either up and down, across, or from corner to corner, call out Bingo!"

- Watch for the student's accuracy as you play.
- Call out the words in the following order: sure, said, friend, their, where, floor, some, are, was, what, one, does. The student should Bingo by the time all the words have been called out.
- Collect the tokens (or colored pencil) and the spelling sound sheet. If you used tokens and the spelling sound sheet is unmarked, keep it available for practice.

NEW LEARNING

- Pull **Picture Card 95** from the Review Deck.

  "I'm going to say some words. Echo them back to me and listen for the sound that is the same in the final position of each word."

- Point to your mouth as you say each word.

  "Echo after me. Wall." *wall* ***"Fall."*** *fall* ***"Small."*** *small*

  "What sound do you hear in the final position of these words?" *l*

- Write the following on the chalkboard: wall, fall, small.

  "What letter is making the /ä/ sound?" *a*

  "That's right. Do you see anything else these words have in common?" *l follows a*

  "When the letter l follows an a, it causes the a to say /ä/, just like w and qu before a did."

  "How did we code the /ä/ sound of a?" *two dots over it*

- Code the *a*'s with two dots: wäll, fäll, smäll.

  "Can you tell me what any of these words mean, or use them in sentences?"

- Discuss the meaning of each word.

  "Get out your Rule Book and turn to page 14."

  "We have a new rule chart that will help us. You can refer to this chart whenever you need to."

- Point to and explain **Rule Chart 14.** Then point to the words on the chalkboard.

  "There's another rule that applies to these words. It's a rule we already know."

"Can you think of the rule about one-syllable words that end with f, l, or s?" *floss rule*

"That's right. These are all floss words, even though the letter a is making the /ä/ sound."

- Show the student **Picture Card 95.**

"Our keyword today is the same as yesterday's because 'wallet' also has an l after the a to help us remember that l does the same thing w does. They both make the letter a say /ä/."

- Re-insert **Picture Card 95** into the Review Deck.

"When the letter a says /ä/, it is irregular for spelling, so we have a chart in our Irregular Spelling Booklet that lists some of these words. You can use this chart to help you learn how to spell these words correctly."

"Get out your Irregular Spelling Booklet, look in the table of contents for the 'A Before L' spelling chart, and turn to that page."

- Allow time for the student to do this.

"What page is this chart on?" *page 15*

"Let's look at these words."

- If time permits, discuss the spelling and definition of each word on the chart. Then have the student put the booklet away.

BOARDWORK

- Write the following on the chalkboard:

whose /hōōz/

"We have a new sight word today."

"Can you tell me what this word is? Remember, it's a sight word, so it won't follow all of our rules."

- Allow the student to try to pronounce the word. If necessary, say it for him/her.

"This word is 'whose.' Can you use the word 'whose' in a sentence?" *expect various answers*

- Make sure the student uses the word to mean "that which belongs to whom" rather than the contraction "who's" (who is).
- Show the student **Sight Word Card 76.**

"Let's find this word on our sight word charts."

- Help the student locate the word in the Irregular Spelling Booklet.

"We'll add this card to our sight word deck."

"Let's practice coding some words like the ones you'll have on your worksheet."

"The rule charts are in your Rule Book if you need to look at them."

- Write the following sentences (without the coding marks) on the chalkboard, one at a time. Ask the student to help you code them. The correct coding is as indicated:

  Hē´ kēēps his (eye) ŏn thė bäll.

  Our bōat ställed ŏn thė wāy (to) thė dŏck.

- Have the student determine whether each of the items coded is a word, a phrase, or a sentence.
- Add **Sight Word Card 76** to the Sight Word Deck.

WORKSHEET

- The student should be seated where he/she can write comfortably.
- Give the student **Worksheet 128.** Make sure the student turns to the correct side.

  "Let's spell with the /ä/ sound of a again today."

  "Remember that when this sound is followed by a final l, it's a floss word and will be spelled with two l's."

  "Put your finger by #1. The first word is 'ball.' "

  "Unblend 'ball' with me." */b/ /ä/ /l/*

  "What sound do you hear in the final position?" */l/*

  "That should tell you something."

  "Write the word 'ball' on the line by #1."

- Allow time for the student to write the word.
- Repeat the procedure with #2 (call), #3 (salt), #4 (squall), and #5 (stall).

  "Now you're ready to code and read the words on your paper."

  "Code the words by #6 through #10. After you have coded all the words, try to read them."

- Assist the student as necessary.

  "Numbers 11 and 12 are questions about the paragraph just above them. If you find any words you can't read, code them. Then see if you can answer the questions."

- Discuss the pronunciation of the name "Pedro" (pā´·drō), if necessary.
- As the student works, provide help as needed. Help the student correct any incorrect answers. Then initial the worksheet in the space provided.
- Some time during the day, ask the student to read from the worksheet, a controlled reader, your basal reader, or other material of your choice.
- **Note:** Always make sure the worksheet is corrected before the student begins the homework. The worksheet serves as a guide to help complete the homework.

HOMEWORK

"Turn your paper over to the homework side."

"Do you know what to do on the homework side of the paper?"

"When you finish your paper, I will check it for you and initial it in the space provided."

- Either now or later in the day, the student should complete the homework independently (if possible). Help the student correct any incorrect answers. Then initial the homework in the space provided.
- If possible, take time to play the Kid Card games listed in Lesson 125.

Name ______________________

Teacher's Initials ____

Worksheet 128
(for use with Lesson 128)
Phonics 1

äl

1. ball
2. call
3. salt
4. squall
5. stall
6. ballpark
7. chalkboard
8. stalled
9. teenage
10. pound

Pedro, a small boy, was getting ready to go play at the park. As he rushed down the hall, he heard his mother call, "Be home in time for supper!" Before he left, he went to the carport to get his football. When he got to his friend Carlton's house, he knocked on the door. A tall boy, Carlton's brother, opened it.

11. What was Pedro getting ready to do?

play at the park

12. To whose house did Pedro go?

Carlton's

P1-WS-128a

Parent's Initials ____

Homework 128
(for use with Lesson 128)
Phonics 1

äl

1. hall
2. salt
3. roasted
4. pitched
5. huge
6. age
7. treehouse
8. sleeve
9. keep
10. seek

Carlton came to the door with all of his gear. They talked until they reached the walk that led to the park. Carlton began to bounce his basketball with the palm of his hand. He was trying to learn to dribble the basketball better. Pedro had brought some chalk, so he started to draw football plays on the sidewalk. They played football and basketball and drew (droo) with chalk until supper, when it was time to go home.

11. What was Carlton trying to learn to do better?

dribble the basketball

12. What did Carlton and Pedro do until supper?

played football and basketball and drew with chalk

Parents: Your child has been taught that when the letter a precedes l, it takes the sound of ä.

P1-WS-128b

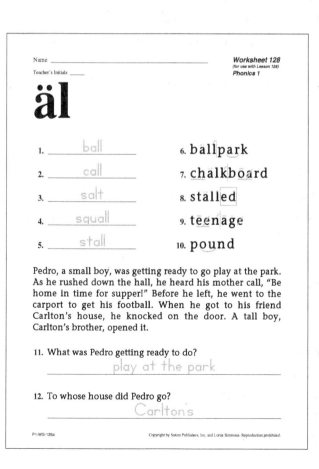

LESSON 129 — Prefix *un-*

lesson preparation

materials

Alphabet/Accent Deck (any section)

Review Decks

Spelling Sound Sheet 90

Affix Card 9

Worksheet 129

Reader 48 (*A Long Car Trip*)

colored pencils

new concepts

prefix

ALPHABET ACTIVITY

"We're going to work with one of the Alphabet/Accent Decks again today."

"Let's stand. When you say the accented letters, I want you to stand up on your tiptoes, and then drop back down as you say the unaccented letters."

- Go through the **Alphabet/Accent Deck** (any section you choose), moving as quickly as possible.
- **Optional:** If you use Section 1 or 2, shuffle the deck before the activity. Do not shuffle Section 3.

REVIEW OF DECKS

- The student should be seated where he/she can write comfortably.
- Show the student **Letter Cards 1–75** in random order. The student should name the letter on each letter card.
- Review **Affix Cards 1–8.**
- Show the student **Picture Cards 1–95** in random order. The student should name the keyword and sound for each picture card.
- Review **Sight Word Cards 1–76.**
- Give the student **Spelling Sound Sheet 90.**
- Call out the sounds on **Spelling Cards 1–48** in random order. The student should echo each sound and name the letter or letters that make the sound as he/she writes the letter(s) on the spelling sound sheet.
- Have the student put the spelling sound sheet away.

New Learning

"I'm going to say some words. Echo them back to me and listen for the sound that is the same in the initial position of each word."

- Point to your mouth as you say each word.

"Echo after me. Unclear." *unclear* ***"Unable."*** *unable* ***"Unzip."*** *unzip*

"What is the same?" *un*

- Write the following on the chalkboard: unclear, unable, unzip.

"What do all of these words have in common?" *un*

"Does this remind you of something we've studied before?"

"Each of these words has something added to it that changes its meaning, like a suffix does. Where do we add a suffix?" *at the end of a word*

"Then this is something new. This is something that is added to the beginning of a word and changes its meaning. If it is added to the beginning of a word, it's called a 'prefix.' 'Pre' means 'before'; a prefix comes before the word."

"What do you think prefix un- means?" *not, the opposite of*

"A prefix is coded just like a suffix, with a box, so we can separate it from the root word."

- Code the words, boxing the prefixes first: [un]clēar′, [un]ā′[blé, [un]zip′.

"Can you tell me what these words mean, or use them in sentences?" *expect various answers*

- Discuss the meaning of each word.
- Show the student **Affix Card 9.**

"What do we say when we see this card?" *prefix un-*

- Have the student say the sound /ŭn/ rather than spell it. He/She will recognize and understand it more readily when it appears at the beginning of words.
- **Note:** Add the new affix card to the Affix Deck.

Boardwork

"Let's practice coding some words like the ones you'll have on your worksheet."

"The rule charts are in your Rule Book if you need to look at them."

- Write the following sentences (without the coding marks) on the chalkboard, one at a time. Ask the student to help you code them. The correct coding is as indicated:

Thăt [un]mādé′ bĕd căn wāit ŭn|tĭl′ nīné.
v c|cv

Wĭll wătch[ed] thé clŏck.

- Have the student determine whether each of the items coded is a word, a phrase, or a sentence.

WORKSHEET

- The student should be seated where he/she can write comfortably.
- Give the student **Worksheet 129.** Make sure the student turns to the correct side.

"Let's spell today with our new prefix, 'un.' "

"Put your finger by #1. The first word is 'uncooked.' "

"Unblend 'uncooked' with me." */ŭ/ /n/ /k/ /o͝o/ /k/ /t/*

- Hold up one finger for each sound.

"Now spell those sounds." *u … n … c … digraph oo … k … suffix -ed*

- Point to each finger as the student spells each sound.

"Now write 'uncooked' by #1."

- Allow time for the student to write the word.

"What word did you write?" *uncooked*

- Repeat the procedure with #2 (unfed), #3 (unpacked), #4 (unlined), and #5 (unsafe).

"Now you're ready to code and read the words on your paper."

"Code the words by #6 through #10. After you have coded all the words, try to read them."

- Assist the student as necessary.

"Look at the picture at the bottom of the page. Write a story about what has happened in the picture. Don't worry about spelling. When you are finished, we will take time to check spelling and correct mistakes."

- As the student works, provide help as needed.
- Then have the student read the story silently and check for spelling errors. Help the student correct any mistakes. A perfect paper is not as important as the student putting his/her thoughts on paper and being able to recognize spelling errors that can be corrected (e.g., *k* and *c* spelling). Be sure to correct the rest of the worksheet as well. Then initial it in the space provided.
- Have the student read the story to you. It is important that children learn to feel comfortable speaking in front of others.
- **Note:** Always make sure the worksheet is corrected before the student begins the homework. The worksheet serves as a guide to help complete the homework.

HOMEWORK

"Turn your paper over to the homework side."

"Do you know what to do on the homework paper?"

"Look at the picture at the bottom of the page. Use the lines beside the picture and write a story telling what's about to happen in the picture."

"When you finish your paper, I will check it for you and initial it in the space provided."

- Either now or later in the day, the student should complete the homework independently (if possible). Help the student correct any incorrect answers. Then initial the homework in the space provided.
- **Note:** When accenting the second syllable of a two-syllable word containing a suffix, the student may place the accent mark immediately before the suffix or after it. Either placement is acceptable.

READER

"We have another new book today."

- Give the student **Reader 48 (*A Long Car Trip*)** and some colored pencils.

"Can you tell me this book's title?" *A Long Car Trip*

- Assist the student as necessary as he/she constructs the book.
- When the student finishes, staple or put a rubber band around the book's spine.

"The title of this book is _________?" *A Long Car Trip*

"I want you to read your book to yourself. When you are finished reading, color the pictures. Write your name on the book so I will know who colored it."

"Keep your book handy because I will be asking you to read it for me."

- Some time during the day, have the student read the reader to you.
- If possible, take time to play the Kid Card games listed in Lesson 125.

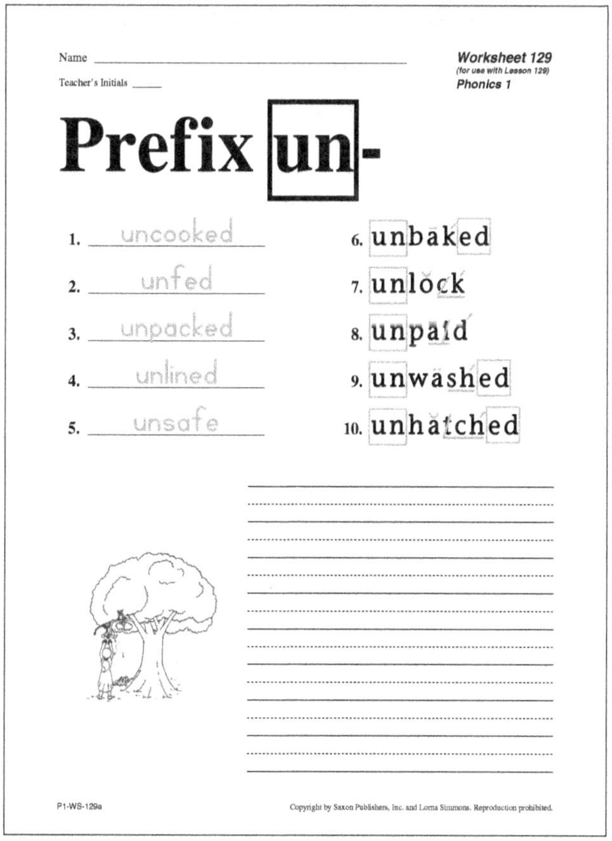

Name __________
Teacher's Initials ____

Worksheet 129
(for use with Lesson 129)
Phonics 1

Prefix un-

1. uncooked
2. unfed
3. unpacked
4. unlined
5. unsafe
6. unbaked
7. unlock
8. unpaid
9. unwashed
10. unhatched

P1-WS-129a

Copyright by Saxon Publishers, Inc. and Lorna Simmons. Reproduction prohibited.

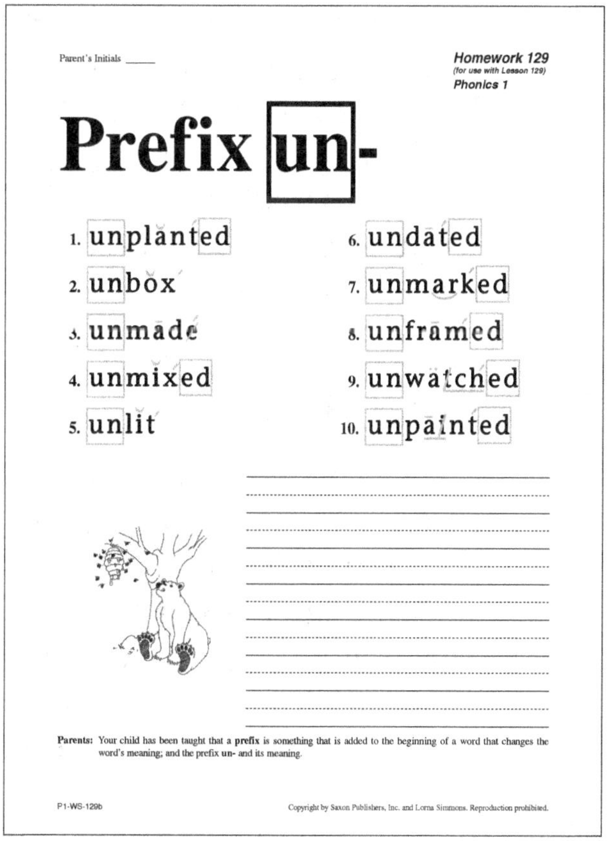

Parent's Initials ____

Homework 129
(for use with Lesson 129)
Phonics 1

Prefix un-

1. unplanted
2. unbox
3. unmade
4. unmixed
5. unlit
6. undated
7. unmarked
8. unframed
9. unwatched
10. unpainted

Parents: Your child has been taught that a **prefix** is something that is added to the beginning of a word that changes the word's meaning; and the prefix **un-** and its meaning.

P1-WS-129b

Copyright by Saxon Publishers, Inc. and Lorna Simmons. Reproduction prohibited.

LESSON 130 Assessment

lesson preparation

materials

Alphabet/Accent Deck (any section)

Review Decks

Assessment 25

Spelling Test 23

Assessment 25 Recording Form

Kid Cards

tokens

the night before

- Separate the Kid Cards marked "Lesson 130."

ALPHABET ACTIVITY

"We're going to work with one of the Alphabet/Accent Decks again today."

"Let's stand up. When you say the accented letters, I want you to stand up on your tiptoes, and then drop back down as you say the unaccented letters."

- Go through the **Alphabet/Accent Deck** (any section you choose), moving as quickly as possible.
- **Optional:** If you use Section 1 or 2, shuffle the deck before the activity. Do not shuffle Section 3.

REVIEW OF DECKS

- The student should be seated where he/she can write comfortably.
- Show the student **Letter Cards 1–75** in random order. The student should name the letter on each letter card.
- Review **Affix Cards 1–9.**
- Show the student **Picture Cards 1–95** in random order. The student should name the keyword and sound for each picture card.
- Review **Sight Word Cards 1–76.**

WRITTEN ASSESSMENT

- Have the student sit where he/she can write comfortably.
- Give the student **Assessment 25.**
- **Section I:**

  "Today we are going to write some words for our assessment."

  "I'm going to say a word. Write the letter that makes each sound in that word on the lines by #1."

  "Look at the rule charts if you need to."

  "Here's the first word: future."
- Repeat with the following words in the order shown: #2 (pasture), #3 (explosion), #4 (bridge), and #5 (stretch).
- **Reminder:** While the student spells, be ready to point to appropriate rule charts as necessary.
- **Section II:**

  "Look at the letters by #6."

  "Find the pictures of the keywords for this sound."

  "Draw a line from the letters to the keywords."
- Repeat with #7 and #8. Allow a few minutes for the student to work.
- The pictures (from top to bottom) are as follows: chef, cheese, television, chord, picture.
- **Section III:**

  "Put your finger on #9."

  "Code the words by #9 through #13."
- Allow a few minutes for the student to work.
- **Section IV:**

  "Turn your paper over and read the paragraph. If you find any words you can't read, code them to help you figure them out. Then answer the questions by #14 through #17."
- **Reminder:** If the student absolutely cannot read the paragraph, read it to the student to see if he or she can answer the questions.

  "When you are finished, show your paper to me."
- This paper will be used during the oral portion of the assessment.

Spelling Test

- Give the student **Spelling Test 23.**
- Call out the following words (in the order shown). Sound them out, if necessary.

  #1 (smiled), #2 (mention), #3 (melted), #4 (wishes), #5 (boxes),
  #6 (marching), #7 (shiny), #8 (saving), #9 (sending), #10 (dusty),
  #11 (early), #12 (floor)
- Grade and record the test in any manner that suits your needs.

Oral Assessment

- It is important to complete the oral assessment promptly (today, if possible) in order to identify any areas of weakness and begin remediation.
- Use the assessment and the following dialogue to complete the oral portion.
- **Section V:**
- Point to the sight word by #18.

  "Read this sight word for me."
- Record the student's response by placing a check mark by each word he/she reads correctly.
- Repeat with #19 and #20.
- **Section VI:**
- Show the student the letters by #21.

  "Tell me the name of these letters and the sounds they make."
- Write the student's response on the adjacent line.
- Repeat with #22 and #23.

Assessment Evaluation

- Grade the assessment and record the results on **Assessment 25 Recording Form.** Check off the boxes to indicate mastery (i.e., the section was completed with 100% accuracy).
- **Reminder:** Try to give as many points as possible for work attempted. Do not grade the coding marks too severely. The most important coding marks to look for are breves, macrons, and syllable division lines.
- Use the assessment results to identify those skills in which the student is weak. Practice those skills by playing Kid Card games.
- Add the Kid Cards marked "Lesson 130" to the existing decks. Listed below are games appropriate for remediation in selected areas. See "Games and Activities" for the directions for each game.
- **Section I:** Play "Spelling Deck Perfection," "Sound Scamper," "Spell Out #1 or #2," or have the student use the letter tiles to spell words you give from the Spelling Word List.
- **Section II:** Play "Keyword and Sound" or "Letter/Sound Identification."

- **Section III:** Play "Chalkboard Challenge."
- **Section IV:** Either have the student read the controlled readers and then ask questions for comprehension, or play "Acting Out" with the green Kid Cards.
- **Section V:** Play "At First Sight."
- **Section VI:** Play "Letter/Sound Identification."
- When the student seems more secure in areas that had previously proven difficult, retest him/her (in those areas only) and indicate on the recording form any sections the student has subsequently mastered.
- Try to help the student achieve mastery of all the sections before the next assessment.
- If the student is having difficulty with a particular skill, keep his or her practice activities at the most basic level so the chance of success is greater.

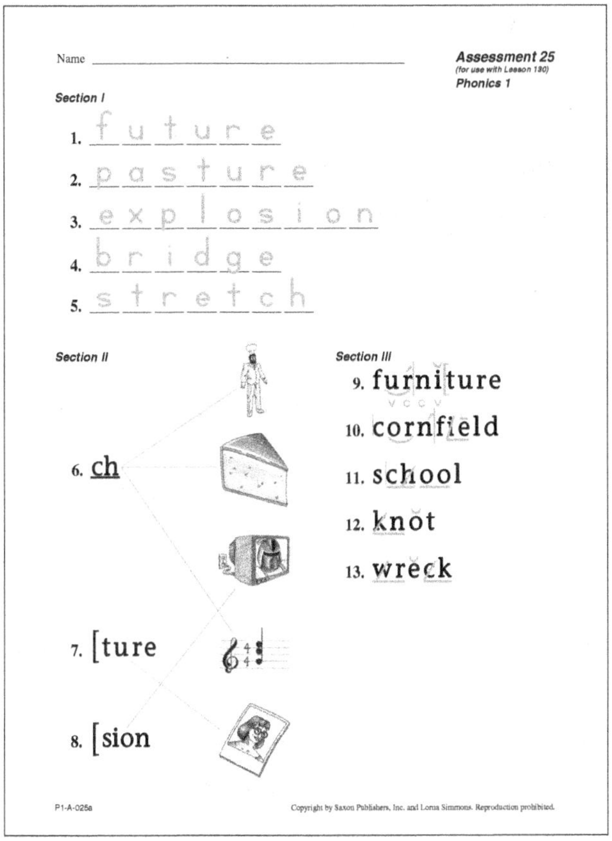

Name ______________________

Assessment 25
(for use with Lesson 130)
Phonics 1

Section I

1. future
2. pasture
3. explosion
4. bridge
5. stretch

Section II

6. ch
7. ture
8. sion

Section III

9. furniture
10. cornfield
11. school
12. knot
13. wreck

P1-A-025a

Copyright by Saxon Publishers, Inc. and Lorna Simmons. Reproduction prohibited.

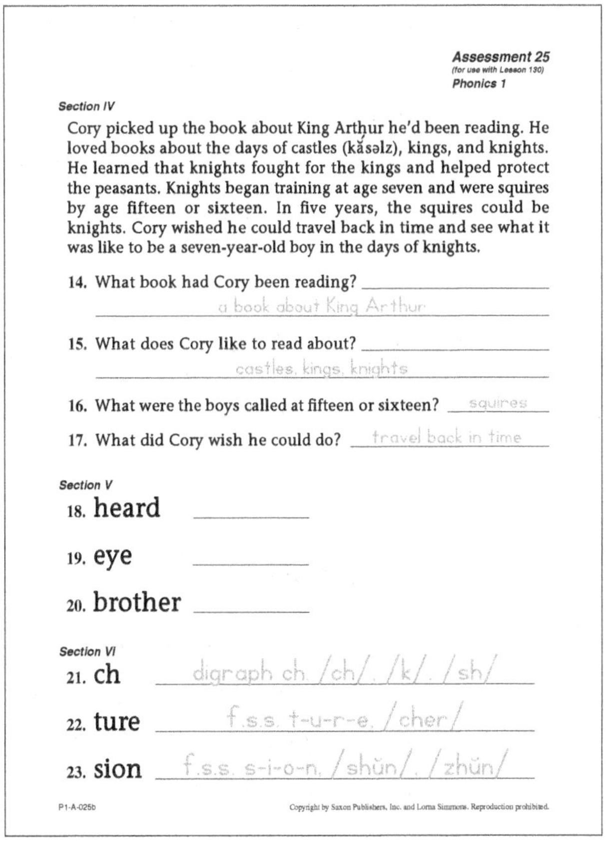

Assessment 25
(for use with Lesson 130)
Phonics 1

Section IV

Cory picked up the book about King Arthur he'd been reading. He loved books about the days of castles (kăsəlz), kings, and knights. He learned that knights fought for the kings and helped protect the peasants. Knights began training at age seven and were squires by age fifteen or sixteen. In five years, the squires could be knights. Cory wished he could travel back in time and see what it was like to be a seven-year-old boy in the days of knights.

14. What book had Cory been reading? a book about King Arthur
15. What does Cory like to read about? castles, kings, knights
16. What were the boys called at fifteen or sixteen? squires
17. What did Cory wish he could do? travel back in time

Section V

18. heard ________
19. eye ________
20. brother ________

Section VI

21. ch digraph ch, /ch/, /k/, /sh/
22. ture f.s.s. t-u-r-e, /cher/
23. sion f.s.s. s-i-o-n, /shŭn/, /zhŭn/

P1-A-025b

Copyright by Saxon Publishers, Inc. and Lorna Simmons. Reproduction prohibited.

LESSON 131 Suffixes -*er*, -*est*

lesson preparation

materials

container of letter tiles

Review Decks

Affix Cards 10–11

Worksheet 131

Spelling List 24

ALPHABET ACTIVITY

- The student should be seated with the container of letter tiles.

  "Before we start, let's say the alphabet together so it is fresh in our minds."

- Recite the alphabet with the student.

  "Today, I'm going to let you put the letter tiles in alphabetical order again. When I say 'go,' dump your tiles on the desk, turn them to the capital (green) side, and begin working."

  "Ready, set, go!"

- Allow enough time for the student to complete the sequencing.
- Have the student replace the tiles in the container and put it away.

REVIEW OF DECKS

- Let the student select a deck (or decks) and play "teacher" with you as the student.

NEW LEARNING

"I'm going to say some words. Echo them back to me and listen for the sound that is the same in the final position of each word."

- Point to your mouth as you say each word.

  "Echo after me. Softer." *softer* ***"Richer."*** *richer* ***"Older."*** *older*

"What do you hear at the end of these words?" */er/*

- Write the following on the chalkboard: softer, richer, older.

"What is the same at the end of all of these words?" *er*

"Look at these words. Can I cover up the 'er' on them and still have a root word?" *yes*

"What do we call something that is added to the end of a root word?" *a suffix*

"This is suffix -er. What do you think it means when it's added to a root word?" *more (more soft, more rich, more old)*

"Suffix -er is used to compare two things and show which one is more: more soft, more rich, more old, or more anything else you might want to describe."

- Let the student experiment with suffix *-er* by comparing items in the room.

"Suffix -er has a second meaning."

- Write the following on the chalkboard: singer, baker, hanger, fryer.

"Look at these words and see if you can figure out the other meaning of suffix -er." *someone who or something that (sings, bakes, hangs, fries, etc.)*

"Suffixes are either vowel or consonant suffixes. They are named according to their first letter. What kind is this one?" *a vowel suffix*

"What word can I make from the word 'smart' that means more smart?" *smarter*

"What word can I make from the word 'help' that means someone who helps?" *helper*

- Show the student **Affix Card 10.**

"What do we call this?" *suffix -er*

- Have the student say the sound /er/ rather than spell it. He/She will recognize and understand it more readily when it appears at the end of words.

"Let's try another one."

"Echo these words and tell me what you hear at the end. Fastest." *fastest* ***"Greatest."*** *greatest* ***"Slimmest."*** *slimmest*

"What do you hear at the end of these words?" */ĕst/*

- Write the following on the chalkboard: fastest, greatest, slimmest.

"What is same at the end of all of these words?" *est*

"Look at these words. Can I cover up the 'est' on them and still have a root word?" *yes*

"This is suffix -est. What do you think it means when it's added to a root word?" *most (most fast, most great, most slim)*

"Suffix -est is used to compare more than two things and show which one is the most: most fast, most great, most slim, or most whatever you want to describe."

- Show the student **Affix Card 11.**

  "What do we call this?" *suffix -est*

- Have the student say the sound /ĕst/ rather than spell it.

  "What word can I make from the word 'quick' that means the most quick?" *quickest*

- **Note:** Add the new affix cards to the Affix Deck.

BOARDWORK

"Let's practice coding some words like the ones you'll have on your worksheet."

"The rule charts are in your Rule Book if you need to look at them."

- Write the following sentences (without the coding marks) on the chalkboard, one at a time. Ask the student to help you code them. The correct coding is as indicated:

  The stōre ōwn´[er] răng ŭp the īce crēam.

  Mĭtch pĭck[ed] ŭp the thĭck´[est] book[s].

- Have the student determine whether each of the items coded is a word, a phrase, or a sentence.

Lesson 131

WORKSHEET

- The student should be seated where he/she can write comfortably.
- Give the student **Worksheet 131.** Make sure the student turns to the correct side.

  "Some of the words we spell today will be with these new suffixes."

  "Put your finger by #1. The first word is 'louder.' "

  "What is the root word?" *loud*

  "What is the suffix?" *er*

  "Try to spell the word and write the letters on the line by #1."

- Allow time for the student to write the word. You may need to repeat the word a few times since you did not take the student through the unblending process. Hopefully, the student will be unblending in his/her head by now.

  "What word did you write?" *louder*

- Repeat the procedure with #2 (thinker), #3 (softest), #4 (farmer), and #5 (sweetest).

  "Now you're ready to code and read the words on your paper."

  "Code the words by #6 through #10. After you have coded all the words, try to read them."

- Assist the student as necessary.

"Numbers 11 and 12 are questions about the paragraph just above them. If you find any words you can't read, code them. Then see if you can answer the questions."

- As the student works, provide help as needed. Help the student correct any incorrect answers. Then initial the worksheet in the space provided.
- Some time during the day, ask the student to read from the worksheet, a controlled reader, your basal reader, or other material of your choice.
- **Note:** Always make sure the worksheet is corrected before the student begins the homework. The worksheet serves as a guide to help complete the homework.

HOMEWORK

"Turn your paper over to the homework side."

"Do you know what to do on the homework paper?"

"Watch for our two new suffixes."

"When you finish your paper, I will check it for you and initial it in the space provided."

- Either now or later in the day, the student should complete the homework independently (if possible). Help the student correct any incorrect answers. Then initial the homework in the space provided.

SPELLING LIST

- Fold **Spelling List 24** in half lengthwise (with the printed side facing out).

"Leave your paper just like I give it to you."

- Give the student **Spelling List 24,** folded with the blank lines facing up.

"Let's spell some more words."

- Call out the following words (in the order shown). Sound them out, if necessary.

  #1 (age), #2 (patch), #3 (bridge), #4 (stitch), #5 (fudge), #6 (protect), #7 (July), #8 (erase), #9 (injection), #10 (rescue), #11 (bush), #12 (push)

"Now unfold your paper and check your words."

- Check the student's work to see if he/she needs extra help with spelling.

"I want you to practice these words. We'll have a spelling test in a few days."

- If possible, take time to play the Kid Card games listed in Lesson 130.

Name ______________________
Teacher's Initials _____

Worksheet 131
(for use with Lesson 131)
Phonics 1

-er, -est

1. louder
2. thinker
3. softest
4. farmer
5. sweetest
6. wildest
7. thickest
8. strŏnger
9. preācher
10. căţcher

I rode my bike with my dog, Whiskers, down to the beach on the hottest day of the year. The wheels on my bike were faster than Whiskers, so I went slower until he could catch up. I got a whiff of salty sea air as we neared the water. Soon we were standing on the hot sand of the beach.

11. When did I go to the beach?
on the hottest day of the year

12. Which is faster, the bike or Whiskers?
the bike

P1-WS-131a

Parent's Initials _____

Homework 131
(for use with Lesson 131)
Phonics 1

-er, -est

1. rănchĕr
2. neārest
3. măţch
4. skĕţching
5. rĭcher
6. kīndest
7. kĭcker
8. lŏngest
9. speāker
10. sĕller

The sand was so hot that it began to hurt our feet. We made a dash for the cooler, wet sand at the water's edge. This time Whiskers was faster, and he did not wait for me. But I was not angry at Whiskers. After all, he had four (for) feet to cool and I only (ōn´ lē) had two.

11. Where was the sand cooler?
at the water's edge

12. How many feet does Whiskers have?
four

Parents: Your child has been taught **suffixes** -er and -est and their meanings.

P1-WS-131b

Lesson 131

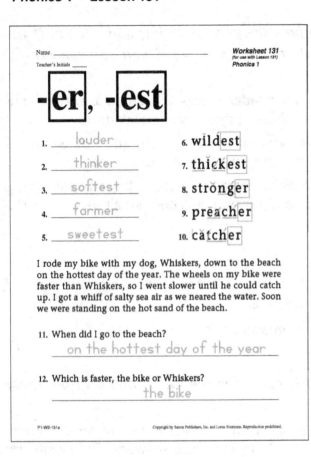

LESSON 132 — Unaccented *ar* and *or*

lesson preparation

materials

Alphabet/Accent Deck (any section)

Retired Decks

Affix Deck

Spelling Sound Sheet 91

Picture Cards 96–97

dollar in a sack (see *the night before*)

Sight Word Cards 77–78

Worksheet 132

Reader 49 (*The Big Fight*)

colored pencils

the night before

- Put a dollar bill in a sack for the student to use to "discover" the new keyword.

ALPHABET ACTIVITY

"We're going to work with one of the Alphabet/Accent Decks again today."

"Stand up. Let's say the unaccented syllables in a normal voice, but karate punch on the accented syllables."

- Go through the **Alphabet/Accent Deck** (any section you choose), moving as quickly as possible.
- **Optional:** Shuffle the deck before the activity.

REVIEW OF DECKS

- The student should be seated where he/she can write comfortably.
- Show the student the retired letter cards in random order. The student should name the letter on each letter card.
- Review **Affix Cards 1–11.**
- Show the student the retired picture cards in random order. The student should name the keyword and sound for each picture card.

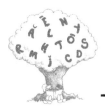

- Review the retired sight word cards.
- Give the student **Spelling Sound Sheet 91.**
- Call out the sounds on the retired spelling cards in random order. The student should echo each sound and name the letter or letters that make the sound as he/she writes the letter(s) on the spelling sound sheet.
- Have the student put the spelling sound sheet away.

NEW LEARNING

"I'm going to say some words. Echo them back to me and listen for the sound that is the same in the final position of each word."

- Point to your mouth as you say each word.

"Echo after me. Collar." *collar* ***"Grammar."*** *grammar* ***"Tartar."*** *tartar*

"What sound do you hear that is the same in the final position of these words?" */er/*

- Write the following on the chalkboard: collar, grammar, tartar.

"What do you see that might be making the /er/ sound?" *combination ar*

"Is combination ar supposed to say /er/?" *no, /ar/*

"Help me code these words. Maybe we can figure out what is happening."

- Have the student help you code each word:

cŏl′|lar (vc|cv)   grăm′|mar (vc|cv)   tar′|tar (vc|cv)

"What is it about the ar's that's making them say /er/ instead of /ar/?"

"Let's look at the word 'tartar.' It has two combination ar's, one in each syllable. Which one says /ar/?" *the one in the first syllable*

"Which one says /er/?" *the one in the second syllable*

"That's right. In fact, the /er/ sound of combination ar comes in the second syllable of each of these words. What do the second syllables have in common?" *they are unaccented*

"That's right. Combination ar says /er/ in unaccented syllables. Let's try some more words."

"Echo after me. Favor." *favor* ***"Odor."*** *odor* ***"Horror."*** *horror*

"What sound do you hear that is the same in all of these words?" */er/*

- Write the following on the chalkboard: favor, odor, horror.

"What do you see that might be making the /er/ sound?" *combination or*

"Is combination or supposed to say /er/?" *no, /or/*

"Help me code these words."

- Have the student help you code each word:

fā´|vor (v|cv)   ō´|dor (v|cv)   hor´|ror (vc|cv)

"Is there anything happening to the or's to cause them to say /er/ instead of /or/?"

"Let's look at the word 'horror.' It has two combination or's, one in each syllable. Which one says /or/?" *the one in the first syllable*

"Which one says /er/?" *the one in the second syllable*

"That's right. In fact, the /er/ sound of combination or comes in the second syllable of each of these words. What do the second syllables have in common?" *they are unaccented*

"That's right! Combination or says /er/ in unaccented syllables."

"What rule can we make about reading with combination or and combination ar?" *"or" says /or/ and "ar" says /ar/ unless they are in unaccented syllables, when they both say /er/*

"There is one other unusual situation involving combination or."

"Echo these words. Word." *word* ***"Worm."*** *worm* ***"Work."*** *work*

"What sound do you hear that is the same in all these words?" */er/ or (/wer/)*

- Write the following on the chalkboard: word, worm, work.

"What do you see that is alike in all of these words?" *wor, or*

"Last week we learned that the letter w can be rather bossy. This is another time when it is bossy. When combination or follows the letter w, it doesn't say /or/ as it should; it says /er/. In this case, the accent doesn't affect it; the w does."

NEW DECK CARDS

- Pull **Letter Cards 48** and **50** from the Review Deck.
- Show the student **Letter Card 50.**

"What do we call this?" *combination or*

- Hold up **Picture Card 96** but keep the picture covered with your hand (or the letter card).

"I have a card with a picture on it that contains the /er/ sound."

"I am going to describe it for you. See if you can guess what the picture is."

"This is a person who tries to keep us healthy. We visit these people quite often when we are babies. As we get older, we visit them mostly when we are feeling ill. What do you think the picture is?" *doctor*

"That's right. The keyword is 'doctor' and the sound is /er/."

- Show the student **Picture Card 96.**
- Show the student **Letter Card 48.**

"What do we call this?" *combination ar*

"I have another sack today. It contains a clue to our new keyword. Don't look in the sack, but put your hand inside and see if you can guess what is inside the sack. Keep in mind that the object in the sack contains the /er/ sound."

- Allow the student a chance to feel inside the sack.

"Can you guess the new keyword?" *dollar*

"That's right. The keyword is 'dollar' and the sound is /er/."

- Show the student **Picture Card 97.**

"These spellings for the /er/ sound are irregular, so it is better not to use them unless you feel pretty sure that the word you are trying to spell contains 'ar' or 'or.' Let's look in the Irregular Spelling Booklet for words that contain these letters."

"Get out your Irregular Spelling Booklet."

"Look in the table of contents and see if you can find the pages showing words that are spelled with combinations ar and or." *pages 21 and 23*

"Turn to page 21. All of the words on page 21 use combination ar to spell the /er/ sound. They don't follow our regular rules, so we must memorize them."

- Allow time for the student to examine the list of words. If time permits, discuss the definition and/or pronunciation of some or all of the words.

"Do you know any other words that belong on this list?"

- If the student offers any appropriate words, write the words on the chalkboard and have the student copy them into the booklet.

"Turn to page 23. The words on page 23 use combination or to spell the /er/ sound. They don't follow our regular rules, so we must memorize them."

- Allow time for the student to examine the list of words. If time permits, discuss the definition and/or pronunciation of some or all of the words.

"Do you know any other words that belong on this list?"

- If the student offers any appropriate words, write the words on the chalkboard and have the student copy them into the booklet.

"Use your Irregular Spelling Booklet to help you learn how to spell with combinations ar and or. For now, put your booklet away."

- **Note:** Add the new picture cards to the Review Decks (and re-insert **Letter Cards 48** and **50**).

BOARDWORK

- Write the following on the chalkboard:

buy /bī/ taste /tāst/

"We have two new sight words today."

- Point to the first word.

"Can you tell me what this word is? Remember, it's a sight word, so it won't follow all of our rules."

- Allow the student to try to pronounce the word. If necessary, say it for him/her.

"This word is 'buy.' Can you use the word 'buy' in a sentence?" *expect various answers*

- Repeat with "taste."
- Show the student **Sight Word Cards 77** and **78.**

"Let's find these words on our sight word charts."

- Help the student locate the words in the Irregular Spelling Booklet.

"We will add these cards to our sight word deck."

"Let's practice coding some words like the ones you'll have on your worksheet."

"The rule charts are in your Rule Book if you need to look at them."

- Write the following phrase and sentence (without the coding marks) on the chalkboard, one at a time. Ask the student to help you code them. The correct coding is as indicated:

words (of) wĭs′|dŏm
vc|cv

(Do) mē′ å fā′|vo͟r ănd păss the̶ mŭs′|ta͟rd.
v|cv vc|cv

- Have the student determine whether each of the items coded is a word, a phrase, or a sentence.
- Add **Sight Word Cards 77** and **78** to the Sight Word Deck.

WORKSHEET

- The student should be seated where he/she can write comfortably.
- Give the student **Worksheet 132.** Make sure the student turns to the correct side.

"We are going to spell with the /e͟r/ sound using combination ar on the first three words today. This is irregular for spelling, so only use it when I specifically say to do so, like right now."

"Put your finger by #1. The first word is 'nec … tar.' "

"Write 'nec' by #1."

"Now after 'nec,' write 'tar.' "

- Allow time for the student to write the word.

"What word did you write?" *nectar*

- Repeat the procedure with #2 (standard) and #3 (hangar).

"The last two words will be with bossy w."

- Continue with #4 (word) and #5 (work).

  "Now you're ready to code and read the words on your paper."

  "Code the words by #6 through #10. After you have coded all the words, try to read them."

- Assist the student as necessary.

  "Now read the word by #11. If you have trouble reading the word, code it. Then draw a line from the word to the picture it matches."

- Repeat with #12 through #14.
- As the student works, provide help as needed. Help the student correct any incorrect answers. Then initial the worksheet in the space provided.
- Some time during the day, ask the student to read from the worksheet, a controlled reader, your basal reader, or other material of your choice.
- **Note:** Always make sure the worksheet is corrected before the student begins the homework. The worksheet serves as a guide to help complete the homework.

HOMEWORK

"Turn your paper over to the homework side."

"Do you know what to do on the homework paper?"

"Watch for combinations ar and or that say /er/. Always code suffixes and final, stable syllables before coding the rest of the word."

- Discuss the homework pictures to make sure the student understands the word each one represents: #11 (tractor), #12 (runner), #13 (whale), and #14 (bookworm).

  "When you finish your paper, I will check it for you and initial it in the space provided."

- Either now or later in the day, the student should complete the homework independently (if possible). Help the student correct any incorrect answers. Then initial the homework in the space provided.

READER

"We have another new book today."

- Give the student **Reader 49 (*The Big Fight*)** and some colored pencils.

  "Can you tell me this book's title?" *The Big Fight*

- Assist the student as necessary as he/she constructs the book.
- When the student finishes, staple or put a rubber band around the book's spine.

  "The title of this book is ________?" *The Big Fight*

"I want you to read your book to yourself. When you are finished reading, color the pictures. Write your name on the book so I will know who colored it."

"Keep your book handy because I will be asking you to read it for me."

- Some time during the day, have the student read the reader to you.
- If possible, take time to play the Kid Card games listed in Lesson 130.

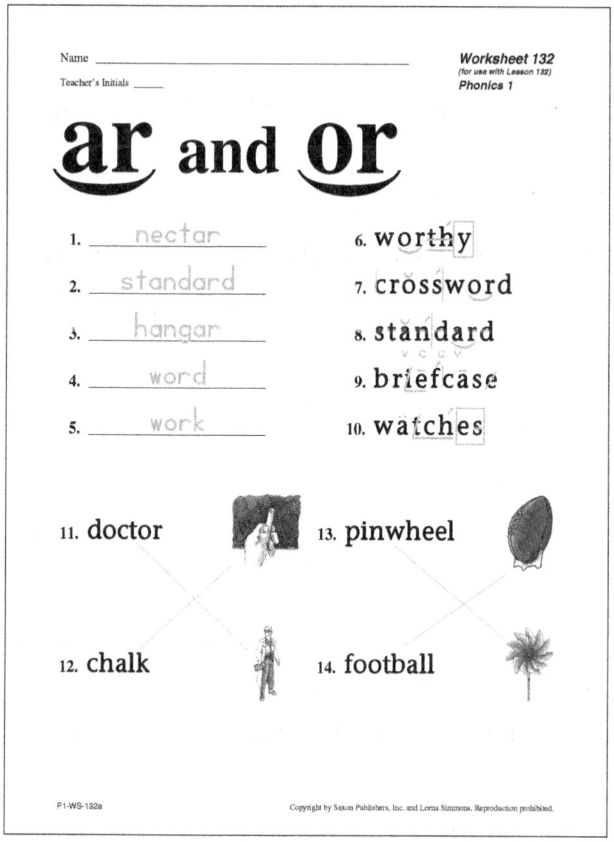

Name ______________________

Teacher's Initials _____

Worksheet 132
(for use with Lesson 132)
Phonics 1

ar and or

1. nectar
2. standard
3. hangar
4. word
5. work
6. worthy
7. crossword
8. standard
9. briefcase
10. watches
11. doctor
12. chalk
13. pinwheel
14. football

P1-WS-132a

Copyright by Saxon Publishers, Inc. and Lorna Simmons. Reproduction prohibited.

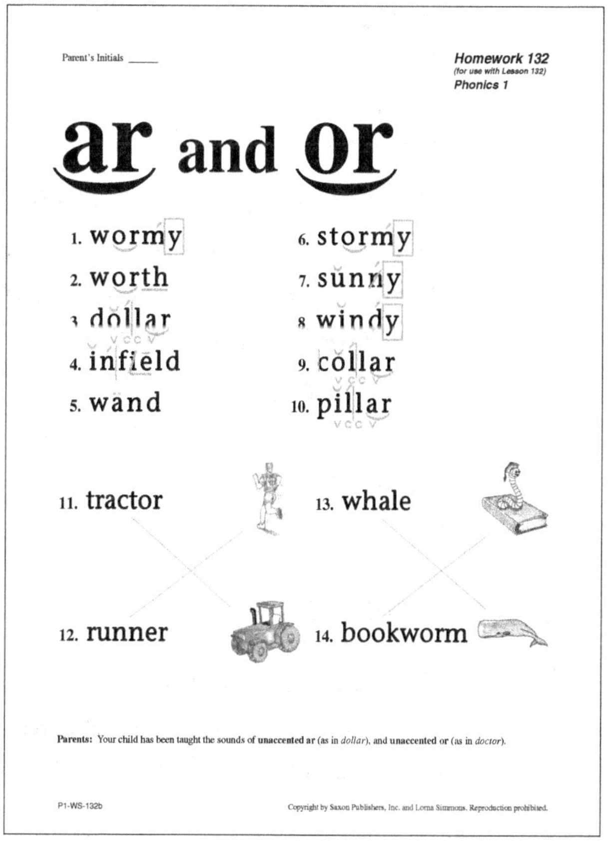

Parent's Initials _____

Homework 132
(for use with Lesson 132)
Phonics 1

ar and or

1. wormy
2. worth
3. dollar
4. infield
5. wand
6. stormy
7. sunny
8. windy
9. collar
10. pillar
11. tractor
12. runner
13. whale
14. bookworm

Parents: Your child has been taught the sounds of **unaccented ar** (as in *dollar*), and **unaccented or** (as in *doctor*).

P1-WS-132b

Copyright by Saxon Publishers, Inc. and Lorna Simmons. Reproduction prohibited.

Lesson 133 — Scribal *o*

lesson preparation

materials

purple Kid Cards
Review Decks
Spelling Sound Sheet 92
tokens or colored pencil
sponge in a sack (see *the night before*)
Picture Card 98
Worksheet 133

new concepts

scribal *o*

the night before

- Put a sponge in a sack for the student to use to "discover" the new keyword.

Alphabet Activity

- The student should be seated.

  "Today we are going to alphabetize some of our Kid Cards again."

- Give the student four or five purple word cards. Make sure that each card begins with a different letter.

  "When I say 'go,' say the alphabet out loud."

  "The first time you say a letter that one of your cards begins with, lay that card down. Lay each card to the right of the previous one. When you finish, the words should be in alphabetical order."

  "Ready, set, go!"

- Repeat with different Kid Cards if time permits.
- Collect the Kid Cards.

Review of Decks

- The student should be seated where he/she can write comfortably.
- Show the student **Letter Cards 1–75** in random order. The student should name the letter on each letter card.

- Review **Affix Cards 1–11.**
- Show the student **Picture Cards 1–97** in random order. The student should name the keyword and sound for each picture card.
- Review **Sight Word Cards 1–78.**
- Give the student **Spelling Sound Sheet 92** and at least twelve tokens (or a colored pencil).
- If you can use "fun" markers, such as goldfish-shaped crackers or cereal pieces, it is much more enjoyable for the student.

"Let's play Bingo!"

"When I call out the spelling sounds today, I want you to cover (or X out) the space that spells that sound on your spelling sound sheet."

"When you cover (or X out) all of the letters on one line, either up and down, across, or from corner to corner, call out Bingo!"

"Don't forget to refer to your rule charts if you need to."

"Are you ready?"

"Cover (or X out) the letters that spell the initial sound in 'whale.'" *wh*

"Cover (or X out) the letters that spell the final sound in 'lecture.'" *ture*

"Cover (or X out) the letters that spell the final sound in 'snitch.'" *tch*

"Cover (or X out) the letters that spell the final sound in 'version.'" *sion*

"Cover (or X out) the letters that spell the initial sound in 'chimney.'" *ch*

"Cover (or X out) the letters that spell the final sound in 'blue.'" *ue*

"Cover (or X out) the letters that spell the final sound in 'carnation.'" *tion*

"Cover (or X out) the letters that spell the final sound in 'boy.'" *oy*

"Cover (or X out) the letters that spell the final sound in 'stage.'" *ge*

"Cover (or X out) the letters that spell the final sound in 'fudge.'" *dge*

"Cover (or X out) the letters that spell the final sound in 'glow.'" *ow*

"Cover (or X out) the letters that spell the medial sound in 'coil.'" *oi*

"Cover (or X out) the letter that spells the medial sound in 'ball.'" *ä*

- The student should Bingo by the time all the sounds have been called out.
- Collect the tokens (or colored pencil) and the spelling sound sheet. If you used tokens and the spelling sound sheet is unmarked, keep it available for practice.

Lesson 133

NEW LEARNING

"I'm going to say some words. Echo them back to me and listen for the sound that is the same in each word."

- Point to your mouth as you say each word.

"Echo after me. Son." *son* ***"Month."*** *month* ***"Wonder."*** *wonder*

"What sound do you hear that is the same in all of these words?" */ŭ/*

- Write the following on the chalkboard: son, month, wonder.

"What is making the /ŭ/ sound?" *o*

"This is called scribal (scrī′ bəl) o."

"Before there were printing presses and copy machines, men called 'scribes' used to copy books by hand. They used pens that had to be dipped in ink every few words. Sometimes the ink would run and a lot of people think this is how some u's got changed to o's by mistake."

- Demonstrate closing the top of the letter *u* to make an *o*.

"The next scribe looked at the letter and thought it was an o, and therefore we have a lot of o's that sound like a short u, or schwa."

- Code the *o* in each word with a schwa: so̊n, mo̊nth, wo̊nder.

"Scribal o's appear most often before the letters m, n, and v."

"You need to remember that o's can often sound schwa. Try that sound if the word doesn't sound right with the usual 'o' sounds."

- Finish coding the words:

so̊n mo̊nth wo̊n′|der
VC|CV

- Leave the words on the chalkboard for the remainder of the lesson.

NEW DECK CARDS

- Pull **Letter Card 2** from the Review Deck.
- Hold up **Letter Card 2.**

What is this called?" *o*

"I have another sack today. It contains a clue to our new keyword. Don't look in the sack, but put your hand inside and see if you can guess what is inside. Keep in mind that the object in the sack contains the /ŭ/ sound."

- Allow the student a chance to feel inside the sack.

"Can you guess the new keyword?" *sponge*

"Can you hear the /ŭ/ sound in 'sponge'?"

- Show the student **Picture Card 98.**

"Get out your Irregular Spelling Booklet."

"Look in the table of contents and see if you can find the page showing words that are spelled with scribal o." *page 20*

"Turn to page 20. All of the words on page 20 use scribal o. They don't follow our regular rules, so we must memorize them."

- Allow time for the student to examine the list of words. If time permits, discuss the definition and/or pronunciation of some or all of the words.

"Do you know any other words that belong on this list?"

- If the student offers any appropriate words, write the words on the chalkboard and have the student copy them into the booklet.

"Use your Irregular Spelling Booklet to help you learn how to spell with scribal o. For now, put your booklet away."

- **Note:** Add the new picture card to the Review Deck (and re-insert **Letter Card 2**).

BOARDWORK

"Let's practice coding some words like the ones you'll have on your worksheet."

"The rule charts are in your Rule Book if you need to look at them."

- Write the following sentences (without the coding marks) on the chalkboard, one at a time. Ask the student to help you code them. The correct coding is as indicated:

Her com´|pass (was) found ĭn the yard.
v c | c v

Jāke wĕnt dīv´ing ănd saw fĭsh (of) all kīnds.

- Have the student determine whether each of the items coded is a word, a phrase, or a sentence.

Lesson 133

WORKSHEET

- The student should be seated where he/she can write comfortably.
- Give the student **Worksheet 133.** Make sure the student turns to the correct side.

"Today, let's spell with our new sound for 'o.'"

"Put your finger by #1. The first word is 'son.'"

- Use the word in a sentence, if necessary.

"Let's sound it out together and I will hold up a finger for each sound." */s/ /ŭ/ /n/*

"Remember that we are spelling with scribal o."

"Write the word 'son' on the line by #1."

- Allow time for the student to write the word.

"What word did you write?" *son*

- Repeat the procedure with #2 (ton), #3 (month), #4 (cover), and #5 (front).

  "Now you're ready to code and read the words on your paper."

  "Code the words by #6 through #10. After you have coded all the words, try to read them."

  "You may notice that your worksheet contains some words that used to be sight words. Since we've learned scribal o, you can code these words now instead of just circling them."

- Assist the student as necessary.

  "Numbers 11 and 12 are questions about the paragraph just above them. If you find any words you can't read, code them. Then see if you can answer the questions."

- As the student works, provide help as needed. Help the student correct any incorrect answers. Then initial the worksheet in the space provided.
- Some time during the day, ask the student to read from the worksheet, a controlled reader, your basal reader, or other material of your choice.
- **Note:** Always make sure the worksheet is corrected before the student begins the homework. The worksheet serves as a guide to help complete the homework.

HOMEWORK

"Turn your paper over to the homework side."

"Do you know what to do on the homework paper?"

"Watch for scribal o. Remember to code it with a schwa."

"When you finish your paper, I will check it for you and initial it in the space provided."

- Either now or later in the day, the student should complete the homework independently (if possible). Help the student correct any incorrect answers. Then initial the homework in the space provided.
- If possible, take time to play the Kid Card games listed in Lesson 130.

Name ______________________ **Worksheet 133**
(for use with Lesson 133)
Teacher's Initials _____ **Phonics 1**

scribal o

1. son
2. ton
3. month
4. cover
5. front
6. color
7. seatcover
8. marble
9. picked
10. cooking

The scouts are planning a camping trip in the month of November. The trees in the woods will be changing colors to red, yellow, and orange so they will be really pretty. The scouts plan to leave on Friday and return Monday morning. They need to be sure to pack shovels, flashlights, and some covers for bedtime comfort.

11. What will the scouts do in November?

go on a camping trip

12. When will they return?

Monday morning

P1-WS-133a

Parent's Initials _____ **Homework 133**
(for use with Lesson 133)
Phonics 1

scribal o

1. wonder
2. comfort
3. compass
4. weak
5. streak
6. beast
7. carsick
8. bundle
9. looking
10. wood

The scout leader's older son is going to teach us how to use a compass. We hope to discover some neat things out in the woods. We will build a fire underground to make an oven for our hobo dinners. When dinner is done, we'll put out the campfire and bed down in our sleeping bags.

11. What will the scout leader's son teach us?

how to use a compass

12. Where will we bed down?

in our sleeping bags

Parents: Your child has been taught the sound of **scribal o** (as in *sponge*); and that it is coded with a schwa.

P1-WS-133b

Lesson 133

LESSON 134 The Rule v|cv′ with *i*

lesson preparation

materials

Alphabet/Accent Deck (any section)

Review Decks

Spelling Sound Sheet 93

Sight Word Cards 79–80

Worksheet 134

Reader 50 (*Hudson Goes to Work*)

colored pencils

ALPHABET ACTIVITY

"We're going to work with one of the Alphabet/Accent Decks again today."

"Stand up. Let's say the unaccented syllables in a normal voice, but karate punch on the accented syllables."

- Go through the **Alphabet/Accent Deck** (any section you choose), moving as quickly as possible.
- **Optional:** Shuffle the deck before the activity.

REVIEW OF DECKS

- The student should be seated where he/she can write comfortably.
- Show the student **Letter Cards 1–75** in random order. The student should name the letter on each letter card.
- Review **Affix Cards 1–11.**
- Show the student **Picture Cards 1–98** in random order. The student should name the keyword and sound for each picture card.
- Review **Sight Word Cards 1–78.**
- Give the student **Spelling Sound Sheet 93.**
- Call out the sounds on **Spelling Cards 1–48** in random order. The student should echo each sound and name the letter or letters that make the sound as he/she writes the letter(s) on the spelling sound sheet.
- Have the student put the spelling sound sheet away.

NEW LEARNING

- Write the word "divide" on the chalkboard.

  "What do you think we should code first on this word?" *expect various answers*

  "There are no suffixes or final, stable syllables to code. What do we look for next?" *vowels*

  "That's right. We look for the vowels."

- Write small *v*'s under each vowel (except the silent *e*):

```
divide
 v v
```

  "What is the next step?" *look between the vowels*

  "What do we have between the vowels?" *only one consonant*

- Write a small *c* under the consonant:

```
divide
 vcv
```

  "Where is the best place to divide this word?" *after the first vowel*

- Refer to **Syllable Division Chart 3,** if necessary.
- Put the dividing line between the *i* and the *v*:

```
di|vide
 v|cv
```

  "Which syllable is usually accented?" *first*

- Accent the first syllable:

```
di′|vide
 v |cv
```

  "How do we code the vowels in the second syllable?" *mark out the silent e; put a macron over the i*

- Code the second *i* and the silent *e*:

```
di′|vīdɇ
 v |cv
```

  "How would we code the i in the first syllable?" *with a macron because it is open and accented*

- Code the *i* in the first syllable with a macron:

```
dī′|vīdɇ
 v |cv
```

  "So this word would be 'dī′ vīde.' "

  "Have you ever heard of the word 'dī′ vīde'?" *no*

  "The next best way to try the word is to divide it after the consonant. That would make the i short."

Lesson 134

- Erase the dividing line and redraw it after the *v*. Replace the macron with a breve:

  dĭv′|īde̸
  vc|v

"This word would be 'dĭv′ īde,' which is so close that you would probably get the word anyway."

"The last place you can try to divide this word is after the first vowel. If you change the accent to the second syllable, the first i is open and unaccented."

- Recode the word:

  dĭ|vīde̸′
  v|cv

- Point to the unaccented (first) *i*.

"This i usually says its short sound, so the word is pronounced 'dĭ vīde̸′.' "

"Get out your Rule Book and turn to Rule Chart 9."

"This chart will help you remember what sound the letter i usually makes when it is in an open, unaccented syllable."

"Look at this word."

- Write "silliness" on the chalkboard.

"What do we code first?" *suffixes or final, stable syllables*

"Do you see any?" *suffix -ness*

- Box suffix *-ness*: silli[ness].
- Point to the second *i*.

"This i was a y before suffix -ness was added."

- Write "silly" on the chalkboard.

"This was the root word. Can you help me code this word?"

- Code the word as the student instructs:

  sĭl′|lẏ
  vc|cv

"Can you read this word?" *silly*

"What sound does y have in this word?" */ē/*

"I have a new spelling rule for you. It's quite easy."

"When a word ends in y after a consonant, change the y to i before adding the suffix, except suffixes that begin with i."

- Point to "silliness."

"See how the y changed to an i in this word? But the i still says /ē/."

"The letter y sometimes sounds like /ē/, and when that y changes to i, the i keeps the long e sound."

"Now that you know the letter i can do this, you can read these kinds of words with no trouble at all."

- Write "player" and "annoying" on the chalkboard.

  "What does the y come after in these words?" *a vowel*

  "The y's in these words are part of a digraph and a diphthong. The y does not change to i in these words. The y must follow a consonant for this rule to work."

  "I have a rule chart to help you remember this spelling pattern."

  "Get out your Rule Book and turn to page 15."

- Briefly discuss **Rule Chart 15.**

  "You can refer to this chart whenever you need to."

BOARDWORK

- Write the following on the chalkboard:

  busy /bĭz´ ē/ only /ōn´ lē/

  "We have two new sight words today."

- Point to the first word.

  "Can you tell me what this word is? Remember, it's a sight word, so it won't follow all of our rules."

- Allow the student to try to pronounce the word. If necessary, say it for him/her.

  "This word is 'busy.' Can you use the word 'busy' in a sentence?" *expect various answers*

- Repeat with "only."
- Show the student **Sight Word Cards 79** and **80.**

  "Let's find these words on our sight word charts."

- Help the student locate the words in the Irregular Spelling Booklet.

  "We will add these cards to our sight word deck."

  "Let's practice coding some words like the ones you'll have on your worksheet."

  "The rule charts are in your Rule Book if you need to look at them."

- Write the following sentences (without the coding marks) on the chalkboard, one at a time. Ask the student to help you code them. The correct coding is as indicated:

  Dĭ|vīde´ the book[s] bȳ´ the book´|cāse.
  (v|c v)

  Māil the fŭn´|ni[est] book (to) Brŏck Grēen.
  (v c|c v)

- Have the student determine whether each of the items coded is a word, a phrase, or a sentence.
- Add **Sight Word Cards 79** and **80** to the Sight Word Deck.

Lesson 134

WORKSHEET

- The student should be seated where he/she can write comfortably.
- Give the student **Worksheet 134.** Make sure the student turns to the correct side.

  "Let's spell with some words in which the root word ends in consonant y and see if you can change the 'y' to 'i.' "

  "Put your finger by #1. The first word is 'rustier.' "

  "What is the root word?" *rusty*

  "Let's sound out and spell 'rusty' first. The first syllable is 'rus.' Write that on the line by #1."

  "The second syllable is 'ty.' Write that after 'rus.' "

  "Now the word is actually 'rustier.' How do we spell suffix /er/?" *er*

  "The root word, 'rusty', ends in vowel y, so we have to change the 'y' to 'i' before we add the /er/."
- Demonstrate on the chalkboard.

  "Erase the 'y' on your paper and write 'ier.' "
- Allow time for the student to write the word.

  "What word did you write?" *rustier*
- Repeat the procedure with #2 (bumpiness), #3 (friskier), #4 (shininess), and #5 (crispiest).

  "Now you're ready to code and read the words on your paper."

  "Code the words by #6 through #10. After you have coded all the words, try to read them."
- Assist the student as necessary.

  "Look at the picture at the bottom of the page. Write a story about what has happened in the picture. Don't worry about spelling. When you are finished, we will take time to check spelling and correct mistakes."
- As the student works, provide help as needed.
- Then have the student read the story silently and check for spelling errors. Help the student correct any mistakes. A perfect paper is not as important as the student putting his/her thoughts on paper and being able to recognize spelling errors that can be corrected (e.g., *k* and *c* spelling). Be sure to correct the rest of the worksheet as well. Then initial it in the space provided.
- Have the student read the story to you. It is important that children learn to feel comfortable speaking in front of others.
- **Note:** Always make sure the worksheet is corrected before the student begins the homework. The worksheet serves as a guide to help complete the homework.

HOMEWORK

"Turn your paper over to the homework side."

"Do you know what to do on the homework paper?"

"Look at the picture at the bottom of the page. Use the lines beside the picture and write a story telling what's about to happen in the picture."

"When you finish your paper, I will check it for you and initial it in the space provided."

- Either now or later in the day, the student should complete the homework independently (if possible). Help the student correct any incorrect answers. Then initial the homework in the space provided.

READER

"We have another new book today."

- Give the student **Reader 50 (*Hudson Goes to Work*)** and some colored pencils.

"Can you tell me this book's title?" Hudson Goes to Work

- Assist the student as necessary as he/she constructs the book.
- When the student finishes, staple or put a rubber band around the book's spine.

"The title of this book is _________?" Hudson Goes to Work

"I want you to read your book to yourself. When you are finished reading, color the pictures. Write your name on the book so I will know who colored it."

"Keep your book handy because I will be asking you to read it for me."

- Some time during the day, have the student read the reader to you.
- If possible, take time to play the Kid Card games listed in Lesson 130. Try to see that the student is prepared for tomorrow's assessment.

Name ______________________

Teacher's Initials ____

Worksheet 134
(for use with Lesson 134)
Phonics 1

ĭ|cv́

1. rustier
2. bumpiness
3. friskier
4. shininess
5. crispiest
6. dilemma
7. hairline
8. crook
9. messiness
10. freeze

P1-WS-134a

Parent's Initials ____

Homework 134
(for use with Lesson 134)
Phonics 1

ĭ|cv́

1. divide
2. grain
3. bait
4. nine
5. score
6. happiness
7. greediest
8. muddier
9. funniest
10. sloppier

Parents: Your child has been taught the syllable division rule **v|cv′** with ĭ (*i* is usually short, as in *divide*, but can say "*e*" as in *silliness*); and the **changing rule:** if a root word ends with vowel *y* (not *y* as part of a digraph or diphthong), change *y* to *i* before adding a suffix (except for suffixes beginning with *i*).

P1-WS-134b

Lesson 134

LESSON 135 — Assessment

lesson preparation

materials

Alphabet/Accent Deck (any section)
Review Decks
Assessment 26
Spelling Test 24
Assessment 26 Recording Form
Kid Cards
tokens

the night before

- Separate the Kid Cards marked "Lesson 135."

ALPHABET ACTIVITY

"We're going to work with one of the Alphabet/Accent Decks again today."

"Let's stand up. When you say the accented letters, I want you to stand up on your tiptoes, and then drop back down as you say the unaccented letters."

- Go through the **Alphabet/Accent Deck** (any section you choose), moving as quickly as possible.
- **Optional:** Shuffle the deck before the activity.

REVIEW OF DECKS

- The student should be seated where he/she can write comfortably.
- Show the student **Letter Cards 1–75** in random order. The student should name the letter on each letter card.
- Review **Affix Cards 1–11.**
- Show the student **Picture Cards 1–98** in random order. The student should name the keyword and sound for each picture card.
- Review **Sight Word Cards 1–80.**

Written Assessment

- Have the student sit where he/she can write comfortably.
- Give the student **Assessment 26.**
- **Section I:**

  "Today we are going to write some words for our assessment."

  "I'm going to say a word. Write the letter that makes each sound in that word on the lines by #1."

  "Look at the rule charts if you need to."

  "Here's the first word: wheel."
- Repeat with the following words in the order shown: #2 (whale), #3 (whiff), #4 (whisker), and #5 (why).
- **Reminder:** While the student spells, be ready to point to appropriate rule charts as necessary.
- **Section II:**

  "Look at the letters by #6."

  "Find the picture of the keyword for this sound."

  "Draw a line from the letters to the keyword."
- Repeat with #7 and #8. Allow a few minutes for the student to work.
- The pictures (from top to bottom) are as follows: sleigh, whale, wallet.
- **Section III:**

  "Put your finger on #9."

  "Code the words by #9 through #12."
- Allow a few minutes for the student to work.
- **Section IV:**

  "Read the paragraph. If you find any words you can't read, code them to help you figure them out. Then answer the questions by #13 through #16."
- **Reminder:** If the student absolutely cannot read the paragraph, read it to the student to see if he or she can answer the questions.

  "When you are finished, show your paper to me."
- This paper will be used during the oral portion of the assessment.

Spelling Test

- Give the student **Spelling Test 24.**
- Call out the following words (in the order shown). Sound them out, if necessary.

  #1 (age), #2 (erase), #3 (rescue), #4 (bridge), #5 (patch), #6 (protect), #7 (July), #8 (fudge), #9 (injection), #10 (stitch), #11 (push), #12 (bush)
- Grade and record the test in any manner that suits your needs.

Oral Assessment

- It is important to complete the oral assessment promptly (today, if possible) in order to identify any areas of weakness and begin remediation.
- Use the assessment and the following dialogue to complete the oral portion.
- **Section V:**
- Point to the sight word by #17.

  "Read this sight word for me."
- Record the student's response by placing a check mark by each word he/she reads correctly.
- Repeat with #18 through #22.
- **Section VI:**
- Show the student the letters by #23.

  "Tell me the name of these letters and the sound they make."
- Write the student's response on the adjacent line.
- Repeat with #24 and #25.

Assessment Evaluation

- Grade the assessment and record the results on **Assessment 26 Recording Form.** Check off the boxes to indicate mastery (i.e., the section was completed with 100% accuracy).
- **Reminder:** Try to give as many points as possible for work attempted. Do not grade the coding marks too severely. The most important coding marks to look for are breves, macrons, and syllable division lines.
- See the introductory material for detailed information regarding grading and recording procedures.
- Use the assessment results to identify those skills in which the student is weak. Practice those skills by playing Kid Card games.
- Add the Kid Cards marked "Lesson 135" to the existing decks. Listed below are games appropriate for remediation in selected areas. See "Games and Activities" for the directions for each game.
- **Section I:** Play "Spelling Deck Perfection," "Sound Scamper," "Spell Out #1 or #2," or have the student use the letter tiles to spell words you give from the Spelling Word List.
- **Section II:** Play "Keyword and Sound" or "Letter/Sound Identification."
- **Section III:** Play "Chalkboard Challenge."
- **Section IV:** Either have the student read the controlled readers and then ask questions for comprehension, or play "Acting Out" with the green Kid Cards.
- **Section V:** Play "At First Sight."
- **Section VI:** Play "Letter/Sound Identification."

- When the student seems more secure in areas that had previously proven difficult, retest him/her (in those areas only) and indicate on the recording form any sections the student has subsequently mastered.
- Try to help the student achieve mastery of all the sections before the next assessment.
- If the student is having difficulty with a particular skill, keep his or her practice activities at the most basic level so the chance of success is greater.

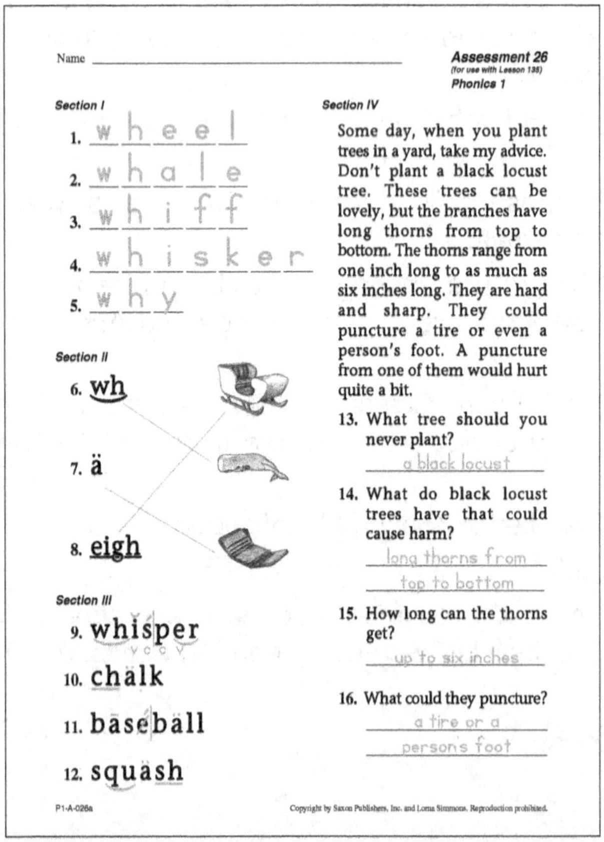
Name ______________________

Assessment 26
(for use with Lesson 135)
Phonics 1

Section I

1. w h e e l
2. w h a l e
3. w h i f f
4. w h i s k e r
5. w h y

Section II

6. wh
7. ä
8. eigh

Section III

9. whisper
10. chalk
11. baseball
12. squash

Section IV

Some day, when you plant trees in a yard, take my advice. Don't plant a black locust tree. These trees can be lovely, but the branches have long thorns from top to bottom. The thorns range from one inch long to as much as six inches long. They are hard and sharp. They could puncture a tire or even a person's foot. A puncture from one of them would hurt quite a bit.

13. What tree should you never plant?
a black locust
14. What do black locust trees have that could cause harm?
long thorns from top to bottom
15. How long can the thorns get?
up to six inches
16. What could they puncture?
a tire or a persons foot

P1-A-026a

Copyright by Saxon Publishers, Inc. and Lorna Simmons. Reproduction prohibited.

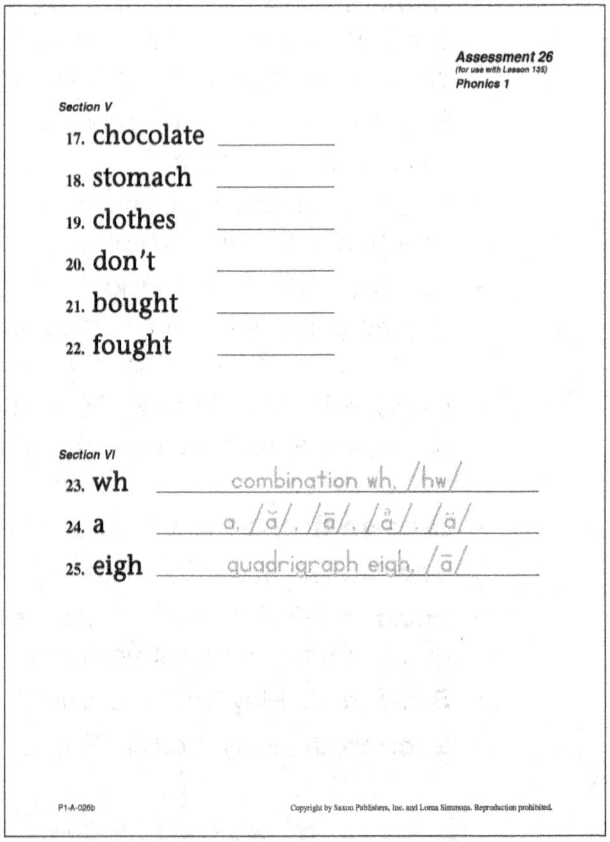
Assessment 26
(for use with Lesson 135)
Phonics 1

Section V

17. chocolate ________
18. stomach ________
19. clothes ________
20. don't ________
21. bought ________
22. fought ________

Section VI

23. wh combination wh, /hw/
24. a a, /ă/, /ā/, /ȧ/, /ä/
25. eigh quadrigraph eigh, /ā/

P1-A-026b

Copyright by Saxon Publishers, Inc. and Lorna Simmons. Reproduction prohibited.

LESSON 136

Suffix *-ful*

lesson preparation

materials

container of letter tiles

Review Decks

Affix Card 12

Worksheet 136

Spelling List 25

ALPHABET ACTIVITY

- The student should be seated with the container of letter tiles.

  "Before we start, let's say the alphabet together so it is fresh in our minds."

- Recite the alphabet with the student.
- Give the following instructions one at a time, allowing time for the student to accomplish each task before giving the next instruction.

  "Take all of the letter tiles out of your container."

  "Flip all of the letters over so that you are looking at the lowercase letters. If they are flipped correctly, they will all be blue."

  "Now we're ready. See if you can put all your letters in alphabetical order."

- When the student has finished, continue by saying the following:

  "Quickly pull down the vowels."

  "Put together two letters that make a digraph."

- Have the student replace the tiles in the container and put it away.

REVIEW OF DECKS

- Play "Twenty Questions" or let the student select a deck and play "teacher."

NEW LEARNING

"I'm going to say some words. Echo them back to me and listen for the sound that is the same in the final position of each word."

- Point to your mouth as you say each word.

"Echo after me. Playful." *playful* ***"Restful."*** *restful* ***"Healthful."*** *healthful*

"What do you hear at the end of these words?" */ful/ (/fo͝ol/)*

- Write the following on the chalkboard: playful, restful, healthful.

"What is the same at the end of all of these words?" *ful*

"Look at these words. Can I cover up the 'ful' and still have a root word?" *yes*

"What do we call something that is added to the end of a root word?" *suffix*

"This is suffix -ful. What do you think it means when it is added to a root word?" *"full of" or "the amount it takes to fill"*

"Suffixes are either vowel or consonant suffixes. They are named according to their first letter. What kind is this one?" *a consonant suffix*

"What word can I make from the word 'harm' that means 'full of harm'?" *harmful*

- Show the student **Affix Card 12.**

"What do we call this?" *suffix -ful*

- Have the student say the sound /fo͝ol/ rather than spell it. He/She will recognize and understand it more readily when it appears at the end of words.
- **Note:** Add the new affix card to the Affix Deck.

BOARDWORK

"Let's practice coding some words like the ones you'll have on your worksheet."

"The rule charts are in your Rule Book if you need to look at them."

- Write the following word and sentences (without the coding marks) on the chalkboard, one at a time. Ask the student to help you code them. The correct coding is as indicated:

tū′|tor|ing

The pitch′er chāsed the hard′est hit.

Wē′ found a spī′|der in the sho′|vel|ful of dirt.

- Have the student determine whether each of the items coded is a word, a phrase, or a sentence.

WORKSHEET

- The student should be seated where he/she can write comfortably.
- Give the student **Worksheet 136.** Make sure the student turns to the correct side.

"Today, some of the words we spell will contain this new suffix."

"Put your finger by #1. The first word is 'wishful.' "

"What is the root word?" *wish*

"What is the suffix?" *-ful*

"Try to spell the word and write the letters on the line by #1."

- Allow time for the student to write the word. You may need to repeat the word a few times since the student was not led through the unblending process. The student will probably be unblending in his/her head by now.

"What word did you write?" *wishful*

- Repeat the procedure with #2 (trustful), #3 (boxful), #4 (helpful), and #5 (hopeful).

"Now you're ready to code and read the words on your paper."

"Code the words by #6 through #10. After you have coded all the words, try to read them."

- Assist the student as necessary.

"Numbers 11 and 12 are questions about the paragraph just above them. If you find any words you can't read, code them. Then see if you can answer the questions."

- As the student works, provide help as needed. Help the student correct any incorrect answers. Then initial the worksheet in the space provided.
- Some time during the day, ask the student to read from the worksheet, a controlled reader, your basal reader, or other material of your choice.
- **Note:** Always make sure the worksheet is corrected before the student begins the homework. The worksheet serves as a guide to help complete the homework.

HOMEWORK

"Turn your paper over to the homework side."

"Do you know what to do on the homework paper?"

"Watch for the new suffix. What is it?" *suffix -ful*

"When you finish your paper, I will check it for you and initial it in the space provided."

- Either now or later in the day, the student should complete the homework independently (if possible). Help the student correct any incorrect answers. Then initial the homework in the space provided.

SPELLING LIST

- Fold **Spelling List 25** in half lengthwise (with the printed side facing out).

  "Leave your paper just like I give it to you."
- Give the student **Spelling List 25,** folded with the blank lines facing up.

  "Let's spell some more words."
- Call out the following words (in the order shown). Sound them out, if necessary.

  #1 (future), #2 (mixture), #3 (adventure), #4 (pasture), #5 (explosion), #6 (lotion), #7 (fiction), #8 (section), #9 (margin), #10 (large), #11 (once), #12 (any)

  "Now unfold your paper and check your words."
- Check the student's work to see if he/she needs extra help with spelling.

  "I want you to practice these words. We'll have a spelling test in a few days."
- If possible, take time to play the Kid Card games listed in Lesson 135.

Name ______ **Worksheet 136** (for use with Lesson 136) *Phonics 1*

Teacher's Initials ____

-ful

1. wishful
2. trustful
3. boxful
4. helpful
5. hopeful
6. richest
7. whirling
8. catcher
9. flavorful
10. wonderful

Sue was joyful about art class tonight. All of the skillful students were asked to finish the wonderful statues they'd been making from colorful paper and glue. The statues were due to be turned in tonight. Then the students will pursue another project. The class ended this evening with a barbecue. Sue arrived a bit early to see if the instructor would help her select a color. She didn't argue with him when he suggested painting her statue a deep blue.

11. What were Sue and the other students doing in art class? making statues
12. What happened at the end of class this evening? a barbecue

P1-WS-136a

Parent's Initials ____ **Homework 136** (for use with Lesson 136) *Phonics 1*

-ful

1. glassful
2. comfort
3. swirling
4. opening
5. scratcher
6. ovenful
7. discoverer
8. whispering
9. scratching
10. whizzing

Sue had a clue that to get a high grade, she needed to be skillful. One student needed help to rescue her statue from the trash where she dropped it by mistake. By eight o'clock, all of the students were finished and had given their projects to the helpful teacher. They ended the evening with a barbecue meal and time to talk to each other about their next projects.

11. What happened to one student's statue? it fell in the trash
12. When did the students finish giving their projects to the teacher? eight o'clock

Parents: Your child has been taught suffix -ful and its meaning.

P1-WS-136b

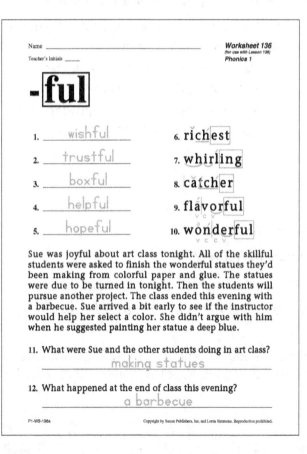

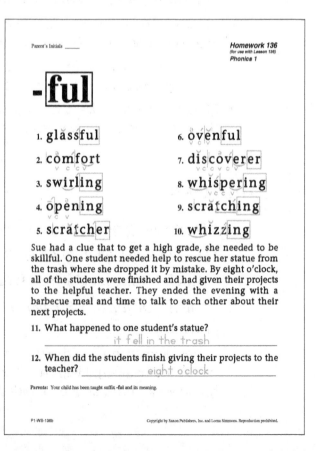

Lesson 137 — Digraph *ei*

lesson preparation

materials

Alphabet/Accent Deck (any section)

Retired Decks

Affix Deck

Spelling Sound Sheet 94

Letter Card 76

receipt in a sack (see *the night before*)

Picture Cards 99–100

Sight Word Cards 81–82

Worksheet 137

Reader 51 (*Grandpa John*)

colored pencils

the night before

- Put a receipt in a sack for the student to use to "discover" the new keyword.

Alphabet Activity

"We're going to work with one of the Alphabet/Accent Decks again today."

"Stand up. Let's say the unaccented syllables in a normal voice, but jump up on the accented syllables."

- Go through the **Alphabet/Accent Deck** (any section you choose), moving as quickly as possible.
- **Optional:** If you think the student is ready, mix two different decks together before the activity. Warn the student that something will be different this time and that he/she must pay very close attention to the cards.

Review of Decks

- The student should be seated where he/she can write comfortably.
- Show the student the retired letter cards in random order. The student should name the letter on each letter card.

- Review **Affix Cards 1–12.**
- Show the student the retired picture cards in random order. The student should name the keyword and sound for each picture card.
- Review the retired sight word cards.
- Give the student **Spelling Sound Sheet 94.**
- Call out the sounds on the retired spelling cards in random order. The student should echo each sound and name the letter or letters that make the sound as he/she writes the letter(s) on the spelling sound sheet.
- Have the student put the spelling sound sheet away.

NEW LEARNING

"I'm going to say some words. Echo them back to me and listen for the sound that is the same in the medial position of each word."

- Point to your mouth as you say each word.

"Echo after me. Neither (/nēther/)." *neither* ***"Protein."*** *protein* ***"Seize."*** *seize*

"What sound do you hear that is the same in all of these words?" /ē/

- Write the following on the chalkboard: neither, protein, seize.

"What letters do you see that might be making the /ē/ sound?" *ei*

"Do you know what this is called?" *digraph ei*

"How do we code a digraph?" *underline it*

Lesson 137

- Underline digraph *ei* in each of the words: n<u>ei</u>ther, prot<u>ei</u>n, s<u>ei</u>ze.

"How can we code this digraph so it will say /ē/ in these words?" *put a macron on the e, mark out the i*

"Can you help me code these words?"

- Code the words as the student instructs: nē̲i̸̲´|t̶h̶er, prō´|tē̲i̸̲n, sē̲i̸̲ze̸. (V; C V; V; C V)
- Assist the student, if necessary.

"Can you read these words?"

"Can you use 'neither' in a sentence?" *expect various responses*

- Repeat with "protein" and "seize."

"Now listen to these words."

- Point to your mouth as you say each word.

"Echo after me. Veil." *veil* ***"Vein."*** *vein* ***"Reindeer."*** *reindeer*

"What is the first vowel sound you hear in these words?" /ā/

- Write the following on the chalkboard: veil, vein, reindeer.

"What do you see that might be making the /ā/ sound?" *ei*

"Can we code this digraph so it will say /ā/?" *no*

"We can't really code the 'ei' to help us remember /ā/, so we will just underline it."

- Underline digraph *ei* in each of the words: veil, vein, reindeer.

"Do these words need anymore coding?" *yes, divide and code "reindeer"*

- Finish coding "reindeer": rein|deer. (vc cv)

"Digraph ei makes two sounds, /ē/ and /ā/."

"Is this a vowel digraph or a consonant digraph?" *vowel digraph*

- Leave the words on the chalkboard for the remainder of the lesson.

NEW DECK CARDS

- Show the student **Letter Card 76.**

"What is this called?" *digraph ei*

"I have another sack today. It contains a clue to our new keyword. Don't look in the sack, but put your hand inside and see if you can feel what is inside. Keep in mind that the object in the sack contains the /ē/ sound."

- Allow the student a chance to feel inside the sack.

"Can you guess the new keyword?"

- If the student cannot guess, give these hints: "This is what is at the bottom of your grocery sack after you take everything out." "Grown-ups keep these as a record of what they have bought."

"The keyword is 'receipt' and the sound is /ē/."

- Show the student **Picture Card 99.**

"Our second keyword makes the other sound of digraph ei, /ā/."

- Hold up **Picture Card 100** but keep the picture covered with your hand (or the letter card).

"I have a card with a picture on it that contains the /ā/ sound."

"I am going to describe it for you. See if you can guess what the picture is."

"This is something that is worn over the head. You usually see them on brides on their wedding day. They are usually made of very light cloth or a type of fine netting. What do you think the picture is?" *veil*

- Do not be surprised if the student does not know this word. You might even show the picture card as a clue. Use this opportunity to add a new vocabulary word.

"The keyword is 'veil' and the sound is /ā/."

- Show the student **Picture Card 100.**
- **Note:** The digraphs and their pictures are also shown in the Rule Book on page 21.

Lesson 137

"These are irregular spellings, so we won't add them to our spelling deck responses. Let's look in the Irregular Spelling Booklet for words that contain this digraph."

"Get out your Irregular Spelling Booklet."

"Look in the table of contents and see if you can find the pages that show words spelled with digraph ei." *pages 3 and 6*

"Turn to page 6. All of the words on the bottom of page 6 use digraph ei to say /ē/. They don't follow our regular rules, so we must memorize them."

- Allow time for the student to examine the list of words. If time permits, discuss the definition and/or pronunciation of some or all of the words.

"Do you know any other words that belong on this list?"

- If the student offers any appropriate words, write the words on the chalkboard and have the student copy them into the booklet.

"Now turn to page 3. In the middle of the page are a few words that use digraph ei to spell the /ā/ sound."

- Allow time for the student to examine the list of words. If time permits, discuss the definition and/or pronunciation of some or all of the words.

"Do you know any other words that belong on this list?"

- If the student offers any appropriate words, write the words on the chalkboard and have the student copy them into the booklet.

"Use your Irregular Spelling Booklet to help you learn how to spell with digraph ei. For now, put your booklet away."

- **Note:** Add the new letter and picture cards to the Review Decks.

BOARDWORK

- Write the following on the chalkboard:

enough /ĭ nŭf′/ laugh /lăf/

"We have two new sight words today."

- Point to the first word.

"Can you tell me what this word is? Remember, it's a sight word, so it won't follow all of our rules."

- Allow the student to try to pronounce the word. If necessary, say it for him/her.

"This word is 'enough.' Can you use the word 'enough' in a sentence?" *expect various answers*

- Repeat with "laugh."
- Show the student **Sight Word Cards 81** and **82.**

"Let's find these words on our sight word charts."

- Help the student locate the words in the Irregular Spelling Booklet.

  "We will add these cards to our sight word deck."

  "Let's practice coding some words like the ones you'll have on your worksheet."

  "The rule charts are in your Rule Book if you need to look at them."

- Write the following sentences (without the coding marks) on the chalkboard, one at a time. Ask the student to help you code them. The correct coding is as indicated:

  The bride'|groom (said) (to) wring out the bride's wět slip'|per[s].
  vc | c v

  The weird măn gāve mē' ăn arm'[ful] (of) the worst art Ī' hăd ěv'|er seen.
  v c | v

- Have the student determine whether each of the items coded is a word, a phrase, or a sentence.
- Add **Sight Word Cards 81** and **82** to the Sight Word Deck.

WORKSHEET

- The student should be seated where he/she can write comfortably.
- Give the student **Worksheet 137.** Make sure the student turns to the correct side.

  "We are going to spell with digraph ei on the first two words today. This digraph is one in which the words will have to be learned, since this is not the regular spelling pattern for this sound."

  "Put your finger by #1. The first word is 'ei … ther' (/ē' ther/)."

  "Write digraph ei by #1."

  "Now write /ther/ after it."

- Allow time for the student to write the word.

  "What word did you write?" *either*

- Repeat with #2 (vein).

  "The last three words will be words where the y might change to an i, according to the changing rule."

- Continue with #3 (frostier), #4 (player), and #5 (saying).

  "Now you're ready to code and read the words on your paper."

  "Code the words by #6 through #10. After you have coded all the words, try to read them."

- Assist the student as necessary.

  "Now read the word by #11. If you have trouble reading the word, code it. Then draw a line from the word to the picture it matches."

- Repeat with #12 through #14.

Lesson 137

- As the student works, provide help as needed. Help the student correct any incorrect answers. Then initial the worksheet in the space provided.
- Some time during the day, ask the student to read from the worksheet, a controlled reader, your basal reader, or other material of your choice.
- **Note:** Always make sure the worksheet is corrected before the student begins the homework. The worksheet serves as a guide to help complete the homework.

HOMEWORK

"Turn your paper over to the homework side."

"Do you know what to do on the homework paper?"

"Be sure to watch for the two sounds of digraph ei."

"When you finish your paper, I will check it for you and initial it in the space provided."

- Either now or later in the day, the student should complete the homework independently (if possible). Help the student correct any incorrect answers. Then initial the homework in the space provided.

READER

"We have another new book today."

- Give the student **Reader 51 (*Grandpa John*)** and some colored pencils.
- Write "John" on the chalkboard.

"Sometimes people's names are not spelled phonetically. This name contains a silent h. Can you read this word?" *expect various answers*

"This is the name 'John.' You'll see this word in your reader today."

"Can you tell me this book's title?" *Grandpa John*

- Assist the student as necessary as he/she constructs the book.
- When the student finishes, staple or put a rubber band around the book's spine.

"The title of this book is __________?" *Grandpa John*

"I want you to read your book to yourself. When you are finished reading, color the pictures. Write your name on the book so I will know who colored it."

"Keep your book handy because I will be asking you to read it for me."

- Some time during the day, have the student read the reader to you.
- If possible, take time to play the Kid Card games listed in Lesson 135.

Name ______________________

Teacher's Initials ____

Worksheet 137
(for use with Lesson 137)
Phonics 1

ēi, ei

1. either
2. vein
3. frostier
4. player
5. saying
6. conceited
7. veil
8. harmful
9. wrote
10. homework

11. worm 

12. oven 

13. veil 

14. mustard 

P1-WS-137a

Parent's Initials ____

Homework 137
(for use with Lesson 137)
Phonics 1

ēi, ei

1. weird
2. skein
3. boxful
4. write
5. skillful
6. wrap
7. worm
8. worse
9. tapeplayer
10. gumdrop

11. reindeer 

12. world 

13. dollar 

14. receipt 

Parents: Your child has been taught the two sounds of **digraph ei** (as in *receipt* and *veil*).

P1-WS-137b

Lesson 137

Lesson 138 — Digraphs *ew* and *ou*

lesson preparation

materials

purple Kid Cards

Review Decks

Letter Card 77

Picture Cards 101–102

cashew nuts (see *the night before*)

Worksheet 138

the night before

- Purchase some cashew nuts for the student to use to "discover" the new keyword.

Alphabet Activity

- The student should be seated.

  "Today we are going to alphabetize some of our Kid Cards."

- Give the student four or five purple word cards. Make sure that each card begins with a different letter.

  "When I say 'go,' say the alphabet out loud."

  "The first time you say a letter that one of your cards begins with, lay that card down. Lay each card to the right of the previous one. When you finish, the words should be in alphabetical order."

  "Ready, set, go!"

- Repeat with different Kid Cards if time permits.
- Collect the Kid Cards.

Review of Decks

- The student should be seated where he/she can write comfortably.
- Show the student **Letter Cards 1–76** in random order. The student should name the letter on each letter card.
- Review **Affix Cards 1–12.**

- Show the student **Picture Cards 1–100** in random order. The student should name the keyword and sound for each picture card.
- Review **Sight Word Cards 1–82.**

  "Let's review our spelling cards orally today."
- Give the sounds on **Spelling Cards 1–48** in random order. The student should echo each response and then skywrite it.

NEW LEARNING

"I'm going to say some words. Echo them back to me and listen for the sound that is the same in the final position of each word."

- Point to your mouth as you say each word.

  "Echo after me. Flew." *flew* ***"Brew."*** *brew* ***"Stew."*** *stew*

  "What sound do you hear in the final position in 'flew'?" */o͞o/*

  "Is this sound voiced or unvoiced?" *voiced*
- Write the following on the chalkboard: flew, brew, stew.

  "What do you see that might be making the /o͞o/ sound?" *ew*

  "How many letters are making that one sound?" *two*

  "What is this?" *a digraph*

  "Is digraph ew a vowel digraph or a consonant digraph?" *a vowel digraph because it contains vowels; w is a vowel when it is part of a digraph*

  "Echo after me. Pew." *pew*
- Write the word "pew" on the chalkboard.

  "What does digraph ew say in this word?" */yo͞o/*

  "Digraph ew usually says /o͞o/, but sometimes it says /yo͞o/. We code digraph ew by underlining it."
- Code the words: flew brew stew pew.

  "We have another digraph that says /o͞o/. Let's see if you can figure it out."

  "Echo after me. You." *you* ***"Youth."*** *youth* ***"Group."*** *group*
- Write the following on the chalkboard: you, youth, group.

  "Look at these words. Do you see something they all have in common?" *ou*

  "That's right. This is digraph ou. It's not found in a lot of words, but some of them are words we use all the time. We learned some of them as sight words because we needed them early in the year."

  "We code digraph ou by underlining it, crossing out the o since it's silent, and putting a macron over the u."
- Code the words: yøū yøūth grøūp.

NEW DECK CARDS

- Show the student **Letter Card 77.**

  "What do we call this?" *digraph ew*

- Hold up **Picture Card 101** but keep the picture covered with your hand (or the letter card).

  "Our first keyword ends with the /ōō/ sound."

  "Close your eyes. I'm going to put the keyword on your desk."

- Put a few cashews in front of the student.

  "Okay, open your eyes! Do you think you know the new keyword?" *expect various responses*

  "That's right, the new keyword is 'cashew.' If you want to eat your cashews, go right ahead!"

- Show the student **Picture Card 101.**

- Hold up **Picture Card 102** but keep the picture covered with your hand (or the letter card).

  "I have a card with a picture on it that contains the /ōō/ sound."

  "I am going to describe it for you. See if you can guess what the picture is."

  "This is something you eat. It is usually served in a bowl with crackers and is good on a cold day. It can be vegetable, chicken noodle, or other flavors. Do you know what the picture is?" *soup*

  "That's right. The keyword is 'soup' and the sound is also /ōō/."

- Show the student **Picture Card 102.**

- **Note:** The digraphs and their pictures are also shown in the Rule Book on page 21.

  "These are irregular spellings, so we will not add them to our spelling deck responses. Let's look in the Irregular Spelling Booklet for words that contain digraph ew and digraph ou."

  "Get out your Irregular Spelling Booklet."

  "Look in the table of contents and see if you can find the pages that show words spelled with digraphs ew and ou." *pages 18 and 19*

  "Turn to page 18. All of the words on page 18 use digraph ew. They don't follow our regular rules, so we must memorize them."

- Allow time for the student to examine the list of words. If time permits, discuss the definition and/or pronunciation of some or all of the words.

  "Do you know any other words that belong on this list?"

- If the student offers any appropriate words, write the words on the chalkboard and have the student copy them into the booklet.

  "Look at page 19. All of the words on page 19 use digraph ou. They don't follow our regular rules either, so we must memorize them."

- Allow time for the student to examine the list of words. If time permits, discuss the definition and/or pronunciation of some or all of the words.

 "Do you know any other words that belong on this list?"

- If the student offers any appropriate words, write the words on the chalkboard and have the student copy them into the booklet.

 "Use your Irregular Spelling Booklet to help you learn how to spell with digraphs ew and ou. For now, put your booklet away."

- **Note:** Add the new letter and picture cards to the Review Decks.

BOARDWORK

"Let's practice coding some words like the ones you'll have on your worksheet."

"The rule charts are in your Rule Book if you need to look at them."

- Write the following sentences (without the coding marks) on the chalkboard, one at a time. Ask the student to help you code them. The correct coding is as indicated:

 Thĕ farm´|er| is grōẇ´|ing| rīçȩ.

 Cặs´|sǐē| knew shē´ hăd bur|n|ed thĕ stew.
 v c|c v

- Have the student determine whether each of the items coded is a word, a phrase, or a sentence.

WORKSHEET

- The student should be seated where he/she can write comfortably.

- Give the student **Worksheet 138.** Make sure the student turns to the correct side.

 "Let's spell with the /ōō/ sound using digraph ew."

 "Put your finger by #1. The first word is 'chew.' "

 "Now spell the word and write it by #1."

- Allow time for the student to write the word.

 "What word did you write?" chew

- Repeat the procedure with #2 (few), #3 (grew), #4 (new), and #5 (drew).

 "Now you're ready to code and read the words on your paper."

 "Code the words by #6 through #10. After you have coded all the words, try to read them."

- Assist the student as necessary.

 "Numbers 11 and 12 are questions about the paragraph just above them. If you find any words you can't read, code them. Then see if you can answer the questions."

- As the student works, provide help as needed. Help the student correct any incorrect answers. Then initial the worksheet in the space provided.
- Some time during the day, ask the student to read from the worksheet, a controlled reader, your basal reader, or other material of your choice.
- **Note:** Always make sure the worksheet is corrected before the student begins the homework. The worksheet serves as a guide to help complete the homework.

HOMEWORK

"Turn your paper over to the homework side."

"Do you know what to do on the homework paper?"

"Watch out for digraph ew. Always code suffixes before coding the rest of the word. Also, watch for words that need to be divided."

"When you finish your paper, I will check it for you and initial it in the space provided."

- Either now or later in the day, the student should complete the homework independently (if possible). Help the student correct any incorrect answers. Then initial the homework in the space provided.
- If possible, take time to play the Kid Card games listed in Lesson 135.

Name ____________

Teacher's Initials ____

Worksheet 138
(for use with Lesson 138)
Phonics 1

ew and ou

1. chew
2. few
3. grew
4. new
5. drew

6. curfew
7. cashew
8. youth
9. landowner
10. accent

When Sally was nine years old, she flew to Vermont to stay with her great-grandmother, Jewel Parker. Jewel lived in a house with a few friends. Jewel was a fine, elderly lady who knew a lot. Sometimes she would brew a pot of coffee and put on a pot of stew for supper. Then they would sit for a long time and Jewel would tell Sally tales of what life was like when she grew up.

11. Where did Sally's great-grandmother live?
in Vermont; in a house with a few friends

12. What did Jewel talk about?
what life was like when she grew up

P1-WS-138a

Parent's Initials ____

Homework 138
(for use with Lesson 138)
Phonics 1

ew and ou

1. blew
2. knew
3. stewing
4. grown
5. brace

6. sunburn
7. group
8. cancel
9. renter
10. clipper

Sally also liked to play in her great-grandmother's big barn. She could hear some tiny newborn kittens mew. Sally looked for them but never found them. When it was time to go, it was hard to leave. Great-Grandmother Jewel gave Sally a hug and threw kisses as she left. "See you next summer."

11. What did Sally like to do at her great-grandmother's house?
play in the barn

12. What did Sally look for in the barn?
newborn kittens

Parents: Your child has been taught the two sounds of **digraph ew** (as in *cashew* and *few*), and the sound of **ou** (as in *soup*).

P1-WS-138b

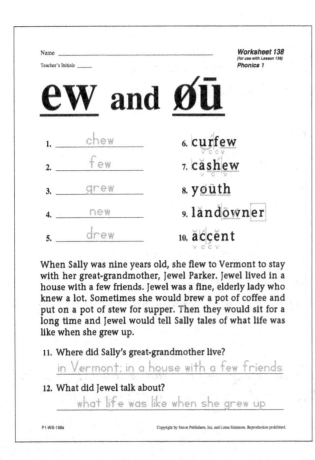

LESSON 139 Prefixes *pre-*, *dis-*

lesson preparation

materials

Alphabet/Accent Deck (any section)
Review Decks
Spelling Sound Sheet 95
Affix Cards 13–14
Sight Word Cards 83–84
Worksheet 139
Reader 52 (*A New Home*)
colored pencils

ALPHABET ACTIVITY

"We're going to work with one of the Alphabet/Accent Decks again today."

"Stand up. Let's say the unaccented syllables in a normal voice, but jump up on the accented syllables."

- Go through the **Alphabet/Accent Deck** (any section you choose), moving as quickly as possible.
- **Optional:** If you think the student is ready, mix two different decks together before the activity. Warn the student that something will be different this time and that he/she must pay very close attention to the cards.

REVIEW OF DECKS

- The student should be seated where he/she can write comfortably.
- Show the student **Letter Cards 1–77** in random order. The student should name the letter on each letter card.
- Review **Affix Cards 1–12.**
- Show the student **Picture Cards 1–102** in random order. The student should name the keyword and sound for each picture card.
- Review **Sight Word Cards 1–82.**
- Give the student **Spelling Sound Sheet 95.**

- Call out the sounds on **Spelling Cards 1–48** in random order. The student should echo each sound and name the letter or letters that make the sound as he/she writes the letter(s) on the spelling sound sheet.
- Have the student put the spelling sound sheet away.

NEW LEARNING

"I'm going to say some words. Echo them back to me and listen for the sound that is the same in the initial position of each word."

- Point to your mouth as you say each word.

"Echo after me. Precook." *precook* ***"Preheat."*** *preheat* ***"Prepay."*** *prepay*

"What do you hear that is the same in all of these words?" *pre*

- Write the following on the chalkboard: precook, preheat, prepay.

"What do all of these words have in common?" *pre*

"Can we cover the 'pre' on these words and have a root word left?" *yes*

"What do you think this is?" *a prefix*

"A prefix is something that is added to the beginning of a root word and changes its meaning. A suffix is something added to the end of a root word that changes its meaning."

"What do you think prefix 'pre' means? I will give you a hint. Think about the word 'prefix.' "

- Allow time for the student to make suggestions.

" 'Pre' means 'before.' So what does 'precook' mean?" *to cook before*

"What about the word 'preheat'?" *to heat before*

"What does 'prepay' mean?" *to pay before*

"Let's try another prefix. Echo these words and listen for the sound that is the same in the initial position of each word."

- Point to your mouth as you say each word.

"Echo after me. Disobey." *disobey* ***"Disbelieve."*** *disbelieve* ***"Distrust."*** *distrust* ***"Disconnected."*** *disconnected*

"What is the prefix?" *dis-*

- Write the following on the chalkboard: disobey, disbelieve, distrust, disconnected.

"What do you see might be making the 'dis' sound?" *dis-*

"What do you think 'dis' means in the words 'disobey,' 'disbelieve,' 'distrust,' and 'disconnected'?" *"not" or "the opposite of"*

"A prefix is coded with a box so that we can separate it from the root word."

- Point to the word "disconnected."

"Do you see something that needs to be coded at the end of this word?"
suffix -ed

"A word can have a prefix and a suffix. Words can also have more than one suffix at the end, as in 'restlessness.' Putting boxes on these suffixes and prefixes makes it easy to find the root word and then read the word, even if it is long."

- Code the words on the chalkboard. Be sure to box affixes first:

[pre]cook´ [pre]hēat´ [pre]pāy´

[dis]bē|lēve´ (v c v) [dis]trŭst´ [dis]cŏn|nĕct´[ed] (v c | c v)

- **Note:** "Disobey" contains the /ā/ sound of digraph *ey*, which the student has not learned. If desired, box the prefix and circle the root word as a sight word.

"Can you read these words?"

- Allow time for the student to read the words.

New Deck Cards

- Hold up **Affix Card 13.**

"What will we say when we see this card?" *prefix pre-*

- Hold up **Affix Card 14.**

"What will we say when we see this card?" *prefix dis-*

"We will add these prefixes to our Review Decks."

- **Note:** Add the new affix cards to the Affix Deck.

Boardwork

- Write the following on the chalkboard:

country /kŭn´ trē/ move /mo͞ov/

"We have two new sight words today."

- Point to the first word.

"Can you tell me what this word is? Remember, it's a sight word, so it won't follow all of our rules."

- Allow the student to try to pronounce the word. If necessary, say it for him/her.

"This word is 'country.' Can you use the word 'country' in a sentence?"
expect various answers

- Repeat with the remaining word.
- Show the student **Sight Word Cards 83** and **84.**

"Let's find these words on our sight word charts."

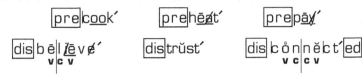

- Help the student locate the words in the Irregular Spelling Booklet.

  "We will add these cards to our sight word deck."

  "Let's practice coding some words like the ones you'll have on your worksheet."

  "The rule charts are in your Rule Book if you need to look at them."

- Write the following words and sentence (without the coding marks) on the chalkboard, one at a time. Ask the student to help you code them. The correct coding is as indicated:

  [un][crowd]′[ed][ness]

  [pre]school′

  Hē′ (said) ēach băd̸ge is round with thrē sĕc′[tion][s].

- Have the student determine whether each of the items coded is a word, a phrase, or a sentence.
- Add **Sight Word Cards 83** and **84** to the Sight Word Deck.

WORKSHEET

- The student should be seated where he/she can write comfortably.
- Give the student **Worksheet 139.** Make sure the student turns to the correct side.

  "Today, let's spell with our new prefixes."

  "Put your finger by #1. The first word is 'prescribe.' "

  "Spell the word and write it on the line by #1."

- Allow time for the student to write the word.

  "What word did you write?" *prescribe*

- Repeat with #2 (premix), #3 (disorder), #4 (disgrace), and #5 (dislike).

  "Now you're ready to code and read the words on your paper."

  "Code the words by #6 through #10. After you have coded all the words, try to read them."

- Assist the student as necessary.

  "Look at the picture at the bottom of the page. Write a story about the picture on the lines beside it. Don't worry about spelling. When you are finished, we will take time to check spelling and correct mistakes."

- As the student works, provide help as needed.
- Then have the student read the story silently and check for spelling errors. Help the student correct any mistakes. A perfect paper is not as important as the student putting his/her thoughts on paper and being able to recognize spelling errors that can be corrected (e.g., *k* and *c* spelling). Be sure to correct the rest of the worksheet as well. Then initial it in the space provided.

- Have the student read the story to you. It is important that children learn to feel comfortable speaking in front of others.
- **Note:** Always make sure the worksheet is corrected before the student begins the homework. The worksheet serves as a guide to help complete the homework.

HOMEWORK

"Turn your paper over to the homework side."

"Do you know what to do on the homework paper?"

"Look at the picture at the bottom of the page. Use the lines beside the picture and write a story about it."

"When you finish your paper, I will check it for you and initial it in the space provided."

- Either now or later in the day, the student should complete the homework independently (if possible). Help the student correct any incorrect answers. Then initial the homework in the space provided.

READER

"We have our last new book today."

- Give the student **Reader 52 (*A New Home*)** and some colored pencils.

"Can you tell me this book's title?" *A New Home*

- Assist the student as necessary as he/she constructs the book.
- When the student finishes, staple or put a rubber band around the book's spine.
- Demonstrate how to separate the pages and check page order.

"The title of this book is __________?" *A New Home*

"I want you to read your book to yourself. When you are finished reading, color the pictures. Write your name on the book so I will know who colored it."

"Keep your book handy because I will be asking you to read it for me."

- Some time during the day, have the student read the reader to you.
- If possible, take time to play the Kid Card games listed in Lesson 135. Try to see that the student is prepared for tomorrow's assessment.

Name ______________________

Teacher's Initials _____

Worksheet 139
(for use with Lesson 139)
Phonics 1

pre-, dis-

1. prescribe
2. premix
3. disorder
4. disgrace
5. dislike
6. pretreat
7. prejudge
8. discounted
9. dismiss
10. preconditioning

P1-WS-139a

Parent's Initials _____

Homework 139
(for use with Lesson 139)
Phonics 1

pre-, dis-

1. prepaid
2. predate
3. prefix
4. preheat
5. precalculations
6. disestablished
7. discredit
8. disorder
9. fudge
10. strain

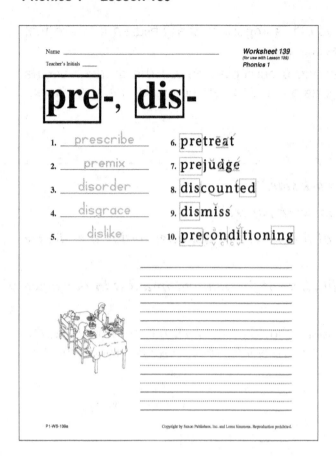

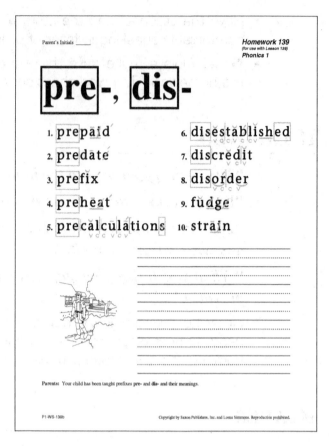

Parents: Your child has been taught prefixes **pre-** and **dis-** and their meanings.

P1-WS-139b

Lesson 139

LESSON 140 — Assessment

lesson preparation

materials

container of letter tiles

Review Decks

Assessment 27

Spelling Test 25

Assessment 27 Recording Form

Kid Cards

tokens

the night before

- Separate the Kid Cards marked "Lesson 140."

ALPHABET ACTIVITY

- The student should be seated with the container of letter tiles.

  "Before we start, let's say the alphabet together so it is fresh in our minds."
- Recite the alphabet with the student.
- Give the following instructions one at a time, allowing time for the student to accomplish each task before giving the next instruction.

  "Take all of the letter tiles out of your container."

  "Flip all of the letters over so that you are looking at the lowercase letters. If they are flipped correctly, they will all be blue."

  "Now we're ready. See if you can put all your letters in alphabetical order."
- When the student has finished, continue by saying the following:

  "Quickly pull down the vowels."

  "Put together two letters to make a diphthong."
- Have the student replace the tiles in the container and put it away.

Review of Decks

- The student should be seated where he/she can write comfortably.
- Show the student **Letter Cards 1–77** in random order. The student should name the letter on each letter card.
- Review **Affix Cards 1–14.**
- Show the student **Picture Cards 1–102** in random order. The student should name the keyword and sound for each picture card.
- Review **Sight Word Cards 1–84.**

Written Assessment

- Have the student sit where he/she can write comfortably.
- Give the student **Assessment 27.**
- **Section I:**

  "Today we are going to write some words for our assessment."

  "I'm going to say a word. Write the letter that makes each sound in that word on the lines by #1."

  "Look at the rule charts if you need to."

  "Here's the first word: wettest."
- Repeat with the following words in the order shown: #2 (runner), #3 (biking), #4 (careful), and #5 (July).
- **Reminder:** While the student spells, be ready to point to appropriate rule charts as necessary.
- **Section II:**

  "Look at the letters by #6."

  "Find the pictures of the keywords for these letters."

  "Draw a line from the letters to the keywords."
- Repeat with #7 and #8. Allow a few minutes for the student to work.
- The pictures (from top to bottom) are as follows: arm/dollar bill, fork/ doctor, sponge.
- **Section III:**

  "Put your finger on #9."

  "Code the words by #9 through #12."
- Allow a few minutes for the student to work.
- **Section IV:**

  "Read the paragraph. If you find any words you can't read, code them to help you figure them out. Then answer the question by #13."
- **Reminder:** If the student absolutely cannot read the paragraph, read it to the student to see if he or she can answer the questions.

"When you are finished, show your paper to me."

- This paper will be used during the oral portion of the assessment.

SPELLING TEST

- Give the student **Spelling Test 25.**
- Call out the following words (in the order shown). Sound them out, if necessary.

  #1 (margin), #2 (fiction), #3 (explosion), #4 (section), #5 (adventure), #6 (lotion), #7 (mixture), #8 (pasture), #9 (future), #10 (large), #11 (any), #12 (once)
- Grade and record the test in any manner that suits your needs.

ORAL ASSESSMENT

- It is important to complete the oral assessment promptly (today, if possible) in order to identify any areas of weakness and begin remediation.
- Use the assessment and the following dialogue to complete the oral portion.
- **Section V:**
- Point to the sight word by #14.

  "Read this sight word for me."
- Record the student's response by placing a check mark by each word he/she reads correctly.
- Repeat with #15 through #22.
- **Section VI:**
- Show the student the letters by #23.

  "Tell me the name of these letters and the sounds they make."
- Write the student's response on the adjacent line.
- Repeat with #24 and #25.

ASSESSMENT EVALUATION

- Grade the assessment and record the results on **Assessment 27 Recording Form.** Check off the boxes to indicate mastery (i.e., the section was completed with 100% accuracy).
- **Reminder:** Try to give as many points as possible for work attempted. Do not grade the coding marks too severely. The most important coding marks to look for are breves, macrons, and syllable division lines.
- Use the assessment results to identify those skills in which the student is weak. Practice those skills by playing Kid Card games.
- Add the Kid Cards marked "Lesson 140" to the existing deck. Listed below are games appropriate for remediation in selected areas. See "Games and Activities" for the directions for each game.

- **Section I:** Play "Spelling Deck Perfection," "Sound Scamper," "Spell Out #1 or #2," or have the student use the letter tiles to spell words you give from the Spelling Word List.
- **Section II:** Play "Keyword and Sound" or "Letter/Sound Identification."
- **Section III:** Play "Chalkboard Challenge."
- **Section IV:** Either have the student read the controlled readers and then ask questions for comprehension, or play "Acting Out" with the green Kid Cards.
- **Section V:** Play "At First Sight."
- **Section VI:** Play "Letter/Sound Identification."
- When the student seems more secure in areas that had previously proven difficult, retest him/her (in those areas only) and indicate on the recording form any sections the student has subsequently mastered.
- If the student is having difficulty with a particular skill, keep his or her practice activities at the most basic level so the chance of success is greater.

FURTHER REVIEW

- For further practice, continue to use the games and activities to reinforce learning.
- Continue to review any of the Review Decks you think would be of benefit.
- Work with the student so that he/she can read all of the readers easily.

Lesson 140

Name ______________________

Assessment 27
(for use with Lesson 140)
Phonics 1

Section I

1. w e t t e s t
2. r u n n e r
3. b i k i n g
4. c a r e f u l
5. J u l y

Section II

6. or
7. ar
8. o

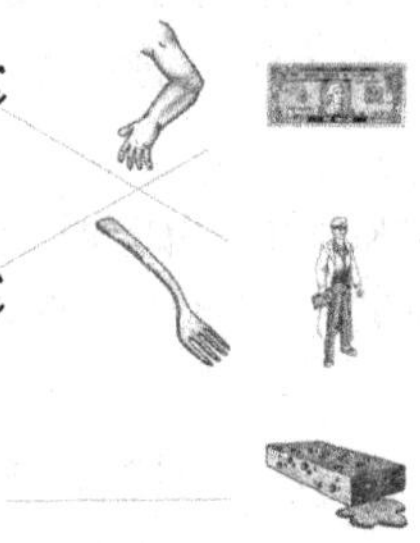

Section III

9. oven
10. mustard
11. crossword
12. tractor

Section IV

School will soon be out. Students will begin to make plans for the many things they hope to be involved in during these months off. Some older students will attend summer school. Most kids will be eager for more exciting things. Swimming tops the list for most. Others look forward to vacations with their moms and dads to places that are exciting to them. Some children are eager to go to summer camp. Others may get to spend a week or so with their grandparents. It will be great if everyone gets to do something fun during summer vacation.

P1-A-027a

Assessment 27
(for use with Lesson 140)
Phonics 1

13. What are your plans for summer?

Section V

14. thought ________ 19. only ________
15. whose ________ 20. enough ________
16. buy ________ 21. laugh ________
17. taste ________ 22. country ________
18. busy ________

Section VI

23. or combination or, /or/, /er/
24. ar combination ar, /ar/, /er/
25. o o, /ŏ/, /ō/, /ə/

P1-A-027b

READING WORD LIST

This is a list of words arranged in the order the letters, letter clusters, sounds, and other concepts are introduced. The list is composed of words first-grade students might be able to read. Lesson numbers indicate the lesson during or after which those words may be used. Use this list to quickly select appropriate words when doing extra boardwork, homework, games, or other activities.

n, o
(Lesson 2)

on

o
(Lesson 3)

no

t
(Lesson 4)

not
tot

p
(Lesson 5)

pop
pot
top

i
(Lesson 6)

I
in
inn
it
nip
pin
pip
pit
tin
tip

l
(Lesson 7)

ill
lint
lip
lit
lop
lot
pill
plot
till
tilt

a
(Lesson 8)

a
lap
nap
pal
pan
pat
plan
plant
tan
tap

z
(Lesson 9)

zap
zip

s
(Lesson 11)

as
is
last
lisp
list
loss
lost
pass
past
sap
sass
sat
sill
silt
sip
sit
slant
slap
slat
slip
slit
slop
slot
snap
snip
snot
so
sop
span
spat
spill
spin
spit
splat
split
spot
still
stilt
stop
toss

Suffix -s
(Lesson 12)

laps
lips
naps
nips
pans
pills
pins
pits
pops
pots
slips
slits
slots
snaps
snips
spills
spins
spits
spots
stops
tans
taps
tips
tops
tots

d
(Lesson 13)

ad
add
dad
did
dill
dip
doll
don
dot
lad
land
lid
nod
odd
pad
pod
pond
sad
sand
slid
sod
stand

f
(Lesson 14)

fad
fan
fast
fat
fill
fin
fist
fit
fizz
flap
flat
flint
flip
flop
fond
if
lift
loft
off
sift
sniff
soft
staff
stiff
tiff

h
(Lesson 16)

had
hand
has
hat
hi
hid
hill
hint
hip
his
hiss
hit
hop
hot

g
(Lesson 17)

dig
dog
fig
flag
fog
gag
gap
gas
gasp
gig
gill
glad
gland
glass
gloss
go
golf
got
hog
lag
log
nag
pig
tag
zag
zig

r
(Lesson 18)

draft
drag
drift
drill
drip
drop
frog
frost
graft
grand

grant
grasp
grass
grin
grip
grit
print
prod
prop
raft
rag
ran
rap
rasp
rat
razz
rid
rig
rip
rod
rot
sprint
strap
strip
trap
trip
trod
trot

k
(Lesson 19)

kid
kill
kiln
kilt
kin
kiss
kit
risk
silk
skid
skill
skin
skip
skit

c
(Lesson 21)

act
can
cap
cast
cat
clan
clap
clasp
class
cliff
clip
clog
clop
clot
cod
con
cop
cost
cot
craft
crisp
crop
cross
fact
pact
scalp
scan
scant
scrap
strict

b
(Lesson 23)

bad
bag
ban
band
bask
bass
bat
bib
bid
big
bill
bin
bit
blast
bliss
blob
blond
blot
bob
bond
boss
brag
bran
brand
brisk
cab
cob
crab
crib
dab
fib
gab
grab
lab
nab
rib
rob
scab
slab
slob
sob
stab
tab

vc′|cv
(Lesson 24)

bobbin
classic
coffin
contact
fabric
frantic
gossip
napkin
picnic
plastic
poplin
rabbit
traffic

m
(Lesson 26)

am
blimp
brim
camp
clam
cramp
dam
damp
dim
film
gram
grim
ham
him
impact
lamp
limp
mad
man
map
mascot
mask
mass
mast
mat
mid
milk
mill
mint
miss
mist
mitt
mob
mom
mop
moss
prompt
ram
ramp
rim
romp
skim
slam
slim
smog
stamp
stomp
tramp
trim

e
(Lesson 27)

absent
be
bed
beg
bell
belt
bend
bent
best
bet
blend
bless
bonnet
contest
crept
dell
den
dent
desk
dress
ebb
egg
elf
elk
elm
end
fed
fell
felt
fled
get
happen
he
held
help
hen
hidden
inlet
insect
keg
kelp
kept
kitten
led
left
leg
lend
lens
lent
less
let
mallet
me
melt
mend
mess
met
mitten
nest
net
peg
pelt
pen
pest
pet
press
red
rest
sell
send
sent
set
sled
slept
smell
sped
spell
stem
step
stress
tablet
tell
ten
test

ck
(Lesson 28)

back
black
block
brick
click
clock
crack
deck
dock
fleck
flick
flock
hack
hock
kick
lack
lick
lock
mock
neck
nick
pack
peck
pick
rack
rick
rock
sack
sick
slack

slacks
slick
smack
smock
snack
sock
stack
stick
stock
tack
tick
track
trick

th
(Lesson 31)

than
that
then
this

th
(Lesson 31)

bath
broth
cloth
fifth
froth
math
moth
path
thick
thin
thrill
throb

ng
(Lesson 32)

bang
bong
bring
cling
ding
dong
fang
fling
gong
hang
king
long
pang
ping
pong
prong
rang
ring
sang
sing
sling
song
sprang
spring
sting
string
strong
tang
thing
thong
tong
zing

nk
(Lesson 32)

blink
drank
drink
honk
link
mink
pink
rank
sank
slink
spank
stink
thank
think

Suffix -ing
(Lesson 32)

acting
adding
backing
bagging
banding
banging
basking
batting
begging
bending
betting
bidding
billing
blasting
blending
blessing
blocking
blotting
bobbing
bonding
bossing
bragging
branding
bricking
brimming
bringing
camping
canning
capping
casting
clamming
clapping
clasping
clicking
clinging
clipping
clocking
clogging
clopping
clotting
conning
contacting
costing
cramping
crossing
dabbing
denting
digging
dimming
dinging
dipping
docking
dotting
drafting
dragging
dressing
drifting
drilling
drinking
dripping
dropping
ending
fanning
fibbing
filling
filming
fitting
fizzing
flapping
flinging
flipping
flocking
flopping
frosting
gabbing
gagging
gasping
gassing
getting
golfing
grabbing
grafting
granting
grasping
grinning
gripping
gritting
hacking
hamming
handing
hanging
happening
helping
hinting
hissing
hitting
hogging
honking
hopping
kicking
kidding
killing
kissing
lacking
lagging
landing
lapping
lasting
lending
letting
licking
lifting
limping
linking
lisping
listing
locking
logging
manning
masking
melting
mending
messing
milking
missing
misting
mopping
nabbing
nagging
napping
nesting
netting
nipping
nodding
packing
passing
patting
pecking
pelting
picking
pinning
planning
planting
plotting
popping
potting
pressing
printing
prodding
propping
rafting
ramming
rapping
razzing
resting
ribbing
ridding
rigging
ringing
ripping
risking
robbing
rocking
romping
rotting
sacking
sanding
sassing
scalping
scanning
scrapping
selling
sending
setting
sifting
singing
sinning
sipping
sitting
skidding
skinning
skipping
slamming
slanting
slapping
sledding
slicking
slimming
slinging
slipping
smacking
smelling
smocking
snacking
snapping
sniffing
snipping
sobbing
sopping
spanking
spanning
spelling
spilling
spinning
spitting
splitting
spotting
springing
sprinting
stabbing
stacking
stamping
standing
stepping
sticking
stinging
stinking
stocking
stomping
stopping
strapping
stressing

stringing
stripping
tacking
tagging
tanning
tapping
telling
testing
thanking
thinking
thinning
thrilling
throbbing
ticking
tilting
tipping
topping
tossing
tracking
trapping
tricking
trimming
tripping
trotting
zagging
zapping
zigging
zipping

Suffix -ed = /d/
(Lesson 33)

banged
belled
billed
ebbed
filled
filmed
gonged
hanged
killed
milled
pilled
pinged
smelled
spelled
spilled
thrilled
tilled

Suffix -ed = /t/
(Lesson 33)

backed
banked
camped
clamped
cramped
cranked
decked
gasped
glossed
grasped
helped
hissed
inked
kissed
lacked
limped
locked
masked
milked
missed
passed
pecked
romped
sassed
sniffed
spanked
stacked
stamped
tacked
ticked
tossed
tracked
tramped
tripped

Suffix -ed = /ĕd/
(Lesson 33)

acted
belted
blended
branded
dented
drafted
drifted
ended
frosted
granted
handed
hinted
landed
lasted
lifted
listed
melted
mended
nested
panted
planted
ranted
rented
rested
sanded
sifted
slanted
tilted
tinted

ee
(Lesson 34)

bee
beef
beep
bleed
breed
creed
creep
deed
deep
deer
eel
fee
feed
feel
feet
flee
fleet
free
freed
greed
Greek
green
greet
heed
heel
keep
meek
meet
need
peek
peel
peep
peer
reed
reef
reek
reel
screen
see
seed
seek
seem
seen
seep
sleep
sleet
sneer
speed
steel
street
tee
teen
teeth
three
tree

u
(Lesson 37)

bluff
blunt
bug
bulb
bulk
bump
bun
bunk
bus
bust
but
buzz
cactus
club
clump
clung
crust
cub
cuff
cup
cut
drug
drum
dug
dump
dusk
dust
fun
fund
fuss
fuzz
grub
gruff
grump
grunt
gulf
gull
gulp
gum
gun
gust
hiccup
hub
hug
hull
hum
hump
hunt
lug
lump
mud
muff
mug
mumps
must
nun
nut
nutmeg
plug
plum
plump
plus
puff
pump
pun
pup
rub
rug
run
rust
rut
scrub
scuff
skull
slug
slump
snug
spun
strum
stub
stuck
stuff
stump
stun
stunt
sudden
sum
sun
sunk
thrust
thud
thump
trust
tub
tug
tusk
up

w
(Lesson 38)

swam
sweep
sweet
swept
swift
swim
swum
tweet
twig
twill
twin
twist
wag
we
web
wee
weed
week
weep
weld
well
went
wept
west
wet
wig
will
wilt
win

wind
wing
wink
wisp
wit

vc|cv´
(Lesson 39)

accuse
admire
admit
affect
compel
confess
consist
discuss
submit
unless
until
upset

ā–e̸
(Lesson 41)

ale
ape
ate
babe
bake
bale
bare
base
blade
blame
blare
blaze
brake
cake
came
cane
cape
care
case
crane
crate
dare
date
daze
drake
drape
fade
fake
fame
fare
fate
flake
flame
flare
frame
gale
game
gate
gaze
glade
glare
grade
grape
grate
graze
hare
hate
lake
lame
lane
late
made
make
male
mane
mate
mistake
name
pale
pare
plane
plate
rake
rare
rate
safe
sake
sale
same
sane
scale
scare
scrape
skate
slate
snake
snare
spade
spare
stake
stare
state
take
tale
tame
tape
trade

ō–e̸
(Lesson 42)

bone
broke
close
code
cone
cope
dope
dose
dote
doze
drone
froze
globe
grope
hole
home
hope
hose
mode
mole
more
nose
note
poke
pole
pope
pore
pose
probe
prone
robe
rode
role
Rome
rope
rose
scope
score
slope
smoke
snore
sore
spoke
spore
stoke
stole
stone
store
strode
stroke
those
throne
tone
tore
tote
zone

ū–e̸
(Lesson 42)

confuse
costume
cube
cure
cute
dude
duke
dune
flute
fume
fuse
lube
mule
mute
prune
pure
rude
rule
tube
tune
use

ī–e̸
(Lesson 43)

bike
bite
bribe
crime
dime
dine
dire
fife
file
fine
fire
glide
hide
hike
hire
kite
life
like
lime
line
mile
mine
mire
mite
nine
pile
pine
pipe
pride
prime
prize
ripe
rise
scribe
side
size
slide
smile
spike
spine
spite
stride
strike
stripe
swine
swipe
tide
time
tire
tribe
twine
wide
wife
wine
wipe
wise

ē–e̸
(Lesson 43)

eke
here
theme
these

Silent e
(Lesson 43)

dense
dispense
eclipse
else
geese
impulse
intense
lapse
offense
pulse
response
rinse
suspense

x
(Lesson 46)

ax
box
fax
fix
flax
flex
flux
fox
lox
mix
ox
pox
sax
sex
six
tax
tux
wax

y
(Lesson 47)

yak
yam
yank
yap
yell
yelp
yen
yes
yet
yip
yo-yo
yuck
yule

sh
(Lesson 48)

ash
brush
cash
clash
crash
crush
dash
dish
fish
flash
flesh
flush
fresh
gush
hash
hush
lash
mesh
publish
rash
rush
sash
shade
shake
shale
shame
shape
share
she
shed
shelf
shell
shift
shin
shine
ship
shock
shone
shop
shore
shot
shred
shrill
shrimp
shrink
shrub
shrunk
shut
slash
slush
smash
splash
swish
trash
wish

oo = /o͝o/
(Lesson 49)

book
brook
cook
crook
foot
good
hood
hoof
hook
look
shook
soot
stood
took
wood

oo = /o͞o/
(Lesson 49)

bloom
boo
boom
boost
boot
booth
broom
cool
coop
doom
drool
droop
food
fool
gloom
groom
hoop
hoot
loom
loop
loot
mood
moon
noon
pool
proof
room
roost
root
scoop
shoot
smooth
soon
spool
spoon
stool
stoop
swoop
tool
toot
tooth
troop
zoo
zoom

j
(Lesson 51)

jab
jack
jacket
jade
jag
jagged
jam
jazz
jest
jet
jig
jilt
job
jog
joke
jot
jug
jump
junk
just
jut

Floss Words
(Lesson 52)

bass
bell
bill
bless
bliss
bluff
boss
brass
class
cliff
cross
cuff
doll
drill
dress
fill
fluff
fuss
gill
glass
gloss
grass
grill
gruff
gull
hill
hiss
ill
kill
kiss
lass
less
loss
mass
mess
mill
miss
moss
muff
off
pass
pill
press
priss
puff
scuff
sell
shall
shell
shrill
sill
skill
skull
smell
sniff
spill
staff
stiff
still
stress
stuff
swell
tell
thrill
till
toss
twill
well
will
yell

v || ve
(Lesson 53)

brave
cave
crave
five
gave
give
grave
grove
jive
live
pave
save
solve
vampire
van
vane
vast
vat
velvet
vent
vest
vet
vim
vine
vote

ble
(Lesson 56)

able
babble
bobble
bubble
bumble
cable
crumble
dabble
dribble
fable
feeble
fumble
gamble
gobble
grumble
humble
mumble
nibble
nimble
pebble
ramble
rubble
rumble
scramble
scribble
stable
stubble
stumble
table
thimble
tremble
tumble

fle
(Lesson 57)

baffle
muffle
raffle
rifle
ruffle
scuffle
sniffle
stifle
trifle
truffle

ple
(Lesson 57)

ample
apple
cripple
crumple
dapple
dimple
grapple
maple
ripple
rumple
sample
simple
steeple
supple

topple
trample

dle
(Lesson 57)

bridle
bundle
candle
cuddle
fiddle
fondle
fuddle
handle
huddle
kindle
ladle
middle
muddle
needle
paddle
puddle
riddle
saddle
spindle
straddle
toddle
trundle

tle
(Lesson 58)

battle
beetle
cattle
kettle
little
mottle
rattle
settle
tattle
throttle
title

gle
(Lesson 58)

angle
bugle
bungle
jangle
jiggle
juggle
mangle
mingle
single
smuggle
snuggle
spangle
strangle
struggle
tangle

cle
(Lesson 59)

uncle

zle
(Lesson 59)

dazzle
drizzle
frazzle
guzzle
muzzle
puzzle

sle
(Lesson 59)

hassle
tussle

kle
(Lesson 59)

ankle
buckle
cackle
crackle
crinkle
fickle
freckle
heckle
pickle
speckle
tackle
tinkle
trickle

y = /ī/
(Lesson 61)

by
cry
dry
fly
fry
my
pry
shy
sky
sly
spry
sty
try

y = /ē/
(Lesson 62)

belly
berry
bonny
candy
dandy
fifty
filly
flimsy
folly
frenzy
granny
guppy
happy
husky
kitty
penny
puppy
silly
sixty
twenty

Suffix -y
(Lesson 62)

baggy
beefy
bulky
bumpy
crispy
crusty
drippy
dusty
filmy
fishy
floppy
fluffy
foggy
frisky
frosty
funny
fussy
grassy
greedy
gritty
gummy
handy
hilly
lucky
lumpy
messy
misty
mushy
musty
needy
rocky
runny
rusty
sandy
sleepy
sloppy
sticky
stringy
sunny

er
(Lesson 63)

after
banner
batter
berth
better
bitter
bladder
blister
blubber
blunder
bluster
butler
butter
clatter
clerk
copper
dinner
expert
fender
fern
finger
fluster
foster
glitter
hammer
hamper
her
herd
hermit
hinder
hunger
jerk
lantern
latter
litter
manner
master
mister
number
per
perfect
perfume
perk
person
rubber
rudder
serve
shatter
shelter
shutter
silver
slender
slipper
slumber
soccer
splinter
sputter
stern
suffer
summer
supper
tender
term
tern
thunder
trigger
verb
winter

igh
(Lesson 64)

bright
fight
flight
fright
high
light
might
nigh
night
plight
right
sigh
sight
slight
thigh
tight

Compound Words
(Lesson 66)

afternoon
backbone
backdrop
backfire
backhand
backpack
backstop
backstroke
bagpipe
bankbook
barefoot
bathrobe
bathroom
bathtub
bedroom
bedtime
beehive
bookstore
bridegroom
campfire
candlestick
cannot
carefree
cupcake
dishcloth
dishpan
drugstore
drumstick
dustpan
eggnog
eggplant
eggshell
fingerprint
fireman
fishhook
flagpole
flashlight
footprint
footstool
grapevine
grasshopper
gumdrop
handbag
handcuff

homemade
jackpot
lampshade
lifetime
mixup
moonlight
nightmare
nosebleed
noseplugs
nutshell
pancake
pickup
pinecone
roommate
rosebud
salesman
setup
skyline
sparerib
stepladder
sunlight
textbook
toothbrush
weekend
windmill

Suffix -ly
(Lesson 67)

badly
barely
crisply
gladly
glumly
likely
madly
manly
purely
rarely
sadly
safely
softly
suddenly
weekly

Suffix -less
(Lesson 67)

backless
beltless
blameless
bottomless
endless
hatless
helpless
jobless
lifeless
nameless
restless
sleepless
sleeveless
spotless
strapless
sunless
thankless
timeless
tireless

Suffix -ness
(Lesson 67)

blackness
dampness
dimness
dullness
fastness
flatness
fondness
gladness
goodness
hotness
illness
likeness
plumpness
redness
rudeness
sadness
sickness
softness
soreness
stiffness
thickness
wetness

ai
(Lesson 68)

affair
aid
ail
aim
air
airplane
bail
bait
braid
brain
claim
drain
fail
faint
fair
faith
fingernail
flair
gain
gait
grain
hail
hair
hairbrush
haircut
hairline
jail
laid
lain
lair
maid
mail
main
nail
paid
pail
pain
paint
pair
plain
raid
rail
rain
sail
saint
slain
snail
Spain
sprain
strain
tail
trail
train
trait
upstairs
vain
waist
waistband
waistline
wait

ay
(Lesson 69)

bay
bray
clay
day
daylight
driveway
gray
hay
highway
jay
lay
may
pay
play
playmate
playroom
pray
ray
say
slay
splay
spray
stay
stray
sway
tray
way

ar
(Lesson 71)

arc
ark
arm
art
artist
bar
barb
bark
barn
barnyard
bookmark
boxcar
car
card
cargo
carp
carpet
cart
dark
darkroom
darling
dart
far
farm
garden
gargle
garland
garlic
garment
garnish
garter
hard
harm
harness
harp
harsh
harvest
jar
junkyard
landmark
lard
lark
marble
mark
market
marsh
martin
park
part
scar
scarf
scarlet
shark
sharp
smart
snarl
spark
sparkle
star
starfish
starlight
starling
start
tar
tart
varnish
yard
yardstick
yarn

ch
(Lesson 72)

arch
branch
bunch
chain
chair
champ
chant
chap
charm
chart
chase
chat
chatter
check
chess
chest
chick
chill
chime
chin
chip
choke
chop
chore
chose
chunk
crunch
flinch
hunch
inch
lunch
March
march
much
munch
parch
perch
pinch
punch
ranch
rich
starch
such
winch

or
(Lesson 73)

absorb
airport
assort

border
born
brainstorm
cord
cork
corn
corner
for
forget
fork
form
former
fort
forth
horn
hornet
horrid
horse
inform
lord
north
or
orbit
order
organ
popcorn
porch
pork
port
scorch
scorn
short
shortcut
shortstop
snort
sort
sport
stork
storm
thorn
thunderstorm
torch
torment
torn
worn

qu
(Lesson 74)

banquet
inquire
quack
quail
quaint
quake
quaver
queen
quell
quench
quest
quibble
quick
quicksand
quill
quilt
quint
quintet
quip
quit
quite
quiz
quote
square
squeeze
squelch
squid
squiggle
squint
squire
squish
vanquish

ir
(Lesson 76)

birch
bird
birth
birthday
chirp
dirt
fir
firm
first
flirt
girl
irk
shirk
shirt
sir
skirt
squirm
squirt
stir
swirl
third
thirst
thirteen
twirl

ur
(Lesson 77)

blur
blurt
burden
burn
burp
burst
church
churn
curb
curl
curry
curt
fur
hurl
hurt
murder
murmur
purse
spur
spurt
turf
turn
turnip
urn

Soft c
(Lesson 78)

accent
accept
access
ace
advice
brace
cancel
cancer
cell
cellar
cent
center
cinch
circle
circus
cite
citrus
concept
concern
concert
dice
excel
except
excite
face
fancy
force
grace
ice
lace
lice
mace
mercy
mice
nice
pace
parcel
place
price
race
rice
sincere
space
spice
succeed
success
trace
twice
ulcer
vice

ow = /ō/
(Lesson 79)

arrow
barrow
blow
bow
bowl
crow
elbow
fellow
flow
follow
glow
grow
hollow
low
minnow
mow
own
pillow
rainbow
row
shadow
shallow
show
slow
snow
sow
stow
throw
tow
willow
window
yellow

a′|cv
(Lesson 81)

acorn
baby
bacon
basic
basin
canine
crater
crazy
gravy
haven
hazel
lady
lazy
navel
navy
paper
raven
zany

i′|cv
(Lesson 82)

crisis
fiber
final
idol
iris
Irish
item
minus
pilot
silent
spider
tidy
tripod

e′|cv
(Lesson 82)

even
evening
evil
female
fever
legal
meter
regal
Venus
zenith

o′|cv
(Lesson 83)

bonus
clover
cozy
donate
focus
frozen
moment
open
oval
over
profile
robot
rodent
Roman
rotate
slogan
spoken
total
vocal

u′|cv
(Lesson 83)

duty
music
pupil
stupid
super
tulip

a|cv′
(Lesson 84)

abandon
abide
adapt
adopt
adorn

adult
ago
ajar
alarm
alike
awake
aware
away

ea = /ē/
(Lesson 86)

beach
bead
beak
beam
bean
beard
beast
beat
bleach
breathe
cheap
clean
clear
cleat
creak
cream
deal
dear
dream
each
ear
east
easy
eat
fear
feast
freak
gear
grease
heal
hear
heat
lead
leaf
leak
lean
leap
leash
least
leave
meal
mean
meat
near
nearby
neat
pea
peach
peak
peal
please
pleat
reach
read
real
really
rear
reason
scream
sea
seal
seam
season
seat
smear
sneak
speak
spear
squeak
squeal
steal
steam
streak
stream
tea
teach
team
tear
tease
teaspoon
treat
weak
weave
year
yeast

ea = /ĕ/
(Lesson 87)

ahead
bread
breakfast
breast
breath
dead
deaf
dealt
death
dread
feather
head
headlight
health
heaven
heavy
lead
leather
meadow
meant
peasant
pleasant
read
ready
spread
steady
sweat
sweater
thread
threat
tread
wealth
weapon
wear
weather

ea = /ā/
(Lesson 87)

break
great
steak
yea

Dropping Rule
(Lesson 88)

baked
baking
blamed
blaming
blazed
blazing
bony
braked
braking
cared
caring
closed
closing
coded
coding
coped
coping
crated
crating
cubed
cured
curing
dared
daring
dated
dating
faded
fading
flamed
flaming
framed
framing
fumed
fuming
glared
glaring
graded
grading
grated
grating
grazed
grazing
hated
hating
hoped
hoping
laced
lacing
lacy
making
named
naming
nosed
nosing
nosy
noted
noting
poked
poking
poky
pruned
pruning
raked
raking
rated
rating
roped
roping
rosy
ruled
ruling
scared
scaring
scary
scored
scoring
shaded
shading
shady
shined
shining
shiny
skated
skating
snaked
snaking
stated
stating
stored
storing
stroked
stroking
taking
tamed
taming
taped
taping
toned
toning
toted
toting
traded
trading
tuned
tuning
waded
wading
zoned
zoning

oi
(Lesson 89)

avoid
boil
broil
coil
coin
foil
hoist
join
joint
loin
moist
oil
point
poison
soil
toil

oy
(Lesson 89)

ahoy
annoy
boy
coy
enjoy
joy
soy
tomboy

vc|cvc|cv
(Lesson 92)

absentee
amnesty
Atlantic
ballistic
embargo
establish
fantastic
hamburger
important
intercept
nocturnal
organdy
personnel
September

tion
(Lesson 93)

action
attention
calculation
caption
circulation
collection
completion
conversation

corporation
deletion
devotion
dictation
direction
education
election
emotion
exception
fiction
fraction
friction
function
indentation
information
interruption
intervention
junction
location
lotion
mention
motion
nation
notion
operation
option
population
portion
potion
preparation
presentation
prevention
promotion
proportion
resolution
satisfaction
sanction
section
station
suction
taxation
traction
vacation
vaccination

ue
(Lesson 94)

argue
avenue
barbecue
blue
clue
continue
cue
due
flue
glue
pursue
rescue
residue
revenue
subdue
sue
Tuesday
value

Suffix -es
(Lesson 96)

ashes
beaches
benches
bosses
boxes
branches
brushes
bunches
bushes
clashes
classes
crosses
crunches
crushes
dashes
dishes
dresses
fizzes
flashes
foxes
glasses
gushes
hunches
hushes
inches
kisses
lashes
lunches
marches
misses
mixes
passes
pinches
punches
ranches
rashes
rushes
sashes
sixes
slushes
smashes
splashes
suffixes
swishes
taxes
waxes
winches
wishes

ou = /ou/
(Lesson 97)

about
account
amount
around
blouse
bound
cloud
clout
couch
count
crouch
douse
flour
foul
found
foundation
grouch
ground
groundhog
grouse
grout
hound
house
joust
loud
lout
mound
mount
mouse
mouth
noun
ouch
our
oust
out
outcast
playground
pouch
pound
pout
proud
round
scour
scout
shout
slouch
snout
sound
sour
south
spout
sprout
stout
trout
underground
wound

ow = /ou/
(Lesson 97)

bow
brown
clown
cow
cowboy
cowgirl
crowd
crown
dowel
down
downstairs
drown
flower
fowl
frown
gown
how
howl
now
owl
plow
scowl
sow
town
vow
wow

vc|ccv
(Lesson 99)

address
burglar
complete
conflict
congress
distress
district
emblem
employ
enclose
inflate
instant
instead
lobster
subtract

vcc|cv
(Lesson 99)

arctic
empty
kingdom
ointment
partner
plankton

au
(Lesson 101)

auction
August
author
auto
because
cause
clause
faucet
fault
flaunt
fraud
gauze
haul
haunt
launch
launder
laundry
pause
sauce
saucer
vault

aw
(Lesson 102)

bawl
claw
crawl
dawn
draw
drawl
drawn
fawn
flaw
hawk
jaw
law
lawn
lawyer
paw
pawn
prawn
raw
saw
scrawl
shawl
slaw
squawk
straw
thaw
yawn

"Wild Colt" Words
(Lesson 103)

bind
blind
bold
both
child
cold
colt
find
fold
gold
grind
hold
host
jolt
kind
mild
mind
mold
old
pint

poll
post
rind
roll
scold
scroll
sold
told
toll
troll
volt
wild
wind

oa
(Lesson 104)

aboard
afloat
board
boast
boat
cardboard
charcoal
coach
coal
coast
coat
cocoa
croak
float
foam
goal
goat
groan
lifeboat
load
loaf
loan
meatloaf
moan
oak
oar
oath
oatmeal
oats
poach
railroad
raincoat
roach
road
roam
roar
roast
rowboat
sailboat
scoreboard
skateboard
soak
soap
soar
throat
toad
toadstool
toast

oe
(Lesson 104)

doe
hoe
oboe
tiptoe
toe
woe

ey
(Lesson 106)

alley
barley
chimney
donkey
galley
honey
key
kidney
medley
money
monkey
trolley
turkey
valley
volley

vc′|v
(Lesson 107)

acid
body
cabin
city
clever
comic
decade
denim
dragon
ever
exit
finish
habit
lemon
lily
limit
mimic
never
oxen
profit
rapid
river
robin
salad
seven
sliver
solid
talent
topic
valid
value
visit
vivid
vixen
volume

ph
(Lesson 108)

diphthong
dolphin
gopher
graph
graphic
graphite
orphan
phase
phone
phonics
phrase
telephone

Soft g
(Lesson 109)

agent
congest
digest
digit
frigid
gee
gel
gelatin
gem
gene
genetic
gentleman
general
generate
germ
gigantic
ginger
longitude
magic
margin
passenger
plunger
tragedy
tragic
urgent

Doubling Rule
(Lesson 111)

bagged
bagging
baggy
batted
batting
batty
begged
begging
betted
betting
bidded
bidding
bobbed
bobbing
bragged
bragging
brimmed
brimming
bugged
bugging
buggy
canned
canning
capped
capping
clipped
clipping
clogged
clogging
clopped
clopping
cutting
dabbed
dabbing
digging
dimmed
dimming
dipped
dipping
dotted
dotting
dragged
dragging
dripped
dripping
drippy
dropped
dropping
drummed
drumming
fibbed
fibbing
fogged
fogging
foggy
gabbed
gabbing
gabby
getting
grabbed
grabbing
grabby
gritted
gritting
gritty
gummy
hitting
hogged
hogging
hopped
hopping
hugged
hugging
kidded
kidding
lagged
lagging
lapped
lapping
letting
logged
logging
mopped
mopping
nabbed
nabbing
nagged
nagging
netted
netting
nipped
nipping
nippy
patted
patting
pinned
pinning
plotted
plotting
popped
popping
prodded
prodding
propped
propping
rammed
ramming
rapped
rapping
ribbed
ribbing
rigged
rigging
ripped
ripping
robbed
robbing
rotted
rotting
rubbed
rubbing
running
scrapped
scrapping
setting
sipped
sipping
skidded
skidding
skipped
skipping
slammed
slamming
slapped
slapping
slimmed
slimming

slipped
slipping
snapped
snapping
snappy
snipped
snipping
snippy
sobbed
sobbing
spinning
spitting
stepped
stepping
stopped
stopping
thinned
thinning
throbbed
throbbing
tipped
tipping
topped
topping
trapped
trapping
trimmed
trimming
tripped
tripping
trotted
trotting

kn
(Lesson 112)

knack
knead
knee
kneel
knickers
knife
knight
knit
knob
knock
knot
know
knuckle

gn
(Lesson 112)

align
assign
campaign
design
gnash
gnat
gnarl
gnaw
gnome
gnu
malign
sign

wr
(Lesson 112)

wrangler
wrap
wreath
wreck
wren
wrench
wring
wrinkle
wrist
write
written
wrong
wrote
wrung

e|cv′
(Lesson 114)

because
beside
debate
depend
eject
elect
erase
erupt
event
evict
pretend
recite
reduce
refer
reserve

o|cv′
(Lesson 114)

hotel
omit
produce
propel
protect
provide

u|cv′
(Lesson 114)

brunet
humane
July
superb
unite

tch
(Lesson 116)

batch
blotch
botch
catch
clutch
crutch
ditch
Dutch
etch
fetch
hatch
hitch
hutch
itch
kitchen
latch
match
notch
patch
pitch
pitcher
pitchfork
Scotch
scratch
sketch
snatch
snitch
splotch
stitch
stretch
switch
thatch

twitch
witch

dge
(Lesson 117)

badge
bridge
budge
cadge
dodge
dredge
edge
fudge
grudge
hedge
judge
ledge
lodge
nudge
pledge
ridge
sledge
sludge
smudge
wedge

ge
(Lesson 117)

age
barge
bilge
binge
bulge
cage
charge
cringe
dirge
flange
forge
fringe
gorge
hinge
huge
large
lounge
lunge
merge
page
plunge
purge
rage
sage

serge
singe
splurge
stage
teenage
tinge
twinge
verge
wage

ie = /ī/
(Lesson 119)

die
lie
pie
tie

ie = /ē/
(Lesson 119)

brief
briefcase
chief
diesel
field
fierce
grief
niece
piece
pier
pierce
priest
shield
shriek
thief
yield

sion = /shŭn/
(Lesson 121)

admission
concussion
confession
discussion
expression
impression
permission
possession
succession

sion = /zhŭn/
(Lesson 121)

conclusion
confusion

decision
division
explosion
incision
invasion
occasion

ture
(Lesson 122)

adventure
capture
creature
culture
denture
departure
feature
fixture
fracture
furniture
future
gesture
lecture
mixture
moisture
nature
nurture
pasture
picture
posture
puncture
rupture
scripture
sculpture
structure
suture
texture
torture
venture
vulture

ch = /k/
(Lesson 123)

ache
character
chord
chorus
chrome
chronic
schedule
scheme
scholar
scholarship

scholastic
school
schooner

ch = /sh/
(Lesson 123)

chaise
chaps
charade
chef
chiffon
chivalry
chute

wh
(Lesson 124)

whale
wheat
wheel
when
whet
whether
which
whiff
while
whim
whimper
whine
whip
whirl
whirlpool
whirlwind
whisk
whisper
white
whiz
why

eigh
(Lesson 126)

eight
eighteen
eighty
freight
neighbor
sleigh
weigh
weight

wa
(Lesson 127)

swallow
wad
waffle
walk
wall
wallet
wallop
wallow
wand
wander
wasp
watch
water

qua
(Lesson 127)

aquatic
equality
quad
quarrel
quality
quantity
squabble
squad
squadron
squall
squander
squash
squat

al
(Lesson 128)

all
bald
balk
ball
call
chalk
chalkboard
fall
false
hall
halt
mall
malt
salt
scald
small
squall
stall
tall
wall

Suffix -er
(Lesson 131)

banker
barber
batter
bigger
blender
bookkeeper
buzzer
catcher
colder
cooler
deeper
dresser
drummer
farmer
faster
helper
hunter
kicker
longer
marker
mixer
nutcracker
older
planter
player
preacher
rancher
renter
richer
runner
sander
seller
shorter
sifter
singer
skyscraper
smaller
spender
stronger
sweeter
taller
trucker
washer
worker
zookeeper

Suffix -est
(Lesson 131)

freshest
hottest
loudest
maddest
saddest
shortest
smoothest
softest
strongest
sweetest
thickest
warmest
wettest
wildest

ar = /er/
(Lesson 132)

beggar
buzzard
collar
custard
dollar
grammar
hangar
hazard
mustard
nectar
pillar
standard

or = /er/
(Lesson 132)

actor
author
doctor
donor
error
favor
harbor
horror
labor
major
odor
sailor
splendor
terror
tractor
tutor
vendor

wor = /wer/
(Lesson 132)

word
work
world
worm
worse
worth

Scribal o
(Lesson 133)

color
come
comfort
compass
cover
discover
done
front
govern
Monday
month
oven
recover
shovel
son
ton
won
wonder

i|cv′
(Lesson 134)

dilute
direct
divide

Changing Rule
(Lesson 134)

bulkier
bulkiest
cozier
coziest
cozily
coziness
flimsier
flimsiest
flimsily
grassier
grassiest
handier
handiest
handily
handiness
happier
happiest
happily
happiness
luckier
luckiest
luckily
merciless
prettier
prettily
sillier
silliest
silliness
sleepier
sleepiest
sleepiness
sleepily
tidier
tidiest
tidily
tidiness
zanier
zaniest

Suffix -ful
(Lesson 136)

armful
bagful
basketful
boxful
capful
careful
fateful
fitful
glassful
gleeful
handful
harmful
hateful
heedful
helpful
hopeful
joyful
playful
restful
sackful
scornful
shameful
skillful

spiteful
tactful
tankful
thankful
trunkful
trustful
tuneful
wakeful
willful
wishful
wonderful

ei = /ē/
(Lesson 137)

ceiling
conceit
deceive
either
neither
protein
receipt
receive
seize
weird

ei = /ā/
(Lesson 137)

rein
reindeer
veil
vein

ew
(Lesson 138)

blew
brew
cashew
chew
crew
curfew
dew
drew
few
flew
grew
jewel
knew
mew
mildew
nephew
new
news
newspaper
pew
screw
sewer
stew
threw

ou = /ōō/
(Lesson 138)

group
route
soup
wound
youth

Prefix pre-
(Lesson 139)

precook
prefix
preflight
preform
preheat
prehistoric
prejudge
premix
prepaid
prepay
prerecord
preregister
preschool
preshrink
preteen
pretreat

Prefix dis-
(Lesson 139)

disability
disable
disadvantage
disagree
disallow
disapprove
disassemble
disband
disbelieve
disclaim
disclose
discolor
disconnect
discontent
discontinue
discredit
disengage
disgrace
disinfect
disinterest
dislike
dislocate
dislodge
dismantle
dismount
disorder
disown
displace
displease
disproof
disqualify
disrepair
disrespect
dissatisfactory
distrust

Sight Words

again
against
any
are
been
bought
brother
brought
build
built
bush
busy
buy
certain
chocolate
climb
clothes
color
come
could
country
cover
do
does
don't
door
early
earth
enough
eye
father
floor
fought
friend
from
full
goes
guess
heard
heart
into
laugh
learn
love
many
mother
move
of
oh
once
one
only
other
people
pull
push
put
said
says
shoe
should
some
stomach
strange
sure
taste
their
there
they
though
thought
through
to
two
want
was
were
what
when
where
who
whose
would
you

Three-Syllable Words

acrobat
alfalfa
alphabet
appendix
apprehend
Atlantic
atmosphere
ballistic
banana
circumvent
comprehend
consonant
cucumber
December
diplomat
embargo
establish
estimate
fantastic
festival
harmony
hibernate
improvise
innocent
intercept
kangaroo
laminate
lavender
microphone
momentum
musketeer
mystery
nocturnal
nostalgic
November
occupy
October
organic
Pacific
personal
represent
romantic
September
signature
statistic
thermostat
uniform
utensil
vanilla
violin
volunteer

Four-Syllable Words

academy
accelerate
administer
advertisement
aluminum
anticipate
barracuda
calculator
capacity
category
decoration
delivery
democratic
demonstration
experiment
fundamental
hexagonal
identical
interesting
kindergarten
legislature
majority
military
numerical
optimistic
percolator
resolution
responsible
security
spectacular
territory

Spelling Word List

This list of words is arranged in the order the letters, letter clusters, sounds, and other concepts are introduced. The list is composed of words that follow regular spelling patterns and that first-grade students might be able to spell. Lesson numbers indicate the lesson during or after which the words may be used. Use this list to quickly select appropriate words when doing extra boardwork, homework, games, or other activities.

n, o
(Lesson 2)

on

o
(Lesson 3)

no

t
(Lesson 4)

not
tot

p
(Lesson 5)

pop
pot
top

i
(Lesson 6)

I
in
it
nip
pin
pip
pit
tin
tip

l
(Lesson 7)

lint
lip
lit
lop
lot
plot
tilt

a
(Lesson 8)

a
lap
nap
pal
pan
pat
plan
plant
tan
tap

z
(Lesson 9)

zap
zip

s
(Lesson 11)

as
is
last
lisp
list
lost
past
sap
sat
silt
sip
sit
slant
slap
slat
slip
slit
slop
slot
snap
snip
snot
so
sop
span
spat
spin
spit
splat
split
spot
stilt
stop

Suffix -s
(Lesson 12)

laps
lips
naps
nips
pits
pops
pots
slips
slits
slots
snaps
snips
spins
spits
spots
stops
taps
tips
tops
tots

d
(Lesson 13)

ad
dad
did
dip
dot
lad
land
lid
nod
pad
pod
pond
sad
sand
slid
sod
stand

f
(Lesson 14)

fad
fan
fast
fat
fin
fist
fit
flap
flat
flint
flip
flop
fond
if
lift
loft
sift
soft

h
(Lesson 16)

had
hand
hat
hi
hid
hint
hip
hit
hop
hot

g
(Lesson 17)

dig
dog
fig
flag
fog
gag
gap
gas
gasp
gig
glad
gland
go
golf
got
hog
lag
log
nag
pig
tag
zag
zig

r
(Lesson 18)

draft
drag
drift
drip
drop
frog
frost
graft
grand
grant
grasp
grin
grip
grit
print
prod
prop
raft
rag
ran
rap
rasp
rat
rid
rig
rip
rod
rot
sprint
strap
strip
trap
trip
trod
trot

k
(Lesson 19)

kid
kiln
kilt
kin
kit
risk
silk
skid
skin
skip
skit

Spelling with k and c
(Lesson 22)

act
can
cap
cast
cat
clan
clap
clasp
clip
clog
clop
clot
cod
con
cop
cost
cot
craft
crisp
crop
fact
pact
scalp
scan
scant
scrap
strict

b
(Lesson 23)

bad
bag
ban
band
bask
bat
bib
bid
big
bin
bit
blast
blob
blond
blot
bob
bond
brag
bran
brand
brisk
cab
cob
crab
crib
dab
fib
gab
grab
lab
nab
rib
rob
scab
slab
slob
sob
stab
tab

vc′|cv
(Lesson 24)

contact
napkin
poplin

m
(Lesson 26)

am
blimp
brim
camp
clam
cramp
dam
damp
dim
film
gram
grim
ham
him
impact
lamp
limp
mad
man
map
mask
mast
mat
mid
mint
mist
mob
mom
mop
prompt
ram
ramp
rim
romp
skim
slam
slim
smog
stamp
stomp
tramp
trim

e
(Lesson 27)

absent
be
bed
beg
belt
bend
bent
best
bet
blend
contest
crept
den
dent
desk
elf
elk
elm
end
fed
felt
fled
get
he
held
help
hen
inlet
insect
keg
kelp
kept
led
left
leg
lend
lens
lent
let
me
melt
mend
met
nest
net
peg
pelt
pen
pest
pet
red
rest
send
sent
set
sled
slept
sped
stem
step
tablet
ten
test

ck
(Lesson 29)

back
black
block
brick
click
clock
crack
deck
dock
fleck
flick
flock
hack
hock
kick
lack
lick
lock
mock
neck
nick
pack
peck
pick
rack
rick
rock
sack
sick
slack
slacks
slick
smack
smock
snack
sock
stack
stick
stock
tack
tick
track
trick

~~th~~
(Lesson 31)

than
that
then
this

th
(Lesson 31)

bath
broth
cloth
fifth
froth
math
moth
path
thick
thin
throb

ng
(Lesson 32)

bang
bong
bring
cling
ding
dong
fang
fling
gong
hang
king
long
pang
ping
pong
prong
rang
ring
sang
sing
sling
song
sprang
spring
sting
string
strong
tang
thing
thong
tong
zing

Suffix -ing
(Lesson 32)

acting
backing
banding
banging
bending
blasting
blending
blocking
bonding
branding
bricking
bringing
camping
casting
clasping
clicking
clinging
clocking
contacting
costing
cramping
denting
dinging
docking
drafting
drifting
ending
filming
flinging
flocking
frosting
gasping
golfing
grafting
granting
grasping
hacking
handing
hanging
helping
hinting
kicking
lacking
landing
lasting
lending
licking
lifting
limping
lisping
listing
locking
melting
mending
misting
nesting
packing
pecking
pelting
picking
planting
printing
rafting
resting
ringing
risking
rocking
romping
sacking
sanding
scalping
sending
sifting
singing
slanting
slicking
slinging
smacking
smocking
snacking
springing
sprinting
stacking
stamping
standing
sticking
stinging
stocking
stomping
stringing
tacking
testing
ticking
tilting
tracking
tricking

Suffix -ed = /d/
(Lesson 33)

banged
filmed
gonged
hanged
pinged

Suffix -ed = /t/
(Lesson 33)

backed
camped
clamped
cramped
decked
gasped
grasped
helped
lacked
limped
locked
milked
pecked
romped
stacked
stamped
tacked
ticked
tracked
tramped

Suffix -ed = /ĕd/
(Lesson 33)

acted
belted
blended
branded
dented
drafted
drifted
ended
frosted
granted
handed
hinted
landed
lasted
lifted
listed
melted
mended
nested
panted
planted
ranted
rented
rested
sanded
sifted
slanted
tilted
tinted

ee
(Lesson 34)

bee
beef
beep
bleed
breed
creed
creep
deed
deep
deer
eel
fee
feed
feel
feet
flee
fleet
free
freed
greed
green
greet
heed
heel
keep
meet
need
peel
peep
peer
reed
reef
reel
screen
see
seed
seem
seen
seep
sleep
sleet
sneer
speed
steel
street
tee
teen
teeth
three
tree

Final /k/
(Lesson 36)

bank
blink
brisk
crank
creek
desk
drank
drink
elk
Greek
honk
ink
kink
link
mask
meek
milk
peek
pink
rank
reek
rink
risk
sank
seek
silk
sink
slink
spank
stink
tank
thank
think
wink

u
(Lesson 37)

blunt
bug
bulb
bulk
bump
bun
bunk
bus
bust
but
cactus
club
clump
clung
crust
cub
cup
cut
drug
drum
dug
dump
dusk
dust
fun
fund
grub
grump
grunt
gulf
gulp
gum
gun
gust
hub
hug
hum
hump
hunt
lug
lump
mud
mug
mumps
must
nun
nut
nutmeg
plug
plum

plump
plus
pump
pun
pup
rub
rug
rum
run
rust
rut
scrub
slug
slum
slump
snug
spun
strum
stub
stuck
stump
stun
stunt
sum
sun
sunk
thrust
thud
thump
trust
tub
tug
tusk
up

w
(Lesson 38)

swam
sweep
sweet
swept
swift
swim
swum
tweet
twig
twin
twist
wag
we
web
wee
weed
week
weep
weld
went
wept
west
wet
wig
wilt
win
wind
wing
wink
wisp
wit

vc|cv′
(Lesson 39)

admit
consist
submit
until
upset

ā–e̸
(Lesson 41)

ale
ape
ate
babe
bale
bare
base
blade
blame
blare
blaze
came
cane
cape
care
case
crane
crate
dare
date
daze
drape
fade
fame
fare
fate
flame
flare
frame
gale
game
gate
gaze
glade
glare
grade
grape
grate
graze
hare
hate
lame
lane
late
made
male
mane
mate
name
pale
pare
plane
plate
rare
rate
safe
sale
same
sane
scale
scare
scrape
skate
slate
snare
spade
spare
stare
state
tale
tame
tape
trade

ō–e̸
(Lesson 42)

bone
close
code
cone
cope
dope
dose
dote
doze
drone
froze
globe
grope
hole
home
hope
hose
mode
mole
more
nose
note
pole
pope
pore
pose
probe
prone
robe
rode
role
Rome
rope
rose
scope
score
slope
snore
sore
spore
stole
stone
store
strode
those
throne
tone
tore
tote
zone

ū–e̸
(Lesson 42)

costume
cube
cure
cute
dude
dune
flute
fume
fuse
lube
mule
mute
prune
pure
rude
rule
tube
tune

ī–e̸
(Lesson 43)

bite
bribe
crime
dime
dine
dire
fife
file
fine
fire
glide
hide
hike
hire
kite
life
like
lime
line
mile
mine
mite
nine
pile
pine
pipe
pride
prime
prize
ripe
rise
side
size
slide
smile
spine
spite
stride
stripe
swine
swipe
tide
time
tire
tribe
twine
wide
wife
wine
wipe
wise

ē–e̸
(Lesson 43)

Irregular Spelling

Silent e
(Lesson 43)

Irregular Spelling

Spelling with ke
(Lesson 44)

bake
bike
brake
cake
duke
flake
hike
lake
like
make
mistake
poke
rake
sake
smoke
snake

spike
spoke
stake
strike
stroke
take

x
(Lesson 46)

ax
box
fax
fix
flax
flex
flux
fox
lox
mix
ox
pox
sax
sex
six
tax
tux
wax

y
(Lesson 47)

yak
yam
yank
yap
yelp
yen
yes
yet
yip
yuck
yule

sh
(Lesson 48)

ash
brush
cash
clash
crash
crush
dash
dish
fish
flash
flesh
flush
fresh
gush
hash
hush
lash
mesh
publish
rash
rush
sash
shade
shake
shale
shame
shape
share
she
shed
shelf
shift
shin
shine
ship
shock
shone
shop
shore
shot
shred
shrimp
shrink
shrub
shrunk
shut
slash
slush
smash
splash
swish
trash
wish

oo = /o͝o/
(Lesson 49)

book
brook
cook
crook
foot
good
hood
hoof
hook
look
shook
soot
stood
took
wood

oo = /o͞o/
(Lesson 49)

bloom
boo
boom
boost
boot
booth
broom
cool
coop
doom
drool
droop
food
fool
gloom
groom
hoop
hoot
loom
loop
loot
mood
moon
noon
pool
proof
room
roost
root
scoop
shoot
smooth
soon
spool
spoon
stool
stoop
swoop
tool
toot
tooth
troop
zoo
zoom

j
(Lesson 51)

jab
jack
jade
jag
jam
jest
jet
jig
jilt
job
jog
joke
jot
jug
jump
junk
just
jut

Floss Words
(Lesson 52)

bass
bell
bill
bless
bliss
bluff
boss
brass
class
cliff
cross
cuff
doll
dress
drill
fill
fluff
fuss
gill
glass
gloss
grass
grill
gruff
gull
hill
hiss
ill
kill
kiss
lass
less
loss
mass
mess
mill
miss
moss
muff
off
pass
pill
press
priss
puff
scuff
sell
shall
shell
shrill
sill
skill
skull
smell
sniff
spill
sluff
stiff
still
stress
stuff
swell
tell
thrill
till
toss
twill
well
will
yell

v || ve
(Lesson 53)

brave
cave
crave
gave
give
grave
grove
have
jive
live
pave
save
solve
vampire
van
vane
vast
vat
velvet
vent
vest
vet
vim
vine
vote

Final c
(Lesson 54)

Atlantic
drastic
fabric
frantic
picnic
plastic
rustic

ble
(Lesson 56)

able
babble
bobble
bubble
bumble
cable
crumble
dabble
dribble
fable
feeble

fumble
gamble
gobble
grumble
hobble
humble
mumble
nibble
nimble
pebble
ramble
rubble
rumble
scramble
scribble
stable
stubble
stumble
table
thimble
tremble
tumble

fle
(Lesson 57)

baffle
muffle
raffle
rifle
ruffle
scuffle
sniffle
stifle
trifle
truffle

ple
(Lesson 57)

ample
apple
cripple
crumple
dapple
dimple
grapple
maple
ripple
rumple
sample
simple
steeple
supple
topple
trample

dle
(Lesson 57)

bridle
bundle
candle
cuddle
fiddle
fondle
fuddle
handle
huddle
kindle
ladle
middle
muddle
needle
paddle
puddle
riddle
saddle
spindle
straddle
toddle
trundle

tle
(Lesson 58)

battle
beetle
cattle
kettle
little
mottle
rattle
settle
tattle
throttle
title

gle
(Lesson 58)

angle
bugle
bungle
jangle
jiggle
juggle
mangle
mingle
single
smuggle
snuggle
spangle
strangle
struggle
tangle

cle
(Lesson 59)

uncle

kle
(Lesson 59)

ankle
crinkle
tinkle

sle
(Lesson 59)

hassle
tussle

zle
(Lesson 59)

dazzle
drizzle
frazzle
guzzle
muzzle
puzzle

y = /ī/
(Lesson 61)

by
cry
dry
fly
fry
my
pry
shy
sky
sly
spry
sty
try

y = /ē/
(Lesson 62)

candy
dandy
fifty
flimsy
frenzy
husky
sixty
twenty

Suffix -y
(Lesson 62)

bulky
bumpy
crispy
crusty
dusty
filmy
fishy
frisky
frosty
greedy
handy
lucky
lumpy
misty
mushy
musty
needy
rocky
rusty
sandy
sleepy
sticky
stringy

er
(Lesson 63)

after
berth
blister
blunder
bluster
butler
clerk
expert
fender
fern
finger
fluster
foster
hamper
her
herd
hermit
hinder
hunger
jerk
lantern
master
mister
number
per
perfect
perfume
perk
person
serve
shelter
silver
slender
slumber
splinter
stern
tender
term
tern
thunder
verb
winter

igh
(Lesson 64)

Irregular Spelling

Compound Words
(Lesson 66)

afternoon
backbone
backdrop
backfire
backhand
backpack
backstop
backstroke
bagpipe
bankbook
barefoot
bathrobe
bathroom
bathtub
bedroom
bedtime
beehive
bridegroom
campfire
candlestick
carefree
cufflink
cupcake
dishcloth
dishpan
drumstick
dustpan
fingerprint
fireman
fishhook
flagpole
footprint
footstool
grapevine
gumdrop
handbag
handcuff
lampshade
lifetime
nosebleed
noseplugs
nutshell
pancake
pickup
pinecone
rosebud
setup
skyline
sparerib
toothbrush
weekend
windmill

Suffix -ly
(Lesson 67)

badly
crisply
gladly
glumly
likely
madly
manly
purely
sadly

softly
weekly

Suffix -less
(Lesson 67)

backless
beltless
blameless
bottomless
endless
hatless
helpless
jobless
lifeless
nameless
restless
sleepless
sleeveless
spotless
strapless
sunless
thankless
timeless
tireless

Suffix -ness
(Lesson 67)

blackness
dampness
dimness
dullness
fastness
flatness
fondness
gladness
goodness
hotness
illness
likeness
plumpness
redness
rudeness
sadness
sickness
softness
soreness
stiffness
thickness
wetness

ai
(Lesson 68)

Irregular Spelling

ay
(Lesson 69)

bay
bray
clay
day
driveway
gray
hay
jay
lay
may
pay
play
pray
ray
say
slay
splay
spray
stay
stray
sway
tray
way

ar
(Lesson 71)

ark
arm
art
artist
bar
barb
bark
barn
barnyard
bookmark
boxcar
car
card
cargo
carp
carpet
cart
dark
darkroom
darling
dart
far
farm
garden
gargle
garlic
garment
garnish
garter
hard
harm
harness
harp
harsh
harvest
jar
junkyard
landmark
lard
lark
marble
mark
market
marsh
martin
park
part
scar
scarf
scarlet
shark
sharp
smart
snarl
spark
sparkle
star
starfish
starling
start
tar
tart
varnish
yard
yardstick
yarn

ch
(Lesson 72)

arch
branch
bunch
champ
chant
chap
charm
chart
chase
chat
check
chess
chest
chick
chill
chime
chin
choke
chop
chunk
crunch
flinch
hunch
inch
lunch
march
much
munch
parch
perch
pinch
punch
ranch
rich
starch
such
winch

or
(Lesson 73)

border
born
cord
cork
corn
corner
for
forget
fork
form
former
fort
forth
horn
inform
lord
north
or
orbit
order
popcorn
porch
pork
port
scorch
scorn
short
shortcut
shortstop
snort
sort
sport
stork
storm
thorn
thunderstorm
torch
torment
torn
worn

qu
(Lesson 74)

equate
equip
inquire
quack
quake
quaver
queen
quell
quench
quest
quibble
quick
quicksand
quill
quilt
quint
quintet
quip
quit
quite
quiver
quiz
quote
square
squeeze
squelch
squid
squiggle
squint
squire
squish

ir
(Lesson 76)

Irregular Spelling

ur
(Lesson 77)

Irregular Spelling

Soft c
(Lesson 78)

cancel
cancer
cell
cent
center
cinch
citrus
concept
concern
concert
fancy
mercy
parcel
sincere
ulcer

Final /s/
(Lesson 78)

ace
advice
brace
dice
face
grace
ice
lace
lice
mace
mice
nice
pace

place
price
race
rice
space
spice
trace
twice
vice

ow = /ō/
(Lesson 79)

blow
bow
crow
elbow
flow
glow
grow
low
mow
row
shadow
show
slow
snow
sow
stow
throw
tow
window

a′|cv
(Lesson 81)

acorn
baby
basic
basin
canine
crater
crazy
gravy
haven
hazel
lady
lazy
navy
paper
raven

i′|cv
(Lesson 82)

crisis
fiber
iris
Irish
minus
silent
spider
tripod

e′|cv
(Lesson 82)

even
evening
evil
female
fever
meter
Venus
zenith
zero

o′|cv
(Lesson 83)

bonus
clover
donate
focus
frozen
moment
open
oval
over
profile
robot
rodent
rotate
spoken
total
vocal

u′|cv
(Lesson 83)

duty
jury
music
stupid
super
tulip

a|cv′
(Lesson 84)

abide
adapt
adopt
adorn
adult
ago
ajar
alarm
alike
awake
aware
away

ea = /ē/
(Lesson 86)

Irregular Spelling

ea = /ĕ/
(Lesson 86)

Irregular Spelling

ea = /ā/
(Lesson 87)

Irregular Spelling

Dropping Rule
(Lesson 88)

baked
baking
blamed
blaming
blazed
blazing
bony
braked
braking
cared
caring
closed
closing
coded
coding
coped
coping
crated
crating
cubed
cured
curing
dared
daring
dated
dating
faded
fading
flamed
flaming
framed
framing
fumed
fuming
glared
glaring
graded
grading
grated
grating
grazed
grazing
hated
hating
hoped
hoping
laced
lacing
lacy
making
named
naming
nosed
nosing
nosy
noted
noting
poked
poking
poky
pruned
pruning
raked
raking
rated
rating
roped
roping
rosy
ruled
ruling
scared
scaring
scary
scored
scoring
shaded
shading
shady
shined
shining
shiny
skated
skating
snaked
snaking
stated
stating
stored
storing
stroked
stroking
taking
tamed
taming
taped
taping
toned
toning
toted
toting
traded
trading
tuned
tuning
waded
wading
zoned
zoning

oi
(Lesson 91)

avoid
boil
broil
coil
coin
foil
hoist
join
joint
loin
moist
oil
point
soil
toil

oy
(Lesson 91)

ahoy
boy
coy
enjoy
joy
soy

vc|cvc|cv
(Lesson 92)

amnesty
Atlantic
embargo
establish
fantastic
September

tion
(Lesson 93)

action
calculation
caption
conversation
corporation
devotion
dictation
election
emotion
exception
information
intervention
location
lotion
mention
motion
nation
notion
operation
option
population
portion
potion
prevention
promotion
proportion
satisfaction

station
suction
traction
vacation

ue
(Lesson 94)

argue
blue
clue
glue
rescue
sue

Suffix -es
(Lesson 96)

ashes
beaches
benches
bosses
boxes
branches
brushes
bunches
bushes
clashes
classes
crosses
crunches
crushes
dashes
dishes
dresses
flashes
foxes
glasses
gushes
hunches
hushes
inches
kisses
lashes
lunches
marches
misses
mixes
passes
pinches
punches
ranches
rashes
rushes
sashes
slushes
smashes
splashes
suffixes
swishes
taxes
waxes
winches
wishes

ou = /ou/
(Lessons 97, 98)

about
amount
around
blouse
bound
cloud
clout
couch
count
crouch
douse
flour
foul
found
foundation
grouch
ground
grouse
grout
hound
house
joust
loud
lout
mound
mount
mouse
mouth
noun
ouch
our
oust
out
outcast
playground
pouch
pound
pout
proud
round
scour
scout
shout
slouch
snout
sound
sour
south
spout
sprout
stout
trout
underground
wound

ow = /ou/
(Lessons 97, 98)

bow
cow
how
now
plow
sow
vow
wow

vc|ccv
(Lesson 99)

conflict
congress
distress
district
employ
lobster
subtract

vcc|cv
(Lesson 99)

empty
partner

au
(Lesson 101)

Irregular Spelling

aw
(Lesson 102)

Irregular Spelling

"Wild Colt" Words
(Lesson 103)

Irregular Spelling

oa
(Lesson 104)

Irregular Spelling

oe
(Lesson 104)

Irregular Spelling

ey
(Lesson 106)

Irregular Spelling

vc′|v
(Lesson 107)

Irregular Spelling

ph
(Lesson 108)

Irregular Spelling

Soft g
(Lesson 109)

agent
congest
digest
digit
frigid
gel
gem
gene
genetic
general
generate
germ
gigantic
ginger
longitude
magic
margin
passenger
plunger
tragic

Doubling Rule
(Lesson 111)

bagged
bagging
baggy
batted
batting
batty
begged
begging
betting
bidding
bobbed
bobbing
bragged
bragging
brimmed
brimming
bugged
bugging
buggy
canned
canning
capped
capping
clipped
clipping
clogged
clogging
clopped
clopping
cutting
dabbed
dabbing
digging
dimmed
dimming
dipped
dipping
dotted
dotting
dragged
dragging
dripped
dripping
drippy
dropped
dropping
drummed
drumming
fibbed
fibbing
fogged
fogging
foggy
gabbed
gabbing
gabby
getting
grabbed
grabbing
grabby
gritted
gritting
gritty
gummy
hitting
hogged
hogging
hopped
hopping
hugged
hugging
kidded
kidding
lagged
lagging
lapped
lapping
letting
logged
logging
mopped
mopping
nabbed
nabbing
nagged
nagging
netted
netting
nipped
nipping
nippy
patted
patting
pinned
pinning
plotted
plotting
popped
popping
prodded
prodding
propped

propping
rammed
ramming
rapped
rapping
ribbed
ribbing
rigged
rigging
ripped
ripping
robbed
robbing
rotted
rotting
rubbed
rubbing
running
scrapped
scrapping
setting
sipped
sipping
skidded
skidding
skipped
skipping
slammed
slamming
slapped
slapping
slimmed
slimming
slipped
slipping
snapped
snapping
snappy
snipped
snipping
snippy
sobbed
sobbing
spinning
spitting
stepped
stepping
stopped
stopping
thinned
thinning
throbbed
throbbing
tipped
tipping
topped
topping
trapped
trapping
trimmed
trimming
tripped
tripping
trotted
trotting

kn, gn, wr
(Lesson 112)

Irregular Spelling

e|cv′
(Lesson 114)

beside
debate
depend
eject
elect
erase
erupt
event
evict
pretend
reduce
refer

o|cv′
(Lesson 114)

hotel
omit
produce
propel
protect
provide

u|cv′
(Lesson 114)

brunet
humane
July
superb
unite

tch
(Lesson 116)

batch
blotch
botch
catch
clutch
crutch
ditch
Dutch
etch
fetch
hatch
hitch
hutch
itch
latch
match
notch
patch
pitch
pitcher
pitchfork
scratch
sketch
snatch
snitch
splotch
stitch
stretch
switch
thatch
twitch
witch

dge
(Lesson 117)

badge
bridge
budge
dodge
dredge
edge
fudge
grudge
hedge
judge
ledge
lodge
nudge
pledge
ridge
sledge
sludge
smudge
wedge

ge
(Lesson 117)

age
barge
bilge
binge
bulge
cage
charge
cringe
dirge
flange
forge
fringe
gorge
hinge
huge
large
lounge
lunge
merge
page
plunge
rage
sage
serge
singe
stage
teenage
tinge
twinge
verge
wage

ie = /ī/
(Lesson 119)

Irregular Spelling

ie = /ē/
(Lesson 119)

Irregular Spelling

sion = /shŭn/
(Lesson 121)

admission
confession
concussion
discussion
expression
impression
permission

sion = /zhŭn/
(Lesson 121)

confusion
division
explosion
invasion

ture
(Lesson 122)

adventure
capture
culture
departure
fixture
fracture
future
lecture
mixture
moisture
nature
pasture
picture
posture
puncture
rupture
sculpture
structure
texture
torture
suture
venture
vulture

ch = /k/
(Lesson 123)

Irregular Spelling

ch = /sh/
(Lesson 123)

Irregular Spelling

wh
(Lesson 124)

whale
wheel
when
whether
which
whiff
while
whim
whimper
whine
whip
whisk
whisper
white
whiz
why

eigh
(Lesson 126)

Irregular Spelling

qua, wa
(Lesson 127)

Irregular Spelling

al
(Lesson 128)

Irregular Spelling

Suffix -er
(Lesson 131)

banker
barber
batter
bigger
blender
catcher
colder
cooler
deeper
dresser
drummer
farmer
faster
helper
hunter
kicker
longer

marker
mixer
nutcracker
older
planter
player
preacher
rancher
renter
richer
runner
sander
seller
shallower
shorter
sifter
singer
skyscraper
smaller
spender
stronger
sweeter
taller
trucker
washer
worker
zookeeper

Suffix -est
(Lesson 131)

freshest
hottest
loudest
maddest
saddest
shortest
smoothest
softest
strongest
sweetest
thickest
warmest
wettest
wildest

ar = /er/
(Lesson 132)

Irregular Spelling

or = /er/
(Lesson 132)

Irregular Spelling

wer = /wer/
(Lesson 132)

Irregular Spelling

Scribal o
(Lesson 133)

Irregular Spelling

i|cv´
(Lesson 134)

dilute
direct
divide

Changing Rule
(Lesson 134)

bulkier
bulkiest
cozier
coziest
cozily
coziness
grassier
grassiest
handier
handiest
handily
handiness
luckier
luckiest
luckily
merciless
sillier
silliest
silliness
sleepier
sleepiest
sleepily
sleepiness
tidier
tidiest
tidily
tidiness
zanier
zaniest

Suffix -ful
(Lesson 136)

armful
bagful
basketful
boxful
capful
careful
fateful
fitful
grateful
glassful
gleeful
handful
harmful
hateful
heedful
helpful
hopeful
joyful
playful
restful
sackful
scornful
shameful
skillful
spiteful
tactful
tankful
thankful
trunkful
trustful
tuneful
wakeful
willful
wishful
wonderful

ei = /ē/
(Lesson 137)

Irregular Spelling

ei = /ā/
(Lesson 137)

Irregular Spelling

ew
(Lesson 138)

Irregular Spelling

ou = /o͞o/
(Lesson 138)

Irregular Spelling

Prefix pre-
(Lesson 139)

precook
prefix
preform
prehistoric
prejudge
premix
prepay
prerecord
preregister
preshrink
preteen

Prefix dis-
(Lesson 139)

disable
disagree
disband
disclaim
discontent
discredit
disgrace
disinfect
disinterest
dislike
dislocate
dislodge
dismantle
dismount
disorder
disown
displace
disproof
disrespect
distrust

Sight Words

again
against
any
are
been
bought
brother
brought
build
built
bush
busy
buy
certain
chocolate
climb
clothes
color
come
could
country
cover
do
does
don't
door
early
earth
enough
eye
father
floor
fought
friend
from
full
goes
guess
heard
heart
into
laugh
learn
love
many
mother
move
of
oh
once
one
only
other
people
pull
push
put
said
says
shoe
should
some
stomach
strange
sure
taste
their
there
they
though
thought
through
to
two
want
was
were
what
when
where
who
whose
would
you

Phonics 1

Games and Activities

KID CARD GAMES

Kid Cards provide a recreational way to review concepts being taught. The purpose of each game varies. Kid Cards may be used to review letter names, sounds, keywords, blending, word matching, spelling, and rhyming. Use of these games is recommended to improve problem areas or to give additional exposure to the written language. After each weekly assessment, specific games are suggested to strengthen the student's skills; these games should be practiced daily until the student masters the concepts missed on the assessment. Kid Card games also can be played to boost abilities or just for fun.

All of the games may be played with two or more people. If desired, occasionally enlist the help of siblings or playmates to make the games more fun. Please note that while the games are "won" by some players, the others must not be made to feel that they have "lost." Players who are unsuccessful are never eliminated from play.

Games that use the orange Kid Cards are especially beneficial for students who are less secure with letter names and sounds. Games that use the white Kid Cards are beneficial for teaching how to blend letter sounds. Games that use the purple, red, or blue Kid Cards are beneficial for students who need practice reading. Finally, games that use the green Kid Cards, which are the most advanced cards, are beneficial for students who are ready to read and comprehend phrases and sentences.

Tokens are used to reward both correct answers and overall effort. They provide motivation for the student to try the different tasks involved in the games and also give the student concrete evidence of his or her abilities.

All games are played with only those Kid Cards containing letters/pictures/words to which the student has been exposed. As the school year progresses, the decks will grow larger and the games will take longer. However, each playing session should last no longer than fifteen minutes.

ABC Trade Out

Objective: To alphabetize letters

Materials: Orange letter cards

# of Players: 2–4

Preparation: Give each player three orange cards. Place the cards face up in a vertical row in front of each player. The cards must remain in the exact order in which they were dealt. Form a draw pile with the remaining cards, and turn the top card face up beside the draw pile to form a discard pile.

Directions: The objective of this game is to trade out cards as necessary in order to get the three cards in alphabetical order (from left to right). The first player should draw one card from either the draw pile or the discard pile and trade it for one of his/her cards. The new card must be placed in the same position as the card that is discarded. Play continues around the circle until one player is able to alphabetize his/her cards.

Variation: As the student's alphabetizing ability improves, increase the number of cards dealt. Give the student blue or purple word cards and have him/her alphabetize words.

Level of Difficulty	Concept(s) Reinforced	Variation
Easier	———	———
Average	Alphabetizing letters	Use orange letter cards
Advanced	Alphabetizing words	Use blue or purple word cards

Acting Out

Objective: To be able to read, act out, and comprehend instructions

Materials: Green action cards (sets of matching cards)

# of Players: 2–4

Preparation: Give each player two different green cards. Make sure matching cards are dealt to the other players. (As the student's reading ability improves, more cards may be dealt.)

Directions: Ask the first player to read one card silently, and then "act out" the instructions on the card. The other players should check to see if one of their cards describes the action the "actor" demonstrated. If so, they should raise their hands and read their cards. If a match is made, each player, both the "reader" and the "actor," receives a point. If no match is made, the "actor" should "act out" again. Once a match is made, play continues to the next person. If desired, pass out more cards to players once they have read and demonstrated the instructions on their cards correctly.

Variation: If the above directions are too difficult for the student, have him/her simply read the phrases or sentences on the cards.

Level of Difficulty	Concept(s) Reinforced	Variation
Easier	Comprehending phrases and sentences	Student reads card
Average	Comprehending phrases and sentences	Student reads card and acts out the instructions for the other players
Advanced	Comprehending phrases and sentences	Student reads card; acts it out; other players check to see if they are holding the card describing that action

Blend It

Objective: To read blends with short or long vowel sounds

Materials: White blend cards

# of Players: 2–4

Preparation: Give each player one blend card.

Directions: Ask the first player to read his or her card with a designated vowel sound. For example, if the player is holding the "pl" card, ask him or her to read it with a long *i*, as in "pli." If the player reads the blend correctly, award him or her a point. Continue to the next person. Once every player has attempted to add the designated vowel sound to his or her blend, give the players a new vowel sound.

Variation: (You will need the orange vowel cards for this variation.) Place 3–6 blend cards that the student is having difficulty with on the table, face up. Hand each player a vowel card. One at a time, have each player add his or her vowel sound to one of the blends on the table. If the player combines the sounds correctly, award him or her a point. When each player has had a turn, have them exchange vowel cards with one another. Continue as long as time permits.

Level of Difficulty	Concept(s) Reinforced	Variation
Easier	Blending sounds with blends	Blend with one vowel sound
Average	Blending sounds with blends	Blend with more than one sound (i.e., a vowel and a consonant)
Advanced	Blending sounds with blends	Blend with more than one sound and determine if the resulting combination is an actual word or not

Capital/Lowercase Letter Match

Objective: To match capital letters with lowercase letters, and vice versa

Materials: Orange letter cards (matching capital and lowercase letters)
Tokens

# of Players: 2 or more

Preparation: Lay the lowercase letter cards on the floor or table face up and place a token on each one. Hold the capital letter cards in your hand.

Directions: One at a time, give the student a capital letter card and have him or her place the capital letter on the matching lowercase letter. If the student is correct, give him or her the token. Remove the capital letter cards as they are correctly matched and add them to your stack. Continue as long as time permits; then allow the student to count the tokens.

Variation: Place the capital letter cards on the floor or table and have the student lay the matching lowercase letter cards on them.

Level of Difficulty	Concept(s) Reinforced
All	Matching capital and lowercase letters

Letter Pairs

Objective: To match letters

Materials: Orange letter cards (lowercase and/or capital letters)
Tokens

# of Players: 2–4

Preparation: Give each player one or two cards. Players should hold their cards so no one else can see them. Use any leftover cards as a draw pile. (*Note*: As the student becomes more experienced, more cards may be dealt.)

Directions: Have players check their cards; if any have been dealt a pair, have them lay the pair aside and award them a token. Instruct the first player to read a card in his or her hand and then ask another player for the matching letter. Matches may be made between lowercase letters, lowercase and capital letters, or capital letters, depending on which cards are being used. If a match is made, give each player whose card helped to make the match a token and allow him/her to draw a new card. Set the matching cards aside. If no match is made, the first player may draw a card from the draw pile (if there is one). Play continues to the next person. Make sure players understand that they can only ask for cards to match what they already have. The player with the most tokens at the end of the game wins.

Level of Difficulty	Concept(s) Reinforced	Variation
Easier	Matching lowercase letters or capital letters	Use only lowercase letters or capital letters
Average	Matching lowercase and capital letters	Use both capital and lowercase letters
Advanced	Asking for specific letters (e.g., a capital *H*)	Use both capital and lowercase letters

Letter/Sound Identification

Objective: To identify letters and letter sounds

Materials: Orange letter cards (lowercase and/or capital letters)
Tokens

# of Players: 2 or more

Preparation: Lay the letter cards face up on the table or floor. Place two tokens on each card, not covering the letter.

Directions: Ask the student to select a letter and say the name and sound of the letter. Give the student one token for the correct name of the letter and another token for the correct sound of the letter. Continue as long as time permits. Have the student count the tokens.

Level of Difficulty	Concept(s) Reinforced	Variation
Easier	Identifying letters/letter sounds	Use lowercase letters only; ask for the sound or the letter name
Average	Identifying letters/letter sounds	Use capital and lowercase letters; ask for the sound and the letter name
Advanced	Identifying letters/letter sounds; identifying initial sounds	Ask for a word that begins with the sound or letter name

Make a Match

Objective: To make matches between facedown cards

Materials: Orange letter cards (matching capital and lowercase letters) or
Green action cards (matching cards) or
Blue word cards (matching cards) or
Purple word cards and red picture cards (matching words and pictures)
Tokens

# of Players: 2 or more

Preparation: Use either the orange cards, the blue cards, the green cards, or the purple and red cards. (Choose a level appropriate to the student's reading ability.) Lay the cards face down on the table or floor.

Directions: Ask the student to turn over two cards in an effort to make a match. If the cards match, remove them from the table and give the student a token. If the cards do not match, instruct the student to lay them back face down exactly where they were. Continue by giving yourself a turn. If necessary, shuffle the cards that have been matched and add them to the table, face down. The player with the most tokens at the end of the game wins.

Level of Difficulty	Concept(s) Reinforced	Variation
Easier	Matching capital and lowercase letters; matching words	Use the orange Kid Cards; use the blue Kid Cards
Average	Matching sentences	Use the green Kid Cards
Advanced	Matching words and pictures	Use the purple and red Kid Cards

Picture/Word Match

Objective: To match pictures with words, and vice versa

Materials: Matching purple word and red picture cards
Tiny candies, crackers, or tokens (optional)

# of Players: 2 or more

Preparation: Give the student two or three purple word cards. Hold the remaining word cards in your hand. Lay the matching red picture cards for the word cards used face up on the table.

Directions: The student should read the word cards and place them on the matching picture cards. When the student makes correct matches, pick up the word cards and replace them in your stack. Give the student more word cards, and continue. Play as long as time permits.

Level of Difficulty	Concept(s) Reinforced	Variation
Easier	Matching words and pictures	Student holds word cards; places them on picture cards
Average	Matching words and pictures	Student holds picture cards; places them on word cards
Advanced	Matching words and pictures	Student holds both picture and word cards; places them on word and picture cards

Rhyme It

Objective: To think of rhyming words

Materials: Red picture cards
Tokens

# of Players: 2 or more

Preparation: Lay the picture cards face up on the table or floor.

Directions: Have the student pick a card and tell you as many words as he or she can that rhyme with that picture. Specify whether the words must be actual words or can be "nonsense" words. Give the student one token for each correctly rhymed word. If desired, you may pick the next card and think of rhyming words, or have the student pick a different card. Count the tokens when the game is over.

Level of Difficulty	Concept(s) Reinforced	Variation
Easier	Rhyming words	Student uses "nonsense" words
Average	Rhyming words	Student may use "nonsense" or real words
Advanced	Rhyming words	Student must use real words only

Sound Solutions

Objective: To identify the initial, medial, and/or final sounds in words

Materials: Red picture cards
Tokens

# of Players: 2 or more

Preparation: Lay the picture cards on the floor or table face up. Place a token on each card.

Directions: Point to a picture and ask the student to name the picture and tell you what sound he or she hears in the beginning position of that word. If the student correctly identifies the sound, give him or her the token. Continue with a different picture. Count the tokens when the game is over.

Level of Difficulty	Concept(s) Reinforced	Variation
Easier	Identifying the initial or final sound	Student identifies the sound in either the initial or the final position
Average	Identifying the initial, medial, or final sound	Student identifies the sound in any one of the three positions
Advanced	Identifying the initial, medial, and final sound	Student identifies the sounds in all three positions

Spell Out #1

Objective: To identify pictures and to spell words

Materials: Orange and red cards (Use the letter cards that spell the words that name each picture card used.)

# of Players: 2 or more

Preparation: Lay the orange letter cards face up on the table or floor. Place the red picture cards face down in a pile in front of you.

Directions: Turn over the first picture card and ask the student to use the letter cards to spell the word that names the picture. When the word is correctly spelled, continue with a new picture card.

Level of Difficulty	Concept(s) Reinforced	Variation
Easier	Identifying initial sounds	Student finds the initial sound only
Average/Advanced	Identifying pictures; spelling words	Student spells entire word

Spell Out #2

Objective: To identify pictures and to spell words

Materials: Orange and red cards (Use the letter cards that spell the words that name each picture card used.)

# of Players: 2 or more

Preparation: Lay the orange letter cards and red picture cards face up on the table or floor.

Directions: Ask the student to choose a picture card on the table without telling you what it is. The student should then use the letter cards to spell the word. When the student is finished, identify the picture he or she spelled. Then you choose a picture, spell it using the letter cards, and ask the student to identify the picture. Continue as long as time permits.

Level of Difficulty	Concept(s) Reinforced	Variation
All	Identifying pictures; spelling words	Student spells entire word

Word Blend

Objective: To blend sounds into words

Materials: Purple or blue word cards
Tokens

# of Players: 2 or more

Preparation: Lay the word cards face up on the table or floor. Place one token on each card, not covering the word.

Directions: Ask the student to select a card, think about how the word would be coded, and read it. Give the student the token if he or she reads the word correctly. If necessary, help the student blend the sounds. Continue as long as time permits.

Level of Difficulty	Concept(s) Reinforced	Variation
Easier	Blending words	Teacher blends all sounds but the final sound
Average	Blending words	Student reads independently
Advanced	Blending words; providing definitions	Student reads the word, defines it, and/or uses it in a sentence

Word Building

Objective: To change initial or final letters in words in order to make new words

Materials: Orange letter cards
Tokens

# of Players: 2 or more

Preparation: Lay all the cards face up on the table or floor.

Directions: Select one vowel card and one consonant card (for example, *i* and *t*). Move the cards together to form a word or word part (*it*). Select another consonant card (*p*) and move the card in front of the two other cards to form a word (*pit*). Ask the student to read the word. If the student correctly reads the word, award him or her a token. If the student does not read the word correctly, help him or her blend the sounds. Once the word is read correctly, continue, but this time remove the final letter (*t*) and replace it with another consonant (*n*). Continue to add and remove letters as necessary to form new words. Once all combinations have been exhausted, start over with two new letters. (*Note*: Be sure to use only the letters and sounds that have been taught.)

Level of Difficulty	Concept(s) Reinforced	Variation
Easier	Reading word after letter in final position is changed	Teacher changes letter in final position
Average	Reading word after letter in initial position is changed	Teacher changes letter in initial position
Advanced	Spelling own words following instructions	Teacher calls out a word; student must change the appropriate letter(s) to make the word

Word Find

Objective: To find a specific word in a group of words

Materials: Purple word cards
Tokens

# of Players: 2 or more

Preparation: Lay three word cards face up on the table or floor. Hold the remaining word cards in your hand so the student cannot see them.

Directions: Read one of the words aloud and ask the student to point to the appropriate card, read it, and then pick up the card and hand it to you. If the student hands you the wrong card, say the word again and help the student unblend the sounds. Give the student a token when he or she reads the word correctly. Continue with another word. When the three cards have been read, lay out three more cards and continue.

Level of Difficulty	Concept(s) Reinforced	Variation
Easier	Reading words	Use two- or three-letter words
Average	Reading words	Use three-letter words
Advanced	Reading words	Use three-letter words or longer

Word Pairs

Objective: To match pictures with words, and vice versa

Materials: Matching purple word and red picture cards
Tokens

# of Players: 2–4

Preparation: Shuffle the red and purple decks together and give each player one or two cards. Players should hold their cards so no one else can see them. Use any leftover cards as a draw pile. (Note: As the student becomes more experienced, more cards may be dealt.)

Directions: Have players check their cards; if any have been dealt a pair, have them lay the pair aside and award them a token. Instruct the first player to read a card in his or her hand (either a word card or a picture card) and then ask another player for the matching picture or word card. If a match is made, give each player whose card helped to make the match a token and allow him or her to draw a new card. Set the matching cards aside. If no match is made, the first player may draw a card from the draw pile (if there is one). Play continues to the next person. Make sure players understand that they can only ask for cards to match what they already have. The player with the most tokens at the end of the game wins.

Level of Difficulty	Concept(s) Reinforced	Variation
Easier	Matching pictures	Deal only red Kid Cards
Average	Matching words and pictures	Deal one or two cards to each player
Advanced	Matching words and pictures	Deal three or more cards to each player

Write Out

Objective: To read and act out instructions, and to write sentences describing those actions

Materials: Green action cards
Handwriting paper

# of Players: 2–4

Preparation: Give each player two or three green cards and some handwriting paper.

Directions: The first player should read his/her card silently and begin acting out the instructions. The other players should try to guess what the first player is doing, and write a sentence describing those actions. Encourage players to begin their sentences with capital letters and to use ending punctuation. Once every player has written a description of the action, have them read their sentences aloud and check them against the actual instructions the first player received. If desired, award one point to each player who correctly describes the action. Continue to the next person.

Variation: Collect the sentences and check the student's spelling.

Level of Difficulty	Concept(s) Reinforced	Variation
Easier	Writing descriptions	Players describe action using one or two words
Average	Writing descriptions	Players describe action using phrases
Advanced	Writing descriptions	Players describe action using complete sentences

Alphabet Games

Alphabet Add On

Directions: Begin by saying, "For lunch I had an apple (or any food item that begins with the letter *a*). Then select the student to repeat the sentence and add a food item that begins with *b*. For example, the student might say, "For lunch I had an apple and a banana." Continue as long as time permits. Provide hints if the student cannot think of food items (**c**ola, **d**eviled egg, **e**ggplant, **f**rench fries, **i**ce cream, **o**range, **p**izza, **s**paghetti, etc.).

Alphabetizing Objects

Materials: Alphabet strip (optional)

Assortment of small items, each of whose name begins with a different letter. Examples of items to use for each letter are as follows: A: acorn, apple, atlas, avocado, (toy) ax B: badge, bagel, bandage, belt, boat, book, bottle, bow, button C: can, candle, candy, carrot, (paper) clip, cork, crayon, crown, cup D: die, dime, dirt (in a plastic sack), doll, dollar, doughnut E: earring, egg (hard-boiled), elastic, elephant, envelope, eraser F: fan, feather, felt, fig cookie, (nail) file, (roll of) film, fish, flag, fork G: garlic, glasses, glitter, globe, glue, goggles, grape, gum H: hair (wig or doll's), hanger, harmonica, hat, heart, honey, horse I: ice tray, ink, insect, ivy J: jar, jawbreaker, (costume) jewelry, joker (playing card), jump rope K: kangaroo, key, king (playing card), kite L: lace, leaf, lemon, licorice, light bulb, lime, lint, lipstick, lock M: magazine, magnet, magnifying glass, map, mask, mint, muffin, mustard N: nail, napkin, necklace, newspaper, nickel, nut O: oatmeal (uncooked), olive, orange, ostrich, owl P: paper plate, pear, pen, pencil, penny, piggy bank, pinecone, ping pong ball, pinwheel, puzzle piece Q: quail, quarter, quartz, queen (playing card) R: raisin, rattle, ribbon, rice (uncooked), ring, rock, rope, rubber band S: salt shaker, sandpaper, screwdriver, seed, (rubber) snake, soap, sock, softball, sponge, spoon, spring, strawberry, sucker T: tape measure, teddy bear, ticket, tie, tomato, toothbrush, triangle, tweezers U: "U" letter tile, umbrella (miniature parasols), umpire, unicorn V: valentine, vanilla, velvet, violin, volcano W: watch, wax, whistle, wolf, wood X: "X" letter tile (or three-dimensional letter *X*), x-ray Y: yarn, yeast, yo-yo, yogurt Z: "Z" letter tile, zebra, zipper, zucchini

Directions: Give the student a few of the items and ask him or her to alphabetize them. The student may refer to the alphabet strip, if necessary. As the student becomes more experienced, you may increase the number of items given to alphabetize.

Alphabet Roll

Materials: Ball

Directions: You and the student should be seated on the floor. Begin by saying a letter of the alphabet and then rolling the ball to the student. The student should catch the ball, say the next letter in the alphabet, and roll the ball back to you. Continue until the alphabet is complete.

Variations: Start the alphabet in various places. (Say "*L*"; on the next turn, say "*B*," etc.)

Have the student identify the letter before the letter you say instead of the letter after.

Instead of rolling a ball, gently toss a stuffed animal or soft toy back and forth.

Write all of the letters in the alphabet in random order on the ball, toy, or stuffed animal and have the student locate various letters on the item following your instructions (e.g., "Find a capital *H*," or "Find the letter that comes after *B*.").

Battle

Materials: Orange Kid Cards
2 large containers

Directions: Separate the two sets of lowercase and capital orange letter cards. Place one set of lowercase cards face down in each container. You and the student should be seated on the floor or at a table with the containers in front of you. Each person should draw one card from his/her container. The person who draws the card that is closest to the letter *Z* (or *A*, middle of the alphabet, etc.) wins both cards. In the event of a tie, lay the two cards aside and draw two new cards; the winner of this round wins all four cards. Play continues until no more cards are left to draw. The person with the most cards at the end of the game wins.

Dictionary Hunt

Materials: Dictionary

Directions: Call out guide words (the words located at the top of the dictionary columns) and have the student locate some or all of the following: the pages those words are found on, their definitions, their spellings, their word origin, etc. After the student has practiced awhile, call out words at random and have the student find them.

Variation: As the student becomes more adept at finding words in the dictionary, call out certain letter combinations and have the student locate words that fulfill those specifications. For instance, have the student look for words that contain digraph *th* and a short vowel (*moth*, *path*, *with*, *cloth*, etc.).

LETTER TILE ACTIVITIES

- Have the student hold up an appropriate letter tile whenever you say a certain sound. For example, read the poem "The House That Jack Built" and have the student hold up the *j* letter tile every time he or she hears the /j/ sound in the poem.
- Have the student use the letter tiles to identify the initial, medial, and/or final sounds in a variety of words. For example, say the word "bat" and have the student move the letter tile that names the initial sound in the word to a new row. Then have the student move the letter tile that names the final sound in the word to a new row, etc.
- Have the student lay the appropriate letter tiles on a variety of pictures in order to identify the initial (or medial or final) sounds in the words that name those pictures. Use the pictures on the red Kid Cards or any other available pictures in books, catalogs, or posters.
- Have the student lay the letter tiles in a row face up. One at a time, have the student select a letter, say its sound, and drop it back into the container. This is an excellent way to review the spelling sounds.
- Follow the procedure above, but have the student say the letter's name instead of its sound.
- Have the student use the letter tiles as Bingo markers.
- Have the student spell designated words with the letter tiles.
- Have the student alphabetize the letter tiles.
- Have the student lay the letter tiles in a row face up. Call out the names of a variety of consonants, digraphs, combinations, etc., and have the student hold up the appropriate letter(s).

REVIEW DECK GAMES

At First Sight

Materials: Sight Word Cards
tokens

Directions: Play this game with two to four players. Lay the sight word cards on the floor or table face up, and place a token on each one. One at a time, have each player read a word. If he or she is correct, give the player the token. Add tokens as necessary to give players more than one chance to play, but place them on those words that are the most difficult for players to remember. The player with the most tokens at the end of the game wins.

Variation: Place the sight word cards on the floor or table face down, and have players select a card and read the word. After reading the word, the player then places the card face down on the table again.

Keyword and Sound

Materials: Letter Deck (use only those cards that have been reviewed)

Directions: Hold up one of the letter cards and ask the student to tell you the keyword and sound of the letter. This provides a good way to judge how well the student knows the keywords.

Letter Deck Data

Materials: Letter Deck (use only those cards that have been reviewed)

Directions: Hold up a letter card and ask the student to tell you as many facts as possible about the letter on that card. For example, if you hold up the *i* letter card, the student could tell you that it is a vowel, it has two sounds, it is the ninth letter of the alphabet, it is in the first half of the alphabet, one of its keywords is "igloo," etc. For each fact the student tells you about the letter, award one point. If desired, set a time limit. When the time limit expires, or when the student can no longer think of any new facts about a particular letter, hold up a new letter card. Continue as long as time permits. Help the student count his or her points at the end of the game.

Seven Questions (or Twenty Questions)

Materials: Letter Deck (use only those cards that have been reviewed)

Directions: Choose a letter card but do not tell the student what it is. The student should try to guess what the card is by asking up to seven questions. Each of the questions may only be answered with "yes" or "no." The first few times the student plays, he or she will probably ask questions like "Is it a *b*?" or "Is it a *t*?" As the student continues playing (and with your guidance), he or she will learn to ask more productive questions like "Is it a vowel?" or "Is it part of a digraph?" in order to eliminate more than one letter at a time. Keep track of the number of questions asked. If the student guesses the letter before asking seven questions, he or she wins. If the student does not guess the letter in seven questions, show the card; then continue to the next one. The overall objective is to help the student learn strategies for asking productive questions. Allow the student to ask more questions (up to twenty) about each card as the deck grows larger.

Spelling Deck Perfection

Materials: Spelling Deck (use only those cards that have been reviewed)

Directions: Hold up a spelling card and give the sound to the student. If the student gives the correct response, give him or her the card. If the student cannot give the correct response, lay the card in your stack. Continue to the next card, and play until there are no more cards left. At the end of the game, see whose stack contains more cards.

Student as Teacher

Materials: Review Decks

Directions: Allow the student to play "teacher" with you as the "student." Review one or all of the three decks (letter, picture, spelling). The review of the spelling deck will be the most difficult for the student but will also be the most beneficial activity.

Spelling Games

Spelling Bee

Materials: Spelling Word List

Directions: Have the student stand at the chalkboard. Call out a word from the Spelling Word List for the student to spell on the chalkboard. Use only those words whose letters and sounds have been taught. **Do not ask the student to spell words that contain twin consonants.** If the student spells the word correctly, award him or her a point or token. Continue as long as time permits.

Spelling Sounds

Materials: Spelling Word List
Container of letter tiles

Directions: Give the student a letter tile from the container. Using the Spelling Word List, call out a two- or three-letter word whose letters and sounds have been taught. Ask the student if the word contains the sound of the letter tile he or she is holding. If it does, ask the student in what position (beginning, middle, or end) that sound occurs. (If the word does not contain the sound, give a new word.) Continue giving new words and letter tiles as long as time permits.

Spelling Toss

Materials: 2–4 containers (bucket, waste-paper basket, etc.)
Purple Kid Cards
Ping pong ball, bean bag, or other soft ball
Tokens

Directions: Place a few purple word cards in each container, face down. The student should be seated in front of the containers. Give the (bean bag) to the student and ask him or her to try to gently toss it into one of the containers. Once the student successfully tosses the object into a container, pull out a word card from the container, read the word, and ask the student to spell it. If the student spells the word correctly, give him or her a token. If the student does not spell the word correctly, provide hints until he or she does. Remove the card from the container and give the (bean bag) back to the student. Continue until all the words have been spelled.

Chalkboard Games

Chalkboard Challenge

Materials: Tokens

Directions: Write a word on the chalkboard containing only those letters and sounds that have been taught. (If desired, use the Reading Word List.) Ask the student to go to the chalkboard, code the word, and then read it aloud. If the student codes and reads the word correctly, give him or her a token. Continue as long as time permits.

Sound Scamper

Directions: Have the student stand about four feet from the chalkboard with a piece of chalk. Call out the sound of a letter the student has learned, and ask him or her to echo the sound and then "scamper" to the chalkboard. The student should write and name the letter that makes the sound. Observe the student carefully to determine if he or she writes the letter independently or if he or she must copy the answer from somewhere else. Continue with another letter sound. For those letters the student has difficulty remembering, provide extra practice. Play this game often to help the student learn to write letters independently.